DATE DUE

DEMCO 38-296

Judicial Policy Making and the Modern State

Between 1965 and 1990, federal judges in almost all of the states handed down sweeping rulings that affected virtually every prison and jail in the United States. Without a doubt judges were the most important prison reformers during this period. This book provides an account of this process, and uses it to explore the more general issue of the role of courts in the modern bureaucratic state. In doing so, it provides detailed accounts of how the courts formulated and sought to implement their orders, and how this action affected the traditional conception of federalism, separation of powers, and the rule of law.

The authors argue that judges have always made policy, and will continue to do so, especially in the modern administrative state. The modern administrative state embodies notions of government as an active policy maker, rather than a passive adjudicator of conflicts. This concept, the book argues, applies to courts as well. The modern administrative state requires an active, policy-making judiciary and, perhaps more importantly, a different and more activist concept of law.

Cambridge Criminology Series

Editors
Alfred Blumstein, *H. John Heinz School of Public Policy and Management, Carnegie Mellon University*
David Farrington, *Institute of Criminology, University of Cambridge*

The Cambridge Criminology Series aims to publish the highest quality research on criminology and criminal justice topics. Typical volumes will report major quantitative, qualitative, and ethnographic research, or make a substantial theoretical contribution. There will be a particular emphasis on research monographs, but edited collections may also be published if they make an unusually distinctive offering to the literature. All relevant areas of criminology and criminal justice are to be covered, including, for example, the causes of offending, juvenile justice, the development of offenders, measurement and analysis of crime, victimization research, policing, crime prevention, sentencing, imprisonment, probation, and parole. The series is global in outlook, with an emphasis on work that is comparative or holds significant implications for theory or policy.

Other books in the series:

Life in the Gang: Family, Friends, and Violence, by Scott H. Decker and Barrik Van Winkle

Delinquency and Crime: Current Theories, edited by J. David Hawkins

Recriminalizing Delinquency: Violent Juvenile Crime and Juvenile Justice Reform, by Simon I. Singer

Mean Streets: Youth Crime and Homelessness, by John Hagan and Bill McCarthy

Criminality and Violence among the Mentally Disordered, by Sheilagh Hodgins and Carl-Gunnar Janson

Crack Selling: The Political Economy, "Get Tough" Policies, and Marketing of Crack Cocaine, by Bruce D. Johnson and Eloise Dunlap

The Framework of Judicial Sentencing: A Study in Legal Decision Making, by Austin Lovegrove

The Criminal Recidivism Process, by Edward Zamble and Vernon L. Quinsey

Judicial Policy Making and the Modern State

HOW THE COURTS REFORMED AMERICA'S PRISONS

Malcolm M. Feeley
*University of California
at Berkeley*

Edward L. Rubin
*University of California
at Berkeley*

CAMBRIDGE
UNIVERSITY PRESS

PUBLISHED BY THE PRESS SYNDICATE OF THE UNIVERSITY OF CAMBRIDGE
The Pitt Building, Trumpington Street, Cambridge, United Kingdom

CAMBRIDGE UNIVERSITY PRESS
The Edinburgh Building, Cambridge CB2 2RU, UK   http://www.cup.cam.ac.uk
40 West 20th Street, New York, NY 10011-4211, USA   http://www.cup.org
10 Stamford Road, Oakleigh, Melbourne 3166, Australia
Ruiz de Alarcón 13, 28014 Madrid, Spain

© Malcolm M. Feeley and Edward L. Rubin 1998

First published 1999
Reprinted 2000
First paperback edition 2000

Printed in the United States of America

Typeset in ITC New Baskerville 10/12 pt. in Penta ™ [RF]

A catalog record for this book is available from the British Library

Library of Congress Cataloging in Publication data
Feeley, Malcolm.
Judicial policy making and the modern state: how the courts
reformed America's prisons / Malcolm M. Feeley, Edward L. Rubin.
p.   cm. – (Cambridge criminology series)
1. Prisons – Law and legislation – United States. 2. Judicial
process – United States. 3. Political questions and judicial power –
United States. I. Rubin, Edward L., 1948 – . II. Title.
III. Series.
KF9730.F44   1997
344.73'035 – dc21   97-25523

ISBN 0 521 59353 0 hardback
ISBN 0 521 77734 8 paperback

To Jacob, Miriam, Amir, and Rivka
and
Alexander, Gregory, Juliette, Timothy, and Ilene

Contents

What the Courts Accomplished
What the Courts Did Not Accomplish

Preface

In academic year 1989–90, the authors jointly taught a seminar to graduate and law students on prison conditions litigation. Feeley, a political scientist, had long taught a course, Courts and Social Policy, which at times had examined the judicial reform of conditions in prisons and jails. Rubin, a lawyer, had focused on prison conditions in his course on administrative law. The joint seminar, in which many students adopted a local prison or jail that was under court order, allowed us to share our perspectives and explore the process of judicial policy making. This book was born from that collaborative effort.

In producing such a large book over such a long period we have incurred a great many intellectual debts, too many to enumerate and properly credit. Yet both jointly and individually we feel obliged and pleased to record our debts and thanks to those people who have played a central role in helping shape our ideas and facilitating the completion of this book. Feeley wishes to thank Dennis Curtis, Daniel J. Freed, Roger Hanson, Jim Jacobs, Shelly Messinger, Kenneth Schoen, and Jon Silbert, who over the years have influenced his thinking about prisons and prison litigation. Rubin is grateful to the many colleagues who have influenced his thinking about courts and law, particularly Robert Cooter, Meir Dan-Cohen, and Robert Post. In addition we wish to express our deep appreciation to Allen Breed and Thomas Lonergan, two of the nation's most well-respected corrections experts and special masters, for sharing their time and knowledge with us. Two other experts, Anthony Newland, of the California Department of Corrections, and Thomas Blomberg, of the University of Florida, also provided useful information and insights over the years. More generally, Philip Selznick and Philippe Nonet's ideas about "responsive law" have affected our thinking on the role of law and courts in more ways than we would have realized before we started this project.

Over the years, some of the sections in this book, usually in quite different form, have been presented in seminars, workshops, and at scholarly conferences or have been published in quite different form elsewhere, and we appreciate the comments of all those who have responded to these materials. In addition to several of those already mentioned in this preface who have been helpful in this regard, we also wish to thank Bradley Chilton, Mary Coombs, John DiIulio, Jeffrey Gordon, Robert Kagan, Samuel Krislov, Lynn Mather, Paul Mishkin, Henry Monoghan, Kevin Reitz, Judith Resnik, Paul Rock, Steven Ross, Harry Scheiber, Kim Scheppele, Jerome Skolnick, Peter Strauss, Larry Yackle, and the late Herbert Jacob.

Each of the case studies in this book was the result of an effort, by one or both of the authors, and in turn we were aided by colleagues and officials familiar with each of the research sites. At each site, we talked to dozens of people – judges, correctional officials, lawyers, scholars, inmates, and still others familiar with the cases. The number of people who gave generously of their time are far too many to enumerate here. However, for each site there was a handful of people who facilitated our work enormously, and we must acknowledge them here. In Arkansas, we wish to thank Mary Parker for help in arranging meetings with a great many officials involved in the Arkansas litigation, arranging a tour of that state's prison system, and sharing her own knowledge and her dissertation on that case with us. In Texas, we wish to thank Ben Crouch and James Marquart, Steve Martin and Sheldon Ekland-Olson, authors of two books that chronicle developments in the Texas prison litigation. These books, as well as conversations with these authors, were indispensable to our own work. In Texas we also wish to acknowledge the help of the late George Beto and his colleague Rolando del Carman for hosting one of us at Sam Houston State University and for helping to arrange a visit to the state prison in Huntsville. Research on the Santa Clara County (San Jose, California) case was initially undertaken by a superb research assistant, Deborah Little, whose contribution to that section of Chapter 3 is gratefully acknowledged. In Colorado, we wish to thank Roger Hanson and Karen Feste for helping one of us to establish contacts with correctional officials and lawyers in that state's case, providing us with background information about developments there, and for housing one of us upon occasion. For help on Marion, we thank Norman Carlson, who arranged the visit, and Gary Henman, for hosting one of us.

We also wish to acknowledge the contributions of several other students who aided us in the early stages of this project and have since been launched in careers of their own: Ted Storey, Jutta Lungwitz-Klapisch, Susan Poser, Noga Morag Levine, and Dan Krislov.

The crucible for interdisciplinary research and teaching provided by the Jurisprudence and Social Policy Program at Boalt Hall School of Law at Berkeley is unique and unparalleled in American higher education. Social scientists and lawyers work together, at times jointly offering courses for both law and graduate students. This book emerged from one such joint enterprise, and we hope it serves as a modest testimony to Sandy Kadish and Philip Selznick, who had the vision and the skill to establish this unique experiment in higher education. The authors also received support for their teaching and research from the Daniel and Florence Guggenheim Foundation, which provided funds to support the Law School's Guggenheim Crime Policy Program. The Foundation's award reinforced the philosophy of the Law School's Jurisprudence and Social Policy Program, and helped support the research of both students and faculty, which has resulted in the publication of numerous articles and several books, including this one. We are deeply grateful to the Foundation, and especially to Oscar S. Straus, its president, and Jameson Doig of Princeton University, its liaison with us, for their confidence, support, and responsiveness.

Portions of this book were written when Feeley was a Fellow at the Institute of Advanced Studies at Hebrew University, during 1993–94. He is indebted to the convenors of the criminal justice group there, Mordechai Kremnitzer and Eliyahu Harnon, for hosting him and for bringing together such a stimulating set of colleagues whose interest in this project was contagious.

This book went through several drafts. We are deeply grateful for the typing and editorial assistance of Sheila John, Kiara Jordan, Kay Levine, Margo Rodriguez, and the indefatigable Susan Peabody.

With all the help we have had, there should be a good many people with whom to share the blame for this book's shortcomings. But alas, if we failed to heed their advice, we alone must assume responsibility for its defects.

Introduction

The Problem of Judicial Policy Making

Courts perform three interrelated but distinguishable functions: they determine facts, they interpret authoritative legal texts, and they make new public policy. The first two functions are familiar, but the third is freighted with the force of blasphemy. In our traditional view of government, courts are not supposed to act as policy makers, and the assertion that they do is generally treated as either harsh realism or a predicate to condemnation.

Political scientists, who work in an essentially descriptive mode, originally tended to adopt the harshly realistic stance toward judicial policy making. Their claims that courts are policy makers – indeed, that courts can be empirically proved to be policy makers – were offered as an antidote to the naive, traditional belief that judicial decisions are determined by "applying" existing law. One notable feature of this stance is that the term *policy* is often used as a synonym for "important" or even for "judicial decision making" in general, with no effort to distinguish policy making from other modes of judicial behavior. Even more notably, the term is used as a synonym for "unprincipled"; political scientists generally ascribe the content of judicial policy making to the political or social predilections of the judge, and regard the legal doctrine that is used to express and justify the decision as epiphenomenal, or part of the superstructure, or window dressing, or a Potemkin village, or any other image by which scholars dismiss the accounts that their subjects give for their own actions.[1]

Legal scholars, whose work tends to be more prescriptive, often regard judicial policy making as an abberation to be regretted or condemned.

1

For some, policy making is a legal error, a miasma judges stumble into when they fail to follow proper interpretive principles.[2] It remains an error when judges use it even for the delimited purpose of managing their own case loads.[3] Others recognize policy making as a universal element of judicial action, but treat this acknowledged reality as an indictment of the entire process. Fact-finding and interpretation, they say, are indeterminate, and thus no better than judicial policy making.[4]

Faced with these condemnations, and unwilling to accept the invitation to declare themselves to be mere politicians, judges' principal response has been to insist that they simply do not engage in policy making. They are willing to acknowledge that they use social policy to inform interpretation, but usually insist that their interpretation, whatever its sources, constitutes the most valid reading of the text.[5] Any tendency toward increased candor is likely to be quashed by the lawyers, litigants, and politicians they confront, who are quick to invoke the traditional doctrine, whatever its coherence, to support their own position. This process reaches its apogee during Senate confirmation hearings, when hard questioning invariably compels the nominee for one of our nation's most important policy-making positions to declare that he or she will do nothing more than interpret the law, and would never dream of exercising the very function that renders the position so desirable and the nominee so anxious to obtain approval.[6]

In recent years, more modulated analyses have tried to come to terms with this all-too-evident component of judicial decision making, while maintaining the distinction between it and other modes of judicial action. Some political scientists have argued that explanations anchored exclusively in extralegal factors are insufficient, and have sought a broader model of judicial decision making that incorporates existing legal doctrine. This claim can be limited to ordinary cases, where the judge engages in "routine norm enforcement,"[7] but it can also be extended to the kinds of leading cases that serve as the best evidence of judicial policy making. For example, Lee Epstein and Joseph Kobylka argue that in the death penalty and abortion cases, "it is the law and legal arguments as framed by legal actors that most clearly influence the content and direction of legal change."[8] Similarly, the legal mobilization literature demonstrates how judges make policy by rephrasing the litigants' dispute in legal terms.[9] Public policy literature on agenda setting sometimes treats courts as one participant in the complex process by which ideas are transformed into governmental priorities for policy initiation and implementation.[10]

Legal scholars have also developed a variety of approaches to assimilate judicial policy making into a more complex and less condemnatory account of the judicial process. One approach is to acknowledge policy considerations as a valid guide to interpretation. The courts should treat the

statute or the Constitution as meaning one thing, and not another, because the first comports with current social policy, whereas the second
contravenes it.[11] Another approach is that policy making is justified when
used to formulate a remedy for legal violations that have been established
by interpretive means.[12] Next, there is the view that courts, generally the
U.S. Supreme Court, may legitimately make policy at times of high political debate or crisis; the implication, however, is that in doing so, the
Court abandons its judicial role and enters the lists as a purely political
combatant.[13] A fourth position is that judges inevitably inhabit the realm
of political decision making and that simply nothing can be done but
recognize that they sometimes, or always, reach decisions that are essentially equivalent to those reached by other agencies of government.[14]

These contemporary approaches are illuminating but they tend to treat
judicial policy making as something to be explained away as an activist
version of interpretation, or to be quarantined within a delimited range.
They tell us what judicial policy making does, not what judicial policy
making is. Quite often, the process is treated as being hidden in the black
box of the judge's mind, or descending, like a deus ex machina, to produce its results by external and undefinable sorcery. It is often described
by reference to grand but unelaborated concepts such as experience,[15]
reason,[16] religion,[17] or maturity.[18]

This book adopts a different and, in some sense, more mundane approach. It treats judicial policy making as a separate judicial function with
its own rules, its own methods, and its own criteria for measuring success
or failure. In addition, it moves beyond description to argue that this
function is legitimate because it emerges naturally from the institutional
role of modern courts and does not violate any of our operative political
principles. The normative argument is secondary, however; the mere description of the subject matter is far more important, since it is generally
useful to know what something is before deciding whether one approves
or disapproves of it. Moreover, if the thing will continue to exist despite
one's disapproval – and judicial policy making belongs securely in that
category – the mere description of it will serve a valuable purpose. That
purpose is to demonstrate how the judge's policy-making function conforms to well-accepted, if little-understood, ideas about the nature of law
and adjudication in a modern administrative state. In other words, we
intend to rethink the forms and limits of adjudication.

But the book does not attempt to describe judicial policy making by
offering a comprehensive account. That is too large a task, and its generality precludes much insight into the detailed operation of the process.
In addition, if one restricts oneself to generalities, it is too easy to shift,
or to be perceived as shifting, back into the familiar debates about the
desirability of the process. One need not subscribe to the postmodernist

position that situated description is always more reliable than general theory,[19] in order to regard it as a safer place to start, particularly when venturing into uncharted territory. Consequently, this book begins with an example and constructs a theory of judicial policy making from a single set of decisions – the prison reform cases decided by the federal judiciary between 1965 and the present. These decisions not only illustrate the policy-making process, but also illuminate important features of our legal system that define the contours of this process and establish its significance.

Of course, it would be possible to follow the custom of many other books about judicial decision making and discuss a number of different examples, rather than just one.[20] Apart from prison reform, judicial policy making produced the constitutional right of privacy decisions such as *Griswold v. Connecticut* and *Roe v. Wade*,[21] the common law right of privacy and publicity decisions,[22] the free speech decisions,[23] the mental hospital reform decisions,[24] many federal antitrust decisions,[25] and the decisions creating implied warranties for consumer products.[26] Such an approach would avoid, or at least decrease, the dangers inherent in generalizing from a single case. The difficulty is that all these examples are complex, and consideration of them would tend to inundate a study of any reasonable length with vast quantities of legal detail. The only way to avoid this would be to present the examples in brutally summarized form, and to sandwich the theoretical discussion in among the case studies, with its systematic development consigned to a few concluding chapters. This study adopts a different approach. It presents one example in detail and then pursues what may be called a microanalysis of that example, building a theory of judicial policy making from the different, complex features that the example offers.

The Nature of Judicial Policy Making

Before proceeding, however, it is necessary to provide at least a preliminary definition of judicial policy making and to distinguish it from the more familiar category of interpretation. Judicial policy making, to put the matter most simply, is policy making by a judge. A judge is an adjudicator of particularized disputes belonging to a governmental institution whose primary task is adjudication. In America's federal court system, most judges are authorized under Article III of the Constitution, which means that they have life tenure and salary protection. However, some officials who would generally be described as judges, such as the members of the District of Columbia courts,[27] other territorial courts,[28] and courts martial[29] are Article I officials, and to the extent that they are part of a separate institution, they are included in this study. There are also a number of adjudicators belonging to administrative institutions and some of these, such as the administrative law judges, have a rather formalized, judgelike status.[30] This study is not intended to apply to these officials; the relationship between adjudication and policy making within an administrative agency is a complex subject that we do not address.

Policy making, by a judge or anyone else, is the process by which officials exercise power on the basis of their judgment that their actions will produce socially desirable results. This definition follows Ronald Dworkin.[31] Since Dworkin is a confirmed opponent of judicial policy making, which he regards as lawless, the use of a definition derived from his work provides reassurance that the concept is not being sugar-coated with conciliatory verbiage to facilitate its easier acceptance.

Policy making may be contrasted with interpretation, which is the process by which public officials exercise power on the basis of a preexisting legal source that they regard as authoritative. This does not mean that policy making is entirely disconnected from any established source of law. American constitutionalism, at both the federal and state level, requires that policy making, by a legislator or administrator as well as a judge, must be based upon the authority granted in some legal text. But policy making is distinguished from interpretation because it treats the text as a source of jurisdiction, not a guide to decision. When judges engage in interpretation, they invoke the applicable legal text to determine the content of the decision, whether by examining the words of that text, the structure of the text, the intent of its drafters, or the inherent purpose that informs it. But when judges engage in policy making, they invoke the text to establish their control over the subject matter, and then rely on nonauthoritative sources, and their own judgment, to generate a decision that is predominantly guided by the perceived desirability of its results.

Various methods of policy making have been discussed with respect to legislatures, executive agencies, private businesses, and other organizations for which policy making is regarded as a legitimate activity. The classic analytic method involves five discrete steps: define the problem, identify a goal, generate a range of alternatives for achieving that goal, select the alternative that seems most promising, and implement the selected alternative.[32] Each of these steps possesses its own subsidiary methodologies. In recent years, for example, cost–benefit analysis has become a particularly popular approach for choosing among a range of alternatives. Generating alternatives is the most mysterious step in the process, but has recently become the focus of attention from those interested in human creativity and cognitive psychology.

As might be expected, the aroma – some might say the stench – of scientific analysis that the five-step method carries has made it seem unrealistic or oppressive to many contemporary scholars. Perhaps the best-known and most starkly contrasting alternative is incremental, intuitive decision making, often described in Charles Lindblom's ironic phrase, as "the science of muddling through."[33] A somewhat more analytic approach is the hermeneutic circle, derived originally from the study of textual interpretation,[34] but applied to social science by Hans-Georg Gadamer.[35] In its initial form, the hermeneutic circle is an interpretive technique in which the meaning of any portion of the text can only be discerned from considering the text as a whole, but the meaning of the text as a whole can only be discerned from considering its component parts; as a result, understanding emerges from an interactive process that moves back and forth from part to whole to part. Gadamer argues that the social sciences should not be modeled on the natural sciences, but on humanities or aesthetic theory, including the hermeneutic circle. Anthony Giddens[36] and Charles Fox and Hugh Miller[37] have applied this approach to policy analysis.

Although this study argues that policy making is a normal and legitimate activity of the judiciary, it makes no effort to choose among these various policy-making approaches. This may seem like an omission in a theory of judicial policy making, but it stems from the generality of our theme. We are not attempting to instruct judges about the optimal way to make public policy; rather, we are arguing that policy making should be recognized – by judges and by observers of judges – as an ordinary and a legitimate mode of action. There is no agreed-upon strategy for policy making by a legislature, but very few people argue that legislatures should not make policy for lack of such a theory. There is no agreed-upon theory for the interpretation of legal texts, either; indeed, the disagreements on this subject constitute the biggest single issue in contemporary legal scholarship. Yet the belief that interpreting texts is a legitimate part of the judicial role is absolutely universal in our legal culture.* Both policy making and interpretation are part of what many observers call the "practice" of judicial decision making, but they are separate parts.[38]

With respect to constitutional interpretation, Philip Bobbitt has transformed the lack of agreement about a theory of interpretation into a theory of its own. Bobbitt argues, in effect, that each rival theory constitutes an element of our legal discourse, a modality of judicial decision making.[39] The modalities he identifies are historical (the intent of the framers), textual, structural, doctrinal, ethical, and prudential (cost–ben-

---

* There has been an ongoing debate about whether the Supreme Court should invalidate legislative enactments on the basis of its interpretation of the Constitution. But no American legal scholar doubts that courts may legitimately interpret statutory enactments; indeed, it is difficult to imagine how our government would function in the absence of this power.

efit analysis). A valid interpretation is simply one that uses these modalities in the manner that they are supposed to be used within our legal culture. This theory has been attacked as less than nourishing, because it does not tell us whether a particular decision is correct, or preferable to some other decision, nor does it resolve conflicts between the various modalities.[40] But it certainly does describe the practice of constitutional interpretation, and it indicates that this practice contains a variety of differing approaches. If that is not deemed a significant achievement, the reason is that the existence of this practice is not open to question, and the legitimacy of the practice is no longer a primary source of controversy.

This study advances the same claim for judicial policy making as Bobbitt advances for constitutional interpretation – that it is a standard method of judicial action, displaying a series of distinct modalities. These modalities include muddling through, hermeneutics, and the classic analytic method, plus its sidekick, cost–benefit analysis. When judges use these modalities, they are making public policy in the standard manner that our prevailing legal culture establishes – they are "talking the talk." The difference between the cases of constitutional interpretation and judicial policy making, however, is that the existence of the latter remains open to debate, and its legitimacy is generally rejected by both sides in this debate. Our claim is that there exists, just below the flimsiest fig leaf of judicial denials, a vast realm of judicial policy making, and that this realm represents a standard, legitimate mode of judicial action. Precisely which mode of policy making is preferable, or optional, is a subject for a subsequent discussion.

Policy Making as a Distinct Category

A second definitional question about judicial policy making is whether the distinction between selection of a desirable result and interpretation of an authoritative text really makes a difference. Judges, after all, regularly rely on social policy when interpreting texts, and they regularly invoke texts even in their most result-oriented moods. In fact, there is a substantial overlap between policy making and interpretation, and judges often engage in both modes of decision making within the same opinion. This would be fatal to any theory of judicial decision making that demanded that each decision be unambiguously assigned to separate categories. But theories of this sort belong to physics, not the human sciences. When we study judicial decision making, the primary goal is to understand the essence of that process, the way it feels to the decision maker and is perceived by those who are affected by it. In other words, the goal is to grasp the phenomenology of judicial action. Interpretation and policy making are different experiences for the judge and are perceived differently by others, no matter how extensively they overlap. A theory of judicial decision making is not complete unless it can capture the different nature of those two experiences. The mere fact that there is no bright line between them does not defeat the assertion that policy making is a distinct judicial function.

The tendency to conflate policy making with interpretation does not stem solely from the fuzziness of the boundary between the two, but also from affirmative beliefs about the judicial process. There are at least four such beliefs, based, in succession, on interpretive theory, political theory, legal epistemology, and flat denial. The first belief emerges from the important philosophic insight that all thought is interpretive.[41] At one level this is persuasive, but its relevance to judicial decision making rests on something akin to a pun. The interpretive structure of all human thought, sometimes described as "the social construction of reality,"[42] does nothing to refute the claim that interpreting texts and making public policy mean different things within that generally interpretive framework. All our understandings are based on interpretations that give meaning to the world around us, and that precede and generate our ability for conscious thought. According to Heidegger, picking up a hammer and driving in a nail is an interpretive act.[43] The culturally embedded distinction between policy making and text interpretation is simply one of those understandings. Its "social construction" only means that the distinction is a product of our culture, not an aspect of external or objective reality. Consequently, we cannot be confident that the distinction will exist among intelligent beings from other planets, but that does not detract from its importance here in North America.

A second belief, somewhat homologous with the first, emerges from the equally important social science insight that all judicial action is political.[44] This insight flourished in response to the assertion, proclaimed by the formalists and refurbished by the legal process school, that judges apply neutral principles in reaching their decisions.[45] By now, the idea of neutral principles has become the phlogiston theory of legal scholarship, and few observers would deny that there is at least an element of political judgment in judicial action. But recognizing the inevitability of politics, like recognizing the inevitability of interpretation, does nothing to conflate policy making and interpretation. Legislators are acting politically when they campaign in their home districts and they are also acting politically when they pass legislation, but that does not make campaigning and legislating identical activities. Similarly, while judicial policy making is obviously political, the fact that interpretation is also political does not rob it of its separate, interpretive character. It is political because any action by a government official is political, but it is interpretation nonetheless, and not the same as policy making.

The argument about the political nature of judicial action can be taken one step further, however, by arguing that all judicial action is so political that it is a pure act of will, with no relation to the text at all. This is the argument from legal epistemology, and its central claim is that all legal rules are indeterminate.[46] There is some strong evidence supporting it, but it has an exaggerated quality, as if our excessive expectations for interpretation, once disappointed, have produced the reaction of excessive condemnation or despair. In this study, however, we take no position on the interesting but belabored question of judicial indeterminacy. Regardless of one's position on this issue, indeterminacy does not efface the distinction between interpretation and policy making. To begin with, the claim that it does is excessively positivist; it characterizes judicial actions based upon an external observer's ability to predict the result, rather than upon the participants' construction of meaning. The experience of interpreting a text is different from the experience of declaring social policy, even though an external observer might not be able to predict the outcomes of the interpretive process from her own examination of that text. Perhaps this lack of predictability means that the interpretive process is a failure, but to try and fail at a particular task will still be experienced as part of that task, not as equivalent to a conceptually different task.

Even more importantly, the argument from indeterminacy emerges from an exclusive focus on interpretation; it treats policy making as nothing more than a failure of the interpretive process. This assumes in advance the very point challenged by a theory of judicial policy making: that there are no rules to govern its performance. In other words, the argument that policy making and interpretation are equivalent because texts are indeterminate assumes that only texts can guide the judicial decision-making process, and that there are no separate norms. If there are such norms, however, then policy making cannot be subsumed into some generic stew of indeterminate judicial decision making. This argument also functions in reverse. If judicial policy making occurs, but we fail to recognize it because we lack a theory for it, we will tend to exaggerate the level of indeterminacy in judicial decisions. We will point to certain decisions as evidence that legal texts do not govern the result when the judge was not interpreting a legal text at all, but declaring public policy based on a textual grant of jurisdiction.

The final belief about interpretation that conflates it with policy making is the judges' own argument, the one that the Senate hears from Supreme Court nominees: "It would be wrong for judges to make policy and we don't do it. All we do is interpret the law. Of course, some judges misbehave, as is inevitable with any group of people, but those judges are in error and their opinions, if reviewed by other judges, will be overruled. To describe policy making as a category of judicial thought is like describing bribery as a category of legislative action."[47] At one level, this seems like little more than a logical mistake; saying that a practice could not possibly exist because its existence would violate a publicly promulgated norm is not particularly persuasive. But the argument becomes somewhat more convincing when advanced by those who are carrying out the supposedly forbidden practice. If judges think policy making is wrong, they may actually desist from doing it.

The most obvious alternative, however, is that they may do it but disguise their actions in some other form. In fact, judges seem to have adopted the latter strategy, and they have done so by describing policy making as interpretation. Our classic arena of judicial action is the common law, and common law – undeniably a form of public policy – is created predominantly by judges.[48] The fiction that judges developed to avoid acknowledging that they were making public policy is that general principles are embedded in the common law, and that the creation of new doctrine is nothing more than the application of those principles to novel situations.[49] In other words, judicial policy making was disguised as the interpretation of an unseen text.

Precisely why the judiciary adopted this approach is a question for legal history to answer. It was probably not derived from the concern that judicial policy making is antidemocratic, since England's common-law process antedates its commitment to democracy by many centuries.[50] More likely, the assimilation of policy making to interpretation sprang from the ongoing effort by common-law courts to assert their authority against other courts[51] and against the king.[52] By declaring that they were merely interpreting legal principles that sprang from the immemorial practices and beliefs of the English people, common-law courts could claim superiority over any other governmental institution. Clearly, such a claim relies heavily on the respect accorded to tradition. In a world that regarded innovation with suspicion and legitimated present actions on the basis of their pedigree, it was natural that judges would cast their policy-making efforts as the interpretation of established principles.

Since the Enlightenment, tradition has lost much of its appeal, but the very process that displaced tradition enthroned democracy as the source of political legitimacy and provided judges with a new reason to describe their policy-making efforts as interpretation. Perhaps there was a hiatus in this process of substituting a different motivation for the same result. Nineteenth-century judges, more comfortable with innovation and not yet troubled by their unelected status, were often willing to acknowledge a policy-making role.[53] The development of the modern administrative state, however, engendered the view that policy making is the particular preserve of state's politically accountable branches.[54] This belief is false, since a great deal of public policy is generated by independent agencies, or by other executive bodies whose political accountability is minimal.[55] But a belief need not be true in order to affect people's behavior, and it certainly does need not be true in order to induce cautious people, such as judges, to mischaracterize their actions in accord with that belief.

The result is that judges continue to describe their policy-making role as an aspect of interpretation. They continue to claim that all their decisions are derived from some authoritative text – the Constitution, a statute, or the common law. They acknowledge that they are using public policy arguments, but present these arguments as mechanisms for informing the interpretive process. Sometimes, this is exactly what courts are doing when they invoke public policy. At other times, however, the court is not interpreting the text at all – it is declaring a new public policy and invoking the interpretive function of public policy to avoid conceding that this policy is the dominant consideration.

Judicial policy making and interpretation are thus separate functions, despite their obvious overlaps and frequent simultaneity of operation. One can attract attention or satisfy one's sense of irony by declaring that all thought is interpretive, political, or indeterminate; one can attack the judicial system by asserting that judges do nothing other than make policy, or defend the judicial system by asserting that they do nothing more than interpret the law. But all these claims, while they contain an element of truth, suffer from implausibility. There is no knockdown argument to prove them wrong, but the energy they must expend to swim upstream against the obvious suggests that they are not the most useful explanation. What seems apparent is that interpretation and policy making are separate from each other, as they are separate from judicial fact-finding. Sometimes, judges base their decision on their own best efforts to understand an authoritative text; at other times, however, they base their decision on their sense of the best public policy.

There are, however, a number of terms for judicial decision making that straddle the boundary between policy making and interpretation. This does not mean that the boundary is nonexistent; the situation, rather, is that the terms are imprecise, and are often used for different things. The most notable examples of such terms are gap-filling, social principles, and judicial activism. Gap-filling is a European concept which states that the judge must follow the statute when it speaks to the case at hand, but may create new law when a gap appears in the statutory framework.[56] H. L. A. Hart translates this into Anglo-American law by distinguishing between the core meaning of the statute and the statute's penumbra; in the latter region, Hart asserts, courts may engage in judicial legislation.[57] The distinction is serviceable enough, but it seems unlikely that there is any externally observable difference between statute and gap, or core and penumbra; instead, these two categories are themselves a matter of interpretation.[58] If a judge interprets a statute to deny herself jurisdiction of the issue, she will refuse to decide the case. If she interprets a statute to grant herself jurisdiction, she must further decide whether the statute provides any rules for reaching her decision, again by interpretation. If she decides it does, she will proceed to interpret the statutory text; if she decides it does not, she must resort to the policy-making mode. An even greater difficulty is that equating the metaphor of gaps or penumbras with judicial policy making suggests that policy making is a delimited activity, safely contained on the periphery or in the interstices of real law. In fact, the core of many common-law, statutory, and constitutional doctrines has been fashioned by judges acting in a policy-making mode, while other doctrines have emerged from a combination of the two approaches.

A number of leading constitutional scholars argue that judges should be guided by social principles or public values, and that their most important task is to articulate these values. Philip Bobbitt,[59] Owen Fiss,[60] Frank Michelman,[61] Michael Perry,[62] Cass Sunstein,[63] and Mark Tushnet,[64] despite their many disagreements, all appear to be proponents of this approach. Their reliance on social principles seems allied to policy making, but these scholars generally present it as a means of interpreting the Constitution. In fact, mere invocation of a social principle tells us nothing about the purposes for which these principles are used; the judge can rely on these principles either to discern the meaning of a text or to initiate a policy-making process. As with gaps and penumbras, this distinction cannot be derived from an examination of the values themselves, but only from observing the way that they are employed. Bobbitt and Tushnet, who present the most complete taxonomy of constitutional arguments, both recognize this fact and identify a separate policy-making approach, which they label prudential and antiformalist respectively.[65] These terms give the process a somewhat exotic sound that seems to preclude the development of a coherent theory, however, and neither Bobbitt nor Tushnet develops such a theory.

A final concept that is sometimes equated with judicial policy making is judicial activism, but again the term describes two different categories of decisions. Activism generally refers to the impact of the decision on society or on other governmental institutions, whether or not there is a textual basis on which the decision rests. To be sure, many examples of judicial policy making involve high levels of activism, but some do not. When common-law courts established the rights of publicity or privacy, they were not being particularly activist;[66] it was true that they created a new, judicially enforced right, but it was no more intrusive than familiar rights in other areas. And when federal courts invented the rule of reason in antitrust cases, they limited their involvement, rather than expanding it.[67] More importantly, not all activist decisions involve policy making. The most significant example of judicial activism in our recent history is the school desegregation cases,[68] but these emerged from a perfectly plausible and readily understood interpretation of the equal protection clause. The interpretation can be disputed, as can the remedies the courts imposed, but one must concede that integration of the public schools was at least a plausible reading of the constitutional text rather than an act of policy making by the courts.

Judicial Policy Making in the Prison Reform Cases

The prison reform cases of the past three decades are the most striking example of judicial policy making in modern America. Beginning in the 1930s, prisoners began bringing suit in federal court to challenge their conditions of confinement. These suits, which increased in frequency as time went on, were generally dismissed by the courts on the ground that prison conditions were not subject to constitutional review. A few courts granted habeas corpus relief or damages, and the Supreme Court, while throwing a few fugitives from southern chain gangs back upon the tender mercies of their native state, expressed sympathy for the prisoners' plight. Nonetheless, as of 1964, no American court had ever ordered a prison to change its practices or its conditions.[69]

The following year, however, the United States District Court for the Eastern District of Arkansas declared that certain conditions at Cummins Farm State Prison constituted cruel and unusual punishment in violation of the Eighth Amendment.[70] During the next few years, the court held Cummins Farm unconstitutional in its entirety and issued a series of injunctions that restructured the institution.[71] Within a decade of that decision, prisons in twenty-five of the fifty states and the entire correctional systems of five states had been placed under comprehensive court orders. A decade later these figures had increased to thirty-five states and nine entire prison systems. And one decade later still, in 1995, the ACLU estimated that prisons in a total of forty-one states, as well as the District of Columbia, Puerto Rico, and the Virgin Islands, had at one time or another been under comprehensive court orders, as had the entire correctional systems of at least ten states.[72] Only Minnesota, New Jersey and North Dakota had been entirely exempted from the judicial prison reform process.[73] With respect to jails, even these penologically virtuous states had been found wanting; at least some jails in all fifty states had been placed under court orders.[74] Many of these orders specified such details of institutional administration as the square footage of the cells, the nutritional content of the meals, the number of times each prisoner could shower, and the wattage of light bulbs in prisoners' cells.

This massive intervention into state corrections was an act of judicial policy making. Over the course of a single decade, the federal courts fashioned a comprehensive set of judicially enforceable rules for the governance of American prisons. They derived these rules from existing correctional literature, sociology, and their own perceptions of political morality. Such a new code of legal rules, inspired by general moral and empirical considerations and derived from a model that had been hovering near but had not yet appeared upon any accepted agenda, is a typical product of the policy-making process, not very different from a statute or an administrative regulation. Indeed, it corresponds closely to John Kingdon's analysis of the way that ambient ideas are placed on the policy agenda.[75]

To be sure, judges did not necessarily identify their prison reform decisions in this fashion. More often, they resorted to the usual argument that they were simply interpreting the Constitution, most specifically the Eighth Amendment's prohibition against "cruel and unusual punishment." But the claim that one can find so elaborate a set of standards in a previously nonjusticiable provision makes hash of any coherent theory of interpretation. As previously stated, this study takes no position on whether the interpretation process in general is indeterminate, that is, whether any coherent theory of interpretation exists. The point here is that it would be incorrect to use the prison reform cases to test this proposition because these cases were not interpretation at all, despite the judges' efforts to characterize them as such. The orders that the courts imposed were far too specific to have been derived from four little eighteenth-century words, no matter how carefully those words were read or how long their meaning pondered. Nor could the courts appeal to the justifying force of incrementalism, where a rule that is apparently unrelated to its textual source can be credibly, if not definitively, traced back to that source along a path of previous decisions. The entire conditions-of-confinement doctrine was articulated in little more than a decade, after 175 years of judicial silence on its subject matter.

The Eighth Amendment was relevant to the prison conditions cases, however – not as a source of standards, but as a basis for judicial jurisdiction. The amendment authorized constitutional courts to concern themselves with modes of punishment, thus creating general boundaries within which they could exercise their powers. It did not mention prisons, of course, but this is not determinative, since prisons as we know them did not exist in America when the Constitution was drafted.[76] In subsequent years, they became our dominant means of punishing convicted criminals; thus, extending the clause to include these institutions certainly seems to be a reasonable interpretation. But that interpretation only provides a general authorization for federal courts to be concerned about prisons; it is too vague, as a matter of both its literal language and its historically comprehended meaning, to serve as a source of standards. Since most policy making, even by executives or legislatures, is ultimately grounded in such authorizations, the mere existence of an authorizing legal text does not deprive subsequent decisions of their policy-making character. Unless there is additional content in the text, those decisions must be recognized as policy making, however much the rule maker may try to characterize them as interpretation.

The federal judiciary's enthusiasm for prison reform has subsided somewhat in recent years,[77] perhaps because of its own increasing conservatism, perhaps because of its sensitivity to the populace's increasing displeasure with criminals, and perhaps because many of the worst conditions that previously seared its conscience have been alleviated. As a result, prison reform may be regarded as an historical event, rather than an ongoing process. But even if it is historical, it is not without continuing impact. The decisions of the federal judiciary have established a comprehensive code of detailed rules and regulations that governs every prison in America, a code that is reflected in state statutes, administrative regulations, and internal prison rules, that is understood by virtually every lawyer and corrections commissioner, and that is monitored by compliance officers in every state department of corrections. The fact that two of the Supreme Court's recent prison cases involved claims that a non-smoking prisoner should be protected from secondhand smoke[78] and that a preoperative transsexual prisoner should be protected from his or her fellow prisoners[79] suggests how extensive the impact of the prison reform cases has been. The fact that the present Court, which is widely regarded as conservative, sustained both claims, the second unanimously,[80] suggests the continued vitality of their results, even if forward motion in this field has now slowed or ceased.

While it is not difficult to identify the prison reform cases as an example of judicial policy making, a description of the way that judges proceeded with their policy-making efforts is more daunting. As stated, the cursory and argumentative approach to this judicial function has left us without any conceptual framework for describing it. But we do know how to describe policy-making discourse by other governmental institutions, and this description can be applied to judicial policy making in the prison reform cases, however unfamiliar the result may first appear. Three modes of policy-making discourse have already been identified – classic analysis, incrementalism or muddling through, and hermeneutics. The first, despite its old-fashioned and somewhat mechanistic character, still provides the best way of specifying the component parts of a complex decision-making process and will be used to structure our analysis. At the same time, incrementalism is a rather convincing description of judicial policy making, because it is an informal, intuitive approach that is particularly suited to policymakers like the courts who are uncertain or apologetic about their role. We will rely on this description as counterpoint to the primary analysis, an antidote to the implication that the courts knew what they were doing in advance or acted with single-minded efficiency. Hermeneutics is relatively new and somewhat vague as a description of the policy-making process. But in its reliance on phenomenology and existentialism, it has the great advantage of providing a description that is connected to a general theory of human understanding. Moreover, it has the most impressive jargon, which is a virtue when one's theory is relatively weak, but is also something of a temptation. We apply it as second counterpoint, and as a primary explanation when trying to explain the motivations of the judges as individuals.

In terms of the classic analysis, judges perceived the problem to be solved as the harsh, immoral, un-American conditions that prevailed in many state prisons, particularly, as we will demonstrate, in the prisons in the southern states. This perception led directly to their goal, which was to impose national standards of progressive prison management on the state prisons. The next step in the classic analysis is to generate a range of alternatives from which to choose. This step was largely absent from the prison reform cases, and is generally absent from judicial policy making; while opposing attorneys occasionally suggest options for decision, courts rarely engage in a sort of systematic survey of alternatives. They do, however, select alternatives by intuition, and that is what they did in the prison reform cases. The alternatives selected, which were bureaucratization and rehabilitation, at first may seem to be rather odd choices for reforming prisons, but they enabled judges to draw directly on national correctional values to achieve the goal of imposing national standards on the prisons. These choices were then implemented by a process of direct intervention that combined micromanagement of the prison with cajoling, enticing, intimidating, threatening, disrupting, and all the other strategies that are familiar to administrative agencies.*

At the same time, the prison reform cases were often the result of an incremental, intuitive process of muddling through. There is an element of muddle at every stage into which the classic analysis divides the prison reform process, but the concept also has a more profound, operational effect. In essence, it means that the courts began implementing their solutions before they knew what the solutions were. They had decided on the problem, and at least sensed their goal, but they often felt their way

---

* It should be noted that the implementation stage of judicial policy making, although obviously a major element in the prison reform cases, need not be carried out by the judges themselves; it can be delegated to another government agency. It can also be omitted, but then the policy-making process is incomplete.

along rather blindly after that, trying one set of specific orders, then another. The legal rules they ultimately imposed could be described as bureaucratization and rehabilitation in retrospect, but at the time many judges were proceeding by intuition. This approach, in which implementation precedes the choice of solutions, violates classic policy analysis, but is the essence of muddling through. It means that a description of the way that courts implemented prison reform will possess a dual aspect; it will constitute the final stage in a classic policy analysis, and will simultaneously constitute a redescription of the entire process using a more informal, intuitive approach. This leads to a fairly complex description, but it also enables us to rely on the categories of classic policy analysis as a means of achieving specificity without making excessive claims for the foresight or coherence of the process.

Given the complexity of this simultaneous use of two rival descriptions of policy making, we will not make extensive use of the third, hermeneutic approach. Hermeneutics is not inconsistent with the other two, although it is more closely allied to incrementalism. At the same time, it has a theory and a vocabulary of its own, which threaten to add too many overlapping layers to the description. We will use it only to address those issues where both classic analysis and incrementalism fail to provide any insights, most notably in explaining the motivations of the actors. Courts may have decided upon the goal of imposing national standards on state prisons, but why did they do so? Why precisely did they choose the particular policy options of rehabilitation and bureaucratization, particularly when the first has negative associations and the second was losing its credibility at the very time that courts imposed it? Why were courts prepared to implement these solutions in such an aggressive fashion, and, to shift to the incrementalist description? Why were they prepared to engage in aggressive implementation even before they had a clear notion of what they were implementing? We will rely on the hermeneutic description of policy making to answer these particular questions, but on the other two descriptions for our overall account of the process.

The Conundrum of Judicial Policy Making

But this description, complex as it may seem, does not end our inquiry. Judicial policy making is a somewhat disconcerting concept, and we cannot fully alleviate our sense of unease with the observation that judges actually do it. The various policy-making models have no justificatory force when used even in their familiar setting by entities whose policy-making role is generally acknowledged; no one argues that these models are so effective that they provide an independent justification for an agency that chooses to employ them. When used by the courts, policy making creates a serious legitimacy problem. In fact, as the prison reform cases amply illustrate, the use of this model by the federal courts violated nearly every accepted principle for controlling the judicial branch. To begin with, it violated the principle of federalism. Standard doctrine holds that states have the right to make their own decisions in a variety of fields, and corrections was widely recognized as one of the fields most unambiguously assigned to state authority. But in the prison reform cases, federal courts imposed nationally defined rules on state prisons. All the familiar furniture of federalist doctrine – the virtues of citizen involvement, the division of power among separate jurisdictions, the opportunity for experimentation[81] – was cast aside as federally imposed standards restructured state institutions and displaced state decision makers.

Second, the prison reform process violated the separation of powers principle. In the process of defining and imposing standards, courts undertook the management and micromanagement of these institutions. The appointment of special masters, working full-time in the prisons and answerable directly to the court, was only the most dramatic manifestation of this general trend. Even when courts acted without appointing subordinate officials, they maintained an ongoing, detailed supervision of the institution that diverges from our traditional image of judicial action and judicial standard-setting.

There was still a third principle, more subtle but more significant, that the courts seem to have violated in reforming prisons – the principle that judicial action should be guided and constrained by preexisting law. This is, in effect, the rule of law as it applies to the judiciary. By fashioning their own set of substantive legal rules, the federal courts departed from this principle. They invoked the Eighth Amendment, of course, but the rules were simply too detailed, and their development too sudden, for this explanation to be credible. If the Eighth Amendment did not apply to conditions of confinement in 1964, precisely how did it become the engine for transforming state corrections by 1970? Courts often justify doctrinal alterations by pointing to changed circumstances or to a reassessment of the facts; on occasion, they even concede that they have made an error. All these explanations, however, involve a specific exercise of judgment, the selection of an option that was conceptually available at the time of the original decision but was rejected in favor of the opposing choice. The prison reform cases were different, because the courts had previously held the issue nonjusticiable; the Eighth Amendment, they declared, did not contain cognizable standards that could govern conditions of confinement. By saying so, they made it so, for the federal courts had dismissed virtually every prison conditions case before 1965 without reaching the merits, and there really were no judicially articulated standards for correctional policy. During the course of the prison reform process, the federal courts developed, or made up, those standards, right down to the wattage in the light bulbs.

There is a deep mystery in the violation of these well-established principles of federalism, separation of powers, and the rule of law. The prison cases represented the collective actions of literally hundreds of federal judges, acting individually. These judges were not fire-breathing radicals, or the minions of an occupying foreign power; they were not captured by some narrow special interest group, nor did they meet in secret conclave to concoct their plans. They were middle-of-the-road, upper-middle-class Americans, largely white and male, appointed by Republican and Democratic presidents. They did not even take their cues from the Supreme Court, the usual villain for critics of judicial activism and, in any case, a convenient means of coordinating the otherwise unconnected federal circuits and the fractious trial courts that they contain. There was no *Brown, Miranda,* or *Roe v. Wade*[82] to generate a sudden shift in doctrine and provide the explanation that a few idiosyncratic individuals had exercised their will. Rather, the prison cases constitute a rapid, inexorable procession of discrete decisions, formulated by federal trial courts throughout the nation and affirmed repeatedly at the appellate level. If these cases represented such a wholesale violation of true principles for constraining judicial behavior, why were so many federal judges willing to decide them, and with such apparent unanimity? Clearly, a relatively transparent effort to dress up their policy-making efforts as interpretation would not suffice in making these decisions justifiable, either to external observers or to the judges themselves.

A great deal has been written about the prison reform cases. One body of literature focuses on prisons, asking what was wrong with them and whether the judicial intervention helped. Some of these studies conclude that the remedy was beneficial, although both its incremental value and its side effects remain a matter of debate.[83] Others conclude that the judges did more harm than good.[84] A second body of literature focuses on judges and asks why they behaved the way they did.[85] Although much of this literature has merit, its frequent conclusion that the federal judges overstepped their authority is somewhat implausible.[86] It is implausible that so large a group of government officials, in so many different regions, acting independently of one another over such an extended period of time, would stray so far from the accepted path. One maverick judge might issue an oddball ruling, and perhaps avoid reversal by good fortune or obscurity, but when hundreds of judges rule the same way, and other hundreds uphold their decisions, we are compelled to reconsider our understanding of the applicable constraints on the judicial process.

Judicial Policy Making and the Modern Concept of Law

This book's hypothesis is that the reason judges were willing to engage in policy making, and apparently to violate the long-standing principles of federalism, separation of powers, and the rule of law, is that there is something seriously wrong with all three principles. Both the structural principles – federalism and the separation of powers – are products of the eighteenth century and are now outdated or in need of significant reformulation. Federalism was a pragmatic solution to the prevailing political situation at the time the Constitution was drafted, while separation of powers was part of the Framers' intellectual background, derived from Montesquieu's misinterpretation of contemporary British politics.[87] The entirety of the original Constitution is the product of eighteenth-century thought, of course, but federalism and separation of powers, unlike free speech, just compensation, or checks and balances, may be showing their age in more serious ways. The growth of the administrative state has demanded, or produced, a massive growth in the scope of federal regulation, while spawning a plethora of executive and independent agencies that do not fit within Montesquieu's tripartite structure. Protecting television programs, as well as books and newspapers, from governmental censorship, or compensating property owners for factories as well as farms requires a mere adaptation of a valued principle to changing circumstances. But the eighteenth-century principles of federalism and the separation of powers, as guidelines for organizing government, cannot be readily adopted to a centralized, bureaucratic nation such as ours unless they are extensively reconceptualized. Clearly, the Framers had nothing even vaguely resembling our current government in mind when they ensconced these principles in the Constitution.

None of this, of course, forecloses an interpretation of the Constitution that would give force to these two principles, nor does it preclude the possibility of adapting them to modern circumstances. But the antiquated character of federalism and separation of powers is certainly a sign of trouble. It suggests that these principles cannot be uncritically and unambiguously applied to a group of contemporary court decisions like the prison reform cases. Obviously, these cases violated federalism and the separation of powers as those concepts existed in the eighteenth century. But an entire generation of scholars has acknowledged that the entire structure of modern government violates those principles. In light of this, we might conclude that our modern government is illegitimate and should be restructured or dismantled. Indeed, there are those who make such claims, although no one thinks that the judiciary should undertake the project on its own.[88] But there is another, less cataclysmic possibility – that something about our structural principles is basically defective and that we must reformulate those principles to account for our current practices.

The rule of law appears to be a more enduring principle than federalism or the separation of powers; if anything, its importance increases as the power of modern government expands. Here too, however, our thinking is dominated by concepts of questionable relevance. When we speak of judges following the law, we generally have in mind some preexisting set of rules from which they can derive particular decisions, rules that reside either in the Constitution, statutes, or the common law.[89] In other words, we are thinking of interpretation. It is certainly traditional to regard interpretation as the furthest limit of judicial action comporting with the rule of law. As with federalism and the separation of powers, however, the actual practices of government suggest that there is something wrong with this traditional account.[90]

In fact, we do not even need to rely on contemporary developments in order to identify the limitations of this interpretation-oriented understanding of the rule of law. All legal doctrines must have a beginning, and they often have rather clearly delineated ones. The right of privacy was articulated in the early decades of this century, inspired by Warren and Brandeis's famous article.[91] The First Amendment is part of our Constitution, but the legal doctrine associated with it originated in the 1920s; before then, there were no cases, no general principles, nothing but the bare words of the amendment.[92] The Sherman Act is an enacted statute, but the rule of reason doctrine that flows from it was formulated by the federal judiciary.[93] Even the common law that we received from England, despite its apparently ancient lineage, can often be traced to specific judicial decisions. Negotiable instruments doctrine, for example, was fashioned by eighteenth-century English common-law judges, most notably Lords Holt and Mansfield.[94] This is not to say that legal doctrines are manufactured from thin air; they are products of the surrounding culture, and they often embody preexisting ideas, just like statutes, administrative policies, and works of art. But like these other artifacts, they are shaped and textured by human creativity.

Thus, we can have no complete account of the rule-of-law with respect to judicial decision making unless that account includes the process by which legal doctrines are created. Some decisions fit the standard rule-of-law model, because they involve only fact-finding, and are regarded by all participants as being controlled by precedent or statutory language; some produce varying amounts of uncertainty because they require interpretation, and thus may or may not fit the standard model. But some are simply outside the model, because they create new doctrine. They refer to precedents, or statutes, or the Constitution, but they are not controlled by them in any realistic sense. A theory of the rule of law in judicial decision making that fails to include this final category is simply incomplete.

The judicial discourse that disguises policy making as interpretation is precisely such a theory, and the motivation for it is largely the belief that judicial policy making violates the rule of law. Previously, it was argued that this effort to legitimate judicial action is unpersuasive and that policy making is in fact a separate mode of action in which judges regularly engage. The question that remained was whether the standard model for the rule of law can be restored by rejecting judicial policy making as illegitimate. Among those who share the view that policy making is a separate category, rather than being equivalent to interpretation because of the political or indeterminate character of court decisions, many claim that it is simply an error to be extirpated. As can be seen from the issue of doctrinal creation, however, this view has rather serious consequences. It does not simply assert that judges sometimes, or even frequently, act illegitimately; rather, it implies the view that every series of legitimate judicial decisions has an illegitimate beginning. This is a sort of military conquest theory of law, where an initial act of force becomes legitimate because its perpetrators manage to remain in power.[95] Such an approach may not be demonstrably wrong, but it certainly suggests some difficulties with our traditional conception of the rule of law.

Unlike the difficulties with federalism and the separation of powers, the conceptual problems concerning the rule of law were as applicable in the premodern era as they are today. But contemporary developments have brought these problems to the forefront. Whereas innovation in the law was once regarded with suspicion, it is now hailed as a virtue. Legislators and administrators create law all the time, and the law-creation enterprise occupies a central place in our political discourse. More generally, we view law as an instrument of social policy, not an embodiment of timeless, memory-of-no-man-runneth-to-the-contrary tradition. This renders a theory of judicial decision making that excludes doctrinal creation as rather old-fashioned, and the effort to maintain this theory to secure legitimacy transparent in its insincerity. The assertion that judges did not create doctrine was always false, but at least it was a credible falsehood before the policy-oriented, instrumental character of law became our dominant conception.

The Implications of Judicial Policy Making

A study of judicial policy making, therefore, not only illuminates an underexplored judicial function, but also provides insight into the contradictions and obsolescence of several highly regarded principles for constraining judicial power. The relationship between these two results is far from adventitious. Just as the administrative state provides the model for judicial policy making, it is the principal force behind the decreasing relevance of federalism, separation of powers and our traditional notion of the rule of law.

Administrative agencies regularly transgress the accepted bounds of federalism. In fact, this common observation greatly understates the role of regulation; a central purpose of national regulation is to unify the nation and override its preexisting federalist system. Conversely, the United States effectively abandoned federalism – a notion for which it originally had deep affection – due to its felt need to establish a unified administrative regime. The Reconstruction of the South represented one effort to dispense with federalism, but that effort failed. By the mid-1870s, the South had freed itself from central government supervision and had reinstituted many aspects of its antebellum culture. The growth of the administrative state began shortly thereafter, and it was this process that led to the general demise of state autonomy.

Rejection of the separation-of-powers doctrine is an even more distinctive feature of modern administrative governance. Agencies clearly locate many powers that can plausibly be regarded as legislative or judicial in the executive branch. More significantly, they combine these legislative, judicial, and executive powers into a single institution, with no clearly demarcated divisions between them. The modern administrative agency is a minigovernment that exercises the full range of public power in its area of jurisdiction, but it is a government organized along unified, managerial lines, not the separation of functions into quasi-independent units. These agencies represent a rejection of the eighteenth-century model, designed around the need to control government power, and reflect a newer model concerned with the exercise of that power in a coherent and efficient manner.

Most significant of all, the modern administrative state embodies the concept of the government as a conscious policy maker, rather than a passive adjudicator. The state is held responsible for social problems and is expected to combat them by developing new governmental programs. Law is a major instrumentality for these proactive efforts; conversely, these efforts by Congress or by the administrative agencies generate the vast majority of our laws. Clearly, Congress is not bound by any preexisting set of legal rules or principles, and the agencies are equally free of anything but the Congressional authorization that empowers them. Thus, if the rule of law is to survive in our modern state, it cannot be defined as it has been defined in the judicial context. We must acknowledge the wholesale creation of new legal doctrines and abandon the notion that the rule of law involves fidelity to any preexisting legal principles.

The study of judicial policy making, therefore, is not only the study of one hitherto scorned or hidden function of the judiciary, but also of an emerging legal order. Judges act as policymakers because policy making has become the characteristic mode of governmental action. They ignore the apparent constraints because the validity of those constraints has been eroded by precisely the same developments.

A further implication flows from a recognition of the judicial policy-making process, one that will not be argued for in any systematic fashion, but only illustrated by the specific case that is explored. It is that ideas or conceptions make a difference in government affairs and that the exploration of ideas possesses explanatory power. This is both a substantive and a methodological point. Substantively, federal judges were motivated to depart from the interpretation of legal texts and to make policy in the prison reform cases because of developing conceptions or attitudes about public morality and about the role of the national government in our modern administrative state. They were willing to ignore apparent constraints based on federalism, the separation of powers, and the rule of law because these constraints had lost their conceptual power. And they were able to take action – to carry out a coordinated, consistent, thirty-year-long program of institutional reform – because they succeeded in developing a reconceptualization of the subject institutions.

Admittedly, the structuralist approaches that are in vogue among political scientists these days deny – indeed, deride – the role of ideas in motivating human action. Public choice theory,[96] which relies on microeconomics to predict behavior on the basis of self-interest maximizing, and positive political theory, which uses a broader but equally mechanistic model to explain institutional strategies,[97] argue explicitly and aggressively for the exclusion of ideas as causal explanations for behavior. Both theories provide enormously valuable insights, but their claim that they constitute complete, all-inclusive accounts of their subject matter appears plausible only to their true believers. For purposes of this book, the argument against relying on such structuralist, nonconceptual approaches is contained in the case study and the analysis that accompanies it.

This substantive treatment of ideas as an explanatory force is linked to a methodological one. Political scientists generally describe judicial behavior as a product of judges' attitudes.[98] This is plausible up to a point, but it views the judicial process from afar, without paying much attention to the legal doctrine that judges themselves use. Legal scholars pay great attention to doctrine, but their writing tends to be prescriptive, not descriptive – they frame recommendations to judges about the proper doctrinal arguments to use, rather than analyzing the doctrinal arguments that judges actually employ.[99] In other words, they write from within the doctrinal framework and treat decisions motivated by personal belief as insincere, illegitimate, or requiring reformulation in doctrinal terms.

There is thus something of a methodological gap between the two disciplines. Neither provides a descriptive analysis of judicial decision making that takes full account of legal doctrine and the way that doctrine interacts with other conceptual elements. The result is that beliefs and doctrine are treated as mutually exclusive categories.

Once again, this book adopts the most commonsense hypothesis. It begins from the substantive premise that ideas affect human behavior. They are not the sole determinant, but they are an important one, and will be particularly important for an institution like the judiciary. It then joins a number of contemporary scholars in employing the methodological premise that judicial decisions are determined by two sets of ideas – the judges' personal attitudes and existing legal doctrine.[100] The judicial opinion studies and legal realist critiques, which assert that attitudes control judicial decisions, are partially correct, and the doctrinalists, who assert or assume that legal rules control these decisions, are also partially correct. Thus, there is no attempt to prove anything startling or counterintuitive about the judicial decision making process. The point of the book, rather, is to carry out a microanalysis of the conceptual machinery that constitutes that process – how ideas motivate judicial policy making, how they interact with existing doctrine to produce new policy, how that policy is articulated in doctrinal terms, how the entire process has been affected by conceptual and material developments in our modern, administrative state, and how the interplay between those developments and judicial policy reveals an emerging conceptualization of both law and government.

The Plan of the Book

The structure of this book is straightforward. Part I, comprising Chapters 2, 3, and 4, describes the prison reform cases, and Part II, comprising Chapters 5, 6, and 7, analyzes the cases. Within Part I, Chapter 2 is devoted to an overall history, beginning with a detailed discussion of the pre-1965 cases where the courts refused to intervene, and then proceeding to a brief review of the post-1965 cases. Chapter 3 explores two classic prison reform litigations, Arkansas and Texas, both involving "totality of conditions" orders imposed on the state's entire prison system. In Chapter 4, three shorter case studies explore variations on this basic scheme: the Colorado case, which involved a partial order for a single facility, the Santa Clara County case, which involved a jail, and the Marion case, which involved a federal facility in which the court declined to intervene.

The four chapters in Part II analyze the prison reform cases as an example of judicial policy making. They are organized according to the structure of the classic policy-making model, and invoke the other models to explicate additional aspects of the process. At the same time, these chapters explain why the existing legal principles that the cases seemed to violate proved unpersuasive to the federal judiciary. This simultaneous description and analysis are carried out by linking each legal principle to the stage in the policy-making process that seemed to violate that principle most directly, or most centrally. Thus, Chapter 5 describes how judges identified the problem and selected the goal of imposing a national standard, and then proceeds to explain why they were willing to ignore the principle of federalism that seems to bar a nationalization of this sort. Chapter 6 describes how judges chose the solutions of bureaucratization and rehabilitation as the legal standards for prisons, and simultaneously explains why judges were willing to create such legal standards ab initio, although such an approach seems to violate the rule of law. Chapter 7 describes how judges implemented the solutions they had chosen, and why they ignored the separation of powers doctrine that seems to bar aggressive implementation of this sort. At the same time, it describes how the judges' implementation efforts can be regarded as the policy-making process in its entirety, when the process is viewed from an incrementalist perspective. Finally, Chapter 8 summarizes our description, and suggests some of the more general implications to which the recognition of judicial policy making leads. It also suggests that the legal principles that this process seems to violate are linked by their premodern origins, and owe to these premodern origins the judiciary's willingness to ignore them.

Our final chapter, a coda, not a conclusion, offers some general observations about the effect of the prison reform cases and the future of corrections in America. To end any possible suspense, and to forestall disappointment, it should be noted that we do not offer any conclusion about whether judicial intervention into state prisons was good or bad – that is, whether it achieved a net social benefit. The main reason is that the criteria by which such a determination could be made have not been established. This is an analytic study; its purpose is to provide information and understanding. The conclusions that we do advance involve the nature of the judicial policy-making process and the insights which that process, as it unfolded in the prison reform cases, provides about law and government in our modern, administrative state.

The Case of Judicial Prison Reform

TO UNDERSTAND JUDICIAL POLICY MAKING, it is necessary that the process be described with some particularity. As stated in Chapter 1, this study focuses on a single example of that process, but it is an extremely complex example. Between 1965 and the present time, there have been hundreds of major prison reform cases, many involving multiple decisions, complex orders, and a variety of concomitant events. An added complexity is that these cases do not lend themselves to easy generalizations, and still less to standard images about the way that courts behave. Critics of the prison reform case have correctly pointed out that judicial action in these cases diverges markedly from the traditional dispute resolution role that is ascribed to courts, but it diverges just as markedly from the critics' own image of an imperial, self-righteous judiciary. These diametrically opposed but symbiotic images are familiar enough to exert strong gravitational pulls on decisions that in fact are located in the intervening space; as a result, detailed attention to the facts is necessary if a more complex, modulated description of the cases is to be maintained.

A number of excellent case studies of the prison reform process have been written in recent years, particularly about southern states such as Alabama, Georgia, and Texas. They join another group of studies that describe the entire history of state prison systems, again of southern states such as Louisiana, Mississippi, and Virginia. There is, however, no general history of the prison reform process as it unfolded across the entire nation and over a period of nearly thirty years. In addition, existing case studies do not always focus on the topic of central interest here, namely, the decision-making process that the judges used in dealing with these complex cases.

The next three chapters present a necessarily brief account of the judicial prison reform process. Chapter 2 provides an overview of the entire process. It begins with the period before 1965, when judges regularly rejected the numerous prisoner complaints that were presented to them, sometimes with dismissive contempt, sometimes with agonized regret. It then describes the sudden and dramatic rise of prison reform during the following decade, ending with the current period of ramification, reevaluation, and partial retreat. Chapter 3 focuses on two "classic" cases, Arkansas and Texas. Both are simultaneously typical and extraordinary, which is a reasonably good definition of a classic – typical, in that they represent a larger group of cases in which federal courts reformed the entire prison system of a southern state; yet extraordinary, in that Arkansas was the first of these cases and Texas was by far the largest. Although these two states are neighbors and share certain cultural features that distinguish them even from the other parts of the South, the cases also offer a sharp contrast. The Arkansas litigation was relatively noncontentious, an example of one of the many ways that these cases violate the critics' imagery, while in Texas the conflict between court and prison was unusually intense.

Chapter 4 describes three other cases, representing just some of the many variations on the classic model. The Colorado litigation, which involved a single institution and a less than total set of reforms, is fairly typical of the cases that were litigated in nonsouthern states. The Santa Clara County litigation involves a jail, rather than prison, and a state court, rather than a federal one. Of course, there were also state court cases concerning state prisons, and federal court cases concerning jails, and both patterns occurred both in the South and elsewhere, but this one case identifies some distinctive features of jail (as opposed to prison) litigation, and some distinctive features of state (as opposed to federal) judicial action. Finally, the Marion litigation involved a federal prison, and a particularly notorious one; there were other cases brought against federal prisons, but Marion, despite its extraordinary drama, accurately represents the general pattern.

The term "case," as used in legal education, refers to a written decision, usually by an appellate court, and has been the staple of law school courses since C. C. Langdell introduced the case law method at Harvard in the 1880s. Langdell and his fellow formalists believed that the true and controlling principles of law could be discerned by examining these decisions; no one believes that any more, but his reliance on readily available, primary source material to teach the law has exercised an enormous appeal. To this very day, legal education views common law, statutes, and the Constitution through the lens of written judicial opinions, and casebooks comprised largely of these opinions remain the major teaching tool in nearly every standard law school course.

The five case studies presented in this part are source materials of a rather different nature. Instead of a written judicial decision, they consist of narratives describing a complex, ongoing interaction between a court and a prison or prison system, accompanied by collateral interactions between the court and other governmental agencies, the court and private groups like prisoner's rights organizations, or the court and the appellate courts that reviewed its decision. Instead of being decided at a single moment in time, they extend over periods ranging from five to twenty years. Instead of being contained within the conceptual framework of the law, they involve bargains, negotiations, appeals to public opinion, and a variety of quasi-legal threats and counterthreats.

But it is these descriptions, not the appellate court decisions studied in law school, that constitute the real "cases" of the modern era. Almost every important case involves a story, whether it is a story about business arrangements, social conditions, or institutional relationships. A purely self-contained dispute between two equal, fully competent parties that is resolved by a single decision is probably a rarity, and certainly does not offer much insight into the complexities of our legal system. Perhaps one hundred years of studying written decisions has created the image of the self-contained dispute and single decision as the norm for judicial action, and has thereby fueled the critics' condemnation of the prison cases as deviations from accepted practice, but these extended cases are the real source of insight into modern law. They represent the complex process by which grievances are perceived and articulated, and by which law is mobilized, applied, reconceived, and understood. Everyone acknowledges that law is mixed with politics, at least to some extent, that law is a social process, and that the law as applied is different from the law of the books. The cases found in law school courses mask those realities and engender either the dubious notion that law is autonomous or the opposing view that it is nothing more than a facade for politics, social processes, or exercises of power. The cases presented here reveal those realities, and thus allow for modulated assessments about the relationship of law and social forces.

Consequently, the next three chapters can be viewed as a sort of casebook for the study of law in contemporary society. The cases are perhaps more similar to the case method used in business schools, also developed at Harvard, than to the cases used in law school courses. To be sure, these cases each contain a number of individual judicial decisions, and these decisions will be discussed, but they will be placed in the context of other aspects of the "case." Attention will not be focused on either the statement of facts or the legal reasoning of these decisions, and certainly not on their arguments from text or precedent; rather, the decisions will be viewed as just one component of an ongoing interaction that involves many other elements. It is only through the study of such cases in their entirety, with all their components and complexities, that the true character of judicial policy making can be understood.

An Overview of
Judicial Prison Reform

The Hands-Off Era (1776–1960)

In November 1956, the United States Court of Appeals for the Seventh Circuit affirmed the district court's dismissal of George Atterbury's civil rights suit.[1] Atterbury was a prisoner of the Illinois State Penitentiary at Joliet, commonly known as Stateville. The named defendant in the suit was Stateville's already legendary warden, Joseph Ragen, who had occupied the position for twenty years and had served as the president of the American Correctional Association in 1951.[2] Atterbury's pro se complaint alleged that he had been savagely and systematically beaten by the prison guards, that he had been kept in solitary confinement for two months with no clothes or blankets, that he had been deprived of food for five days, and that his mail had been withheld from him, "including a copy of the Constitution of Illinois sent to him at his request by the Secretary of State."[3] The district court dismissed the suit on its own motion, which meant that, in the court's view, Atterbury had no remedy even if all his allegations were true. In affirming this decision, the court of appeals stated that "such charges of aggression by state prison officials and guards, in spite of the general assertion that they were acting under color of state law, do not state a claim upon which relief can be granted under the federal Civil Rights Act."[4] The court's opinion went on to quote some general principles from other Seventh Circuit cases: " 'The Government of the United States is not concerned with, nor has it power to control or regulate the internal discipline of the penal institutions of its constituent states.' "[5] " 'Inmates of state penitentiaries should realize that prison officials are vested with wide discretion in safeguarding prisoners committed to their custody.' "[6] " 'We think it is well settled that it is not the function of the courts to superintend the treatment and discipline of prisoners in penitentiaries, but only to deliver from imprisonment those who are illegally confined.' '"[7] Atterbury's remedy for his alleged mistreatment was to file a tort suit in Illinois state court against the offending officials.

This was the so-called hands-off doctrine, the dominant federal court approach to prison conditions cases until 1965. Consistent with the principle that we can only perceive and label patterns of our own behavior once that behavior ceases to be natural, the name of this doctrine dates from the early 1960s, when there were already premonitions of its incipient demise.[8] Before then, it was not seen as a doctrine at all, but merely as the proper way for federal courts to respond to the somewhat bewildering flow of prisoner complaints that they received. Most of these complaints were summarily rejected with the casual scorn that courts bestow on pro se petitions advancing untenable legal claims, but there are enough written decisions to illuminate the prevailing rationale.

The hands-off doctrine consisted of both procedural and substantive components. With respect to procedure, claims by prisoners in federal court were necessarily based on violations of the Constitution, and the classic means of bringing such claims forward was to petition for a writ of habeas corpus. In addition, state prisoners could bring suit under the Civil Rights Act of 1871[9] for violation of their constitutional rights[10] and federal prisoners could bring suit under the Constitution itself. All these causes of action, however, were regarded as inappropriate for challenging the conditions of confinement.

Habeas corpus, a venerable English writ, had evolved during the seventeenth century into a means by which courts could review the legality of a prisoner's confinement and order release in appropriate circumstances.[11] Established by statute in the United States,[12] its scope remained narrow until well into the twentieth century.[13] It was not until either *Frank v. Mangum*, in 1915,[14] or *Moore v. Dempsey*, in 1923,[15] that the Supreme Court declared that habeas review was available for constitutional imperfections in the prisoner's trial, and not solely for jurisdictional violations by the trial court. Even after this hurdle had been overcome, federal courts maintained that habeas corpus was directed to the process by which the prisoner had been convicted, and not to the conditions of his subsequent confinement. The standard formulation was that the writ is not designed "to superintend the treatment and discipline of prisoners in penitentiaries, but only to deliver from imprisonment those who are illegally confined."[16] The judges never really explained why this was true; most of them regarded it as a relatively uncontroversial interpretation of the habeas statute.

A further difficulty with habeas corpus was that courts generally believed that the only remedy permitted by the writ was to release the aggrieved prisoner from custody.[17] This seemed perfectly appropriate if there was a due process defect in the trial, for if the conviction was not properly obtained, the defendant should be freed. It was much more problematic for a validly convicted criminal, however; not only were judges reluctant to allow known criminals back on the streets, but the remedy of release bore no obvious relationship to the wrong. A convicted felon who was left naked in an isolation cell for two months should receive clothes and a blanket, and perhaps compensation, not a remission of his validly imposed term of imprisonment.

Finally, habeas corpus was viewed as unavailable to state prisoners unless they had exhausted their state remedies.[18] Prior to the Supreme Court's 1953 decision in *Brown v. Allen*,[19] this meant that, if a remedy was available in state court, including an appeal to the U.S. Supreme Court, the prisoner was required to seek that remedy before applying to the federal court. It also meant that, if the state courts had considered and rejected the prisoner's constitutional objections, federal habeas review was unlikely unless there was a defect in the state's appellate process.[20] Because of the perceived hostility of state courts to prisoners' cases – and since federal courts were generally hostile, state court levels of hostility must have been truly impressive – relegation to those courts was considered a death knell for the prisoner's claim. Even after *Brown*, requiring the prisoner to go through the state appeals process seems to have been viewed as a virtually insurmountable barrier, perhaps because it provided prison authorities with greater opportunity to punish or intimidate the prisoner.

Apart from habeas corpus, state prisoners could also bring actions under the Civil Rights Act, which provides federal remedies against anyone who, acting "under color of" state law, deprives the person of his constitutional rights. This should have been an appealing option because it probably contained no exhaustion requirement, it applied to constitutional violations in any setting, and it provided for a much wider, more flexible range of remedies than habeas, including both injunctions and money damages. But there was also a great procedural impediment to civil rights suits – the phrase "under color of" was often interpreted to mean that the offending conduct had to be authorized by law. A state official who abused a prisoner without specific authorization to do so was regarded as acting on his own authority, and thus subject only to a civil suit in the state courts.[21] Atterbury, for example, asserted that the prison officials who beat him, took away his clothes, and denied him food were acting under color of state law, but, of course, he could not point to any statute authorizing such behavior. Thus, the court dismissed his claim, rejecting his "general assertion" that the prison guards were acting under "color of state law."

The restrictive reading of the Civil Rights Act was challenged by the Supreme Court's 1939 decision in *United States v. Classic,*[22] in which election officials had engaged in fraud, and its 1945 decision in *Screws v. United States,*[23] in which a sheriff lawfully arrested a suspect and then beat him to death. The precise scope of the Civil Rights Act remained uncertain after these decisions, however, allowing the Seventh Circuit to adopt its restrictive reading in the *Atterbury* case. Other federal courts expressed opposing views; the Fifth Circuit read the statute and the Supreme Court cases more expansively, while acknowledging its conclusion to be "paradoxical."[24] The mystery was not definitely resolved until *Monroe v. Pape,*[25] in 1961, held that police officers on duty, no matter how unauthorized or illegal their activities, were clothed with state authority and therefore acting under color of state law.[26]

Unlike state prisoners, federal prisoners could not bring suit under the Civil Rights Act, but in theory they could make the same substantive claims in actions arising directly under the Constitution. But such suits were subject to a limit that resembled the "under color of" state law barrier. While it was clear that a statute repugnant to the Constitution could be invalidated by the federal courts, the remedy for unconstitutional administrative behavior was not clear at all. Injunctions in this area were uncommon until the 1960s[27] and money damages were not available until 1971, when the Supreme Court decided *Bivens v. Six Unknown Agents of the Federal Bureau of Narcotics.*[28]

Quite apart from these procedural barriers, there were serious questions about the scope of the substantive constitutional rights that would provide the basis for a habeas petition, a civil rights suit, or a suit under the Constitution. The most obvious of these questions, although perhaps the least serious hurdle in the prison context, was the controversy about whether the Bill of Rights applied to the states. While this controversy was not resolved until the 1960s,[29] eight members of the Supreme Court were prepared to assume that the Eighth Amendment did apply when they decided Louisiana ex rel *Francis v. Resweber* in 1947.[30]* Moreover, the question was not nearly as central to prison conditions cases as it was to cases based on specific Bill of Rights provisions. Although some of the early

---

* In *Francis v. Resweber,* the State of Louisiana had attempted to execute Francis by electrocution, but had failed to kill him and was now proposing to carry out the execution again, presumably using more electricity. The Court addressed the case on the merits and concluded, by a 5–4 margin, that a second try did not constitute cruel and unusual punishment. The Court's refusal to constitutionalize the age-old taboo about repeating a failed execution – a taboo that frequently resulted in physical attacks on feckless executioners – was based on the unintentional nature of the state's initial failure.

prison cases involved petulant-sounding complaints about disposition of the prisoner's clothing, or participation in a radio program, many contained accounts of neglect or outright torture that would easily satisfy the preincorporation formula that states are forbidden to act in ways "offensive to a decent respect for the dignity of man, and heedless of his freedom."[31] Nonetheless, uncertainty about incorporation did indeed constitute a barrier in certain jurisdictions; as late as 1961, prisoner complaints were rejected on the ground that the Eighth Amendment did not apply to the states.[32]

An apparently more serious substantive barrier was federalism. State prisoner complaints were asking federal courts to intervene in the daily operation of a state administrative institution. There was virtually no precedent for such action, and the courts were reluctant to establish one. Occasionally, the issue of federalism was discussed explicitly in the opinions; more frequently, it was treated as an implicitly understood concern.[33] As the court stated in *Atterbury*, "The government of the United States is not concerned with, nor has it power to control or regulate the internal discipline of the penal institutions of its constituent states."[34]

The heart of the hands-off doctrine, however, was an issue that applied equally to state and federal complaints, and that informed many of the doctrine's more specific limitations. In stating that the "Government of the United States ... [does not have] power to control or regulate the internal discipline of prisoners," or that "prison officials are vested with wide discretion in safeguarding prisoners committed to their custody,"[35] the *Atterbury* court was expressing a deeply held, widespread belief that courts simply should not become involved in the internal management of prisons.[36] This limitation had strong linkages to the separation of powers doctrine, and strong prudential justifications as well, but its basic force was regarded as virtually jurisdictional in nature – internal prison management lay beyond the power of the courts. When the *Atterbury* court spoke of the state's role of "safeguarding prisoners" in response to allegations by a prisoner that he had been beaten, starved, and left naked in an isolation cell, it was not being ironic, but expressing this basic understanding about the allocation of governmental powers.

The Reform Instinct Begins to Emerge (1960–1965)

It is somewhat curious, given the evident hostility of most federal courts to prisoner complaints, that these prisoner complaints kept coming. In fact, there are hundreds of reports of prison cases before 1965, and because courts presumably rejected most of the complaints without bothering to write an opinion, the actual number of complaints must have been many times greater. The most obvious explanation is that time and expense, the two factors that deter people from litigating lost causes, meant relatively little to the prisoners; they had plenty of spare time and most of the complaints cost no money at all when filed pro se. In addition, because convicts frequently harbor an abiding sense that they have been wronged, a lawsuit is a natural way to express that feeling and obtain a welcome trip out of the penitentiary, even if it offers no hope of success. There is also the procedural peculiarity that the traditional habeas corpus petition alleging defects in one's trial names the warden as defendant, because the writ, as it developed in England, instructed the warden to release the prisoner from custody. When a prisoner who was not trained in law sat down to write such a petition, it was natural to point out that the warden had not only refused to release him from custody despite defects in his trial, but also that the warden's guards had beaten the stuffing out of him the day before.[37]

Finally, the prisoner complaints were encouraged by sympathetic language that crept into a number of the federal court opinions. At first, such opinions were rare, but as time went on, they became notably more frequent. In the 1944 case of *Coffin v. Reichard*,[38] a Sixth Circuit panel reversed the trial court dismissal of a federal prisoner's habeas petition. The court briefly noted that the prisoner's claims, if true, revealed actions by the prison guards that were not only cruel, but "contrary to the regulations of the institutions in which he was confined."[39] It then systematically rejected virtually every element of the hands-off doctrine: "The fact that a person is legally in prison does not prevent the use of habeas corpus to protect his other inherent rights," the court said. "The judge is not limited to a simple remand or discharge of the prisoner, but he may remand with directions that the prisoner's civil rights be respected." Most significantly, the court stated that a prisoner retains any rights that have not been specifically taken away from him by law. Far from being a slave of the state, he is merely an incarcerated citizen.[40]

These were grand and, as it turned out, prescient words, although the decision was generally treated as an aberration in the years that followed.[41] There were also several other decisions that, while less definitive than *Coffin*, expressed more human feeling for the prisoners' plight. In *Gordon v. Garrson*, decided in 1948,[42] a state prisoner claimed that he was injured in a prison melee and then mistakenly placed in solitary confinement, where he was denied medical care and subjected to barbarous conditions. The federal district court refused to dismiss his civil rights action, holding that the alleged actions by prison officials occurred under "color of state law." The opinion is not specific about the standard or the remedy, and there is no further decision, but the judge took care to specify the prisoner's allegations – a beating with a blackjack leading to deafness in one ear and ninety-two days in a solitary cell, sleeping on a wet cement floor and being fed only bread and water. Similarly, in ex parte *Pickens*, decided in 1951,[43] the federal court expatiated about the barbarous conditions in an Alaska territorial jail, where forty prisoners were jammed into a tiny, dirty, poorly ventilated room with a coal stove that threatened to incinerate them all. The court denied relief, however, on the ground that it could not instruct the U.S. marshal to create new jail facilities for the prisoners.

The best-known and most dramatic cases of this genre involved fugitives from southern prisons who made their way to the North, were arrested there, and then petitioned for a writ of habeas corpus to prevent being returned to their state of origin. Many of these prisoners were black, and most were fleeing the notorious chain gangs, particularly the ones in Georgia. The exotic cruelties of this peculiarly southern institution had been a fixture in America's public consciousness since the movie *I Am a Fugitive from a Chain Gang*, starring Paul Muni, was released in 1932,[44] and had been regularly featured in the national press. In the leading case, *Johnson v. Dye*, decided in 1949,[45] the Third Circuit ordered the outright release of a fugitive from a Georgia chain gang. After holding that the Eighth Amendment applied to the states, the court stated that it would not "set out . . . the revolting barbarities which Johnson and his witnesses stated were habitually perpetrated as standard chain gang practice."[46] The court went on to observe that recounting these "atrocities in an opinion is to be unfair to the American scene as a whole" – this was, after all, the midst of the cold war[47] – and indicated that it was restoring the "decency and humanity"[48] of that scene by releasing the prisoner from Georgia's clutches.*[49]

The Supreme Court reversed *Johnson v. Dye* in a summary decision[50] consisting entirely of a citation to a single case, which stated the doctrine that a prisoner must exhaust state remedies before petitioning the federal courts.[51] Three years later, in a similar case named *Sweeney v. Woodall*,[52] the Court confirmed this conclusion in a full opinion. There was, however, a spirited dissent from Justice Douglas, who argued that the prisoner should not be returned to Georgia and "forced to run a gambit of blood and terror,"[53] while awaiting the exhaustion of his state court remedies. Although the majority was not prepared to support this breach of standard

---

* The concurring opinion in this case also explains why so many of the fugitive cases happened to involve Georgia prisoners. Apparently, it was Georgia's practice at this time to solve its prison crowding problem by permitting its prisoners to escape to the North. Some 175 prisoners had escaped at the same time that Johnson did; indeed, there were so many that all but one of the witnesses at his trial were also escaped Georgia convicts who happened to be at the very same jail where Johnson was being held.

doctrine in the name of human decency, its silence on the substantive issue could be taken, if one were so inclined, as tacit approval of *Johnson v. Dye*. Thus, several federal trial courts chose to follow the Third Circuit opinion and at least two prisoners were actually released.[54] The tone of these decisions clearly indicates a growing revulsion toward southern penal practices and a growing discomfort with the doctrine that courts should not intervene in the management of prisons. In response, more and more complaints pullulated out of the nation's long-ignored and judicially rejected prison population.[55]

The *Atterbury* case is one of the last federal court decisions to dismiss a prisoner complaint in categorical terms. By the mid 1950s and early 1960s, a different tone had emerged, and all the barriers that had previously seemed so adamantine began to dissipate. A number of courts held that habeas corpus was available for complaints about prison conditions as well as trial procedures,[56] that it could provide remedies other than release,[57] and that it did not invariably require exhaustion of state remedies.[58] Actions by prison officials, even if they were not authorized by state statutes, were held to be under color of state law for purposes of the Civil Rights Acts.[59] The Eighth Amendment was applicable to the states,[60] federalism was not such a serious concern,[61] and the federal courts did indeed seem to have a role in holding prison officials to constitutional standards.[62] There remained, to be sure, at least as many published decisions which relied on these well-established elements of the hands-off doctrine in rejecting prisoner complaints,[63] but they became increasingly qualified and increasingly fact-dependent as the mid-1960s approached.

To some extent, these changes may be attributed to major Supreme Court decisions in nonprison cases, most notably *Brown v. Allen*, the habeas corpus case; *Monroe v. Pape*, the Civil Rights Act case, and *Robinson v. California*, the Eighth Amendment incorporation case. To some extent, they may be attributed to the same changing attitudes that underlay these cases, and were about to produce the Civil Rights Act of 1964.[64] There was, in addition, an internal dynamic in the prison cases themselves. The more the federal courts relented, the more prisoners filed complaints; the more complaints that courts received and seriously considered, the more distressing the conditions in American prisons appeared to the federal judges.

A particular manifestation of this internal dynamic involved the Black Muslim cases of the early 1960s. Most prisoner complaints were brought pro se, by a prisoner whose motivation was a sense of grievance and a lot of spare time; a few were initiated or assisted by individual attorneys. The Black Muslim cases were the first complaints brought by an organized group as part of a consistent strategy. While the existence of this group depended on the Muslims' own organizational abilities, the choice of litigation as a strategy reflected the developing sense that relief could be obtained from the federal courts.

In fact, prison officials who wanted to suppress the Muslims found themselves in a difficult situation. Ever since the inception of American penitentiaries, the inmates had generally been provided with adequate opportunity for religious observance.[65] This was not conceived as a right, but as a means of reform, rehabilitation, or discipline. Since virtually all prisoners were Christians, religious services had seemed like a positive force, administered by law-abiding individuals and encouraging law-abiding conduct.[66] To suppress the Black Muslims, therefore, prison officials were compelled to deny prisoners something that they had always been granted. They advanced the usual claim about internal prison management, but in this case the managerial decision involved distinguishing among religions on the basis of their content. Federal courts were fully accustomed to adjudicating this issue, and they had regularly invalidated such distinctions.[67]

Thus, while some courts continued to accept the internal management rationale,[68] others asserted that "a charge of religious persecution falls in quite a different category" from general claims about conditions in prison.[69] Most notably, the Supreme Court reversed the Seventh Circuit's decision in *Cooper v. Pate*.[70] Cooper, like Atterbury, was a prisoner at Stateville, and his central complaint was that he had been denied a copy of the Koran, while other prisoners received copies of the King James Bible. In rejecting this claim, the Seventh Circuit recited its usual litany – that the courts are not supposed to superintend the treatment of prisoners but only release those who are illegally confined, that state prisons are not under the supervision of the federal courts, and that prison authorities have the responsibility for "safe-guarding the prisons."[71] It also took judicial notice of the violent, antiauthoritarian nature of the Black Muslim movement, on the basis of "authoritative racial studies," and speculated that the Supreme Court would do so as well, since it had, after all, taken cognizance of such social science studies when it decided *Brown v. Board of Education*.[72] In fact, the Supreme Court reversed per curiam in a one-paragraph decision that consisted primarily of citations from two other circuit courts that were apparently able to discern their views about race, religion, and social science somewhat better than the Seventh Circuit.[73]

According to James Jacobs, the decision in *Cooper v. Pate* was the "Supreme Court's first modern prisoners' rights case."[74] As he recognizes, however, the holding was a narrow one; indeed, it seems fair to say that *Cooper* was only a prisoners' rights case, and not a prison reform case. The same is true of all the other decisions that had gradually dismantled the hands-off doctrine during the decade before 1965. Many of these declare that the prisoner had stated a claim on which relief could be granted, and that the complaint should not be dismissed without a hearing. There were very few that actually ordered relief, however, and these were limited to a specific prisoner, or a specific, readily recognized claim like religious discrimination. Something was changing to be sure, but there was little indication that those changes would lead to a comprehensive transformation of American prisons. As late as 1965, few people among the judges, prisoners, and even proponents of judicial intervention[75] imagined that courts could do any more than validate specified rights for specified groups of prison inmates.

The Reform Movement in Full Stride (1965–1986)

The Arkansas prison litigation began in 1965, with the decision by the United States District Court for the Eastern District of Arkansas in *Talley v. Stevens*.[76] That litigation will be described in detail in the following chapter. It was striking from the outset because of the savage and quasi-feral character of the Arkansas prisons that the prisoners' complaints revealed, but its truly extraordinary features became apparent over the course of the next several years, as the court's orders grew in scope. Finally, in 1970, the court held that the Arkansas prison system in its entirety was in violation of the Eighth Amendment, and placed the system under a comprehensive court order that was tantamount to federal receivership.[77] This was the first "totality of conditions" decision. By basing its rationale on the Eighth Amendment, and thus using the Civil Rights Act as its source of legal remedies, the court avoided all the complexities and limitations of habeas corpus and struck directly at the conditions under which prisoners in Arkansas were being held.

Fifteen years before *Talley*, the general view had been that the federal courts lacked jurisdiction over any American prisons, whether state or federal. Even if prisoners were allowed to bring a habeas corpus, Civil Rights Act, or constitutional case, it would be rejected on the merits because the internal management of prisons was the realm of prison officials, not of the judiciary. Five years before *Talley*, views had begun to change, so that courts could imagine granting relief to a particular prisoner who was brutalized by the guards, or to a group of prisoners who had been denied a specific constitutional right that was cognizable in the outside world, such as the right to be free from religious discrimination. Now, unheralded by theory or political demands, and unexpected by those most interested in the outcome, a complete transformation in the position of the federal judiciary was underway.

There followed a dramatic proliferation of prison decisions. In the five-year period after the Arkansas case was decided, federal courts declared prisons in Mississippi,[78] Oklahoma,[79] Florida,[80] Louisiana,[81] and Alabama[82] to be unconstitutional, in whole or part. Five years after that, prisons or prison systems in twenty-eight more jurisdictions had been added to this lugubrious list; at present, forty-eight of America's fifty-three jurisdictions*[83] have had at least one facility declared unconstitutional by the federal courts, and the judicial intervention has produced direct effects of considerable significance in all but a handful of them.[84] Moreover, there have been numerous cases involving jails, as well as prisons, and still other cases decided by state courts.[85] The federal cases against state prisons were the first ones and the most important, but they were only one part of a larger process.

These federal decisions varied in their scope, of course. Sometimes they involved only a single institution in the state, or a single aspect of several institutions. In Iowa, for example, the principal intervention has been against the state penitentiary at Fort Madison;[86] in Maryland, several facilities have been declared unconstitutional, but only on the grounds that they were overcrowded.[87] On the other hand, some decisions, or series of decisions, have been directed at virtually every aspect of every institution in the state; apart from Arkansas, this has been true in at least nine other states: Alabama, Alaska, Delaware, Mississippi, New Mexico, Rhode Island, South Carolina, Tennessee, and Texas.[88]

At the same time that these rather dramatic Eighth Amendment cases were being decided, federal courts were also continuing and expanding the more limited themes that had been sounded toward the end of the hands-off era. They reaffirmed the principle that prisoners deserved some measure of religious liberty[89] and the even more obvious principle that the same measure of religious liberty must be granted to followers of one religion as is granted to followers of another.[90]† They expanded prisoners' First Amendment rights to receive mail and published material.[91] They invoked the equal protection clause to forbid segregated facilities,[92] and the due process clause to require hearings before discipline could be imposed.[93] Most readily of all – since it was recognized even during the height of the hands-off era and was a predicate for any other rights – they guaranteed prisoners access to attorneys, legal materials, and the courts.[94]

The upshot of the Eighth Amendment cases and the more specific

---

* These jurisdictions are the fifty states, the District of Columbia, the Commonwealth of Puerto Rico, and the Virgin Islands, which is a territory.

† Prisoners were quick to test the limits of this principle, based on the metaphysical complexities of deciding what constitutes a religion. Thus, the federal courts adjudicated the rights of Satanists and Eclaterians during this period. Eclaterianism, incidentally, was a religion organized by inmates, and constituted the divine doctrine of the Church of the New Song of Universal Life, or CONS.

decisions based on other constitutional provisions was that the federal courts ended up promulgating a comprehensive code for prison management, covering such diverse matters as residence facilities, sanitation, food, clothing, medical care, discipline, staff hiring, libraries, work, and education. The decisions themselves, and often the resulting body of law, specify many requirements in what can be described, depending on one's perspective, as painstaking or excruciating detail; the wattage of the light bulbs in the cells, the frequency of showers, and the caloric content of meals are all part of the code that the federal courts have promulgated. This code has now been summarized in treatises on "prison law" and in self-help manuals for prisoners themselves.[95] Prison systems and individual prisons throughout the country have hired attorneys to ensure that they are in compliance with it; even states or facilities that escaped direct suits or weathered such suits and obtained favorable judgments know that they can be sued or sued again if they fail to comply with the multifarious provisions of the judicially promulgated code.

Comprehensive as the prison reform process has been, its impact upon prisons themselves has been far from uniform. The process took shape, and exercised its most transformative effects, on prison systems in the southern states. Of the first six cases, five, and arguably six, involved systems in the South.*[96] Ultimately, comprehensive orders involving the totality of conditions in the entire prison system were issued against six of the eleven southern states: Alabama,[97] Arkansas,[98] Mississippi,[99] South Carolina,[100] Tennessee,[101] and Texas;[102] comprehensive orders were issued regarding the principal maximum security facility, as well as numerous smaller facilities, in Georgia[103] and Louisiana.[104] In addition, court orders were entered against the entire Florida system[105] and virtually all the North Carolina prisons regarding overcrowding and certain specified conditions.[106]

In contrast, only four of the thirty-nine states outside the South have been subject to comprehensive orders against their entire system – Alaska, Delaware, New Mexico, and Rhode Island – and since one of these, Rhode Island, has only one major prison, the distinction between a systemwide and single institution case is not meaningful in that context. The nine states where there has been no litigation, or where the litigation has not

---

* The sixth state was Oklahoma, which can be characterized in various ways. Of course, "the South" is not a precisely defined term. Perhaps the most general definition would be the eleven states of the Confederacy; this would include Tennessee, although much of it, particularly the western part where southern sentiment was strongest, was occupied by the Union for most of the Civil War. Oklahoma was not a state during the Civil War, but it was part of the Confederacy for all practical purposes.

produced any significant court orders, all lie outside the South.*[107] To be sure, there has been rather extensive litigation in the remaining twenty-nine or thirty nonsouthern states. The typical pattern was that individual facilities were subjected to court orders, often on specific grounds, although sometimes on their totality of conditions. Quite often, the issue that drove these suits was overcrowding.†[108] This was also an issue in the southern states, but there it tended to merge into more general concerns about the entire range of carceral conditions.

An even more striking contrast involves the federal Bureau of Prisons. Although it is the third largest prison system in the United States, after California and Texas, there has never been a court order against it that significantly affected its operations.[109] The decision that had the potential to produce such an effect was the litigation leading to *Bell v. Wolfish*,[110] in which the district court found unconstitutional crowding in New York City's federal jail. While this decision was upheld on appeal,[111] it was reversed by the Supreme Court in a 1979 opinion that adumbrated the period of retrenchment in judicial prison reform.[112] The federal penitentiary at Marion, a supermaximum facility that, for many years, imposed the strictest control on inmates of any prison in the nation, was under frequent legal attack, but, as will be discussed in Chapter 4, the courts generally declined to intervene.

The difference between the South and the remainder of the nation is also apparent from an examination of correctional expenditures. Since costs for publicly run facilities of all kinds have increased substantially during the past thirty years, and prison costs have necessarily increased as a result of burgeoning inmate populations, any particular impact of the prison cases is rather difficult to measure. William Taggart has carefully examined the first ten conditions cases and concluded that the budgetary impact of the court decisions is somewhat less than what would be expected and substantially less than what the criticisms of judicial intervention would lead one to believe.[113] Of the five states where Taggart found that statistically significant increases occurred, however, four are in the South – Alabama, Arkansas, Louisiana, and Mississippi – and the fifth, Oklahoma, is arguably southern.[114]

The various patterns that characterize the prison reform cases – reliance on the Eighth Amendment, willingness to address a wide range of

---

* No litigation: Minnesota, New Jersey, and North Dakota. Litigation of very limited scope: Maine, Massachusetts, Montana, Nebraska, Vermont, and Wyoming.
† This pattern also applies to Virginia, the only southern state that did not have at least its principal facility declared unconstitutional in its entirety, or its entire system declared unconstitutional on at least one major issue.

conditions and to develop detailed rules, condemnation of the southern state prisons, scrutiny of the nonsouthern state prisons, and deference toward the federal prisons – emerge with clarity because of the virtual unanimity of the decisions in the 1970s and early 1980s. Although they were venturing into unchartered territory, the federal courts moved forward with an apparent lack of uncertainty or regret. There are virtually no decisions that revive the rationale of the hands-off doctrine, or even the reservations about the unprecedented, highly interventionist stance that the courts had adopted. There are, moreover, few cases that diverge very far from the general idea, first articulated in the Arkansas litigation, of what constitutes admirable, passable, and reprehensible correctional practices.

This unanimity was certainly not the product of Supreme Court leadership. The Court, which was basically conservative after Warren Burger became chief justice in 1969, played only a minor role in the prison reform process. It produced several decisions confirming the existence of specific constitutional rights in the prison context in the decade following the initiation of the Arkansas litigation.[115] The most important of these was *Wolff v. McDonnell* (1974),[116] which held that prisoners could not be deprived of "good time" credit for disciplinary infractions without a written notice, a hearing of some sort, and a written statement of reasons for the decision. To reach this issue, the Court was necessarily required to decide whether prisoners had any constitutional rights at all. Justice White, writing for a unanimous Court, declared in ringing phrases that they did, thus confirming the demise of the hands-off doctrine. He said: "But though his rights may be diminished by the needs and exigencies of the institutional environment, a prisoner is not wholly stripped of his constitutional protections when he is imprisoned for crime. There is no iron curtain drawn between the Constitution and the prisons of this country."[117]

This decision was important, for it indicated that the Supreme Court would not use its power to quash the prison reform movement, and it provided a surprisingly strong endorsement to the principle that prisoners have rights. For example, the Fifth Circuit Court of Appeals withheld its ruling on an appeal from the District Court order in the Mississippi litigation until *Wolff v. McDonnell* was decided. Once that decision was issued, it felt free to affirm the order in its entirety.[118] But *Wolff* hardly placed the Court at the forefront of the process or provided guidance for the mass of cases that were just then moving through the lower courts. Justice White followed his "iron curtain" declaration with a list of the rights prisoners had been held to "enjoy," including access to the courts, due process, and equal protection, and a list of prior cases that had recognized these rights, but he did not mention the Eighth Amendment, and he did not cite any of the Arkansas decisions or the recent district court decision in the Mississippi litigation.[119] The only reference to prison conditions in the opinion is to indicate that these conditions provide a rationale for limiting due process rights to a greater extent than would be desirable in other circumstances.[120] In fact, one could view *Wolff v. McDonnell* as being not a prison case at all, but a due process case involving prisoners. It is part of the important line of cases that began with *Goldberg v. Kelly*,[121] which held that due process rights are available in administrative settings such as welfare benefits termination, public employment termination, and license revocation. It followed naturally, if not ineluctably, from two earlier decisions that required a hearing before revocation of probation or parole.[122] The principal issue in the case, and the one that drew dissents from two members of the Court, involved the precise modifications that should be permitted in the disciplinary hearing because it was occurring in a prison context.[123]

A somewhat more direct confirmation of the prison reform process came in 1976 with the Supreme Court's decision in *Estelle v. Gamble*.[124] This was a pro se civil rights action against the Texas prison system – quite separate from the massive litigation that is described in Chapter 3 – claiming that the petitioner had been denied necessary medication. Justice Marshall, writing for the Court, concluded that the facts did not support this claim, but went out of his way to note that "deliberate indifference" to a prisoner's serious illness or injury states a cause of action under § 1983.*[125] Consequently, this case, whose very presence in the Court bewildered Justice Stevens,[126] can be regarded as a sotto voce signal to the lower courts that they should continue on their course. Two years later, the Supreme Court affirmed one of the remedial orders in the Arkansas litigation.[127] Justice Stevens's opinion continues the tone set by *Wolff*, briefly describing the horrors of the pre-1965 Arkansas prisons, affirming the application of the Eighth Amendment to prison conditions, and speaking with approval of the district court. The only issues that were presented in the appeal, however, were the legitimacy of "placing a maximum limit of 30 days on confinement in punitive isolation; and . . . an award of attorney's fees to be paid out of Department of Corrections funds."[128] Most of the discussion in the case involved the attorney's fee award, which was affirmed by a vote of six to three;[129] the thirty-day limit

---

* To distinguish deliberate indifference from an accidental deprivation, such as negligent malpractice, the Court cited *Louisiana ex rel. Francis v. Resweber*, the insufficient electricity case. That case held that subjecting Francis to a second execution did not constitute cruel and unusual punishment because the first failure was not intentional. Thus, the issue of intentionality entered the prison reform cases.

was affirmed much more summarily and drew a dissent only from Justice Rehnquist. He wrote: "No person of ordinary feeling could fail to be moved by the Court's recitation of the conditions formerly prevailing in the Arkansas prison system. Yet I fear that the Court has allowed itself to be moved beyond the well-established bounds limiting the exercise of remedial authority by the federal district courts."[130] That statement clearly summarizes the dominant view, on all sides, of the prison reform cases. The question was whether the Court would conclude that the extraordinary remedies that the district court had imposed were legally impermissible; the Supreme Court of the 1970s and early 1980s did not do.

Congress did not play an active role in the prison reform movement either. Prisoners, of course, are not a particularly influential group with politicians, and not a particularly popular one either; in all likelihood, the legislators were relieved to see the federal courts assume the burden of correcting what virtually everyone regarded as an intolerable situation. It was not until 1980 that Congress took action by passing the Constitutional Rights of Incarcerated Persons Act (CRIPA, unfortunately).[131] Once passed, the act promptly became a dead letter because the Reagan administration refused to enforce it, and occasionally went so far as to use the intervention rights granted by the act to appear on the side of the institutional defendant.

Perhaps the most notable external force that contributed to the actions of the lower federal courts was neither the Supreme Court nor Congress, but the prisoners and prisoners' rights lawyers who supplied the courts with ever expanding numbers of complaints. In 1960, prisoners filed a total of 872 habeas corpus and civil rights claims, less than 2 percent of all federal court filings. By 1965, the number had increased to 5,329, or 12 percent, and by 1971 it reached 12,145, or 18 percent of all filings.[132] The significance of this surge in prisoner filings is not entirely clear, however. To begin with, the bulk of the claims filings were pro se and did not state a justiciable claim; they were reviewed and rejected after just a few minutes of scrutiny by the judges' clerks, student clerks, or secretaries. Second, the causal relationship between the upsurge in claims and the federal court cases is difficult to determine; it is quite possible that the surge in petitioners was a dependent variable, elicited by the judicial decisions.

Some evidence that the upsurge in petitions is indeed a dependent variable is provided in a study by Jim Thomas that disaggregates both state and federal prisoner filings into habeas corpus petitions and civil rights complaints. Comparing 1966 to 1961, the number of habeas filings by state prisoners increased by over five thousand, perhaps because the federal courts had begun to abandon the hands-off doctrine and to award limited relief for specific constitutional violations. The number of civil rights complaints, however, increased by less than two hundred. Between 1966 and 1971, when the federal court in the Arkansas case was issuing the first comprehensive orders on civil rights grounds, the increase in absolute numbers for habeas and civil rights cases was similar – about three thousand – but the rate of increase was 53 percent for habeas petitions and 1,237 percent for civil rights petitions. Between 1971 and 1981, as federal courts throughout the nation issued comprehensive civil rights orders, habeas filings by state prisoners declined 14 percent, from 9,230 to 7,968, but civil rights filings rose another 536 percent, from 2,915 to 15,639. In 1986, as the period of retrenchment set in, both categories of claims had increased at a moderate and roughly equal rate over the 1981 level.[133]

Federal filings exhibit a different pattern. While the number of habeas petitions for each year that Thomas sampled has been about 40 percent of the number of state prisoner petitions, with an increase to 50 percent in 1976, the number of civil rights complaints has risen slowly and remained small. As a result, these complaints were only 7 percent of the number of state prisoner filings in 1971, and declined to 5 percent in 1981 and 4 percent by 1986.[134] The figures appear to reflect the refusal of the federal courts to hold federal prison practices unconstitutional on Eighth Amendment grounds.

It seems unlikely that the distribution of prisoner claims, most of them pro se, is changing in response to some internally generated dynamic. The more plausible hypothesis is that these claims are simply responding to the changes in federal court doctrine. Of course, some of the claims are filed by sophisticated prisoners' rights attorneys, and there is no question that many of these attorneys possess well-developed, independently conceived agendas. As the case studies in Chapters 3 and 4 suggest, however, it was often the judge who selected the attorney, rather than the attorney who selected the judge, the issue, or the case. In short, the prisoner petitions were probably no more of an influence on the pattern of decisions than the Supreme Court or Congress. It was the federal courts themselves that not only initiated the prison reform movement but established its specific contours.

Winding Down – The Reform Movement in Retreat (since 1986)

The history of American prison reform movements has been a cycle of sharp peaks of intense moral indignation followed by broad valleys of quiescence. Prison reform through litigation may be following this time-honored sequence. Since the late 1980s, the decline of momentum in prison conditions litigation has been abundantly evident. Several factors account for this decline: first, many judges (and, quietly, some prisoners' attorneys) acknowledge that the worst conditions have been eliminated and that the challenge has shifted to administrative efforts, not test-case litigation. Certainly the horrors that caused such anguish during the hands-off era which led to such decisive action once that era ended, have now been thoroughly discredited, and a new institutional structure and ethos have emerged. Even the resurrection of the "chain gang" by prison officials in Alabama and the sheriff of Maricopa County, Arizona, bears scant resemblance – other than high public visibility – to their counterparts of the 1950s. Second, changes in the political environment have not been conducive to continued support for a politics of rights, and especially for prisoners' rights. The rights revolution has run its course, although prison conditions litigation was among the last areas to be affected. The cumulative efforts of both the Reagan and Bush administrations – the rhetoric, the policies, and the appointments to the federal bench – were not the stuff to sustain rights litigation as a source of social change. Finally, the dramatic increase in the prison population since the early 1980s represents a harsher response to criminal offenders, which has translated into a growing impatience with court-ordered improvements in prisons and jails.

Although the Supreme Court was not a leader in creating the judicial prison reform effort, it has proved to be a leader in the retrenchment process. Perhaps the first clear sign of this role came in *Bell v. Wolfish* (1979),[135] where the Court reversed a lower-court decision holding the federal jail in New York City unconstitutional on a wide variety of grounds. The reversal itself was not particularly surprising. The federal Bureau of Prisons has always fared well in federal court, and the facility in question was a newly built one that, in the Court's view, "differs markedly from the familiar image of a jail."[136] But Justice Rehnquist, now writing for the six-judge majority, took the occasion to admonish the lower federal courts for their interventionist attitudes: "In recent years, however, these courts largely have discarded this 'hands-off' attitude and have waded into this complex arena. . . . But many of the same courts have, in the name of the Constitution, became increasingly enmeshed in the minutiae of prison operations. . . . But under the Constitution, the first question to be answered is not whose plan is best, but in what branch of the Government is lodged the authority to initially devise the plan."[137] The image of wading into an arena suggests a mud fight, but one cannot really become "enmeshed" in mud; as the last quoted sentence makes clear, the instinct that lies behind Rehnquist's mixed but vivid imagery is the legal process idea that each government institution has its own area of competence, and that the judiciary's area does not include policy making.[138]

A more direct but moderate reproof to the federal courts deciding state prison cases came in 1981 when the Supreme Court reversed the court below in *Rhodes v. Chapman*,[139] which was, significantly, one of the first conditions decisions involving a nonsouthern state.[140] As both the majority and dissent prominently noted, this was the first Supreme Court case to consider the centerpiece of the judicial prison reform process, that is, the application of the Eighth Amendment to conditions of confinement.[141] In his majority opinion for reversal, Justice Powell adopted a more moderate tone than Justice Rehnquist had. He acknowledged that the Eighth Amendment, despite its mere "three words,"[142] imposed limits on state prison practices and strongly implied that Arkansas and Texas, whose prison systems had been before the Court on other grounds, had exceeded those limits.[143] Mere double-celling of prisoners, however, which was the issue in *Chapman*, did not constitute a violation of the Eighth Amendment: "To the extent that such conditions are restrictive and even harsh, they are part of the penalty that criminal offenders pay for their offenses against society."[144] Justice Brennan, joined by Blackmun and Stevens, was satisfied to agree with this decision on the facts and emphasize that "today's decision should in no way be construed as a retreat from careful judicial scrutiny of prison conditions."[145] Perhaps Brennan felt that it should not be construed as a retreat but, of course, it was.[146] Overcrowding has turned out to be the most serious ongoing issue involving the conditions of confinement, and the decision's declaration that double-celling does not violate the Eighth Amendment stands as an impediment to many of the more interventionist solutions to this issue that courts might otherwise have imposed. *Chapman* certainly did not end the judicial reform process, but it suggested that the movement had passed its apogee.

During the course of the past decade, the Court has produced a number of decisions that decrease the scope of the specific constitutional guarantees that federal courts had previously established. Prisoners' rights of free speech,[147] due process,[148] legal access,[149] and free exercise of religion [150] have all been scaled back; in addition, the Court authorized defendants to reopen consent decrees that have become unworkable or counterproductive.[151] But the case that signals a true retrenchment is *Wilson v. Seiter*, decided in 1991.[152] *Wilson*'s specific holding had been anticipated in 1986 by the Court's rather peculiar decision in *Whitley v. Albers*.[153] In *Whitley*, a prisoner argued that being purposely shot during a riot in which he was not participating constituted cruel and unusual punishment. The opinion, which is drenched with dread about the violent nature of prisoners,*[154]

---

* It also employs an incorrect standard for interpreting the facts of the case. The district court granted a directed verdict to the defendant. As Justice Marshall's dissent points out, this means that, on appeal from that verdict, the facts must be viewed in the light most favorable to the plaintiffs. But the Court seems to

holds that the level of intent required to find an Eighth Amendment violation is higher during a prison riot. *Wilson* generalizes the result in *Whitley*; it holds that conditions must be specifically imposed as punishment, or must be the result of wanton behavior by correctional officials.[155] Wantonness, the Court explained, in an opinion by Justice Scalia, depends on the circumstances; demonstrating a real flair for precise moral distinctions, he held that wantonness in an emergency situation would consist of acting "maliciously and sadistically," whereas wantonness in an ordinary situation would consist only of acting with "deliberate indifference" (which is, of course, something of an oxymoron).[156] Since *Wilson* involved the latter type of claim, the Court reversed a summary judgment for the defendants and remanded the case.

Wilson appears to raise a substantial barrier to Eighth Amendment suits against state prisons; it is conceivable that the case could preclude most conditions of confinement suits on the ground that the conditions are the result of an insufficiently trained staff, an insufficiently funded operational budget, an insufficiently large physical plant, or any of the other insufficiencies that genuinely bedevil state prison systems. Certainly Justice Scalia, who adopts his typically snide tone in answering Justice White's concurrence, fails to address White's perceptive observation that "wantonness" is an incoherent notion when dealing with institutional behavior.[157]

But neither the Supreme Court nor the lower federal courts seem to have treated *Wilson* as a watershed. One year later, in *Helling v. McKinney*, the Supreme Court held that the threatened exposure of a nonsmoking prisoner to secondhand tobacco smoke could constitute cruel and unusual punishment.[158] Although insisting that the case must be decided by means of the *Wilson* test of deliberate indifference, the mood of the opinion is certainly more favorable to the idea of prisoners' rights and judicial intervention. Similarly, in *Farmer v. Brennan*,[159] decided in 1994, the Court held that the *federal* prison system could have violated the Eighth Amendment when it placed a transsexual male who "projects feminine characteristics"[160] in the general prison population. There are also a number of important conditions cases that have been decided by the lower courts since *Wilson*, or that are currently under consideration.[161]

Federal officials in the Reagan and Bush administrations also sent a signal that social engineering, at least for society's most vulnerable members, was to be frowned upon. In the late 1980s and 1990s, Justice Department lawyers took the lead in settling several highly visible conditions cases in ways that were advantageous to the defendant institutions.[162] In

balance each side's contentions, pointing out, for example, that the plaintiffs' expert testimony "was controverted by" the defendants.

addition, they were successful in bringing some long-standing cases to a close and in terminating the court's jurisdiction, even as other plaintiffs' attorneys continued to present evidence showing lack of full compliance.

Finally, Congress has taken some bites out of the judiciary's Eighth Amendment jurisprudence. The Violent Crime Control and Enforcement Act of 1994 contains a provision, known as the Helms amendment, which prohibits courts from finding prisons or jails overcrowded unless an individual prisoner can prove that the crowding constitutes cruel and unusual punishment.[163] The Prison Litigation Reform Act extends this principle to all issues, requiring courts to link their remedial orders to specific constitutional violations. In addition, it allows corrections officials to reopen consent decrees to which they had previously agreed, thus codifying the Court's decision to the same effect.[164] Finally, the Anti-Terrorism and Effective Death Penalty Act of 1996 limits the ability of prisoners to file habeas corpus petitions.

Thus, in the 1990s, the judicial prison reform process has suffered a succession of heavy blows from the Supreme Court, the Administration, and Congress. It appears that the era of the big case is over and that the whole process has entered a prolonged period of retrenchment. But the process has also proved to be surprisingly resilient, perhaps because it has become institutionalized. Furthermore, there continue to be serious problems in selected types of institutions, such as women's prisons, the uncounted thousands of local jails, and the vast network of custodial facilities and programs for juveniles. The conditions in women's prisons seem to be a particular source of concern at present.[165] Although complaints against such institutions are not likely to uncover the range of problems found in the earliest and biggest conditions cases, they may reveal serious problems. Such legal challenges are now part of the correctional landscape across the United States, and will probably continue despite the shift in the political and legal climate. In short, the nation's prisons, jails, and juvenile facilities have been constitutionalized, and there is no sentiment to turn back the clock to where it was in 1965, before the Arkansas litigation. In all states, officials have become proactive in inspecting conditions in their custodial facilities, aggressive in trying to resolve shortcomings, and anxious to avoid litigation. Such actions are sustained under a web of rules and procedures that were put in place as a result of the Eighth Amendment and related cases, and they are not likely to wither away and die even during a civil rights drought.

Two Classic Prison Reform Cases: Arkansas and Texas

Arkansas

Introduction: A Legacy of Neglect (1838–1965)

Throughout its history the Arkansas prison system experienced cycles of scandal, response, neglect, and repeated scandal, each scandal triggered by a mixture of corruption, mismanagement, and cruelty. High-level prison officials pilfered desperately needed funds and resources, low-level ones indulged some of humanity's basest inclinations, and all operated with a casual disregard of the prisoners' well-being that often seemed designed to hasten them into the next world rather than to discipline them in this one. Responses, which varied from active reform to cautious retrenchment, were invariably succeeded by extended periods of neglect until some new scandal roused state officials and began the cycle once again.

This lugubrious history began in 1838 when the frontier state of Arkansas, following the fashion that had swept the nation in the Jacksonian era, built itself a modern, stone-walled penitentiary.[1] For several years, the penitentiary was operated as a state agency, but after the inmates revolted in 1846, burning down the main building together with the inmate records, a new, less secure facility was built and turned over to a private contractor. He was expected to relieve state officials of the responsibility for running a prison and to provide them with much-needed revenue by leasing out the able-bodied prisoners as shoemakers, blacksmiths, and butchers. Like most such prisons for profit, this one was riddled with abuse and scandal, and in 1853 Arkansas abandoned convict leasing and built a second penitentiary. Still enamored of the market, however, and

51

still reluctant to assume full responsibility, it turned over day-to-day management to another private contractor.

During the Civil War the penitentiary was used as a hospital and then destroyed; afterward, rather than rebuild its physical facility, the bankrupt state reintroduced convict leasing as an economy move. But once again, the lease system generated scandals stemming from neglect and mistreatment; once again, it failed to produce a profit, as favoritism resulted in awards of no- or low-cost leases to prominent politicians and their friends. An additional factor that contributed to the mistreatment of the prisoners was that they were increasingly black, for the Arkansas criminal justice system was now performing the social function that had previously been carried out by private punishment on slave plantations. The crisis came in 1886, when prisoners at a state-owned coal mine, protesting subhuman conditions, staged a protracted sit-down strike, which generated sympathy from the Arkansas newspapers. It triggered a state-sponsored study commission whose most dramatic discovery was that fully one-fourth of prisoners in custody had died each year between 1873 and 1893.[2]

These revelations led the state to abolish the practice of convict leasing once again, and to adopt a still different strategy. It acquired an old plantation, Cummins Farm, in 1902 and added Tucker Farm in 1912. Together the two farms contained several thousand acres of prime agricultural land, which had become uneconomical to cultivate since the abolition of slavery. With prisoners substituting for slaves, however, state officials hoped to create a self-sufficient correctional system, one that might even produce that long-desired profit for the state. The convicts were expected to build their own housing, produce their own food by working in the fields, and even guard each other. The limited funds that were needed for running the farms were to be generated by selling cash crops, mainly cotton, on the open market. To realize economies, prisoners were housed in cheap, unventilated, overcrowded barracks; food, medical, mental health, and vocational training services were provided at a minimum level, if at all. Of the convicts who survived, many did so only because their families bribed the convict guards, or "trusties," to provide them with the necessities of life.

This system remained more or less unchanged throughout the first six decades of the twentieth century. In important ways, it worked. Despite scandals, public outcries, and quiet criticism from the emerging national corrections profession, the Arkansas prison system caused the state few problems. It was largely invisible – run by independent prison wardens who placed few monetary demands on the state budget. It operated with reasonable efficiency and in some years actually did return a surplus for the state. Only occasionally was its isolation pierced and its barbarities revealed to a wider public. Such revelations precipitated intermittent cri-

ses but yielded slight changes, usually a new building or a few more employees, before things settled down again. Having institutionalized the
cycle of scandal, response, and neglect, the two institutions weathered
these perturbations and continued on their savage, scandal-ridden course
until the 1960s.

Let us pay a visit to Cummins Farm on the eve of the events that were
to transform it and initiate the judicial prison reform process.[3] The institution – which still exists, albeit in much-altered form – lies southeast of
Little Rock, amid flat, green farmlands dotted with tiny, white frame
houses that constituted the insignia of the region's devastating poverty. A
visitor turned in from the highway at a small road with a few houses on
each side that terminated in a chicken-wire fence topped with barbed
wire. There was a gate in the fence at this point and a small wooden
structure on the inside of the gate, from which would issue forth a man
dressed entirely in white and carrying a rifle. This man was a prisoner,
for perimeter security at Cummins Farm was maintained exclusively by
inmates. The inmates selected for these and other positions of authority
were, as the name "trusty" suggests, those whom prison officials regarded
as reliable. They were felons nonetheless, often hardened ones; within the
memory of current Arkansas prison officials, one of them opened fire on
a crop-dusting plane that came too close to the fence in his considered
judgment, while another fired a warning shot at the feet of the lieutenant
governor's wife when she emerged from a building she was inspecting
without giving the appropriate signal.

Upon presenting one's permission for the visit, one followed the road
through some pine woods and came out facing the main part of the
prison. Directly in front was the prison building, a long, white windowless
structure. To the left there were broad, flat fields dotted with lines of
men, dressed in white, who were engaged in various agricultural tasks.
Near each group was a man on horseback and between the lines of working prisoners were other men, armed with shotguns or rifles; these men,
since they were all trusties, were also dressed in white. To the right was a
row of comfortable-looking homes along on a straight, well-paved street.
This was the "free line" where the warden and a number of the other
prison officials lived with their families. A man in white might be digging
in the garden of these homes or entering one with a bag of groceries, for
tractable prisoners worked as house servants for the officers who inhabited
the free line.

Prisoners at Cummins Farm were required to work in the fields six days
per week, ten hours each day, planting, weeding, and harvesting the crops
by hand. They worked in rain or sun, heat or cold, being excused only
when the temperature dropped below freezing; they were given no warm
clothing or bad weather gear, and were sometimes sent into the fields

without shoes. They did not have fixed production quotas, but rather were expected to do their "best," and would be whipped by the trusties with a leather strap if they failed to achieve this amorphous but demanding standard. The trusties were apparently adept at whipping; one of them was confined at Cummins because he had beaten the warden of the Mississippi Penal Farm to death. Each group of prisoners, referred to as a "long line," was supposed to work within a defined but unmarked position in the fields. If a prisoner strayed out of his assigned area, he was informed of this transgression by a warning shot, fired by one of the armed trusties who patrolled the area between the long lines. If he failed to return to his position, the trusties were instructed to shoot him. Judgments about whether a prisoner had strayed and about the alacrity of his return were generally within the trusties' discretion.

The white prison building was and still continues to be known as barracks, but it was simply a large residence structure for the prisoners. It was built on the traditional "telephone pole" plan with a long, wide central corridor and side structures opening out from it at various intervals. In a northern prison each of these side structures would have a corridor of its own lined with two or three stories of separate, bar-fronted cells. At Cummins Farm, however, they consisted of one large, open space, packed virtually solid with double-decker beds. There were eight such barracks; one for white trusties, one for black trusties, and the remainder for the other prisoners, further divided into "rankers" and "do-pops," as well as being segregated by race. During the day, the barracks were nearly empty, since the inmates were all working in the fields, but in the evening bedlam reigned. And as night fell, all but two of the state-employed guards at Cummins Farm would leave the prison; order was kept by a few trusties, armed with their own knives, who patrolled the central corridor without venturing into the depths of the individual barracks. Since the prisoners possessed the usual assortment of home-made or smuggled weapons, and bore each other the usual assortment of grudges and resentments, the lack of supervision gave free reign to the "crawlers" and "creepers" who would stab other inmates while they slept. Homosexual rape was openly practiced – the few guards would rarely intervene, and the trusties were not expected to do so either. To escape these various indignities, some of the inmates would come to the front of the barracks and cling to the bars all night.[4]

What one would not have seen on this tour were prison shops, educational facilities, or a medical and dental clinic, for none of these existed at the old Cummins Farm. There was, however, a commissary store where a variety of small amenities were sold. Since the prisoners were not paid for their fieldwork, employment at this store was one of the two legitimate ways to earn the money needed to make purchases; the other was to sell one's blood at the store, which each healthy prisoner was permitted to do once per week. The items in the store were not the only commodities available, however; since the trusties were often allowed to leave the prison and return without being searched, there was an ample supply of drugs, alcohol, and weapons for anyone who could afford to buy them. The most common purchasers were the trusties themselves; since the rankers and the do-pops had to pay the trusties in order to obtain food, medicine, access to medical personnel, access to outsiders, and immunity from arbitrary punishments, the trusties often had extra money, while the rankers and the do-pops rarely did.

The Beginning: *Talley v. Stephens* and Its Progeny (1965–1969)

In 1965, several jailhouse lawyers, or "writ writers," at Cummins sent a pro se habeas corpus petition to Judge J. Smith Henley of the United States District Court for the Eastern District of Arkansas, alleging that superintendent Dan D. Stephens was holding them under conditions that violated their constitutional rights. Consistent with the general pattern of prisoner complaints at this time, the petitioners requested that they be released, and neither proposed nor envisioned any structural changes in the prison. Judge Henley, who was familiar with the long series of scandals involving the Arkansas prison system, appointed two local attorneys, Bruce T. Bullion of Little Rock and Louis L. Ramsey of Pine Bluff, to serve as pro bono attorneys for the prisoners, and proceeded to hold a hearing on their petition.

As rephrased by their attorneys, the inmates' claim was that they were being denied their rights under the Eighth and Fourteenth Amendments, in violation of section 1983 of the Civil Rights Act of 1871. The prisoners alleged that Superintendent Stephens had denied them access to the courts and to adequate medical services, had exposed them to unduly harsh working conditions, and had subjected them to severe corporal punishment. This claim, as reformulated, represented a departure from the more limited complaints that had been rejected in so many prior cases nationwide. Despite its unprecedented nature, state prison officials were far from eager to contest it. With the defiant segregationist Orville Faubus still occupying the Arkansas governor's mansion and the reverberations of confrontations at Little Rock's Central High School still ringing in their ears, they were fully aware of the implications of a "federal court takeover." They quickly moved the complaining inmates into better housing, dismissed those guards who had been most brutal, and promised to improve the regulations governing the administration of corporal punishment and other forms of inmate discipline. By doing so, they sought to avoid a class action suit that would precipitate more widespread inquiry into the conditions at Cummins Farm.

This strategy appeared to work. To be sure, Judge Henley entered a judgment in this essentially uncontested suit, captioned *Talley v. Stevens*,[5] in favor of the prisoners. But the judgment involved only one limited issue that parties had been unable to resolve – the authority of prison officials to intercept inmate communications to and from the court. While Henley permanently enjoined prison officials from such actions, or from carrying out reprisals against inmate "writ writers," he seemed satisfied with the state's promise that it would make improvements in other areas. He concluded, in deference to the now-breached hands-off doctrine, that the "courts cannot take over the management of the prison system, and they cannot undertake to review every complaint made by a convict about his treatment while in prison."[6]

Far from satisfying Arkansas convicts, however, the small victory in *Talley* encouraged the growing group of inmate writ writers to file still more petitions with the federal courts. Crudely written and often wildly imaginative, these complaints depicted horrible conditions and brutal treatment. For the most part they were routinely denied after a quick glance by a clerk, on the grounds that they did not state a cause of action. However, several petitions making similar but independent claims struck a chord with the clerk, and he passed them to Henley. Henley then appointed additional pro bono counsel to represent the inmates and held more hearings to consider the merits of these claims.

The first of the complaints that Henley had selected for full consideration was *Jackson v. Bishop*,[7] filed in 1967. William King Jackson, a twenty-eight-year-old inmate serving a five-year term for burglary, had filed a pro se habeas corpus petition seeking release from prison because of the repeated beatings to which he had been subjected. Henley consolidated this petition with two others that complained about beatings with leather straps and the use of the notorious "Tucker telephone."* The three cases were heard jointly by two judges, Oren Harris and Gorden E. Young of the United States District Court for the Eastern District of Arkansas. They

---

* The "Tucker telephone" was a device that generated electricity by means of a hand crank. Electrodes from this device were attached to the extremities of the prisoners, including their genitals, and then cranked by guards. The resulting shocks, apart from being excruciatingly painful, could burn their bodies and cause seizures and death. Prominently placed in a small building (the "telephone booth") at Tucker Farm, the "telephone" was a standard punishment for all sorts of infractions. It made quite an impression on the federal courts and, indeed, on the entire nation. To this day, visitors to Tucker Farm ask the warden whether the telephone on his desk is "the Tucker telephone."

received extensive evidence from all three petitioners, as well as from twelve other inmates. Their joint ruling drew heavily on testimony that had been produced in *Talley* and on information that had been revealed in a 1966 state police investigation of the prisons. Despite this evidence, Judges Harris and Young ruled against the inmates. Although they enjoined the use of the Tucker telephone and similar instruments of torture, they noted that the Department of Corrections had dismissed a number of officials implicated in past violations and had instituted new rules to govern corporal punishment. Even though only Mississippi and Arkansas prisons continued to mete out such punishment, they refused to hold that it was per se unconstitutional.

On appeal, then Judge Harry Blackmun of the Eighth Circuit Court of Appeals vacated the district court's judgment and ordered it to enter a new and expanded decree enjoining corporal punishment in its entirety. In an expansive opinion, he ruled that such punishment is easily subject to abuse, that it "generates hate toward the keepers who punish and toward the system which permits it . . . [and that] it frustrates correctional and rehabilitative goals."[8] Drawing on testimony in *Jackson* from James V. Bennet, the former and long-time director of the federal Bureau of Prisons, and Fred Wilkinson, director of the Missouri Department of Corrections and a former Deputy Director of the federal Bureau of Prisons, he ruled that corporal punishment was "unusual" because only two states still permitted it, and "cruel" because "whipping creates other penological problems and makes adjustment to society more difficult."[9]

The second case that followed in the wake of *Talley*, captioned *Courtney v. Bishop*,[10] was a consolidation of several pro se prisoner petitions. Unlike the earlier cases, which had focused on limited and well-identified abuses, the court-appointed attorneys in *Courtney* mounted a sweeping challenge to general conditions in the Arkansas prisons: they asserted that the process for imposing solitary confinement, the treatment in solitary, and the crowded, dangerous and dirty conditions in the prisons as a whole constituted cruel and unusual punishment. District Judge Oren Harris dismissed the petition, and a panel of judges on the Eighth Circuit Court of Appeals upheld him, announcing that "[t]he law to be applied is well-settled. Lawful incarceration necessarily operates to deprive a prisoner of certain rights he would otherwise possess."

Talley, Jackson, and *Courtney* represented the very first cases in which judges gave serious and sustained attention to the general conditions in state prisons. Although the decisions were hardly ringing declarations of prisoners' rights, and *Courtney* was a clear defeat, Henley's opinion in the largely uncontested case in *Talley* and Blackmun's firm language for the court of appeals in *Jackson* did establish important precedents. Even the defeats did not wholly foreclose future litigation. None of these three cases had secured substantial changes in the Arkansas prisons, but they established that inmates could be heard in federal courts and occasionally receive some vindication of their claims. They indicated that neither federalism, nor the prison's primary responsibility for prisoners, nor the procedural aspects of the Civil Rights Act posed insuperable barriers to granting prisoners relief. And they undoubtedly contributed to the upsurge in prisoners' petitions that generated the next phase of litigation.

Between the time Judge Henley handed down *Talley v. Stephens* in 1965 and the time the Eighth Circuit decided *Courtney* in 1969, the inmate writ writers and their court-appointed attorneys acquired a number of unwitting allies. In 1966, the Arkansas prison system, true to form, was rocked by a series of scandals, and Governor Orville Faubus ordered an investigation of Cummins Prison Farm by the state police. The police report documented institutionalized torture, near starvation diets, rampant violence, and widespread corruption. Had this report been produced by civil rights activists or meddlesome federal officials, it could have been discounted, but coming from the state police, it had a galvanizing effect on the Arkansas legislature. In quick succession the legislature appointed two study commissions, both of which recommended increases in funding and extensive reorganization of the prison system.

Rather than responding defensively, the superintendents of the state's two largest prison facilities, Tom Murton and Otis Stephens, endorsed these findings. They held press conferences and gave highly publicized tours of their institutions to call attention to execrable conditions and to campaign for increased funding. Indeed, Murton, the superintendent of Tucker Farm, gained nationwide notoriety at the time for his flamboyant revelations of systematic abuses of prisoners by prisoner trusties and his dramatic "discovery" of a graveyard on prison property, which he claimed had been used to bury murdered prisoners. By all subsequent accounts, this so-called prisoner graveyard was a cemetery that predated the use of the land by the prison. It is marked on old maps and thought to be either a pauper's graveyard or a slave graveyard on the corner of the former plantation. Whatever the actuality, these bygone victims of prior and different injustices had returned to dramatize the present one. Murton's crusade, together with the state police report, captured the attention of Winthrop Rockefeller, who in January 1967 had become the first Republican governor of Arkansas since Reconstruction. Given these revelations and Rockefeller's own inclinations, prison reform quickly emerged as one of his highest political priorities.[11]

Although there was deep antagonism between Rockefeller and the solidly Democratic legislature, the two did agree that the state's prison system was in terrible condition, and they were able to hammer out several agreements for its improvement. For the first time in Arkansas's benighted

history, a single state Commission of Corrections was established to oversee its various institutions, and Tom Murton was appointed commissioner.
As head of this new consolidated agency, he enjoyed the confidence of
the governor for a period, and was able to promote a variety of reforms
over the opposition of many rank-and-file correctional employees. Although he later came to be widely regarded by both friend and foe as
something of a crackpot, he was highly successful for several years in interesting the governor in prison reform and in publicizing the plight of
the state's prisoners. His flamboyant exploits as superintendent and later
as commissioner were widely reported by the national press, so much so
that they became the subject of a popular movie, *Brubaker*, staring Robert
Redford as a thinly disguised Tom Murton. Murton ultimately lost his job
as a result of his willingness – even delight, some said – to go public with
his criticisms of abuses within the prisons. He then moved to Alaska to
serve as its commissioner of corrections, but after losing this job as well,
he returned to his native Oklahoma to raise turkeys. He died in the mid-
1980s, but he is still remembered by many Arkansas prison officials for
his willingness to press so vigorously for correctional reform.[12]

Murton was succeeded as state commissioner of corrections in 1968 by
C. Robert Sarver. Trained as a lawyer, Sarver had practiced in West Virginia and Washington, D.C. His interest in corrections was first kindled
by his experience as a prosecutor in West Virginia, where he became
known as a moderate reformer interested in rehabilitation. When chosen
by Governor Rockefeller to head the Arkansas prison system, he identified
his priorities as expanding rehabilitative opportunities for inmates, ex-
perimenting with administrative reforms, and "taking a hard look" at the
notorious trusty system.[13] He tackled his job with enthusiasm, using the
various reports detailing irregularities to dismiss still more employees and
campaigning tirelessly to secure more funding for the department.

The Turning Point: *Holt v. Sarver* (1969–1971)

It was within this context of scandal and ferment for reform that Judge
Henley consolidated the next batch of prisoner petitions, certified them
as a class action, and thus created *Holt v. Sarver*[14] in May 1969. The two
Little Rock attorneys that Judge Henley appointed, Steele Hayes and Jerry
Jackson, alleged unconstitutional denial of medical and dental care, dis-
criminatory and unreasonable confinement of inmates in isolation cells,
unconstitutionally cruel treatment of inmates in isolation,*[15] failure of of-

---

* The isolation unit was a relatively new feature at Cummins Farm, which had
previously relied almost exclusively on corporal punishment to discipline the
prisoners. It consisted of eleven windowless, eight- by ten-foot cells located in a

ficials to protect inmates from assaults from other inmates, and failure of officials to comply with the earlier court orders regarding the use of corporal punishment.

At trial, Henley ruled against the inmates with respect to medical, dental, and food services, but found that conditions in the isolation units and the failure to protect inmates from assaults by other inmates violated constitutional standards. In a memorable understatement, he observed:

> The Court is of the view that if the state of Arkansas chooses to confine prison inmates in barracks with other inmates they ought at least to be able to fall asleep at night without fear of having their throats cut before morning, and that the State has failed to discharge a constitutional duty in failing to take steps to enable them to do so.[16]

Regarding the isolation cells, he held that packing from four to eleven men into an eight- by ten-foot cell that was dirty, unsanitary, and furnished with possibly infected and contagious bedding constituted a violation of the Eighth Amendment. Having made these findings, Henley responded in a way that would come to characterize his approach throughout this litigation. He did not formulate a detailed remedial order, but issued a series of general "suggestions" to prison administrators about alleviating the constitutional violations he had found. These suggestions were addressed to the state legislature as well as to the prison authorities, since increased funding was one of the necessary conditions for overcoming the problems Henley had identified; new construction, additional guards, more health services, and the like were all well beyond the reach of the department's meager budget. The Department of Corrections was the party before him, however, and he ordered it to produce a plan that was responsive to his suggestions.

Thirty days later, as required, Commissioner Sarver submitted his report documenting the steps he had taken to comply with Henley's ruling. The department had installed an improved system of classification, reduced crowding by transferring some inmates away from the most crowded units, established an inmate council to facilitate prisoner–staff communication, and begun to improve sanitary conditions throughout the institutions. But the commissioner's report also emphasized that the department had no funds to hire additional free-world staff to replace

---

separate building and guarded solely by trusties. An average of four men were confined in each cell, with the number sometimes being considerably more. Many of the men were required to spend twenty-four hours per day in these cells; their meals, consisting of a baked mixture called "grue," were delivered to them through a grating at the bottom of the door.

inmate trusties or to make other improvements identified as necessary by the court.

In responding to this report, Henley was not required to choose between acknowledging the department's efforts and condemning the results. Throughout the trial and in his opinion in the case, Henley had commended Sarver for his efforts in the face of limited resources and departmental resistance. It was Sarver's own testimony, as well as that of other witnesses that he produced for the defendants, that Henley drew on most heavily in his opinion. In fact, it was widely believed at the time – and still is today – that Sarver helped the plaintiffs' attorneys draft their complaints against him. Whatever the truth of this claim, there is no doubt that he welcomed the suit and actively opposed the state attorney general's appeal of the rulings.[17] Years later, Sarver continued to hold Judge Henley in high regard and to assert that he had played a central role in the transformation of the Arkansas prison system.[18]

Thus, Henley could rule against a reformist commissioner without frustrating or undermining him, and that is what he did; he announced that the department's report, although filled with good intentions, fell far short of what was needed. He immediately ordered additional hearings designed to probe still deeper into the issues. Consolidating another batch of the growing number of prisoner petitions, he announced that the challenge was no longer limited to isolated practices or conditions in selected prison units but was an attack on conditions throughout the state's entire prison system. This produced a second *Holt v. Sarver* case, generally known as *Holt II*.[19]

Anticipating the significance of this case, Henley sought out experienced attorneys to handle it. He ultimately chose Philip Kaplan and Jack Holt to serve as cocounsel for the plaintiffs. Kaplan, a northerner and a Jew, was a member of the state's only racially integrated law firm and was a well-known civil rights litigator. Holt, in contrast, was a local lawyer with extensive experience as a criminal prosecutor and impeccable conservative, hometown credentials, as well as a childhood friend of Judge Henley's.[20] Kaplan's appointment brought considerable experience in civil rights litigation and large-scale remedial orders. Holt brought credibility – no small matter given the problem of relying on prisoners' testimony – and instant acceptance by the local establishment, also no small matter given its intense hostility toward the federal courts for their role in the continuing school desegregation cases.* Henley's choice of this unusual, complementary team turned out to be a stroke of political genius;

---

* Holt was not related to the named plaintiff, Lawrence Holt, but given the extent to which the plaintiffs' attorneys controlled the litigation, it was an appropriate coincidence that the case and one of its attorneys were homonymous.

indeed, the *Arkansas Gazette* immediately hailed the appointments as a "brilliant" move.[21] Despite the court's subsequent assault on the entire prison system, its actions were never vigorously attacked as illegitimate by public officials or the press. Jack Holt was later appointed to the Arkansas Supreme Court, an unlikely reward for someone who had injured or betrayed the state, and Kaplan went on to have a successful law career in Little Rock.

Virtually at the invitation of Commissioner Sarver and Judge Henley, Kaplan and Holt launched a full-scale attack on the conditions in the state's prison system as a whole. They amended the original complaint to incorporate three sets of arguments: that the prison's use of forced and uncompensated labor violated the Thirteenth Amendment's prohibition against slavery, that the conditions and practices within the prison were so unsanitary, unhealthy, and dangerous that they constituted cruel and unusual punishment in violation of the Eighth Amendment, and that the prison's racial segregation of inmates violated the Fourteenth Amendment's equal protection guarantee. They then presented the court with a long list of specific practices and conditions that they argued demonstrated one or another of these three assertions. Chief among their allegations were that inmates were denied opportunities for rehabilitation, minimal due process safeguards in decisions affecting administrative punishments, minimally decent housing, clothing and food, minimally decent medical and dental care, protection from predatory inmates and correctional officials, protection against enforced labor, protection against racial segregation, and a variety of other rights.

At trial, witness after witness called by the plaintiffs testified in graphic detail to pervasive abuses and inhuman conditions. Plaintiffs introduced a motion picture made by Philip Kaplan that revealed the decrepit and crowded conditions in the prison. Correctional professionals, including James Bennett, former director of the federal Bureau of Prisons, a witness in earlier cases, and James McCormick, executive director of the Osborne Society, a national prison reform organization, condemned practices in Arkansas and underscored the fact that they were out of step with those in other states.

Defending the Department of Corrections against this barrage of claims were lawyers from the state attorney general's office. They filed a motion to dismiss, asserting that the "suit is in substance an attempt to coerce the State . . . to provide additional funds for the operation and maintenance of the State Prison System." This was, in fact, exactly what the plaintiff's attorneys were attempting to do. Unfortunately for the defense, Judge Henley, who had appointed these attorneys, was attempting to do the same thing, and he refused to dismiss the case. Worse still, the principal witness for the defense was necessarily Commissioner Sarver, who was also attempting to compel the state to provide additional funds. He testified at length, admitting that the Arkansas prison system fell far short of contemporary correctional standards. To the plaintiffs' catalog of abuses he added still others, and underscored the need for additional resources.

Judge Henley announced his opinion in *Holt II* on February 18, 1970. Addressing each of the specific complaints set forth by the plaintiffs, he held the Arkansas prisons to be in violation of the Eighth and Fourteenth Amendments for their lack of medical and dental facilities, the unsanitary conditions in their kitchens (which were "deplorable" according to the testimony of defendants' own medical witness), their inadequate toiletries and clothing, their filthy bedding, the constant physical danger from other inmates, the widespread corruption and intimidation, and the racial segregation and rampant racial discrimination. But what was significant about the opinion was not these individual holdings, unprecedented though they were in scope, but the general conclusions that Judge Henley reached. In *Talley* and *Holt I*, Henley had focused on specific problems – whipping bare-backed inmates for minor infractions, crowding in the isolation unit at Tucker Farm, selected acts of violence by identified trusties, and the like. In *Holt II* he confronted the system as a whole: its structure, organization, philosophy, and consequences. He was well aware of the significance of this approach. "This case," he wrote ". . . amounts to an attack on the system itself. . . . This is the first time that convicts have attacked an entire penitentiary system in any court."[22]

The first part of Henley's frontal attack on the Arkansas prison system challenged the basic notion of a prison-for-profit, a notion that had been an article of faith for Arkansas legislators since the 1840s.*[23] Although he rejected the argument that forced labor constituted slavery in violation of the Thirteenth Amendment, he did hold that it was cruel and unusual punishment to run a prison system as a net income producer for the state. He reasoned that

> [w]hile confinement, even at hard labor and without compensation, is not considered to be necessarily a cruel and unusual punishment, it may be so in certain circumstances and by reason of the conditions of the confinement. In the instant case Petitioners contend that overall conditions in the Arkansas penal system, including but not limited to those relating to inmate safety, may be so bad that it amounts to unconstitutional cruel and unusual punishment to expose men to those conditions, regardless of how those conditions may operate fortuitously on particular individuals.[24]

* According to a state commission report cited by the court, total receipts of the Penitentiary from all sources, including the sale of cotton, vegetables, fruit, and pecans, was $1,763,487.09 for fiscal year 1966. The corresponding figures for fiscal years 1964 and 1965 were $1,566,712.76 and $2,785,570.33.

The Arkansas prison system's effort to make a profit for the state, and the lack of financial support engendered by that expectation, fully justified this contention, in Judge Henley's view.

The second basic issue was the use of inmate trusties as guards. Judge Henley found that Cummins Farm had only thirty-five free-world employees to supervise over a thousand inmates, and that at night only two employees were available to maintain order in barracks holding a thousand crowded bunks. In condemning such conditions, he again drew heavily on the testimony of James Bennett, who stated that "the use of trusty guards is universally condemned by penologists, and the system is used only in Arkansas, Louisiana and Mississippi."* Judge Henley went on to catalog a long list of abuses that naturally arose when the prisons were largely run by a small clique of violent and dangerous criminals. With barely controlled outrage, he wrote, in what became one of the best-known statements of the judicial prison reform movement:

> For the ordinary convict a sentence to the Arkansas Penitentiary today amounts to a banishment from civilized society to a dark and evil world completely alien to the free world, a world that is administered by criminals under unwritten rules and customs completely foreign to free world culture.
>
> It is one thing for the State to send a man to the Penitentiary as a punishment for crime. It is another thing for the State to delegate the governance of him to other convicts and to do nothing meaningful for his safety, well being, and possible rehabilitation. It is one thing for the State not to pay a convict for his labor; it is something else to subject him to a situation in which he has to sell his blood to obtain money to pay for his own safety, or for adequate food, or for access to needed medical attention.[25]

Henley's third sweeping condemnation involved the availability of rehabilitative programs. To be sure, he rejected plaintiffs' claims that inmates had a constitutional right to rehabilitation, arguing that he was "not willing to hold that confinement was unconstitutional simply because the institution does not operate a school or provide vocational training or other rehabilitative facilities and services which many institutions now offer." However, what he rejected with one hand he embraced with the other:

> [This] is not quite the end of the matter. The absence of an affirmative program of training and rehabilitation may have constitutional significance where in the absence of such a program conditions and practices exist

---

* This was not quite true. As will be discussed in the next section, Texas also relied extensively on trusties, but had thus far refused to concede this fact in public.

which actually militate against reform and rehabilitation. That is the situation that exists in Arkansas today. . . . Thus the absence of rehabilitation services and facilities of which Petitioners complain remains a factor in the overall constitutional equation before the Court.[26]

Henley's long catalog of abuses and his rulings that they were unconstitutional constituted an attack on virtually every facet of the prison system. Having satisfied himself that the entire Arkansas prison system violated the Eighth Amendment, he proceeded in what had already become his characteristic manner. He commended the commissioner for his efforts to improve the department and for his willingness to acknowledge and deal with its problems. He commended the governor for calling a special session of the legislature to address correctional issues. He commended the state legislature for increasing its appropriations for the prisons, enacting new laws providing for rehabilitation programs, and commissioning reports that were critical of the prison system and recommended far-reaching changes. Having dispensed these commendations, he then issued a broad ruling that condemned the entire prison system and demanded immediate, accelerated efforts to transform it. He rejected the state's contention that the recent increases in appropriations would improve conditions sufficiently so that there would be no need for further supervision by the court. Even "if the Respondents had unlimited funds at their disposal tomorrow," he wrote, "they could not solve their constitutional problems overnight."[27] The situation required a fundamental reorientation in the nature of the prison system, to be achieved over a lengthy "phase-in" period. He concluded by ordering the department to prepare periodic reports documenting the steps it had taken to correct the continuing constitutional abuses he had found.

Holt v. Sarver II was a resounding victory for reform. Judge Henley had found the prison system to be a brutal world run by brutal people in a manner that was unconstitutional in its entirety, and he had ordered the department to take immediate steps to restructure itself. However, if he had been bold in his condemnation of existing practices and conditions, and in what he regarded as the scope of the response required, he was hesitant in setting out detailed steps to overcome the problem. He left the responsibility to the prison officials themselves, officials who nearly all observers admitted were understaffed and underfunded. However, he did warn that if the department did not show substantial progress in the near future, he would be forced to take more drastic measures.

The state appealed Judge Henley's ruling and in May 1971 the Eighth Circuit Court of Appeals handed down its decision. It affirmed Judge Henley's holding that the system as a whole constituted cruel and unusual punishment, quoting extensively from Commissioner Sarver's testimony to support its reasoning. It also agreed with Henley that the process of transforming the system would be both lengthy and expensive, and it instructed him to retain supervision of the prisons until he could "reasonably assume that incarceration therein will not constitute cruel and inhumane punishment violative of the Eighth Amendment."[28] It ruled that Judge Henley had not erred in ordering the department to produce, at its own expense, detailed progress reports to the court on a regular basis. In sum, the appellate decision was a complete validation of Henley's actions. Its only implicit criticism was that he should act even more aggressively in ordering remedial measures.

The Judge Takes Command: *Holt v. Hutto* and *Finney v. Hutto* (1971–1977)

Apparently buoyed by this vote of confidence, Judge Henley ordered respondents to produce a progress report within six weeks that would describe current conditions, recent improvements, and future plans for three facilities: Cummins, Tucker, and the Arkansas Women's Reformatory, which had been included in the systemwide suit, and whose existing facility had been characterized as "poor" by the Corrections Commission. Unlike the general and gentle "suggestions" that had accompanied his earlier rulings, these orders were more specific, requiring responses in each of nine separate problem areas. Henley also ordered the department to show how it was planning to respond to findings and recommendations in a report the department had recently prepared for the governor.

The task of dealing with this order fell to Terrell Don Hutto, who had just replaced Robert Sarver. By most accounts, Sarver was eased out of the office by the growing number of state legislators who resented his continued criticism of their failure to provide more funds for the prisons, and his not-so-subtle use of the federal court to further his goals. Despite the widespread agreement that something needed to be done about the prisons, the legislators believed that the state had done enough already. They resented the "takeover" by a federal judge and were dismayed by Commissioner Sarver's apparent willingness to be taken over. They could not do anything about Judge Henley, of course, so they had to settle for removing Sarver. But Arkansas officials were far from flatly opposed to changes in the prisons. Indeed, Sarver's replacement, Hutto, was a nationally respected, reform-minded administrator who had held important posts in California, then regarded as being at the forefront of modern American penology.

The report Hutto prepared for Judge Henley asserted that substantial progress had been made in each of the nine areas specified in the court's order. It stated that the department was continuing efforts to dismantle the trusty system. Admittedly, the report declared, the lack of funds had hampered this effort; inmate trusties were still overseeing convicts in the fields and still standing guard with firearms in the prison watchtowers. But these trusties were now under the supervision of free-world employees, and still more new free-world staff members were undergoing crash training programs. The report also claimed that medical and dental services were now available to inmates. Admittedly, their supply was still severely limited, but at the least the inmates no longer had to bribe trusties to gain access to these services. Better classification systems had reduced crowding and improved safety in the isolation units, while clothing, bedding, food services, ventilation, and heating had been upgraded in those units where it had been the worst. Admittedly, conditions for women convicts in the Arkansas Reformatory for Women at Cummins Farm remained poor, but staffing had increased and a new and larger facility in Pine Bluff was under construction.

In accepting the report, Judge Henley noted that these steps constituted a promising beginning, but that he looked forward to further reports documenting still more progress. However, a few weeks later, prompted by continuing complaints by the plaintiffs' attorneys that the department was dragging its heavy feet, he scheduled six more days of hearings. In November and December 1971 he received testimony from more inmates and prison administrators, and a few weeks later he issued what came to be known as the *First Supplemental Decree*. This very detailed decree, in effect, replaced his original order of February 1970, which was much more general. Henley's action generated still more written complaints from inmates, who expanded their allegations of continuing unconstitutional practices as the court expanded its findings. Henley responded by urging Commissioner Hutto to take more aggressive actions to ameliorate conditions; over the next several months he continued to hear still more testimony from inmates about the continuing abuses in the prison system, and he continued to issue orders and to correct those abuses.

In late 1972, a number of these further complaints were consolidated in a new legal action, and in early 1973 Judge Henley held hearings on it. These hearings culminated in a supplemental decree in August 1973, which came to be known as *Holt v. Hutto* or *Holt III*.[29] In this decree, Judge Henley both expanded the range of issues and pressed the department to establish a more precise timetable for resolving them. The ruling also established a pattern that was to continue for some time. The department would submit a report to the court detailing steps it had taken to resolve issues previously identified. In explaining why it had not accomplished more, it would thereby reveal additional, deep-seated problems. Henley would then expand the scope of his concerns and issue a new order, calling for further changes and an additional report.

This process also subtly changed the nature of litigation. At the outset, Superintendents Stephens and Murton and Commissioner Sarver had welcomed the litigation, and the state legislative leaders had grudgingly acknowledged the legitimacy of the court's concerns. No one seriously tried to defend the state's prisons or even to challenge vigorously judicial intervention. But with the passage of time, the elimination of the worst abuses, and the vast increases in prison expenditures, the legislature and the new commissioner grew decidedly more frustrated. The more they did, it seemed to them, the more criticism they received.

Thus, as state officials were deciding that they had already done enough, Judge Henley was coming to appreciate just how deep the problems were and how much more still had to be done. In particular, he realized how important – and difficult – it would be to institutionalize the sorts of changes his decrees envisioned. In his August 1973 *Holt III* opinion, he stated:

> This litigation stands in a position quite different from that in which it stood in 1969 or 1970. In those years the Court was dealing with officially prescribed or sanctioned conditions and practices which were claimed to be unconstitutional, and the controlling facts were essentially undisputed. Today, most of the practices and conditions alleged by petitioners to exist and of which they complain are not officially approved or sanctioned, and a number of them are specifically prohibited by rules and regulations of the Department. . . . Additionally, controlling facts are sharply disputed in many areas.[30]

Indeed, he himself appreciated the irony that as prison conditions were improving, the court was becoming more, not less embroiled in the administration of the prison system. Earlier, Henley had been intent on eliminating the brutality of the trusty system. Now, he had to oversee the hiring, training, and deployment of a new and rapidly expanding freeworld staff. Earlier, he had confronted a system in which inmates had to sell their own blood for funds to bribe trusties so that they could obtain food and medical care. Now, he had to consider the relative quality of medical services available to inmates at different units. Earlier, he had confronted two prisons, one for blacks and one for whites; now, he sought to fine tune the department's inmate classification system and to review affirmative action plans for staff hiring and promotion. Earlier he had expressed revulsion at the near starvation diets for selected groups of inmates, the brutality of unsupervised corporal punishment, the placement of electrodes on inmates' genitals, and other abuses that were tantamount to systematic torture; now, with the worst of such abuses abolished, he reviewed details for the proposed "Inmate Handbook" of rights and examined refinements in procedures to be followed in disciplinary hearings. Earlier he had found it easy to declare that a system with virtually no educational, vocational, and rehabilitative facilities was unconstitutional; now, he dealt with challenges of unfairness brought about by allegations of variations in the quality of these programs at different facilities.

The creation of an administrative structure capable of sustaining the new policies and programs was of special concern to Henley. The department's typical response to his orders was to rush about dealing with whatever problem he had most recently identified, without pausing to develop a long-range plan or to bolster a weak administrative infrastructure. To combat this, Henley devoted considerable time to reviewing the plans he had ordered and to pressing the department to strengthen its organizational capacities. Thus, rather than stepping back in light of progress, he pursued the case with renewed energy, all the while being prodded by Kaplan and Holt.

Given Henley's approach, his supplement to *Holt III*, termed the *Second Supplemental Decree*, contained something of a bombshell. Handed down on August 13, 1974, it detailed a long list of problems the Department still needed to resolve. However, it also announced that "the Court does not consider it either necessary or desirable to retain further supervisory jurisdiction with respect to the Department and such jurisdiction will not be retained."[31] This surprise announcement was coupled with a curious observation: "this release of jurisdiction will not impair the validity and continuing effect of [the court's] injunctions, and if those injunctions are violated, those guilty may be faced with contempt proceedings either civil or criminal."[32] It then went on to remind the defendants that the court had authority to "impose the ultimate sanction" – "closing one or both of the prisons," and other lesser sanctions, such as "enjoining the further reception of inmates at one or both institutions" or "discharging offending employees, . . . or punish[ing] for contempt," but expressed his hope that the department would make the additional improvements he had ordered and avoid these Draconian sanctions.[33] Henley concluded this dramatic revelation with an invitation to the lead plaintiffs' counsel to visit the prisons, talk to inmates, and decide whether to appeal his order. Philip Kaplan and Jack Holt did exactly that. Concluding that compliance with the court's orders was far from complete, they quickly appealed Henley's decision to terminate jurisdiction.

During the time that *Holt v. Hutto* was on appeal, Judge Henley remained actively involved in supervising the prison system. In fact, during the spring of 1974, he visited several prisons for the first time. This served to publicize his continuing concern for the issues, as well as the need for increased funding. In addition, it signaled his willingness to expand his control over the case at a time when some thought he would wind it down. Finally, the visits symbolized his departure from the judge's traditional role. The traditional doctrine is that the only facts a judge can recognize are those that percolate through the adversary process: the direct acquisition of information that has not been presented by a party and subjected to cross-examination by its opponent is called judicial notice, and is generally reserved for straightforward, publicly available data like the distance between Little Rock and Washington.* Judge Henley's personal tour of the prisons indicated that he was no longer adjudicating an adversary process, but was in direct control of remedial effort, at least until his jurisdiction ended.

On October 10, 1974, the Eighth Circuit Court of Appeals decided the plaintiffs' appeal, which was captioned *Finney v. Arkansas Board of Corrections.*[34] It ordered Judge Henley to retain jurisdiction of the case and maintain his efforts to remedy the unconstitutional conditions in the Arkansas prisons.[35] The court identified three areas in need of ongoing attention: the growing problem of overcrowding; the continued lack of medical supervision, equipment, and treatment; and the continued evidence of physical and mental brutality. It then went on to discuss continuing shortcomings of the department in addressing each issue. In a ringing endorsement of the district court's efforts, it concluded:

> Based on the overall record before us, it is our firm conviction that the Arkansas correctional system is still unconstitutional. We are fully cognizant of the considerable progress which has been made by the Board of Correction with the minimal resources at hand. However, we confront a record and factual history of a sub-human environment in which individuals have been confined under the color of state law. The effort to make *some* amelioration of those conditions will simply not suffice. The fact that an individual has violated the criminal law, is generally uneducated and in poor health is no justification for inhumane treatment and brutality. Segregation from society and loss of one's liberty are the only punishment the law allows.[36]

The appellate court then suggested that Henley consider appointing a special master or a "visiting committee" to help gather facts, develop remedial plans, and monitor compliance.

---

* The traditional doctrine, it should be noted, is a myth. Every opinion incorporates innumerable factual statements which are neither proved at trial nor straightforward and uncontestable. A more realistic statement of this traditional doctrine is that the judge must obtain such facts unobtrusively, by using his memory or by reading a book, rather than by an open, explicit mechanism such as personal inspection of the defendant's facilities.

We can never know whether Henley's decision to terminate jurisdiction was a strategic move to bolster his own sagging authority over state officials or a heartfelt expression of his preference for a more traditional approach to the judicial role. He had certainly demonstrated his strategic acumen earlier by appointing Kaplan and Holt as plaintiffs' attorneys and by enlisting the support, or at least the acquiescence, of the state's correctional leaders. It would not be out of character for him to have devised the attempt to relinquish jurisdiction as a means of strengthening his hand vis-à-vis the department and the state officials at a time when their enthusiasm for continued judicial supervision was clearly waning. Certainly, the curious wording of his opinion, which warned of continued oversight and more drastic remedies even as it announced termination of jurisdiction, suggests that he was not quite done with the Arkansas prisons.

Whatever his views, Judge Henley plunged into the quagmire with renewed enthusiasm once the court of appeals insisted that he retain jurisdiction. He initiated a lengthy series of hearings on existing conditions and progress, conducting some of these hearings himself and turning the remainder over to his magistrate, Robert W. Faulkner. Rather than bringing large numbers of inmates to the court, Faulkner heard evidence at the prisons themselves and provided Judge Henley with transcripts of the testimony. This significantly expanded the court's capacity to gather evidence; in short order, nearly seventy-five witnesses testified on virtually every facet of prison life. Part of the reason for Henley's burst of activity and his use of the magistrate to hold hearings was that he had been appointed to the Eighth Circuit Court of Appeals by President Gerald Ford on March 24, 1975. Even after his elevation, he continued to sit as a trial court judge in the case, no doubt in the hope that he could soon complete it. Whatever the reason for his renewed burst of energy – the vote of confidence by the court of appeals, his elevation to that court, or the innovativeness of his magistrate – he had once again greatly expanded the issues in the case.

This burst of judicial activity in late 1975 and early 1976 resulted in Judge Henley's final order, *Finney v. Hutto*,[37] handed down in two parts in February and March of 1976. The ruling, which subsequently became know as *Finney I,* has been characterized as the "most comprehensive, thorough examination" of a prison system ever undertaken by a court.[38] It followed Judge Henley's familiar format. As before, he began with praise for the progress the department had made; as before, he went on to catalog a long list of continuing problems and to insist that good intentions had to be accompanied by concrete results. Specifically, the opinion addressed thirteen different issues: overcrowding, medical services and health care, rehabilitative services, mail and visitation regulations, access to legal services, inmate safety, race relations, racial discrimination, grievance procedures, special needs for Black Muslims, continued brutality, disciplinary procedures, and conditions in punitive isolation and administrative segregation. Each issue was broken down into a series of parts, and each part contained detailed lists of steps required for the department to meet constitutional standards.

But Henley's opinion in *Finney I* was more than a catalog of shortcomings or a set of suggestions to corrections officials. Once again, he had produced a carefully crafted document that addressed several different messages to several different audiences. It ordered the department to rectify a host of continuing deficiencies – to develop plans for expanding early release, using temporary facilities for housing, and to develop a more flexible system of inmate classification to relieve overcrowding. It spoke directly to the legislature and governor, urging them to provide still more appropriations for additional construction, new personnel, and other improvements. It hinted at still stronger measures to come – court-ordered early release of inmates – if additional efforts and resources were not forthcoming. But after waiving this stick, Henley offered all the Arkansas officials a carrot; he ended his opinion with a reminder that it was within their power to terminate the court's jurisdiction. All they had to do was to comply with the constitutionally mandated improvements he had specified in his orders.

A theme that recurred in many aspects of the court's orders was crowding. Although present from the outset, it had only lingered on the fringes of earlier rulings. But in *Finney I* it came to dominate the court's concerns. Between 1970, when *Holt II*, was decided, and late 1975 when hearings for *Finney I* were held, the population of Cummins Farm had increased by 50 percent, from just under 1,000 to 1,518, and Tucker's population had increased over 60 percent, from 325 to 501. According to the department's own testimony, the 1970 population figures already constituted twice the number of inmates who could safely be housed in these facilities. Noting these figures and the fact that there had been little new construction in the interim, Judge Henley argued that unless this growth was slowed or more funds quickly appropriated for new housing units, the improvements that had so painstakingly been instituted over the past five years were in danger of being swept away.

The state appealed Judge Henley's ruling, and on February 3, 1977, the Eighth Circuit Court of Appeals, in a brief opinion, affirmed his decision. To move ahead of the narrative a bit, the U.S. Supreme Court reaffirmed this decision fifteen months later in an 8-to-1 ruling.[39] Justice Stevens's majority opinion discretely but pointedly summarized some of the leading horrors of the prereform Arkansas prisons in five footnotes, and made clear, although the state of Arkansas had not raised the issue, that such treatment was indeed cruel and unusual. He commended Judge

Henley for his handling of the case, emphasizing the many opportunities Henley had offered the defendants to correct the violations on their own. But most of the opinion dealt with the issue of attorneys' fees and rejected the state's contention that the lower court had been too generous in awarding them.

These two decisions had a significant effect in Arkansas; they seemed to energize Judge Henley and chasten state officials. Following the Eighth Circuit's ruling, Henley set about ordering more changes in the prison system and requesting still more reports from the department. And throughout 1977, in comments both on and off the bench, he continued to remind officials that he was anxious to close the case if they would only make the necessary effort. A number of state officials had hoped that they would benefit from the growing conservatism of the federal judiciary and that the Eighth Circuit or the Supreme Court would slow Judge Henley down, if not stop him altogether. But in light of their dual defeats, they were forced to reconcile themselves to Henley's actions and to adopt a more cooperative stance. Their new goal was to do "whatever it takes to get out from under" the control of the federal court.*[40]

The appellate court decision affected other state officials as well. Anxious to end the federal court takeover and to return prison reform to state officials, the legislature created the "Arkansas Prison Study Commission" in April 1977. Knox Nelson, the single most powerful state legislator at the time, sponsored the enabling legislation, which demanded that the commission review "all aspects of the Department of Corrections." In short order, the commission was established, members appointed by the governor and the legislature, and its first meeting convened. It immediately divided itself into eight subcommittees, each focusing on a different concern raised by the litigation. Within a few weeks, it issued a report that found the department seriously deficient in virtually every area it had examined. The report concluded with a long list of recommendations for far-reaching changes and called for a significant increase in funding. At the same time, a study group commissioned in 1975 by the American Bar Association was completing its report. It too was highly critical and concluded, with lawyerly circumspection, that "after 10 years of . . . continuous litigation, the Arkansas prison system is somewhat less than ideal." These two reports, particularly the Prison Study Commission's, received considerable publicity and served to heighten public concern over conditions in the prisons. They also reinforced the whatever-it-takes-to-get-out-from-under mentality of state officials.[41]

---

* In our interviews with some of the department's attorneys and other state officials years later (January 1992) this phrase was used repeatedly to characterize their attitude at the time.

The Compliance Coordinator Goes to Work (1977–1982)

As the appeal in *Finney I* was pending in the Eighth Circuit, Judge Henley realized that the litigation was still far from over and announced his withdrawal. The case was then reassigned to G. Thomas Eisele. A 1970 Nixon appointee to the federal bench, Eisele had served as campaign manager for Winthrop Rockefeller's first bid for the Arkansas governorship in 1964, and had been Rockefeller's chief of staff between 1966 and 1969, a period when prison reform was the governor's top priority. He took over the case just as the court of appeals declared its support of Judge Henley's sweeping ruling and Senator Knox's Prison Study Commission was completing its own highly critical report.

There was barely a pause in the transition as Eisele quickly established firm control of the litigation. Because of his assignments on Governor Rockefeller's staff, he was intimately familiar with conditions in the state's prisons, perhaps even more so than Henley had been.[42] As a result, he may have accelerated the momentum established by Henley's final opinion. He ordered Magistrate Faulkner to hold more hearings regarding allegations of inmate beatings. The magistrate ruled against the inmates, and the court was flooded with mail alleging still more beatings, which led Judge Eisele to reject Faulkner's findings, expand the inquiry, and conduct hearings of his own. All this encouraged the plaintiffs' attorneys to file an amended complaint expanding their challenge to conditions and practices in the prisons. They alleged continued use of excessive force, inadequate procedures for confining inmates in punitive isolation, racial discrimination, poor living conditions, and continued retaliation against inmates who asserted their legal rights. Still another amended complaint attacked overcrowding. In dealing with these complaints, Judge Eisele employed various innovative devices to expedite testimony, devices that represented a greater departure from traditional practice than anything Henley had done. For example, he limited discovery to reduce the likelihood of witness intimidation, agreed to keep identity of witnesses secret prior to their testimony, and had his magistrate hold more extensive hearings at the prison.

In his subsequent decision in *Finney v. Mabry (Finney II)*,[43] handed down on June 16, 1978, a week before the U.S. Supreme Court upheld Judge Henley's earlier decision, Judge Eisele held that the department's disciplinary procedures were still woefully inadequate. This was a dramatic ruling since some of these procedures had been drafted by the department in light of Henley's earlier rulings, had received Henley's blessing, and had been upheld by the court of appeals. In thus rejecting procedures that had received the federal court seal of approval, Eisele introduced still another dimension into the case – the issue of the actual administration and effect of the department's newly promulgated rules and regulations. Although seemingly acceptable on their face, Eisele found that the new disciplinary hearings were often shams, perfunctory affairs whose outcomes were foregone conclusions. In quasi-biblical terms, he intoned, "[w]hen arrogant, unprincipled, and evil men are in control, the rule of law becomes meaningless."[44] Then, shifting to the more instrumental, meliorist discourse, he added, "It seems not such a hard lesson to learn: basic fairness by prison officials will, in the long run, greatly simplify their management problems and enhance the possibility of attaining their correctional goals."[45]

Judge Eisele was also vigorous in his efforts to persuade the parties to negotiate their remaining differences. With respect to the Department of Corrections, his devastating decision in *Finney II*, together with the Supreme Court's resounding affirmance of *Finney I*, proved wonderfully persuasive. Thus, after his initial show of force, Eisele was able to step back somewhat. Rather than holding further hearings, he met intermittently with the opposing lawyers throughout 1977 and most of 1978, at times helping them to identify subjects in need of further negotiation. On October 5, 1978, after several months of intense discussions, the parties announced that they had hammered out an agreement. In short order, it was approved by Judge Eisele – the first time a consent decree was used in the Arkansas prison cases.

Eisele's consent decree, which embodied the agreement that the parties had reached, contained thirty-nine separate provisions, each stating a specific problem and presenting a detailed plan for solving it. It allowed plaintiffs' attorneys unlimited access to all department facilities so that they could speak to inmates and conduct their own inspections. Perhaps most significant, it provided for the appointment of a "compliance coordinator" to evaluate the department's progress reports and to recommend the actions necessary to implement the terms of the decree.[46]

The power to appoint a compliance coordinator, more familiarly known as a special master, is traditionally regarded as an inherent power of an equity court and is explicitly authorized by the Federal Rules of Civil Procedure.[47] Throughout the nineteenth century, the Supreme Court had used special masters for various purposes, most notably to define state boundaries in cases that arose in the Court's original jurisdiction; since the 1960s federal courts had relied on special masters in civil rights cases to draw up detailed school desegregation plans in the face of continued recalcitrance by local school boards. By the time Judge Eisele made his appointment, masters had already been used in several other prison cases, including Rhode Island and neighboring Alabama.[48]

The person chosen for this role in the Arkansas case was Stephen C.

LaPlante, a former ombudsperson and staff researcher with the San Francisco Sheriff's Department. He came highly recommended by Allan Breed, then the Director of the National Institute of Corrections, as well as by Vincent Nathan, with whom he had worked, and whom we will meet at length in the next section of this chapter. The term "compliance coordinator" was Breed's; he felt that "master" possessed unfortunate connotations for the prison inmates, a large proportion of whom were black.[49]

Having made this appointment, Judge Eisele withdrew into the background, preferring to let the parties work out details either by themselves or under guidance and prodding from LaPlante. But despite the judge's apparent reticence, issues in the case continued to expand. The terms of LaPlante's appointment were extremely vague; he did not purport to speak for the judge, and, indeed, no one knew exactly for whom he spoke or precisely what the limits of his powers were. But everyone knew that he had Eisele's confidence and his recommendations consequently carried considerable weight.

Over the course of the next three years, LaPlante monitored the Arkansas prison system and issued a series of increasingly lengthy and detailed reports to Judge Eisele regarding the system's compliance with the consent decree. As an expert in correctional administration, unconstrained by the rules and procedures governing judicial fact-finding, and able to devote a substantial part of his time to the prisons, LaPlante probed at greater length and depth than had either of the judges or their magistrates. His reports covered minute details of almost every aspect of institutional life. He expressed approval of some of the department's practices and procedures, but far more often he called the department's efforts into question. For instance, in September 1979, LaPlante submitted a "complete list" of all relevant *Finney* issues that identified eighty-seven separate items grouped under thirteen different headings, a considerable expansion of the thirteen issues listed in *Finney I*, or even the thirty-nine separate issues identified in the consent decree. LaPlante's reports touched on virtually every area of prison administration. They dealt with health and sanitation, overcrowding, racial discrimination, Muslim inmates, punitive segregation, access to the courts, rehabilitation, mail and visiting, inmate safety, grievance procedures, and discipline. Overall, this list was not really a compliance report on the limited set of issues that had been agreed upon in the consent decree, but a plan for overall administrative reorganization of the prison system.[50]

As LaPlante's list of concerns grew, and as his attempts to address them expanded, he came into increasing conflict with correctional officials. By some accounts, this conflict was exacerbated by his willingness to "go public" with his criticisms rather than report quietly to the court and work behind the scenes with correctional officials. By other accounts, the real irritant was that his compensation, even on a part-time basis, quickly came to exceed that of the corrections commissioner. Many were antagonized by what they considered to be LaPlante's high-handed manner – a feeling that he was too quick to see the department's shortcomings and too slow to acknowledge its substantial accomplishments. But underlying all these concerns was a growing sense of institutional frustration. After years of litigation, vast increases in funding, a dramatic expansion of staff, extensive new construction, and, in general, a sustained effort to remake the state's prison system, Arkansas correctional officials resented the continuing criticisms of an "out-of-state compliance coordinator" who, they felt, knew little of their history and accomplishments. Although framed in terms of compliance with constitutional minimums, LaPlante's reports were easily recognized for what they were – efforts to implement far-reaching changes and to reorient virtually every facet of the department's administration.[51]

In the spring of 1981, this conflict reached a crisis. Without the court's authorization or the department's knowledge, LaPlante invited federal authorities to investigate allegations of corruption by corrections officials that implicated A. L. Lockhart, then the acting commissioner of corrections. The response to this reappearance of Arkansas's perennial problem – the one that the legislature had so decisively addressed in 1853 – was predictable. The Board of Corrections, the oversight or governing board of the department, announced that LaPlante's contract, which was to expire on March 31, 1981, would not be renewed.

Both LaPlante and the plaintiffs' attorneys challenged this "dismissal," asserting that despite the fact that LaPlante was under contract with the department for purposes of payment, he was an "agent of the court" and not an employee of, or consultant to, the board. But Judge Eisele upheld the dismissal, saying that the case was winding down and that he would now monitor its final stages himself. He was convinced that the Department of Corrections was doing all it could to comply and he saw no need to complicate matters by allowing a personality conflict to emerge.[52] He did extend LaPlante's appointment for another few months in order to allow him to complete two more reports that were in progress at the time. LaPlante's reports, which were submitted to the court on May 27 and June 1, 1981, contained a list of issues on which compliance with court orders had been reached, as well as a long list of issues that remained problematic.

Judge Eisele was true to his word. He resumed an active role in overseeing the compliance process and, using LaPlante's reports as guides, ordered corrections officials to submit quarterly assessments that addressed the remaining, unresolved issues. Even as he appeared to give ground by upholding LaPlante's dismissal, he also used the occasion to expand the case once again. He went beyond LaPlante's recommendations and directed the department to develop plans to reduce the population in the barracks at Cummins, to develop tighter procedures before confining an inmate in administrative segregation, and to improve the operation of the segregation unit. In addition, he ordered the department to continue to report on its compliance with the host of other issues that had previously been raised. Throughout the fall and winter of 1981–82, Eisele received a series of reports from the department and held frequent hearings to determine compliance regarding the nearly one hundred different issues that had been cataloged in LaPlante's last two reports.

Whether consciously or not, Judge Eisele shaped the dynamics of this last stage of litigation. By denying plaintiffs' request to appoint another compliance coordinator, he shifted the burden of reporting directly to the department itself. And by once again immersing himself in the day-to-day issues, he created a sense of urgency and a belief that closure was within the department's grasp. This produced a final burst of energy by department officials in late 1981 and through the summer of 1982. Relying on LaPlante's catalog of concerns, the court urged department officials to do what was necessary to comply with the standards contained in his reports, and the officials concentrated their efforts on doing so. In a series of reports they convinced the court that the department was finally in compliance. This denouement was anticlimatic. In the past when department officials had made concentrated efforts to address one of the court's demands, the effort came at the expense of other priorities or revealed other violations. But at this juncture, no such concerns were even raised; it was as if everyone involved in the case was simply exhausted and ready to call it quits. On August 20, 1982, after only half a day of a hearing that had been scheduled to last two days, Judge Eisele gave the department a clean bill of health. Seventeen years after the writ writers at Cummins Farm had sent their desperate complaint against Superintendent Stephens to Judge Henley, the case unceremoniously came to a conclusion.[53]

It is fruitless to try to determine precisely when and why the department overcame its constitutional defects. Indeed, any effort to frame the question this way had long been abandoned both by the department and by the court. Rather, the question was whether the department was doing a good enough job, and whether it was capable of sustaining this level of performance without continuous judicial oversight. The reason this question could be answered affirmatively in 1982 was that top corrections administrators had come to regard the courts as both inevitable and desirable.

Looking back on the case two years after it had been terminated, A. L. Lockhart, commissioner of corrections during its final phase, observed that he had quarreled with the court about details and felt the case had dragged on longer than it should have, but that "There is no question that the litigation has been beneficial – it prodded the Department and the legislature when they needed it."[54]

Some judges in the prison reform cases terminated jurisdiction the way Richard Nixon ended the Vietnam War; after a period of battle they declared victory and departed, hoping that they would not be dragged back into the morass once more. Others preferred more clear-cut victory and seized on one or more indicators by which to define compliance. In either case, the decision is, as almost all would admit, somewhat arbitrary, since the overarching concern is whether prison authorities will be able to do things differently in the future. The proof of structural institutional reform can only be measured by the long-term performance, not by any readily identifiable indicator or set of indicators at some moment in time.

Judge Eisele's approach fell somewhere between these two poles. Despite his concerns and rulings, some issues, such as crowding and inmate safety in large, open barracks, were not resolved by any of his orders. When the court terminated its jurisdiction, the prison population was still rising rapidly, although, as a result of his rulings, the state did have an early-release statute to help control it. Inmates were still housed in large open barracks, something the court had opposed almost from the outset, although bunks were not stacked so closely together and professional employees, not a few armed prisoners, patrolled them.

More generally, there is no doubt that the prison system Judge Eisele left in 1982 was significantly different from the one that had greeted Judge Henley seventeen years earlier. If the quondam chaos and cruelty had not been replaced by compassion, at least the worst elements of the chaos and cruelty themselves were largely gone. Inmates no longer had to bribe brutal inmate overlords to obtain basic necessities. They no longer had to fear for their lives every time they went to sleep. They no longer were capriciously deprived of food and medical services. They no longer had to worry that their genitals might be taped to electrodes or their knuckles cracked with pliers. They were no longer stripped to the waist and whipped for failure to pick a sufficient amount of cotton or okra. They were no longer segregated by race. Black Muslims could read the Koran and eat a pork-free diet. There was a statewide Department of Corrections, governed by written rules and regulations, with strong central leadership, a staff, free-world guards, a budget, and a personnel policy. The Arkansas prison system had entered the twentieth century.

Texas

The *Ruiz* Complaint and Trial (1972–1980)

The Arkansas litigation was the first and, in many ways, the most significant of all the prison cases, but the largest, longest, and most acrimonious involved the Texas prison system. The events that triggered it occurred in 1965, shortly after Frances Jalet decided to return to law practice after having raised a family. After spending a year at a University of Pennsylvania program to train legal services lawyers, she accepted a position in a federally funded legal services office in Austin, Texas. Almost immediately, she was drawn to some of the office's work involving the legal problems of state prisoners. A few months later, she filed a petition on behalf of a writ writer in the Texas prison system who claimed he was being denied access to legal services.

As if acting on a premonition, officials of the Texas Department of Corrections (TDC) fiercely resisted Jalet's efforts at every turn. They prevented her from visiting the prison on the grounds that she was not a criminal defense attorney representing inmates on appeal. They retaliated against the writ writers who tried to contact her. Eventually, they filed a rather unique suit against Jalet herself, seeking to bar her permanently from access to the prisoners on the grounds that she was "indoctrinating them with revolutionary ideas." As anyone with an even vaguely Cro-Magnon sensibility might have guessed, this bit of legal creativity by the TDC not only failed to intimidate Jalet, but spurred her, and others, to further action. By the time TDC's suit was finally and decisively rejected by the Fifth Circuit, Jalet had been joined by a number of colleagues who were busily filing dozens of petitions against the Texas prison system, challenging the lack of access to legal services and the harsh treatment of inmate writ writers. The writ writers, in turn, were beginning to file complaints about their conditions of confinement, the computation of good time, the prison disciplinary procedures, and a host of other issues.

These petitions were accumulating in disconcerting numbers by the early 1970s. Many of them were directed to Judge William Wayne Justice of the United States District Court for the Eastern District of Texas, who sat in Tyler, home of two state prison units.* Appointed to the district court by Lyndon Johnson in 1968, Judge Justice had quickly gained a reputation as an activist. By the time he began to address conditions in the state prisons, he had already handed down landmark rulings involving bilingual education, voter and employment discrimination, desegregation

* Texas, which has its own names for so many things, calls its prisons "units."

of schools and public housing, and conditions in custodial facilities for juveniles, the accused, and the mentally retarded.[55] Prison reform was thus a natural extension of his abiding concern with the rights of legally marginalized individuals.

In 1972, because of this interest and involvement, Judge Justice was invited to speak at a Practicing Law Institute Seminar on prisoners' rights at Dallas's Southern Methodist University. At the seminar, a young San Francisco lawyer named William Turner gave an impassioned speech on the same topic. Turner, a native Texan and a graduate of Harvard Law School, had litigated desegregation cases in the South for the NAACP Legal Defense Fund. Impressed, Judge Justice resolved to develop a prisoners' rights case of his own and to contact Turner to see if he would represent the complainants. As he later recalled, "I decided that I'd have a little test case to see what a first-class lawyer could do with the state's contentions and what he could develop in favor of the inmates, because I wanted to find out if there was any substance to what [the prisoners] were saying."[56] To develop the issues in the case, Judge Justice asked his clerks to locate "typical" petitions for each type of complaint.[57] Of the several such petitions they directed to him, one had been filed by David Ruiz on June 29, 1972. Ruiz, serving a twenty-five-year term for armed robbery, was known as a troublemaker by prison authorities because of his efforts in helping a number of other inmates file petitions in federal court. In his handwritten petition to Judge Justice, Ruiz alleged that he was being harassed by prison officials and was being denied his constitutional right to medical services and access to the courts. His petition was one of seven that Judge Justice ultimately selected for his "little test case."

Judge Justice's office tracked Turner down in Nepal, where, in true 1970s style, he was trekking, and invited him to handle the case. Upon his return Turner met with the judge, reviewed the petitions, and agreed. On April 12, 1974, he filed a revised version of Ruiz's complaint, now consolidated with the complaints of several other inmates and titled *Ruiz v. Estelle*. The resulting case quickly escalated into a class action suit on behalf of every Texas prisoner against every Texas prison. This was unique at the time, and remains unique to this day; no other system of this magnitude has been the subject of a comprehensive prison conditions suit.* Other prison cases have either involved much smaller systems, like Arkansas's or Rhode Island's; single institutions, like the Colorado Penitentiary and the Santa Clara County Jail; or particular practices in larger systems, like the California visitation rules. But Texas, which so often prides itself

---

* In 1974, Texas had the largest prison system in the nation in terms of inmate population. At present, California's growing enthusiasm for incarceration has dropped Texas into second place.

on having things that are large, was now embarked on a longhorn-sized litigation involving a host of conditions in all twenty-four of its "units."

Judge Justice quickly recognized the need for rather extensive investigatory resources, far beyond the limited capacities of a legal services office. Displaying a willingness to improvise that was to continue for the duration of the case, and determination that was born from prior experience in massive class action cases involving school desegregation, he took the unusual step of ordering the U.S. Department of Justice to appear as amicus curiae for the plaintiffs. He also ordered it to use its substantial investigatory powers and resources "to investigate fully the facts alleged in the prisoners' complaints, to participate in such civil action with the full rights of a party thereto, and to advise this court at all stages of the proceedings as to any action deemed appropriate."[58] The department's Office of Civil Rights was already involved in a suit challenging racial discrimination in the Texas prisons, and was thus familiar with the situation. Still staffed by lawyers recruited in the heyday of its civil rights activity, the Justice Department attorneys welcomed the request and enthusiastically joined the litigation. Attorney Gail Littlefield was named cocounsel along with Turner, and the department's resources were deployed to investigate conditions in the Texas prisons.[59] Like dozens of other innovative rulings that Judge Justice would make in *Ruiz*, the decision to draw the U.S. Department of Justice into the suit was appealed by the state to the Fifth Circuit Court of Appeals; like almost all the others, the decision was upheld.[60]

As the pretrial proceedings got under way, another distinctive aspect of the Texas litigation quickly became apparent. Arkansas prison officials had recognized that they were part of a backward, corrupt, mismanaged system in an impoverished little state, and were consequently apologetic about the practices revealed by the litigation against them. Other southern prison officials, while they varied in their levels of voluntary self-abnegation, generally displayed similar reactions. But Texas and the TDC were different. Texas was a large, wealthy, and rapidly growing state, located at the geographic juncture where the South became the Sunbelt. And Texas prisons were regarded by their own officials – and by many outsiders – as not only well managed, but as paragons of stern, effective punishment.

This belief in the exemplary nature of the Texas prison system had been carefully cultivated during the previous twenty-five years.[61] It began with the appointment of Oscar Ellis as the commissioner of the Texas Department of Corrections in 1947, a reaction to the usual southern-state scandals over corruption and abuse. Ellis began his adult life as a shoe salesman in Memphis and had backed into corrections. Elected to the Shelby County Board of Commissioners in the late 1930s, he was assigned responsibility for overseeing maintenance of the county roads. This required coordination with the county Department of Corrections, whose inmates worked on the road gangs. Ellis found that he had a gift for disciplining and controlling prisoners, and in short order was running the county corrections work program.[62] His model of a highly regimented, self-sufficient correctional system attracted general notice, and a few years later he was called to apply his approach in Texas. As the state's first systemwide prison manager, he was supposed to clean up the mess, and to a considerable extent he did. For the next fourteen years, until his death in 1961, Ellis reigned over the Texas prisons with an iron hand. He gained widespread respect within the state because he was an efficient administrator who ran orderly institutions and made few demands on the state budget. The prisoners were marched into the fields six days a week where they worked from "day clean to first dark"[63] growing cotton and a variety of other crops on the more than 100,000 acres of agricultural land owned by the TDC. They were guarded largely by "building tenders," armed inmate trusties who were compensated with a variety of costless goods such as special privileges and the opportunity to abuse the other inmates. If they failed to work, or failed to work hard, or sometimes failed to work ferociously hard, they were beaten with a rawhide strap. They were fed cheap food, housed in substandard facilities, and denied all but the most rudimentary medical care.[64] Between the late 1940s and 1958, the average daily cost of maintaining an inmate in the Texas prisons declined from $4 to less than $1.25, and in some years the system even returned funds to the state.[65] This was greatly appreciated by the state legislature, and was no doubt one of the reasons legislators were so willing to defer to Ellis and to abstain from "meddling" in TDC affairs.

Ellis's successor, George Beto, formerly president of a Lutheran college in Austin, not only maintained this tradition, but elevated it to near mythology. Fully six foot, seven inches tall, Beto was a man of tremendous charm and energy, known, with fearful admiration by staff and inmates alike, as "walking George" for his unannounced, personal inspections of the prisons under his command.[66] During his nearly twelve years in office, from 1961 until his retirement in 1972, the TDC came to be regarded as a model prison system: efficient, orderly, and inexpensive.[67] This view was widely held throughout the United States, as evidenced by Beto's election in 1970 as president of the American Correctional Association.[68] In 1972, just as the *Ruiz* case got under way, he was succeeded by James Estelle, his former assistant and handpicked successor.

Although the litigation ultimately revealed the Texas prisons as something of a Potemkin village, the initial reaction of TDC officials to the prisoner complaints must be understood in light of this twenty-five-year myth that had been painstakingly fostered by two powerful, charismatic, and morally self-assured commissioners. TDC officials were proud of their traditions, viewed their authoritarian regime with its insistence upon cleanliness, order, and strict discipline as the epitome of penological success, and resented outside interference. The bizarre lawsuit under Beto's leadership against Frances Jalet, on the grounds that she was a "troublemaker" intent on "indoctrinating [prisoners] with revolutionary ideas," was not an aberration, but a product of this self-righteous mentality.

The TDC's position in the *Ruiz* litigation, therefore, was predictably one of fierce, no-holds-barred resistance. Because Estelle lacked the charisma and creativity of his predecessors, as Beto himself acknowledged to one of the authors,[69] he felt all the more determined to maintain the regime they had established. He categorically denied any wrongdoing by the TDC, denied that "building tenders" did anything other than janitorial work, and continued to resist and protest at each step of the case.[70] In fact, during the lengthy pretrial phase between 1975 and 1977, Judge Justice had to issue a number of orders to protect the safety of inmates who were cooperating with the plaintiff's attorneys.

The trial finally began in Houston on October 2, 1978, and its massive scale reveals the intensity of the conflict between the plaintiffs and the TDC. The trial lasted 159 days, as the court heard 349 witnesses and reviewed 1,565 exhibits. This mother of all prison trials concluded nearly a year later on September 20, 1979. Fourteen months later, on December 12, 1980,[71] Judge Justice issued a 118–page opinion that amounted to a wholesale condemnation of the Texas prison system. In his conclusion, he could hardly contain his anger at what he had found and his contempt for the officials who had categorically denied these facts:

> [I]t is impossible for a written opinion to convey the pernicious conditions and the pain and degradation which ordinary inmates suffer within the TDC units–the gruesome experiences of youthful first offenders forcibly raped; the cruel and justifiable fears of inmates, wondering when they will be called upon to defend the next violent assault; the sheer misery, the discomfort, the wholesale loss of privacy for prisoners housed with one, two or three others in a forty-five foot cell or suffocatingly packed together in a crowded dormitory; the physical suffering and wretched psychological stress which must be endured by those sick or injured who cannot obtain adequate medical care; the sense of abject helplessness felt by inmates arbitrarily sent to solitary confinement or administrative segregation without proper opportunity to defend themselves or to argue their causes; the bitter frustration of inmates prevented from petitioning the courts and other governmental authorities for relief from perceived injustices.[72]

Judge Justice held that TDC was in violation of the Constitution in six areas: space per inmate, security and supervision, health care, disciplinary procedures, access to legal services, and sanitation and safety conditions. He also indicated a strong preference for the parties to negotiate a settlement rather than relying on the court to formulate its own remedial order. The plaintiffs' attorneys were quite willing to do so, but the TDC officials were seething with rage. While they acknowledged that health services, disciplinary procedures, access to legal services, and sanitation conditions were less than optimal, they argued that these services met constitutional minimums. They thus felt that the judge was holding them to unreasonably high standards and did not fully appreciate the need for security and control. And throughout the trial TDC officials had steadfastly denied plaintiff's allegations that inmate building tenders – the TDC's own name for trusties – were used for security and supervision of other inmates. Nothing in Judge Justice's ruling caused them to change their stance. Although TDC and state officials were bitter that Judge Justice had given them virtually no credit for doing anything right, it was this condemnation of the building tender system that made them truly apoplectic.[73]

Nevertheless, the TDC officials finally did agree to negotiate, believing that they were probably better off participating in the formulation of a consent decree than relying on Judge Justice to formulate one on his own. For them, in other words, negotiations were simply the lesser of two evils. After three months of arm-twisting, Judge Justice finally got the parties to agree to a brief document outlining a procedure for correcting most of the violations found by the court. It contained a list of improvements that had been made since the trial in the areas of health care, provisions for special-needs prisoners (retarded, physically handicapped, developmentally disabled, or mentally ill), work safety and hygiene, the use of chemical agents, the terms and conditions of solitary confinement, and the terms and conditions in administrative segregation. It also specified that the TDC would prepare additional plans to address problems in these areas in light of "the relevant facts and conclusions contained in the court's Memorandum Opinion of December 12, 1980."[74] In all likelihood, this agreement could only have been reached because it was brief and couched in very general language, a tactic that, while successful in the short run, guaranteed that the intense conflict that had characterized the trial would subsequently reemerge.

The Consent Decree, the Special Master, and the Building Tenders (1981–1983)

The draft settlement agreement was submitted to Judge Justice in spring of 1981 and received his swift approval. Judge Justice also persuaded the parties to agree to the appointment of a special master to monitor the preparation and implementation of the plans. A few months later, on July 21, 1981, after reviewing nominations submitted by the parties, he selected Vincent Nathan.[75] Nathan had once taught contracts at the University of

Toledo School of Law. In 1974 District Judge Timothy Hogan had appointed Nathan, who then had had no experience or special interest in prisons, as the master in *Rhodes v. Chapman*.[76] Although the resulting decision was ultimately reversed by the Supreme Court, as noted in Chapter 2, Nathan's intelligence and natural courage had gained him respect from the attorneys for both sides in the case. After his work on *Rhodes*, he was appointed in several other cases, and by the end of the decade he was, along with Allen Breed, one of the two best known masters in the field. He was widely regarded as knowledgeable, businesslike, and well organized, but even his admirers described him as arrogant.

Justice's order gave Nathan sweeping powers and, rather unusually, granted him authority to appoint several assistants. Although the order emphasized that he could not "intervene in the administrative management of the Texas Department of Corrections," or "direct the defendants or any of their subordinates to take or to refrain from taking any specific action to achieve compliance," it provided that Nathan and his assistants could

> observe, monitor, find facts, report or testify as to his findings, and make recommendations to the court concerning steps which should be taken to achieve compliance. The special master may and should assist the defendants in every possible way, and to this end he may and should confer informally with the defendants and their subordinates on matters affecting compliance.[77]

The Court also granted the special master access to TDC files and the authority to conduct confidential interviews with staff and inmates, to attend all formal meetings of TDC officials, to require written reports from any TDC staff member, and to "order and conduct hearings with respect to the defendants' compliance with this court's orders."

Although TDC officials had been consulted regarding the idea of appointing a special master, and welcomed the appointment of Nathan because of his known expertise in corrections, the sweeping powers he received were viewed as one more gratuitous insult by Judge Justice. And almost immediately after Nathan commenced his work, TDC officials realized that they had made a mistake by not opposing his appointment.[78] To assess the adequacy of the TDC plans, Nathan and his associates held hearings and conducted their own investigations. In doing so they almost invariably found the TDC's plans to achieve compliance with the consent decree to be woefully deficient. TDC officials typically acknowledged minor violations, but Nathan's investigations revealed major ones. The TDC proposed modest, incremental reforms; Nathan saw the need for sweeping change. When such disagreements occurred, as regularly they did, the special master would ask the TDC to revise its plans in light of his findings and offer "suggestions" about what would be required to make the new plans satisfactory. This pattern occurred so frequently that the sequence – submission of plans followed by the master's review and then revision and resubmission – became confused and perhaps even reversed. Nathan gradually came to be perceived as directing the scope and substance of the TDC's plans, rather than simply responding to them.

From Nathan's perspective it was the recalcitrance of the defendants that forced him and his staff to become increasingly involved in ferreting out issues and problems, and in determining the concrete steps needed to meet the requirements of the consent decree. From the defendants' perspective, Nathan was reveling in his power to "run the institution," and nothing they did could ever satisfy him. The final authority to resolve the ensuing disputes belonged to Judge Justice, and he almost always exercised it in favor of his special master. Throughout the process, TDC officials continued to challenge Nathan's findings and requests for more comprehensive planning, but Justice invariably supported Nathan and chastised the TDC for its recalcitrance. Indeed, as TDC resistance to the court continued, Justice's confidence in the special master seemed to grow, and the size and resolve of the master's office grew apace. At its apogee, the office had three monitors, a staff of thirteen, and an annual budget of well over one million dollars. It also had the collective determination to compel the TDC to abide by both the letter and the spirit of the consent decree, by persuasion if possible but by force if necessary.[79]

As a result, Nathan was able to pry out of the TDC a series of increasingly detailed plans which covered virtually every facet of prison life, including delivery of health services, inmate access to law libraries, vocational training programs, space requirements, diets, heating and ventilation, inmate classification systems, plans to deal with inmate gangs, correctional officer hiring, promotion policies, early release options, and architectural plans for new construction in the face of the mushrooming prison population. Each of the plans, together with the special master's reports on them, could run into the hundreds or even thousands of pages, and involve extraordinary levels of detail. Many of the recommended actions depended on vast funding increases for hiring and training new correctional officers, renovating large, old facilities, building still larger new ones, and expanding health, education, and other services. The court routinely approved these recommendations and ordered TDC officials to comply with them. The not-so-hidden audience for many of these recommendations and court orders was the governor and state legislature. The master's findings and recommendations emboldened plaintiffs' attorneys, who continued to expand their inquiry and to unearth new issues. For a period, it seemed, the more TDC acted to respond to these criticisms, the more additional problems were revealed and the more the court's concerns expanded.

The most divisive issue in the entire process, and the one that best reveals the deep hostility between plaintiffs and defendants, involved the building tenders. At trial the plaintiffs' attorney Bill Turner had alleged that the building tender system, which placed prisoners under the discretionary control of other prisoners, had subjected them to a regime of "totalitarian brutality." The judge agreed, and the issue had been included in his consent decree, although the nature of the defendant's response had not been specified. Because the TDC continued to deny the very existence of the building tender system, one of the first things Vincent Nathan did after receiving his appointment was to assign his monitor, David Arnold, to conduct an investigation into the plaintiffs' allegations. Within short order, Arnold produced a lengthy report documenting the building tenders' role in guarding prisoners and maintaining general security. Even after this report, TDC officials continued to deny the findings, and successfully enlisted then Attorney General Mark White to their cause, who at the time was preparing an appeal of Judge Justice's rulings on behalf of the TDC. White had gubernatorial ambitions, which were shortly to be realized, and he and then Governor William Clements were seeking to outdo each other in their support for the TDC and their condemnation of Judge Justice's meddlesome orders.

At this juncture, however, a dramatic turning point occurred in the Texas prisons case. One of the TDC lawyers who was coordinating the appeal was Steve Martin. For many years prior to going to law school, Martin had worked as a guard in Texas prisons, and he was intimately familiar with their procedures, including the actual operation of the building tender system. As he recounts in his coauthored book about the case, he initiated his own quiet investigations in the wake of Arnold's report, the TDC's denials, and the attorney general's plans for the appeal. Drawing on his extensive contacts among both inmates and guards, Martin learned that the system was still intact and that, if anything, Arnold, as an outsider, had been unable to uncover many of its most egregious features. There followed a series of meetings with the attorney general's office, and with the Houston law firm of Fulbright and Jaworski, which had been retained to assist with the appeal, and later to assist the attorney general himself. Martin quietly informed them that Arnold's report was essentially accurate; if anything, it had understated the problem.[80] Attorney General White and his staff were incredulous at first and continued to rail against Judge Justice, but Martin's actions did sow the initial seeds of doubt. The first member of the defense team to seize upon Martin's evidence, however, was not one of the TDC's fancy lawyers, or the Texas attorney general, but Dick Whittington, a member of the Texas Board of Corrections.

Until *Ruiz* forced the TDC into the limelight, the board had been an inactive oversight body, rubber-stamping whatever actions the commissioners proposed. Now it was beginning to take an active role in trying to protect the TDC from the court's ever escalating attacks. As the only lawyer on the board, Whittington, a conservative Republican, had been charged with keeping abreast of the litigation, and thus learned about Martin's confirmation of Arnold's findings. At a meeting with Fulbright and Jaworski lawyers and TDC officials, he confronted Commissioner Estelle. Within a few days, Attorney General White was asking tough questions of Estelle and the TDC, angry that he had been lied to, and no doubt angrier still that he had embraced the lie in public. As time went on, the extent of the TDC's prevarications became increasingly apparent; with surprising rapidity, state officials began to place more credence in the court's findings and were motivated to conduct their own investigations, which in turn uncovered still other problems and abuses.[81]

As these events were transpiring, the TDC suffered another serious defeat – the loss of its appeal from Judge Justice's order. Even as the parties were hammering out the provisions of the settlement agreement and taking the first steps toward its implementation, state officials had been preparing to mount a full-scale appeal of the court's ruling, challenging the court's findings and the scope of the special master's authority. The appeal grew with the case, as the TDC added challenges to the detailed changes that the court demanded. In December 1982, the Circuit Court of Appeals for the Fifth Circuit handed down a unanimous opinion upholding Judge Justice's sweeping rulings, and the broad powers he had granted to the special master.[82] The TDC had drawn heavily on its vast reservoir of political support among Texas lawmakers in mounting this appeal and the concomitant effort to discredit Judge Justice, the special master, and the lead plaintiff's attorney. It had trifled with that support by lying about the building tender system, apparently hoping that Judge Justice would be reversed and the TDC could withdraw into its prior insularity and independence. Now the appeal was lost, the lie exposed, and their political support was crumbling.

Implementation of the Court Order (1983–1990)

By the mid-1980s, it seemed clear that the old order was passing, although battles continued to be fought and resistance remained fierce. The central features of the system under which it had flourished – income-producing prison labor, the building tenders, paternalistic discretionary control – had all been ground into the Texas dust. *Ruiz* had not found any of these features unconstitutional per se, but the joint implementation efforts of Judge Justice and Vincent Nathan created a regime in which they could not survive. Instead of profit-making labor, Justice and Nathan demanded vocational programs and vastly increased expenditures on food and health care; instead of the inexpensive, sadistic convict building tenders, they demanded well-trained, salaried guards; instead of paternalism, they demanded due process and formally enacted legislation. These changes were each extensive by themselves; collectively, they produced a complete transformation of the methodology and style of the Texas prisons.

The collapse of the old order created a crisis within the TDC, as many of the most experienced managers were forced to resign or chose to do so. Those disillusioned few who remained were compelled to oversee the work of a rapidly growing cadre of inexperienced and hastily recruited guards who filled the role once occupied by the building tenders. With the court, its special master, and increasingly disgruntled state officials scrutinizing them, the TDC's leaders initiated a series of administrative shake-ups, which resulted in still more resignations, dismissals, and reassignments, plus a regime of micromanagement from the top down that further undermined staff effectiveness and morale. During 1983 and 1984, over two hundred disciplinary actions were brought against the remaining correctional officers. Citing frustration with the court and an inability to obtain funding from the state legislature, James Estelle resigned in 1983.[83]

He was replaced in May 1984 by Ray Procunier, the first TDC director who accepted the court orders as a given and was prepared to work within the framework established by them. Procunier had a solid record as a tough, reform-minded correctional administrator, whose strength was turning problems around quickly. He had held a series of important positions in California and, at the time of his appointment, was deputy director of corrections in New Mexico, specifically appointed there to bring order and discipline to that state's prison system in the wake of the 1980 rioting that had left thirty-three inmates dead. In Texas Procunier only served a little more than one year, but during that time he agreed to a second major settlement of outstanding issues that included crowding, visitation, staffing, construction, and classification. In reaching these agreements, Procunier alienated Attorney General White, who had continued to use the prison litigation as a campaign issue and had attacked any proposals, including his own earlier ones, to spend more funds on prisons. Rather than waiting to be fired by soon-to-be Governor White, Procunier resigned.

This administrative and political turmoil had its counterpart among the inmates. The problem had been anticipated by both Judge Justice and various state officials, but they were unable to prevent it. Guarded by an inexperienced and ill-prepared staff and freed from the brutal repression of the building tenders, inmates began to prey on each other with increasing frequency, while inmate gangs battled each other through every section of the Texas prisons. These gangs were part of a nationwide development unrelated to events in Texas, or even prison reform generally, but in Texas they had clearly seized an opportunity presented by the lacuna in control. As Ben Crouch and James Marquart observe in their study of Texas prisons in the aftermath of *Ruiz*, to "protect themselves in an increasingly uncertain world, many inmates resorted to violent self-help, and in the process violence became a mechanism of social control."[84] The net result was that inmate-to-inmate violence escalated to an all-time high. The number of recorded fights among prisoners more than doubled, from thirty-eight per thousand prisoners in 1983 to eight-seven per thousand in 1986. Inmate deaths caused by other inmates skyrocketed, jumping from one or two per year throughout the 1970s to twenty-five in 1984 and twenty-seven in 1985.[85]

Following Procunier's resignation, state officials turned to another non-Texan to run the TDC: Lane McCotter. McCotter had been both a career soldier and a career corrections administrator, having spent his entire time in the Army – over twenty years – running military prisons. His last posting had been commander of the military barracks at Fort Leavenworth, Kansas, the toughest of the Army's several maximum security facilities. Among his colleagues McCotter was known as someone who was firm, fair, and ran a tight operation for both his staff and inmates. The significance of his selection could not have been lost on either the TDC administrators and correctional officers or the inmates – everyone knew that he had been selected to restore order and discipline to both these now unsettled groups. McCotter moved quickly, adopting the strict style that had characterized his administration at Leavenworth. He instituted frequent twenty-four-hour lockdowns and introduced massive numbers of new guards who had been subjected to an intense regimen of training. By 1986, the level of inmate violence began to decline. Indeed, Crouch and Marquart report that after McCotter's changes, long-term inmates felt safer than ever before, not only in comparison with the immediately previous period of heightened violence, but in comparison to life under the old order and the building tender system.[86]

This new regime was also harsh, however. Crouch and Marquart characterize it as "hyperlegalistic," by which they mean that the new director insisted that every detail in the prison's operations had to run "by the book," a book that he himself had written.[87] At times, some observers have commented, this meant that compliance with picayune, hastily conceived rules took precedence over common sense. But it did produce immediate results, and it eventually began to mature into a new order modeled along military lines rather than upon autocratic and personalistic rule.

Although everyone recognized the need to restore order, other features

of the court-ordered changes faced fierce resistance and daunting com-
plications, as TDC officials continued to be truculent and uncooperative.
Writing of his experience as a monitor for the special master, Samuel
Brackel described the difficulties in implementing the seemingly straightforward task of providing prisoners access to legal materials:

> [T]he very introduction of the access [to legal materials] rules into the
> prison system generated – like any other new set of rights or rules would –
> considerable conflict and controversy. Inevitably, the availability of these
> new rights led to a spirited assertion of them by inmates and an explosion
> of charges that they were being violated by prison staff. The staff in turn
> reacted to these charges, often in a fashion that matched the unproductive
> and frivolous character of too many of the inmate complaints.[88]

This problem was complicated still further when the new library, with its
relatively easy access, became a convenient rendezvous for homosexual
liaisons, which at times crowded the limited space beyond capacity and
initiated yet another round of conflict among inmates, staff, the prison
system, and the Court.* Such spiraling problems were repeated hundreds
of times, each time a new program or a new policy was put in place.

The situation was further complicated by the emergence of an additional problem that was clearly not attributable to either the TDC or the
court order – the prison population explosion. Between 1972, when the
case was first filed, and 1982, when the trial ended, Texas's prison population jumped from fifteen thousand to over twenty-six thousand. By the
time the court terminated jurisdiction over *Ruiz*, in December 1992, it
had risen to nearly fifty thousand. As in Arkansas, what began as a suit
challenging practices and conditions eventually turned into a crowding
suit, with the court, along with plaintiffs' attorneys and the defendants,
scrambling to devise ways to accommodate the hundreds of new inmates
who arrived each day at the doors of the state's already overcrowded
prisons.

During the course of the litigation, this pressure grew even more acute
as a result of separate federal court orders dealing with crowding in Texas
county jails. For instance, in a suit against the Harris County (Houston)
jail, a different federal judge ordered the TDC to stop its practice of refusing to accept newly sentenced offenders and leaving them to languish
in the still more crowded county jails. Although this was a strategy devised
by the TDC to meet its own court-ordered population caps, its compliance

---

* This pattern ultimately led Brackel to question the value of highly intrusive court
  orders. Repeatedly, he argues, such changes "led to a situation in which the level
  of mutual psychological harassment and the inclination to engage in other petty
  tests of power [were] raised to new heights."

was purchased at the price of keeping inmates in even worse conditions. The Harris County jail suit precipitated a crisis regarding this arrangement, but despite sustained litigation, the matter was never fully resolved and as of this writing TDC officials still try to delay acceptance of offenders sentenced to their custody.

The court's response to the crowding problem was to obtain the parties' agreement to a separate stipulation. In its original version, established in 1985, this stipulation provided for a system capacity of 40,134, but it was regularly amended as new facilities opened, and had reached 77,213 by 1995. The TDC's response to crowding took a variety of forms. Nudged by the court, it entered into a massive building campaign, greatly expanding its housing capacity throughout the 1980s. It turned to private contractors who quickly built and began to run facilities for low-security offenders. It developed a classification system that allowed it to house offenders more efficiently. It delayed acceptance of newly sentenced offenders, the court orders notwithstanding, thereby decreasing intake. It constructed tent cities within the walls of existing facilities to house inmates temporarily. Throughout all this, there was constant friction with the plaintiffs, the special master, and the court, as the population of various facilities approached the numbers provided for in a crowding stipulation.* [89] But there was also a sense that all parties were addressing the same problem, and that they perceived that problem in roughly equivalent ways.

In fact, by the late 1980s, there was a new attitude toward the court in evidence among TDC officials, largely because the officials themselves were new. These new officials grudgingly accepted the court's jurisdiction and embraced the views of modern correctional professionals. They no longer sought to defend the old order, or saw a need to lie about the discredited building tender system. It may have been this change in attitude, more than anything else, that led Judge Justice to begin winding down this elephantine case. On March 6, 1990, Justice ordered the parties to begin negotiations for a comprehensive final order. He required that the parties address "compliance problems, ensure that unconstitutional conditions do not recur, eliminate unnecessary detail, institutionalize reforms, improve defendant's internal monitoring mechanisms, and establish remedies and timetables for termination of the court's jurisdiction."

---

* Early in this process, after Judge Justice had released inmates on his own in order to relieve crowding, the legislature in Texas enacted the Texas Prison Management Act in order to permit the TDC to select the inmates to be released. This act, which provided a mechanism for early release whenever crowding reached a specified level (95 percent of capacity as defined in the act) was invoked twelve times in the first two years of its existence.

Needless to say, the path toward this final order was not always smooth, and the negotiations took over two years to complete. The proposed final judgment that emerged was divided into twenty-two sections, each covering an issue that had been central to the litigation. Rather than establish a timetable for the complete termination of the court's jurisdiction, the proposal included certain permanent injunctions that prescribed defendant's future actions with regard to crowding and to selected services.*

On December 11, 1992, Judge Justice signed the final order. In it he observed that "Deputy Director Scott . . . testified that the dramatic increases in staffing since the court entered its Amended Decree in 1981 have permitted the TDC to replace the building tender system with uniformed security staff, . . . and the record reflects that . . . officials effectively have dismantled the building tender system, and . . . that those officials intend to maintain their current policies in this area."[90] This was a dramatic turnabout from the first several years of the litigation, when TDC officials steadfastly denied the existence of the building tender system while trying to maintain it in actuality. Although the final judgment covered a host of issues, it may have been the significance of this acknowledgment and the changes that it implied that led Judge Justice to conclude his opinion with the following observation:

> Over twenty years ago, a handful of brave prisoners set in motion a process that even defendant's highest officials acknowledge has improved all aspects of the TDCJ-ID. TDCJ-ID has remade itself into a professionally operated agency whose goals are to achieve the highest standards of correctional excellence.
>
> Equally important, the measures taken by TDCJ-ID officials to meet their constitutional obligations have been memorialized and institutionalized in numerous internal rules and regulations that have replaced this court's orders as the agency's "road map" to success. The court is satisfied that the defendants not only will maintain and implement these rules and regulations, but also will continue to strive to improve on them and their implementation despite the absence in many areas of detailed court orders.[91]

But even as he took great satisfaction in the department's change of attitude and positive accomplishments, Judge Justice's opinion sounded two

---

* Sections of the final order addressed the following issues: staffing, support services, disciplinary procedures, health and safety, use of force, access to courts, maintenance of facilities, heating and ventilation, programmatic and recreational opportunities, crowding, bilingual staff, internal monitoring by defendants as to the conditions of the final agreement, programs for mentally retarded inmates, health services, psychiatric services, and conditions on death row.

themes he regarded as ominous. Noting that the department agreed to be permanently enjoined from exceeding population caps for those institutions identified in the plan, he nevertheless observed that the state appeared to have an "insatiable appetite" for incarcerating people. He also noted two recent, retrenchment-era cases, *Rufo v. Inmates of the Suffolk County Jail*[92] and *Freeman v. Pitts*,[93] which were handed down by the Supreme Court as the proposed settlement agreement was being negotiated. In *Rufo* the Supreme Court had substantially weakened the importance of consent decrees, establishing a "flexible" standard for the modification of such decrees in place of the more restrictive "grievous wrong" standard that had been in effect since 1932,[94] and that had applied to this case until its final months. Thus even as Judge Justice hailed the dramatic improvements in the state's prisons and the professionalism of its new administrators, he noted two developments that threatened to unravel the complex, painfully achieved agreement that had brought *Ruiz* to its conclusion.

In the twenty years since David Ruiz filed his petition and, more particularly, the twelve years that the Texas prisons had been placed under comprehensive judicial supervision, massive changes had occurred. The patriarchal regime, the building tenders, and the primitive living conditions were gone; professional guards, medical personnel, educational programs, and a federally trained superintendent had appeared in their place. Hundreds of millions of dollars, perhaps as much as a billion, had been spent as a result of the court's orders. In the largest, most bitterly contested prison case in American history, and almost certainly one of the largest and most bitterly contested legal cases in the history of Anglo-American law, the court had won a decisive, if potentially unstable victory.

Three Variations on the Theme: Colorado State Penitentiary, the Santa Clara County Jails, and Marion Penitentiary

Colorado State Penitentiary

Crisis and Inaction at Old Max (1970–1977)

In 1977 the Colorado Department of Corrections was a modern, progressive correctional system. Unlike many southern prisons at the time, it had a cadre of full-time guards who received training before they began work. Its administrators subscribed to modern penological practices endorsed by the American Correctional Association (ACA). Colorado law required the department to provide treatment, rehabilitation, and employment opportunities for prisoners.*[1] The department had working arrangements with state hospitals to provide physical and mental health services to inmates who needed them. State health and safety regulations explicitly applied to the state prisons and were regularly enforced by state inspectors. There was even a law requiring the state librarian to provide library services to prisoners.[2] Corrections administrators embraced and actively supported the progressive ideology of the ACA and regularly turned to the association for advice and evaluation. Thus, in the statute books and in the regulations, Colorado had a model prison system.

Unfortunately, a substantial number of Colorado prisoners were not confined in the statute books or in the regulations, but at "Old Max,"

---

* The law provided in part that the department had a duty to "assume responsibility for training offenders in general work habits, work skills, and specific training skills that increase their employment prospects when released," and to "develop industries that provide forty hours of work activity each week for all able-bodied offenders."

96

the maximum security Colorado State Penitentiary at Canon City. Established in the 1860s, when Colorado was still a territory, Old Max had been renovated and expanded numerous times since then, and now consisted of a conglomeration of ill-matched buildings that angled up the side of a hill in crazy-quilt fashion. Most of these buildings dated from the turn of the century, and by all accounts the entire facility, with the exception of the administration building, was in a fairly advanced state of decay. It was a maze of open areas, closed cells, hidden nooks and dark crannies that were unsupervisable and unsecurable. Due to age and lack of maintenance, roofs leaked, toilets overflowed and backed up into sinks, and shower areas dripped with mold and slime. High ceilings and open-tiered cell blocks made it impossible to control noise, to provide heat in winter or ventilation in summer.

But antiquated buildings, deteriorating facilities, and inadequate security were only part of the problem at Old Max. Essential services were woefully inadequate, and had declined markedly since the mid-1960s. A principal reason was that resources earmarked for medical, educational, and occupational services had been diverted to support the additional security that Old Max's antiquated facility demanded.[*3] The increased safety that resulted in the short run was purchased at a severe price, however. Eliminating the educational, vocational, and rehabilitation programs that occupied the inmates' time and provided them with pocket money engendered anger and frustration. Prison officials responded by increasing cell time and cutting back Old Max's programs even further. They tore down a substantial portion of the prison's industry row, eliminating the cannery, mattress factory, brick plant, shoe repair shop, tin shop, soap plant, blacksmith shop, and tailor shop. In 1977, as further economy and safety measures, they terminated the laundry service, which employed fifty inmates, closed the library and stopped all library services, discontinued meetings of numerous inmate organizations, including Alcoholics Anonymous, banned the inmate council, and shut down the inmate radio station and newspaper. Colorado's enlightened state law requiring that all eligible inmates work in training-related jobs was mocked by the fact that there were few jobs to be had. Most of those in the general population were locked down twenty or more hours a day with nothing to do. By 1977, inmates were not even collecting the prison's garbage.[4]

---

* A host of studies in the early and mid 1970s all pointed to antiquated design as one of the causes of security and safety problems. Old Max's design required high concentrations of security officers and led officials to terminate or suspend many programs in order to reduce inmate circulation through the mazelike prison complex. Thus, for instance, positions earmarked for teachers were filled by security personnel.

This already incendiary situation was made still more explosive by the demographic changes in the prison population. By 1977, Colorado prison officials were confronting a situation for which they were not prepared: a substantial increase in the number of prisoners, a more violent population, and inmates of more varied ethnic backgrounds. Instead of being predominantly white, as it had been in previous decades, Colorado's inmate population was now 30 percent Hispanic and 28 percent black.[5] The staff remained overwhelmingly white, however; few guards spoke Spanish and none received any continuing training in multicultural issues. Non-English language publications were prohibited from entering the prison and the 1977 cutbacks on inmate organizations included both the Black Cultural Development Society and the Latin American Development Society.[6] This combination of insecure facilities, inadequate programming, and escalating racial tensions led to the predictable results, as violence increased and neither the guards nor the inmates felt safe. The guards responded by leaving, and since new replacements were inexperienced, security declined still further. The inmates, for the most part, did not have this option, but a high proportion asked to be placed in protective custody because they were afraid to remain in the general population.

Over the course of the early to mid 1970s, a succession of reports had documented all these problems with Old Max – the dilapidated facilities, the inadequate programming, the absence of basic services, the lack of security, and the increasing levels of violence. In 1973 the facility was criticized by a state grand jury and the U.S. Department of Civil Rights for failure to provide adequate medical and mental health treatment.[7] In that same year, an inspection team of the American Correctional Association (ACA) characterized the prison as "outdated" and "unmanageable," and recommended that it be demolished.[8] This report also warned that pervasive inmate idleness was a potentially explosive problem. In 1975, one of the prison's largest cell blocks was condemned and closed by state health and safety inspectors due to problems of crowding, noise, and ventilation.[9]

The almost inevitable riot broke out at Old Max on May 18, 1975, leaving one inmate dead and sixteen severely injured. Governor Richard Lamm immediately appointed a commission to investigate the causes of the riot and to frame recommendations, while the state legislature conducted an investigation of its own. Chaired by the state's attorney general, the governor's commission issued a report in fall 1975, which characterized Old Max as "antiquated" and "insecure," and recommended demolishing all but one of its buildings or completely gutting their interiors and reconstructing them.[10] Echoing the 1973 ACA report, the attorney general laid much of the blame for the riot on inmate idleness due to lack of facilities, staff, and programs. In response to the report, the governor called the legislature into special session and asked it to support the commission's recommendations with increased funding. Instead, the legislature responded by enacting a law declaring that participation in a prison riot was a felony. Having thus provided that prisoners who engaged in prison riots would be sent to prison, the legislature grudgingly appropriated some funds for a consultant to assess the prison's problems yet again. In late 1976, the consulting firm Touche-Ross was commissioned to render this assessment. It issued its report in February 1977, which – to no one's surprise – called for substantial renovations and recommended the transformation of Old Max into a medium-security institution with far fewer inmates.[11]

In that same year, another committee appointed by Governor Lamm tied the increase in inmate suicides, and in assaults on inmates and guards, to inadequate staffing. A further report issued in 1978 found: that the prison's small medical staff was overwhelmed; that, contrary to every medical recommendation, the department relied heavily on untrained inmate aides to dispense medical services; and that the prison had virtually no capacity to diagnose the suicidal tendencies that festered in Old Max's grim environment. Still another report concluded that the prison's classification system was outdated, and that its diagnostic unit was both understaffed and undertrained.

In February 1978 the Department of Corrections commissioned its own study and issued its own master plan. It rejected the possibility of renovating Old Max and instead proposed that it be demolished and replaced with a new maximum-security facility.[12] This report was issued after the start of the litigation described in the next section. But that process had just begun and the February 1978 report seems to have been formulated independently of the litigation. Other experts were consulted, and all agreed that a full-scale renovation would be extremely expensive, $38 million according to one estimate. It would be better – and probably cheaper – to raze Old Max and start from scratch.

Again, none of these findings came as a surprise to corrections officials; indeed, a number of them had been initiated or sponsored by the department itself. But despite this willingness to acknowledge the problems, department officials were unable to get control of them. Most of their energies seemed to be consumed by commissioning the tsunami of reports that had washed over Old Max and by coping with day-to-day crises that the reports themselves did nothing to alleviate. Part of the reason for this was the turmoil caused by continuing instability in the leadership of the department. Between 1973 and 1979, the department had four different executive directors and Old Max had six different wardens. Policies and practices were constantly changing, leaving both prisoners and staff in a state of confusion.[13] Nor was the governor or the state legislature able to remedy this situation. Although the 1975 riot had made prison conditions and corrections a highly visible issue, the Democratic governor and Republican-controlled legislature found it difficult to work together on this as well as other issues. Thus, throughout the early and mid-1970s Old Max remained heavily studied, widely condemned, and largely unchanged.

Ramos v. Lamm and the End of Old Max (1977–1979)

During the mid-1970s, and especially after the 1975 riot, various prisoners' rights advocates met periodically with corrections officials, urging them to implement the recommendations of the committees that had assessed conditions in the Colorado prisons. These advocates came from several different groups; some were members of local prisoners' rights organizations, others were attorneys for legal services offices, and still others were attorneys for the Colorado branch of the American Civil Liberties Union (ACLU). All of them had been deluged with complaints by inmates at Old Max and the state's other prisons. They began by being optimistic about their negotiations. On paper, at least, the state was committed to a progressive correctional system, and officials were candid at meetings about the prisons' shortcomings. However, because many of those on the advocates' side of the table were lawyers, and all were receiving a growing number of complaints, the threat of litigation always hovered in the background. As the complaints accumulated, and the prison system's inability to deal with its problems became more apparent, these lawyers began to talk seriously about a class action against Old Max.

The class action suit that actually emerged, however, was initiated by a federal judge. In fall of 1977, Judge John Kane of the District Court for Colorado invited the Colorado ACLU to bring a class action suit on behalf of all inmates at Old Max. The recipient of a steady stream of pro se petitions from inmates at Old Max, Kane was also well aware of the problems at the institution through the less formal mechanism of reading the local newspaper. The petition that finally gave rise to the case was filed in his court on November 30, 1977. It was a handwritten document by Felix Ramos, presenting the seemingly mild complaint that he was being denied employment which was guaranteed to him under state law.*[14] In fact, the complaint implicated several larger issues; inmates sought jobs

---

* Ramos was a "transitional worker," a term used in the Colorado prison system to denote an inmate who is unemployed but eligible for employment, and thus, presumably, in transition. The problem at this time, however, was that the vast majority of inmates at Old Max were in the permanent position of being "transitional workers." After the prison's industry row had been dismantled, there was simply no place into which they could "transition."

to obtain a respite from Old Max's crowded, noisy, stuffy, smelly cells, in which they were otherwise locked down as much as twenty-three hours per day. In addition, they were not eligible for social and educational programs unless they were employed, even if their unemployment was due to no fault of their own. Ramos was in fact eligible for employment, but there were no jobs available.

In mid-December, Kane assigned Ramos's petition to James Hartley and Hugh Gottschalk of the Colorado ACLU, and asked them to consider developing a class action suit. Two months later, on February 15, Hartley and Gottschalk dutifully appeared, along with attorneys from the ACLU's Washington, D.C.–based National Prison Project, and filed an amended complaint, captioned *Ramos v. Lamm*, alleging a wide range of unconstitutional conditions and practices at Old Max. In addition, they petitioned the court to certify the complaint as a class action, naming Governor Richard Lamm and then Commissioner of Corrections Allen Ault as defendants. Not surprisingly, Kane agreed; he consolidated the Ramos petition with a number of others and certified the cases as a class action on behalf of "all persons who are now or in the future may be incarcerated in the maximum-security unit of the Colorado State Penitentiary at Canon City."[15]

Over the next several months the ACLU attorneys filed a series of amended complaints broadening their attack. They alleged that the "totality of conditions" at Old Max constituted cruel and unusual punishment in violation of the Eighth Amendment, and that limitations on access to counsel and unnecessary censorship of mail violated inmates' Sixth and First Amendment rights. On May 17, 1978, the defendants moved to dismiss on grounds that the problems alleged, however real, did not rise to the constitutional level, and that at any rate the state legislature had recently committed still more funds to address the problems. This motion was denied, but Kane strongly urged the parties to settle and offered to facilitate the process. He was optimistic about the possibility of a settlement because he believed there would be few if any factual disputes. By and large, corrections officials agreed with criticisms of the prison and had expressed a willingness to make improvements. As was true in Arkansas, the commissioner of corrections – Allen Ault, in this case – may not have been at all unhappy about a suit that threatened to punish him for constitutional violations by recommending an increase in his department's budget.

Whatever the reason, Judge Kane's instinct proved to be correct. During the next year and a half, from June 9, 1978, to October 5, 1979, the parties negotiated with each other to reach a settlement. The process went relatively smoothly and ultimately generated a 250-page document containing proposed stipulations of fact, excerpts from sworn testimony, summaries of statistics, and a rather impressive list of mea culpa's by the

Department of Corrections. In their testimony, the department officials acknowledged that "according to their own corrections studies, the housing facilities at Old Max are totally obsolete and continued use can only lead to an ongoing series of challenges to the constitutionality of [such] use," and that "the old maximum-security prison is below current correctional standards for housing and programming." In addition, Paul Silver, a well-respected corrections architect called by the defendants, characterized Old Max as "unfit for habitation." Still other uncontradicted evidence, introduced at the hearings and cited in the draft agreement, showed that the department did not meet minimum professional standards in a number of areas; for instance, medical standards required that a physician be on duty at Old Max for at least forty hours a week, but, in fact, one was available for only ten hours or less. Given the department's willingness to flagellate itself, it is not surprising that the parties were able to formulate a draft settlement agreement.

This agreement did not extend to all issues however. Lawyers in the state attorney general's office were adamant about not admitting to any constitutional violations. Encouraged by the recent Supreme Court decision in *Bell v. Wolfish*,[16] which had reversed a lower-court decision that conditions in New York City's federal pretrial detention center were unconstitutional, they took the position that none of the problems in the state's prisons were constitutional in nature and insisted that the proposed settlement agreement contain a provision denying any legal violations. But the parties were able to agree upon the nature of the problems, if not their legal characterization, and they were able to outline a plan for remedying the situation at Old Max.

There was a final hurdle to be overcome, however, and it proved to be the settlement's undoing. Governor Lamm, the named defendant in the case, insisted that legislative leaders support the settlement. He argued that since the legislature would have to appropriate funds to pay for the improvements that the agreement called for, it should go on record as supporting the settlement. In a letter to the court dated October 9, 1979, he wrote: "I believe that an agreement negotiated by the parties in good faith in this matter should be given a chance to succeed, which it can if there is a legislative consensus in support of it. But I cannot agree to the document which I have reviewed absent such a consensus, and I do not believe that it would be in the interest of the court or the parties for me to do so."[17] In light of his history of strained relations with the Republican-controlled state legislature, Lamm, a Democrat, undoubtedly insisted on this additional condition as a way of protecting himself against criticism from the legislature for being fiscally profligate and soft on criminals. But the legislators saw the governor's ploy for what it was – an attempt to neutralize the settlement as a partisan issue – and refused to go along. As a result, Lamm would not approve it, and despite the lack of any real controversy, the agreement could not be finalized and the case went to trial.

The trial began on October 15, 1979, and lasted five weeks. Inmates, state corrections officials, and numerous expert witnesses testified and thousands of pages of documentary evidence were submitted. But the proceedings were anticlimactic, as well as otiose; they consisted largely of efforts by the plaintiffs' lawyers to introduce into evidence the state's uncontested reports and the opinions of the several expert witnesses who had been called by the defendants during the pretrial process. As Judge Kane later wrote in his opinion, "the testimony was credible and largely uncontradicted."[18]

On December 20, Kane announced his ruling from the bench, and a week later he distributed a written opinion.[19] The major portion of his opinion was devoted to an assessment of ten sets of issues and his analysis of each issue followed the same pattern. First, he reviewed testimony about conditions in Old Max, often noting that it had been supplied by the defendants themselves or their experts, or was uncontested. He then posed the question, whether these conditions or practices met "any known professional or constitutional standard – or state law or regulations," and invariably answered his own question in the negative. Living units in Old Max were severely overcrowded, decrepit, and unsanitary, he found. They failed to meet standards enunciated in prior court rulings, Colorado state health codes and safety regulations, accepted architectural standards, American Correctional Association standards, and standards employed by numerous experts in their testimony. Inmate idleness and isolation pervaded Old Max; opportunities for employment and participation in organized activities had declined markedly in recent years, and almost all inmates were left idle twenty or more hours a day in disgusting, overcrowded cells. This situation ran counter to recommendations that had been articulated by the American Correctional Association, by correctional experts from other states who had been called by the defendants, and by reports issued by the department itself.

Judge Kane also found that the prison's education budget and programming were virtually nonexistent, the prison library was at best inadequate, and the staff positions for these functions were unfilled or had been reassigned to other duties.*[20] Yet Colorado state law mandated ed-

---

* He noted, "Despite the fact that the vast majority of inmates lack a high school diploma, there is only one full-time civilian teacher at Old Max for a population of 800–900 prisoners . . . , that the other teacher . . . spends little or no time teaching prisoners, . . . [and that] the education department has a budget of $6,000, half of which has been diverted to other departments."

ucational opportunities for inmates, and the Colorado state librarian had a legal obligation to provide general library services to prisoners at Old Max. Medical care at Old Max was terrible. "The prison is today ill-equipped and unable to provide essential health services," Kane wrote. "Both in terms of physical and mental health delivery, the conditions in the penitentiary amount to an emergency situation. One expert described the poor conditions as a 'time bomb ready to explode into disaster.' "[21] Such conditions violated "all known standards," including those of the American Medical Association, Colorado's own health code, the Colorado Dental Association, policies established by the Colorado State Hospital, and the department's own regulations.

Old Max overclassified inmates both into and within the maximum-security prison, Kane held. Overclassified inmates were not only housed under stricter security than was necessary, but as a consequence of their inappropriately formidable classification they were denied opportunities to participate in educational and rehabilitative programs. Everyone agreed that these policies and practices were irrational and failed to conform to any known professional standards. In addition, all inmates were deprived of reasonable access to their families, and inmate correspondence was subjected to gratuitous censorship. Visitation periods were severely restricted, and conditions in the visitation rooms were substandard. The prison refused to deliver mail in any language other than English, even though one-third of the prison population was Spanish-speaking. Letters from inmates to lawyers and courts were routinely opened by prison officials. The law library was virtually empty and access to it extremely limited. Here too practices failed to meet minimal standards established by the American Correctional Association, the American Bar Association, the American Library Association, the National Advisory Commission on Standards and Goals, the federal Bureau of Prisons, the prison system's own regulations and, as noted earlier, Colorado state law.

Finally, Kane found that the lack of personal safety at Old Max violated every known correctional standard. Suicides, attempted suicides, self-mutilation, and violence against fellow inmates were regular occurrences. Medical reports, logs, and shift reports all documented unusually high numbers of problems of this sort, but poor record keeping and high turnover did not even permit their full documentation. Despite the special session of the legislature called by Governor Lamm in 1976 to deal with the "reign of terror" at Old Max, and despite the preparation of the two master plans (one by Touche-Ross and the other by the department itself), an attorney general's report, and several other studies, the prison's safety and security were worse three years after the 1975 riot than they had been immediately before.

In this litany of Old Max's specific failures, Judge Kane sounded two recurring themes. The first involved the criteria he used to assess the conditions at Old Max, and the second concerned the purposes of imprisonment. His opinion is replete with such phrases as "grossly inadequate by any standards," "fail to meet any known standards," "do not conform to [a state law or regulation]," and the like. He repeatedly contrasted descriptions of current practices with standards employed by corrections experts in their testimony, written standards developed by various professional associations (he identified at least ten such associations in his opinion), the state's own statutes, and the Corrections Department's own regulations. He emphasized that he was not imposing his own personal views, but simply observing that the prison system fell far short of what was expected by a consensus of professionals in the field, particularly the American Correctional Association. As he wrote, "[e]very report which has been issued in the last ten years had described the inadequate facilities and sporadic rehabilitation of Old Max."

Perhaps in an effort to give even more support to this conclusion concerning professional standards, his opinion also developed a second theme. He asked, in effect, "Why should we be concerned about idleness or isolation or any of the other many problems that have been identified – what penological principle is involved?" While emphasizing that there is no explicit constitutional right to rehabilitation, he nevertheless made an effort to identify the basic goals of incarceration that lay behind the standards he invoked when assessing the prison's conditions. For example, after recounting the various educational and employment opportunities that had been discontinued and pointedly noting that Colorado law required inmates to work, he observed, "I cannot, and will not, 'second-guess' the prison administrators in trying to say which of the individual decisions might have been unjustified. The fact is that the overall effect is to create conditions of idleness and lockdown that made degeneration likely and self-improvement impossible."[22] In assessing mail censorship, he asserted that Old Max's practices served no "legitimate penological purposes." Elsewhere, he asked how a particular noxious practice could possibly conform to "one or more of the substantial governmental interests of security, order, and rehabilitation." And in a number of other places, he noted that the various standards and state laws that mandated specific features of prison life (inmate employment, mental health treatment, programs for alcohol and drug abuse, and the like) were anchored in a concern with rehabilitation, or at least with "doing nothing that would lead to further deterioration." In short, Kane constructed a penological vision through which he could assess practices in the prison and on which he could ground his own ruling.

Judge Kane's remedy for all these problems was simple and direct: he ordered Old Max closed within forty-five days.[23] He further ruled that the state should take immediate and continuing steps to correct the violations identified in his opinion, and to present a detailed plan that would "set forth the means by which the plaintiff class would be forever protected from further violations." In response to the state's objection that there was no need for such an order because it was making "wrenching good faith" efforts to correct its prison "problems," including constructing a new prison that would open within two years, Kane responded that the history of the state's approach to its prison problem was one of "confession and avoidance." Time and time again, he observed, state officials had agreed that severe problems existed, promised to take remedial steps, and failed to do anything. Furthermore, he continued, most of the improvements he had ordered involved increases in staffing and programming, changes that could easily be transferred to the new facilities once they had opened. As for physical improvements at Old Max, he asserted that it would be possible to deal with them without great additional expense, especially if some of the inmates could be transferred to other facilities. By way of encouragement, he also emphasized that nothing in his order would prevent further stays of the closure order if the state pursued the changes vigorously and in good faith.*[24]

The Aftermath of *Ramos* and the Successors to Old Max (1979–1990)

Angry at his insistence upon a host of expensive improvements in a facility that would soon be closed, and at the size of the award for attorneys' fees – especially the award to Alvin Bronstein and other out-of-state attorneys from the ACLU's Washington D.C.–based National Prison Project – the state appealed Judge Kane's ruling. Two years later the ruling was upheld on appeal by a two-to-one vote in the Tenth Circuit Court of Appeals.[25] Although the attorneys' fees were trimmed back somewhat, the majority commended his handling of the case and supported it in every other aspect. Meanwhile, during the long interval between his decision and the

---

* Judge Kane was well aware that Old Max was to be replaced by a new facility that was already under construction. His actions here were clearly designed to force officials to develop programs and appoint staff – institutional arrangements that could be transferred to the new facility. Undoubtedly, he was concerned that a shiny new facility would be ready for occupancy, but that it too would lack staffing, programs, and the resources necessary to overcome the problems he had identified. As he warned at the conclusion of his opinion, "The meager evidence [regarding plans for staffing and programming in the new facility] suggests that the new facility may very well aggravate rather than mitigate the problems which presently exist."

court of appeals ruling, Kane continued to press the defendants to make the changes he had ordered. He announced that he would not appoint a special master, but that the department should submit periodic progress reports directly to him. Two months after his decision, in a motion to stay execution of his order pending the appeal, the department submitted a plan that it claimed showed further good-faith efforts to make improvements in the prison, thus rendering his order unnecessary. In fact, the department's submission was nothing more than a thinly veiled restatement of Kane's own order two months earlier, and not a detailed plan of action. Kane was not fooled; he expressed his satisfaction that the department now recognized these matters as constituting problems, but indicated that much more than verbal gestures were required. He did not close Old Max, however, and the department eventually submitted sufficiently detailed plans to satisfy him. Furthermore, the battle between the governor and legislature that some had expected did not occur. Apparently the trial had its desired effect of transforming prison reform from a fiscally profligate, socially overpermissive public policy into a legal obligation. The legislature approved the building plans for new facilities and, more importantly, authorized the funds needed to implement the plans.*[26]

The new facilities were built in accordance with the 1978 master plan and were opened in 1982. They consisted of three separate prisons – the Centennial Correctional Facility, the Shadow Mountain Correctional Facility, and the Colorado Territorial Correctional Facility, all located in Canon City and graded as minimum-, medium-, and maximum-security, respectively. As these facilities were completed and inmates transferred to them, Old Max finally closed. The court now shifted its attention to the three new prisons; at the urging of the ACLU, Judge Kane sought assur-

---

* In his dissent in the court of appeals, Judge Barrett argued that the five-week trial, the long list of findings, and the order to make costly improvements on a soon-to-be-closed prison made no sense. He took Judge Kane to task for letting the plaintiffs draw out the case so long, for awarding them such large attorneys' fees, and for issuing such detailed orders, when he should have been satisfied only to deal with "emergency" matters in the old facility. As if anticipating this sort of criticism, Kane argued in his initial opinion that the state and the department had a long history of acknowledging problems and doing nothing or very little other than "planning" to deal with them. In approving the department's detailed plans, he noted that it now appeared that the state was in fact going to provide substantial funds for new construction and staffing; he justified his ruling, however, by saying that in the past the state had expressed good intentions but not acted on them, and under this decision it could not back down. He also noted that the state would not have made these decisions had it not been for the litigation.

ances that these prisons would provide the services and maintain the conditions that he had established in his order.

Despite their resentment at being held in violation of the Constitution, the successive directors of the Department of Corrections were willing, if somewhat ineptly so at times, to make the sorts of changes Kane had ordered. Although there were public disagreements between the various agencies involved, the issue of improvements in the prisons did not deteriorate into a contest of wills between Kane and corrections officials, or between him and the governor or legislature. One indication of the department's willingness to comply was that, in 1984, without prompting, it appointed a lawyer, Brad Rockwell, as its "legal affairs coordinator." His role was to facilitate communication between the department and its lawyers in the attorney general's office, and to assemble materials required by the court to show compliance with its order. Rockwell stayed on after termination of the case to draft regulations for the department and to provide continuing liaison.

From 1981 to 1985, the department submitted a number of reports to the court, documenting improvements in each of the ten areas covered by the order. On August 7, 1985, three years after the new facilities had opened, Judge Kane pressed the parties to try to bring the case to a close. He asked them to review the changes that had occurred and to identify those areas of prison administration now in compliance with the court order, those areas where they could agree that still more had to be done, and those areas where disagreements remained. By doing so, he hoped to narrow the scope of the suit and induce the department to concentrate on the areas that remained problematic. This effort succeeded; within a relatively short period, the parties negotiated a settlement calling for termination of the case in eighteen months. The agreement tracked Kane's tripartite division of the issues, identified the areas where substantial work was required, and specified what had to be done in those areas during the next eighteen months in order for the prisoners' attorneys to agree to termination of the court's jurisdiction. The court incorporated their agreement into a new order, which required the defendants to continue to provide to inmates in the new facilities "services and staffing of a quality and quantity substantially similar to that provided at the time this consent order is entered."[27] To this end, the order contained a detailed set of plans describing staff functions and programming. It also required that various state and local health and safety agencies, such as the fire and health departments, inspect the prisons on a regular basis, and committed the department to correct all problems found in these inspections. The order provided for the appointment of a number of new staff within 120 days, including staff for employment, educational, and rehabilitation programs for at least 90 percent of all eligible prisoners at each of the three facilities. Somewhere in the process, department officials seem to have realized the value of the consent order in obtaining new resources, for they appear to have promised much more than was necessary to obtain this agreement of the plaintiffs' attorneys.

As in many lengthy prison and jail cases, crowding loomed larger as the case dragged on and the number of inmates increased. Responding to this, the final consent order limited the number of single and double cells in each of the facilities. It also outlined a grievance procedure for handling inmate complaints and a procedure for resolving disputes arising under the order.

The agreement failed to resolve two issues, prisoner access to legal materials and to the courts, and the perennial sore point of attorneys' fees, so the parties agreed to litigate them separately. However, two months later, on November 29, 1985, they were able to produce a document on legal access that specified the contents of the prison's law library and provided for easier access to it.[28] This was quickly accepted by Judge Kane. They were never able to agree on the issue of attorneys' fees and had to argue the matter before Kane. On March 27, 1986, he issued a memorandum order that compensated the plaintiff's attorneys for nearly all billable hours that they had submitted.[29]

Between August 1985 and February 1987, defendants made periodic reports to the ACLU attorneys and the court detailing progress they had made in light of the plans contained in the 1985 consent agreement. In addition to reviewing these reports, Kane visited the new prisons and reviewed plans prepared by the department. Brad Rockwell, the legal affairs coordinator for the department, was responsible for much of this "mopping up" process, interpreting provisions in the consent agreement to department officials, pointing out to them what still needed to be done, and working with them to provide reports that were responsive to the issues.

In February 1987, Kane held another hearing to review the status of the agreement pending a motion to terminate jurisdiction. The ACLU lawyers reported that, although the department had made substantial progress on many fronts and they were pleased that the new prisons were open and that Old Max's quondam inmates had been transferred to them, a number of problems remained unresolved. In an effort to narrow the case to its vanishing point, Kane once again encouraged the parties to specify those areas where conditions of the consent order were being met and to pinpoint areas of continuing disagreement. Once again the parties negotiated, and once again they reached an agreement. In a document submitted to the court on September 18, they declared that "all issues in this case not objected to by plaintiffs in their objections to the closure of the case dated February 9, 1987 are deemed closed."[30] The document then identified seven issues of the initial list of over thirty where there was more work to be done: fire inspections, provision of necessities for indigents, food service and health inspections, health services, programs for inmates, security, and legal access. In addition there were still the attorneys' fees, where the parties once again agreed to disagree.

The agreement and stipulation specified the additional steps required in each area to satisfy the ACLU lawyers that the department was in compliance with the court's order. Most of these were easily accomplished; the parties crafted a procedure whereby the area in question would be inspected or reviewed by a neutral, independent agent, the agent would issue a report with copies to the plaintiffs, and the department would correct any identified violations of the established standards. Fire safety, food service, medical service, programs for inmates, and legal access were all addressed by this procedure; with respect to legal access, the Colorado litigation acquired its first special master, Donald E. Abram, who was to perform the monitoring function for a six-month period.

The remaining issues were readily resolved as well. For example, the ACLU argued that the department had failed to provide indigent inmates with toiletries and underwear as specified in the earlier agreement. This was disputed by the department; the basis for the disagreement, and a chastening thought for anyone who asserts that broad terms such as "law" or "justice" have culturally established meanings, was the uncertainty about the meaning of the terms "toiletries" and "underwear" as used in an earlier court-approved plan. The new stipulation described these terms in more detail (e.g., "the term 'underwear' shall include undershorts and undershirts"), and the department agreed to supply what it considered supernumerary items.[31]

On this inspiring note, the Colorado litigation came to an end. Interviews with ACLU attorneys and corrections officials in 1990 indicated that over the next year they did receive the materials called for in the order and were generally satisfied. Both ACLU lawyers and department officials expressed no doubt that the prisons were in much better shape following the litigation and that there was a better system for continuous review and inspection of programs and facilities. But the ACLU lawyers were not wholly satisfied; the remaining problems, they emphasized, were the lack of resources and the possibility of a decline in will. And both they and department officials were concerned that, as the prison population continued to grow, major problems would reappear if adequate funding was not forthcoming. The ACLU attorneys pointed out that there was no mechanism that would permit the prison's bed space to expand proportionately, or trigger a reassessment of sentences and an early release of some inmates as maximum capacity was approached. There is thus the possibility that the gap between demands and resources will once again widen. Still, as a result of *Ramos*, Colorado obtained three new facilities in place of a dilapidated century-old prison, improved the security and safety in the prisons, expanded its medical and health services to inmates, improved a host of other services including legal access and employment, expanded the web of standards and regulations by which its policies and practices are assessed, and institutionalized an expanding process of inspection by relevant state and local health and safety agencies. An unnecessary five-week trial was required to reach this result, but there was otherwise relatively little excess posturing or wasted resources. The entire case lasted just under ten years' time, which is mercifully brief for prison conditions litigation. But then again, it involved only a single facility.

The Santa Clara County Jails

Introduction: A Deteriorating Situation (1970–1981)

As is generally known, jails hold those presumed to be innocent; as is less generally known, they also hold those found guilty, but not so guilty that they are sentenced to more than a year's incarceration. Unlike prisons, most jails are administered by counties and financed from county budgets. The administrator in charge of a county's jail or jail system is typically called the sheriff, a title that harkens back to the romance of the wild west, and still further back to the shire reeve of Saxon and Angevin England, but which now designates a low-level elected or appointed official enmeshed in the grimy bureaucracy of American local government.

Jails presently hold significant numbers of people – about 450,000, or 45 percent as many inmates as are in American prisons. Very often, conditions in jails are worse than those in prison. Because their inmates are not convicted, or are serving relatively short sentences, jails have proportionately fewer educational programs, vocational programs, recreational facilities, and medical services. Because they are funded by counties, not states, their resources tend to be more constrained. Despite these chronic problems, most of the early litigation involved prisons. The relatively short terms that jail inmates serve make the abuses in jail less dramatic (they attract attention only when an inmate converts his short term into the ultimately long one by committing suicide), and since their decentralized administration precludes statewide lawsuits, any relief obtained against them will be less dramatic as well. As time went on, however, and the prison reform process became well established, more attention came to be focused upon jails, and lawsuits against them proliferated.[32]

Santa Clara is the fourth most populous county in the state of California; an urban–suburban agglomeration wrapped around the southern end of San Francisco Bay, it is dominated by the city of San Jose, but it also includes Palo Alto, Stanford University, a substantial part of "Silicon Valley," and Gilroy, the garlic capital of America. Prosperous on average, Santa Clara contains some of the nation's wealthier towns, and while it has its share of slums as well, these appear relatively benign in comparison with many of our more blighted urban landscapes.

At the beginning of the 1980s, when the litigation that forms the subject of this section began, the Santa Clara jail system consisted of three facilities. The main jail, built in downtown San Jose in 1954, had a Board of Corrections–rated capacity of 598 medium- and maximum-security inmates. The Elmwood Rehabilitation Facility, in the suburban town of Milpitas, consisted of barracks for male prisoners, a medical annex, and the Women's Detention Facility, while the North County Jail consisted of a small facility attached to the auxiliary courthouse in Palo Alto. Like other California counties, Santa Clara had experienced huge increases in its jail population through the 1970s and 1980s. During the beginning of this period, populations rose steadily, and during the latter part they exploded. In 1976–77, Santa Clara had the fifth largest average daily jail population in the state, with 1,195 inmates; by 1986, it ranked third, with 3,289.[33]

Throughout the 1970s, conditions in the Santa Clara jails had been the subject of periodic investigations and criticisms by the grand jury, occasional complaints by judges, and controversy in the press. In 1971, the San Jose office of the Public Interest Law Foundation (PILF) filed a suit in federal district court challenging conditions in the San Jose jail. The case, *Batchelder v. Geary*,[34] alleged the usual litany of complaints: overcrowding, inadequate medical care, food, and clothing, punishment without due process, lack of access to law books and legal periodicals, lack of rehabilitative educational, vocational, and recreational programs, and unequal treatment of prisoners. But the suit was never vigorously litigated, in part because the county acknowledged the problems and promised that it was in the midst of rectifying them with a major, ongoing expansion program. In fact, this was actually true; between 1971 and 1975, the jails were significantly expanded and improved. Capacity was increased through new construction and remodeling, medical care, food, recreational facilities, and access to the law library were upgraded, and the Women's Detention Facility was constructed. In addition, inmates were afforded privacy rights, due process rights, and access to counsel. During this same period, using funding from the Law Enforcement Assistance Administration, the county also expanded pretrial release, pretrial diversion, and community-based sentencing alternatives.[35] The court took note of all these changes, but never probed into the management of the jail or into the ultimate quality of services available to inmates; in 1975, after gaining assurances that the planned construction was in fact taking place, it terminated jurisdiction of *Batchelder*.

In October 1976, the PILF filed suit in U.S. District Court, alleging constitutional violations in the Women's Detention Facility in Milpitas. The primary issue was crowding, but the court also found a host of other deficiencies involving bedding, food services, showers, and staff supervision. Again the county confessed error and entered into a settlement agreement.[36] It promised to respond by expanding the capacity of the facility and by increasing its resources and staff.*[37] In addition, in 1979 it formed a Jail Overcrowding Task Force, which commissioned a study of incarceration trends and initiated a general discussion about constructing a new jail. But neither the task force nor the county itself formulated any concrete plans.

The courts' apparent confidence in the ability of the San Jose jail system to address its problems turned out to be misplaced. All the county's new construction, improved programming, and upgrading of physical conditions were little more than pictures drawn in the loose sand of an unstable administrative situation. Jails had never been high priority items for the county's cost-conscious Board of Supervisors, and in the wake of the state's tax-restricting Proposition 13,[38†] they ranked even lower. Furthermore, responsibility for administering jails in Santa Clara County, and throughout California, is structured in ways that exacerbates funding and administrative problems. Sheriffs are independently elected, but their budgets are provided by county boards of supervisors, which have no direct responsibility for jail management. The obvious tensions that this division of roles and functions generates are increased when the sheriff and board members belong to different political parties, as was the case at the time in Santa Clara County.‡ Furthermore, the Santa Clara

---

* Because so few women – in relation to men – are incarcerated, conditions in women's facilities tend to be neglected. In addition, women's institutions pose special problems that officials tend to overlook, such as women's health, prenatal care, and maternity services.

† California's Proposition 13, the fruit of a number of "tax revolts" in the state, fixed property taxes for personal residences as of 1970. The result was a significant decrease in revenues for the state's counties. Criminal justice expenses, including jails, have traditionally been paid for by counties; accordingly, they were hard hit.

‡ Shortly after he was elected in the spring of 1978, Sheriff Robert Winter opposed construction of a proposed "reception center" (a facility to hold new arrestees for up to seventy-two hours), and instead proposed construction of a larger facility for long-term detention. The Democratic supervisors responded by can-

County sheriff, Robert Winter, had risen from the ranks of law enforcement, and despite the fact that the jails were his department's single largest responsibility, he continued to think of himself primarily as a "peace officer," not a correctional administrator. Since he had little enthusiasm for running jails, as he readily acknowledged, jail administration received an inadequate share of his department's inadequate resources.[39]

The predictable result was barely controlled chaos. The Santa Clara County jails had no classification system to speak of; placement was carried out on an ad hoc basis, determined by the available beds and the inclinations of the particular deputy on duty at the time. There were few operational rules and procedures, and few middle-level supervisors. The physical plant was in poor shape. Necessary services – food, visitation, exercise, medical care – were inadequate. Most serious of all, by the end of the decade, the county jail population had reached record highs, and the already crowded, unsanitary cells had overflowed, producing a disorganized bivouac of prisoners in corridors, storage areas, and a variety of other ancillary spaces. Despite an expensive pretrial diversion program and alternative sentence programs that had been expanded in response to crowding, the burgeoning jail population still threatened to overwhelm the system's capacity to cope.[40]

The Court Intervenes (1981–1983)

On March 27, 1981, when Ervin Branson, who had been incarcerated at the main jail while awaiting trial, appeared before the Santa Clara County Superior Court to plead guilty to grand theft, he handed Judge David Leahy a petition for a writ of habeas corpus against Sheriff Winter, signed by seventeen inmates. His petition complained of overcrowding; defective plumbing, lighting, ventilation, heating and fire safety conditions; inadequate nutrition, medical care, recreation, visitation privileges, and law library facilities; improper classification and screening of inmates; and various due process violations. Judge Leahy had not invited this petition, but he found it welcome nonetheless, for he had previously been openly critical of the crowding at the San Jose jail. He responded by inviting the Public-Interest Law Foundation, now a veteran of Santa Clara County Jail litigation, to represent the inmates in a class action suit. The invitation was accepted by Eileen Matteucci, head of the one-person PILF office in San Jose. Matteucci, a young legal-aid lawyer, had no experience with jail or prison conditions litigation, and, in fact, had not been looking for a case of this nature. The judge initially defined the plaintiff class as "all

celling plans for the reception center, but did not move forward on Sheriff Winter's alternative.

pre-trial detainees at the main jail,'' although it later expanded the class to include all detainees in the county's jail facilities except the county jail at Elmwood, which was subject to litigation in the federal court. Named as defendants in *Branson v. Winter* were Sheriff Robert Winter and the five members of the County Board of Supervisors. Not named, although later a crucial participant in the litigation, was the county executive, Sally Reed.

Both the sheriff and the board were represented by the same lawyer from the county counsel's office. The plaintiffs were represented by the Public Interest Law Firm (PILF), which, for all practical purposes, meant Eileen Matteucci. In developing her case, Matteucci focused on the most obvious and egregious abuses, such as forcing inmates to sleep on the floor of the jail's malodorous corridors.[41] The facts were largely uncontested and five months later, on August 21, 1981, Judge Leahy held that the Santa Clara County jails were unconstitutionally overcrowded.[42] At the time of his ruling the jail was holding 900 inmates, well over California State Board of Corrections capacity limit of 598. He ordered early releases, a more vigorous pretrial release program, and set a provisional maximum limit of 700. His order prohibited the county from forcing the inmates to sleep on mattresses on the floor and required it to come up with a plan within four months that would further reduce the jail's population to no more than 637 inmates, the figure supplied to him by the sheriff after a bed count and classification survey. In December, after the county failed to meet this deadline, Judge Leahy ordered the early release of sentenced inmates in order to reduce the population to the level specified in his earlier order. When the district attorney challenged this decision and moved to have Judge Leahy taken off the case, the judge removed himself.*[43] Although his decision was subsequently upheld upon appeal, Leahy, the first of several judges to be worn out by the litigation and withdraw from the case.[44]

In his efforts to obtain compliance with his order, Judge Leahy quickly realized that the problem of overcrowding was only symptomatic of a wide array of much more basic difficulties in the county's jails. Even when provided with the amenity of a cell, inmates found themselves sleeping on dirty mattresses, inside crumbling walls, and next to leaking toilets; they continued to eat bad food, and they still received inadequate medical care and lacked educational, vocational, recreational, and law library facilities. Leahy and Matteucci were both cognizant of these additional problems,

* The district attorney argued that the judge could not release sentenced inmates without making the district attorney a party so that he could challenge the judge's actions. When he moved to intervene, he challenged the judge at the same time.

but they hoped that population reductions would alleviate them as well. In Matteucci's case, the reason for this expectation was her lack of familiarity with the subject matter and PILF's lack of resources for investigation. But she was learning quickly, and when the initial solution revealed still more problems, she amended her complaint and brought these problems to the attention of the court.[45] Thus, the litigation expanded slowly as the jail's many physical inadequacies and weak, or virtually nonexistent, management systems were exposed. As in Arkansas and Texas, complaints by prisoners made at the right time in history, to a moderate but sympathetic judge, had begun a process that moved inexorably forward, fueled by the perceived horror of conditions, the intransigence or disorganization of prison administrators, and the internal dynamics of the litigation process.

Matteucci soon acquired a somewhat unusual ally, although not an entirely surprising one in the light of the experience in Arkansas. This was Sheriff Winter, the county's only elected Republican, who had long been at odds with the entirely Democratic Board of Supervisors. The Board did not think highly of Winter's skills as an administrator and attributed many of the jails' difficulties to his mismanagement. Winter disagreed with this assessment, and thought that the problems stemmed from the board's unwillingness to appropriate sufficient funds. In fact, he believed this so strongly that after a few weeks of hearings, he began to sit next to Eileen Matteucci at the plaintiffs' table in the courtroom, rather than with the county counsel who ostensibly represented him as the named defendant.*[46]

In March 1982, Judge Brice Allen inherited the case from Judge Leahy. Like Leahy, Allen had a background in local politics and, in fact, had once served on the county Board of Supervisors. Soon after his assignment to the case, and at Matteucci's request, he toured the county's jail facilities. To a newspaper reporter, he later described the conditions he found as "demoralizing, inhumane, and debilitating," which was not a good sign for the defendants.[47] Following this tour, he issued three orders in rapid succession to implement Judge Leahy's decision; these established population caps, appointed a special master to investigate "all aspects" of jail administration, and expanded the case to include all the detention facilities in the county other than the Women's Detention Facility, which was already the subject of litigation titled *Fischer v. Geary*[48] in federal district court. Over the course of two years these orders reduced the jails' population, improved their physical facilities plant, upgraded services, and secured promises to expand capacity.

But Judge Allen did much more than issue an order, appoint a master,

---

* Eventually, he retained separate counsel to avoid a conflict of interest problem with the supervisors.

and expand the case. Frustrated by the disorganization and passivity of the county's jail administration, he undertook what may be called an adventure in judicial micromanagement. To remedy the overcrowding in the jails, he had conferred explicit authority on Sheriff Winter to ignore state laws regarding conditions of pretrial release and early release of sentenced inmates. When Winter balked at exercising this authority, Allen personally reviewed inmate files and ordered the releases himself. When Allen was unable to obtain sufficient information from the sheriff about the implementation of these early releases, he demanded that other members of the jail staff appear in court, where he interrogated them and issued orders directing them to comply with his demands. When cumbersome county procedures delayed court-ordered appointments of maintenance staff, he ordered the sheriff to personally hire independent contractors and bill the county for their work. When the county balked at paying the contractors, he ordered the county comptroller to issue checks to them. Upon learning that an earlier order to improve sanitary conditions in the jail had not been implemented, he ordered Winter to retain six plumbers until all the plumbing defects were repaired. When his general order to develop a visitation plan failed to produce results, he wrote out his own plan, which required the jail to provide three hours of visitation seven days a week.[49] At one hearing, he ordered Winter to obtain additional beds for the inmates; at a later hearing, when the sheriff reported that the beds had arrived, but that the new beds were not being used because there were no bed linens, Judge Allen ordered the Sheriff to go to J. C. Penney "this afternoon" and purchase sheets.[50] All told, Allen issued over ninety written orders, and several times as many oral ones.*

---

* These orders, it should be recalled, were based on a finding that the jails were unconstitutionally overcrowded. Neither Leahy nor Allen had ever actually held that conditions in general were unconstitutional. A sampling of his – and other judges' – many orders gives a flavor of the degree of the court's involvement in managing the jail in this case:

May 7, 1982: Order (7) Release 12 named sentenced inmates immediately.

May 7, 1982: Order (8) Release 8 named sentenced inmates between 5/9 and 6/12.

May 12, 1982: Further Hearing (12) Respondents to fix, install mirrors.

May 12, 1982: Order (11) Prepared by Pl. Beginning 5/12 at 9 am, Respondents to begin to replace, repair toilets in main jail and complete by 5 pm on 5/21/82. Same order for lighting fixtures and stainless steel mirrors.

May 28, 1982: Orders (19–25) (nos. 1–7) Sheriff, County Exec and Bd to promptly: supply Sheriff with 100 gal. appropriate paint for use inside main jail and 150 gal./year thereafter. On failure of prompt compliance and approval of County Exec. Sheriff authorized and directed to buy from a commercial vendor

Judge Allen's special master, appointed to help monitor compliance with his orders and to press the sheriff into more vigorous action, was Charles Romey, then the criminal division coordinator for Superior Court and a trusted court employee.[51] Romey, however, was of limited use. Although close to Judge Allen, he had no special expertise in law enforcement or corrections; moreover, as a career county employee, he was concerned about his future with the county and was thus reluctant to embrace Judge Allen's aggressive and confrontational stance. The special master's lack of aggressiveness meant that Allen had to do the work himself, and as time went on, he did so at increasing levels of detail. By February 1983, he had placed the jail in virtual receivership; no funds over $1,000 could be spent without his approval.[52]

These hands-on tactics were effective to a point; things got done, and the jail population remained within its court-imposed limits. But Allen's methods generated resentment and increasing resistance from the Board of Supervisors and from County Executive Sally Reed.*[53] They did not object to actions that they interpreted to be criticisms of the sheriff's management; indeed, they evinced a certain enthusiasm for orders that could be interpreted in this manner.[54] Nor did they object strenuously to Allen's various release orders designed to keep the jail population within state-mandated limits. But once Allen began issuing rulings that involved substantial expenditures and affected the board's budget-setting prerogatives, their attitude changed. Now it was Sheriff Winter's turn to display equanimity; far from taking exception to the judge's budget-forcing or-

and submit invoice to Treasurer (without compliance with County bid procedure) and Treasurer to pay from County funds as a priority expenditure. Court reserves jurisdiction to modify order on one day's notice.

May 28, 1982: Order (20), No. 2: maintain 6 qualified plumbers, 1 foreman in main jail until plumbing fixed, procure additional material, reduce work force only as supplies or work are exhausted (plus payment and reservation paragraphs).

May 28, 1982: Order (21) No. 3: maintain work force of electricians in jail until defects repaired (plus . . .).

May 28, 1982: Order (22) No. 4: maintain continuing repairs/replacement services to jail for electrical fixtures, plumbing, kitchen equipment, ventilation equipment (plus . . .).

June 3, 1982: Order (28) No. 10: procure, maintain, replace appropriate drinking fountains (plus . . .).

June 3, 1982: Order (29) No. 6: inmate pop cap of 664 "housed" and 100 "unprocessed." Statement that the County is able to comply by 10 am on 6/10.

* Together, they constituted the executive and legislative authorities of Santa Clara County. The sheriff was elected, just like the board members, but he functioned as an administrator.

ders, he often used the occasion of a new order to comment publicly that such orders would not be necessary if the board had provided him with satisfactory funding.

Eventually, the growing resentment of both Sally Reed and the Board of Supervisors boiled over, and they directed the county counsel to take one of Allen's orders to the appellate courts. This order involved an effort to circumvent cumbersome county hiring provisions and to alter the county's plans for creating additional bed space in the jails. Although Reed and the board acknowledged the court's power to find conditions unconstitutional, they were adamant in their belief that they should be the ones to formulate detailed remedies and order substantial expenditures. More generally, Reed viewed the court's orders as starting points for negotiation, rather than as final decisions to be followed without question. In addition, she categorically rejected the court's implicit argument that if the county decided to incarcerate someone, it was obligated to meet minimal constitutional standards regardless of cost. In her view, all public decisions require trade-offs, and the board, not a judge, was best situated to make these decisions. "Who says," Reed asked one of the authors rhetorically, "that a judge is in a better position to decide that our limited funds should be spent on inmates rather than battered children?"[55]

On October 21, 1982, the California Court of Appeals rejected the county's appeal, thereby upholding Judge Allen's population caps and his various orders for the release of inmates once these limits were reached. In this same decision, the appellate court also rejected the county's contention that Judge Allen had a conflict of interest (his son worked for the county), and that he had exceeded his authority when he appointed a special master to review the jail classification system.[56] This decision indicated to county officials that their theories of legitimate power distribution in a democratic government were not going to prevail, and that Judge Allen, not the plaintiff's attorney or Sheriff Winter, was their most formidable enemy. Their response was to initiate secret settlement discussions with Eileen Matteucci and an appellate judge familiar with the case. The county offered sufficient concessions to reach an agreement. When county counsel, Sheriff Winter's attorney, and Matteuchi presented this agreement to Judge Allen for approval in early December, he was flabbergasted at the effort to circumvent his authority and refused to consider the document, claiming that it ignored most of his thirty-three orders, violated the fire marshal's order that no new beds could be added to one of the facilities, and failed to guarantee that funding for an agreed-upon new facility would be forthcoming.[57] Later, Judge Allen called the proposed settlement "disgraceful," commenting that the county had done nothing unless he personally "dragged [it] by the hair."[58] The county appealed and this time the court of appeals, not surprisingly given its involvement in formulating the settlement, ruled in its favor. Judge Allen's response was immediate and decisive; he resigned from the case, bitterly condemning the appellate court for undermining his authority.

Despite Judge Allen's outrage, the concessions that the county had offered to secure this settlement were substantial. It had agreed to translate its vague promises for building a new jail into a definite plan for a new 850-bed facility, with a timetable for its financing and construction. In addition, the board agreed to shift funds from other county programs to cover repairs and improvements of the existing jails. It also promised to expand the Sheriff's Department staff, and to make immediate purchases of modular temporary facilities to cope with the rapidly increasing jail population. But the big item was the new jail. Although the county would no doubt have built a new jail without the litigation, the agreement forced it to act much more quickly and more conscientiously than it would have otherwise.

The settlement agreement ignored one of Judge Allen's central concerns, however. Allen had come to believe that a crucial problem with the jail was the sheriff's lack of administrative and managerial competence. Although he had repeatedly addressed this issue in dealing with the parties and in framing his own orders, he had not attempted any far-reaching structural reform of the county's administrative system. Neither did the proposed settlement agreement; it focused on bricks and mortar, not organizational structure or managerial capacity. So when Allen withdrew from the case, his increasing focus on management issues was lost, and, predictably enough, many of the specific changes he had ordered did not survive his tenure.*[59]

The Compliance Officer Takes Charge (1983–1989)

After Judge Allen's withdrawal in May 1983, the case was assigned to Eugene Premo, still another Santa Clara Superior Court judge. Premo inherited a settlement agreement that, despite its unusual provenance, had been approved by a court of appeals. But Judge Allen's reaction to it had caused Matteuchi to have second thoughts, and she was now somewhat embarrassed that she had agreed to less extensive relief than Allen had thought necessary.[60] Accordingly, she asked Judge Premo to broaden the relief provided by the settlement agreement. In response to her concerns, Judge Premo decided to recast the order; during the summer and fall of

---

* When a compliance officer who was appointed several months later first began to investigate the jails, he found the same problems that Judge Allen had addressed: overcrowding, lack of maintenance and repair procedures, and inadequate provision of services.

1983 he met with the parties in an effort to secure a revised "comprehensive" agreement. Despite the county's understandable irritation at these renewed negotiations, he succeeded; that fall the parties agreed to a new settlement.[61] In addition to the provision for new construction that had been reached behind Judge Allen's back, it included new provisions that fixed the jail population limits and provided for still more bed space beyond the 850 beds already promised by the county. It also stipulated that the sheriff would expand the pretrial "cite and release" program, and that he would have more authority to control the early release of sentenced inmates and to direct selected types of offenders to alternative sentencing programs without court approval.

Another notable feature of the new agreement was that it established clear, rule-governed compliance mechanisms. It required the county to submit periodic reports documenting its population controls, to permit semiannual inspections by health officials, and to report any significant violations to the court. But it also provided for termination of the court's order as soon as the new jail became "operational," a provision that the county attorney had insisted upon.[62] While this was an important concession, it meant that at a minimum the court would retain jurisdiction of the case for several years while financing was arranged, plans drawn up, bids let, and construction carried out.

The final component of this much revised settlement agreement was the appointment of a compliance officer, a decision that was to significantly reshape the entire case. The person Premo selected for this role was Thomas Lonergan, a former deputy sheriff and jail commander in Los Angeles. Lonergan was granted sweeping access to jail facilities and staff, authority to hold meetings and issue recommendations necessary to enforce the agreed-upon conditions, and the right to petition the court for orders to enforce, supplement, or modify the agreement. All the parties were enthusiastic about his appointment. Matteuchi, skeptical about the good faith and capacity of the sheriff and board, wanted assurances that the defendants would conform to the agreement, and she welcomed the appointment of an experienced, reform-minded jail administrator to help guide the process. The county board also welcomed the appointment since it removed the court from day-to-day involvement with the jail. The sheriff, continuing to maintain a somewhat passive stance, did not object and in retrospect said that he too welcomed Lonergan because he was an experienced jail administrator. Finally, the appointment satisfied Premo, since in his view it was an acknowledgment by the sheriff that there remained significant weaknesses in the administration of the jails.

With everyone looking to him for leadership in resolving the litigation, Lonergan got off to a good, quick start. The day the settlement agreement was signed, the jails were, as usual, over capacity, and Judge Premo ordered him to take immediate steps to bring the population down to the judicially established maximums. Within twenty-four hours, Lonergan had developed a plan to redistribute the inmates and release a number of them. Soon thereafter, there were vacant beds in each facility and the jail population was down to the court-imposed limits.

But Lonergan knew that the real problems would not be resolved so readily. Despite the provisions in the agreement, the jails still had no classification system and orders for repair and maintenance work were being ignored. Lack of funds was part of the problem, but lack of administrative capacity was, he felt, an even larger part. Orders often did not even reach relevant staff because there were not enough middle-level managers to disseminate new policies. Deputies resisted some changes, especially those regarding inmate discipline and classification,* and no one ever bothered to check up on them. Indeed, Lonergan found that each subunit and shift within the jail had its own procedures, and that new rules promulgated under the settlement agreement either never reached the staff or were simply ignored once they did. The responsibility for these failures, in Lonergan's view, belonged largely to Sheriff Winter.[63]

Lonergan's response to this disarray was to take charge, and neither Winter nor any of the other parties objected. Whether they were weary of the responsibility for this complex problem, or felt that they had already been deprived of their administrative autonomy, they were clearly willing to be ordered around by a judicially appointed officer, and perhaps even pleased by the prospect of submitting to the authority of an expert. Lonergan was thus able to institute a number of administrative changes: he moved middle-level management from the Sheriff's Department into the main jail and improved the jail's systems of communication and supervision.[64] A short time later, he returned to the court, where he requested and received an amended order of reference that greatly expanded his powers.[65] He was given authority to meet with any of the parties or the court ex parte, to design the jail's classification and population management systems, to order as many releases as necessary to keep the population within the established limits, and to exercise the full authority of the court unless his action was appealed to it within three days. He was even granted authority to hire his own experts at county expense. Once again, the parties' principal reaction to this far-reaching usurpation of their powers was relieved acquiescence.

During this period, which lasted for most of 1984 and 1985, few hear-

---

* Both of these policies affect the placement of inmates. Staff may have perceived the new procedures as threatening to safety or as conflicting with goals of security and order. In January 1984, the sheriff blamed the new classification system, imposed by the court in December, for an overcrowding crisis.

ings were held. When there were hearings, Premo sought to resolve matters informally in chambers because he believed that the situation required bargaining and management, not adversarial proceedings.[66] In his view, the two most basic needs that the jails faced were for more space and better management, and he felt that both were gradually being met. With respect to the first, the county was now moving swiftly to renovate the old San Jose jail and to build the new one. With respect to the second, he was pleased that Lonergan was actively and effectively in command. Lonergan continued to refine the system for early releases, and he expanded pretrial release, diversion, and alternative sentences to keep within the court-imposed population caps. He developed procedures for discipline, for maintaining the dilapidated facilities, and for providing medical care, exercise, and mental health treatment. New staff members were added and trained. Security was improved and escapes declined.

Despite these improvements, the basic conflict between the county board and the sheriff had not been resolved. Both were content to let Lonergan take charge, but each continued to follow different agendas and to respond to different political pressures. The sheriff's commitment remained with law enforcement and not jail management. The county was primarily interested in containing costs and escaping from the lawsuit as quickly as possible. Lonergan bridged this chasm, but he was not able to convince the sheriff and the board to work together in a more constructive fashion, nor was he able to interest the sheriff in assuming greater responsibility. Nor was he able to escape all criticism.*[67] It was under these conditions that Lonergan ran the county's jails for almost two full years. He issued twenty-seven written findings of fact and notices of noncompliance or recommendation in 1984, and fifteen in 1985.

In retrospect, the period when Lonergan ran the jails was the calm before the storm. That storm finally broke in June 1985, when he reached an impasse with the Board of Supervisors. After having agreed with his recommendation to build a unit with two hundred single-bed cells as part of his comprehensive jail construction plan, the board, without consulting him and in an attempt to economize, voted to build a dormitory facility instead.[68] Lonergan was furious and asked the court to impose sanctions against the board for violation of the settlement agreement.[69] In turn, the board countered that it had agreed to undertake an expansion program of a specified magnitude, but not to implement every "detail" of the preliminary plans. On December 20, 1985, Judge Premo ruled in favor of Lonergan, ordering the county to provide the two hundred single-bed

---

* For instance, in January 1984 the jail reached capacity and some inmates had to be released early. When questioned about it, Sheriff Winter put the blame on Lonergan's newly implemented classification system.

cells as originally called for in the plans and to do so within the next six months.[70] He followed this dramatic ruling with an ever more dramatic announcement that he was withdrawing from the case, owing to the demands of his other work.

After his withdrawal, every single other judge in Santa Clara County refused to take the case. Their ostensible reason was conflict of interest, since they might be asked to rule on fiscal matters that might impact on their own judicial budget. But many observers speculated that the judges feared that the direct confrontation with the county that the case seemed to require would ruin their careers, or that the case's contentious and seemingly endless character would ruin their health. Premo had indeed been passed over for a court of appeals appointment while he was presiding in the case, and Allen's health had deteriorated. Moreover, the board had delayed acting on long-standing plans to build a new county courthouse for the entire judiciary during *Branson*'s pendency. This could be interpreted as either budgetary caution or puerile retaliation; given the county's prior history, the balanced, circumspect view is that both motivations were present, with puerile retaliation being predominant.

Contempt, Reorganization, and Uncertain Results (1986–1995)

Faced with the refusal of the entire Santa Clara judiciary to handle the quagmire that was *Branson*, the State Judicial Council appointed Judge Spurgeon Avakian, a highly respected retired judge from neighboring Alameda County. Avakian immediately began meeting with the parties in an effort to calm everyone down and negotiate a resolution to the disagreement. He attempted to convince the board to provide more single-bed cells, but once he found that it was adamant in its refusal, he himself became significantly less calm and held the entire Board of Supervisors in contempt. In March 1987, he sentenced each of the supervisors to five days in their own inadequate jail and "tentatively" fined the county $9,396,000, an enormous sum when measured against the county's annual criminal justice budget of $75 million.[71] But he stayed the execution of his order, and between March and June 1987 he continued to press the county to agree to the original plans or to a suitable alternative. He also continued to offer Lonergan his full support, and Lonergan in turn developed and implemented plans to expand the numbers eligible for early release and noncustodial sentencing alternatives. The county agreed to the appointment of additional staff, but the central issue[72] – the plans for new facilities – could not be resolved. Finally, in June 1987, Judge Avakian resigned from the case, citing frustration and a belief that county officials were engaged in endless, purposeful delays.[73]

The county had appealed his contempt order, and on September 17, following Avakian's resignation, the court of appeals set it aside.[74] The court found that the particular plan for the single-bed cells, however desirable, had not been explicitly provided for in the settlement agreement. It also emphasized that during the previous three and a half years the county had undertaken extensive construction that had significantly expanded its jail capacity and relieved overcrowding. About the same time as the appellate court ruling, the Judicial Council reassigned the case to Judge Henry Ramsey, the presiding judge of the Alameda County Superior Court.

The contempt hearing represented a watershed in the Board of Supervisors' attitude toward the case. Not only did it strain relations with Lonergan, but it produced a permanent rupture with the sheriff, who had testified against the board in the hearing. Although they could do little to alter Lonergan's responsibilities, they could and did do something about the sheriff's. In effect, they fired him, despite his independently elected status. They established a "Department of Corrections," and transferred full responsibility for managing pretrial and sentenced inmates to the newly created agency. This relieved the sheriff of all responsibility for jails and reduced his department's budget by about two-thirds. The board publicly defended its actions as an economy move, arguing that there was no need for jail guards to be trained peace officers who were entitled to carry guns and make arrests, and who received high pay and advantageous retirement benefits. Although there was some truth to this position, everyone understood the move for what it was – an effort to wrest control of the jail from the sheriff. Winter immediately challenged the board's actions as a violation of his constitutionally mandated responsibilities. But a fast-acting court of appeals, citing other, earlier such arrangements in other California counties, upheld the county's actions, and some time later the California Supreme Court affirmed this decision.

In October 1988, only a few months after having enacted the legislation creating the new department, the board appointed Ed Hall as commissioner of corrections. Hall was a highly regarded and experienced career corrections official whose most recent position had been with the Maryland Department of Corrections. His first tasks were to organize the new department and to staff it with correctional officers. Many of these new officers were the former sheriff's deputies who had chosen to transfer to the new department, thereby retaining their previous position. Since the basis for the board's economy move was to avoid the use of trained, highly compensated peace officers, this created some complexities. The new "correctional officers" felt that they were entitled to retain both their old status as peace officers and the higher salaries and pensions that come with it. In keeping with the general approach in Santa Clara County corrections, they filed suit to prevent the reorganization. The board was determined to proceed, but it had learned a lesson about the unpredictability of the state courts and, in any case, could not afford to further antagonize the deputies when it needed their help to effect a smooth transition. Consequently, it grandfathered them in, allowing the transferring deputies to retain both their guns and their butter, but insisted that all new employees would not be granted any of these dignitary or financial benefits. This, in turn, created obvious morale problems among the newly hired staff. Despite the appointment of an experienced and well-regarded corrections administrator as commissioner, the department's first few months of operations were thus a difficult time. The old organization had been disbanded, but these status and financial issues took some time to resolve. Both the deputies and Sheriff Winter's suits were still wending their way through the courts. During this period the administrative instability in the jail was severe, and some believe that it may have contributed to the increasing number of suicides and suicide attempts among the inmates. Whatever the case, Commissioner Hall and his aides had to scramble to create and implement procedures to prevent such incidents in the future.

The confusion was further exacerbated when Tom Lonergan, the compliance officer, more or less withdrew from active participation in the case. Lonergan felt that the September 1987 court of appeals ruling had undermined his authority when it rejected his recommendations for constructing two hundred single-bed cells and reversed the finding of contempt.[75] In addition, the new commissioner was an aggressive hands-on manager who did not feel he needed Lonergan's help the way his more passive predecessor had. Finally, Lonergan became one more entry on the lugubrious list of people whose health or careers suffered during their involvement in *Branson*; in the winter of 1988 his long-standing heart condition took a turn for the worse. He had previously commuted to Santa Clara County by plane from his home in Los Angeles, but after an unsuccessful operation, he could only travel by train, which significantly impeded his ability to make frequent short-term trips to monitor the details of compliance.

Despite the uncertain state of affairs, Judge Ramsey seized upon the opening of the county's new jail in September 1989 as a basis for terminating the court's jurisdiction in the case. This was the long-awaited jail the county had first promised in a 1972 report and later in the settlement agreement, but without the additional two hundred single-bed cells that Lonergan had recommended. Eileen Matteucci asked the court to postpone termination of its jurisdiction on the grounds that the creation of the new department had generated a host of problems that had not yet been resolved. The county, she argued, was still experiencing rapid increases in its jail population that were only being dealt with by the court's emergency release orders, orders that would necessarily cease if the case were terminated. Matteucci focused on the term in the settlement agreement calling for termination when the new jail was "operational," and argued that because all the planned equipment was not installed, such as the dental clinic, and all the cells on all the floors of the ten-story building were not completed, the required criterion – an "operational" jail – had not yet been satisfied. But the county was adamant about ending the case, and Judge Ramsey, perhaps fearful of his health, his career, or both, was anxious to comply. He indicated that the resources for the jail system had increased significantly in recent years, and that the new jail was already housing substantial numbers of prisoners.

Ramsey scheduled a tour of the new jail in mid-September 1989 and set a hearing to consider a motion for termination shortly thereafter. He took the tour as planned, but the night before the hearing one of the jail's inmates committed suicide. At the conference in his chambers early the next morning, before the scheduled hearing, county counsel was subdued. Lonergan gently reminded Ramsey that state law required a complete inspection of the jail, that the Board of Corrections had not done so, and that a design defect that should have been detected in that inspection had been a direct cause of the suicide.* Ramsey then postponed the hearing, with the county's abashed acquiescence, until the inspection could be completed. Two months later, with a green light from Lonergan, Ramsey quietly ruled that the new jail was operational and that the case was closed.

This ruling also had the effect of terminating the court's population caps and emergency release orders, which had been used to maintain the jail's maximum population capacity during the previous five years. When asked by one of the authors what would happen in the absence of these safety valves, Sheriff Winter, who was still litigating his case and hoping for a victory in the appellate courts that would restore his control over the jail, responded that since the court no longer had control over the jails, he could return to the practice of double-celling and putting mattresses on cell floors. Soon after, the court of appeals upheld the county's authority to create a new Department of Corrections and Winter resigned his post as sheriff.

A number of significant and lasting changes occurred as a result of *Branson*. A new jail was constructed. Older facilities were improved and expanded. The county's jail capacity grew from 1,635 beds in 1981 to

* The inmate had strangled himself with a telephone cord. Cords on telephones in jails are supposed to be only two feet long, specifically to prevent self-strangulation, but the ones at the new Santa Clara jail were considerably longer.

3,848 beds in 1988, with more scheduled to be added through the 1990s.[76] Classification systems were improved. Pretrial release was expedited and expanded, and a host of new alternative community-based sentences were put into operation. Social, medical, and food services were markedly upgraded, and a new Department of Corrections was established, headed by a professional corrections administrator. This newly constituted department is the largest agency in the county, surpassing welfare and transportation.*[77]

Despite these changes, however, there is ample reason to be wary. Once the jail was no longer subject to the court's order, the county immediately moved to increase bed space by transforming the new jail's single cells into double ones. Indeed, it had long planned to do this; when the cells were originally built, the walls were fitted with built-in bolts for double bunks; the upper bunk simply had to be attached and bolted into place. The county also canceled plans to close the outmoded old jail, which had previously been scheduled for demolition, and since then has continued to use it, albeit at a significantly reduced capacity.

Throughout the 1980s, the court had aggressively monitored the court-ordered release of sentenced inmates to keep crowding under control. With the authority for early release eliminated, the population of the Santa Clara jails has again begun to swell, and facilities are beginning to reach their maximum capacities. Even if the county continues to use the old central jail, despite the fact that its outmoded design and facilities triggered the original suit, it will not be long until it reaches maximum capacity again. As a result, many observers feel that a second *Branson* case is virtually inevitable.

Marion Penitentiary

A Brief History of America's Toughest Prison

The federal Bureau of Prisons, administered by the U.S. Department of Justice, is the third largest prison system in the nation, with sixty-eight detention facilities and over three hundred halfway houses holding a total of 70,000 federal offenders.[78] These facilities are organized in six levels, generally based on the amount of perimeter security that they maintain.

---

* A rough estimate of the change can be seen in the percentage of expenditures in the area of law and justice which go to corrections. In 1981, the county's law and justice expenditures were approximately 15% of its total operating budget and corrections/custody (not including probation) was 17% of that total. In 1989, law and justice was slightly more than 15% of the budget, but corrections now took up 35% of that amount.

Level-one facilities, sometimes referred to as "Club Fed," are open camps with virtually no security; their prototypical inhabitants, by an irony of language, are securities defrauders. At the opposite end of the scale, level-five facilities, which currently include prisons at Leavenworth, Lewisburg, Lompoc, and Atlanta, are maximum-security institutions, surrounded by high walls or fences topped with concertina wire, overlooked by officers in gun towers with "shoot to maim" instructions, and entered only through multiple locked gates. They hold bank robbers, kidnappers, and murderers of federal officials.*[79] Inside all these facilities, however, the regime is relatively similar. The prisoners, who generally sleep in two-bed cells or open dormitories, leave these accommodations in the morning and return to them at night. During the day, they eat in the prison cafeteria, exercise in the gym or the yard, and watch television in a common room. Some work, either in prison industries or by providing services for the prison itself, some attend educational programs, and others pump iron or just hang around.

There is one level-six facility in the federal system, located until recently at Marion, Illinois, and its regime was different. All inmates were single-celled, and most were locked in that cell between twenty-two and twenty-three hours a day. The beds in the cells were made of poured concrete, and the ventilator gratings were concrete as well. Inmates exercised in small groups or alone, often inside metal cages; their meals were served on a tray passed through a slot in their cell door, and when they left their cells, they were escorted by three prison guards and they wore handcuffs, waist chains, and leg manacles. The metal shop at Marion had been abandoned; the gym, the yard, and the inmate cafeteria were often empty.

Hardly anyone was sent to Marion directly; most of the inmates had been transferred from other prisons where they killed a guard or inmate, tried to escape, dealt drugs, actively participated in a violent prison gang, or otherwise impressed authorities as being particularly dangerous.[80] Many were serving life or multiple life sentences; some were subject to state detainers or convictions, which meant that after they completed their federal sentence, they would be returned to their home state, where they would be tried, and often reimprisoned or executed for additional offenses.[81]

Marion became a famous place, but it is the successor to a still more famous one. Until 1963, the federal Bureau of Prisons maintained a supermaximum facility on Alcatraz Island in San Francisco Bay. A former military prison, Alcatraz was taken over by the bureau in 1934 to hold the worst cases from its existing facilities at Leavenworth, Atlanta, and MacNeil

* As of 1991, 12 percent of all federal prisoners were held in high-security, level-five facilities.

Island.[82] Joseph Conrad observes that an island is simply the top of a mountain, just as conspicuous and just as isolated.[83] Alcatraz was both. It was located within plain sight of Fisherman's Wharf in San Francisco, where all the tourists go, and, in an era fascinated by personalities, it held some of America's most famous criminals: Al Capone, Machine Gun Kelly, Alvin Creepy Karpis and Doc Barker of the Ma Barker gang, Roy Gardner, the escape artist, and, later, "Birdman" Robert Stroud (without his birds).[84] But it was separated from the mainland by choppy frigid water,*[85] and the only person who ever successfully escaped from Alcatraz was Clint Eastwood.†[86] Running an island prison is expensive, however, and by the 1960s the expense, combined with a growing discomfort about the harshness of its regimen, persuaded the bureau to close its most notorious institution.[87]

For the next decade or so, the federal prison system managed without a supermaximum facility. Then the bureau, faced with an increasingly disruptive population in its various facilities, began to transfer its most difficult prisoners to Marion, an ordinary, maximum-security prison at the time.[88] Marion was located in the flat, featureless fields of southern Illinois, more isolated than Alcatraz amid this sea of land, since hardly anyone goes anywhere near it without a specific reason. It had previously been distinguished as the site of a relatively mild and notably unsuccessful behavior modification program;[89] now it was to be transformed into the "new Alcatraz." The process culminated in 1979, when the prison was designated as the one level-six facility in the bureau's new, previously five-level classification system. This gaudy designation brought it more transfers of disruptive prisoners, but no change in procedures.[90]

Trouble followed rather quickly. In 1980, the inmates staged a series of strikes, a serious matter since it not only brought Marion's metal shop program to a halt, but also suspended all the cooking, janitorial, and clerical services, which inmates characteristically provide for the institution that contains them.[91] The bureau adjusted, however; it was only too

---

* To prevent the prisoners from becoming inured to this water, the showers at Alcatraz were adjusted so that the hot faucet could never be turned completely off. Just before it was opened, however, three young women swam to the prison from shore, with one of them swimming completely around the island and back to shore again.

† On June 11, 1962, Frank Morris, John Anglin, and Clarence Anglin escaped from the prison house through holes that they had laboriously dug in the rear wall of their cells and headed across the water on homemade rafts. They were never seen again and it is the Bureau's position that they drowned. In *Escape from Alcatraz*, filmed at the prison itself just after it was closed, Clint Eastwood, playing Frank Morris, reaches the shore and heads off to freedom.

happy to eliminate the metal shop, which it regarded as a source of weapons for the prisoners. To replace the inmate labor, it redeployed staff and brought in a more benign set of inmates from the level-one prison camp that it had established nearby.*[92] This enabled the prison to function, but left the prisoners with very few legitimate activities.[93]

An even more severe problem for Marion was the escalating level of violence. Inmates were murdered, guards were stabbed, fires were set inside the cells, and garbage, feces, and other unsavory items regularly came flying out of them. The prison administrators searched for ways to deal with the situation. They locked down the prison for brief periods of time, canceling all activities and feeding prisoners in their cells, only to ease the restrictions until the next incident occurred.[94] They forbade the possession of specified items, razors one day, salt the next.[95] They banned entry to the prison by lawyers and paralegals from the Marion Prisoners' Rights Project, a ban that remained in force only long enough for the federal court of appeals to enjoin the warden from maintaining it.[96]

But the most significant action taken by the Marion authorities was to redesign the Control Unit, the wing of the facility that housed the prison's most disruptive inmates. At the time, Marion had nine wings, creatively designated A through I; H was the Control Unit. Like the others, it consisted of two floors, each with two rows of eighteen cells. The renovation involved the construction of wire cages in the corridor, or range, alongside the cells, so that the prisoners could exercise in a contained, supervised space. In addition, solid plexiglass and steel barriers were built three feet in front of forty-six H-Unit cells to prevent garbage, feces and disruptive comments from coming through the bars. When the door in this outer wall was closed, the inmate could not hear anything from outside, could barely see anything outside, and could not communicate with the guards.[97]

One of the main functions of the newly redesigned Control Unit was to hold members of the Aryan Brotherhood, a prison gang organized by whites to counterbalance the power of the older black and Hispanic gangs.[98] Among the leaders of this neo-Nazi organization were Clay Fountain and, by an irony of patronymics, Thomas Silverstein, both of whom were transferred to the Control Unit for murdering another inmate.[99] On November 22, 1981, when Fountain and Silverstein were free on the range, they strangled Robert Chapelle as he lay on his back with his head propped up against the bars of his cell. The reason, apparently, was that

---

* Marion Camp has held some of Chicago's many corrupt officials, as well as a group of seventy-two Oklahoma county commissioners; a man who served as a guard at the camp told one of the authors that working there and talking with the inmates – which was quite unencumbered given the low level of security – was like attending a graduate school program on local government.

Chapelle, a member of a gang known as the D.C. Blacks, had "disrespected" a member of the Mexican Mafia, a Hispanic gang that was allied with the Aryan Brotherhood.[100] While Silverstein and Fountain were on trial for this murder, the Bureau of Prisons decided that there could be no better place to transfer Raymond "Cadillac" Smith, another member of the D.C. Blacks, than to the Marion Control Unit, in a cell quite near to Thomas Silverstein's. During September 1982, Smith attempted to kill Silverstein two separate times. On September 27, Silverstein and Fountain were in the exercise cage together while Smith was taking a shower. Using a contraband hacksaw blade, they sawed through the cage and attacked Smith as he came back onto the range. Fountain pulled a contraband knife, Smith responded by pulling his own contraband knife and they fought until Fountain and Silverstein overpowered Smith and stabbed him to death.[101]

There was no punishment in the federal system more severe than the Control Unit at Marion, so Fountain and Silverstein remained where they were after these killings. About a year later, on October 22, Silverstein was being escorted from the shower, handcuffed and accompanied by three guards in accordance with the Control Unit's new security procedures. He stopped for a moment to chat with Randy Gometz, a fellow member of the Aryan Brotherhood, placing his hands inside Gometz's cell. Gometz unlocked Silverstein's cuffs with a contraband key and handed Silverstein a contraband knife. Silverstein turned, ran past two of the guards and killed the third, against whom he held a grudge, by stabbing him some forty times. On the upper floor of the Control Unit, Clay Fountain heard about this incident and, according to subsequent reports by prison authorities, became upset that Silverstein was now one murder ahead of him. Later that same day, as he was being escorted along the range with the same security procedure in place, he stopped to talk to one of his friends, who also happened to have a handcuff key and a knife. Fountain attacked all three guards, killing one and permanently disabling another.[102]

It now seemed to the Marion administration that there were just too many knives, hacksaw blades, and handcuff keys floating around the institution, so all the prisoners were locked down for a day. Normal procedures were then restored, and in the four days that followed, an inmate was killed and a group of guards attacked. This persuaded the warden and the Bureau of Prisons administrators in Washington that Marion required special procedures to deal with its special population. On October 28, 1983, a state of emergency was declared by the warden, and the entire prison placed on lockdown status.[103]

To reduce the amount of weaponry that Marion's prisoners possessed, prison officials called in a special operations squad from Leavenworth, known, somewhat questionably in light of subsequent litigation, as the "A

Team" after the popular television show about a group of highly skilled mercenaries who operate outside the law. Together with the Marion officers, the A Team systematically removed the prisoners from their cells, searching both the prisoner and the cell for contraband. The steel frame beds, a potential source of material for weapons, were replaced with poured concrete, as were the steel ventilator covers. Many personal possessions, including hardcover books, were banned, those already in the inmates' possession being sent home or destroyed. Visiting rooms were refitted with a plexiglass divider and a telephone on each side, so that there would be no physical contact during visits. New procedures were instituted to move inmates through the prison; whenever they left their cells, their hands were to be handcuffed behind their backs, with a "black box" covering the handcuffs, and they were to wear waist chains and leg shackles. Whenever they left Marion for court appearances, returned from such appearances, or were otherwise suspected of carrying contraband, they were subjected to a strip search and a digital-rectal examination, colloquially known as a "finger wave."

At the same time, the Bureau began to redesign Marion's physical facility, using the ample resources of the federal government, so that the lockdown could continue for an indefinite period. Microwave ovens were installed in each unit, allowing warm food to be served to prisoners while they were in their cells. "Basic" law libraries were established for each of the four ranges of cells that comprise each unit. The physician's assistants who had previously provided medical care in the prison infirmary were now assigned to walk from cell to cell, dressed initially in full riot gear. Protestant and Catholic chaplains followed the same procedure, although without the riot gear. The outdoor recreation yard was subdivided into separate areas so that prisoners could exercise at the same time without coming into contact and individual television sets were provided for virtually all the inmates.[104]

Finally, the administration designated B-Unit as an honor unit, where prisoners would not be subject to lockdown conditions. They would be permitted to walk around the cell block during the day, to eat together on the range or in the prison dining hall, to watch television in a common room, and to exercise together in the gymnasium. About a year after the lockdown was initiated, A-Unit was turned into a cable assembly workshop, and the B-Unit inmates began working there on a daily basis. Somewhat later, C-Unit was added as an intermediate step between B-Unit and the other housing units at Marion. Prisoners who had served eighteen months at Marion without violating the rules were transferred to C-Unit for six months, then to B-Unit for another six months. At that point, they were eligible to be returned to a normal, maximum-security federal prison.[105]

A History of the Marion Litigation

Shortly after the lockdown was imposed, Marion Penitentiary was sued for violation of the Constitution. In fact, it was sued four different times on a variety of different grounds, invoking several different constitutional clauses. At this point, however, Marion's institutional history diverges from that of the Texas and Arkansas prison systems, the Santa Clara jails, or the Colorado Penitentiary. Marion won all of the suits brought against it after the lockdown; the federal magistrates and judges who decided these cases never required it to change a single one of its procedures. In the most important of the cases, a class action suit challenging the conditions at Marion in their entirety, the federal magistrate was so supportive of the regime at Marion that the district court, while fully adopting his decision, conceded that "the Magistrate's praise of certain government witnesses was perhaps unnecessary."[106]

Marion had been sued before, twice with somewhat less favorable results. In *Bono v. Saxbe*, a class composed of present and future inmates of the Control Unit challenged both the procedures by which they were placed in that unit and the conditions that prevailed there. District Judge James Foreman decided the case in April 1978, just as Marion was undergoing its formal apotheosis as the new Alcatraz. He did not order any sweeping changes, but he did require prison authorities to conduct modified due process hearings, including notice, a chance to present documentary evidence, an impartial decision maker, and a written statement of reasons, before transferring inmates to the Control Unit. He forbid transfers to the Control Unit on the basis of escape attempts, reasoning that this criterion would include most of Marion's population. Finally, Foreman enjoined nonconsensual placement of prisoners in the closed-front cells of the Control Unit.[107]

In response to this decision, prison authorities submitted a proposal regarding procedures for transfer to the Control Unit, periodic review of Control Unit status, and physical exercise by Control Unit inmates. Judge Foreman accepted this proposal, over the plaintiffs' objection, with the sole modification that weekly exercise be increased from four to seven hours.[108] On appeal, Seventh Circuit affirmed the district court opinion on most issues, specifically distinguishing Marion from the Arkansas state prisons and stating that "conditions in the Control Unit (as modified by the district court) do not involve the kinds of punishment which would violate the Eighth Amendment."[109] Not hesitating to involve itself in details, the court remanded the case on the issues of the wattage of the light bulb in each cell and the need for strip searches before and after noncontact visits.[110] Foreman then ordered the prison authorities to provide a forty-, sixty-, or hundred-watt bulb to each prisoner, but upheld the validity of the strip searches.[111]

The final event in the *Bono* litigation came in 1981, when the plaintiffs filed a contempt action claiming that the Marion authorities were continuing to use ten closed-front cells on B-range of H-Unit in violation of the court's previous order. Prison authorities responded by pointing out that two large windows had been added to the door in the barrier closing off the cell front, and that this door was closed only when other inmates were being escorted into or out of their cells, or when the cell's inhabitant threw garbage, feces, or other such items through the bars. The court accepted this explanation, denying plaintiffs' motion for contempt, but ordered the prison authorities to submit a plan governing procedures for closing the outer door. About a month later, such a plan was produced; it provided notice to the inmate explaining why the door was to be closed and under what circumstances it would be reopened, and it prescribed a daily review of the closure by prison authorities. Foreman found this response acceptable and the *Bono* litigation came to an end.[112]

A still less favorable result for prison authorities, although one with even fewer consequences for basic prison operations, followed from the efforts to exclude members of the Marion Prisoners' Rights Project from Marion. The purported grounds for this clever strategy, which allied the enlightened federal authorities with the troglodytes of Texas, was that one member of the project, a paralegal, had made statements to the press supporting the inmates' 1980 strike, that two other members, both attorneys, had helped an inmate formulate a list of strike demands during an attorney–client visit, and that one of them had given the inmates postage stamps and water color paper in violation of the prison rules. In *Abel v. Miller*, the court of appeals issued injunctions against the prison authorities;[113] in a subsequent trial, four members of the project were awarded a total of $36,000 in damages for violation of their constitutional rights.[114]

While the level of judicial intervention that resulted from the *Bono* and *Abel* litigation was rather modest when compared with that of the state prison cases, it was relatively high for a federal facility. More typical was *Garza v. Miller*, an individual suit challenging the restrictions imposed after the 1980 inmates' strike at Marion.[115] The Court held that Garza had no right to work in prison industries, that his security classification was not arbitrary or capricious, and that, in general, "there was nothing to indicate that conditions at the prison constitute wanton and unnecessary infliction of pain or are grossly disproportionate to the severity of the crime warranting punishment, so as to give rise to an Eighth Amendment violation."[116] Additionally, it held that Garza, who was Jewish, was being provided an adequate opportunity to follow his religion, although a rabbi was not provided for him and the Jewish high holy days, not surprisingly, were not observed at Marion.*[117]

A new round of litigation against Marion began shortly after the lockdown was imposed on October 23, 1983. *Caldwell v. Miller*, an individual action, was filed about four and a half months afterward, while *Bruscino v. Carlson*, the comprehensive class action suit, had a nine-month gestation. In addition, *Campbell v. Miller*, an ongoing suit at the time of the lockdown, was amended some three months later to include a challenge to the new procedures. A fourth suit, *Miller v. Henman*, challenged the procedures for transferring prisoners to a locked-down institution such as Marion. In addition to the judicial oversight that these cases engendered, a congressional subcommittee held two days of hearings on the situation at Marion and commissioned Allen Breed, previously the director of the National Institute of Corrections, and David Ward, a sociologist from the University of Minnesota, to report on these conditions.

The *Bruscino* class action was assigned to Judge Foreman, who had previously decided *Bono v. Saxbe*; sensing the scale of the case, Foreman designated a magistrate, Kenneth Meyers, to conduct the hearing and submit proposed findings of fact and recommendations for disposition. The hearing Magistrate Meyers conducted possessed the massive proportions that had become common in this area of law: 28 days, 90 witnesses, 150 exhibits. In addition to challenging the lockdown and associated practices such as the finger waves, plaintiffs claimed that they had been systematically beaten and abused by the A Team and by the regular Marion guards. Meyers found that one guard, David Hale, had mistreated several prisoners, but held that this constituted an isolated incident, not a pattern or practice.[118] Otherwise, he found, the evidence "reflects the professional manner in which institution staff have handled belligerent and assaultive inmates."[119] He also concluded that Marion met constitutional requirements in every other area; the transfer of prisoners to Marion without due process protection, the amount of time that the prisoners were confined to their cells, the use of physical restraints when they were out of their cells, the confiscation of personal property, the access to medical care, the access to legal materials – all were constitutional. Even the finger waves, "a repugnant necessity" in the magistrate's view, were constitutional.[120]

But Meyers did more than merely reject the plaintiffs' claims; he did his best to grind those claims into the dust. "[T]he Court," he wrote, "is

---

* The authors were informed by Bureau of Prisons officials that a number of federal prisoners had converted to Judaism because Judaism, given its arcane rituals and numerous dietary restrictions, creates even more difficulties for prison authorities than Islam does.

of the firm conviction that this litigation was conceived by a small group of hard-core inmates who are bent on the disruption of the prison system in general and USP-Marion in particular." He was correspondingly supportive of the Marion administration, describing then Warden Jerry Williford as "enthusiastic and energetic in his pursuit to establish programs and opportunities at USP-Marion while still maintaining adequate security for the protection of staff and inmates alike." Meyers concluded that it was "abhorrent that correctional staff and officers have been subjected to so many vicious and unjustified attacks on their integrity. Such exploitation is an abuse of the judicial process."[121]

The plaintiffs, not surprisingly, filed objections to Meyers's recommendations, triggering a de novo review by Judge Foreman in accordance with the terms of the Magistrates Act.[122] Foreman did not repeat the entire twenty-eight-day hearing, of course, but he reviewed the transcript and held four days of additional hearings to update the information that the magistrate had received. He also made an unannounced visit to Marion itself, as he had during the remand stage of the *Bono* case.*[123] On the basis of this review, Foreman adopted the magistrate's report in its entirety and rejected the plaintiffs' objections. He did not reiterate either the magistrate's glowing encomium of the Marion staff or his growling condemnation of the plaintiffs and their attorneys – indeed, he expressed some concern about the heightened rhetoric of Meyers's opinion – but he ultimately made the same judgment and reached the same result. The plaintiffs then appealed to the Seventh Circuit; that court, in an opinion by Judge Richard Posner, affirmed the district court's decision in its entirety and brought the *Bruscino* litigation to a relatively rapid end, four years and a mere three opinions after it was filed.[124]

Related litigation followed a similarly short trajectory. In *Campbell v. Miller*, the ongoing suit that was amended after the lockdown, the district court rejected the plaintiff's claim of illegal impoundment of his property on summary judgment, and rejected his claim of restricted access to his attorney and the courts after an evidentiary trial. The Seventh Circuit affirmed both parts of the opinion.[125] *Miller v. Henman* challenged the constitutionality of transferring a prisoner to Marion without a due process hearing on the inmate's conduct. The argument was that such transfers were not mere administrative actions, as transfers between ordinary prisons might be, but impositions of additional punishment, like transfer

---

* In *Bono*, Judge Foreman was still sufficiently uncomfortable with this mode of judicial conduct to refer to himself as "the Court," for example, "This Court actually stood inside one of the controlled visiting booths and observed the layout of the visiting room area." Seven years later, in *Bruscino*, he could write: "My law clerks and I made an unannounced visit and toured the institution.

to the control unit within a single prison. The district court rejected this claim, however, and the Seventh Circuit, in an opinion by Judge Frank Easterbrook, affirmed.[126]

The fourth lawsuit, *Caldwell v. Miller*, was brought by a single inmate. Its particular assortment of complaints was that the lack of exercise and contact visits resulting from the lockdown constituted cruel and unusual punishment, that the lack of congregate religious services violated the free exercise clause, that access to a law library had been improperly restricted, that the plaintiff's legal and religious books had been improperly confiscated, and that the lockdown itself had been imposed without due process of law. The case was submitted to a magistrate, this time by consent of the parties; following argument, the district court granted summary judgment to the defendants on all claims.[127] On appeal, however, only the Eighth Amendment and due process claims were sustained.[128] The free-exercise claim, the access-to-law claim, and the confiscation claim were remanded for further proceedings. The court of appeals went to some length, however, to reassure the defendants about the limited nature of its holding. With respect to the free-exercise claim, for example, it emphasized that the Marion authorities "need not demonstrate that group religious services pose a 'present danger' to security and order," and then went on to specify the kind of evidence that was needed in order to defeat the plaintiff's claim.[129] It was relatively easy for the authorities to comply with the demands of this gentle reproof. They established a law library within the prison that contained nearly ten thousand volumes by the time of the congressional hearings, and they eased the confiscation practices, returning some of the confiscated material. The showing that the court requested regarding the risk of congregate religious services was made and ultimately accepted in *Bruscino*. Thus, *Caldwell* joined the other cases in demanding no real changes in the Marion regime.

Some Reasons for the Government's Success at Marion

The outcome of the Marion litigation stands in striking contrast to the other cases that have been considered thus far. This does not appear to be the product of any general trend disfavoring prisoners' rights, or any particularized squeamishness about the issue among judges in the Seventh Circuit. The *Bruscino* case was contemporaneous with a number of major litigation efforts, including those in Texas, and as it was proceeding, the district court awarded money damages against the *Marion* authorities in the *Abel* case, a sanction that was never imposed on the monsters of penal vice in the Texas Department of Corrections. Some of the reasons why the Marion litigation reached such a divergent result involve the underlying motivations of the federal judiciary and will be discussed at length in Chapter 5. There are several more specific reasons, however, relating to the particular course the litigation followed, and these are worth exploring at this juncture, since they shed light on the dynamics of the litigation process. In addition, the implications of this litigation for modern penal practices, while not directly relevant to our inquiry, also merit brief consideration.

Many of the state prison and jail cases initially pitted a sophisticated, committed plaintiff's attorney against a state attorney who had little knowledge and little enthusiasm for the prison, and against a group of prison officials who were bewildered and enraged by this unprecedented intrusion into their previously sacrosanct domain. As time went on, the defendants gained sophistication, but this produced a concomitant sense of embarrassment about the regime they represented, as in Arkansas and Colorado, or the strategic realization that they could gain resources by siding with the plaintiffs, as in Arkansas and Santa Clara County. In the Marion litigation, however, the alignment differed. The leading plaintiffs' counsel was the Marion Prisoners Rights Project; while certainly committed, their contemporaneous printed statements – some of which were submitted to the congressional subcommittee – imply that every inmate in America is a political prisoner who has been unjustly incarcerated.[130] This attitude may be right or wrong, but it does not readily generate a winning litigation strategy. The defendants, on the other hand, were represented by the U.S. Attorney's Office, an institution with a well-deserved reputation for tough, effective lawyering. The regime at Marion had been recently and consciously designed, and was regarded as the best approach to a difficult situation by a group of sophisticated, self-confident prison officials with ample resources at their command.

These characteristics of the plaintiffs' and defendants' counsel manifested themselves in various strategic decisions by each side. The plaintiffs' attorneys adopted a highly combative, scorched-earth approach to the litigation. They moved to recuse both the magistrate and the district judge – a maneuver whose downside risks are notoriously high – for no better reason than that both seemed to possess more respect for prison authorities than for convicted felons. They advanced an enormous number of claims, including complaints that prisoners in the Control Unit were placed in alternate cells, thus interfering with their ability to socialize with one another by tapping on the walls, that the amount of hobbycraft material that prisoners could keep inside their cells was improperly restricted, that toilet paper was only distributed on specified days, and that the guards did not engage in small talk, or "chitchat" with the prisoners, but spoke to them exclusively in harsh and callous tones.[131] They were unwilling to compromise and reach a settlement with the defendants, thus foreclosing the possibility of salvaging a minor victory and risking what was ultimately a complete defeat.

The prison authorities and their attorneys, on the other hand, seemed to have learned from their experience in the *Bono* and *Abel* litigation. They treated the federal courts with great respect and approached the litigation as an opportunity to validate their program, not as an unwanted intrusion on their private realm. Wardens Williford and Henman consistently took the position that they had nothing to hide; they provided Magistrate Meyers with massive quantities of prison documents, encouraged Judge Foreman to visit the Marion facility when the magistrate's decision was under reconsideration by him, and gave him a comprehensive tour when he arrived.[132] A legal advisor was appointed to the Marion staff shortly after the *Bruscino* litigation started; he served as a liaison between the prison authorities and the U.S. Attorney's Office, monitoring the collection of information in response to the plaintiffs' discovery requests.[133] Every claim was taken seriously and answered in detail; when the plaintiffs asserted that there was a lack of chitchat between guards and inmates, the defendants, showing remarkable restraint, presented testimony indicating that the amount of chitchat had in fact been increasing as the lockdown became institutionalized.[134] Indeed, the only minor defeat that the Marion authorities suffered occurred when they responded to the free-exercise claim in *Caldwell* with a four-page affidavit written by a paralegal – a fact that was prominently and disapprovingly noted by the Seventh Circuit.[135]

As every lawyer knows, the most important rule of litigation is that the good guy always wins and the bad guy always loses, and both of the opposing sides seemed fully conscious of this courtroom bromide. The plaintiffs' attorneys attempted to portray Marion as the harshest prison in America, a brutalizing, dignity-depriving institution that would naturally provoke explosive violence from its perpetually caged and regularly humiliated inmates. They asserted that the prisoners were no worse than the inmates of any other institution, that their security ratings were often much lower than "six," and that many of them had been transferred to Marion because they had asserted their rights in other institutions. In contrast, the defendants argued that the Marion inmates were some of the most vicious people on the planet. The prison, they asserted, was not their idea of an optimal institution, but it enabled other federal prisons to maintain more open, positively oriented regimes by jettisoning their most disruptive inmates. Marion itself, they asserted, was a well-run, efficient institution that was only as harsh as its vicious inmate population warranted.

The prison authorities won this debate in every courtroom where they appeared. To begin with, they had a good deal of assistance from the inmates. Conditions in Marion's Control Unit were rigorous even prior to the lockdown, but they were no worse than those in many other institutions, whereas Silverstein's and Fountain's conduct was truly extraordinary. Indeed, both these inmates were well known to the Seventh Circuit, which had heard and rejected their appeals from their convictions for the murder of Chapelle and for the double murder of the guards; Judge Posner, who wrote the opinion in *Bruscino*, also wrote the opinions in both murder cases.*[136] Randy Gometz, the inmate who had unlocked Silverstein's handcuffs and given him the knife, testified to Magistrate Meyers that he wanted "to kill and mutilate guards, open up their bellies, and play in their guts."[137] While this testimony presumably made Mr. Gometz feel wonderful, it did not produce a good impression on the Magistrate.

But the Marion authorities also succeeded in presenting an affirmative case for the value of their institution. To begin with, the food, sanitation, and sleeping conditions at Marion met the highest standards for a correctional institution. As Meyers noted, the plaintiffs never questioned this and were complaining about entirely different things, but the fact that Marion excelled in the very areas where so many prisons had failed obviously counted in its favor.[138] Second, Marion's postlockdown regime, however harsh, was not the product of inadvertence, corruption, inefficiency, or resource shortages; it was intentional. In fact, the Bureau of Prisons sent a special committee to Marion a few days after the lockdown to develop a comprehensive plan for the institution. Meyers noted this with approval, referring to the committee as "an elite group of some of the most qualified correctional administrators in the Bureau."[139]

Finally Marion, despite its severe regime and reputation, did not have "abandon all hope" emblazoned on its doorway. Rather, it was designed to prepare its inmates to return to normal life – normal life for them, since most were serving multiple long-term sentences, being life in the general population at a level-five facility.[140] This admittedly modest goal

* In the Chapelle case, Posner made use of his famed expertise in law and economics to argue that "because there is no applicable federal death sentence, because the Control Unit at Marion imposes the most rigorous confinement in the federal system, and because many of the inmates confined there are serving long prison terms without the prospect of early parole . . . the price of murder . . . must be close to zero" – in other words, that there was no rational reason for Silverstein and Fountain not to kill again if given the opportunity. Incidently, this turned out, like so many behavioral predictions based on a rational actor theory of human behavior, to be incorrect. After Silverstein was transferred out of Marion into a special cell at Atlanta Penitentiary, a group of Cuban detainees at that institution rioted and took control. They released a number of the other prisoners into the yard, among them Thomas Silverstein. "Terrible Tom" then had the opportunity to kill several of the guards who had been taken hostage, but he desisted. The Bureau of Prison authorities ultimately persuaded the Cubans, during the course of negotiations, to drug Silverstein's coffee and turn him over to them as a gesture of good faith.

was to be achieved through the use of B- and C-Units. B-Unit maintained a regime that was essentially equivalent to general population at a normal prison; the inmates were free to move around during the day, they ate in a common dining area, and they worked in an industrial shop. C-Unit was essentially halfway between B-Unit and the remainder of the prison, which was locked down all day. These two units were mentioned several times by the courts, and they figured prominently in the Ward-Breed report to Congress.[141] They constituted the most convincing response to the claim that the Marion prisoners were being treated like animals, and that the institution, in the words of plaintiffs' attorney Howard Eisenberg, was a "morgue for the living."[142]

Whatever the reasons for the judiciary's positive response to Marion, the correctional establishment chose to interpret it as validating the concept of a supermaximum-security prison. The Bureau of Prisons became persuaded that Marion was essential to the general maintenance of order in its other institutions. It proceeded to construct Marion's sister institution, with the equally and inappropriately dainty name of Florence, in Colorado; Florence is specifically designed to be a supermaximum facility from the ground up, thus replacing the retrofitted Marion.[143] At the same time, it built a supermaximum facility for female prisoners, located, by an irony of place names, in Marianna, Florida.[144] Some thirty-six states have followed the example of Marion, and of Oak Park Heights in Minnesota, building supermaximum facilities that vary from one renovated wing of an existing structure to specially designed, punitively expensive new facilities in remote locations.[145] Of the latter, the most elaborate is California's Pelican Bay – another irony of place names, since Alcatraz means "island of the pelicans," thus continuing the transformation of the pelican from a symbol of Christian mercy to an emblem of supermaximum-security incarceration. All the legal challenges to the basic regime established by these institutions have been defeated. Pelican Bay was held to be in violation of the Constitution for a variety of ordinary abuses, such as boiling prisoners in hot water and denying them adequate health care, but the prison itself, despite the scrutiny it had attracted by virtue of these vices, survived the challenge.[146]

The American Friends Service Committee and Human Rights Watch regard the "Marionization" of American prisons as the most important and most sinister trend in American penology.[147] This seems a bit overdrawn. Marion holds less than a half of 1 percent of federal prisoners, and other supermaximum facilities generally contain even a lower proportion of the prisoners in their respective states. Claims that these institutions have been an organizational ball and chain, dragging other institutions into more restrictive methodologies, are at least as speculative as the opposing claim that they have freed others to create a more genial, rehabilitative atmosphere. Facilities like Marion are certainly spectacular – spectacularly effective in the eyes of their supporters, spectacularly oppressive in the eyes of their opponents – and are thus a natural object of attention in a field which often punishes everyone involved in it with its numbing routinization. It is clearly true that supermaximum facilities have become a prestige item that state prison systems strive to acquire, and willingly maintain with disproportionate resources. But the burgeoning populations of virtually all prison systems, their increasing inability to deliver services that they themselves view as desirable, their failure to decrease the crime rate, and the lack of viable alternatives all seem like more basic problems for the prisons than any direct or indirect effects of these relatively tiny supermaximum facilities.

For purposes of this study, the significance of the Marion litigation lies elsewhere. The judicial decisions in this litigation serve as a reminder that federal judges are a rather traditional group of people. By and large, they dislike criminals, they favor established institutions, they respect government officials, and they think they live in the greatest nation on earth. The Marion decisions, like the pre-1965 decisions, are thus precisely what one would expect. What needs to be explained are the cases that lie between the first and last sections of this part – the willingness of the federal courts to comprehensively restructure entire state prison systems like Arkansas and Texas, and individual institutions, like Santa Clara Jail, to restructure others partially, like Colorado State Penitentiary, and in general, to adopt the most interventionist, policy-oriented judicial posture in the history of our nation.

The Theory of Judicial Policy Making

A COMPLEX SERIES OF EVENTS like the prison reform process can always yield a variety of different stories. The stories told by most commentators concern the horrors of the southern prison or the unprecedented intrusiveness of the federal courts, or, for those cursed with a sense of irony, the combination of the two. But what seems most striking about the entire process, from the perspective of a quarter century since its inception, is the deliberate, almost tidal force with which so many separate and uncoordinated federal courts moved in the same uncharted direction. Where one would have expected uncertainty, disagreement, and retrenchment, there was only a relentless unanimity.

Even more remarkable, this movement occurred with no centralized control or guidance. The first case involving prisoners to be decided by the Supreme Court after the hands-off doctrine was abandoned came in 1973 and dealt with parole revocation. The Court did not decide a prison conditions case until 1977, and did not deal with the major issues in these cases until the mid- to late 1980s. Moreover, this was the Burger-Rehnquist Court, which was hardly inclined to exercise leadership in the area of human rights in general, or prisoners' rights in particular. In fact, it is remarkable that the Court did not begin cutting back on lower-court decisions until the late 1980s, when the reform process had largely run its course. Perhaps this testifies to the force of the prison reform cases, but, in any event, that force was present, and it moved a disparate group of judges forward in unison, without any coordination from above.

But if this sustained, insistent force did not originate with the Supreme Court, neither did it arise from the constitutional language that the judges invoked as their basis of decision. For many people, including three Supreme Court justices, the lack of textual authority renders the prison reform cases illegitimate. This may condemn the decisions, but it does not explain them; while an illegitimate action by a single judge, or even by a few judges who constitute the majority of a single court, presents no great explanatory problem, the idea that the entire federal judiciary, without external coordination or command, would violate basic norms of governance seems implausible at best. It works well as a normative condemnation, but fails as descriptive social science.

The argument in the second part of this book, as noted in Chapter 1, is that the prison reform cases represent a standard mode of judicial action, that is, policy making of the same kind that the legislature or the executive pursues. When acting in this mode, judges treat the applicable text as a grant of jurisdiction, much as an administrative agency treats a vaguely worded authorizing statute, and then fashion a decision that they believe will yield the most socially desirable results. In addition, this part argues that judicial policy making is normatively justifiable. The charge of illegitimacy arises from outmoded concepts of governance, combined with the erroneous assumption that, apart from fact-finding, the only valid basis for judicial action is the interpretation of texts.

Three questions, each with a descriptive and normative component, come to mind in connection with these claims. First, under what circumstances do judges utilize the policy-making mode, rather than resorting to the familiar process of interpretation? The startling suddenness of judicial intervention into prisons demands a more robust description than the mere assertion that judges "sometimes" engage in policy making. Precisely what motivated them to do so in this situation but not in others? The normative implications of the question quickly follow. If we have no rule to determine when policy making is appropriate, and when interpretation should be used instead, then recognition of the policy making mode becomes little more than a license for careless thought and self-indulgent action.

Second, what are the particular procedures, or mechanisms, that judges employ when formulating public policy? While discussion thus far has established that judicial policy making is not interpretation, a complex governmental activity cannot be adequately described by a negation. In fact, judicial policy making is a distinctive process, involving both conceptual and operational mechanisms. Identification of these mechanisms is clearly a descriptive effort, but it also possesses normative implications. There is no point making public policy if it cannot be done with some degree of effectiveness, and effective governance depends on established mechanisms. The recent emphasis of legal scholars on practical reason in judicial decision making does not contradict this view; established mechanisms are the sinews of a practice and distinguish the reliance on practical reason from blind intuition.

The third question about judicial policy making implicates a tremendous issue, perhaps the central theme in legal and political science scholarship on the judiciary. How is the policy making process constrained – what renders the policy making judges lawful government officials, rather than petty autocrats imposing their unfettered will on the unfortunate litigants who fall within their jurisdictional grasp? The usual answer is that a legal text constrains the judge (although legal realists, critical legal scholars, and other cynics would argue that these texts are indeterminate and provide no significant constraint). But this answer obviously will not serve for judicial policy making – not even as a source of cynicism – because it is limited to judicial interpretation; policy making is not based on a text, and so cannot be constrained by one. The general view has been that it is therefore unconstrained in its entirety. But, as noted in Chapter 1, this treats policy making as failed interpretation. Since it is in fact a separate judicial function, the question that remains is whether it is constrained by separate, nontextual forces. This begins as a descriptive question, but its normative implications follow immediately and obviously, given our theory of limited government as a source of political legitimacy.

Part II of this book is an effort to answer these questions about judicial policy making. As Chapter 1 suggests, the best way to describe judicial policy making, and thus to approach the descriptive aspect of these questions, is to rely on the familiar descriptions of public policy making by other governmental institutions, particularly executive or administrative agencies. The classic description divides the process into five discrete steps: defining the problem, identifying the goal, generating alternatives, choosing the solution from among these alternatives, and implementing the chosen solution. An alternative approach is to treat policy making as an intuitive, incremental process, where each step is based upon the decision maker's observations about the prior step's success. Finally, one can view policy making as a hermeneutic process, where a vision of the whole issue leads to perceptions of particular problems, and the response to these problems then changes the decision maker's view of the totality, which in turn generates new perceptions of particular problems.

The chapters in Part II answer the descriptive questions about judicial policy making by using these models. In Chapter 5, we discuss the judiciary's definition of the problem and identification of its policy making goal. The problem, as federal judges perceived it, was that state prisons, particularly those in the South, were being run in violation of national standards for the treatment of prisoners. The goal was to impose such standards, as defined by two national institutions – the American Correctional Association and the federal Bureau of Prisons. Chapter 6 describes the next stage in the classic model, but it involves a complexity. The judges never really considered alternatives, but simply proceeded from their goal to the solution by imposing national standards. These standards could not be imposed directly, however, because they were not stated in legal or doctrinal terms. To constitute a solution that the courts could impose, it was necessary to develop a legal doctrine of prison conditions that would embody the national standards. Since there is no existing account of the way judges create new legal doctrine, we first address that issue. We then use our model of judicial creativity to explain how judges fashioned the prison conditions doctrine from the institutional conceptualization of a rehabilitative, bureaucratic prison. In Chapter 7, we describe the way this doctrinal solution was implemented through administrative-style intervention. At this point, we also invoke the incremental model, and show how implementation can also be regarded as the entirety of the policy making process by using this model. We summarize the description of judicial policy making in Chapter 8, the last chapter in Part II.

In describing these aspects of the policy making process, we necessarily confront the major normative objections that have been raised against it. As noted in Chapter 1, the prison reform cases violated an impressive array of established legal principles: federalism, the separation of powers, and the rule of law. Chapter 5 explains why federal courts, in imposing national standards on the states, were willing to ignore the principle of federalism. This discussion also responds to the normative question about the motivation of judicial policy making: judges will initiate a policy making effort when motivated by strong moral sentiments of the community, a community defined by considerations linked to the decline of federalism as an operative norm. Chapter 6 discusses how the courts, in creating new legal doctrine as their solution, apparently violated the rule of law. It argues that it is only a premodern concept of the rule of law, and not the rule of law itself, that the judges violated. It further argues that judicial policy making is justified because courts can effectively create new legal principles. Chapter 7 explains why federal courts, in implementing their solution, were willing to ignore the separation of powers principle, and simultaneously addresses the normative issue of judicial effectiveness in crossing this boundary and acting in a managerial mode. Both chapters address the normative aspect of constraint; they assert that the intrinsic constraints in the judicial policy making process yield decisions that are as principled and legitimate as decisions that interpret legal texts. Chapter 8 summarizes these arguments and explores their implications for our general conception of the state.

CHAPTER FIVE

Defining the Problem, Identifying the Goal, and Rejecting the Principle of Federalism

THE FIRST TWO STEPS in the classic analysis of policy making are to define the problem and to identify the goal. These steps are clearly present in some of the prison cases, most notably Arkansas and Texas. They are only implicit in later cases, but that is also characteristic of policy making: once the problem has been defined and the goal established, subsequent decision makers can proceed directly to the later stages of the process. The goal that was identified involved the imposition of national standards on state prisons. As will be discussed in this chapter, this goal was articulated in a series of cases dealing with prisons in the South and then applied to institutions in other parts of the nation.

But the goal of imposing national standards on state institutions collided directly with the principle of federalism, for nothing can be more central to that principle than the ability of states to operate their own institutions. Recent Supreme Court cases that have treated federalism as a barrier to national policies have involved rather peripheral matters, such as the freedom of state agencies from comprehensive federal rules that apply to all employers,[1] or the limits on the federal government's ability to reach private conduct.[2] The prison cases were a direct attack on state institutions, a series of decisions holding that the state could not operate these institutions according to its own established policies, but was required to follow national norms identified and imposed by the national judiciary. Yet having thus collided with the apparent barrier of federalism, the judicial prison reform effort simply appeared on the other side, unscathed and unabated, like some strange, relativistic particle. This suggests that the extent or composition of this barrier is rather different than we picture it, and leads in turn to some more general questions about the meaning of federalism in our modern, administrative state.

149

Defining the Problem: The Plantation Model of the Southern Prisons

Throughout the hands-off era that has been described in Chapter 2, courts were clearly troubled by the prisoner complaints that they received. These complaints, often generated by the peculiarities of the ancient habeas corpus writ,[3] revealed what they would later characterize as a "dark and evil world."[4] The hands that were scrupulously restrained from interfering with correctional administration were sometimes wrung in anguish at the perceived injustice of the result; this is often palpable in the federal court decisions of the postwar era.[5]

Despite this felt sense of unease, the courts of this era did not perceive prison conditions as a problem; more precisely, they did not perceive these conditions as their problem, as a matter that might trigger the search for goals and solutions that characterizes judicial policy making. People were suffering in prisons, they were being subjected to conditions that judges found personally repulsive, but people were suffering in Watts and Harlem, or in Mexico and India for that matter, and none of these were seen as problems for the judiciary in the specific and crucial sense of being the basis for judicial action.

The situation that finally induced judges to perceive prison conditions as a problem, and a basis for action, was the discrepancy between southern prisons and those in the remainder of the nation. This may seem odd, because the judicial prison reform occurred in virtually every state, but the process of defining the problem was a hermeneutic one. First, the judges became troubled by the treatment of American prisoners in general. In this context, they were ultimately able to perceive one set of prisons – those in the South – as embodying a divergent and particularly objectionable approach to punishment. Enlightened by this perception, they were then able to identify a more general problem that was applicable to state prisons throughout the nation.

The judiciary's definition of the problem that initiated their policy-making efforts was based on a striking dichotomy which existed among American prisons. To be sure, every jurisdiction relied on incarceration as its basic form of punishment for serious offenses.[6] There were no truly dramatic variations – no state relied on psychological counseling, corporal punishment, or thought reform. In fact, most states, specifically those in the Northeast, Midwest, and West, adopted a single approach to incarceration, which may be described as control and rehabilitation.[7] It was an amalgam of the practical need to incapacitate the criminal with the Progressive Era ideal of individual treatment and rehabilitation articulated by reformers such as William White, Austin MacCormick, and Alfred Lewisohn.[8] Some states emphasized control, placing a larger portion of

inmates in maximum-security institutions and relying heavily on administrative segregation, while others were more rehabilitative, encouraging
education, job training, and more personal responsibility for inmates. A
few even experimented with behavior modification through psychological
regimes and aversion therapy, but only in isolated instances;[9] by and large
the similarities outweighed the differences.

But prisons in the southern states followed a distinctly different approach to incarceration; they were modeled on the slave plantation.[10] This
model, like segregation, was the lineal descendant of the South's separate
culture. As both a mode of production and a style of life, the plantation
was perceived as the source of the region's prosperity during its culturally
formative years. For those who have grown up in an industrial or mercan-
tile environment, it is difficult to imagine the sense of rightness and well-
being that many Southerners derived from seeing people, particularly
people they regarded as inferior to themselves, working in bondage on
large, agricultural establishments. The Civil War ended the slave plantation itself, but certainly did not destroy its appeal.

One indication of the plantation's continuing durability was the crop
lien system that evolved in the postbellum period. Throughout the
South, small landowners or tenant farmers, lacking the cash to buy basic
necessities and agricultural supplies, would mortgage their expected
crop. When the crop was harvested, it was delivered to the creditor, and
if it turned out to be worth less than the outstanding debt – as it invariably did – the farmer would be required to mortgage the following year's
crop and the cycle would continue.[11] While driven primarily by economic
conditions, particularly the collapse of the South's financial sector following the Civil War, the crop lien system developed in a manner distinctly
reminiscent, if not positively modeled on, the antebellum plantation.
Since the farmer had no security beyond the crop he mortgaged, he
could only obtain further credit for daily necessities from the particular
creditor who held his mortgage. That creditor, doling out overpriced
supplies to the hapless farmer, became known as the "furnishing man,"
or as black farmers called him with a directness born of all-too-vivid familiarity, "the Man."[12] The Man was effectively the farmer's master. Each
one typically had a "run" of fifty to one hundred tenants, either blacks
who had never owned their land or whites who had lost title as their
debts increased. Instead of controlling his farmers by owning them as
chattel, an unholy practice extirpated in the Civil War and forbidden in
the Thirteenth Amendment, the Man controlled his run of farmers
through credit and contract, two central features of the North's commercial credo. That the South could recreate the plantation, using the
North's legal system in place of its own, indicates the staying power of its
"peculiar institution."

The South's approach to the punishment of criminals represented another recreation of the slave plantation. Before the Civil War, southern states had built prisons at about the same rate and along roughly the same lines as their northern counterparts.[13] These institutions, termed penitentiaries because of their emphasis on silence, discipline, and repentance, were populated by whites and a few free blacks; slaves were generally disciplined on the plantation as a matter of their private relationship to their owner.[14] The physical destruction of the penitentiaries by northern troops during the Civil War, and the need to rely on law and public punishment to suppress blacks once they had ceased to be slaves, created a correctional crisis for the economically exhausted southern states. In response, most of these states began leasing convicts to private entrepreneurs – first with reluctance, then with some enthusiasm.[15] The model for this system was not the antebellum penitentiary but slave labor. In part this was because the penitentiaries had been small, while the plantations were pervasive; in part, the reason was that so many of the postbellum prisoners were black and the plantation was the mode of treatment that came naturally to mind. If there was any distinction between prewar slavery and postwar convict leasing, it was that the leasing system was harsher; as a southerner observed in 1883: "Before the war we owned the negroes. If a man had a good negro, he could afford to take care of him; if he was sick, get a doctor. . . . But these convicts: we don't own 'em. One dies, get another."[16]

Toward the end of the nineteenth century, a combination of public outcry, objections from free laborers in competition with the convicts, and the declining profitability of the leases led the southern states to abandon the convict-leasing system and return the convicts to state institutions, now termed prisons. But these prisons, like the convict leases and the crop lien system, continued to be modeled on the slave plantation. At first, the use of the slave model was explicit. The Supreme Court of Virginia declared, in 1871:

> A convicted felon whom the law in its humanity punishes by confinement in a penitentiary instead of with death, is subject while undergoing that punishment, to all the laws which the Legislature in its wisdom may enact for the government of that institution and the control of its inmates. For the time being, during his term of service in the penitentiary, he is in a state of penal servitude to the State. He has, as a consequence of his crime, not only forfeited his liberty, but all his personal rights except those which the law in its humanity accords to him. He is for the time being the slave of the State.[17]

As time went on, the terminology became less explicit but the basic status of the southern prisoner did not change. Prisoners, after all, are the one group of people explicitly excluded from the Thirteenth Amendment's prohibition against slavery, and southerners took this obscure detail of constitutional prose very much to heart.[18]

The primary factor that linked southern prisons to plantations, and that distinguished them from their northern counterparts, was that they were designed to function as moneymaking enterprises.[19] The prisoners were required to work – not to learn skills, not to develop steady habits, not to occupy their time or to divert their energies – but to produce a return. They were required to "turn out" every morning for a long day of back-breaking manual labor on the roads – this was the notorious chain gang – or, more often, on the prison's own agricultural land.[20] There is nothing edifying about working ten hours a day, six days a week in the fields under the observation of armed guards, nothing that produces a sense of personal responsibility, but southern prison officials neither conceived nor offered any such rationale for the regime that they imposed. The acknowledged purpose of prison work was to produce crops that could be sold or used. The only justification was that the prisoners had given up their freedom by committing crimes; they were slaves of the state, and slaves are supposed to provide for their own upkeep and return a profit to their owner.[21]

Accompanying this view of prison labor as a resource was the belief that prison expenses were an economic input whose magnitude must be minimized, rather than a necessary if regrettable part of the state's general budget.[22] All state prisoners suffered from their prison system's shortage of resources, but southern prisoners were maintained at the absolute minimum level needed to keep them working. They were housed in open barracks, despite obvious security problems, or in substandard cells, fed meager rations, and denied basic medical care.[23] This was the way that plantation owners kept their slaves; one had to provide the minimal sustenance needed for survival – it would be foolish to have one's asset and one's work force dying off – but every dollar spent on maintaining them was regarded as one dollar less of profit. Some plantation owners were more conscientious, of course, whether from enlightened self-interest or a genuinely humane sense of responsibility, but most, under the lash of competition, followed the capitalist's general tendency to keep costs as low as possible.[24]* The southern warden, held by the legislature to the

---

* Richard Fogel and Stanley Engerman, in *Time on the Cross*, portray the slave system as more benign and rational than is common among modern writers. But the authors leave no doubt that the motivation for the relatively decent treatment they perceive was economic in origin. Their point is that relatively few slaveholders were irrationally cruel to the slaves, not the older and now generally discredited view that slaveholders were motivated by feelings of benevolence. In other words, there is fairly wide agreement that the general treat-

same economic discipline that the market held the southern planter, followed the same fiscal strategy.

Beyond the basic economic organization of the southern prisons, there was a variety of other features reminiscent of the slave plantation. To begin with, many of these prisons actually consisted of former plantations that had been purchased by the state.[25] This was often eminently practical, there being a large number of agricultural establishments in the South whose owners, finding themselves short of labor, were willing to sell cheap. But a good price on a stretch of river-bottom cotton land, perhaps complete with barracks and a nice plantation house, seemed like a good deal only if state officials conceived of a prison as an agricultural establishment. The direct conversion of plantations into prisons, therefore, betokens a conceptual link between the two that extends beyond the opportunities offered by the postbellum land market.

Even if the state were not fortunate enough to acquire land with a plantation house in place, the warden of a southern prison – the "Man," as he was sometimes called – generally lived in a government-owned house on the prison grounds.[26] More tractable prisoners were assigned to serve him as cooks, waiters, gardeners, and handymen,[27] just as the plantation master had his staff of relatively compliant house slaves.[28] Some wardens in other parts of the country exercised a patriarchal form of control during this period, but southern wardens projected an immediate and personal presence that lent their authority the distinctive cast of the plantation master.

The trusty, or building tender system that was prevalent throughout the South but rarely found in other sections of the country,[29] was also reminiscent of the slave plantation. On large plantations, slaves were used as bosses, or drivers, of the field hands. They generally worked under the supervision of a white overseer, a position roughly comparable to the assistant warden, but possessed substantial authority of their own.[30] According to one South Carolina rice planter, "Drivers are, under the Overseer, to maintain discipline and order on the place. They are to be responsible for the quiet of the negro-houses, for the proper performance of tasks,

---

ment of slaves was motivated by the desire for the profit, despite the inevitable existence of occasional saints and sadists; the disagreement centers only on whether this motivation produced generally decent treatment, designed to protect the long-range value of the slaveholders' asset, or whether it produced harsh, debilitating treatment, designed to realize a quick profit. In all likelihood, both patterns were common, for slaveholders would have lacked information on the most effective economic strategy. The market had some disciplining effect, to be sure, but half of the slaves lived on small farms, which often operated at a subsistence level, and were thus partially insulated from market forces.

for bringing out people in the morning, and generally for the immediate inspection of such things as the overseer only generally superintends."[31] Frederick Law Olmsted, in his extensive description of the slave states, noted that: "[The driver's] authority is not limited to the direction of labor in the field, but extends to the general deportment of the negroes. He is made to do the duties of policeman, and even of police magistrate. It is his duty, for instance, on Mr. X's estate, to keep order in the settlement; and, if two persons, men or women, are fighting, it is his duty to immediately separate them, and then to 'whip them both.' "[32] In addition to these tasks, the black driver often served as the master's agent among the subject population. He was given special privileges – small crumbs of status that seemed like feasts compared to the complete subjugation of his compatriots.[33] In exchange, he was expected to take the master's side among the slaves and to report their disaffections and disloyalties.[34] As Chapter 3 of this book indicates, the convict trusty in a Southern prison fulfilled precisely these same roles, and was paid in precisely the same coin.

Southern prisons also followed the tradition of the slave plantation in their fondness for corporal punishment as a mode of discipline. Thorsten Sellin notes that plantation owners often relied upon the kinds of punishments that were later to be found in all American prisons – denial of privileges, confiscation of property, transfer to other locations, and solitary confinement; a few even had a little jail on their property.[35]* But their principal form of discipline was the lash.[36] Slaves were regularly whipped for serious infractions with a rawhide or a leather strap; sometimes they were whipped for minor infractions, and sometimes, a tradition of whipping having been established, they were whipped because the owner or the overseer liked to whip them.[37] Indeed, the entire tenor of life on the southern plantation was a violent one. Olmsted reported that the plantations used mules instead of horses because mules could stand the phys-

---

* According to Sellin, the punishments originally reserved for slaves have been gradually extended to the general population, in ancient Rome and Renaissance Europe as well as in America. But the southern prison was modeled on the slave plantation in its entirety, not on the particular punishments to which the slaves were subjected, and the same is true for the convict lease system. Backbreaking field work, substandard living conditions, and comprehensive physical restriction – the hallmarks of the southern prison – were not punishments for slaves, but intrinsic aspects of their basic status. It is true that favored slaves were exempt from many of these disabilities, but so were favored prisoners. The primary punishment used for slaves in the antebellum South was whipping, and this, contrary to Sellin, was not extended to the general population. Rather, it was only used as a punishment within the prison, thus contributing to the analogy between slavery in its entirety and the postbellum southern prison.

ical abuse they regularly received. He added: "I do not need to go further than to the window of the room in which I am writing, to see, at almost any time, treatment of cattle that would insure the immediate discharge of the driver, by almost any farmer owning them at the North."[38] This tradition of beating any animate creature that did not do exactly what one wanted became an ingrained feature of southern life, characterizing its prisons as well as its plantations. To this very day, a rawhide whip is proudly featured in a display case at the main administration building of the Texas Department of Corrections.[39]

While most prisons try to prevent prisoners from escaping and to re-capture those who do so, it was mainly southern prisons, like southern plantations, that pursued their escapees with dogs.*[40] The "Negro dogs" that were bred to catch fugitive slaves[41] were almost certainly the canine ancestors of the dogs that were used to catch escaping convicts in a later era. Dogs were not only used to retrieve escapees, but also as a means of retribution for escape attempts. A Louisiana planter, after having "treed" a runaway slave with dogs, "made the dogs pull him out of the tree, bit him very badly, think he will stay home a while."[42] This practice continued as well; an official of the Texas Department of Corrections told one of the authors that it had been common, after catching an escaped prisoner with dogs, "to let the dogs chew on him for a while." "We probably shouldn't have done that," he added.[43]

Now the use of dogs by both plantation owners and southern prison wardens may be an insignificant and adventitious correspondence. There may even be some practical reason why dogs are useful in the piney south-ern woods, and not on the Great Plains or in the crowded Northeast. But such correspondences are also evidence of a particular mindset at work, an approach to the problem of incarceration that reflects deep-seated cultural habits. When southerners thought about catching someone who is running through the woods – whether that person was a slave in 1860 or a prisoner in 1960 – their instinctive reaction was, "Go get the dogs." Elsewhere in the country, people simply did not think this way. On a more general level, the experience of the plantation established certain atti-tudes in this most insular and tragic section of the country – certain ways of doing things that were readily translated to other correctional institu-tions.

Of course, the most basic pattern was nationwide, because we are ul-

---

* This practice was subject to the surreal variations that reflexively accepted insti-tutions often display; Mississippi's Governor James Vardaman, founder of its no-torious Parchman prison farm, would occasionally release a few convicts into the woods and send the dogs out after them, following on horseback like an English baron on a fox hunt, until the convict was "treed."

timately a single nation. The nineteenth-century penitentiary and the twentieth-century prison both proliferated throughout all the states until they became the dominant means of dealing with all serious offenders.[44] But the South infused this institution with a particular meaning of its own, drawn from its unique experience. Just as it used the accoutrements of the dominant society, credit and contract, to recreate the slave plantation through the crop lien system, it used the correctional philosophy of that society to recreate the plantation through the prison. Within the overarching framework of the penal institution, southern institutions became qualitatively different from those in other sections of the country. The divergence was normative; it was based on a distinctly different attitude toward convicts and correctional institutions.*[45]

The problem then, as federal courts initially perceived it, was that southern prisons were following a divergent and reprehensible approach to incarceration. As described in Chapter 2, the prison reform movement had its first full expression in the attacks on the southern prisons, and exercised its greatest impact there. The first case was Arkansas and the largest case was Texas, both of which involved comprehensive orders directed at the entire prison system. Arkansas was followed in short order by statewide cases in Alabama and Mississippi, and later by South Carolina and Tennessee. In addition, comprehensive orders were issued against many institutions in Louisiana and Georgia, more limited orders were entered against the entire system in Florida and North Carolina.

Thus, it was the southern prison that first elicited judicial horror and broke through the long-standing doctrinal and prudential barriers that had prevented courts from adjudicating prison conditions cases. It was the southern prison that sustained the movement; the body of forbidden practices that created Eighth Amendment jurisprudence was derived from the South's negative example.[46] Finally, it was the southern prison systems that were most commonly subjected to comprehensive orders designed to alter every aspect of their correctional administration.

All these efforts were focused on the distinctive aspects of the planta-

---

* In his classic study of the history of American penal policy prior to 1915, Blake McKelvey begins his chapter, "Southern Penal Developments," with the observation, "The Southern states from a penological point of view never really belonged to the Union." He accounts for this in terms of the Civil War, the turmoil of Reconstruction, and continuing social and economic problems. What McKelvey wrote in 1936 about pre–World War I southern prisons could have been written in 1965 about post–Korean War southern prisons, and the assessments he made of southern prisons were not much different from those offered by Judge Henley when he finally confronted the Arkansas prison system and the philosophy of penology that underlay it.

tion model, the aspects that distinguished southern prisons from prisons in other sections of the nation. This was the problem that the judiciary had defined as its basis for action. Over time, the judges declared that "driving" the prisoners to perform agricultural labor was unconstitutional,[47] that plantation-style barracks, subsistence diets, and minimal medical care were unconstitutional,[48] that using prisoners as guards was unconstitutional,[49] and that relying on the whip as the major method of discipline was unconstitutional.[50] Less explicitly, but just as definitively, the entire concept of prisoners as a pool of labor, sentenced to sustain the institution that held them in bondage, was declared to be a violation of the Eighth Amendment.

As the prison reform movement progressed, of course, prisons and jails in other sections of the nation came under judicial scrutiny and, in many cases, were found to be in violation of constitutional standards.[51] Once judges had used their general concern about prisons to perceive the particular difficulties with the southern prisons, they were then able to apply the standards developed in the southern cases to prisons in other sections of the nation. Virtually all state prisons, after all, were parsimoniously funded and inadequately managed. But the cases involving nonsouthern prisons came later, generally involved a smaller proportion of the total number of institutions in each state, and were less comprehensive. Most significantly, they tended to involve a failure to meet the correctional administrator's own acknowledged standards, as in Colorado and Santa Clara County, rather than a failure to adopt the proper standards in the first place, as in Arkansas and Texas.

The Judiciary's Motivation for Its Definition of the Problem

One of the most striking features of the prison reform process was the suddenness with which it started. By 1965, federal judges had been rejecting prisoner complaints about conditions of confinement for at least thirty years. Within a single decade, they not only reversed their position, but proceeded to issue massive orders that restructured the entire prison system in a dozen states. This naturally raises a question about the judges' motivation: what induced them to perceive prison conditions as a problem, and to do so at a particular moment in time?

The hermeneutic process by which the judges defined the problem helps explain their motivation and their timing. If one thinks of the prison reform process as being directed toward prisons in general, the judges' motivation and timing seems mysterious. By recognizing that they defined the problem in terms of southern prisons, and then applied this problem definition to the remainder of the nation, the process can be placed in a more general political and legal context. The prison reform cases were part of a wide-ranging, nationally initiated attack on southern institutions that took place in the decades following World War II, and also part of an even larger process that forms a central theme in our entire history, and that has led to our most violent social and political upheavals. In essence, it was the last and least glorious battle of the Civil War.

The Civil War abolished slavery and subjected the South to military occupation, but the North's enthusiasm for a sustained and total transformation of southern culture quickly waned. During the latter decades of the nineteenth century, that culture gradually knit itself together; blacks were banished from government positions and virtually reenslaved by means of segregation laws, the crop lien system, and other forms of political and economic subjugation.[52] Their gradual progress toward a second, much delayed emancipation is too familiar to be recounted here. It need only be noted that during the first half of the twentieth century much of this emancipation occurred only for those who left their home states and migrated to the North. The federal government did not commit itself to achieving equality for southern blacks, and thus to extirpating the most divergent feature of southern culture, until after World War II. The judiciary was the first to take action against the South, deciding *Brown v. Board of Education* in 1954.[53] The executive followed, as John F. Kennedy abandoned his predecessor's reluctant enforcement of Supreme Court decrees and announced his commitment to an independent, proactive enforcement strategy.[54] Congress, where the southern states were most fully represented, acted last, but perhaps most effectively, with the Civil Rights Act of 1964.[55]

The judicial prison reform process began in 1965. While the precision of this time sequence is probably coincidental, the basic relationship between the civil rights movement and prison reform is causal, not adventitious. This is reflected in the doctrinal basis of the prison reform cases, and, more importantly, in their underlying moral motivations. Doctrinally, implementation of prison reform by the federal judiciary depended on a series of important Supreme Court decisions in the early 1960s, as has been described in Chapter 2. *Mapp v. Ohio*[56] held that the Fourth Amendment was applicable to the states through the due process clause of the Fourteenth Amendment. *Robinson v. California*[57] held that the Eighth Amendment is also applicable to the states, and that it is justiciable. Finally, *Monroe v. Pape*[58] held that violations of constitutional rights by state agents acting without explicit legal authorization can constitute action under color of state law within the meaning of the Civil Rights Act of 1871. None of these cases involved prisons, not even *Robinson*, which invalidated a statute criminalizing the status of being a drug addict. Rather, they were part of the effort to secure decent treatment for black citizens in general. They belonged to the second generation of civil rights cases, the one that followed the abolition of de jure segregation. In fact, all three of these cases concerned police practices that were clearly perceived, if not explicitly identified, as a means of harassing and intimidating black urban populations, and that would need to be eliminated before social justice for all races was achieved.

But the case that was most important for placing prison reform on the judicial agenda was *Brown* itself, whose moral message was the fountain-head of our postwar constitutional jurisprudence. While *Brown* held that "separate but equal was inherently unequal,"[59] its real meaning was that America would finally fulfill the broken promise of its founding, that the full panoply of rights would be extended to everyone, including the people it had formerly enslaved. The notion that even convicted felons had rights could not have been accepted without *Brown*; it may not have followed inevitably from *Brown*, but *Brown* was its necessary precursor. Ironically, *Brown's* specific holding was less relevant to prisons than to virtually any other southern institution. It is true that southern prisons were often segregated, but that was not the primary source of their injustice; the problem, rather, was that they treated everyone like slaves. What is truly significant for prisons is that, in holding racial segregation unconstitutional, *Brown* constituted a retroactive invalidation of the racial distinctions on which American slavery was based, and on which the separate social system of the South had rested.

These doctrinal and moral forces acted together to produce a sort of legal epiphany for federal judges. These judges saw the conditions in southern prisons repeatedly, every time they rejected a complaint about these conditions during the hands-off era; what they perceived, however, were the inevitable oddities of one section of the nation that had different social values. Once those social values were decisively rejected by all three branches of the federal government, the scales fell from the judges' eyes, and they found themselves gazing on "a dark and evil world."[60] Suddenly, the physical abuse of prisoners, the squalid conditions and severe overcrowding, the lack of medical care, the use of armed inmates as guards, and the blatant, endemic corruption seemed the product of another time and place, and to be so repugnantly "un-American" as to compel decisive action. All these conditions had existed for a century, of course; what changed suddenly, in 1965, was the judiciary's perception of them.

There may also have been more general forces of morality at work. Two recent studies of penal practice, David Garland's *Punishment and Modern Society* and Pieter Spierenburg's *The Spectacle of Suffering*, apply Norbert Elias's idea that sensibilities in Western society have gradually become more civilized since the early Middle Ages.[61] The result, Garland and Spierenburg suggest, is that people are increasingly unwilling to witness or to tolerate the purposeful application of pain.*[62] Judges are traditionally viewed as representing the general public's attitudes, and their efforts to end the barbarities of southern prisons may well have been motivated by the civilizing tendencies Elias notes. This is an intriguing explanation, but it cannot be a complete one. There must be some further factor, some specific trigger, that led judges to take action in 1965 on the basis of a sensibility that had, according to Elias, been developing since the eleventh century. That factor was the civil rights movement and the general attack upon the South by federal officials.

The judiciary's motivation for its intervention in state prisons provides the answer to the first question about judicial policy making. Judges tend to engage in policy making when confronted with a practice that violates a widely held principle of social morality. The general role of courts in defining moral values has been emphasized by a number of leading scholars, including Philip Bobbitt,[63] Ronald Dworkin,[64] Owen Fiss,[65] and Michael Perry.[66] They perceive such values as a source of both content and legitimacy; in their view, social morality possesses a particular, definitive content, and reliance on it serves as an independent and possibly sufficient justification for judicial activism. That is not the position that is being suggested here, however; we treat social morality as playing a much more limited role. In descriptive terms, it does not determine the content of judicial policy making, but merely serves as a threshold condition, a motivation to define a problem that initiates the policy making process. In normative terms, it does not justify policy making, but merely limits the policy making process to a certain range and thus makes the effort to justify it a bit easier. The reasons for this more limited role are the ones that are usually given: that social morality is too vague, and the judges' ability to perceive it too uncertain, for it to perform the heavy labor that some scholars have assigned to it.

In the prison cases, our developing social morality about minimal conditions of treatment triggered the judicial realization that prevailing conditions in the southern prisons presented a problem to be solved. Social morality need not be behind the judiciary's perception of problems in the more general, nontechnical sense in which the term "problem" is used in ordinary language; for example, two converging lines of cases may reveal to judges that there are contradictions within a given body of doctrine. But "problems" such as these are typically resolved by interpretative means. It is only where judges begin to perceive some situation as violating

---

* Elias recognizes that this process does not preclude the application of rather vast amounts of pain by specialists like prison administrators, but points to the increasing tendency to conceal such practices from the general public as evidence of evolving sensibilities.

social morality that they are likely to define it as a problem for judicial policy-making efforts. While this sense of restraint does not, by itself, legitimate judicial policy making, it does suggest that the resort to policy making will be delimited, and not continual, as some political scientists suggest. Courts did not resort to policy making as soon as they were confronted with a challenge to the conditions of confinement. Their initial reaction, while just as politically motivated as their subsequent one, was expressed in interpretive terms. It was only when the conditions became outrageous – outrageous due to a change in the idea of outrage, not a change in the conditions – that the judges were willing to abandon interpretation and begin the more activist process of making public policy.

For the concept of collective morality to have any substance, however, the collectivity that generates the moral principles must be defined. People with power have been confusing "I" with "we" for several millennia at least; it is easy for a judge to assume that his own views reflect those of the collectivity, particularly when other people treat that person as important. In an age that has become more pessimistic about the potentialities of wisdom, we tend to look to the principle of representation, rather than objectivity or rationality, to provide assurance that the decision makers's reactions are homologous with the collectivity's. But to decide whether the federal judiciary was representative, in this sense, we need to know the nature of the collectivity, the definition of the "we" that decision makers so readily invoke. That question will be addressed here, as part of the analysis of federalism.

Identifying the Goal: The Imposition of National Standards

Having defined the problem as the discrepancy between southern prisons and those in the remainder of the nation, the goal that the courts selected was a straightforward one – southern prisons must conform to national standards. While this may seem obvious, it was not inevitable. The courts, at least in theory, might have devised some markedly new institution or new form of punishment. Alternatively, they could have drawn the remedy directly from the rights that southern prisons had been found to violate, which is the standard that both the Supreme Court and Congress have insisted on during the retrenchment phase of the prison reform process. Instead, they simply demanded that these prisons conform to existing national standards. They derived these standards from two principal sources: the American Correctional Association[67] and the federal Bureau of Prisons.[68]

The American Correctional Association, a voluntary organization of prison administrators, was founded in 1870 as the National Prison Association (NPA), its first president being then Governor Rutherford B.

Hayes.[69] From the outset, it has been committed to fostering progressive reforms and professionalism in prison administration by means of technical assistance, inspections and assessments of member institutions, workshops, publications, and intentional exchanges of information. During the 1930s and 1940s, it became heavily involved in promoting rehabilitation as the goal of punishment, changing its name to the American Correctional Association to signal this new mission.[70] This policy placed it at odds with some of its members, particularly those from the South; in fact, its publications during these years reveal a gentle but consistent criticism of the "backward" penal practices in southern institutions.[71]

An important part of the association's drive to increase professionalism in prison administration was its successful effort to develop written standards during and immediately after World War II. Its first *Manual of Correctional Standards* was published in 1946 and quickly became a basic reference tool.[72] But it was the third edition, commissioned in 1956 and published in 1959, that exercised the greatest influence on the prison reform decisions. Most notably, it contained a new chapter entitled "Legal Rights of Probationers, Prisoners and Parolees."[73] After acknowledging the "vague and spotty" nature of the existing legal doctrine, the chapter enumerated a set of "legal rights" for prisoners, actually policy standards drawn from various international sources.[74] These were presented as a discussion of ten separate topics including due process in disciplining prisoners, limits on the types of administrative punishment, prohibitions against racial and other status discrimination, minimal standards for accommodations, facilities, and services, standards for a safe environment, and free access to legal materials. The following section, entitled "Prisoner Remedies" discussed how these standards could be implemented, and listed five avenues for securing redress against prison authorities: a tort action for inmates, initiation of a criminal proceeding, a suit for an injunction under the Civil Rights Act, a writ of habeas corpus, and a contempt action.[75] The section concluded with a catalog of the obstacles that rendered such actions impractical and ended where it began, with a call for the development of more effective forms of legal redress for prisoner grievances.

As a statement by the nation's leading organization of prison administrators, and one definitively associated with progressive, enlightened thought about the subject, the ACA manual became a leading resource for the federal courts in the prison reform cases.[76] Judge Henley's ruling in *Holt v. Sarver*, for example, addressed all ten issues in the manual, following virtually the same order in which they appeared, and incorporated many of the specific standards.[77] This is hardly surprising, since some of the expert witnesses in the cases were among the officials who had advised the preparation of the manual.[78] Similarly, the manual's list of remedies served as a validation of the legal strategies that would be employed during the decades which followed.

The second source of standards for remedies in federal prison reform cases was the federal government itself, specifically the Bureau of Prisons.[79] The Bureau of Prisons was created in 1930 to centralize and nationalize the supervision of the casually and sometimes corruptly run federal prisons.[80] With Sanford Bates, a noted correctional administrator, as its first director, and Austin MacCormick as assistant director of training, the bureau rapidly moved to the forefront of progressive prison practice. Inmate classification systems were implemented, vocational programs developed, and all employees placed under the federal civil service system. Even the establishment of Alcatraz as a supermaximum facility, which might seem somewhat regressive today in light of Alcatraz's sinister reputation and even more sinister successor, was regarded at the time as an innovative extension of the classification concept. Drawing on the resources and access to talent that the federal government possesses, and benefiting from the fortuity of stable and effective leadership,* the bureau maintained its high reputation and solidified its institutional ethos of firm but forward-looking administration.[81] Federal courts deciding prison cases regularly referred to the bureau's practices and gave enormous credence to bureau officials, such as longtime director James V. Bennett, when they were called as expert witnesses.†[82] Thus, these two national institutions provided a ready source of applicable standards – the American Correctional Association because it was promulgating its standards explicitly and the federal Bureau of Prisons because it was setting an example by its own treatment of a similar population. By adopting these standards, the federal courts were consciously imposing national norms on state prison systems.

To be sure, the national standards articulated by the American Correctional Association and the federal Bureau of Prisons interacted with more general notions of prison reform. The national standards were regarded as "reforms" – that is, progressive and enlightened ideas about corrections – because prestigious national institutions adopted them. Conversely, these institutions adopted the standards they did because the standards

---

* Bates's successor, James V. Bennett, served as director for twenty-seven years. He was succeeded by Myrl Alexander, who served for six and then by Norman Carlson who served for seventeen. Thus, the current director, J. Michael Qunilan, is only the fifth that the bureau has had in the sixty-five years of its existence.

† In *Jackson v. Bishop*, Judge Henley's opinion notes that "the court had benefit of expert testimony of a recognized expert on prisons and their administration," and goes on to observe that Bennett, who had been called as an expert by the defense, found that the Arkansas prisons failed to meet modern correctional standards.

were seen as progressive and enlightened. The political constituencies of the American Correctional Association and the Bureau of Prisons were receptive to such standards, and their practical situation gave them the leeway to adopt them – the Association because it was free of the grimy obligation to operate actual prisons, the Bureau because it had the funding it needed to do so. Thus, one might argue that the prison reform movement did not represent the nationalization of state prisons, but a more general process of reform based on standards that had simply become associated with national institutions. The existence of such standards, as Deborah Stone suggests, is often a major incentive for decision makers to define and address a particular problem.[83]

One illustration of this point is the state-sponsored prison reform efforts that occurred independently of the federal judiciary. In Louisiana, for example – the heart of plantation model country – a citizen's committee was appointed by Governor Earl Long (Huey's brother) in 1951 to investigate Angola, the state's principal prison farm. This committee, finding that conditions at Angola were as miserable as those in its colonial namesake, reiterated some of the major recommendations from an earlier report: creation of a comprehensive program of rehabilitation, abolition of corporal punishment, segregation of first offenders, a merit system for employees, and the appointment of a qualified penologist as warden. Many of these reforms were actually carried out by Long's successor. Thus, two decades before the first comprehensive judicial decision regarding prison conditions, Louisiana, one of the most conservative of southern states, had articulated and implemented a reform program with many of the same elements as the subsequent, nationalizing effort.[84] Similar initiatives appeared in other southern states, with the most notable being the Florida reforms in the 1960s under the leadership of Commissioner of Corrections Louis Wainwright.[85]

There was thus a complex interplay between the general reform agenda, shared by many people in a variety of institutions, and the standards developed by national institutions like the American Correctional Association and the federal Bureau of Prisons. If the question were whether the reform agenda were "truly" national, that interplay would need to be explored in depth, or one would need to acknowledge that the question was impossible to answer. But the issue here is a somewhat different one – not the character of a social process, but the behavior of a group of federal judges. Because these judges are conscious beings, the relevant desideratum is revealed social meaning, not underlying social causes, and this social meaning is quite clear. By 1965, the reform agenda was widely associated with national institutions, particularly the American Correctional Association and the U.S. Bureau of Prisons. When federal judges adopted this agenda as the basis for their remedial orders for southern prison systems, they were consciously imposing national standards on state prisons, whatever the provenance of these standards. That is why the judges repeatedly referred to national organizations as a means of validating or specifying the standards that they were imposing.

In an open, interacting culture like America, it was quite natural that southern decision makers, despite their adherence to a different model, would be aware of the prevailing reform agenda and apply it or claim allegiance to it when the situation warranted. But these incipient efforts generally succumbed to the dominant southern norm. Florida was the exception; Wainwright's reforms took hold, and by the 1980s it was the only state whose prisons had all been certified as conforming to the standards of the American Correctional Association.[86] Although there have been a number of important federal court decisions involving Florida prisons, its correctional system has never been subjected to the kind of comprehensive judicial orders characteristic of other southern states.*

Louisiana's experience proved to be more typical. By 1965, the state had virtually abandoned its reforms. A new governor, James H. Davis – nicknamed "Singing Jimmie" and composer of the popular song "You Are My Sunshine" – had slashed Angola's budget. Professional staff resigned, convicts were restored to positions of authority, and gloom, not sunshine, descended upon all the local proponents of reform.[87] The task of instituting lasting changes at Angola, and extirpating the plantation model root and branch, fell to the federal courts. In 1975, District Judge Gordon West held that conditions at Angola "shock the conscience of any right-thinking person" and "flagrantly violate basic constitutional requirements."[88] He issued a fifteen-page list of requirements for the continued operation of the facility, covering "inmate protection, medical care, maintenance, repair, construction and safety, food and sanitation, religious freedom, censorship of mail, conditions of punitive or administrative confinement and procedural due process."[89] This decision was upheld in its entirety by the Fifth Circuit Court of Appeals.[90]

In short, despite the crosscurrents that are to be expected in a complex, everchanging situation, the reform agenda was essentially national in character. When federal judges imposed this agenda on the states, they were rejecting the plantation model that still dominated southern thinking about prisons and insisting that those prisons conform to the standards

---

* This does not appear to have been caused by Florida's changing demography, although south Florida, a sparsely populated swamp during the antebellum period, had filled up with Jewish retirees, Cuban emigrés, and other distinctly non-southern people. The state legislature was dominated by the North, and Wainwright himself was a "good ol' boy" from the Panhandle. The explanation awaits a comprehensive study of the Florida prison system.

that prevailed elsewhere in America. Like other federal policy makers, they were imposing national standards on divergent states.

The fact that the goal identified by the judges in the first prison cases was to impose national standards helps explain the rapid acceptance of their decisions at the appellate level and, after some time, by state judiciaries as well. As noted at the outset of this inquiry, the federal judiciary was not some small cabal of left-wing activists that had insinuated itself into power to undermine our well-accepted institutions. Although it had acquired a somewhat liberal cast during the Kennedy and Johnson administrations, it was a group of rather traditional American officials whose primary motivation was to do justice as they conceived it. Moreover, by the time prison cases began moving up to the appellate level, the Supreme Court had acquired a decidedly conservative cast – Earl Warren was gone and the Burger Court was in full stride when the first certiorari petitions were filed. Had the prison decisions seemed like the work of a left-wing fringe group, or even like the policy of the Democratic National Committee, the Burger Court could certainly have reversed them in their totality and brought the entire prison reform movement to a halt. Instead, as described in Chapter 2, it validated lower court decisions because it recognized that these decisions were based on prevailing national standards. To be sure, it did so largely by taking these decisions for granted, rather than by any ringing affirmation, and it hastened to add cautionary reminders about the need for physical security, thereby deepening the existing doctrinal confusion on a number of issues rather than providing moral leadership.[91] But the minor retrenchments that it imposed on the lower courts presumed and acknowledged the underlying body of decisions. In some cases, moreover, the Court affirmed the lower court decisions outright,[92] and it gave us one memorable phrase when Justice White wrote that "[t]here is no iron curtain drawn between the Constitution and the prisons of this country."[93] In short, the entire prison reform movement was the work of a moderate, rather traditional group of federal judges, acting under the wary, but generally supportive scrutiny of a conservative Supreme Court.

Nor did decision makers in other branches leap to the defense of the plantation model prison. The courts claim to speak with the voice of the Constitution, but they cannot mobilize public opinion by themselves, and a novel enterprise like prison reform could easily have given way in the face of determined opposition. In fact, there was hardly any opposition at all from Congress, from elected state officials, or from state administrators. Congress certainly took no steps to constrain the national judiciary. In fact, it reinforced the judicial initiative by establishing the Law Enforcement Assistance Administration (LEAA) and enacting the Civil Rights of Institutionalized Persons Act of 1980 (CRIPA).[94] The LEAA invested heavily in developing and promoting uniform standards for criminal justice agencies; in the field of prison administration, it prompted the adoption of standards derived from the federal Bureau of Prisons and worked closely with the American Correctional Association to develop a system for accrediting state prisons. CRIPA, an explicit effort to impose national standards on state prisons, presented states with what was essentially a nonchoice: either accept the congressionally approved standards drawn largely from the federal Bureau of Prisons, or run the risk of having the U.S. Department of Justice bring suits in a federal court that will essentially apply those very same standards. Even under the Reagan and Bush administrations, the largely passive Civil Rights Division earned the wrath of state prison officials by its willingness to use CRIPA as a means for challenging state penal practices.

With a few exceptions, southern state governors chose not to make an issue of the judicial intervention in state prisons. State legislators were as often supportive as condemnatory; although faced with rising correctional budgets, which often resulted from the litigation and sometimes were the litigation's major goal, they evinced relatively little enthusiasm for their quondam penal approaches that so obviously diverged from national norms. Southern prison administrators did not offer any serious opposition either. Once they were subjected to scrutiny by a national organization, they proved somewhat apologetic about the norms and practices that they had previously followed. Some, like Arkansas's Robert Sarver, welcomed lawsuits against themselves as a means of extracting money from the legislature. The majority of prison officials opposed the suits but reformed their own practices along national lines in anticipation of the trial. As indicated in the accounts of the Arkansas litigation, many of the leading cases involved procedures that were spanking new, and apparently quite reasonable, as if litigation had unaccountably befallen some the state's most forward-looking institutions. In fact, southern prison authorities suddenly realized how their previous procedures would appear to a federal judge; to put the matter a bit more conceptually, they suddenly saw themselves from the perspective of a national decision maker and perceived the bizarre and foreign character of their own practices.

The closest thing to Governor Ross Barnett's defiant resistance at the schoolhouse door was the actions of the Texas Department of Corrections, which fiercely opposed the prisoners' arguments in federal court and campaigned to vilify the judge once he had decided in the prisoners' favor. But these efforts were self-destructive; they quickly eroded the base of state political support for the department and led state officials to embrace the core position of the federal court. Moreover, even in Texas, prison administrators themselves underwent a change of heart. While the department did not go so far as to change its practices prior to the litigation, it did proceed to lie about these practices during the course of the trial. In particular, it categorically denied the existence of the building tender system, despite irrefutable evidence to the contrary. Apparently, the use of armed felons to discipline other prisoners was no longer a practice that Texas prison officials cared to defend before a federal court, however reasonable it had seemed to them a few years before.

But if the support for the plantation model rapidly gave way once national norms were identified and invoked, the converse effect also occurred: once the southern states abandoned that model and adopted the national norm, the federal courts had little more to say. The apparently endless cases ended when a college-educated warden from outside the South was appointed, when the trusties were replaced by professional civil service guards, when there was decent medical care and decent food – often provided by independent contractors, when the chain gang and the hoe squad gave way to industrial labor and educational programs, when the rawhide strap was replaced with administrative segregation controlled by a due process hearing, and when the prison, rather than making a profit, was being run at enormous cost, supported by ever-increasing state appropriations.

These changes were significant, and in some cases so widely viewed as beneficial that they seem to have their origin in simple human decency. Taken together, however, they do not represent some generalized reform agenda but the specific correctional model that prevailed in the rest of the United States. This becomes more apparent when one considers what the federal courts did not require. They did not require that the prisons eliminate double-celling, since nonsouthern prisons double-celled their inmates; they did not demand the reduction of inmate-to-inmate violence because such violence was endemic everywhere; they did not require that prisoners be incarcerated near their home, as opposed to being sent to remote rural locations; and, most significantly, they did not require any prison to produce the results that the Progressive model claimed as its guiding principle, namely, rehabilitation of the prisoner. In other words, the basic pattern of the prison cases was to compel one group of outlying institutions to conform to the prevailing standard.

Of course, many of the prison cases involved institutions in nonsouthern states. It may appear somewhat odd that institutions throughout the nation could diverge from national standards, but this follows from both the nature of the process and the nature of the standards. The process was a hermeneutic one, in which the goal was identified in relation to a group of divergent institutions, that goal was then applied throughout the nation, and then further divergences from the generalized goal were discerned. The standards, moreover, were not derived from some sort of complex averaging of prevailing conditions in nonsouthern prisons, but from the written standards of national organizations, primarily the federal Bureau of Prisons and the American Correctional Association. Thus, it is not surprising that there were many nonsouthern state prisons that fell short of these standards.

When suits were brought against nonsouthern prisons, however, one would expect that the remedial orders would be more delimited. Even comprehensive suits, such as the Colorado litigation, tended to involve a single institution rather than the state's entire prison system,*[95] and to challenge the operation of the prison, rather than the entire basis on which the prison was organized. There were exceptions, of course, like the Santa Clara jails, which were subject to judicial orders as comprehensive as those visited on any southern prison. But even there, the source of the court's displeasure seemed to be the lack of resources and management skills – two virtually universal features of American local government – rather than any basic disagreement about correctional philosophy.

If the federal courts imposed only delimited remedies on most nonsouthern prisons, they imposed none at all on the federal prison system. The only comprehensive conditions case that the Bureau of Prisons ever lost involved its New York City jail, and that decision was reversed in its entirety in the 1977 Supreme Court case of *Bell v. Wolfish*.†[96] In *Thornburgh v. Abbott*, a somewhat more conservative Supreme Court concluded that restrictions on communications with prisoners, which it had held unconstitutional in 1974 when enacted by the State of California, now appeared perfectly acceptable when enacted by the Bureau of Prisons, and overruled its prior holding.[97] Marion Penitentiary, with its permanent lockdown, its twenty-three hours of cell time per day, its concrete beds and its digital rectal searches not only survived repeated challenges, but won plaudits from the federal courts. This too is hardly surprising, since the federal institutions were the inspiration and embodiment of the standards that the courts imposed upon the states; holding a federal prison unconstitu-

---

* The only two nonsouthern states whose prison systems were declared unconstitutional in their entirety were Rhode Island and Hawaii, both of which have systems consisting largely of a single institution.

† Mr. Wolfish, however, was more successful elsewhere. After finishing his term for fraud in the federal prison in New York, he made aliyah to Israel, where he resumed his dubious career, and once again was caught, convicted, and sentenced to prison. Still in possession of his writ writing skills, Wolfish petitioned the Israeli Supreme Court to expand his conjugal visits, citing the commandment to "be fruitful and multiply." The court agreed, drawing on religious law and delicately ignoring the fact that Mrs. Wolfish was in her late fifties. Thus, Wolfish is one of the few prisoners whose name is connected with important prison law precedents on two continents.

tional would have been a bit like claiming that God had violated the Ten Commandments. The Bureau of Prisons could have been subjected to judicial intervention only for a failure to follow its own standards in specific circumstances, an administrative gaffe that it generally had the wit and the resources to avoid.

The Judicial Rejection of Federalism

The goal identified by the federal judiciary – imposing national standards on state institutions – is a perfectly sensible one, but it would appear to be precluded by the principle of federalism. This principle establishes the states as separate sovereignties and assigns them general responsibility for the welfare of their citizens. In the American system, the federal government is granted important but delimited powers; one of these, of course, is the power to punish violators of the laws it promulgates, and it has established an extensive prison system, the Bureau of Prisons, to do so. But the federal government is not granted authority to control the punishment imposed on violators of state laws. This unchallenged interpretation of the constitutional text is confirmed by history, for the states developed and administered their own prison systems to punish state offenders, and the federal government restricted its correctional policy to its own institutions prior to 1965.

When the federal courts acted, therefore, they were acting in violation of the federalist principle. In fact, their intervention could be regarded as a direct rejection of that principle; it was the insistent need to break through the barriers established by our governmental structure that impelled the courts to assume their activist role. They took charge of the process because the federal system limited the ability of other federal instrumentalities to do so. While limitations on national power have been steadily eroded during the course of the past century, they were still in place with respect to prisons as of 1965; in contrast to most major industrial nations, the United States had no national institution that exercised a legally coercive jurisdiction in this area. The judiciary was thus acting as a national policy maker by default. Judges took action because they believed that national standards should be imposed on southern prisons and they perceived that no other national institution would do so. They were able to take action, within the limits of their designated powers, because the Eighth Amendment served as a grant of jurisdiction in the area of punishment, a jurisdiction that, being grounded on a specific constitutional provision, contained none of the limits to which Congress or the president were subject.

Although the courts were the only federal institution that could exercise direct coercive authority over prisons, Congress might have achieved the same effect by offering federal grants conditioned on specified behaviors by the state recipients. As Seth Kreimer notes, this stratagem for circumventing our inherited federal structure has been employed in a number of areas and has drawn substantial criticism for its indirection and, ironically, for the heavy-handedness that accompanies that indirection.[98] But Congress chose not to use this most potent of its powers to reform state prisons, perhaps because of the unpopularity of prisoners, perhaps because it did not want to appropriate the necessary funds. The explanation for congressional inaction is an interesting question, but it is tangential to this inquiry. What is significant, for present purposes, is simply that Congress did not act, and that the federal courts were prepared to fill the breach, in specific and conscious violation of federalist doctrine.

It might appear, however, that the federal judiciary's rejection of federalism was not a thoroughgoing one. While the courts imposed national norms in their policy-making efforts, they left the operation of prisons in control of state officials. Once they had remedied the divergent situation that prevailed in the South, they withdrew, leaving the state prisons under the unaltered control of state officials. Thus, it might appear that the judiciary's rejection of federalism was limited to one specific and extraordinary situation: the effort to abolish the plantation model in American corrections.

In fact, the prison reform cases represent a direct and total rejection of the federalist principle, despite the continued state authority over state prisons. To see why this is so, it is necessary to distinguish between federalism and the related but independent principle of decentralization. Decentralization is an instrumental, managerial concept; it refers to the delegation of centralized authority to subordinate units of either a geographic or a functional character.[99] There are many reasons to decentralize, but the principal one is probably managerial effectiveness.[100] Very often, a manager who is relatively close to the subject matter will be more knowledgeable, more responsive, and more involved than a higher-ranking administrator ensconced in some distant central office. An industrial corporation might decentralize authority to factory managers, or a state university system might decentralize authority to the head of each constituent campus. The British army employs decentralization as a military strategy; whereas French or German field commanders are expected to follow detailed instructions, a British commander in the field possesses virtually complete autonomy.

But none of this has anything to do with federalism.[101] All these decentralized systems are hierarchically organized and the leaders at the top, or center, have a plenary power over the other members of the organization. Decentralization represents a deliberate policy that the leaders select, or at least approve, based on their view of the best way to achieve their goals. Thus, a decentralized system can be, and often is, the product of a purely managerial decision by a centralized authority.

Federal systems share certain structural features with decentralized ones. The most basic is that, within a single system of governance, decisions are made by subsidiary units and the central authority defers to those decisions. But in a federal system, the subordinate units possess prescribed areas of jurisdiction that cannot be invaded by the central authority, and leaders of these units draw their political power from sources independent of that central authority.[102] Federalism is not a managerial decision by the central decision maker, as decentralization can be, but a structuring principle for the system as a whole.

In the United States, we conceptualize federalism's principle of partial independence in terms of rights. Roughly speaking, a right is a legally defined claim that can be asserted against others, including, where relevant, the prevailing governmental power. Individuals in our society can assert certain claims against all governmental institutions, while states can assert certain claims against the federal government. In fact, states stand in essentially the same relationship to the federal government as individuals stand to all governments; they are subordinate, but partially independent by virtue of their rights.

The point of granting partial independence in this way, and thus the point of federalism, is to allow normative disagreement among the subordinate units so that different units can subscribe to different value systems. Purely instrumental disagreements can be resolved within a unitary system because the criteria for judgment are shared by or imposed on those within the system. Similarly, the adaptation of a single norm or goal to different circumstances can be readily achieved by managerial decentralization. Once everyone agrees that the goal is to produce more wheat, there may nonetheless be disagreement about whether one growing method is better than another. But the standard way to resolve this question is to investigate the merits of each method, not to give different farmers the right to grow wheat any way they please. When the investigation is complete, moreover, it may turn out that the growing conditions are crucial, and that these vary markedly from place to place. A natural resolution would be to decentralize the regulation of wheat growing – not to give subordinate farm administrators independence, but to enable them to adapt to the differing conditions of each region in their efforts to achieve a single goal.*[103]

Federalism becomes relevant only when the people in one region want

---

* Jonathan Macey suggests, on public choice grounds, that American federalism can be explained as a decentralizing strategy by which national legislators obtain enhanced political support.

to grow wheat, while those in another want to build factories on farmland or turn all the wheat fields into ecological preserves. It is possible, and indeed quite common, to resolve such normative disagreements by a centralized decision maker's fiat. The point is that it is also possible to resolve this problem by federalism, that is, by recognizing that each area has a right to control the use of its own land. More importantly, federalism only makes sense in this context; there is no need to grant such rights in order to choose more effective instrumentalities, or to adapt the selected instrumentalities to local circumstances.

This relationship between the rights of governmental units and the normative basis of their choices is an organic one. Rights are deontological, not instrumental claims. Although we may justify the existence of rights by an instrumental argument, a right, once recognized, stands independent of that argument and permits the rights holders to act whatever way they choose, regardless of the practical result. Of course, no society is blind to results or willing to tolerate unlimited frustration of its collective purposes. When the collectivity acts to obtain the results that it desires, however, the right is abrogated. As long as rights exist they represent the willingness of the society to subordinate its purposes to those of the rights holders, or, alternatively, to recognize the rights holders' choices as a purpose that transcends the pragmatic choices of the collectivity. If the society does not permit deontological choices of this nature by constituent governmental units – if it recognizes only instrumental strategies for achieving its collective goals – then it has not established rights, but has simply developed a specific mechanism for selecting strategies. In that case, federalism will not be needed as a structuring principle or, if already in place for historical reasons, will be otiose.

Clearly, only federalism can operate as a bar to national policy, and only federalism can justify the imposition of that bar by the judiciary. Decentralization, being an instrumental, managerial strategy, is no different in degree from any other policy; like cost, or administrative convenience, it is simply one factor that political decision makers should take into account. Their failure to do so could lead to the charge that they are unwise, but everyone agrees that such debates over policy alternatives are consigned to the ordinary political process. To declare a policy beyond the power of government and to enforce that position by judicial action requires the assertion that a right has been infringed. That right, in the case of federalism, is the right of states to act independently, according to goals the national government does not share. The notion that an admittedly valid national policy is best implemented by decentralizing its administration cannot support either the rhetoric of federalism or the remedy of judicial intervention.

This distinction between federalism and decentralization permits a fuller account of the reasons for the Constitution's allocation of state and national powers. One reason is related to federalism; the states were separately governed entities at the time the Constitution was adopted and their separate status was partially preserved under the new regime. Precisely how to characterize this result in more anthropormophic terms depends on one's theory of the process, as Samuel Beer suggests. The federalist, or states' rights, account is that the states relinquished only part of their power to the central government; the nationalist account is that the Framers and the populace created a new government that preserved part of the preexisting power of the states.[104] Both accounts agree, however, that the states survived as decision-making entities, with the authority to follow different norms in certain areas of governance.

The second reason for the Constitution's allocation of state and federal powers was decentralization. Even if the Framers or the populace had wanted to create a unitary regime, or if the states had been willing to relinquish all their powers, the technological and social conditions to operate such a regime did not exist. In 1789, the United States still consisted of a scattered set of clearings in a vast, primeval forest. There was no central metropolis from which to govern this far-flung, sparsely settled realm, and no existing administrative apparatus to carry out the tasks of governance. Thus, the only practical strategy for governing the new nation was to decentralize; because the eighteenth century's understanding of management strategies and public administration was still rudimentary, this pragmatic solution was naturally and imperceptibly merged into the more familiar principle of federalism. The fact that it was a separate motivation becomes apparent when one recognizes that government is not only decentralized among the states but also highly decentralized among various localities within the states, whose existence is not guaranteed by any federal right.

The way in which the prison cases represent a complete rejection of federalism now becomes apparent. By preserving the state governance of their prison systems, the federal courts were continuing the pragmatic strategy of decentralization that remains so characteristic of American government. But in imposing national norms on the state prisons that were following distinctly different models, the courts were rejecting the essential principle of federalism. As stated, federalism is distinguished from decentralization because it allows governmental subunits to follow separate norms rather than simply following separate managerial strategies for achieving a single, centrally established norm. The prison cases decisively rejected the state's power to follow separate norms in prison administration. The states could continue to govern their own prisons, in accordance with the managerial principle of decentralization, but only if those prisons conformed to the standards established by the federal Bureau of Prisons and the American Correctional Association.

What renders the prison cases a complete rejection of federalism, and not merely a rejection of federalism in a specific area, is that prison administration was probably the last vestige of true normative divergence, and thus true federalism, in the American polity. Originally, the great divide between the American states was slavery. At the time of the Revolution, to be sure, abolitionism was largely restricted to the Quakers, but as the northern states gradually abolished slavery in the post-Revolutionary period, a clear divergence developed between the economic system, cultural attitudes, and normative beliefs of the North and South.[105] The South's response, advanced under the banner of states' rights, was that each state should be able to determine its own norms. As discussed earlier, this was rejected in the Civil War, partially reestablished as a result of the Redeemer movements in the South and the failure of Reconstruction, and then finally rejected in the civil rights movement of the 1950s and 1960s. With the Civil Rights Act of 1964, any normative divergence among American states regarding race relations was abolished, at least de jure. By 1965, the most striking normative divergence among American states that was still legally permitted involved the treatment of prisoners. The same forces that motivated judges to recognize prisoners as America's final minority impelled them to reject the federalist principle that their divergent treatment represented.

The point becomes still clearer when one considers that the judiciary's decisive action on behalf of prisoners was, in the larger public policy context, somewhat gratuitous. Race relations is perhaps the central problem of our nation, one that has continually threatened to tear us apart. The need to resolve this problem, therefore, could readily overcome any other consideration, including federalism. But this is not true of prison reform. There was only very limited political agitation over the rights of prisoners during the 1960s, and it is not difficult to imagine our polity surviving rather nicely without altering the southern prisons.

In other words, the prison reform movement, unlike the civil rights movement, was not compelled by political or social forces. When federal judges took action, they were motivated by the mere fact of normative divergence. It was not the effects of the southern prison that horrified them, but the southern prison itself, and its divergence from the national standard that they had come to regard as essentially American. The extraordinary aggressiveness of their response betokens a complete rejection of the federalist principle that different states are allowed to follow different norms. Thus, when critics of the prison reform cases assert that the courts violated the principle of federalism, they are understating the actual situation. The courts were not simply violating federalism in a particular instance; they were trying to obliterate it in its entirety.

Instrumental Arguments for Federalism

But why were the federal courts so antagonistic toward federalism? After all, we Americans love federalism, or, as the Court has affectionately christened it, "our federalism."[106] It conjures up images of Fourth of July parades down Main Street and family farms with tire swings in the front yard. Imagery aside, a number of powerful arguments are made on its behalf. Federalism, as Justice O'Connor so grandiloquently wrote in the process of interpreting a minor implication of a specialized federal labor statute, "increases opportunity for citizen involvement in democratic process," "allows for more innovation and experimentation in government," and "makes government more responsive by putting states in competition for a mobile citizenry."[107] A related argument, popular among law and economics writers, is that this competition among states generates efficient regulatory laws because firms will choose the optimal regime in which to operate. But the greatest virtue of federalism, in Justice O'Connor's view, is that it constitutes "a check on abuses of government power" by diffusing that power among separate sovereigns.[108] To this already formidable litany, contemporary writers have added still another argument: that federalism fosters community – that vague but vibrant something that both constitutes individuals and provides them with an opportunity for self-expression. Given all the many virtues that the principle of federalism is said to possess, it is surprising to see the federal courts so assiduously squelching it.

As stated in Chapter 1, explanations based on collective brain-fever should be avoided. If hundreds of federal judges were willing to reject federalism, they must have perceived or sensed that this principle is not as hallowed as our public rhetoric suggests. There must be something wrong with federalism, something that should be observable from studying the prison cases. In fact, what is wrong with federalism is that it has become obsolete. Over the course of the past century, our country has been transformed into a national, administrative state, responsible for managing major portions of our social and economic systems. This state, and the political developments it embodies, have condemned the principle of federalism to irrelevance by virtue of the central government's normative engagement with virtually every area of political controversy. The judiciary's willingness to conceive of itself as a policy maker is a reflection of this more general trend. Its decision to make policy and its decision to reject federalism were not separate, successive steps, but aspects of a single set of developments that have transformed both the judges' understanding of their role and their interpretation of the constraints upon their actions.

It is possible to describe the decline of federalism in terms of brute empirics, of course; the massive growth of the central government in absolute magnitude and in areas of operation is a matter of agreement among both critics and proponents of the process. But this does not explain why federalism lost its appeal to the judiciary. Federal judges are insulated from the political forces that produce such trends, in part because of the explicit expectation that they will be a countervailing force in certain instances. More importantly, judges inhabit a conceptual and normative realm. If federalism lost its appeal for them as a result of political developments, those developments must have undermined the normative appeal of the principle as well as its political practicality. They must have generated an answer to Justice O'Connor's formidable list of federalism's virtues and to the persuasive force of the imagery that underlies them.

This is precisely what has occurred. The Supreme Court's attitude toward federalism during recent decades has been decidedly negative. Indeed, the intensity of its enthusiasm for this principle seems inversely related to the significance of the issue at hand; the less politically significant the issue, the greater the Court's insistence on the virtues of federalism. The Court has validated the division of political power and secured the "promise of liberty" in areas of minor political significance, such as the power of states to compel the retirement of elderly judges, or in areas where Congress can readily design alternative ways to accomplish the same substantive goals, such as hazardous waste disposal.[109] It has remained silent, or explicitly rejected federalism, every time it really mattered, that is, every time it permitted genuine normative variation. In fact, the Court's intermittent embrace of the federalist principle can best be understood as a form of symbolic politics,[110] one that in fact undermines rather than enhances federalism itself. The Court's opinions play a minor, but much noted role in the continuing national dramaturgy that fosters the myth of small-town America, with its self-contained communities, its family values, and its part-time lawmakers. All of this is condensed, or smuggled, into the term "federalism." Even as political and social conditions make these institutions infeasible, they remain powerful and reassuring symbols, part of the myth that we have not really changed as much as we have really changed. The Court's continued insistence upon "our federalism" is an important means for fostering this myth, thereby obscuring the replacement of its factual referent by a nationwide culture and a complex administrative state.

The Court's recent and somewhat unexpected decisions in *United States v. Lopez*[111] and *Printz v. United States*,[112] may indicate a turn toward more substantive implementation of federalism, but, at this juncture, serve largely to underscore the symbolic nature of the Court's decisions in this area. *Lopez* involves the Gun-Free School Zones Act of 1993, which declares that knowing possession of a firearm within a school zone is a federal offense. By a narrow majority, the Court held the statute unconstitutional because it exceeds Congress's authority under the Commerce Clause. Justice Rehnquist's opinion, however, takes great pains to emphasize that the decision does not challenge either *Wickard v. Filburn*, which held that Congress could use its commerce power to regulate a farmer who grows wheat for his own use, or *Heart of Atlanta Motel, Inc. v. United States*,[113] which held that Congress could use that power as the basis for the Civil Rights Act. Having preserved the outer limits of national authority, the Court then stated its two principal objections to the statute in question: that Congress had offered no explicit findings about the effects of gun possession in a school zone on interstate commerce, and that proponents of the statute's constitutionality had declined to offer a concrete example of any activity that would be beyond the reach of national authority if the statute were upheld.[114] The symbolic character of this dual request for offerings is unmistakable. The Court is saying, almost explicitly, that Congress should not be so transparent about the decline of federalism, that it should, through an explicit finding, perform the old-time act of obeisance when passing by federalism's august but unattended shrine, and leave a little something, in the form of a counterexample, in the hands of the impecunious old druid who is standing in its doorway.

In *Printz v. United States* the Court, again by a narrow margin, invalidated portions of the Brady Handgun Violence Prevention Act that required local officials to perform background checks on prospective gun purchasers. This requirement, the Court said, violates the Tenth Amendment because it commandeers state officials to perform a federal function, something for which there is no precedent in two hundred prior years of federal legislation. Justice Scalia's majority opinion flounders around quite a bit in its effort to explain why the admittedly numerous statutes requiring state judges to enforce federal law and even to perform administrative functions – statutes that date back to the quasi-constitutional First Congress – do not fall within this forbidden category. His final explanation is that judges are different from administrators, although he never explains how they are different, or why any difference would be relevant to the issue in the case. He also goes on to distinguish the Brady Act requirement from the common requirement that state officials report various kinds of information to federal officials, again without explaining the basis for making this distinction. By the time he has finished, he does not have a coherent opinion, but he certainly has a limited one. Moreover, Justice O'Connor, usually federalism's most grandiloquent defender, goes out of her way in a concurrence to point out that states could still participate in the Brady Act program voluntarily, and that the use of state officials was only an interim measure until full federal enforcement could be instituted. Once again, the opinion seems to demand that Congress perform some act of obesiance at federalism's shrine, in this case by asking the states to participate, rather than simply telling their subordinate officials to do so. It may also contain the even more symbolic, golden-bough-type implication, that Congress may invade the shrine of federalism if it acts in the full war armor of conditional funding or federally employed bureaucrats, but not in the bourgeois, somewhat disheveled guise of administrative instructions.*

The reason that the Court's federalism decisions have been so peripheral, despite the sweep of the majority's rhetoric, is that most of Justice O'Connor's grand justifications for federalism do not apply to federalism at all, but to the managerial policy of decentralization. In other words, they do not truly contemplate that norms will vary from one state to another, but articulate a single norm and argue that this norm is best implemented by decentralized management. Implementing a single norm through decentralization is an administrative or bureaucratic approach, however. It involves a central government with articulated and wide-ranging social policies that makes strategic decisions about the best strategy for implementation of those policies. Political action of this nature can be confused with federalism because federalism was our historical means of decentralization in the era before the administrative state developed. Now that the two can be distinguished, it is apparent and quite significant that most of the common arguments for federalism actually refer to managerial decentralization. This indicates the conceptual dominance of the administrative state, with the very nature of the arguments that are advanced to support federalism providing evidence of federalism's continuing decline.

Four of the standard arguments for federalism that in fact relate to administrative decentralization are increasing public participation, maximizing citizen utility through competition among jurisdictions, achieving economic efficiency through competition among jurisdictions, and encouraging the development of new approaches through experimentation. Of the four, the public participation argument is the most complex because it overlaps with genuine arguments for federalism that will be discussed later in connection with the concept of community. For present purposes, the claim is that locating various decisions at the regional or local level will enable more people to participate in these decisions. As

---

* The two decisions may also reflect the justices' dislike of gun control legislation, which may be at least strong enough to test the growing, but still tentative, national majority that seems to favor it.

Justice O'Connor stated, federalism "increases opportunity for citizen involvement in democratic processes."

Participation of this sort may not be as unambiguous a benefit as the Court and many commentators imply. In our present political context, participation is generally a middle- and upper-middle-class activity, which is as likely to exclude and disadvantage less fortunate citizens as it is to help them.[115] In any event, if one wants to implement a program of ensuring and increasing local participation, decentralized decisions may well be a valid way to proceed, but this would be a national policy, not a federalist one. The goal would be to encourage participation in every state or locality. Federalism does not necessarily increase participation; it simply authorizes a set of specified political sub-units – states in our case – to decide for themselves how much participation is desirable. Some might choose to encourage participation, but others might choose to suppress it. There are, moreover, a variety of other methods that national policy makers could adopt for achieving the same goal, such as hiring community organizers, funding local organizations, and requiring approvals for government decisions from different sectors of the population.[116] None of these have anything to do with federalism, or even decentralization, but if participation is a real goal, rather than a post hoc rationalization for federalism, they should be given equal consideration. More generally, participation is a complex process that must be fostered by specific, carefully constructed mechanisms; it will not be secured by large-scale structural arrangements whose relevance is based on vague and unproven assumptions.

One might argue that the states, being "closer to the people" than the federal government, are more likely to foster local participation. As Richard Briffault points out, however, there is simply no reason why an intermediate political unit would be more favorable to local units than the nation's central authority.[117] In practice, actual alignments are likely to depend on the correspondence of substantive policies. For example, the white-dominated governments of the southern states undoubtedly fostered the autonomy of white-dominated towns against federal intervention; on the other hand, the federal government was correspondingly more solicitous of black communities, at least during the Reconstruction and civil rights eras.

One might also argue that federalism fosters public participation by enabling citizens to choose their own rulers. But this merely combines decentralization and the independent norm of electoral politics, without involving federalism at all. In a truly federal regime, some states might opt for elections, while others might not; it is the Guarantee Clause, a nationalizing provision, that probably requires states to choose their leadership by election. As a matter of political reality, elections are deeply ingrained in our political culture. We do not need the Guarantee Clause because every state, no matter how much normative latitude it is given, grants its citizens the power to choose their own leaders by election, at the local level as well as the state level. This phenomenon cannot possibly be attributed to federalism, since federalism does not protect the political systems of localities. Indeed, it has the reverse effect, for it subjects these localities to the plenary control of state government and precludes or limits the ability of the national government to set standards for local politics. Thus, if the electoral principle were under attack in certain states, and Americans decided at a national level that we needed to make sure that every locality held elections, true federalism would constitute a barrier to the implementation of this policy.[118]

Nothing illustrates the disjunction between federalism and citizen involvement better than the history of American prisons. Prior to 1965, there was probably no area of state authority more insulated from the national government than correctional management. But this did not lead to any particular increase in accessibility for ordinary citizens; state prisons, to the extent that they were controlled by any outside authority, were generally administered by a state department of corrections that was as remote and self-contained as any regional branch of a national prison administration would have been. The principal result of state control was that the correctional departments were underfunded, low-prestige governmental entities, which lacked the will or the resources to supervise individual prisons, and that these departments were themselves supervised by underpaid, understaffed, part-time legislators, rather than the U.S. Congress. As a result, the typical state prison – and this was true throughout the nation – was a virtual satrapy of the warden, and a testament to the lack of any necessary link between federalism and citizen participation.

A second standard argument for federalism, again in the words of Justice O'Connor, is that it "makes government more responsive by putting the states in competition for a mobile citizenry."*[119] The claim, as

---

* On its face, these statements seem contradictory, because they elide Hirschman's distinction between voice and exit. Responsiveness is generally regarded as allied to voice; a government, for example, responds when those within its jurisdiction express their dissatisfaction with its policies. Competition for a mobile citizenry, on the other hand, seems allied to exit; the government attracts those dissatisfied with other jurisdictions, while accepting, or celebrating, the departure of those dissatisfied with its own policies. These arguments can be reconciled, however, through an understanding of exit and voice as alternative ways in which individuals relate to organizations. Individuals will seek organizations that are responsive to their needs, or voice; if their present organization fails to respond, they can exercise their exit option to locate a more responsive one. Conversely, an orga-

articulated more precisely by Charles Tiebout, is that a group of government jurisdictions can offer varying packages of government services with varying means of funding those services, and varying costs to their citizens;[120] citizens can then choose among these jurisdictions, so that they come to rest in one that matches their personal preferences, or utility function. This argument has found much favor in the economic and law and economics literature.[121] There is something a bit fanciful in the image of people choosing a place to live the way shoppers choose their favorite breakfast cereal, and critics have pointed out that the transaction costs of obtaining information and transplanting one's life may well overwhelm the utility gains from the selection process.[122] But there is much truth to the argument as well in our mobile, restless society.

This argument is unrelated, or only tangentially related, to the concept of federalism, however. The package of government services and costs that a particular jurisdiction offers is only one element in its overall appeal to potential citizens. Climate, size, location, employment opportunities, and a variety of other factors are likely to loom larger in the utility function of our wandering citizen, even apart from affective considerations that discourage mobility like family ties, nostalgia, local loyalty, and baseball. In addition, government service packages involve a number of factors, such as education, police protection, social welfare, and recreation, all of which can vary, and all of which can be funded by a variety of mechanisms that produce differential impacts on people of different economic positions. The net result, in economic terms, is that the supply of jurisdictions from which citizens can choose is likely to be less than perfectly elastic.[123]

The difficulty can be partially resolved if there are a large number of such jurisdictions and, indeed, if there are a large number in each region of the nation. Thus, the concept of government service packages seems to apply to localities, like counties, cities, or towns. States are just too large to produce the necessary range of choices; telling wheat farmers in Kansas that they can obtain the kinds of schools they want by moving to New Jersey is unlikely to provide an increase in their overall utility function. What would help them, if one assumes the entire concept makes sense, is a choice of jurisdictions with different educational policies within their own region, state, or city. Eric Nordlinger's discussion of decentralization in a single city, for example, is more relevant for people's realistic choices among government service packages than any of the literature on the juridical autonomy of states.[124]

nization can generate a self-selected membership by resisting some divergent voices, and then being more responsive to those with more desirable views who have remained or entered.

But federalism only protects the autonomy of states, not the autonomy or variability of local governments.[125] Indeed, the very essence of American federalism is that the national government is forbidden to interfere with state policies for managing and controlling local governments. Federalism does not secure the kind of governmental variability that would provide any realistic choice for citizens; instead, its principal effect in this area is to create a legal barrier against the imposition of such variability as a matter of national policy.*[126] Again, if we are truly serious about providing people with choices, we should provide those choices universally, through a national program, rather than relying on the adventitious impact of a tangentially related policy like federalism.

A third argument for federalism, closely related to the preceding one, is based on competition among jurisdictions, rather than on choice by citizens.[127] The idea is that federalism will increase the economic efficiency of our system, and thereby maximize the material wealth of the nation as a whole, because jurisdictions will compete for productive assets, such as factories, and desirable people, such as chemical engineers, by creating a favorable economic climate. Asset managers and individuals will then choose among jurisdictions, voting with their well-heeled feet in favor of the most efficient states, thus ensuring the efficiency of the nation as a whole. This argument, in contrast to the argument regarding citizen choice, does apply to states. Firms, unlike individuals, have a relatively simple utility function based on profit maximization. They do not need to consider their preference for a particular climate, size of community or community location, to say nothing of family ties or local loyalty. Such factors affect the individuals within the firm, and they only matter to the firm, as a decision-making entity, to the extent that they affect the firm's single criterion of profitability. As a result, America's fifty-three jurisdictions may be enough to provide the requisite variation for interjurisdictional competition. To be sure, the competition argument leaves open an interesting question about the fate of undesirable facilities, like radioactive waste dumps, and of undesirable people – chemical dependents rather than chemical engineers – in the absence of central government control;[128] nonetheless, a central authority might well choose to decentralize certain aspects of the economy to generate this salutary competition.

---

* Proponents of federalism frequently confuse it with localism in arguing for its virtues. One argument offered by Charles Fried and Lino Graglia is that federalism confines the erroneous governmental policies of places like Santa Monica or New York City (or, worse still, Berkeley), thus avoiding their imposition on the entire nation. But these benighted places are cities, not states. Their boundaries are not fixed by federalism, and the forces that keep them contained are thus political, not constitutional.

Once again, however, the arguments cannot really be viewed as favoring federalism, because federalism allows a multiplicity of norms, and not simply a multiplicity of rules. In a truly federal system, some subunits might not be interested in economic efficiency or social welfare at all; they might be primarily motivated by the desire to preserve an agrarian life-style, or to protect the environment, or to encourage individual spirituality. These particular subunits might lose out in the competition for factories and chemical engineers, as the economic analysis predicts. But rather than perceiving their losses as a chastening lesson that induces them to change their laws, they might perceive them as a necessary cost or as a positive advantage. Clearly, this would not achieve the single goal that the proponents of efficiency desire. What they really want is a unitary system, devoted to efficiency, which delegates instrumental decisions to decentralized subunits but retains normative control to make sure that every subunit is committed to the general goal.

To put the analysis of all three arguments more generally, true federalism cannot be regarded as a means of favoring any specific, first-order norm because its essence is to permit a multiplicity of norms. It favors only the second-order norm that no first-order norm should dominate the polity. In practice, of course, a federal regime may turn out to be a means of achieving a specific, first-order norm such as participation, citizen choice, or economic efficiency. This will occur when that norm is so widely shared that every subunit will adopt it, even if left to its own normative devices. The United States, despite its federal structure and its self-image as a vast and variegated nation, is in fact a heavily homogenized culture with high levels of normative consensus.[129] It displays less regional variation than Great Britain or Italy, to say nothing of China, India, or the erstwhile Soviet Union; the more appropriate comparisons might be Finland or Venezuela.[130] In political structure, every state has a popularly elected governor, a regionally elected legislature, independent courts, and similar decision-making processes. In economic structure, every state has the same general goal of maximizing material welfare, and has chosen the same mixed, free-enterprise economy for doing so. Compared with the range of political and economic systems found worldwide, to say nothing of those found throughout recorded history, the variations among states are insignificant. This is the reason why the Guarantee Clause can be safely declared nonjusticiable. If some American state were to establish a monarchy or adopt communism, national institutions, in particular the U.S. Marine Corps, would quickly respond, and the Supreme Court would approve that response.

The disjunction between federalism and any first-order norm is further emphasized by a fourth and somewhat different argument for federalism: that federalism gives the states an opportunity to experiment with different policies.[131] The reason this is desirable, presumably, is not because of an abiding national commitment to pure research, but because the variations may ultimately provide information about a number of governmental policies and enable us to choose the most desirable one. To quote no less of an authority than Justice Brandeis: "It is one of the happy incidents of the federal system that a single courageous state may, if its citizens choose, serve as a laboratory; and to try novel social and economic experiments without risk to the rest of the country."[132] This has a certain ring to it, but on further examination, experimentation also turns out to be a happy incident of managerial decentralization, not of federalism.

In a unitary system, the central authority will generally have a single goal, but it may be uncertain about which of several policies will best achieve that goal. To resolve this uncertainty, it could order different subunits to experiment with different strategies until the best way to achieve the goal emerges.*[133] Experimentation of this sort is an instrumentality, useful only when the subunits share a single goal. It is not particularly relevant to subunits whose goals are different from each other. But true federalism allows governmental subunits to choose different goals, and not merely to experiment with different mechanisms for achieving a single one.

The experimentation argument for federalism, therefore, is an effort to justify a normative regime by invoking the appeal of an instrumental one. The instinct to do so is understandable in this instrumental age, but the argument, like the argument for participation, citizen choice, or competition, supports only managerial decentralization. A unitary manager can experiment with different policies for achieving the same goal, just as it can encourage different subunits to compete against each other in pursuit of that goal. But these arguments would be inapplicable to federalism if our country consisted of subunits with truly different goals. For example, precisely what experiment would one design to tell the antebellum southerners that slavery was morally repugnant? The experimentation argument, like the competition argument, seems applicable to federalism only when there is no normative disagreement among subunits, so that federalism merges into administrative decentralization. The fact that this is true in the United States today is what gives these arguments their surface plausibility.

---

* An interesting example is the People's Republic of China's experiment with essentially unrestrained capitalism in the Shenzhen Economic Zone. A more unitary regime than the PRC would be hard to find; it is so committed to central control that it has placed China's entire 3,000 mile expanse on Beijing time. Yet it is fully capable of establishing a local regime that is virtually a polar opposite of its more general mode of governance.

In fact, even decentralization creates problems for the kind of experimentation that is needed to select policies in a highly regulated administrative state. To experiment with different approaches for achieving a single, agreed-upon goal, one subunit must be assigned an option that initially seems less desirable, either because that option requires changes in existing practices, or because it offers lower, although still-significant, chances of success. Allowed to choose their own strategies, as they are in a decentralized system, no subunits would choose these unappealing options;[134] they must be forced or encouraged to do so by the centralized authority. Economic theory underscores this conclusion. Experiments are likely to be public goods because the information that they generate will be available to all states regardless of each state's individual investment. As a result, individual states will have no incentive to invest in experiments that involve any substantive or political risk, but will prefer to wait for other states to generate them; this will, of course, produce relatively few experiments.[135]

The standard solution to this dilemma is either coercion or coordination through some inclusive entity, such as the central government. If the decentralized states are rational actors who desire to experiment (a heroic assumption, but certainly one that is required for the entire states-as-laboratories argument), they might agree among themselves to share the costs of such experiments. More typically, they might agree to subject themselves to coercive discipline to overcome the free-rider problem, just as a patriotic citizenry that supports strong national defense might opt for a military draft and a system of taxation, rather than a voluntary army supported by individual contributions. In either case, the natural consequence of their agreement would be centralization. It is thus hardly surprising, even given the most favorable assumptions about the rationality and conscientiousness of state governments, that most significant "experimental" programs in recent years have in fact been organized and financed by the national government. Some of these efforts, like the National Center for State Courts and the National Institute of Corrections,[136] are organized as advisory bodies because the residual influence of federalism discourages more direct involvement. Thus, the effect of federalism, to the extent that it is still operative, has not been to encourage experimental state programs or state-sponsored coordinating agencies, but simply to keep some truly innovative national efforts limited, tentative, and vaguely apologetic.

Finally, even if decentralized states establish a mechanism by which they can coerce themselves to experiment, they will need to collect massive amounts of data if proper choices are to be made; in technical areas particularly, the virtues of a specific policy are unlikely to be self-evident. Decentralized states, acting on their own, will have little incentive to generate this information; they may be motivated to articulate politically palatable justifications for their chosen policy, but they are unlikely to gather data directed to its replication or modification. And if the information is gathered and assimilated, it is not likely to be useful unless the original policy choices are coordinated by a centralized authority. Even in the absence of normative, truly federalist variations, state-initiated experiments are unlikely to be particularly useful to other states because they will tend to vary along specific, technical dimensions. Of course, data and experience developed for one set of conditions can be applied to another, but such applications require information and analysis that no state is likely to undertake on behalf of others. Thus, centralization is not only necessary to initiate the experimental process, but also to implement that process in any reasonably effective fashion.

All of this is implicit in the imagery of scientific experimentation, once that imagery is taken seriously. Experiments generally involve variations among subsets of a total population, but those variations are carefully and minutely prescribed by the researcher – a centralized authority if ever there is one. In medical research, for example, it would be unusual for the researcher to authorize her subjects to follow whatever course of treatment they desire, even if all the subjects agree on the general goal of finding a medical cure. The more common practice is for the researcher to prescribe the treatment for each group, which allows the use of therapies that would not otherwise be chosen and provides comparable data regarding their effects.

Liberty-Based Arguments for Federalism

Since many of the standard arguments that favor federalism really refer to a managerial policy of decentralization, it is not surprising that these arguments, however much rhetorical respect is paid to them, did not persuade the federal courts to contain their policy-making efforts. There remain, however, two important arguments that genuinely support the basic principle of federalism; an older one that emphasizes federalism's role in protecting liberty by diffusing governmental power, and a more recent one that emphasizes its support of communitarian values. These arguments, unlike the argument for participation, citizen choice, governmental competition, or experimentation, do not champion one substantive policy; instead, they favor the rights of political subunits to adopt whatever policy they choose, and they justify this position on the basis of overarching moral values like liberty or community. This section deals with the diffusion of power argument; the community argument is considered in the following section.

The idea that federalism secures liberty by diffusing power[137] depends on two separate assertions: first, that federalism actually does diffuse power; and, second, that the diffusion of power protects liberty. The development of the modern administrative state is virtually a direct denial of both claims. Our present governmental system is based on the idea that national policy making itself diffuses power, at least in certain areas, and that the diffusion of power in other areas – specifically those which would frustrate national policy making – constitute a denial of liberty, not a guarantee of it. Given the centrality of these ideas, it is hardly surprising that federal judges found the claim that federalism secures liberty by diffusing power unpersuasive.

To assess the relationship among the doctrine of federalism, the diffusion of governmental power, and the protection of liberty, one needs to know what is meant by power and how the process of diffusion operates. The term "power" is an ambiguous one;[138] at the very least, it is necessary to distinguish between the political and administrative power of the government.* The political power of a governmental subunit involves its ability to choose its own officials, to structure its own institutions and to determine its own internal units. The natural implication of federalism is to grant these powers to the states. Clearly, political power is more diffused in a federal regime because the leaders and representatives of each subunit possess a legally protected political base from which they can voice their opposition to the central authority.[139] As stated earlier, this argument can be readily overstated; elections are part of our political culture and flourish at the local level without the protection of federalism. In any event, political power cannot be the subject of our concern about the growth of the national government, or serve as a basis for invoking federalism. Despite the current scholarly emphasis on state autonomy, the political power of the states, whether cultural or constitutional in origin, is not under attack.[140] No one is suggesting that state governors be appointed by the president, or that the U.S. Department of Agriculture can-

---

* The term power could also refer to the physical power of the government, but current concern about diffusing power cannot have physical power in mind. There is no period of history when a central government has possessed such overwhelming physical power, compared with its governmental subunits, as the present time. Our federal armed forces have the capacity to turn any state, any segment of humanity, or humanity in general into a thin gas, and to do so, like the seventh seal's silence, in "about the space of half an hour" (Revelations 8: 1). This situation will not change. Even the rapidly dispersing republics of the former Soviet Union quailed before the possibility that they would secure their independence from the center by maintaining nuclear arsenals of rival strength; the likelihood that, within our infinitely more cohesive union, Nebraska would develop a deterrent force of nuclear missiles, or New Jersey would launch a fleet of nuclear submarines to patrol its seacoasts, is not particularly great.

cel state legislative elections in rural areas. The political independence of the states has not changed over the course of this century and has not been challenged since the Reconstruction era.

The issue of federalism arises, and the jeremiads about its demise seem plausible, because of concerns about administrative, rather than physical or political, power. If physical power is control over soldiers, airplanes, missiles, and artillery, and political power is control over votes, offices, and public opinion, then administrative power is control over appointed officials, public resources, and regulatory rules.[141] While complaints about the demise of federalism often speak in terms of political power, they invoke the centralization of administrative power as their principal evidence.[142] The vast growth of federal regulatory programs, from the banking, antitrust, and conservation programs of the Progressive era, through the labor, agricultural, and social programs of the New Deal, to the consumer, environmental, social welfare, and civil liberties programs of the Great Society era, all involved administrative power. The current federalization of criminal law can be understood in the same terms.[143] These programs left the political structure of the states entirely intact; their effect was to expand the central government's administrative apparatus.[144]

The prison reform cases illustrate this distinction between political and administrative power. Although the federal courts clearly disapproved of the entire process by which southern states made correctional decisions, there was never even the slightest intimation that their political decision-making process should be changed. No court ever contemplated such strategies as federal appointment of prison administrators, or federally managed taxation schemes to fund the prisons, to say nothing of federal initiatives to reform the legislature or executive branches of state government. Rather, the courts acted as Congress acted in so many other areas; they required state decision makers to use different rules and different standards in exercising their existing powers. In many cases, the court decisions were designed to force these state decision makers to act in designated ways; in others, particular decisions were simply dictated by federal authority. This had no effect on the political structure of the state, but it did represent a dramatic increase in the administrative power of the federal government – its power to instruct appointed officials, to control the use of funds, and to prescribe prevailing rules.

The administrative power that the federal courts exercised in the prison cases, and that the federal government has exercised in so many fields, is the defining characteristic of the modern state. When the courts rejected federalism in the prison cases and imposed national policy on state correctional institutions, they were simply participating in the general process of modern administrative governance. No doubt, the more usual approach would have involved the creation of a large, well-funded bureaucratic agency of the sort that has generated all the anguish on behalf of federalism. But since Congress was unwilling to act, the task of wielding the modern state's administrative power fell to the federal judiciary.

Thus, the idea that federalism considerations should constrain the judiciary's policy-making efforts would imply that federalism should constrain the basic administrative power of the central government. Proponents of federalism might favor this approach – they might seek a major reversal of the national policy that has prevailed for the past century – but the federal judiciary was unlikely to agree. The judges understood that the nation was irretrievably committed to the use of national administrative power, particularly during the Great Society era, and more particularly in relation to the divergent southern states. By imposing national standards on state prisons, they were replicating a process that national policy makers had undertaken in so many other areas, a policy that is inconsistent with the use of federalism as a constraint on central government initiatives.

Quite apart from the fact that the expansion of national administrative power implied the rejection of federalism, the mode of this expansion tended to undercut the claim that federalism diffuses governmental power. To begin with, the growth of federal administrative power, dramatic though it is, has not necessarily detracted from the administrative power of the states.[145] There is no fixed supply of governmental power such that increases in federal power ineluctably cause decreases in state power through a zero-sum exchange. Rather, the administrative power of government at all levels has been steadily increasing in our culture for a substantial period of time. One hundred years ago, the work place was essentially unregulated, other than by judicial enforcement of individual contracts. We now have a truly formidable panoply of labor, health, and safety regulations by both the federal government and the states. Similarly, the government's involvement in environmental matters once consisted essentially of selling off the environment in quarter-section parcels; now governments at all levels monitor the quality of air and water and regulate the emissions of factories, which once spewed their fumes into the unmeasured air with laissez-faire abandon.

But even if we assume that national power is growing at the direct expense of states, we cannot conclude that this growth decreases the dispersion of governmental control over the people, and thereby threatens liberty. With respect to this inquiry, the crucial question is not the gross aggregation of power, but the way power is exercised in each area of human life. Edward Corwin and, more recently, Harry Scheiber and David Walker, characterize the first seven decades of our republic as the classic period of "dual federalism,"[146] when national and state governments exercised authority in virtually exclusive spheres. The essence of their relationship was jealous protection of their legally established jurisdiction, rather than interpenetration or cooperation. As Scheiber recounts, the Civil War began a gradual but inexorable expansion of the areas where the federal government exercised authority, with cooperation, grants-in-aid, parallel administrative systems, and outright competition displacing the prior exclusivity of state control.[147] Again, this does not mean that the state governments exercised less overall power, given the general growth in the power of government. What clearly decreased, however, were the number of areas where state power was unaffected by federal authorities.

Thus, the expansion of federal administrative power generally means that two governmental hierarchies will be involved in a particular area of governance instead of one. This is sometimes described as cooperative federalism; Milton Grodzins invokes the image of a marble cake, with state and federal power intertwined in innumerable, complex ways.[148] Whether it is cooperative, competitive, or simply convoluted – whether it is marble cake or mush – there seems little doubt, as Stephen Gardbaum suggests, that state and national powers overlap, and that national policy is regularly implemented by state officials.[149] The Supreme Court's recent decision in *Printz v. United States* seems to challenge this approach but, as just observed, it does so only marginally: continued evidence of Congress's recognition that American administration consists of overlapping bureaucracies can be found in the decentralization of welfare payments and the authorization of congressional challenges to unfunded federal mandates.[150] This may not be efficient or even generally beneficial, but it seems difficult to characterize it as a dangerous concentration of the national government's power.* Rather, it is precisely the sort of balance between

---

* Perhaps it could be argued that the aggregation of federal power across a broad range of governmental areas represents a dangerous concentration of power, even if its effect, in individual areas, is to disperse power among multiple authorities. But this assumes the point at issue – whether federalism has moral force that justifies its invocation as a constraint on governmental action. If one wants to argue this point, rather than to assert it, one must show that federal aggrandizement impinges on some independent value, such as individual liberty. As indicated, however, federal intervention tends to increase liberty in each area of governance. One might argue that the general size of our federal government creates the danger that it will act oppressively in each area by virtue of its elephantine bulk, but this is an abstract argument that relies on little besides metaphor for its plausibility. Does the existence of Social Security or the Environmental Protection Agency really affect the Federal Reserve Board's regulation of banks or the behavior of the federal courts in prison cases? Would the federal government's program in any area become more extensive if its budget in other areas were doubled, or less extensive if its budget in other areas were halved?

opposing forces, with each checking and challenging the other, that is regarded as the Madisonian guarantor of liberty.[151]

Southern prisons, as already noted, were holdovers from the antebellum period in their design and operation. Similarly, prison administration, in the South and elsewhere, was a holdover from the dual federalism of this antebellum era. While the federal government had interceded in banking, industrial structure, welfare, health, agriculture, energy, and innumerable other areas, it had contented itself with establishing and managing its own prison system for violators of its own statutes, leaving state prison systems as untouched as other state functions had been in the days of mutually exclusive state and federal jurisdiction. As a result, state prisons were under the complete and exclusive control of their respective states. Within those states, and particularly in the southern states, these prisons were under the equally complete control of corrections officials, often the wardens of the individual institutions. It is difficult to think of any other American institution that continued, as late as the 1960s, to be governed in a more absolute and insulated manner than state prisons.

The entry of the federal courts into state corrections, therefore, represented a significant diffusion of governmental power. The courts did not displace state decision makers, all the excoriations of a federal "takeover" or "judicial imperialism" notwithstanding. Rather, they became fully involved with a group of decision makers who remained in place – the state legislature, its corrections department, the individual prisons, the governor's office, and others. This involvement was sometimes cooperative, more often adversarial, and almost always intense, producing all the advantages associated with diffusion of power. New standards were introduced, old ones were subjected to debate, popular awareness grew, arbitrary power was diminished, corruption was restrained, and public scrutiny increased.

To be sure, the absolutism of state prison governance was not the necessary result of a federal system. Within a given state, power can be dispersed among various agencies and subjected to various forms of public scrutiny. But the brute fact is that federalism also permits the complete lack of power dispersion that characterized state prisons. It was federalism that had enabled these correctional toadstools to sprout in the dark, unexplored recesses of state government, and this phenomenon, as much as any other, that impelled the federal judiciary to take action. The judges could see how unconstrained and absolute the power of state prison wardens was, and that such power had produced its usual, unfortunate effects. They knew – and who can disagree – that their intercession was increasing the liberty of the inmates, whatever other consequences it might have had.

The second aspect of the argument that federalism secures liberty by diffusing governmental power involves the concept of liberty. As Franz

Neumann points out, the empirical case for linking federalism and liberty is rather weak.[152] One important reason for this disjunction is that any definition of liberty must involve the individual's freedom from both government and private power. Underlying federalism's claim to secure liberty by diffusing power is the belief that government is a threat to liberty, and that the more diffuse, conflictual, and inefficient government control, the more the liberty of the people will be secure. But the theory of an administrative state is that government plays a positive role in securing liberty, that its function is to protect its citizens from private power: to protect workers from their employers, consumers from oppressive merchants, depositors from bankers, minorities from private discrimination.[153] If government is conflicted or ineffectual, according to this view, the liberty of the populace will be decreased. Because the modern administrative state is based on the idea that government protects liberty, it cannot rely on the structured inefficiency that federalist theory contemplates to protect citizens from government oppression. Instead, such protection is secured by the political process and by more direct constitutional guarantees involving human rights.

From this perspective, one of the most serious threats to liberty involves a state's failure to protect its citizens from private power. This was, of course, the precise rationale for the Civil War and the civil rights movement. In light of this historical experience, national decision makers, including the judiciary, properly view federalism itself as a threat to liberty. That threat becomes actualized when a state, following the true federalist principle, tolerates behavior that contravenes the national consensus about individual liberty. Of course, as Akhil Amar suggests, the national government might also fail to protect individual liberty, and state governments might step into the breach.[154] This has in fact occurred, but the predominant pattern in our history has involved federal initiatives and state inaction. The national government may not always choose to act, but when it does, federalism is much more likely to function as an impediment to increased liberty than a protector of it.

In the prison cases, of course, no private power was involved. But the personalistic, corrupt, arbitrary regimes imposed by southern wardens resembled private power in their character and in their effect, a resemblance that was only emphasized by the direct modeling of southern prisons on the private slave plantation. Federal judges saw the prisoners as requiring protection from this quasi-private power, and they saw state governments as unwilling to take action on the prisoners' behalf. Sharing the general mentality of the national administrative state, they felt obligated to provide the requisite protection in the name of liberty. This naturally led them to reject any federalist claim to state autonomy, and it made any liberty-based argument for such action seem contradictory and insincere. In short, the proactive, modern state had made federalist objections to national administrative power obsolete.

Community-Based Arguments for Federalism

The long-standing argument that federalism diffuses government power has recently been joined by another – that federalism secures community.[155] The argument, in essence, is that our community determines who we are; it is the context in which we exist and which gives meaning to our actions. When communities are empowered, therefore, decisions about people's lives are made within their own individual context, within their own system of relationships and meaning, not by a remote, external force. To some extent, the argument that federalism activates this process overlaps with the argument that federalism facilitates participation in government decision making. But disaggregating the term "community" into specific elements such as participation underestimates its true significance. The value of participation can be fully reconciled with traditional liberalism by noting the relatively apparent point that participation is part of many people's individual utility functions. True communitarian arguments begin from a different conception of the self – that the self is not an aggregation of identifiable preferences that exist prior to or apart from any group, but a member of a group with a sense of identity, meaning, and personal fulfillment constituted by that membership.

Thus conceived, the argument for community is a complex claim, sounded in modern scholarship by epistemologists like Richard Rorty[156] and Stanley Fish,[157] political philosophers like Michael Walzer,[158] Michael Sandel,[159] Robert Paul Wolff[160] and Hannah Arendt,[161] political scientists like Benjamin Barber,[162] historians like J. G. A. Pocock,[163] sociologists like Philip Selznick[164] and Robert Bellah,[165] and legal scholars like Cass Sunstein[166] and Frank Michelman.[167] Obviously, a principle so large that it encompasses so many disciplines and so slippery that it can be invoked by such divergent thinkers cannot be analyzed within the confines of the present study. The immediate question is why this principle proved unpersuasive to the federal judiciary. The easy answer is that most judges had never heard of it and would have viewed it as peculiar had it been described to them. This is much too quick, however, for the real claim is that the communitarian principle is deeply embedded in our more explicit beliefs about federalism, and explains their normative appeal. It is necessary, therefore, to consider this communitarian analysis in more detail.

Many different types of community are possible, but there are two that seem particularly relevant in connection with federalism. First, a group of people may be regarded as a community because its members feel a personal, emotional connection to one another. Borrowing a term from Robert Wolff, this may be called an "affective community."[168] Alternatively, a group may function as a community because its members engage in a collective decision-making process regarding major questions of self-governance. This is sometimes referred to as a "dialogical" community by emphasizing the element of public debate; Wolff uses the term "rational" community because he, like Bruce Ackerman and Jürgen Habermas, regards uncoerced persuasion as essential to true collective decision making.[169] A safer term might be political community, which acknowledges the sense of a shared enterprise, while not imposing such high standards that it precludes any real-world examples.

The important claims about both types of communities involve the individual's relation to the group: that the community is constitutive of the individual and that individuals achieve fulfillment of some sort through participation in that community.[170] While affective and political communities serve many of the same functions with respect to individuals, they do so in crucially different ways. Affective communities necessarily consist of small groups; emotional attachments, like the strong force in nuclear physics, are very powerful but tend to operate only over short distances. As described in a number of standard sociological studies, including those by Baker Brownell,[171] Robert Nisbet,[172] and Robert E. Park,[173] one generally establishes affective relationships through some form of personal contact, often through ongoing, day-to-day relationships. It is possible, of course, to become emotionally attached to a remote figure, like "the king," or an abstract entity, like "France," but such relationships lack mutuality. Since the usual image of an affective community involves mutual attachments, personal contact is virtually obligatory. Thus, affective communities constitute that part of the individual consciousness that involves concepts of group membership, personal loyalty, and emotional connection. The sense of participation they offer is generated by mutual assistance, sharing, and, less nobly but just as centrally, the exclusion of outsiders.

Political communities can be coextensive with affective communities, but this is rarely the case in advanced societies. Even in ancient Greece, the concept of the self-contained polis that combined affective bonds and political decision making was seriously outdated;[174] Aristotle's *Politics* may have been applicable to his little hometown of Stagira, but it was irrelevant to Athens, to say nothing of his pupil's empire. The other classic example of a political community that also operated as an affective community was the New England town. Such towns seem virtually irrelevant to the modern world because of their diminutive size, but even they may have been too large and pluralistic to function along affective lines. According to David Konig, the Puritan communities experienced too many value conflicts to rely on informal controls, and needed to resort to a system of written law to maintain their integrity.[175] The modern world's ability to mobilize large groups of people through bureaucratic organization and technology has produced further increases in the size of operative political units and the arenas of political decision making. Such larger-scale political communities constitute the individual's sense of self as a political actor, and possibly her sense of social position. Participation in them provides a connection to events that would otherwise be remote and recondite. These are important interactions, but they are qualitatively different from the self-constitution and methods of fulfillment that occur, on a smaller scale, in affective communities.

With this distinction in mind, we can now assess the claim that federalism is justified by the value of community, and thus should operate as a constraint on judicial decision making. We can begin with affective community, and assume that fostering such communities is a desirable goal. This is, incidentally, by no means self-evident. There is a certain sappy pastoralism to much of the communitarian literature;[176] small, tightly knit groups of people with strong affective bonds among themselves are likely to be xenophobic, intolerant, and repressive. But even if they behave more the way that proponents of community envision, that is, like the people in contemporary beer commercials, such communities would not provide an argument for federalism. Federalism, unlike the more general principle of managerial decentralization, only protects the rights of states, and American states are far too large to function as affective communities.[177] If we take the notion of mutual bonds of emotional attachment seriously, it seems clear that we are speaking about small towns or urban neighborhoods, not about our nation-size political subdivisions.

It is true that smaller American states can be controlled by a narrow, political elite that operates as a community for certain purposes. But since communities tend to be exclusionary, and elites remain elite by that same mechanism of exclusion, a political elite of this sort is unlikely to instill communitarian feelings among its state's excluded millions. When proponents of affective community become specific, they tend to speak about volunteer groups, PTAs, church congregations, farm cooperatives, and urban self-help programs – all entities that are considerably smaller than a state. There are undoubtedly affective communities to be found in various parts of the United States: religious groups, Native American tribes, even small towns with relatively homogenous populations. Because of the necessarily small size of such communities, they will generally be located within the borders of a single state. But they have no particular relationship to the state itself, and we cannot identify any of our states as being uniquely composed of, or identified with, such communities, with the possible exception of Utah.

Since this distinction between affective communities and states is readily apparent, the communitarian argument for federalism tends to emphasize a different claim: that state governments are more likely to protect and foster local communities than a more remote federal government.[178] But no theoretical argument or empirical evidence supports this proposition. Indeed, for reasons previously discussed, if one wanted to establish such a program of this sort throughout the nation, one would need to persuade the national government to implement it. Left to their own devices, some states will foster some communities and bedevil others, while other states might be uniformly discouraging to community-based claims. Native Americans are perhaps the prime example; given how cruel our national government has been to them, the fact that it is nonetheless their principal protector testifies to the truly abysmal attitudes that state governments often display toward affective communities within their midst.

If federalism cannot be regarded as protecting or fostering affective communities, perhaps it plays this role regarding political communities. There is no particular constraint on the size of such communities; indeed, looking around the world, or back across the course of history, there appear numerous political communities that were the size of our states or larger. One finds, moreover, impressive empirical evidence to indicate that federalism does protect political communities. Many current nations, as well as ancient empires, are alliances of political communities whose individual existence was secured by the rights that they could assert against the central government. These political communities often preserve linguistic, religious, and cultural features that would be disrupted or submerged by central control – a control that tends to be exercised quite rigorously in diverse nations unless the political communities have a legal right to resist. Conversely, political rights often contribute to people's sense of identity with each other, and to their ability to constitute a political community.

In the early days of our nation, the states may well have functioned as political communities; there is strong evidence that people felt more connected to their state than to the distant federal government and the relatively limited issues it addressed. Certainly, the political community of the antebellum South was distinct from the rest of the nation, whether that community was constituted regionally or state by state. But modern developments in social structure, economic relationships, and politics have largely effaced these distinctions.[179] Most of our states, the alleged political communities that federalism would preserve, are mere administrative units, rectangular swatches of the prairie with nothing but their legal definitions to distinguish them from one another.[180] The differences due to the separate founding of the original thirteen colonies, and the separate political and social system of the antebellum South, have been submerged into the national culture. Of course, citizens of Nebraska know that they live in Nebraska, and can identify themselves as Nebraskans. But this level of identification does not exceed that which people naturally establish with a governmental subunit that administers numerous decentralized services. If that is counted as a political community, then such communities are not only ubiquitous but virtually unavoidable in any moderate-size nation, and the term becomes diluted to the point of insignificance.

American society has internal divisions, to be sure, and the depth of these divisions is a source of ongoing and intense debate – a division in itself. To some, America remains a melting pot, with its various races and nationalities blended into a rather uniform, bourgeois culture; to others, it is more like a stew, consisting of unblended elements. But even if one adopts this latter view, it seems apparent that the ingredients are rather evenly distributed through every region of the country. Perhaps blacks are a distinct, excluded group, but they are no more so in Denver than they are in Baltimore. Perhaps the Irish have clung to a separate cultural identity, but this identity is no different in Brooklyn than it is in San Antonio. The point is that our ethnic and cultural differences do not correspond to geographic sections of the country, and thus cannot be regarded as political communities. They are more properly regarded as interest groups, or affiliations, and thus no different in structure from other widely dispersed groups such as environmentalists, abortion rights advocates, used-car sellers, and fundamentalists.

This nationwide dispersion of ethnic and cultural identities, paralleling the dispersion of economic or ideological identities, does not mean that the concept of political community is inapplicable to the United States. What it means, rather, is that the United States has one political community, and that political community is the United States.[181] The arena in which our political consciousness takes shape and our crucial decisions are made is a national one. It is the nation that constructs our sense of self, that provides a sense of participation in a larger group that constitutes, in Habermas's terms, our public sphere.[182] The reason that American federalism is nothing more than decentralization is that the normative claim of political community is not available to the states. That claim, in any meaningful sense, belongs only to the nation as a single entity.[183] Thus, the concept of community supported federal court intervention in state prison systems, rather than acting as a constraint against it.

The development of this national political community is cocausal with the growth of the administrative state. It was the development of national politics that generated the federal administrative apparatus. The administrative initiatives of the Jacksonian era, including the development of penitentiaries, occurred almost entirely in the states. The reforms of the

Progressive era were divided between the state and federal arenas, with the latter gaining in importance under Woodrow Wilson with the passage of the Clayton Act, the Federal Reserve Act, and the Federal Trade Commission Act. By the time of the New Deal, administrative initiatives were conceived almost exclusively in national terms, a pattern that became even more pronounced with the civil rights, environmental, consumer, and worker safety initiatives of the Great Society. Just as these political initiatives created our national administrative state, so the existence of a national administrative state, with ongoing responsibility in so many areas, created national politics. Debates about the economy, the environment, social welfare, and civil rights are now conceived in national terms, as they always have been in more traditionally national areas like foreign trade and foreign policy.

Of course, the fact that our political community is so vast means that the individual's sense of personal participation is generally quite attenuated. This does not transform the states, or counties, or cities, into true political communities. It simply means that most Americans will not be able to find personal fulfillment by participating in the collective decision process that shapes their consciousness and controls their lives.[184] Perhaps, as Bruce Ackerman suggests, that is not serious, given our other opportunities for fulfillment, including participation in administrative subunits of the polity.[185] Perhaps it is very serious, breeding a sense of personal alienation and undermining the legitimacy or effectiveness of the central government. But that is our present condition, powerfully established and supported by our entire history and culture; it is not going to be changed by granting our administrative subunits juridical rights.

While the decline of states as political communities is a general phenomenon, it acquired a specific and more pointed meaning in conjunction with the South. The South's separate identity as a political community or group of communities was based on slavery, and subsequently on segregation.[186] It did not simply decline as a result of gradual changes in our political and governmental system, but was specifically rejected by means of violent conflict and aggressive, albeit belated, national action. The southern prison was one of the last vestiges of the South's political community. In reforming the prisons, the courts were simply completing the rejection of that community, a rejection based on the moral unacceptability of its distinguishing feature and on the well-developed sense that our real political community was a national one. This is why the notion that federalism fosters community had so little appeal to the federal judiciary.

It is sometimes said that claims of federalism are nothing more than strategies to advance substantive positions or, alternatively, that people declare themselves federalists when they oppose national policy, and abandon that commitment when they favor it. This is true; the term "states" or "federalism" becomes a code word for particular substantive positions because those positions are what people really care about. Many of those who say "federalism" in the 1990s mean gay rights, because the national government's position, as reflected in *Bowers v. Hardwick*[187], is so disappointing to them, just as many of those who said "states' rights" in the 1950s and 1960s meant "no civil rights." The reason is not that federalism is an argument that inherently attracts the cynical or insincere, but that we have a national political community and political claims acquire meaning largely in that context. Federalist claims are simply following this general and unavoidable pattern; their dominant meaning is determined by the national policy they favor or oppose at any given time, not by any deeply felt theory of federalism. To be sure, as Larry Kramer points out, the existence of states themselves plays an important role in the politics and administrative practices of our national community,[188] but the principle of federalism is not part of this role; it stands in opposition to the national character of our policy and has lost its independent meaning as that policy has evolved.

This conception of community circles back to the discussion of decentralization at the beginning of this chapter. An underlying ambiguity in that discussion – and in virtually every other discussion of federalism – is the locus of the crucial decision-making function. One can ask whether "we" want a decentralized or unified regime, but the nagging question is the definition of that small, collective pronoun.[189] The way one goes about answering such a question may well depend on whether "we" are the United States, or "we" are the citizens or government of each state taken separately. Determining the identity of polity to which one speaks is anterior to any issue about the desires or interests of its citizens.

The answer suggested here is that the "we" means our national polity, because that is the real locus of public debate. Federalism, as opposed to decentralization, acts as a constraint on our ability, as a nation, to achieve the policies we want, including policies of participation, local variation, and experimentation. Of course, it may encourage some states to go further with these policies, but, more significantly, it permits other states to fall below the nationally accepted minimum. In the case of prisons, it permitted some states to treat their prisoners like slaves. One can only justify federalism by asserting that there is no "we," that the nation is not a political community. If that is true, then the variation among states, and their commitment to different normative positions, is not problematic because there is no national standard below which they can fall, and, on average, states are as likely to reach the right level as the national government. But our nation is indeed a political community; for better or worse, it does constitute our political sense of self and the arena in which our basic normative positions about government must be argued and resolved. In the prison conditions cases, "we," through the instrumentality of the federal judiciary, insisted that a divergent section of the nation conform to "our" views.

The collective morality that motivated judges to adopt their activist policy-making stance in the prison cases is thus the morality of the nation as a whole, because the nation as a whole structures the political consciousness of its citizens. This morality is embedded in national institutions; it does not consist of the pragmatic strategies of those institutions, but of their animating concepts. Of course, a particular federal agency might violate the national morality, while state governments might champion it.[190] The national principle is not equivalent to a rule that the feds always win. In the prison cases, however, the federal Bureau of Prisons clearly embodied national norms about corrections. Many states did so as well, but there was also a group of states that diverged sharply from these norms, and those were the states where the courts acted earliest, longest, and most comprehensively.

As discussed earlier, this descriptive observation about the prison cases suggests a normative principle: judges should not make policy without the support of nationally established moral principles. What renders this a normative argument, of course, is democratic rule. Many writers argue that the norm of democratic rule precludes judicial policy making in its entirety. As will be discussed in the following chapters, this is an overly literal and unrealistically idealized interpretation of democracy. For the present, it is sufficient to observe that democracy, at the very least, allows judges to make social policy – that is, to formulate new legal rules based on their judgment that these rules will produce socially desirable results – only when they are acting in consonance with other prevailing principles of social morality. They should not do so on the basis of individual conscience or heavily contested norms. This precludes the use of judicial policy making for radical social change, to be sure, but it also renders it a sufficiently cautious approach to negate most of the "horribles" that the concept frequently evokes. As stated, social morality is far too vague to serve as a complete justification for judicial policy making; its essential role is to establish outer limits for the policy-making process.

One of the most famous and unfortunate examples of judicial policy making was *Lochner v. New York*,[191] and all its substantive due process progeny that overturned so much Progressive era legislation. The common criticism of *Lochner* is that it constituted an incorrect interpretation of the due process clause;[192] implicit in this criticism is the claim – rejected here – that interpretation represents the limits of legitimate judicial power. There is no inherent reason why the courts should not make social policy, employing the due process clause as a grant of jurisdiction. Indeed, this is precisely the basis of many decisions that remain not only good law, but uncontroversially good law, including decisions prohibiting involuntary sterilization,[193] bodily intrusion by the police,[194] English-only statutes,[195] or discrimination in the District of Columbia[196] and decisions securing the right to send one's child to a public school,[197] to travel abroad,[198] or to use birth control devices.[199] The more serious fault of *Lochner* was that it emerged from the social morality of the propertied class, not of society in general. National institutions, including Congress and the presidency, had partially embraced the Progressive ideology that the Supreme Court was so intent upon reversing. Of course, perhaps the national commitment to social welfare legislation was not entirely clear in 1905, when *Lochner* was decided. Judgments regarding prevailing morality, like judgments about future eventualities, must be based on guesswork, and it is the fate of all decision makers to be evaluated by the harsh glare of hindsight. But if *Lochner* was only arguably wrong when it was decided, then *Morehead v. New York*,[200] which invalidated a minimum-wage law for women in 1936, was obviously incorrect.

And what of the most controversial substantive due process case of the contemporary era, *Roe v. Wade*?[201] This was certainly an act of policy making, and it was not supported by nationally embedded norms. The short answer is that this is why the legitimacy of the decision has been so tenuous. In fairness, however, the depth of the opposition has only become clear over time, and the Court may have felt that it represented the leading edge of a developing national consensus when it decided the case. Gerald Rosenberg goes so far as to argue that the legalization of abortion was a independent, rapidly growing trend, and that the Supreme Court simply jumped on board.[202]

In all likelihood, what led the federal courts astray in the first third of this century, as John Ely suggests, was that they were not representative with respect to the issue they were confronting.[203] The federal judges were wealthy or upper-middle-class people assessing laws enacted for the benefit of the laboring classes.*[204] Thus, their assessment of national norms tended to be faulty, an error that they could have recognized and counteracted only through an exercise of empathy that was quite beyond them. The prison reform cases, in contrast, involved a conflict between a divergent section of the nation and the nation as a whole. Here federal judges – even those who came from the South and were appointed there – were more representative of the national perspective. As a result, their assessment of national morality was accurate and has been confirmed by history.

---

* In addition, they invalidated laws that favored one group of entrepreneurs over another. These cases were also rejected during the New Deal era but not as fully, and they receive a much more sympathetic reading at the present time.

Creating Doctrine, Choosing Solutions, and Transforming the Rule of Law

Introduction: The Role of Judges and Law Creation in the Prison Reform Cases

According to the classic model of policy analysis, the definition of the problem and the identification of the goal is followed by the generation of alternative solutions, and then by the choice among alternatives according to some decision-making methodology. No list of possible alternatives is to be found, either explicitly or implicitly, in the prison reform cases. If this stage is to be regarded as a critical one for an effective policy-making process, then judicial policy making in these cases must be counted as a failure. To be sure, it would not be the only failure in the realm of policy making. Government decision makers of all kinds, not only judges, operate with limited time, limited resources, and limited opportunities to explore alternatives without attending to the howls of every interest group that would be disadvantaged by those particular alternatives. The dispassionate, methodical consideration of all possible options is probably found more frequently in policy texts than in the real world of government decision making. This fact does not necessarily render the judicial policy making any less a failure, but it does render it a familiar failure, no different from the shortcomings that nonjudicial policy makers display.

While they did not generate alternatives, the judges in the prison reform cases did select particular solutions. In the absence of a systematic survey of the options, they chose these solutions by an informal, intuitive process – in other words, by muddling through. In Chapter 5, it was suggested that federal judges derived many of the standards they imposed on state prisons from national organizations such as the federal Bureau of

Prisons and the American Correctional Association. They were motivated to do so by their moral revulsion at the prevailing conditions in state prisons; the justification for their motivation was the strong social consensus that condemned these conditions, particularly those that were modeled on the slave plantation and diverged so dramatically from national norms. It might appear, therefore, that these observations provide an explanation for the judiciary's actions. The difficulty with this explanation is that it seems incomplete; it may account for the substance of the standards that the courts imposed, but it does not explain the relationship between their decisions and the concept of law.

Such an incomplete account is normatively troubling, but, even more importantly, it is descriptively inaccurate. The reason lies in our general concept of law and its relationship to the judiciary. For purposes of this discussion, law can be viewed as either a framework or a constraint; in fact, it fulfills both functions simultaneously in the judicial process. In its role as a framework, or a conceptual procedure for judicial decision making, it is generally called legal doctrine.[1] This is simply the set of all statements recognized as authoritative legal rules. As Duncan Kennedy suggests, legal doctrine is perceived by judges "as a medium in which one pursues a project, rather than as something that tells us what we have to do."[2] For a new statement to become a part of this doctrine, it must be built out of this medium – connected with existing doctrine in some recognizable fashion. The precise nature of the connection is a source of controversy – perhaps the leading source of controversy in legal scholarship – but the need to establish a connection of some sort is well accepted. A judge cannot say, "I am imposing this standard because the American Correctional Association uses it," anymore than she can say, "I am imposing this standard because my mother mentioned it to me" or "because it is my sovereign will."

A judge could say, "I am imposing this standard because it is implicit in the Eighth Amendment." That is a recognizable legal statement, being connected with an existing element of doctrine by an accepted mode of argument. But it is not a particularly convincing legal statement for the prison conditions cases, and the authors of these cases do not appear to have relied on it. This brings us face to face with an issue that is central to the entire concept of judicial policy making. As stated in Chapter 1, we traditionally view judges as interpreters of preexisting law or as finders of facts, not as policy makers and law creators. Virtually everyone acknowledges, however, that interpretation is not a mechanical act and will often, if not invariably, involve the creation of new doctrinal elements. Because doctrine creation is so ubiquitous in the interpretive process, it is often treated as an integral component of that process, a feature that sophisticated, realistic people readily acknowledge, even if it is glossed over in junior high school textbooks and decried by fringe-group academics. At some point, however, the legal text becomes so vague and the judge-made law so comprehensive and precise that the term "interpretation" seems like more of a conceit than a description. At some further point, the conceit fails, the fig leaf falls, and the judicial action is revealed as naked public policy making and law creation.

When courts held that prisoners had the right to send and receive mail without its being censored by prison authorities, their decision could reasonably be regarded as an interpretation of the First Amendment. One might disagree with them, arguing that the First Amendment does not apply to prisoners, or mail, or whatever. Nonetheless, the interpretation is plausible enough to be both persuasive to outsiders and to serve as a credible explanation of the courts' behavior. We can reasonably assume that the judges who held that mail opening violated the First Amendment believed precisely that and were acting upon that belief.

But this is simply not true of most of the prison conditions orders promulgated under the authority of the Eighth Amendment. The broad language of the cruel and unusual punishment clause must be seen as a grant of jurisdiction, a mandate that courts should somehow concern themselves with prisons because prisons are a form of punishment. Of course, it could – and did – lay dormant, serving largely as an admonition. But even after it was invoked and applied, it could be understood only as a jurisdictional provision that invited the courts to construct a set of rules, for it provided no meaningful guidance about the content of these rules. The problem is not simply that the prohibition against cruel and unusual punishment is so elliptical. Other constitutional provisions like "freedom of speech" or "due process of law" are equally succinct, but they have a history that reaches back before the Constitution and forward through a succession of interpretations. This is simply not true for the Eighth Amendment. To be sure, the term "cruel and unusual punishment" also had a preconstitutional history, but the reference is to those sanguinary practices, like drawing and quartering, garroting, gibbeting, and mutilation, that blossomed like heather through the length and breadth of England.[3] These practices, together with the closely related practice of investigatory torture, were being actively debated in western Europe during the last half of the eighteenth century[4] and were almost certainly what the Framers of the Eighth Amendment had in mind.[5] The clause is not likely to have referred to the treatment of prisoners, however, since imprisonment was rarely used as a punishment for felons until after the Constitution was drafted.[6]

This certainly does not preclude the application of the cruel and unusual punishment clause to prisons; indeed, the term "unusual" suggests that it is explicitly intended to cover the barbarisms of a vaguely imagined future. Justice Thomas's dissent in *Helling v. McKinney* was simply wrong in declaring that "when members of the founding generation wished to make prison conditions a matter of constitutional guarantee, they knew how to do so."[7] His only evidence for this assertion is that the Delaware Constitution of 1792 refers explicitly to conditions in jails as part of an analogous provision.[8] But there are two fairly obvious reasons why a provision drafted in the early 1790s regarding methods of punishment would not be intentionally excluding prisons because it referred explicitly to jails, and did not mention prisons. The first is that jails, then as now, were primarily a means of pretrial detention, not punishment, so a specific reference would be required to include jails, but not prisons, in a clause concerning punishment. The second reason is that the Framers would not necessarily have mentioned prisons in any case, since unlike jails, there were few prisons in existence at the time. Punishment by incarceration was highly unusual, and it would require extraordinary prescience to make specific reference to one particular means of punishment because it would become dominant some forty years later.

Thus, the prison conditions cases are permissible under the cruel and unusual punishment clause, contrary to Justice Thomas's textual exegesis. The problem is that they are not an interpretation of that clause; they are public policy promulgated by the courts under the grant of jurisdiction that the clause provides. No thoughtful observer – indeed, no thoughtless observer either – has ever been persuaded that federal judges were simply interpreting the Eighth Amendment in the prison cases. Antagonistic scholars like John DiIulio[9] and Robert Wood,[10] sympathetic scholars like Bradley Chilton[11] and Larry Yackle,[12] and outraged participants like the old-time wardens who were hounded from their posts (after the courts had chewed on them for a while) all recognized that the federal courts were creating new law in this area. The judges themselves could hardly have believed that their decisions were guided by the constitutional text. But what did they then believe and how – again rejecting the collective brain-fever hypothesis – did they justify their actions to themselves?

In its role as a constraint, rather than a framework, law is generally described as the "rule of law." This is a phrase of many meanings, but one common definition is that public decision makers must be subject to some external control that is general, clear, well-accepted, and congruent with the legal order that applies to private citizens.[13] All our government officials are bound by broad constitutional rules governing their procedures for decision, of course, but the rule of law also demands some substantive constraints on the decisions that they can reach. For legislators, elections serve as the requisite constraint; we allow legislators to make law, within constitutional limits, because we regard elections as a legitimate means of limiting their power. For administrators, who are not elected and who dominate our government, the constraint is the enabling statute enacted by the legislature. They can make laws by regulation, but the statute defines the purpose and scope of these regulations, while supervision by the president, Congress, the courts, or the administrative hierarchy keeps administrative lawmaking within its proper boundaries. If judges make law, according to this approach, they too should be constrained. They are not constrained by either election or supervision, however. This can be regarded as an aspect of Bickel's countermajoritarian difficulty;[14] the problem is not that the courts are invading the preserve of the majoritarian branches, but that they are exercising the same level of discretion as those other branches without being subject to the same majoritarian constraint. The traditional answer is that judges satisfy the rule of law by limiting themselves to legal doctrine; it is the doctrine itself that acts as a constraint on the substance of their decisions.

For other legal actors, legal doctrine and the rule of law are separate concepts; the first comprises a body of promulgated rules, while the second comprises the legal constraints that operate on them as political actors. But the two concepts merge in the arena of judicial decision making, where reigning theory is that nonelected judges satisfy the rule of law by limiting themselves to legal doctrine.[15] For judges, legal doctrine takes the place of elections or hierarchial supervision. Legislators and administrators are not limited by legal doctrine – in fact, legislators are specifically empowered to amend or abolish it – but they must answer to the electorate or to elected supervisors. Judges are not subject to this same constraint, the argument goes, so they must limit themselves to the framework formed by legal doctrine. Hart and Sacks described this limitation as the noncontinuing discretion of the judge, as opposed to the continuing, or less legally constrained discretion of a legislator.[16] The relationship between judicial discretion, legal constraint, and the rule of law was most fully explored by Hart and Sachs, Bickel, Fuller, and other members of the legal process school as they tried to reconstruct an account of legitimate judicial action in response to legal realism's challenge.[17]

The normative and descriptive inadequacies of the analysis thus far are now apparent. Normatively, the question is what constrains judges when they create new legal doctrine, as they did in the prison reform cases, rather than following or interpreting existing doctrine. In general, judicial policy making often involves the promulgation of substantive standards by creating legal doctrine; if this is truly an unconstrained process, it would appear to violate the rule of law. As stated in Chapter 1, such a conclusion carries serious jurisprudential consequences; in fact, this was precisely the issue on which the legal process theory foundered. Most legal doctrines are created by judges at some point; common law certainly was, despite the formalist mythology, but so were virtually all constitutional law and a good deal of statute-based law. Once created, the doctrine can certainly be elaborated by the more familiar process of interpretation, but most doctrines have the skeleton of judicial creativity hidden somewhere in their past. The prison cases based on free-speech considerations, for example, are plausibly regarded as interpretive because the extent and density of First Amendment doctrine allowed its extension to new circumstances by familiar interpretive methods. But there were no free-speech decisions before 1919, just as there were no prison conditions cases before 1965, and all the well-established pieces of First Amendment furniture – the clear and present danger test, overbreadth, the chilling effect, the public forum doctrine, the actual malice standard, and the restrictions based on time, place, and manner – can be traced to specific and relatively recent judicial decisions.[18]

A common view among political scientists, and increasingly among legal scholars as well, is that judges regularly violate the rule of law. This is frequently presented as a descriptive truth, while the normative difficulties that it raises are conceded or gleefully declared. But an appreciation of the phenomenological experience of judges themselves suggests that there are also serious descriptive problems with this position. Whatever judges thought they were doing when they decided the prison reform cases, for example, it must have possessed some recognizable relationship to law. Judges, after all, are conscious beings, and they must have had some means of justifying their decision to themselves, some conceptual process that assimilated their decisions to their existing understanding of their role. The cynical position must fall back on hypotheses such as confusion, conspiracy, or automatism to explain what was going on inside the judges' minds, but none of these is particularly plausible when applied to hundreds of judges over a twenty-five-year period. In some cases, one can rely on judicial self-delusion to make the account appear more plausible, as Cardozo observed;[19] what is interesting about the prison cases is that they were such a naked act of judicial policy making that this option is simply unavailable. The judges who decided the prison cases never persuaded anyone that they were deriving their standards from the Eighth Amendment and, for most part, they did not bother claiming that they were doing so. Yet, unless they were suffering from collective brain fever, they must have possessed some workable rationale for their decisions.

This chapter provides an account of the relationship between the prison reform cases and the concept of law. Again rejecting the brain fever hypothesis, it argues that federal judges were operating within the framework of law in the prison cases. The reason is that doctrine creation fits within the doctrinal structure of the law, just as interpretation does. New doctrine can be derived from existing doctrine by accepted modes of thought, and consists of recognizable legal statements that judges can articulate within their recognized role. This is the conceptual process of judicial policy making, and it provides an answer to the second question about judicial policy making that was posed at the beginning of Part II, namely, What are the procedures or mechanisms by which judicial policy making is carried out? That mechanism, in essence, is the creation of new legal doctrine. It possesses two essential characteristics. First, it must be new; if it is not, then the court is engaged in interpretation, not policy making. Second, and the central argument of the present chapter, it must be doctrine; while the courts can identify their goal in general, policy-oriented discourse, they must achieve that goal with solutions stated in doctrinal terms. The translation of policy goals into legal doctrine is the basic procedure, or mechanism, of judicial policy making.

In addition, this chapter provides most of the answer to the most insistent question about judicial policy making, namely, How is the process constrained or limited? We argue that it is limited, like other judicial decisions, by the rule of law. Of course, this answer is precluded in advance if one asserts that only judicial fact-finding and interpretation satisfy the rule of law, but this is not the current understanding of our legal system. Principles such as the rule of law are now treated in functional, not categorical terms – the operative question is whether the policy-making process is subject to constraint. Our claim is that the process of creating doctrine, when performed properly, is inherently constrained. When judges engage in this process, they do not feel unconstrained at all, but feel subject to powerful forces limiting their range of action. The methods that judges use to create new legal doctrine are simultaneously a framework or conceptual process that empowers them to do so and a set of constraints that guide their actions. The unity of legal doctrine and the rule of law in judicial decision making generate constraints that are inherent, or in-dwelling, in the process of doctrine creation.

Thus, we do not argue, as we did for federalism, that the rule of law is an outmoded principle; it is as relevant and as important in the administrative state as it was in prior centuries. The advent of the administrative state does make a difference to rule of law analysis, however, because it establishes policy making as a norm of governance; consequently, it allows judges to adopt this role more consciously and more decisively. Specifically, judges have become more willing to promulgate substantive standards and to invoke social policy considerations when they do so, at least in comparison with their predecessors during the "formalist" or legal process eras. In the prison cases, they still saw themselves as operating within a legal framework, but they were quite aware that they were creating a great deal of law in a relatively short period of time.

Unfortunately, the prevailing attitudes toward the judicial creation of legal doctrine, which consist largely of denial, condemnation, or grudging recognition, have left us without an account of the ordinary mechanism by which doctrine is created. Before proceeding with a description of the way that the prison conditions doctrine was created, therefore, it will be necessary to describe the process in general terms. The first section of this chapter provides that description, and explains how that process is consistent with legal doctrine and why judges view it as comporting with the rule of law. In essence, it consists of a microanalysis of the judiciary as an institution, that is, an account of the institution's behavior that is constructed from the behavior of the individual actors who compose it. The following two sections describe the policy solutions that the courts imposed in the prison cases as part of their new doctrine. These rules were based on two institutional conceptualizations: that prisons are supposed to be designed to rehabilitate the prisoner, and that prisons are supposed to be bureaucratically organized. Both may appear rather odd, the first because very few people believe that prisons really rehabilitate, and the second because most people do not believe that bureaucratization is particularly desirable. Nonetheless, they are the conceptualizations that judges had in mind, for reasons that will be discussed.

The Process of Creating Legal Doctrine

Doctrine

An immediate difficulty in formulating a theory of doctrinal creation is that the process, as Martin Shapiro has pointed out, involves the conceptual behavior of an institution.[20] The judiciary, after all, is an institution; at issue here is not one particular decision by a single judge or court, but hundreds of decisions over a period of thirty years. Modern scholars have much to say about the structure of institutions, but relatively little about their conceptual processes. Mary Douglas has written an insightful book entitled *How Institutions Think*,[21] but her topic is the way institutions structure individual thought, not the way that institutions solve problems or develop new ideas. Yet most political and governmental action these days springs from ideas generated in the institutional context itself, not from either individual theory or charismatic leadership.

Whatever its origin, this lack of theory about the conceptual process of institutions is generally replaced with two different, rather unconsidered views. The first is the naive attribution of human thoughts or feelings to institutions in their entirety – the assertion that the institution "behaved" or "reacted" in such and such a manner.[22] This sort of anthropomorphism does not aid us in understanding the way that individuals in institutional roles think individual thoughts and take individual actions that produce institutional consequences; rather, it obscures this process behind a set of metaphors that range from the conspiratorial to the miraculous.

But if the fanciful animation of institutions as big, complicated people is unhelpful, the second view, which separates the institution into self-enclosed individuals with no institutional concerns, is equally unhelpful. This approach has become quite popular of late. It serves as the basis of the public choice movement, for example, which treats all public officials as motivated solely by their own self-interest.[23] The result is to exclude, as a preempirical assumption, any possibility that the individual official will think on behalf of the institution and that some collective conceptual process will emerge.[24] It depicts the institution as a set of preestablished roles into which interchangeable individuals are inserted or removed.

We are confronted, therefore, with a complex situation that has not been sufficiently assessed. On the one hand, institutional action, including action based on ideas, must be located within the minds of individuals. On the other hand, those individuals cannot be treated as generic persons with undifferentiated motivations like self-interest, but must be recognized as highly contextualized beings acting in accordance with their institutional positions. What is required, in other words, is a phenomenology of institutional thought. This would provide a way of understanding how individual human beings, on the basis of their own thoughts and actions, are shaped by their institutional context, and how, in turn, they shape that context in response to changing circumstances or conceptualizations.

The general project is obviously beyond the scope of this study, but a more narrowly focused inquiry about the institutional phenomenology of judicial decision making is a necessity. In the prison cases, a group of federal judges created a new body of doctrine. This raises a simple, brute descriptive question: how did they actually do it? Political science offers no answer, and hides its embarrassment over this lacuna (to lapse into anthropomorphic discourse for the moment) by exploring the social motivations of the judges. Legal scholarship offers no answer either, and hides its embarrassment by debating the normative implications of the result. We have already discussed the motivations in Chapter 5, and will discuss the normative implications later. But in order to explain the process of judicial policy making, in the prison cases or in general, we must first explain how doctrinal creation actually occurs.

We can begin the analysis of doctrinal creation by identifying three major motivations that act upon judges in carrying out their institutional roles. These can be described as doctrine, attitude, and integration. The first two are familiar elements in most theories of judicial decision making; indeed, they restate the debate that has dominated political science scholarship about judicial decision making and has figured prominently, at the very least, in legal scholarship. According to the leading school of thought in political science, represented by Joel Grossman, Harold Lasswell, Glendon Schubert, Jeffrey Segal, Harold Spaeth, Sidney Ulmer, and others,[25] judicial decisions can be predicted by nonlegal factors such as the judges' personal backgrounds or values. The opposing school, which includes John Gruhl, Fred Kort, Charles Johnson and Ronald Kahn, argues that these decisions can be frequently, although not always, predicted by examining doctrinal precedents.[26] The contrast is less stark in legal scholarship because this scholarship tends to be prescriptive, rather than descriptive, but the debate has been all the more intense as a result. Generally speaking, critical legal studies,[27] critical race theory,[28] and law and economics[29] all claim that nonlegal influences predominate, while interpretivists of various sorts, including Philip Bobbitt, Ronald Dworkin, Melvin Eisenberg, and Owen Fiss recognize an important role for the legal tradition, although disagreeing about the scope and nature of its influence.[30]

Given the long-standing nature of this debate, and the desirability of avoiding either cynicism or panglossianism, it seems most likely, as Karl Llewellyn argued in the *Common Law Tradition*,[31] and as John Poulos has discussed in his articles about Roger Traynor,[32] that both factors are at work and it would be more productive to explore their interaction than to choose between them. For present purposes, the concern is how these factors interact to generate new doctrine. Before exploring this issue, however, it is necessary to define both doctrine and attitude from a more phenomenological perspective, that is, from a perspective that takes account of the judge's experiential position. There have, of course, been a number of efforts to describe the process of judging, including notable recent efforts by Ronald Dworkin,[33] Melvin Eisenberg,[34] William Eskridge,[35] Kent Greenawalt,[36] Richard Posner,[37] and Frederick Schauer.[38] The one that bears the closest resemblance to our approach is Duncan Kennedy's,[39] which also relies upon phenomenology. But all these efforts, including Kennedy's, concern the interpretive process, and thus necessarily address the extent to which legal texts function as constraints. The question here is how judges reach their decisions when there is no text, when they are creating an entirely new doctrine. This is the question that is central to an understanding of the judicial policy-making process.

The first force, or motivation, that acts upon judges when they are creating new doctrine is existing legal doctrine – not a particular text, but existing doctrine as a whole. Since judges are supposed to decide cases by following legal doctrine, the inclination to do so is part of their more general desire to act in the proper fashion. This is a well-recognized motivation; Alisdair MacIntyre defines it as a mode of thought organized around appropriateness and concerned with obligatory action, as opposed to thought that is organized around consequences and concerned with anticipatory choice.[40] In a recent work, James March and Johan Olsen explicitly link it with the process of legal reasoning, by which they mean doctrinal interpretation.[41] While institutional propriety is a familiar concept, its operation in a given institution is generally far from simple. Every institutional role carries with it a remarkably complex set of behavioral expectations, expectations that exist in the minds of the institution's members.[42] As Niklas Luhmann observes, these institutionalized expectations make communication and collective action possible in a complex, uncertain world.[43] They involve the way in which each job is done, but also extend to informal interactions: how to run a meeting, what to talk about at the beginning of the day, where to eat lunch, how to behave toward one's superiors and one's subordinates. In one sense, the expectations are continuous; the formal ones, relating to the task to be performed, and the informal ones, relating to one's personal comportment in the institution, are established and enforced by other members of the institution and perceived by the individual role occupant as a single continuous set of requirements.[44] In another sense, however, these sets of expectations, despite their obvious overlaps, are discontinuous because they are established and perceived as such; that is, one of the institutional understandings involves the collectively perceived distinction between formal and informal rules.

Because of the individualistic, antiinstitutional elements in our belief system, we tend to associate the concept of role behavior with conformism, conventionality, and repression. We see it, in other words, as an imposition on individuals that suppresses many of their natural, healthy inclinations. As a normative matter, this may be useful, but if we are to understand institutional thought and behavior, we must recognize that such behavior is not only an external constraint but an internal relation or conceptual framework. This is true in two senses. First, the rules of behavior construct the individual's institutional role in its entirety – they constrain but they also empower.[45] The chief administrator who initiates a massive reform program for her agency may be no less bound by role expectations than the night watchman who follows a precisely defined route around the perimeter of the agency's building. With respect to courts, the obligation to relate one's decision to legal doctrine not only limits action but makes action possible; it provides a deep and strong system of meaning that confers both contour and legitimacy on judicial decisions. Thus, institutional actions are like a language.[46] The English language has rather strict rules about word formation, which function as constraints on what we can say, but also enable us to speak; they are not oppressive because there is no natural or primeval speech that they preclude. It is possible to break some of the rules, of course – Ira Gershwin broke the rule for forming contractions when he wrote "'swonderful, 'smarvelous, that you should care for me" – but it is the background of other rules that gives the violation meaning.[47]

The second way in which role expectations are relational is that the individual is not only their object, but also their origin. They do not come from "the institution" itself – that would be anthropomorphism again – but from the individuals who compose the institution. Each individual responds to the expectations of others and also projects expectations to which others must respond. These expectations are learned, but they are learned from others who project them and thus transmit them over space and time. They constitute the network of relations that, in a very real sense, constitutes the institution. Role expectations, in other words, are intersubjective; they exist within each individual member of the institution, but are generated by a social learning process. Collectively, they form the preempirical structure that makes possible the individual expectations that are then projected onto others.[48] This does not mean that every member of the institution will behave identically in a given situation, but only that the set of individual views regarding appropriate institutional behavior will tend to converge because relatively powerful intersubjective forces shape those views.[49]

The role expectations for judges include both the aspects of law identified earlier: law as a doctrinal framework and law as a constraint on decision-making discretion. In short, they involve the process of following legal doctrine.[50] We tend to apotheosize the law, and the resulting glow obscures the very mundane, law-following process. In effect, legal doctrine is part of the manual for new employees that judges receive when they begin their job. Following established legal rules is simply the right way for judges to do this job, and is thus continuous with the rules about how to behave on the bench or in judicial conferences. In thus demoting doctrine from an overarching ethos to a portion of the judge's job instructions, however, we should not stereotype it. As Eisenberg points out, the doctrine that constitutes part of the judge's sense of institutional propriety is the entire corpus of the law, including conflicts between rules, principles of legal change, and theories about law derived from secondary sources.[51] In addition, different judges will perceive doctrine differently; the intersubjective, culturally embedded nature of the role will produce a high level of convergence in their views, but will not determine these views with unvarying precision.

While a judge's role will include a vast range of rules, principles, practices, and habits, it also involves the interpretation of legal texts. The concern here is the way that judges fashion legal doctrine when they decide, for one reason or another, that existing texts provide them only with a grant of jurisdiction, and not with any particularized guidance for the case at hand. This does not mean, of course, that texts are irrelevant.

Legal doctrine in general is still perceived as being derived from texts in some systematic, nonarbitrary manner; it is only the particular issue in the case at hand that is bereft of textual support. Of course, the judicial and cultural belief that doctrine is derived from texts has been the subject of much recent controversy. This analysis asserts no claim about the extent to which texts control judicial decisions; all that it asserts is that there will generally be a prevailing interpretation of various texts that will be incorporated into the judge's understanding of doctrine. There may be nothing more to textual interpretation than this consensus view,[52] or there may be somewhat more,[53] or there may be a great deal more.[54] But, as an empirical matter, there is generally a consensus; when scholars speak of indeterminacy, they are referring to an uncertainty about the meaning of the text itself, not an uncertainty about the prevailing view. Although some interpretations will be contested at any given time, judges tend to be fairly clear about the standard interpretation of most texts, even if they cannot justify that interpretation in persuasive terms. Of course, such agnosticism about the role of texts deprives this consensus of any justificatory force. We cannot say that the judge's behavior in following the accepted interpretation embodies the rule of law, or constitutes the product of legitimate decision making; it is simply the interpretation that is in place at a given time.

With respect to the prison reform cases, the judges' sense of their proper role has been discussed at length in the preceding chapters. It is nothing more than their perception of existing legal doctrine with respect to this particular subject matter. Prior to 1965, it consisted of the hands-off doctrine, the belief that conditions of confinement were outside the jurisdiction of the courts and within the complete discretion of correctional officials. There were, however, conflicting elements that indicate the complexity of doctrine, and cast doubt on any simple, binary judgment about its certainty or uncertainty. As described in Chapter 2, the scope of habeas corpus seemed to be increasing, while the interpretation of the phrase "under color of" state law in the Civil Rights Act was becoming more expansive. There was a growing sense that the Eighth Amendment was directly applicable to the states, but since the Supreme Court had not spoken definitively on this matter, each federal circuit was free to adopt its own interpretation. In addition, there were a few scattered cases indicating that some remedy might be available in extreme situations and, as the 1960s arrived, a growing consensus that outright religious discrimination was unconstitutional. The great weight of doctrinal authority, however, continued to instruct judges that they could not intervene in the regular administration of state prisons.

Beyond doctrine itself, however, there was another component of the judges' sense of their role that prepared the ground for the prison reform cases. This was the growing, albeit implicit, recognition that policy making was the dominant approach to modern governance and thus a valid mode of action for the judiciary. Since there was no legal doctrine stating this in terms, it could not function independently. It could attach itself to an established legal doctrine, however, providing courts with a rationale for framing expansive, administrative remedies. This process, which dates back to the premodern era, was occurring in school desegregation cases by the 1960s. It could not occur in prison cases, however, until the development of an accepted legal doctrine provided courts with a basis for remedial action.

Attitude

The second basic motivation for the behavior of individuals in institutions is their personal beliefs, or their attitude. Roughly speaking, if role expectations determine the relationships among members of the institution, then attitudes or beliefs determine the relationship between each person's institutional role and certain other aspects of that person's life.*[55] The precise texture that one ascribes to this relationship depends upon one's theory of the self.[56] It may be seen as a relationship between the person's institutional role and the other roles a person plays, or it may be seen as a relationship between the institutional role and the individual's core identity. In either case, this interaction introduces a significant amount of variability into the individual's behavior as a member of the institution. Often, role expectations operate as a centripetal or cohesive force, and beliefs as a centrifugal or dissociative one, but this is not invariable. To be sure, people's beliefs can lead them to pursue personally defined goals, rather than those established by institutional expectations, and to carve out areas of individual privilege and advantage. But it is also true, at least in an open, democratic society, that high levels of commitment to the institution's goals can only result if the person's attitudes are at least generally consistent with the expectations that the institution generates.

Like role expectations, attitudes are intersubjective. Although they are part of the individual's personal thought process, and stand apart from her institutional role, they are socially constructed, as are all individual thought processes.[57] While both political scientists and legal scholars gen-

---

* David Rhode and Harold Spaeth define attitude as a set of interrelated beliefs that are relatively enduring and produce behavioral consequences. In this discussion, the terms "attitude" and "belief" are used interchangeably, since no effort is made to distinguish beliefs from sets of beliefs. Where attitudes or beliefs are organized in a more general construct of which the judge is consciously aware, the term "ideology" is used instead.

erally recognize the social nature of judicial attitudes, they hold a range
of views about the specific character of these attitudes. Political scientists
often imply that judicial attitudes are instinctive or reflexive, the product
of personal background and social class.[58] Legal scholars, on the other
hand, tend to emphasize the conscious or ideological character of judicial
beliefs, an emphasis that can be either positive or negative. For some,
such as Philip Bobbitt, Ronald Dworkin, Melvin Eisenberg, Owen Fiss, and
Michael Perry, judicial beliefs serve as a pathway by which important social
principles, shared by the great majority of citizens and reflecting widespread norms or values, are incorporated into law.[59] For others, often
associated with critical legal studies[60] or critical race theory,[61] judicial beliefs reflect the political ideology of society's dominant group, and become
a vehicle for maintaining that group's power at the expense of ordinary
citizens or people of color.

The analysis presented here does not require any choice among these
views, and the subject is far too complex to address by way of a digression.
It is necessary, however, to reject two somewhat extreme variations of these
views in order to proceed. First, the implicit suggestion in the political
science literature that these attitudes are reflexive cannot mean that
judges are literally unaware of them. The judges may be unaware of their
provenance, and unable to organize them into a systematic theory, but it
would be bizarre to suggest that these attitudes were actually unavailable
to the judge's conscious mind. A typical judicial attitude scale for the 1990
Court, for example, ranks the justices' attitudes toward civil liberties, with
Marshall and Blackmun on the liberal side, Kennedy and Rehnquist on
the conservative side, and all the other justices except for Stevens leaning
toward the conservatives.[62] Obviously, all these justices could have constructed the same ranking, and placed themselves quite accurately within
it. Perhaps they have thought about the reasons why they have these attitudes and perhaps they have not; perhaps they could give a consistent
account of them, although none of them would be able to satisfy Kant in
this respect. But they are all fully aware of their attitude toward civil liberties, and fully able to articulate it, assess it, and consciously change it if
motivated to do so.

The second extreme that must be rejected is the notion, sometimes
implied in critical legal studies or critical race theory, that the federal
judiciary constitutes a conscious conspiracy. Their attitudes may reflect
the ideology of society's dominant elite, but that elite is necessarily a
large and rather variegated one. It might well exclude people of color,
and might well favor the middle and upper classes over the working
class and the poor, but it cannot be much narrower than that. Judicial
beliefs cannot be ascribed to a self-conscious, collectively developed plan
by power holders to perpetrate the status quo because the assumptions

necessary to sustain such a claim are simply too baroque to be plausible.*[63]

Judicial attitudes are clearly related to the considerations of social morality that were discussed in Chapter 5 as motivations for defining a problem. While it is hardly surprising that personal beliefs would appear at each stage of a discretionary decision-making process, there is a distinction between these two uses of belief. The decision to initiate policy making is a conscious one, and it is one that is disfavored by judges because of its inherent activism. Judges prefer to rely on legal texts; they will generally abandon those texts, and make decisions designed to achieve beneficial results, only when they have some assurance that the beliefs that motivate them are strongly felt and widely held, that is, that these beliefs are truly elements of social morality. In contrast, the beliefs that mix with doctrine, once the decision to engage in policy making has been reached, will be the entire range of beliefs that the judges possess. Judges will no longer be trying to assure themselves that they are invoking beliefs that represent generalized norms. Rather, they will be acting more instinctively, or naturally, as part of their ordinary decision-making process. Their beliefs will still be intersubjective, and thus widely shared, but they will not be consciously delimited.

Once again, but even more decisively, the beliefs that figure in the judicial policy-making process play a much more modest role than principles do in the works of Bobbitt, Dworkin, Fiss, or Perry. Demoting principles to mere attitudes or beliefs resolves most of the paradoxes that attend the standard invocation of them. There is no question how the judge recognizes social principles or how she chooses among them; she does so instinctively because these principles are what she believes. There is also no question about the justificatory force of these social principles; because they exist as merely individual attitudes, they have no justificatory force at all. We can be partially reassured that the judge's reliance on social principles will fall within a delimited range, since these principles

---

* Duncan Kennedy's insightful discussion of judicial decision making verges close to this position, at least by implication. His example, which he presents as a first-person projection of what his own approach would be, is that of a judge who believes that the workers should prevail in any labor-management dispute, and that the employer should not be allowed to control the means of production. A class-oriented, conscious ideology of this sort, standing in opposition to general social attitudes, implies that most judges subscribe to an equally class-oriented ideology favoring employers. Such an interpretation of the prison cases is certainly conceivable; the judges could have been instituting the reforms to relieve revolutionary pressure on the instrumentalities of social control and to maintain the power of a ruling elite. We find this account implausible, however; there is no direct evidence that the judges were not acting in good faith, and that their beliefs diverged from general social attitudes.

are the intersubjective, socially constructed views of a rather traditional group of people. But, by itself, this does not provide the predictability or sense of external constraint that is required for us to regard judicial behavior as being subject to the rule of law.

The contrary claim – that social principles provide definitive guidance for judges, and thereby legitimate departures from accepted doctrine – has been creatively and forcefully advanced by Ronald Dworkin.[64] Most observers believe that Dworkin has described an important aspect of judicial decision making, but one that simply does not provide the certainty he claims.[65] Dworkin's response is to hypothesize a superhuman judge named Hercules who unerringly discerns and applies those general social principles.[66] This seems like an admission of defeat, but, more importantly, it assumes the very point at issue, namely that social principles exist somewhere beyond the realm of ordinary discourse.* In fact, these principles are produced by real human beings, and are applied by real human judges; the result is the variation and uncertainty that is inherent in all normative debate. Judges regularly rely on their own beliefs – the social principles that they believe are right – but we cannot look to that reliance as a means of subjecting judicial policy making to the rule of law.

Important changes in the attitudes of many federal judges were occurring in the late 1950s and early 1960s, as described in Chapter 5. With respect to prisons, the leading element was probably the judges' personal commitment to human rights and their sense that their particular role in government was to intervene on behalf of the oppressed and powerless. This sounds more closely allied to the Democratic Party than to the Republicans and, in fact, all the big prison cases except Arkansas were decided in the years following 1968, after two terms of Democratic appointments to the federal judiciary. Beyond this, the federal courts had committed themselves decisively to human rights in the *Brown* decision. When the case was decided, it represented a great risk for the judiciary; as time went on and the public support for the concept of desegregation grew, *Brown*, as viewed through that marvelous instrument know to medical practice as a retrospectascope, began to appear indubitably correct. The culmination of this process was the Civil Rights Act, passed in 1964 – the very eve of the prison reform movement – which ennobled and protected the *Brown* decision within vast statutory battlements. For federal judges of this era, therefore, *Brown* provided the heroic image of what

* In addition, by buttressing the concept of unambiguous social principles with the concept of an all-knowing judge, Dworkin violates an epistemological guideline known as Occam's Razor (entities should not be multiplied beyond necessity), which scientists also call the tooth fairy rule (only one mysterious agent per theory).

courts should do; they were supposed to discern, articulate, and implement the rights of individuals against the state. The prisoner's inartful complaint, which had previously appeared to demand that judges intrude into the justifiably closed world of the penitentiary, now seemed like an opportunity to carry out the basic work of the judiciary, the task that judges had signed up for when they took the oath of office.

A second and related attitude that many judges shared involved their image of the South. As discussed, one of the principal elements of the prison reform movement was the nationalization of the South, and the South seemed ripe for nationalization in the 1960s. This was the temporal hiatus between the moonlight-and-magnolia image of the Old South, vibrantly alive well past 1939 when *Gone With the Wind* was produced, and our contemporary go-go image of the New South, with its thriving factories, burgeoning suburbs, and professional sports franchises. The dominant image of the South during this intervening period was of a troubled, backward region in resentful transition, a region of red-necked sheriffs, segregation academies, police dogs, fire hoses, grinding poverty, and the murderers of Martin Luther King, Medgar Evers, and those New York civil rights workers. Federal judges probably felt more personally motivated to displace southern institutions than at any time since the early days of Reconstruction.

Finally, many federal judges seemed to experience strong visceral reactions to prisons once other factors motivated them to regard their inmates as human beings with rights. As Victor Hugo observed, visitors who set foot in a prison almost always ask themselves: "How would I feel if I were confined in these conditions?"[67] They ask this not because they sense within themselves the potential to commit a crime, but because the experience of being confined – of being caged – is one aspect of the human condition that almost everyone perceives. The palpable distress that Dickens's Arthur Clennam felt when he was accidentally locked in the Marshalsea for a single night springs from this perception.[68] As soon as judges began going into these institutions, either imaginatively, by perceiving the prisoners as fellow human beings, or physically, through inspection tours, they began to empathize powerfully with the prisoners' conditions. The personal shock they experienced when they saw the way that prisoners were being treated is apparent from their decisions, breaking through the doctrinal framework and appearing as direct expressions of personal outrage and dismay.

Integration

The third basic institutional motivation, and the one that carries us beyond familiar elements of judicial decision making, can be described as integration. In essence, it involves the relationship between legal doctrine and personal beliefs – the way in which the individual's experience as an individual relates to the individual's experience as a member of the institution.[69] It is essentially an adaptation of some basic insights of cognitive psychology to the institutional setting in which people function as judges.[70] Not all choices based upon a judge's personal beliefs can be described in this manner. For example, if the judge is only interested in maximizing personal self-interest, there will be no occasion for integration. But when the judge's sense of personal beliefs includes action on behalf of the institution, the relationship between that motivation and the demands of doctrine often involve the integration process.

Integration is the starting point for a theory of creativity within an institution, and specifically for a theory of judicial creativity. To see why this is so, it is necessary to consider the interaction of doctrine and belief in greater detail. As stated earlier, the judge's understanding of doctrine and his personal belief will sometimes correspond and at other times diverge. Correspondence is generally unproblematic; it means that the recognized legal doctrine seems satisfying or morally proper to the judge and can be followed without qualm or reevaluation. No process of integration is required. Of course, the judge may be incorrect in this assessment, which, at the very least, means that most other members of the institution would disagree with his perception of correspondence. Since people tend to be accurate in assessing their personal views (and how could we tell if they are not?), the problem usually resides in the judge's assessment of doctrine; that is, he has concluded that existing law corresponds to his personal beliefs about the situation, whereas most people, having heard an account of his beliefs, would say that his views and the law diverge. In this situation, the judge will confidently and unsuspectingly misstate existing law, and his decision will be regarded as a poor one by his colleagues, whatever their own ideology suggests about the situation. Since misperception is a popular means of avoiding intrapsychic conflict, this is likely to occur with some regularity, but need not detain us any further.*

---

* There is another possibility that should be added for the sake of completeness: the judge might believe that existing doctrine and his personal belief diverge, but he might be wrong, just as he might be wrong about their correspondence. Again, his error would presumably lie in his assessment of existing law. As a response to this imagined quandary, the judge might submit to his understanding of the doctrine and reluctantly apply an unaccepted legal rule. That would obviously be regarded as a poor decision, leaving the poor judge with no compensating benefit except the dubious one of having his real beliefs validated by an appellate court reversal of his actual decision. Alternatively, the judge might reject the doctrine, consciously reaching a desirable, but in his mind, unjustifi-

The important situation, for present purposes, is the one where the judge's attitudes are genuinely at odds with doctrine; that is, where the judge finds the institutionally expected answer to be personally distasteful. As a matter of descriptive sociology, this is probably more likely to occur when there are conflicts within doctrine, thereby weakening its force. The hands-off doctrine regarding constitutional challenges to prison conditions was probably in this condition by the 1960s. The crucial conflict, however, is not within doctrine, but between doctrine and the judge's attitudes. Faced with a conflict of that sort, a judge has three possible options. First, she can ignore her beliefs and make the decision that her understanding of the doctrine suggests. This may cause her varying degrees of personal stress, based on the nature of the issue, the breadth of the divergence, and the structure of her own personality. Assuming she is able to control this stress, she will act in a way that is, to an outside observer, virtually indistinguishable from the judge whose beliefs correspond to the existing doctrine. Perhaps there will be more hesitation or humility in her manner, perhaps qualifications will creep into her opinion, but if she has truly resolved to ignore her own beliefs, these evidences of apostasy will often be subtle and relatively insignificant. This seems to have been the situation with the Supreme Court's fugitive-from-the-chain-gang cases.

A second option for the judge is to ignore the doctrine and make a decision that is governed entirely by her attitudes. Presumably, this would involve the conscious thought, and perhaps the explicit statement, that "the law requires me to do one thing, but I find that law objectionable and I have decided to ignore it and do something else instead." Behavior of this nature is extremely rare, given the power of role expectations. As Robert Cover describes in *Justice Accused*, even abolitionist judges enforced the Fugitive Slave Law, rather than engaging in civil disobedience from the bench.[71] During the past few decades, feelings have run high about abortion, but how many lower-court judges, even Republican-appointed ones, have declared that they would not follow *Roe v. Wade?*

The third course of action when doctrine and attitude diverge is to integrate the two. In this process, the judge finds some way to unify her subjective sense that the law as it exists requires one result with her subjective sense that the law ought to be different. The structure of this in-

---

able result. In fact, he would be declaring the accepted law and, in this one case, contrary to what his mother told him, two wrongs really would make a right. Finally, the judge might try to integrate his beliefs with his mistaken understanding of doctrine in a valiant effort to justify changing a doctrine that has already changed. Many of the decisions that appear in law school casebooks probably belong within this final category.

tegrative process is fairly well defined because our legal system contains a variety of principles that recognize and explain doctrinal change. It is generally accepted that the law evolves, that specific constitutional or statutory language can mean different things in different circumstances, that we should look at the underlying purpose or intent of positive legal enactments as well as their literal language. All these principles, being well-recognized, if not universally accepted, are elements of the law itself and are available for use in the integrative process. What is not part of the law as it exists – what could not be, if the concept is to have any meaning – are those changes in the law that would bring it into congruence with the judge's attitudes. Those attitudes, therefore, can be regarded as supplying content or direction to doctrinally accepted notions of legal change.

In the process of integration, the judge has the personal, or phenomenological experience that she is changing the law, or at least stretching the existing doctrine.[72] This experience will tend to demand an explanation; a judge who acknowledged that she had changed existing law on the basis of her own beliefs without writing an opinion, or who was perceived as doing so, would be regarded as doing a poor job. But the two operative motivations in the integrative process demand different kinds of explanations. The judge's attitudes will lead her to justify her conclusion in terms of general normative or social principles. The judge's commitment to doctrine will lead her to justify her decision in terms of the existing law, including the rules for legal change that this existing law incorporates. Frederick Schauer suggests that the act of explaining one's position involves the invocation of more general considerations and a statement of commitment to those considerations.[73] According to this view, the judge's explanation would be the alembic of the integrative process – the place where she states a general consideration that is consistent with the underlying spirit of the law and with generalized normative or social principles.

As described in Chapter 2, some of the prison cases decided during the hands-off era indicate that judges were experiencing a serious conflict between doctrine and belief. The doctrine, as they understood it, included the long-established principle that prison authorities possessed complete discretion regarding the conditions of confinement and that courts had no authority – no jurisdiction – to intervene in this area.[74] But many of these judges, already thinking in terms of human rights, were deeply troubled by the glimpses of the "dark and evil world" that they received from prisoner complaints.[75] The problem was that they were unable to integrate these two divergent motivations, unable to find any appropriate legal discourse that would express their personal concerns. They hazarded vague assertions that prisoners possessed constitutional rights, but they were unable to connect this abstract declaration with any coherent remedial approach.[76]

The vagueness of the formulations and the skittishness of well-meaning judges about specifying the rights involved is striking. In *Coffin v. Reichard*, the 1944 decision much distinguished by other judges in the years that followed, the Sixth Circuit offered the following circular and tortuous definition of prisoners rights:

> A prisoner is entitled to the writ of habeas corpus when, though lawfully in custody, he is deprived of some right to which he is lawfully entitled even in his confinement, the deprivation of which serves to make his imprisonment more burdensome than the law allows or curtails his liberty to a greater extent than the law permits.[77]

Cooper v. Pate,[78] a civil rights suit by Black Muslims against Stateville Penitentiary, was in some sense the Supreme Court's first prisoners' rights decision,[79] but the Court's 1962 opinion was a summary reversal of the dismissal below, without explanation; apparently, the Supreme Court was experiencing similar difficulties in articulating the nature of the prisoners' rights. As late as 1966, *Landman v. Peyton*,[80] a truly odd decision by the Fourth Circuit, affirmed dismissal of a prisoner's complaint that conditions at Virginia State Penitentiary "trenched upon his constitutional rights."[81] Judge Simon Sobiloff declared: "Courts are not called upon and have no desire to lay down detailed codes for the conduct of penal institutions, state or federal."[82] Apparently dismayed by his own conclusion, he proceeded to remonstrate within the state: "We strongly commend to the close scrutiny of higher officials of the state the general problem of effective supervision of prison personnel."[83]

The problem of designing a remedy related to this vague conception of prisoner rights proved as great an impediment for the judges' integrative efforts as the definition of the rights themselves. Habeas corpus was the natural remedy, but it was generally regarded as being limited to the release of the complaining prisoner, which struck most judges as inappropriate. The Civil Rights Act was regarded as being somehow relevant, but no judge at the time perceived that it could be used to issue comprehensive injunctions governing all aspects of prison policy. In *Ex Parte Pickens*,[84] for example, decided in 1951, the judge held that conditions in the Alaska territorial jail did not constitute cruel and unusual punishment. Obviously troubled, he described at length the conditions in the "facility," a single, twenty-seven-square foot room holding forty prisoners – the overcrowding, lack of ventilation, lack of adequate toilets, and the constant danger of fire from the ancient cook stove in the center of the room.[85] But discharging the prisoners would only endanger public safety and there was no other remedy in sight. The judge wrote:

If relief could be had in this proceeding by commanding the [United States] Marshal to furnish other quarters for the prisoners the solution would be easy. But the Marshal has no funds with which to build or construct or lease or otherwise obtain any prison more suitable or more safe for those confined. . . . Those who are responsible for the present condition, the members of the two Houses of Congress of the United States are not subject to the jurisdiction of this Court.[86]

The judge then reassured himself by noting that the soldiers fighting in Korea at that time, who were defending the nation and accused of no crime, were being subjected to even harsher conditions than the prisoners.[87] Clearly, conditions in American prisons clashed with the attitudes of many judges, but they were unable to integrate this sense with the perceived demands of legal doctrine, and were thus incapable of acting on it.

Integration of the developing doctrine of civil rights with this attitude of discomfort and dismay about the conditions in state prisons was first achieved by Judge Henley in the Arkansas litigation. Over a period of about five years, he gradually realized that the totality of the conditions in the prison could be regarded as a generalized violation of the Eighth Amendment. This enabled him to bypass the complex and perhaps insuperable task of matching specific conditions with specific constitutional provisions, or of defining particularized rights that prisoners possessed. But the creativity and elegance of his approval does not explain why that approach became standard doctrine, nor does it explain how the problem of fashioning a remedy was solved. To do so, we must consider the way in which the individual integration process becomes generalized, and the nature of the ideas that can serve this function in the judicial decision-making context.

Coordination

While the interaction of doctrine, attitude, and integration occurs within a single judge's mind, a new doctrine, however conceptual its character, is not an individual idea. The mere fact that one particular judge articulates a new legal concept does not, by itself, render that concept the doctrine of her jurisdiction. In order to achieve that status, the concept must be actualized as a basis for institutional action. It must be something that the institution, as a functioning social entity, is prepared to implement.

To continue avoiding anthropomorphism, however, it is necessary to define institutional implementation in terms of individual behavior. We can begin by assuming that there is some element of inertia built into every decision maker's set of role expectations. It arises from the individual desire for stability and from the institutional or social virtue of continuity. In the legal system, such inertia is associated with the reliability of law and great value is attached to it.[88] In fact, what is notable about judicial institutions in most situations is the relative weakness of an institutional ethos of innovation; other institutions possess more conscious ideologies to encourage change, although most have strong inertial elements as well.

The engine that drives the creation of new ideas within institutions generally, and within the judiciary in particular, is a countervailing set of attitudes among a large proportion of the institution's members. This divergence can result from external forces, internal changes, the entry of new people into the institution, or a variety of other factors.[89] Whatever its origin, its result will be that the members will undertake a variety of efforts at integration, and even those who initially ignore their personal attitudes and act in accordance with their established role will be amenable to integrating ideas. Since attitude is intersubjective, these integrative efforts will frequently be widespread – the more widespread they are, of course, the more they resemble the social principles on which so many accounts of judicial decision making rely. As previously stated, however, the concept is used here as an empirical observation, not a decision rule for individual judges. For a divergence between doctrine and belief to trigger doctrinal change or creation, the divergent attitudes need not be universal or even conceptually available to every judge; they need only be reasonably common.

The idea that will become the new legal doctrine is one that ultimately prevails as a means of integration for the majority of judges. The process by which this occurs can be referred to as coordination. In one sense, coordination represents a further level of abstraction; integration involves the relationship between doctrine and attitude, while coordination can be seen as the relationship among individual integrative efforts. As such, it is quite rarified. Attitude or belief involves the individual's personally lived experience, and role expectations involve a complex, historically developed institutional experience. Integration is the intersection of the two around a specific issue; it is not, in itself, a personally grounded experience but a concept that emerges from those experiences. Coordination is the intersection of various people's integrative processes, removed still further from lived experience because it contains only those elements of the integrative process that can be shared among individuals. It is not necessarily a least common denominator, since one person can learn new things from another, but it is clearly a subset, or abstraction, of the integrative efforts that the various members of the institution undertake.

Coordination is an institutional process; it involves ideas that are necessarily held in common by many, if not all members of a given institution. In defining its operation, there is the ever present danger of anthropomorphism, of simply saying that the integrative process of the institution's members "gets" coordinated, or that the institution coordinates it, without bothering to define the phenomenology of this process. But it remains true that only individuals can think, and if an idea emerges from an institution, that idea must be present in the minds of real human beings who belong to or speak for that institution.

An idea can coordinate individuals' senses of integration while existing within the minds of individuals because the individuals in an organization will generally be committed to that organization as part of their institutional role. Consequently, they will have a specific, often conscious motivation to coordinate their integrative efforts with the other members of the organization. They will recognize that they must simplify, or abstract these individual efforts if the goal of a shared institutional approach is to be achieved. This process involves the distinction between what can be thought and what can be thought in conjunction with others. Coordination, in this sense, is mutual, not intersubjective; it is not a mental process, arising as part of the individual's experience of the world, that is shared with others because of the system of meaning that preempirically structures that experience. Rather, it is a thought or idea that is consciously adopted by individual members of the institution to integrate their ideology and their role expectations in a manner that is consistent with their colleagues.

Without delving too deeply into the phenomenological structure of thought, we can note that coordination is kept separate from integration because judges are able to bracket their entire decision-making process.*[90] In effect, they set their own integrative efforts to one side and examine the conclusions of other judges. Ordinarily, we assume that our own best solution to a problem deemed to be within our area of competence is the solution to be followed. But to the extent judges perceive themselves as members of an institution, they will question this assumption by bracketing their thought process and examining solutions that differ from their own conclusions. Although they may remain persuaded that their own integrative effort best resolves the perceived conflict between existing doc-

---

* The term is used here by analogy; as originally defined by Husserl, it represents the method of transcendence. His description of the mental process, however, is applicable to any conscious effort to suspend one's own belief by moving toward second-order thought. Husserl states: "At the natural standpoint we simply *carry out* all the acts through which the world is there for us. . . . At the phenomenological standpoint, acting on lines of general principle, we *tie up* the *performance* of all such cogitative theses, i.e., we 'place in brackets' what has been carried out, 'we do not associate these theses' with our new inquiries; instead of living *in* them and carrying *them* out, we carry out acts of reflection directed toward them."

trine and their personal beliefs, they can accept a different integrative effort because it possesses a superior capacity for coordination. To put this another way, individuals reconstruct themselves, and more particularly their thought process, as members of the institution to which they belong.

Coordination occurs when judges communicate their ideas to one another. Probably the most common, and certainly the most studied means of doing so is a judicial opinion. We need not inquire, at this juncture, whether the opinion represents a candid account of the judge's thought process, although much interesting work has been done on this subject.[91] In writing the opinion, the judge sets down her public account of the way that her personal beliefs can be integrated with her perception of existing legal doctrine. That is a thought process of its own, born of the need to act consistently with one's role expectations. It represents the judge's real feelings in her institutional role, and the question of whether it represents her real feelings about the integrative effort, apart from the personal attitudes that have already been incorporated in the integration process, is too metaphysical to be productive. There are other ways for judges to communicate, of course, including judicial conferences, personal contacts, service on multimember panels, and contributions to law reviews and similar publications. In a concrete, antiformalist account of judging, such means of communication count just as much as the traditional means of written decisions. As Judge Justice's experience at the SMU conference where he met Bill Turner suggests, informal contacts were probably an important factor in coordinating the concept of a constitutional right to decent prison conditions.

The process of coordination operates either horizontally or vertically, that is, it either emerges from the collective actions of various institutional actors or it is imposed by the leaders of the institution. For horizontal coordination to generate institutional change, it must ultimately become absorbed into the set of role expectations that all the members of the institution experience. This can be regarded as a three-stage process. First, a widespread, though not necessarily universal divergence between the members' role expectations and personal beliefs produces various efforts to integrate the two, and these efforts are communicated to other members of the institution. In the second stage, those members who have made these efforts accept one particular means of integration as a conscious strategy for fulfilling certain institutional goals that their role expectations demand. Finally, when this chosen method, or coordinating idea, becomes sufficiently common, it will begin to seem like appropriate institutional behavior and the conflict between role expectation and belief will be resolved by its generalized adoption. Not all the members of the institution need agree with the coordinating idea in order for it to become enrolled in the repertoire of institutionally proper behaviors. For a complex institution, two different and even conflicting courses of action may be comprised within the ambit of appropriate behavior, at least when one is old and one is new. Over time, of course, we would expect a well-functioning institution to settle on a relatively unified approach.

Vertically or hierarchically promulgated ideas may begin by simply integrating the leader's role expectations and beliefs. The integrative effort can then be issued as an order with no coordinating features, and it will be effective if the members of the institution are willing to obey the leader. More precisely, the members' role expectations often include a principle of obedience; having received an instruction from the leader, they would ignore, or at least bracket, their own beliefs to the extent that these beliefs conflict with the newly promulgated order. This combination of integration and ukase by the leader of an institution is certainly a familiar strategy, but it is not a particularly promising one. To begin with, it underestimates the difficulty of developing integrative ideas that achieve the institution's purposes. In a situation where role expectations and personal beliefs diverge both for the leader and for other members of the institution, the leader will not necessarily be the person who can integrate these two divergent motivations most effectively. Thus, coordination of the subordinate's and leader's integrative efforts may be necessary to generate the best solution. More importantly, the willingness of subordinates to obey an institutional leader is generally limited; the more democratic the society, the more prestigious and "professional" the subordinates, the greater their resistance to outright command will be.[92] When the subject matter of a command is merely routine, the propriety of hierarchical relationships is likely to prevail, but if the command is generated by a divergence between the leader's role expectations and personal beliefs, as it must be to constitute a new institutional idea, it will generally be received by subordinates whose own role expectations and beliefs have diverged. They are likely to resist the command, because the command's authority belongs only to their own role expectations, and that is exactly what the divergence between role expectation and belief has called into question. In other words, the leader's efforts to impose her integrative effort on subordinates will often conflict with her subordinate's own integrative efforts, and these beliefs will then impel her to resist the command.[93] This does not simply mean that an institutional idea is being undermined by truculent subordinates; it means that there will be no institutional idea at all, because an institutional idea is a practice followed by all the relevant members of the institution, not a declaration of the institution's leaders.

The declarations of a leader become institutional ideas by coordinating the integrative efforts of the people who compose the institution, or at least those who determine the institution's actions. This is simply cookbook management theory: "a good leader should obtain the willing cooperation of her subordinates."[94] The important point for present purposes is that this approach is not only an effort to control subordinates; it may also serve a conceptual function, producing cooperation because it generates new ideas that solve a generally felt dilemma by the members of the institution.

The judiciary develops new doctrine by both horizontal and vertical coordination. Some new doctrines, or integrative efforts with the potential to become new doctrines, percolate up through the lower courts and do not reach the supreme court of the jurisdiction until after a coordinating idea has taken shape. Others rise rapidly, generating a supreme court opinion that either coordinates or fails to coordinate the integrative efforts of the lower courts.[95] If it fails, the supreme court is operating purely by command, not coordination. In response, lower-court judges must either suppress their own beliefs or begin developing new integrative efforts that circumvent the force of the high-court opinion. As that opinion ages, these integrative efforts are likely to increase, ultimately generating new coordinating ideas by horizontal action, or inviting the supreme court to do so in a new opinion.

Many discussions of the U.S. Supreme Court tend to overemphasize the Court's role, and thus the verticality of the judicial decision-making process. Ironically, the tendency to do so comes from both sides of the debate about the relative importance of attitude and doctrine. For those who want to emphasize the "imperial" or "political" nature of the Court, an unexpected coup de main, without lower-court precedents or conceptual preparation, is a deliciously unreasonable posture for the Court to adopt. For those concerned with doctrine, a Supreme Court decision renders prior lower-court decisions irrelevant; they become mere historical footnotes that scholars can ignore when analyzing the architecture of prevailing law and that attorneys avoid citing because their reasoning or details may differ from the reigning precedents. In fact, both views are something of a distortion; most major Supreme Court cases represent the culmination of a coordination process that began horizontally, among the federal trial and appellate courts. While this pattern is far from universal, it is much more common than is generally assumed.

An example of the converse phenomenon is the Supreme Court's decision in *Jones v. Alfred H. Mayer Co.*,[96] which held that a post–Civil War statute forbid discrimination by private persons under the authority of the Thirteenth Amendment's abolition of "all badges and incidents of slavery." The statute had been interpreted by federal courts only twice before, and there had been no preparatory cases leading to the Supreme Court decision. The decision itself was clever, and many commentators argued for its extension,[97] but it served no coordinating role for the lower courts;

as a result, they were unable to use the "badges and incidents of slavery" concept in connection with race relations, and regularly rejected any claims based on this concept that went beyond the precise facts of the *Jones* case.[98]

The prison reform cases are an extreme example of horizontal coordination, and acquire additional interest thereby. Not only did they represent an unusually high level of judicial policy making, but they achieved this without hierarchial control or supervision. As is apparent from Part I, and further discussed in Chapter 7, the federal trial courts were the principal architects of the prison reform effort, with the courts of appeals playing a secondary, although significant, role. The Supreme Court did not address the issue of prison conditions until the 1980s, although it implied approval in the course of deciding some related, less important issues. Lacking any hierarchial command or supervision, the federal courts' ability to develop a unified, coherent body of doctrine for prison conditions depended entirely on the conceptual process of coordination. The fact that the courts succeeded in this effort indicates the power of the coordination process for creating legal doctrine.

All this, of course, is a conceptual account of judicial behavior. It explains the judges' motivations in terms of the ideas available to them, and it describes their actions in terms of the ideas that they developed within the context of the legal system. One could search for deeper, more structural explanations. Public choice theory would focus on the self-interest of the judges, ascribing the prison reform cases, perhaps, to their desire to maximize their salaries or their leisure time. While this does not seem to be a particularly promising approach, the closely allied school of positive political theory would explain the cases as an effort to expand the institutional power of the judiciary, which is substantially more plausible. Marxist scholars might attribute the judiciary's actions to the elite's desire for more efficient mechanisms to control the lower classes, mechanisms that operated more systematically and were purged of the evident abuses that might draw attention to this system's oppressiveness or incite open rebellion. A neo-Marxist account might stress the rhetoric of rights and reform as a means of masking the socially oppressive nature of the prison. The plausibility of these accounts is increased when one recognizes that American prison populations are disproportionately black and, even controlling for race, disproportionately poor.

While these explanations can be illuminating, they are not sufficiently specific to answer the question that this inquiry addresses. That question is why a particular institution, the judiciary, adopted a particular reform strategy at a particular time. An analysis of underlying motivations is unhelpful because it is equally applicable to all governmental actors at all the relevant times. To explain a particular event, it becomes necessary to factor in the very same conceptual, contingent developments that have been invoked without relying on these deeper motivations. In addition, these deeper explanations, whether based on public choice, Marxism, or a variety of other theories, do not describe the terms in which the actors themselves thought. Yet these actors – the judges – were not bugs or boulders, but senscient, indeed intelligent beings who participated in creating a complex system of meaning through the legal system. That process is worth describing, and its internal dynamics provide at least a necessary and perhaps sufficient explanation for the events in question.

An emphasis on the actual thought processes of judges does not imply the claim that these processes can be described in some pure, objective form, anterior to any theory. The conceptual account given here is itself a theory, and it is derived from the more general phenomenological idea that people construct systems of meaning to control both their perceptions and their actions. The claim is that this theory is anterior to any deeper one; people do not act automatically, but as part of a conscious process that intervenes between their structural position and their actual behavior. One can then proceed to a deeper theory if one chooses, but the gain in explanatory power is often counterbalanced by the interpretive nature of the effort. For example, judicial behavior is described here as being motivated, in part, by the judge's personal attitudes. One could then argue that these attitudes are always generated by personal self-interest, institutional self-interest, class interest, or whatever. If any of these explanations could be persuasively demonstrated, they would add genuine depth to the analysis; while they remain contested, they may only add complexity. Whether they are right or not, however, they still must operate through conceptual mechanisms like a decision maker's attitudes, and it is those mechanisms that this study explores.

The Character of Coordinating Ideas

Because coordination is an institutional process, the character of the ideas that instantiate it will vary depending on the nature of the institution. The institution that we are concerned with here is the judiciary. In that context, coordinating ideas must have a specific and distinctive set of characteristics – they must be fully realized, delimited, and directional.

The most basic feature of a coordinating idea for the judiciary is that it must be fully realized at the time of its creation. It cannot be an argument or a provisional approach that awaits delineation in the future, but must be presented as an end state, a definitive right, obligation, qualification, or exception. One reason for this is structural; because the judiciary is highly dispersed and loosely organized, coordination involves action at a distance. Judges do not meet together very often except on panels at the appellate level. For the most part, they communicate through their written opinions, and the opinion needs to present a clear and fully formulated solution if that solution is to appeal and take hold. In other words, coordination must occur in real time and real space, where the quantity of information that can be communicated is restricted by the institutional structure. In an institution like the American judiciary, the ideas that judges will find applicable or usable will generally be limited to a single, fully realized concept.

A second reason why coordinating ideas must be fully realized is conceptual. Our system of law does not possess an overarching theoretical framework from which particular decisions are derived. Apparently, there was a time when legal scholars thought it did, or at least were willing to assert it did in order to get law schools accepted on university campuses.[99] If so, they maintained this belief for the first twenty or thirty years after law schools achieved this status and they have been assiduously making fun of it for the ninety years that followed.[100] Many scholars now believe that judges proceed by practical reasoning, that they employ a mixture of various techniques informed by intuition, political experience and knowledge drawn from other disciplines to reach decisions in situations of uncertainty.[101] In such a system, new doctrines are likely to be introduced as discrete, fully defined units because there is no method of inductive or deductive argument, no analytic procedure, syllogism, or rule that can serve the purpose. Judges must be presented with the end product, the change itself, and must decide by their intuitive, experiential method whether that change is desirable.

Finally, coordinating ideas must be fully realized because previous coordinating ideas were fully realized. That is, once doctrinal change takes place by means of fully realized legal concepts, for the reasons just described, the process becomes powerfully self-reinforcing. This is not only because judges like to do things the way their predecessors did, but also because the process of development, in law as in so many other fields, is path dependent;[102] the means by which the result is reached affects the nature of the result itself. All doctrine was created at some time, and the judge-made parts of it were generally created through the process of conceptual coordination. As a result, the doctrine consists, almost in its entirety, of a linked collection of end states that once served as coordinating ideas. Absent codification, this collection of ideas will not be extensively reconstituted, or "smoothed out"; no judge has time or means to do so. Consequently, the law retains the imprint of its generative process, and strongly encourages that process to continue.

A second feature of a coordinating judicial idea, apart from its fully realized character, is that it represents a delimited change in doctrine, generally involving a single right or obligation. Coordination is a response to a particular divergence between role expectations and attitudes, and it provides a way of unifying various individual efforts to integrate that divergence. Although each judge will probably experience a variety of such divergences at any given time, it is unlikely that the group of judges who experience this divergence on one issue will be the same as the group who experiences it on another. Even if there is a substantial overlap, it is also unlikely that a fully realized idea that resolves the integrative efforts of these judges on one issue can be linked to a second idea, resolving a second set of integrative efforts. Because of the particularized nature of the coordination process, that process will generally proceed on a retail basis.

The result is incremental change, of course, and as Martin Shapiro and others have suggested, incremental change is in fact a familiar feature of judicial decision making.[103] For present purposes, the important point is that incrementalism is not only a tradition within the judiciary, or a personal preference of the middle-class, middle-of-the-road individuals who constitute it; it is not simply an empirical observation about judges' institutional role expectations or personal beliefs. Rather it is a structural feature of the coordination process. Even if some judges were smitten with the desire for comprehensive, root-and-branch reform, they could not coordinate this desire with the rest of the judiciary and they probably could not coordinate it with each other. In effect, the organization's bulk precludes the lambency of individual thought; individuals can change their minds in an instant, like Paul on the road to Damascus, but institutions generally change only by degrees. This is not invariably the case, but it is generally true, and all the more so when the change agent is the judiciary, rather than an agency with more staff, economic resources, or hierarchial control.

The idea of incremental, step-by-step development, with each step being fully realized or complete, resembles punctuated evolution. This is not surprising; incrementalism by fully realized steps would seem to be the method of change built into any process that is not directed by a controlling force that stands above the individual participants. A controlling force can either instruct the participants to follow a comprehensive long-range plan or provide a general vision that the participants follow on their own. Absent such a force, change must proceed step by step, with each step justifying itself as an improvement that should be accepted on its own terms, just as each evolutionary alteration must confer a competitive advantage in order to be genetically preserved. There is no person or belief system that can reassure the participants that a currently unappetizing change will yield good results at some time in the future.

It should also be noted that the step-by-step development of legal doctrine represents substantive incrementalism rather than the methodological incrementalism, or muddling through, discussed earlier as an alternative to the classic mode of policy analysis. As such it is a universal feature of judicial policy making, regardless of whether the judge uses the classic model or just muddles through.[104] It emerges from the need to translate the policy goals, no matter whether clearly defined or dimly sensed, into legal doctrine. Thus, judicial incrementalism is similar to an administrator's decision to achieve a goal by adopting an existing program, rather than abolishing the program, retraining all the staff members, and initiating something new. It is the past, not the choice of methodology, that commands this form of incrementalism.

The final feature of coordinating ideas may be referred to as directionality. Although doctrinal creation proceeds on an incremental basis, without overarching control, the individual decision makers do have some sense of the general contours of the law. Guido Calabresi uses the image of the legal landscape,[105] while William Eskridge describes the phenomenon as horizontal coherence;[106] in phenomenological terms, each judge feels the totality of the law the way a person in one particular location feels the totality of her surroundings, and makes sense of her particular location in relation to that feeling. A somewhat more modest version of this idea is teleology, or if that sounds less than modest, directionality. The law may not be truly consistent at any given time, but it does tend to move in a particular direction, perhaps in response to general social principles that are actuated through the judges' beliefs. Judges will be aware of that direction, and it will shape their choice of coordinating ideas. Karl Llewellyn captured this notion in *The Common Law Tradition*, his magnum opus in which he significantly modified his legal realist belief in the unpredictability of judicial decisions. He argued that judges' decisions are predictable if one places them in social context, a process made easier when judges write in the Grand Style and themselves seek to locate their decisions in the prevailing legal context.[107] In short, a coordinating idea must not only be fully realized and delimited, but it will generally move in the direction that judges perceive prior doctrinal innovations as establishing.

This is the weakest of the three features of coordinating ideas because it is the most subject to changes in judicial attitudes. When a new political party gains control of the executive, it will often begin appointing judges whose attitudes differ from the previously appointed ones. These new judges are not likely to have beliefs that affect the fully realized character of coordinating ideas, and they are relatively unlikely to have beliefs that affect the delimited or incremental quality of these ideas. But they may well believe that the direction of the law is wrong, and their efforts at coordination may involve a change in the law's previous directionality. It seems plausible, however, that legal development has an inertial character, so that changing direction requires more time and energy than continuing along the prior path. In addition, some of the doctrine's directionality may involve technical issues that are not located on contested political terrain; this was true, for a long time, of the steady expansion of tort liability that common-law courts effectuated. Thus, coordinating ideas will generally need to reflect the directionality of legal doctrine, even though they can sometimes abandon this feature as a result of changes in judicial attitudes.

The Categories of Coordinating Ideas

In order to identify and assess the coordinating ideas that constituted the prison conditions doctrine, it is necessary to consider the kinds of ideas that serve this function. For anyone familiar with contemporary legal scholarship, the two types of legal reasoning that will come almost immediately to mind are analogy and metaphor. The role of these techniques in legal thought has long been recognized, and the level of interest in them continues to increase, with major contributions in the last few years from Steven Burton,[108] Melvin Eisenberg,[109] Steven Winter,[110] Cass Sunstein,[111] and Roberto Unger.[112] While these discussions often refer to legal thought in its entirety,[113] they seem to possess particular relevance to the process of doctrine creation. In fact, the most obvious role for analogy and metaphor in legal decision making is as a means of generating coordinating ideas for the creation of new doctrine.

A notable feature of both analogy and metaphor, as opposed to deductive reasoning, is that they produce fully realized ideas. When using an analogy, one takes a complete and established approach to one subject and applies it, in its entirety, to another. Thus, a court might argue that the considerations that underlie the right of privacy are just like those involving libel, and right then, without any further elaboration, an entire doctrinal apparatus has been imported into a new realm, started up, and set to work. Similarly, when using a metaphor, one takes a complete image and applies it to a situation as means of conceptualizing that situation in its entirety.*[114] There is a visual quality to metaphor; it is like a picture, where one sees the totality at a glance and then fills in the details on closer examination. This can be contrasted with a necessarily linear verbal

---

* This follows John Serle, who argues that a metaphor is a statement whose literal meaning can call to mind a different meaning for the purpose of telling us about the object of the metaphor, but not about the metaphorical expression. Thus, the sentence "Richard is a gorilla" tells us something about Richard, not about gorillas. An analogy asserts that two legal situations resemble each other; a metaphor uses an image, not necessarily legal, to characterize a given legal situation.

argument, where one proceeds point by point, filling in the details of each step before proceeding to the next.[115] The metaphor of a chilling effect in First Amendment law, for example,[116] brings to mind, in an instant, a complete mental image of a cold wind emanating from the offending governmental agency and of potential speakers, like pedestrians in Chicago, withdrawing in discomfort to protect themselves from its effect.

To this fully realized quality of analogy and metaphor can be added their delimited effect. While both can vary in their scale from large doctrines to minor emendations, neither can function as a comprehensive theory, resolving questions not yet asked or situations not yet encountered or imagined. Both methods have a specificity that limits them to a particular issue, whether small or large; when the next issue arises, one must begin anew, seeking the most felicitous analogy or metaphor. Of course, there can be a connection between analogies or metaphors, due to the association of ideas, but the value of each new one must be demonstrated in the specific context it is used. Since these methods are not fully logical, there is no underlying argument that can definitively carry them beyond their context. Put another way, the applicability of analogies or metaphors must be apparent on their surface, for that immediate applicability is the source of their appeal. They are thus restricted to the issues they address at the time they are applied.

Analogy and metaphor do not necessarily possess directionality – that must be supplied from elsewhere – but their fully realized and delimited quality makes them natural methods for the generation of coordinating concepts. They are not the only methods, however; instead, they represent the middle range of a continuum that extends in either direction to smaller-scale and larger-scale efforts. A small-scale but still significant means of generating doctrine is a process that can be called "labeling" – the mere giving of a name to a vaguely discerned but previously unarticulated legal idea. The right of privacy (adopted from Warren and Brandeis's famous article),[117] the right of publicity (invented by a judge),[118] the doctrine of unconstitutional conditions (developed over time by many judges),[119] and the doctrine of irrebuttable presumptions (invented and abandoned by the U.S. Supreme Court)[120] were all products of felicitous labeling. They are not analogies, since they imply no comparison, nor are they metaphors, since they conjure up no mental images. Rather, they exemplify the primordial act of naming, by which one takes mental control of something and perhaps creates it as a separate entity.[121] It is the label itself that gives this technique its fully realized character, and the inherent specificity of labeling is the source of its delimitation.

At the other end of the continuum is an institutional conceptualization, a fully realized concept of an entire institution's legal status. Carried too far, of course, this can become a legal theory of the institution, which might be too extensive and controversial to coordinate the judiciary's integrative efforts. What renders the concept usable as a coordinating idea is that it is limited to one specific institution. It represents a conceptualization of the institution, an image that coordinates individual judges' efforts to integrate their sense of proper judicial behavior with their personal attitudes about the way the institution is supposed to operate. In some sense, therefore, the concept of an institution is just a large-scale metaphor. Metaphor, however, is a heavily visual notion, and institutions are often too complex to visualize in the usual manner. A fully realized but delimited concept of an institution's legal status may be capable of articulation only in terms of that institution, and not in terms of any particular image.

The coordinating idea that generated the new doctrine regarding prison conditions is clearly an institutional conceptualization. The judges were doing more than attaching a label to inchoate but existing principles, transferring one body of law to a new subject area, or even creating a new image to characterize a situation. Rather, they were establishing a new legal concept of a social institution – to be specific, they were creating the idea of a moral, legally justifiable prison. It was a fully realized conceptualization; rather than occurring step by step, with one aspect of the prisons and then another being reformed, the entire idea emerged from the very first case – the Arkansas litigation – and was simply refined and clarified in subsequent decisions. The image of the moral prison was delimited. It was not part of a general theory of institutions; the prison cases, however great their influence on prisons, exercised relatively little effect on other areas of law. Yet the concept that the courts developed clearly embodied the directionality of constitutional law, which steadily granted justiciable rights to new groups of people throughout the 1950s and 1960s.

Because metaphor and analogy are regarded as common elements in legal thought, labeling is clearly common, and even institutional conceptualizations have become familiar, their centrality in the process of doctrine creation raises a question about the extent to which the process is distinct from legal thought in general. The answer will depend on one's position on what is perhaps the leading legal question of our age – namely, the extent to which legal doctrine is indeterminate. There is clearly a high level of indeterminacy inherent in the process of doctrinal creation because the search for labels, metaphors, analogies, or institutional conceptualizations is necessarily an open-ended one. While a good analogy or metaphor, for example, may possess a sense of "rightness," it would be implausible to insist that there was only one right metaphor for a given legal question.

If one believes that legal doctrine is relatively certain, then one would regard it as being controlled by techniques different from those needed to create new doctrine. Statutory language could be applied to specific fact situations based on standard canons of interpretation, and precedents could be followed on the basis of their rationale. In this case, the use of more impressionistic methods such as metaphor or analogy would be limited to the creation of new doctrine, and the process described earlier would be only one part of judicial decision making, albeit an important part. On the other hand, if one believes that legal doctrine is largely indeterminate, then judges are creating it much more often, perhaps as often as every time that they reach a decision. In that case, the process described is the essence of legal thought and all else is apology and facade.

For present purposes, there is no need to adopt a position on this much debated question. The creation of doctrine clearly represents a mode of legal decision making where doctrine is indeterminate; how much deeper this indeterminacy extends does not necessarily affect the analysis of that core area. It seems likely, however, that judges' experience when creating doctrine is different from their experience in deciding more ordinary cases. Because of our preexisting myth that judges are merely discovering the law, there is really no domesticated theory of indeterminacy. Commentators tend to reinvigorate the concept that the law is definitively determined, or to shatter it and concede the entire field to the forces of untrammeled willfulness. In all probability, however, there are degrees of indeterminacy, and the level of indeterminacy is sufficiently greater when new doctrine is created so that this process may be regarded as a distinct judicial activity.

The most plausible account is that legal decision making forms a continuum that extends from relatively determined decisions on the one hand to the highly indeterminate process of doctrinal creation on the other. Many decisions will strike judges as compelled; this does not mean that an individual judge cannot reach a different conclusion, but only that certain conclusions, once reached, will be regarded as correct by the great majority of other judges. Such consensus may be merely the result of social conventions, as Stanley Fish asserts,[122] or it may follow what Owen Fiss calls disciplining rules.[123] In any case, the continuum extends from these "easy cases"[124] through increasing levels of uncertainty, with the process of doctrinal creation and its attendant techniques of labeling, analogy, metaphor, and institutional conceptualization playing an increasingly important role.

Within this continuum, however, there would seem to be at least two discontinuous transitions; in other words, to invoke one of the dominant metaphors of our own century, the continuum is quantized. The first transition occurs at the point where the level of indeterminacy can call forth a coordinating idea. Below that point, judges will not perceive a sufficient divergence between existing doctrine and their own beliefs to require integration, or they will experience that divergence, but will regard doctrine as so compelling that it will demand obeisance and foreclose the integrative process. Without individual efforts at integration, coordinating ideas cannot develop. There is no motivation to adopt such ideas, which only function as a conscious response to the felt need to coordinate the judges' integrative efforts. Once this first transition has occurred, however, judges become aware that they need to integrate the existing doctrine with their personal beliefs. This means that they are conscious of the integration process and that coordinating ideas provide the means by which that process can be implemented. The second quantum shift in the continuum occurs at the point that judges consciously recognize that the coordination process is not simply interpreting some existing legal source, but is creating a new doctrine. In other words, they recognize that the coordinating idea is an indeterminate creation of judicial thought and not an emanation of existing law. At present, judges' understanding of their role motivates them to resist this recognition, even when it most accurately reflects their decision-making process. To the extent they do, the continuum appears relatively smooth, but still extends beyond interpretation to doctrinal creation; to the extent they recognize the process, the second quantum shift in the continuum becomes apparent.

Doctrinal Creation and the Rule of Law

This, then, is a description of the conceptual process by which judges create new legal doctrine. Based on this description, one could naturally proceed to consider the way that this process was used in the prison cases to generate the doctrine that reformed the prisons, and that prevails to the present day. As indicated at the beginning of Part II, however, the descriptive questions about the nature of judicial policy making are joined by normative questions about its legitimacy. Before proceeding to describe the particular coordinating ideas in the prison cases, therefore, we will discuss the legitimacy of the doctrinal creation process in general.

The challenge to legitimacy of doctrinal creation is whether it conforms to the rule of law. As stated earlier, the rule of law demands that judges be subject to external constraints that are general, clear, well accepted, and congruent with the legal order. It affects judges because it is part of their set of role expectations, their institutionally induced beliefs about the way they should carry out their official functions. Judges, being a rule-abiding group of people by and large, are not likely to ignore such beliefs. The prison cases have regularly been regarded as indicating that they did, since these cases are not guided by a legal text, but this is not the impression one receives from reading them. In their decisions and their orders, the judges seem to be groping toward some image of a just, efficient prison, rather than expressing their desires or exercising their will. The megalomania of tropical dictators and the self-righteous, bureaucratic willfulness of the Important Personage in Gogol's *Overcoat*[125] are absent from these records of judicial decision making. The impression is that these are the same judges who decide contract cases and construe the Securities Exchange Act, and that they feel the same sense of constraint as they do in these more traditional activities.

The constraint the judges experienced in the prison cases did not derive from a text, but from the internal dynamics of the coordination process. As stated, coordination involves the conscious decision to displace one's own efforts at integration with an integrative effort that can be communicated to, and followed by, a large number of dispersed individuals within the judiciary. For an idea to coordinate individual judges' integration processes, it must be continuous with existing legal doctrine; that is, it must be perceived by judges as a natural outgrowth of that doctrine, rather than a radical departure. To use Gadamer's phrase, it must be part of the judiciary's effective historical consciousness.[126] Only certain ideas possess the simplicity, clarity, and continuity to serve this purpose. These ideas are necessarily legal, in a recognized social sense, because legal training is the main thing judges share, and judges know that.

To be more specific, coordinating ideas in the judicial context must be fully realized, must be incremental, and must usually reflect the prevailing directionality of law. Thus, they consist of a small step in a particular direction, a step that is formulated as a specific doctrinal element that is recognizably similar to preexisting doctrine. These are severe, albeit not determinative, constraints. The judge who is subject to them is unlikely to experience a sense of unrestrained freedom; instead, she will perceive herself as struggling to find the most persuasive formulation from among a very limited range of possibilities. That sense of limitation – of conscientious striving to find an acceptable solution, rather than of self-indulgent exultation at imposing one – constitutes the rule of law for the judiciary.[127]

Thus, the constraints on judicial policy making are internal to the process by which policy making is carried out. This is neither an oddity nor an accident, but derives from the independent character of the judiciary. As stated previously, law functions as both a framework that engenders judicial decision making and a constraint that disciplines it. The concept of an independent judiciary demands that the same conceptual structures perform both these functions. If the doctrinal framework that engenders decisions did not provide the constraint on those decisions, then the constraint would need to come from elsewhere, that is, from another decision maker. But the judiciary, being independent, must constrain itself; it must generate the limits on its actions from the same practice that constitutes those actions. Because the framework and constraint overlap, judges can only be constrained by the inherent dynamics of the law itself, as they themselves formulate it. That is why the demands of doctrine creation – of the coordination process – can be understood as securing the rule of law.

This process of self-constraint is consonant with the views of many commentators, including Philip Bobbitt,[128] Dennis Patterson,[129] and Steven Winter,[130] who regard judicial decision making as a socially situated practice legitimated by the well-established rules that are internal to that practice. The discussion here asserts that, within that social practice, judges themselves, as a matter of their phenomenological experience, perceive particular constraints upon their actions. Quite often, that perceived constraint comes from a text or, more precisely, from their agreed-upon perception of a text. In the case of policy making, the constraint comes from the demands of the coordination process. The text may seem more external to the decision-making process, and thus more of a constraint, but the current debate about interpretation casts serious doubt on this impression. Besides, there can be varying degrees of constraint, and the fact that policy making is less constrained than some interpretations does not mean that it is unconstrained in its entirety.

The self-constraint of the coordination process is also consonant with what Niklas Luhmann[131] and Gunther Teubner[132] call the autopoiesis of law. In their view, law is a self-describing, self-reproducing system that generates new elements within the framework of that system. This is not a return to the much scorned idea that legal doctrine is autonomous or apolitical; the notion, rather, is that law is a system of meaning, and that political or moral values only affect law when they are translated into legal terms and evaluated in accordance with existing legal criteria. "Their normative content is produced from within the law itself, by constitutive norms which refer back to these values," as Teubner says.[133] Thus, the judges' own personal ideologies are not law, as judges themselves well know. They become part of law through a process of integration and coordination whose contours are established by existing legal categories. The autopoietic structure of the legal system means that this process is subject to a set of internally generated constraints that are recognizable as the rule of law. Indeed, it means that only such internally generated constraints could satisfy the rule of law, for no legal standard exists outside the autopoietic system that generates such standards.

It may be objected that the internal dynamics of the coordination process do not provide clear guidance for an individual judge or definitive constraints on her decisions. That is true. What is being constrained is not each individual judge but the judiciary as an institution. The individual judge, like the individual legislator or administrator, is an official who is granted a significant amount of discretion. We can no more expect the rule of law to control comprehensively and unambiguously each judicial decision than we can expect the need for reelection to control each individual legislator or the supervision of the president to control each federal administrator.*[134] It is not the individual decision maker who is constrained, but the institution in its general operation.

For some reason, we tend to forget that the judiciary is an institution when considering the rule of law. Although descriptive political science has long recognized this apparent fact,[135] and several law and economics scholars, most notably Lewis Kornhauser, have employed resource utilization issues to model judicial structure,[136] jurisprudence tends to speak of "the judge," as if America had only one of them, operating in lordly isolation.[137] Jurisprudential theories are invariably framed as descriptions of, or prescriptions to, a single judge, who is supposed to perceive the constraint of law or the demands of justice as a matter of individual perspicacity. Ronald Dworkin goes so far as to call his ideal judge Hercules,[138] and we all know that Hercules did not have supervisors, colleagues, or staff members when he set out to perform his labors.[139] Indeed, he was a self-conscious loner; he originally joined Jason's expedition on the Argo, but wandered off one day and went on to pursue more solitary adventures.[140] This image of the judge as an isolated hero, cutting off and cauterizing the hydra-heads of injustice,† is an appealing one, but it is hardly realistic. Judges are members of institutions, which means they interact with and are constrained by other judges. Each individual judge will be aware that the judiciary as a whole, not its individual members taken one by one, is the proper locus of operation for the rule of law.

It is only from the outside that this process seems potentially or actually unconstrained, as if "the judiciary" – this mystic collectivity – could cavalierly decide to do whatever it desires. From the inside, from the phe-

---

* Some legislators are lame ducks, or come from safe seats; some administrators function largely on their own, even though their supervisor's supervisor was appointed by the president. Moreover, the ultimate penalty for disobedience is not death, but simply the loss of one's job; consequently, legislators and administrators will decide to disobey whenever their personal beliefs make that act of disobedience more valuable to them than their position. There are also legislative decisions that are too technical for any significant group in the electorate to police, and administrative decisions too detailed or fact-dependent to be controlled by a superior. In addition, as Mortimer and Sanford Kadish indicate, societies like our own may grant public officials a certain range of discretion, including the discretion to disobey the orders that their superiors issue.

† Hercules did obtain some help from his charioteer in defeating the Lernaean Hydra, but, as a result, the ever begrudging Eurystheus refused to count this labor toward the originally required ten.

nomenological perspective of individual judges, the creation of new legal doctrine is a complex, arduous endeavor. Perhaps the judge can reach a specific result on the basis of her personal preferences, although few judges really do this. But she cannot create new doctrine without coordinating her ideas with other judges, either in different courts and, at the appellate level, on her panel. Thus, the multimember nature of the judiciary, often regarded as an unfortunate impediment to principled decision making,[141] is in fact an important mechanism for securing the rule of law in the judicial decision-making process. Existing doctrine, moreover, forms an enclosing shell around the judge, toughened by institutional demands and made opaque by the judge's legal training.*[142] It is difficult to push this shell outward at any point, and because actions must be performed in coordination with other judges, it is particularly difficult. In other words, doctrinal creation, far from being an act of an unfettered judicial will, is inherently constrained. Judges understand this intuitively, as part of their personal experience in their position, and thus do not perceive doctrine creation as raising insuperable difficulties for the rule of law.

While the coordination process provides constraint, it also permits movement; over time, coordinated judicial creativity will reposition the enclosing shell, even if it does not shred its fabric. The possibility of movement is essential for descriptive purposes, because the law indeed evolves, and most people would regard this possibility as equally essential for normative purposes as well. To be sure, the constraint provided by coordination will not satisfy those for whom the rule of law involves fealty to fixed principles of natural or positive law origin, but this failure only means that we are dealing with an evolutionary theory. Many of our leading theories of less controversial judicial activities, such as interpretation or common-law decision making, are also evolutionary. If the rule of law depends upon unchanging principles, Eskridge's[143] or Aleinikoff's[144] theory of statutory interpretation, Ackerman's[145] or Bobbitt's[146] theory of con-

---

* The image of doctrine as a shell that limits legal meaning to a subset of all culturally available meanings has been suggested by Patricia Williams. It is not a Gadamerian horizon. Gadamer's horizon represents the limits of our understanding at our own historical moment; the shell of existing doctrine lies well within that horizon. As an ordinary person, the judge can see beyond it, but when she performs her role, the shell constrains her thought processes if she does not ignore role expectations. The creation of doctrine, then, must take place within the doctrinal framework in which the judge has been placed by her specialized training, not within the larger space that is limited by her horizon as a human being. She brings her broader attitudes into the shell, of course, as part of her attitudes or ideology, but she must actuate that sense from inside the doctrinal system.

stitutional interpretation, and Eisenberg's[147] theory of common-law decision making fail just as badly as the theory of doctrine creation outlined earlier. To put the matter another way, this theory of doctrine creation, like most contemporary theories of judicial decision making, limits the acceptable results at a given time on the basis of the preexisting doctrine, but does not prescribe any absolute limitations. As Justice E. W. Thomas has observed, "The exercise of judicial discretion is constrained, not by the operation of the doctrine of precedent, but by the felt presence of all the factors which make up the discipline that binds the judiciary."[148]

Our federal and state judiciaries, while more collegial than most of our institutions, are ultimately hierarchical, headed by a supreme court whose decisions possess authoritative force. This creates the possibility, as previously described, that the jurisdiction's supreme court will dispense with the coordination process and operate by ukase. Confronted with a situation that creates a conflict between their understanding of doctrine and their personal beliefs, the supreme court justices may develop their own integrative solution and then impose it on the lower courts, relying on their institutional power rather than on the coordination process. Of course, as research on small-group behavior in the judicial context suggests,[149] coordination remains necessary among a sufficient number of the supreme court's judges to comprise a majority of the institution. But sometimes a smaller group, or even a single judge, will have a decisive voice, and in any case the opportunities for direct interaction among the judges on a single court will tend to weaken the requirements of coordination. Thus, a supreme court, like an agency head or chief executive officer, has the power to preempt the process of coordination.

According to the account just given, this approach appears to deprive doctrine creation of the constraint inherent in coordination and thus revive the doubts about whether doctrine creation violates the rule of law. In fact, that probably occurs in many circumstances, *Roe v. Wade*[150] being the most notable example, and the concern about its occurrence probably leads the supreme courts to hesitate in many others. Much of Alexander Bickel's analysis in *The Least Dangerous Branch*[151] is devoted to the argument that precipitous decisions weaken the Supreme Court's legitimacy. The reason why the Court's legitimacy is vulnerable, in Bickel's view, is the "countermajoritarian difficulty," a rather dubious notion that will be criticized at length in the following chapter. But Bickel is certainly correct in observing that the Supreme Court exhibits a healthy solicitude for its political legitimacy, even if that legitimacy rests on firmer ground than he believed. To be sure, his area of concern is broader than doctrine creation; any decision that is likely to elicit controversy or that generates a conflict between high principle and practical politics challenges the

Court's legitimacy in Bickel's view.[152] But doctrine creation is generally the starkest assertion of authority by the judiciary, the time when it sticks out its proverbial neck the furthest. Creating doctrine precipitously, without waiting for the coordination process to generate a solution that seems relatively continuous with preexisting legal doctrine, is thus the situation that would raise the most serious legitimacy problems.

Bickel's recommendation is that the U.S. Supreme Court should employ a variety of procedural devices to avoid making definitive decisions prematurely.[153] Many criticisms have been voiced about his views, but two that are particularly relevant are that Bickel turns the Supreme Court into a political actor – and not just any political actor, but a craven, poll-watching, dispute-dodging political actor – and that he sanctions insincere subterfuges.[154] If Bickel's technique is limited to doctrine creation, however, these objections lose much of their force. There is nothing craven, or even excessively "political," about saying that one is not in a position to articulate a new legal doctrine until the lower courts have decided more cases, generated possible approaches for the Supreme Court to adopt, and indicated what sorts of ideas would be accepted by the judiciary as a whole. Similarly, there is nothing insincere about refusing to decide a case when one does not possess the legal doctrine required for decision. Of course, the lower courts do not have this luxury, but lower-court decisions do not have the same capacity to terminate the ongoing process of coordination – they do not, in Robert Cover's memorable phrase, possess the "juris-pathic" potential of a supreme court decision that operates by command and not coordination.[155] As noted earlier, judges of supreme courts sometimes abandon the inherent constraints of the coordination process, most notably the constraint of directionality, when they are appointees of a newly victorious political party. In effect, these judges are looking to the political mandate of that party for their legitimacy, and thus exchanging the inherently judicial rule of law, which is based on the constraints of coordination, for its popular or electoral equivalent.

We might speculate that the U.S. Supreme Court declined to rule on the basic issue of prison conditions because of a Bickelian concern about its legitimacy. It denied certiorari in all the major cases, preferring to lurk in the background and nibble at the edges of the rapidly developing doctrine. While this could have been a conscious strategy, it could also have manifested itself as the justices' felt experience of unease when confronted by yet one more certiorari petition from yet one more colossal prison litigation. The massive record, the innumerable issues, the lengthy retention of jurisdiction, and the fantastic level of detail made these cases look like vast and trackless quagmires. In addition, the Court might have been motivated by concerns less cosmic than its ultimate legitimacy. Sometimes people refuse to wade into a quagmire because they fear for their lives, but at other times they simply realize they will get their clothes dirty and need to spend an inordinate amount of energy to get across it. Both instincts presumably rank among the possibilities that would have motivated the justices to leave the prison conditions cases to the lower courts.

There are countervailing motivations, of course. One of the most common triggers, or "cues," or signals for the Supreme Court to address an issue being litigated in the federal court system is a conflict among the circuits.[156] This could be viewed as an effort to remedy defects in the coordination process, providing a definite resolution in cases where the lower courts were unable to settle upon one doctrinal idea that would coordinate their various integrative efforts. There were no such conflicts in the prison conditions cases, however; the doctrine developed smoothly and steadily, thus granting the Supreme Court the option of remaining uninvolved. Another reason the Supreme Court intervenes is that a majority of its members disagree with a particular lower-court decision.[157] But that did not happen either; the Supreme Court justices, even in the Burger–Rehnquist era, were federal judges after all, subject to the same motivations to nationalize the South, the same sense of revulsion toward the conditions that the cases had revealed, and, ultimately, the same human rights orientation of the post–*Brown* era.*[158] Perhaps they felt these motivations somewhat less strongly than the average lower-court judge, particularly those who had direct experience with state prisons, but the divergence was not nearly great enough to overcome their virtuous passivity.

Institutional Conceptualizations as Law

Of the four types of coordinating ideas that have been described, the type involved in the prison cases, institutional conceptualizations, seems to raise specific problems for the rule of law. These conceptualizations differ markedly from the labels, analogies, and metaphors that also serve a coordinating function. A label like "the right of privacy," a metaphor like "the chilling effect," and an analogy, like treating medical malpractice as an assault, all lead to recognizable legal rules. But institutional conceptualizations produce large arrays of rules, many of which possess a managerial, detailed quality that seems distinctly nonlegal. Thus, even if the other types of coordinating ideas are accepted as consistent with the rule of law, for reasons just presented, an institutional conceptualization might

---

* This was also true of the solicitor general, the attorney general and the president. Federal government request for review is another important cue for granting certiorari, but there was no such request in the state prison cases during the 1970s.

be regarded as failing to provide constraints that are general, clear, well accepted, and congruent with the existing legal order.

The reason an institutional conceptualization is recognizable as law, that is, as an element of legal doctrine and a constraint on judicial discretion, lies in the nature of the administrative state. To begin with, the administrative state has changed our views about the pace and scope of doctrinal innovation generally. This is not because it has diminished the importance of the rule of law the way it has diminished the importance of federalism. If anything, the rule of law seems increasingly important as the power and discretion of government expands. Federal courts were prepared to promulgate legal standards for prisons in the face of apparent rule-of-law constraints because creating doctrine is a standard role for American courts. As practicing judges, they recognized this role as inherently constrained and legal – in other words, as being consistent with the rule of law.

While the concept of law preceded the administrative state, the advent of that state tends to amplify it, attenuating the force of traditionalism and recharacterizing doctrine as an evolving structure that responds to changing circumstances. The doctrinal framework in general empowers judges to act, but our modern reinterpretation of it allows for more wide-ranging, comprehensive action. As a result, the role of doctrine as a constraint on the judiciary is reconceived in functional, rather than substantive terms. As Francis Mootz suggests, we now regard the rule of law as a principle for limiting the discretion of government agents, not as a fixed framework of either substantive or procedural principles.[159]

These changes in our concept of the doctrinal framework and the rule of law, like the changes in the doctrine of federalism, affect judges by being incorporated into their role expectations. Thus, modern judges have begun to believe that it is appropriate for them to develop new legal doctrines, at least within the limits set by the coordination process. They respond by making more conscious efforts to conceive or adopt coordinating ideas that create such doctrines. In other words, the governance style of the modern state motivates judges to overcome their traditional view that interpretation is the limit of judicial creativity, and to abandon their clandestine approach to judicial policy making. This process represents the second quantum shift in the continuum of legal decision making described earlier. The increasing acceptability of conscious policy making generates a greater willingness to engage in larger-scale efforts to move from labeling, through analogy and metaphor, to the more comprehensive approach of institutional conceptualization. This is probably a nascent, rather than a fully developed trend; most judges continue to be reluctant to see themselves as policy makers, but their reluctance seems to be decreasing. While they still struggle to portray all their actions as interpretive, the gradual abandonment of this legal fiction encourages the development of institutional conceptualizations.

The second way that the administrative state enables institutional conceptualizations to function as legal doctrine is more direct. The modern state's administrative or regulatory approach to governance makes institutional conceptualizations necessary by creating the large, public institutions and the comprehensive regulatory programs that serve as the subject matter of these conceptualizations. When the judges' attitudes produce a strong reaction to these institutions, they must develop institutional conceptualizations to translate those reactions into legal doctrine. To preclude this process would purchase simplicity at the price of effectiveness. If courts were to avoid developing coordinating ideas that related to the programs and institutions of an administrative state, they would hobble themselves from addressing contemporary problems in a way that their predecessors in the preadministrative era never did.[160] In other words, once we have an administrative state, it is virtually inevitable that many of the conflicts between doctrine and belief will involve large institutions; the only way for judges to coordinate their individual efforts to integrate this conflict will be to develop a conceptualization of the institution in question.

Despite the unfamiliarity of these conceptualizations, they are law in the sense that they are engendered by legal doctrine. They are, after all, not simply policy judgments about institutions, but a subset of those judgments that can function as coordinating ideas because they integrate judges' beliefs with preexisting legal doctrine. Like other types of newly created legal doctrine, institutional conceptualizations are constrained by the requirements of coordination. Those requirements are at least as stringent in the institutional context as they are in the often more familiar legal settings; in fact, they may be more stringent because of the complexity and controversiality of their subject matter. One indication of this is the apparent difficulty of developing such institutional conceptualizations, even in modern judicial decision making. The prison cases, after all, represent the clearest, most dramatic case. Their only rival is the mental institution decisions,[161] where courts adopted the Progressive era model championed by Adolph Meyer[162] and Clifford Beers[163] as their image of a well-run institution.*[164] Federal courts seemed to be on the verge of developing a similar concep-

---

* The coordinating idea in the mental institution cases was the "right to treatment," which was first articulated by Morton Birnbaum in a bar association journal. Its development paralleled that of the prison conditions cases, consisting largely of lower federal court cases decided in the late 1960s and 1970s. When the Supreme Court finally addressed the central issue, in 1982, it endorsed the

tualization regarding urban police departments in the 1960s. The elements of rationalized, externally supervised, rights-oriented police departments were beginning to emerge from various federal court cases, and models developed by the U.S. Department of Justice and fostered by the administration were available.[165] But in 1975, the Supreme Court quashed these developments in *Rizzo v. Goode*,[166] apparently because the attitudes of the Burger Court justices did not impel them to take such an interventionist approach on behalf of accused persons and inner-city communities. In other areas, such as broadcast regulation, no conceptualization ever developed. Despite rampant dissatisfaction with the Federal Communication Commission's highly discretionary mode of granting and monitoring broadcast licenses,[167] the federal courts have not been able to impose effective controls on this process. One possible reason is that no institutional conceptualization of a good radio or television station was available – indeed, First Amendment doctrine may have incorporated into the judges' role expectations a disinclination to develop such a concept.

Although institutional conceptualizations are law in the sense that they are generated by the doctrinal framework and constrained by the rule of law, they may not seem like law. As coordinating ideas, they seem different from labels, analogies, or metaphors, and the doctrine that results seems different from the rules for tort or contract. But on reflection, these reactions appear to be the product of preadministrative traditionalism. There is no general, theoretical reason to deny that the rules for a lawful institution or lawful agency behavior can constitute a body of law.

It is true that these rules are specific to an institution. But traditional, common-law rules are specific to an interaction; we have separate sets of rules governing consensual business relationships, blameworthy injuries, nonblameworthy injuries, bequests, the sale of real property, and a variety of other matters. Aficionados of the common law often claim that all these rules are derived from the same general principles, but that is a jurisprudential theory, not an accurate description of existing doctrine. Moreover, it is possible that the rules governing prisons, schools, and administrative agencies can also be traced back to general principles with the help of a similarly abstract theory. The common law operates at a level of generality no greater than the law of prisons, and there is no theoretical reason to assume that any claim to higher levels on the former's behalf could not be met by equivalent claims on behalf of the latter.

concept, but established the qualification that the patient's rights must be balanced against the state's interest in exercising its professional judgment. This is reminiscent of the Court's more restrictive rulings in recent prison cases, but the qualification came earlier, and was more broadly stated.

One might argue that common law possesses an internal logic that the law of prisons lacks. Contract law, it can be argued, consists of rules clustered around basic elements – offer, acceptance, performance, breach, and damages; because these elements are logically connected, and the rules that govern them derived from the concept of contract in general, they constrain the judge and preclude the expression of personal prejudice or political preference. The difficulty with this argument is that it fails to indicate what counts as logic. Precisely what is the internal relationship among a set of rules that would satisfy this criterion? In fact, the logic of contract law is approximately equivalent to the logic of a lasagna recipe. The individual elements relate to a definable entity and are comprehensible as a single body of rules, but they are not derived from each other or from some overarching principle. Perhaps offer and acceptance may be implied by our basic concept of a voluntary contract, but all the operative rules that determine whether offer or acceptance has occurred are prudential judgments that have become entrenched through time. What constrains the judge is not the fact that all the operative rules can be derived from general principles, but the mere fact that these rules have been established and now must be followed or explained away. The rules that the federal courts developed to govern prison conditions have at least this level of coherence. In fact, they may have more, for they can be traced to two coordinating ideas derived from general theories about punishment and modern institutions.

The Rehabilitative Model

Rehabilitative Design as a Coordinating Idea

We are now in a position to describe the way that federal judges created the legal doctrine of prison conditions as part of their policy-making process. Motivated by a conflict between the existing hands-off doctrine and their personal beliefs, they developed two institutional conceptualizations that coordinated their integrative efforts. These two ideas were that prison conditions should be designed to rehabilitate the prisoner, and that prisons should be bureaucratically organized. Both seem like odd choices, although for different reasons. Rehabilitation is a well-established goal for prisons, and usually regarded as a noble one, but by the time of the prison reform movement few people thought it could be achieved. Bureaucratization can certainly be achieved – indeed, we seem to achieve it as readily as wharves achieve barnacles – but we generally do not regard it as inherently desirable. The next two sections explore the reasons why these two coordinating ideas appealed to the courts, and the way that they generated the standards that the courts imposed on prisons.

The concept of rehabilitation, as a correctional philosophy, was a personal belief of most judges; for people who regarded themselves as enlightened – and federal judges generally did – it was the proper purpose of incarceration. This has been true ever since America adopted incarceration as its primary mode of punishment. The earliest penitentiaries, which developed during the Jacksonian era, were designed to teach virtue and good citizenship to their inmates.[168] The reforms of the Progressive era, which included parole, indeterminate sentences, education programs, vocational training, and grading prisoners for differential treatment, were all intended to rehabilitate.[169] Efforts to establish separate facilities for women and juveniles sprang from this same motivation.[170]

In fact, rehabilitation is virtually implicit in the idea of incarcerating convicted felons. Premodern Europe and America incarcerated people they wanted to control – those awaiting trial, those awaiting punishment, those who failed to pay their debts, or those who posed a political risk to the state – but they punished people convicted of a crime by means of physical pain, mutilation, execution, exile, or penal servitude.[171] Imprisonment was widely recognized as a possible mode of punishment[172] and occasionally used,[173] but it was probably not common. Most felons who were being punished by incarceration were actually sentenced to penal servitude; the reason they were confined in a building, as opposed to a maritime galley or a mine, was due to the particular nature of the tasks they were being compelled to perform.[174] In rustic, loosely administered America, imprisonment was virtually unknown.[175] Once reformers convinced the general society that other punishments, particularly corporal punishment and mutilation, were barbaric, incarceration became the dominant technique, the notion being that the criminal would be punished and potential criminals deterred by loss of liberty.[176] In exploring the development of penitentiaries, John Bender, borrowing the anthropological terminology of Victor Turner,[177] describes premodern incarceration as "liminal."[178] In entering the facility, the prisoner crossed a threshold from civil society into another world, cut off from that society and beyond the scope of its concern. "Randomness was one of the rules in the old prisons: the squalor, the disease, the possibility of escape, the periodic jail deliveries voted by Parliament. . . ."[179] The growth of the modern penitentiary, according to Bender, occurred when society developed the conceptual resources to penetrate that previously liminal world with a narrative scheme for the criminal's life, a scheme conceived as a progress from disobedience and degeneracy to responsive citizenship.[180] The story, of course, is the story of rehabilitation, and it is the concept of rehabilitation that gives the modern penitentiary its form.

The difficulty is that depriving a person of his liberty takes time; one can inflict as much pain, or perform as much mutilation, as the most bloodthirsty person would demand within the space of a few hours, but the deprivation of liberty for that length of time is a punishment appropriate for children who shoot spitballs in school, not for serious felons. To punish felons by depriving them of their liberty, the deprivation must last for years, or, according to our current thinking, years and years, and the question then arises: what does one do with the convicts during all this time? To inflict pain would be too harsh – a return to barbarity*[181] – but to entertain them would be unacceptably lenient. The most viable options are either to rehabilitate them or to use them as labor, and both approaches were common in American prisons. Rehabilitation was the enlightened approach, the one that embodied society's aspirations to reduce crime and create a better world.[182] The prisoner-as-source-of-labor model was, of course, the one used in the South. Confronted by the inhumanity that this approach produced in practice, and that seemed implicit in its design, federal judges naturally thought in terms of rehabilitation as the only proper way to treat incarcerated convicts.

But this attitude produced a conceptual dilemma for the judges, a dilemma that they were unable to resolve for several decades. Rehabilitation was a familiar element of Progressive politics, with no established or apparent relationship to legal doctrine. The judges could not simply declare that rehabilitation was constitutionally required; this would have allied them with one side of the dominant political debate of their formative years, which they could only have experienced as a purely political act. Moreover, they had learned in law school, or soon thereafter if they were elderly, that the courts had been wrong when they allied themselves with the opposing side of this very same debate in the substantive due process cases. To be sure, the judges were not immune from politics or motivated exclusively by neutral principles and undefiled doctrine. But neither were they willing to advance their political beliefs by taking actions they themselves perceived as lawless and unjustified. In order to act, they needed a coordinating idea that would integrate their attitudes with established legal doctrine.

Many of the complaints that prisoners had presented to the federal courts during the decades before 1965 invoked specific constitutional guarantees. The most common were that particular conditions violated the free-speech clause,[183] the free-exercise clause,[184] the due process clause,[185] or the equal protection clause.[186] In some cases, the courts held

---

* This prevailing view is challenged by Graeme Newman. His arguments are intriguing, but, as he readily acknowledges, they run contrary to a very prevalent and well-established set of contemporary beliefs.[186]

in favor of the prisoner; it was clear, for example, that prisoners had a right to consult their attorney, regardless of the hands-off doctrine, and that a writ of habeas corpus could be granted to secure this right.[187] None of these provisions seemed sufficient to address the basic issues, however, or to overcome the prevailing, doctrinally based belief that the general conditions in the prisons did not raise constitutional concerns. This was even true of the equal protection clause, the doctrinal workhouse of the Warren Court. Mississippi's Parchman Farm, for example, housed prisoners in a number of widely spaced barracks, called cages, all of which were strictly segregated.[188] As might be predicted, and as the Supreme Court held in *Brown v. Board of Education*,[189] such separation naturally led to worse treatment for the blacks and was thus unconstitutional.[190] But Mississippi could have remedied this violation by mixing the prisoner population of the cages and treating all the prisoners equally, and this would hardly have eliminated the great majority of Parchman's sins – its primeval housing, savage discipline, rudimentary or nonexistent medical care, and use of all the prisoners, black and white, as slaves.

The obvious solution was to rely on the cruel and unusual punishment clause, the one constitutional provision that directly and explicitly addresses criminal sanctions. But that clause had long been regarded as lacking any justiciable standards. In addition, the remedy that would follow from its violation was unclear. Had some state legislature passed a statute authorizing offenders to be drawn and quartered, a federal court could have readily invalidated it. But no court was going to issue an injunction against the use of prisons, and it was not apparent how any more specific injunction could be framed, since it would have involved administrative practices, not legislative policy. Habeas corpus seemed like a more obvious remedy, but because it evolved as a means of correcting an improper trial, the common remedy that it provided was release. As previously stated, there was some discussion about using it for more delimited relief, but the lack of standards seems to preclude that possibility.[191] Until Judge Henley's decisions in the Arkansas litigation, there was still no way for judges to integrate their Progressive beliefs, and their consequent dismay about conditions in the southern prisons, with the Eighth Amendment.

What Judge Henley held, in effect, was that a prison whose separate components were not designed to rehabilitate its inmates was engaged in cruel and unusual punishment. He specifically declared that rehabilitation itself was not constitutionally required, and that the absence of a rehabilitative program did not violate the Eighth Amendment.[192] Instead, he divided prison conditions into their components, and held that the failure of each component to be designed upon a rehabilitative model was a violation. He introduced this concept by stating:

> The absence of an affirmative program of training and rehabilitation may
> have constitutional significance where in the absence of such a program
> conditions and practices exist which actually mitigate against reform and
> rehabilitation. That is the situation that exists in Arkansas today, completely
> at Cummins and to a lesser degree at Tucker.[193]

By proceeding in this fashion, Henley immediately generated standards
for the cruel and unusual punishment clause that rendered it justiciable.
In effect, he penetrated the liminal world of the plantation-model prison
with the dominant narrative of rehabilitation. He also generated a remedial approach; using the authority established by *Monroe v. Pape*,[194] he
could enjoin prison administrators from maintaining any feature of the
prison that failed to meet the rehabilitative standard. Precisely how he
happened upon this concept is unclear; perhaps his step-by-step approach
to an egregious situation led him to parcel the prison's condition into its
component parts. In retrospect, the idea may seem obvious, but so does
Newton's law of gravitation.

However it originated, Judge Henley's idea clearly coordinated many
federal judges' efforts to integrate their personal beliefs with doctrine,
since it spread like wildfire. In the years following his 1970 decision in
Holt v. Sarver,[195] a number of federal courts adopted the idea that rehabilitation, while not constitutionally mandated per se,[196] was nonetheless
a principal aim of imprisonment and a crucial component of a constitutionally acceptable prison. Nor did this general instinct weaken over time.
Judge Kane's 1979 decision in the Colorado litigation was exceptional only
because it was so explicit on this point;[197] general use of a rehabilitative
model continues to this day. As in the Arkansas case, none of the cases
hold that rehabilitation was constitutionally required. But also as in Arkansas, they generally held that individual elements of the prison violated
the Eighth Amendment unless they were designed along rehabilitative
lines. Prisoners must be graded on the basis of their offense because mixing hardened criminals with first-time offenders was not conducive to
the latter's rehabilitation.[198] Due process was required before prisoners
were punished because it would teach respect for law rather than fear
and resentment of arbitrary power;[199] educational programs were desirable, if not required, because of their rehabilitative potential;[200] professional guards, not convict trusties, had to be used because the trusties
established a brutalizing, counterrehabilitative regime;[201] nutritious food,
competent medical care, and decent sleeping quarters were required because a starving, sick, or miserable prisoner will not be open to rehabilitative efforts.[202]

The constitutionally required model of rehabilitative design possessed
all the basic attributes of a coordinating idea. To begin with, it was fully
realized. Far from being an abstract legal argument, it constituted a com-

plete, fully developed set of standards for its subject matter. By the 1960s, the Progressive reform agenda for creating rehabilitative prisons was so well established and widely known that its attributes were conceptually available to most people, and certainly most judges, without reflection or research. Indeed, it had been explicitly endorsed by both the federal Bureau of Prisons and the American Correctional Association. This approach did not resolve every question federal judges faced – it said little about the physical design or administrative organization of the prison, for example – but it presented a clear, comprehensive set of standards for vocational programs, education, inmate classification, and staff training and contained clear implications in areas like food, medical treatment, cell conditions, discipline, and visitation rights.

Second, the rehabilitative model was delimited by its own terms. Had courts relied on a concept such as the due process right to individualized treatment[203] as the basis of prison reform,* the resulting doctrine would have contained vast implications for other areas such as probation, mental health, and education. The concept of rehabilitative design, in contrast, applied exclusively to prisons and other closely related institutions for the incarceration of the blameworthy, such as juvenile institutions. Although many larger legal trends contributed to the creation of this approach, none emerged from it; the whole concept was a sort of doctrinal sink. Thus, in the 1976 case of *Ingraham v. Wright*, the Supreme Court held that corporal punishment in public schools, no matter how severe, is not cognizable under the Eighth Amendment.[204] This newly stated hands off doctrine, at the height of the judicial prison reform movement, indicates the highly delimited nature of the prison reform standards.

Finally, the rehabilitative design approach possessed directionality. Although it led nowhere beyond its subject matter, it certainly emerged from a general development in legal doctrine. During the 1940s, the Supreme Court's focus shifted from questions of governmental power to questions of human rights.[205] The following decades saw a sustained effort by the federal courts to provide constitutional protection to specific groups of people, such as racial minorities, religious minorities, women, and aliens,[206] and to specific governmental activities, such as police practices, voting rules, and benefit distribution.[207] Prisoners were both a specific, victimized group and the subjects of a specific governmental policy; ex-

---

* The right to treatment was a coordinating idea for mental hospitals that developed simultaneously with the prison reform cases. The conceptual appeal of a right to treatment seemed to be as great as the right to a rehabilitative design, but it lacked the same long-term success. The reason may have been its less delimited character, although it may also have been its lack of implementability, a criterion that is discussed in the following section.

tending constitutional protection to them was thus a natural outgrowth of the developing doctrine. This does not mean that the prison reform cases were inevitable. Every doctrine has its stopping points; equal protection doctrine, for example, stopped short of holding wealth to be a suspect classification at the precise moment that the prison reform cases began.[208] Prisoners would have been easy to distinguish from minority groups or aliens had the judges not been motivated to include them. But given their motivation, the congruence of rehabilitative design with larger doctrinal developments facilitated the judges' use of this concept as a coordinating idea for creating a new Eighth Amendment doctrine.

The Implementability of the Rehabilitative Design

Coordination is one element of the process by which the judiciary develops solutions, and this, in turn, is one part of the classic mode of policy making. The development of a coordinating idea enables judges to promulgate rules for the subject matter in question; those rules operationalize the standards described in Chapter 5 and are elaborated through the implementation process that will be described in Chapter 7. In order to make public policy, the implementation process must be able to proceed and must produce identifiable changes. This means that the coordinating idea must possess a certain level of implementability. In theory, therefore, an idea could successfully coordinate the interpretative efforts of the judiciary but fail as a basis of judicial policy making because it could not be implemented. This is not a likely scenario, however, since it implies a highly schematic time sequence where judges develop a coordinating idea as an abstract proposition and then, upon applying it, discover its impracticality. In fact, as discussed in Chapter 1, and as will be elaborated in Chapter 7, a description of policy making that provides an alternative to the classic model is that of incrementalism, or muddling through. According to this approach, implementation efforts proceed as the idea is being formulated; each judge's integrative effort, prior to coordination, emerges from a real case and involves an implementation component. As a result, judges are unlikely to suspend their own integrative efforts and to coordinate their actions by adopting someone else's approach unless the new approach has already demonstrated its possibility of implementation. Even if judges follow the classic model of policy making quite strictly and fully develop the solution before implementing it, their practical experience will generally enable them to anticipate implementation problems; once again, the result is that an unimplementable idea will be unable to coordinate the judges' integrative efforts. This built-in control is likely to preclude the development of any truly farfetched coordinating ideas and suggests that implementability is a basic requirement for any idea to succeed as a basis for coordination.

Thus the implementation stage of judicial policy making not only generates inherent constraints, but also imposes constraints on the conceptual process. These constraints will be particularly severe when the coordinating idea consists of an institutional conceptualization, and thus relies on its relationship to an institution for its entire effect. The two most significant of these constraints can be termed comprehensibility and incrementalism.

Comprehensibility refers to the subject institution's ability to understand the coordinating idea that the judiciary has developed. In the case of prison reform, this was a fairly formidable requirement. Among the public officials of a single nation, there are few groups who inhabited such different worlds as federal judges and prereform southern prison administrators. Judges, as we have seen, thought in terms of rights – the concept of rights, albeit in different forms, was central to both their role expectations and their attitudes. Prison officials thought in terms of administrative responsibilities, the primary one, no matter what their philosophy, being the insistent, minute-by-minute management of a large mass of truculent criminals. For them, running a prison was a task whose extraordinary demands were counterbalanced only by the extraordinary discretion that they exercised. Theirs was a regime of men, not laws, and together with the military, they probably existed in the most law-insulated environment in our litigious, legalistic land. For southern wardens, this task of management was separated further from a prisoners' rights model by their attenuated but still powerful belief in the plantation as the proper way to control a subject population, and by the southern legislators' related belief that prisons should be run at a profit.

In the face of these conceptual differences, judges knew that they had to find a way of communicating with prison officials in order to implement their image of a constitutional prison. Their powers, after all, were limited. As will be described in Chapter 7, they adopted the role of administrators to carry out this implementation function, but their institutional position made them rather weak administrators. They could castigate a warden, hold him in contempt, declare him an enemy of the Constitution, perhaps even drive him crazy, but could not fire him and they could not appoint his replacement. They could not hire new staff. They could not order the construction of new prisons. They could not appropriate money. Thus, judges had to explain what they wanted and use the prison official's comprehension of their message to achieve their goal.

Rehabilitative design proved to be the judiciary's major tool for communicating across the conceptual chasm that separated judges from the targets of their efforts. Unlike prisoner's rights, it was an essentially administrative concept that had been generated within the correctional community and was part of that community's existing mental outlook. In deploying it, the judges were reflecting the aspirations of correctional administrators back to them, forcing the administrators to view themselves in the mirror of their own more progressive inclinations. Prison officials, like judges, are involved in an institutional thinking process, and the rehabilitative ideal served as a major method of integration between their own role expectations and their personal attitudes. In many prison systems, it was already the "party line," the rationale that prison officials themselves would offer as the basis for their actions.*[209] It also constituted the personal ideology of many prison administrators, in part because it was regarded as a reformist idea, an idea that – despite its long pedigree in American penology – retained association with "progressiveness" in many correctional contexts. It thus enabled many prison administrators to integrate their role expectations and their personal attitudes in an effortless manner that did not even demand a conscious coordination process.

To be sure, not every prison system recognized the desirability of the rehabilitative model; in particular, the southern states embraced the plantation model, but this had become a somewhat deviant position within the correctional community by the early 1960s. Thus, the rehabilitative model, although not adopted by southern prison officials, was not as foreign as a prisoners' rights model. The warden in Alabama may not have thought in terms of rehabilitation, but he knew that the warden in Wisconsin did and he could talk to that warden in administrative terms. More significantly, when the time came, the warden from Alabama could be replaced with the warden from Wisconsin, or with a reform-oriented prison social worker from an Alabama juvenile institution. In intermediate states, those less enlightened than Wisconsin but less benighted than Alabama, the judiciary's use of an administrative model had the effect of empowering the reform group within the correctional establishment, to

* The most notable evidence of this attitude, of course, is the American Correctional Association's 1959 version of the *Manual of Correctional Standards*, but there is other evidence as well. In a 1979 survey, prison administrators in Illinois consistently favored rehabilitation by overwhelming margins, invariably greater than any other identified group, including judges. The idea that rehabilitating prisoners is as important as punishing them was supported by 91.7% of prison administrators, compared with 81.8% of judges, 78.8% of prisoners, and 58.3% of the general public. When the question was whether prisoners should be given the chance to be rehabilitated, 76.7% of the public agreed, 93.5% of prison guards agreed, and 98.9% of judges agreed; for prison administrators, the figure was 100%.

the detriment of the old guards who constituted the old guard.*[210] As a result, the courts gained needed allies for producing change in states where they could not point to the extreme and un-American injustice of the plantation model. The partial acceptance of the rehabilitative ideal thus enabled judges to do indirectly what reformist administrators generally need to do – to replace the entrenched, traditional officials with their own people. Yet their own people nonetheless were other prison administrators, because the institutional idea that they adopted was essentially an administrative one. Had the judiciary remained within the confines of the prisoners' rights approach, they would have risked outright disobedience from state officials, or compelled those officials to replace the old warden with a lawyer, and in either case catastrophe would have almost certainly ensued.

Rehabilitative design was thus the central element in a complex, interinstitutional process. First, as we have seen, it enabled judges to coordinate their efforts to integrate their personal beliefs with their role expectations. Second, it enabled them to communicate with many prison officials, because rehabilitation was part of these officials' role expectations, part of their ideology, or both. Third, to the extent the judiciary could impose it, the rehabilitative model exercised a sort of hydraulic pressure on those officials who did not accept it. To live with this model, these officials had to change their views about appropriate institutional behavior. In some cases, these changes took place within the individuals who continued in their positions; in most, the changes proved too great for the individuals involved, and they had to be replaced. They could be replaced, however, with other prison officials who used the rehabilitative model as their own means of integrating their role and their beliefs.

The second form of implementability that an institutional reconceptualization must possess in order to function as an effective coordinating idea is incrementalism. One of the reasons the rehabilitative ideal appealed to judges as a means of creating prison conditions doctrine was because of the incremental character of the changes it produced. It is true that the judges instituted a rather thoroughgoing transformation of the southern prisons, and a virtually total extirpation of the plantation model. But they knew the alternative model they imposed was operationally feasible – it was being used, after all, in the federal prisons and in many states. They sensed that an institution could go from here to there in a

---

* This was also true, although to a lesser extent, in the deep South; there were reform efforts, based on distinctly Progressive ideas, in many southern states. Although these efforts generally had limited success, they indicate that the rehabilitative model was conceptually available to at least some prison administrators in these states.

fairly smooth, continuous pathway, since a number of prisons had done so, and the American Correctional Association was urging the remainder to follow. The significance of this cannot be overemphasized. A federal judge, sitting in his chambers, listening to the claims of some prisoners' rights lawyer who seemed to think all criminals were victims of social oppression, simply would not have intervened if he thought his intervention would rip the institution apart or force it to close and loose its savage inmates on the populace while it was being redesigned. The use of the rehabilitative model by real prison administrators assured the judges that these dire results would not ensue.

This, once again, is substantive rather than methodological incrementalism. It applies whether the mode of policy making is classical, incremental, or hermeneutic. As such, it is allied to the incrementalism of doctrinal changes, as described in the previous section of this chapter. It differs, however, because it applies to the doctrine's subject matter, not to the doctrine itself. The doctrinal form of substantive incrementalism suggests that new doctrine must be continuous with the preexisting body of legal rules, but it does not make any assertions about the doctrine's "real-world" effects. Thus, the Supreme Court's holding in *Reynolds v. Sims,* that unequal representation in state legislatures violates the Fourteenth Amendment, was a natural and delimited extension of equal protection doctrine,[211] but its effect on many states was quite abrupt. The same could be said of the school prayer, abortion, and numerous other decisions. What distinguishes these cases from prison reform was that they involved the creation of new doctrine by labeling, analogy, and metaphor, not by institutional reconceptualization. When an entire institution is being changed by judicial action, rather than by a rule or set of rules, the coordinating idea must not only be delimited, but must be capable of being implemented incrementally. From the judges' perspective, therefore, the new doctrine regarding prison conditions needed to be incremental along two separate axes; first, with respect to their own, preexisting legal doctrine and, second, with respect to the preexisting structure of the prisons that were being changed by virtue of that doctrine. Both forms of incrementalism are instantiated in the coordination process – the first because an idea will not coordinate most judges' integrative efforts if it is not continuous with preexisting doctrine, the second because it will not coordinate these efforts if judges think it is impractical.

There is, nonetheless, an obvious relationship between the delimited character of doctrinal creation and the incremental character of institutional change. As previously stated, the judiciary is an institution also, not a collection of self-contained moral philosophers, literary critics, or self-interest maximizers. When institutional change possesses a conceptual component – when it involves creating or assimilating new ways of thinking about an issue – a coordination process will generally be involved. Both judges and prison officials had to find ways of coordinating the integrative efforts that arose from divergences between their personal beliefs and their role expectations, and this coordination process contains a built-in incrementalism. In other words, the interaction of individual thought with institutional structure produces a demand for incrementalist approaches at both the conceptual and the operational level.

The Empirical Critique of Rehabilitation

Once it is established that an institutional conceptualization is capable of being implemented, the next logical question is whether its implementation will be effective, that is, whether reconceptualizing the institution will produce the desired results. This brings us face to face with the basic conundrum of the rehabilitative model. By the time the judicial prison reform movement hit its stride, there was a growing recognition that rehabilitation simply did not work. Ever since rehabilitative programs assumed their modern form in the Progressive era, empirical data of a decidedly negative sort had been accumulating. In the 1970s, the widely recognized work of Robert Martinson and the American Friends Service Committee reached particularly pessimistic results.[212] When Francis Allen published *The Decline of the Rehabilitative Ideal* in 1981, he concluded that this decline had become an accomplished fact during the 1970s[213] – the very decade when the courts were imposing the rehabilitative model upon American prisons in our nation's most aggressive program of judicial policy making.

Of course, the courts might have been hoping that prisons could find new methods of rehabilitation, but the prison reform movement was clearly not a source for such initiatives. There was never any effort on the part of the plaintiffs' attorneys, the judges, or their specially appointed masters to develop new methods of rehabilitating prisoners. The "better" institutions – the federal prisons, together with those in the belt of penalogical liberalism that ran from Kansas and Nebraska to Minnesota and Wisconsin – were never comprehensively attacked, and rarely attacked at all without their own acquiescence. Yet there was no evidence that they did a significantly better job at rehabilitation than other institutions, and, indeed, their "betterness" was not based on their ability to do so. Similarly, no federal judge ever contemplated a "results test," where the constitutionality of the institution was to be determined by its success in restoring its wayward charges to respectability.

In short, although the prison reform movement was a sustained attempt to impose the rehabilitative model on American prisons, it was undertaken without any empirical evidence that rehabilitation was a real possibility. It continued without any effort to develop new rehabilitative methods and without any evidence that the reforms that were imposed were producing the desired results. Indeed, by the end of the entire process, the assessment of the one million prisoners in America's vast archipelago might be similar to Dostoyevsky's personal assessment, more than one hundred years ago, of his experience in Siberia:

> I have said already that in the course of several years I never saw one sign of repentance among these people, not a trace of despondent brooding over their crime, and that the majority of them inwardly considered themselves absolutely in the right. This is a fact. . . . [P]risons and penal servitude do not reform the criminal; they only punish him and protect society from further attacks on its security. In the criminal, prison and the severest hard labour only develop hatred, lust for forbidden pleasures, and a fearful levity. . . . Of course, the criminal who revolts against society hates it, and almost always considers himself in the right and society in the wrong. Moreover, he has already endured punishment at its hands, and for that reason almost considers himself purged and quits with society.[214]

The explanation for the simultaneous decline and triumph of the rehabilitative design model lies in the function that this model served for the federal judiciary. This analysis is not intended to defend the rehabilitative model but to understand what rehabilitation really means. For surely it means something. The plaintiffs' attorneys, federal judges, and others who fashioned the prison reform movement may have been wrong-headed according to some people's lights, but they were neither crazy nor corrupt. It is all very well to condemn them for being excessively interventionist, but they could hardly have thought of themselves as adopting an impossible or ineffective goal for the sheer sake of intervention.

The difficulty with existing criticisms of the judiciary's approach on the basis of its failure to decrease the rate of recidivism, or to produce some other rehabilitative effect, is that it assumes that the purpose of imposing the rehabilitative model upon prisons was actually rehabilitation. While this may seem obvious, it adopts a criterion established by the rehabilitative design itself. The only other basis for arguing that the purpose of the rehabilitative design must be rehabilitation is a general obligation of sincerity – the idea that if Jane orders Fred to do something, Fred is usually entitled to assume that Jane actually wants that thing done. But the federal courts and the state prison systems are not Jane and Fred; they are complex social institutions, and we cannot assume that they should be assessed by the same criteria we use for individuals.

In fact, consideration of the prison reform cases suggests that the goal of rehabilitative design was not rehabilitation at all but the creation of a prison that judges regarded as morally acceptable. The judges needed an image or model of this type of prison, and the rehabilitative design served that purpose. A prison whose components were designed to facilitate the rehabilitative process was seen as the sort of prison that America should have, not because it would really halt recidivism, but because it corresponded to the national standards that judges had incorporated into their personal beliefs about the way a prison should be run. It is in this sense that Bender's notion of rehabilitation as a modern, narrative approach to punishment, standing in opposition of the premodern approach of quasi banishment to a different world, is more accurate than viewing rehabilitation as a thought reform model. Thus, the rehabilitative model satisfied the social morality that motivated judges and provided content for the previously empty doctrinal category of cruel and unusual punishment. By creating a prison that tried to rehabilitate the prisoners, that organized itself according to this goal, the judges were creating a prison that achieved their real goal of establishing a morally acceptable institution. That is what the judges meant when they held that the individual components of the prison must be designed along rehabilitative lines, but that there was no constitutional right to a rehabilitative program. Francis Cullen and Karen Gilbert observe that rehabilitation, despite the empirical attacks on its effectiveness, is the only correctional strategy that generates an obligation to care for the prisoners' needs, and that it continues to be a major motivation for correctional reform.[215] Norval Morris expresses the same notion when he states that although rehabilitation is no longer conceived as the purpose of imprisonment, nevertheless treatment programs should be continued and expanded during the time an inmate is being punished by incarceration.[216] Despite popular moves to "warehouse" offenders, rehabilitation continues to be embraced by forward-looking prison administrators. "We cannot force anyone to change," they typically declare, "all we can do is provide the opportunities for anyone who wants to change on his own."[217] Indeed, rehabilitation continues to serve as the primary coordinating idea within the move to "professionalize" prison administration.

This means of instituting a moral prison appealed strongly to federal judges because its inherent characteristics enabled it to function as a coordinating idea; it was fully realized, delimited in scope, and consistent with the general direction of the law. Moreover, it was implementable, a requirement for the category of coordinating ideas that conceptualize institutions. Prison officials understood the model – indeed, many of them had helped create it – and it could be imposed on prisons incrementally. In short, the rehabilitative design model, in addition to conforming to the judges' beliefs, provided them with a coordinating idea and reassured them, by its familiarity to correctional officials, that this idea was implementable. It was these purposes that the model was expected to fulfill, not the actual rehabilitation of the prisoners. That explains why Marion Penitentiary, probably our nation's most repressive prison, survived constitutional attack. There is something risible about the notion of rehabilitating prisoners who will never be released so that they can live a normal life in the general population at a level-five facility, but that notion, whatever its effectiveness, enabled federal authorities to constitute a moral prison. It was the morality of Marion – the fact that it was harsh but not cruel, purposive and not random or capricious – that rendered it acceptable to the federal judiciary.

The judiciary's use of the rehabilitative design may thus be described as deontological instrumentalism. The substantive idea of rehabilitation involves the use of various techniques and strategies to alter the prisoner's attitudes, so that he will become a law-abiding citizen upon release. This is an instrumental approach to the correctional process; one selects certain approaches, such as education, job training, and decent physical conditions in order to produce the desired effect of rehabilitation. But judges were not particularly concerned with the effect. They were interested in the techniques themselves, because these techniques, taken together, constituted an image of a moral prison; in other words, the appeal of the techniques was deontological.

Deontological instrumentalism is a category unknown to logic; more precisely, it is a category unknown to the grammar of individual thought, of which logic forms one part. Rehabilitative design was not generated by individual thought, however, but by an institution, specifically by the federal judiciary. Of course, an institution like the judiciary cannot really think; the point, rather, is that individuals think differently as members of an institution when they are deciding upon actions to be taken in the institution's name. In particular, they must coordinate their individual efforts to integrate their role expectations and their personal attitudes. Coordination involves a partial suspension of the individual's own thinking process and the acceptance of another's because of its ability to be agreed upon and implemented by all the members of the institution. It is a process by which individuals restructure their thoughts in response to their institutional position. Thus, an idea that an individual would use for one purpose can be adopted by a group of individuals within an institution for a different purpose if it aids in the coordination process. One can criticize the logic of this conceptual soufflé, but the criticism would only be applicable to the thought of individuals, qua individuals. When individuals think within institutional structures, the concepts they produce fulfill different purposes and respond to different rules.

The Normative Critique of Rehabilitation

But the problems with the rehabilitative ideal are not only empirical. There is also a normative difficulty, one that has produced several of the most thoroughgoing critiques of the entire concept. The effort to cure a criminal of criminality, critics claim, contains no natural limits; any action performed upon the prisoner, for any length of time, can be justified if it leads to rehabilitative results.[218] Thus, the rehabilitative model is nothing other than a special case of the morally unacceptable idea that the end justifies the means – adopting rehabilitation as an end or goal permits any means of punishment that is related to the goal, no matter how severe. This conjures up dramatic images of brainwashing, psychosurgery, and outright torture; more subtly, it suggests a medical model, where the prisoner is manipulated as an object rather than being respected as an autonomous, albeit errant, human being. Of course, one can invoke an independent principle, such as the Eighth Amendment, to provide some limitations – one can say that the rehabilitative program must be neither cruel nor unusual. But this is an unsatisfactory solution because it leaves rehabilitation as a potentially savage regimen that can only be controlled by external concepts, not as a source of Eighth Amendment morality. Moreover, the Eighth Amendment, even as currently interpreted by the federal courts, would allow numerous practices that most proponents of rehabilitation would find unacceptable. For example, it suggests that the length of a person's sentence would be measured by the time required for true rehabilitation, rather than by the seriousness of the original offense.[219]

These normative concerns, when combined with the empirical data indicating that the rehabilitative model does not rehabilitate, have spawned proposals for alternative approaches. Apart from rehabilitation, the classic purposes of punishment are general deterrence, special deterrence, retribution, just deserts, and incapacitation. All of these, with the possible exception of general deterrence, were regarded as social atavisms by the Progressive reformers, and all have experienced revivals as the reformers' rehabilitative model has come under attack.[220] Just deserts and incapacitation currently possess a particular appeal, the former through the rejection of social science explanations of behavior, the latter as a second-best, or least-worst, option in our increasingly cynical times.

The claim that the dark side of the rehabilitative model includes mind control, electroshock, and psychosurgery is a dramatic one, but the reason it exercised virtually no effect on judges is not difficult to discern. That claim applies only to individual thought, where the proponent of an idea is properly charged with its conceivable ramifications.

It is thus a relevant and perhaps persuasive answer to MacCormick and Menninger,[221] but it has little application to the rehabilitative model that the federal judiciary imposed on state prisons. That model was a coordinating idea, a means of conceptualizing a morally acceptable correctional regime. No matter what its theoretical linkages to thought control, it was no more likely to lead judges down that path than their invalidation of school prayer would lead them to demand that schools build marble alters to secular humanism. Moreover, judges understood that this same characteristic of institutional thought eliminated any danger that prison officials who adopted a rehabilitative model would start brainwashing the prisoners. In the institutional context of American prisons, rehabilitation is a coordinating idea for enlightened, reform-oriented officials, not a theory that favors any strategy for changing prisoners' personality structures. As such, it has a great deal more to say about whether the prisoners get a green vegetable with lunch than it does about the use of mind control techniques.

There is an interesting piece of historical evidence that supports and illustrates the status of rehabilitation as an institutional idea allied to decent treatment, not invasive therapies. This evidence is the occurrence of a nonevent. As noted, rehabilitation has long been the explicit philosophy of many American prison administrators. In the early decades of this century, the rehabilitative methods that observers would have identified consisted of an informal and clearly unsatisfactory mixture of work, vocational training, education, and exhortation. Then, in the 1930s, an extraordinary thing occurred; someone developed a scientific method of rehabilitation that actually worked. The person was Ivan Pavlov, and the method, of course, was thought reform, informally know as brainwashing.[222] Pavlov's method was a simple one, consisting largely of the sustained application of stress. Enough stress will generally cause a person to recant; Pavlov's method was to continue applying stress until the person not only recanted but went blank and actually lost his beliefs. The Pavlovian brainwasher thus penetrates all levels of consciousness, the submissive as well as the defiant, and reaches that same subconscious core that Freud had explored with his more humanistic probes. What was remarkable about Pavlovian thought reform was that it provided an objectively verifiable, mechanical method for achieving effects that were previously accessible only to the uncertain, impressionistic process of persuasion. It seemed to work, moreover, on virtually everyone: in Pavlov's terse phrase (his experiments were performed largely upon dogs), "every dog has his breaking point."[223] The real effectiveness of Pavlov's method can be questioned,[224] but at the time it became known in the United States – and at least through the production of *The Manchurian Candidate* in 1962[225] – most Americans were convinced of its effectiveness.

The conundrum, then, is why American prison authorities so rarely adopted Pavlovian methods. Of course, they flirted with behavioral techniques from time to time,[226] but no prison ever adopted Pavlovian thought reform as a comprehensive approach, or even as a particularized response to assaultive or disruptive individuals. Prison officials claimed to believe in rehabilitation, they presumably believed in science because virtually everyone did, and Pavlov had just discovered a scientific method of rehabilitation that actually seemed to work. What held them back would hardly have been squeamishness, or a concern for the rights of prisoners. Prisoners had no rights in those days, and the regime to which they were subjected contained enough verbal degradation, physical abuse, and sensory deprivation to provide the raw materials for any Pavlovian technician. Moreover, the mental patients of the day, more despised than criminals perhaps, but hardly more condemned, were regularly subjected to lobotomies, electroshock, and other procedures that would have made a little darkness-at-noon sleep deprivation seem mild by comparison. The Eighth Amendment, to be sure, prohibited outright torture, but, as we have seen, it was regarded as nonjusticiable. Besides, use of Pavlovian techniques would not have been a mode of torture but a mode of treatment – painful perhaps, but hardly more painful than the punishments that were fully accepted at the time.

The reason that prison officials' commitment to rehabilitation did not lead them in this direction, whatever the internal logic of that connection in the realm of individual thought, is that this approach is essentially an institutional idea, one that operates according to a different grammar than ideas in the realm of individual thought. For prison officials in the first half of the twentieth century, rehabilitation was part of a generalized, progressive approach to corrections, not an abstract goal to be achieved by any conceivable means. In fact, for these officials, the means they perceived as leading to rehabilitation – educational and vocational programs, classification, good-time credits, and parole – were as central to the concept as the goal of rehabilitation itself. That does not necessarily invalidate the critique of rehabilitation, for the effectiveness of the critique depends on the criteria one chooses for evaluation. If one decides that institutional ideas should be evaluated according to their implications in the realm of individual thought, the critique presents an argument many people would find quite persuasive. But if one decides that these implications only matter if they will actually occur in the real, institutional setting to which they refer, then the critique is essentially irrelevant.

This same discontinuity between individual and institutional thought explains the reason the rehabilitative model has displayed continued appeal to judges, while the alternative rationales for imprisonment have exercised little effect. These alternatives may seem persuasive to scholars or legislators, and may even serve the latter as coordinating ideas. But they do not translate into an institutional program, and are thus largely irrelevant for judges who need an institutional conceptualization, or prison administrators who need an operational strategy. Unless we are prepared to impose some punishment other than the loss of liberty, the alternatives to rehabilitation can only affect the length of the prisoner's sentence. It is not difficult to imagine other options; indeed, the lugubrious truth is that punishment has provided one of the most fecund fields for human creativity.[227] We could punish those convicted of assault, for example, according to a general deterrence model (flog them in public), a special deterrence model (flog them a lot), a retribution model (give their victims a chance to assault them), a just deserts model (have state officials assault them), or an incapacitation model (cut off their hands). Since we are not prepared to impose any of the Dantean sanctions, the only variable is the length of the sentence. Deterrence translates into long sentences, retribution into longer ones, just deserts into proportional sentences, and incapacitation into sentences that keep the felon in prison until he is at least thirty-five years old. While the just deserts or justice model would appear to be a general theory of punishment, the only correctional implication that its proponents have been able to derive from it is determinate sentencing.

But it is at this point, once these various theories have completed their work, that the task of prison officials and prison reformers begins. What is one to do with the criminals once they have been locked up in the facility, for however many years one has determined? Only the rehabilitative model seems to provide much guidance for the institution; only that model indicates how the prisoners should be grouped, how they should spend their time in the facility, and what sort of supervision they should receive.*[228] This is the reason, as stated at the outset of this section, that rehabilitation is virtually implicit in the modern concept of incarceration. Deterrence, retribution, just deserts, and incapacitation are all older concepts, and as long as we are unwilling to tolerate their more sanguinary

* Proponents of the just deserts model sometimes assert that their approach will produce more orderly, well-managed prisons. But that is not really just deserts; it is a managerial objective, with no relationship to the nature of the crime that the inmate has committed. Perhaps it could be argued that a just deserts approach to citizens in general also implies a just deserts approach to prisoners, so that prisoners should be strictly punished for disciplinary infractions in the prison. But everyone agrees that prisoners should be punished for disciplinary infractions, including rehabilitationists; the only disagreement involves the severity of the sanctions. The just deserts model does not tell us what should be done with prisoners when they are not committing disciplinary infractions.

implications, they have little to say about the design of penitentiaries. Modern prison officials are confronted with the overwhelming pragmatic task of doing something with the prisoners while they are imprisoned, and federal judges were confronted with the equally pragmatic task of reforming that function so that it satisfied our general standards of morality. Rehabilitation, no matter how often it was criticized, and no matter how many alternatives to it were proposed, remained the only theory that provided guidance, and that was the theory judges used to generate their coordinating idea for reform.

The Bureaucratic Model

Bureaucratization As a Coordinating Idea

The prison reform cases reveal a second coordinating idea that partially overlaps with rehabilitation. This was the concept of bureaucratization. As James Jacobs noted in his study of Stateville Penitentiary,[229] the effect of the judicial decisions was to bureaucratize prisons, to impose the kind of purposive-rational order that Weber identified as the cold soul of modern governance.[230] The case studies in Part I confirm this observation. By the end of the judicial prison reform movement, virtually all state systems had instituted formal hierarchies, written policies, routinized procedures, and fixed credentials for staff positions. They had instituted the requirement that prisoners receive regular due process hearings before being subjected to punishment for misbehavior, a punishment that was now referred to as "administrative segregation." They had acquired legal staffs that were assiduously consulted before changes were made or initiatives were undertaken. This is not to say that these features were "rational" or efficient in any glorified sense. All it means is that prisons had become ordinary departments of an ordinary governmental agency, with all the bureaucratic accoutrements that any modern agency possesses.

The bureaucratizing effects of the prison cases result from the courts' demand for managerial regularity. It was cruel and unusual punishment, they held, to subject prisoners to arbitrary punishment,[231] to use armed trusties rather than paid, hierarchically organized employees,[232] to provide inadequate or disorganized health care,[233] and to use prisoners to support the institution rather than relying on regular state appropriations.*[234] More generally – and this emerges from the remedial orders rather than the liability decisions – it was literally cruel and unusual for prison ad-

---

* Weber specifically notes the dependence of bureaucracy on the money economy. His observation that bureaucratized officials are compensated with money salaries is linked to his characterization of office holding as a vocation.

ministrators to be disorganized, informal, or ad hoc: cruel, because the inevitable result was mistreatment of the prisoners, unusual because that is not the way that institutions in a modern state are managed.*[235] In other words, the Eighth Amendment could only be satisfied by a bureaucratically organized and effectively managed institution.

It is important to recognize that bureaucratization is not coextensive with the process of reform but simply a particular reform conception. Other methods of reform were possible. In the prebureaucratic prison, reform was often achieved by charismatic leadership;[236] a leader who was regarded as incompetent or depraved was replaced by another who was efficient and kind. According to Robert Hughes, when Alexander Maconochie became commander of the notorious prison colony of Norfolk Island, he brought both fairness and empathy with a dramatic suddenness that the bureaucratic model could not possibly achieve.[237] This makes good theater; as recently as 1980, the motion picture *Brubaker* – a fictionalized account of the scandalous conditions which precipitated the Arkansas prison case – presented Robert Redford as a humane but forceful warden who brings his own form of salvation.[†238] We are not likely to see a movie about the judicial reform of prisons, and if we do, we are still less likely to see Robert Redford, even at his present age, playing Judge Henley. Bureaucratization represents a different, less photogenic conception of reform. In place of heroism, it offers regularity; in place of individual leadership, it offers generalized routine. Thus bureaucratization is not reform itself, but only our notion of reform. It is a cultural style, one element, and perhaps the major element, in our repertoire of governance techniques.

The steady and rapid bureaucratization of prisons as a result of the prison cases is recognized by almost all observers,[239] but the general view is that bureaucratization was an undesired by-product of the reform process. It occurred because powerful forces in society move our institutions

---

* Even when cutting back on prisoners' rights, the courts often championed the virtues of bureaucracy. For example, in *Sardin v. Connor*, the Supreme Court argued against finding that prison regulations created liberty interests under the due process clause on the ground that doing so would discourage the promulgation of written guidelines that curb staff discretion. Such guidelines are important, the Court said, because "they confine the authority of prison personnel in order to avoid widely different treatment of similar incidents."

† Hughes reports that Maconochie was probably the only prison administrator who had been in prison himself (as a prisoner of war), and the film depicts Brubaker as beginning his term by masquerading as an ordinary prisoner. This again suggests that empathizing with the prisoners – a common reaction among judges once they had abandoned the hands-off doctrine – is a strong motivation for reform.

inexorably in this direction, generally without our conscious effort and frequently against our conscious desires.[240] The rather negative connotations of the term "bureaucracy" support this view; just as urban developers may create ugliness but do not consciously impose it, or teachers create confusion but do not strive for it, so it is difficult to imagine judges purposely imposing something that we regard as at least a disadvantage and perhaps a disaster.[241]

But this image of inexorable, undesired bureaucratization is a mechanistic one which minimizes the role of institutional ideas. It may be accurate in certain situations, but it is not always accurate, and it does not apply to the judicial prison reform effort. In that setting, bureaucratization was a coordinating idea, a comprehensive, fully realized image of a properly run prison. It enabled federal judges to promulgate rules, one of the basic elements of policy making, by creating a new body of legal doctrine. Overlapping heavily with the rehabilitative design model, it amplified that model's force but it also imposed standards in areas where rehabilitative design provided relatively little guidance.

Bureaucratization possessed all the elements of a coordinating idea. It was fully realized because it constitutes a comprehensive, well-understood image of an institution. The federal Bureau of Prisons certainly provided a clear example of bureaucratized prisons, but in this case an example was not even necessary. Anyone familiar with modern government knows what a bureaucratic institution looks like and, with relatively little mental effort, can easily imagine what would be required to bureaucratize a prison, a liberal arts college, a boy scout troop, or any other organized collection of human beings.

In addition, the bureaucratization concept displayed directionality; it constituted a major theme in modern constitutional and administrative law. The most obvious manifestation of this trend is probably the due process movement, which began in the mid-1960s,[242] received a decisive imprimatur from the Supreme Court in 1969,[243] and continued as one of the dominant themes in the constitutional jurisprudence of the 1970s and 1980s.[244] By holding that public employees could not be dismissed, benefits could not be rescinded, penalties could not be imposed, and licenses could not be revoked without notice and an opportunity for a hearing of some kind,[245] the Court required government agencies to develop written rules and standardized procedures to support their actions and to prepare a record from which they could argue each individual case against an attorney for the other side. Other institutional rights produced similarly bureaucratizing effects in particularized contexts; the Fourth and Fifth Amendment rights of the accused standardized many practices of local police departments,[246] while equal protection rights and affirmative action programs standardized the admissions, personnel, and benefit allocation procedures of innumerable institutions.*[247] Thus, the prison cases fit securely into the contemporaneous developments of administrative due process and related doctrines that were not only well established but steadily expanding in scope.

The delimited character of the bureaucratic ideal is closely related to its directionality. Because the trend toward bureaucratization was so powerful in other areas of law, the use of that idea for prisons posed little danger of unforeseen implications. Of course, the implications of the due process movement generally were quite extensive, but prisons were just a side channel in the vast stream of these decisions. Virtually no one argued that some other institution should be bureaucratized because this process was occurring in the prisons. The bureaucratization model was not intrinsically limited to prisons, as rehabilitative design was, but since the same process was already occurring in so many others areas, the bureaucratization of prisons could be viewed as a delimited process with virtually no collateral effects.

Because bureaucratization was an institutional conceptualization, the most extensive form of coordinating idea, it was subject to the additional requirements of implementability. Again, this posed no particular difficulty. As David Garland indicates,[248] the bureaucratization and routinization of punishment, quite apart from any change in legal doctrine, is a long-term trend that has affected every aspect of the criminal justice system. Almost all prisons were at least partially bureaucratized, and because many were as bureaucratized as the courts would ever demand, the concept was clearly communicable and incremental. Indeed, the insufficiently bureaucratic prisons, the ones being run as personal fiefdoms of the warden or as antebellum plantations, were probably perceived as outliers even before the courts became involved. This meant that imposing a bureaucratic model would not create extensive disruption in existing institutions, and that the courts could obtain support for their initiative, as well as a supply of properly minded prison officials, from within the correctional establishment.

While all of this is reasonably apparent, the hypothesis that judges were using bureaucratization as a coordinating idea does present one rather formidable difficulty. This involves the judges' attitudes. The concept of bureaucracy, however familiar, carries decidedly negative associations; re-

---

* Lauren Edelman has explored the increased bureaucratization that has developed in business organizations in response to antidiscrimination law. As part of a litigation avoidance effort, firms have established expanded personnel departments, developed personnel policies, initiated training programs, and the like. In short, they have bureaucratized their hiring and promotion and employee relations programs in order to conform to the new laws.

habilitation, in contrast, was viewed as a positive although perhaps impractical ideal. Why then would judges want to employ bureaucratization as a coordinating idea for institutional reform? It is certainly understandable that bureaucratization would occur as a by-product of other developments; indeed, given its overlap with ideas about rehabilitation, the imposition of a rehabilitative design model would inevitably have resulted in substantial bureaucratization. The prison reform decisions, however, suggest that bureaucratization was not a by-product of rehabilitative design or any other concept, but a separately motivated coordinating idea, generating rules that neither rehabilitation nor prisoners' rights demanded. Judges did not impose bureaucratization per se – that would hardly have been a tenable position – but only imposed the separate components of bureaucratization that reflected this implicit norm. As a result, it is also necessary to explain why bureaucratization can be described as a coordinating idea when it was not being consciously imposed. This inquiry will provide further insights into the nature of coordinating ideas and their role in creating legal doctrine.

Bureaucratization as an Antidote

To understand the independent force of bureaucratization, one must first understand what it was designed to replace. Identifying the general model that the judges opposed is not difficult; Weber's characterizations of charismatic and traditional organizations serve quite well in this regard. But these are technical-sounding terms, themselves the product of a rationalistic, bureaucratized analysis that places things in categories and enumerates their characteristics. Weber and the sociologists who followed him classify societies the way the bureaucratized prison classifies prisoners. A real understanding of the concerns that underlay the bureaucratic model requires that we not only identify its nonbureaucratic predecessor, but appreciate the appeal that this preceding model possessed.

But the prebureaucratic prison was itself an anachronism, a small tentacle of a long-gone social order whose extension into the twentieth century was so attenuated, so distant from its source, that it could be readily stomped into jelly by a relatively weak governmental institution like the judiciary. In earlier times, however, it possessed great power, power that modern rationalistic, bureaucratically conditioned minds find difficult to grasp. To understand the judiciary's real concern, therefore, we will turn to literature as a means of providing vivid access to bygone sensibilities. In this case, there is a particularly relevant work that deals directly with the exact issue of changing sensibilities and does so using prisons as a context. This is the well-known story by Franz Kafka, ''In the Penal Colony'' (Der Strafkolonie).[249]

"In the Penal Colony" is set in an island prison where the execution of a prisoner is about to occur. The instrument of execution is a complex "piece of apparatus" placed in a "small sandy valley, a deep hollow surrounded on all sides by naked crags."[250] In this harsh arena are the condemned man, an officer of the colony, and an explorer, who is present at the invitation of the colony's commandant. The officer explains the operation of the apparatus to the explorer: it consists of a "Bed," into which the prisoner is strapped, a set of needles called the "Harrow," which move across the prisoner's back, and a "Designer," which controls the needles. Once set in motion, the apparatus cuts an elaborately lettered inscription into the condemned man's back with its needles. The procedure takes twelve hours. At about the sixth hour, as the officer explains, "[e]nlightenment comes to the most dull-witted. It begins around the eyes. From there it radiates. A moment that might tempt one to get under the Harrow oneself. Nothing more happens than that the man begins to understand the inscription, he purses his mouth as if he were listening. You have seen how difficult it is to decipher the script with one's eyes; but our man deciphers it with his wounds."[251]

The particular prisoner in the story has been sentenced to death for shouting at a captain of the prison colony, who had lashed him across the face for his failure to salute the captain's door. For this, he is to die by having the words "Honor thy superiors!" cut into his back by the apparatus. The explorer is astonished to learn that the prisoner does not know the sentence, does not know that he has been sentenced, and never had a chance to present a defense. Instead, he was sentenced by the officer on the basis of a report by the affronted captain. The officer explains that he was appointed as judge by the former commandant, who is now deceased. He continues: "My guiding principle is this: Guilt is never to be doubted. Other courts cannot follow that principle, for they consist of several opinions and have higher courts to scrutinize them. That is not the case here, or at least, it was not the case in the former Commandant's time. The new man has certainly shown some inclination to interfere with my judgments, but so far I have succeeded in fending him off and will go on succeeding."[252] As the officer readies the apparatus, he begins complaining about the new commandant's unwillingness to maintain it properly, and the man's reservations about the colony's overall system of punishment. In former times, the officer wistfully recounts, the executions were events of pageantry. The entire valley was filled with people who came to watch, and who crowded around the condemned man's face as his moment of realization approached. Now, the valley is empty and the new commandant is anxious to institute more modern methods of punishment. But he is reluctant to do so at once, according to the officer, because the old system still has numerous adherents in the colony; indeed, the new commandant is looking to the explorer to provide moral support for his initiatives. This gives the explorer an opportunity to strike a crucial blow to preserve the old system, the officer explains; all he need do is speak out, to announce his admiration for the dignity and justice of the method of execution that is being demonstrated to him.

But the explorer's sympathies lie entirely with the new commandant; indeed, as he listens to the officer, he has been thinking of ways in which he can intervene to abolish the process that he is about to witness. Although impressed by the officer's sincerity, he tells the man, quite decisively: "I do not approve of your procedure."[253] The officer now realizes that he has lost his struggle against the new commandant's reforms. He releases the prisoner, and readjusts the Designer to inscribe a different message – "Be Just." He then removes his clothes, straps himself onto the Bed, and switches on the apparatus. But the mechanism has gone awry; wheels and gears come flying out of the Designer and the Harrow blindly stabs the officer to death.[254]

The story, of course, cannot be taken literally; like most of Kafka's works, it is an allegory about our relationship to God. The underlying theme of "In the Penal Colony," roughly stated, is the desanctification of the modern world and the individual's resulting loss of faith. The old commandant is not necessarily God, but he is surely endowed with both the power and majesty of the divine.* His apparatus of torture is a vivid symbol of a harsh but accessible divinity, which subjects us to a life of suffering but holds out a promise that, through faith, we will perceive a pattern or meaning to our suffering and be redeemed. Our guilt is never to be doubted, as the officer proclaims, and there is no appeal from the sentence, but there is a design to our ordeal, and our ability to perceive that design is our compensation and salvation. To those who believe in such salvation, this is a just regime, and that is why the officer views justice as the motto by which he lives and hopes to die.

But our ability to believe in, or even to perceive this harsh and just path to redemption is fading rapidly. Our rationalism and our lack of rootedness puts us in the place of the aptly titled explorer, or, in the contemporaneous words of Joseph Conrad, "tourists in the lobby of a large, garish hotel."[255]† Our democratic notions of justice illuminate the arbitrary, oppressive nature of the sacerdotal order at the same time that they obscure its promise of redemption. Even if we try to return to the

---

* The old commandant's gravestone asserts that he will rise again and lead his adherents to recapture the colony.

† Even religion has been rationalized, Kafka suggests. The priest of the penal colony will not allow the old Commandant to be buried in the church yard, so his supporters have placed his grave in the floor of a roadside teahouse.

prior world, we find our pathway blocked; we cannot recreate its meaning and its majesty, but only suffer from their disappearance and become mangled by their outdated, inoperative remains.

To express this metaphysical theme, Kafka constructs a parable about a prison reform that bears a remarkable similarity to James Jacobs's account of the changes at Stateville Penitentiary. This is not an accident. Although Kafka is not writing about prison reform, the metaphysical transformation he describes is part of a social process that affects, and indeed is expressed through, changes in social institutions such as prisons. In other words, while the story describes the spiritual journey of the individual, it is a journey that necessarily moves in one direction because it is linked to changes in society at large. With his older contemporary Max Weber, Kafka (who, like Weber, was trained as a lawyer) perceived the demise of traditional society and patriarchal leadership as the triumph of a rational, legalistic order. Kafka unites the individual experience of rationalism and the loss of faith with a social evolution that is exemplified in his parable of penal reformation. He not only tells us about both developments, but, by virtue of his art, he tells us about the link between the two, a link that not only exists from the social observer's point of view, but for us, within our individual experience.

Kafka's story gives us access to the powerful but distant ideology whose lonely outpost in our modern, rationalist culture was the old-time prison. The regimes of Joseph Ragen at Stateville and George Beto in Texas were not depraved repositories of sadism; they were not Devil's Island or Maquarie Harbour, to say nothing of Auschwitz and Dachau. Rather, they represented an entire world view of patriarchal leadership and strongly held values that punished severely but promised purification and redemption. To win the approval and respect of these old-time wardens or their subalterns was to expiate one's crimes and to be validated as a law-abiding citizen again* – hence, both men's well-known kindness to ex-cons who took the "straight path" after their release.[256] In Mississippi, several governors, declaring themselves the judge of a "mercy court," visited the state's prison farms, interviewing convicts and granting pardons; they also tended to issue pardons in batches on Christmas, New Year's Day, Thanksgiving, and the Fourth of July.[257] In both its southern and more general versions, the old-time prison treated the prisoner as a subject and followed the motto of Kafka's officer that guilt will always be assumed. Both versions

---

* Whether true expiation for black prisoners was ever possible in the South, given the culture's endemic racism, is an open question. While class differences would not have precluded this process, since they were even more extreme in premodern culture, race might well have precluded the forgiveness or sense of expiation that traditional society offered its ex-convicts.

emphasized obedience without question and punishment without warning, but offered paternalistic approval as their path to expiation and social reintegration. Whether this was ever actually achieved depends on the psychology of the prisoners and the observer's assessment about the possibilities of rehabilitation. But whatever the results, it would appear that the prebureaucratic prisons possessed their own image of justice, one that our civilization lived with for several millennia. It is a formidable image which we would be hard-pressed to disprove by any objective means lying outside the recently acquired value system that has led to its rejection.

This preexisting ideology, moreover, has an intrapersonal correlative that remains alive today, as a matter of individual psychology. For every person who demands justice and chafes under arbitrary restrictions, there is another who craves fixed rules and the approval of superior authority. This latter personality may well be disproportionately represented among prison populations. While the idea of a prisoner who prefers harsh paternalism to due process is a threatening notion to our liberal ideology, any visitor to a prison cannot help noting the infantalized character of many prisoners and dependence upon the authorities that they display. Something in so many of us inarticulately yearns to relinquish our will in return for guidance and approval. We reject this inclination, as a matter of contemporary ideology, but its continued existence makes the premodern image of the prison all the more threatening to us.

By the 1960s and 1970s, almost any federal judge's personal beliefs would have motivated him to combat the once appealing but now repugnant ideology of the prebureaucratic world that had remained alive in American prisons. As long as judges saw themselves as disabled from intervening, the discretion of the prison authorities seemed to be a solely jurisdictional phenomenon. With the jurisdictional barrier removed by the rejection of the hands-off doctrine, the prebureaucratic prison was revealed as a disturbingly familiar, now unacceptable regime of patriarchal leadership, presumed guilt, harsh punishment, and paternalistic subjugation. As liberal rationalists, judges saw this regime as something that ought to be destroyed.

Since the judges' personal opposition was ideological in origin, it did not matter whether the prebureaucratic prison was well-run or mismanaged, balanced or depraved. In some sense, the well-run prebureaucratic prison was more threatening than its chaotic counterpart. The latter certainly made an easier target; accounts of conditions that even the old-time wardens would agree were inhuman or mismanaged carried a judicial opinion along nicely, while jousting with the vaguely articulated zeitgeist of a bygone era could prove more challenging. But, in the final analysis, a demonstration that the prison was efficiently run did not protect it from a finding of unconstitutionality. The judges were reacting to the moral statement of the old regime, an image of human beings that had survived in the insular environment of prison but was repugnant to their ideology of rights and democratic liberalism.

The prison reform decisions often spoke in terms of rights, not bureaucratization, but the enforcement of rights was generally an instrumental means of achieving the judiciary's larger purpose. Because bureaucratization was a unified conception, implementing one part of it could pull the other parts along. Due process for prisoners was the element most closely linked to individual rights, because it possesses explicit textual support in the Constitution. Written policies were intermediate; there is no clause in the Constitution that could reasonably be viewed as requiring it, but one could argue that a variety of constitutional violations lurked within any system that was informally administered. Classifying prisoners by intuition – a wonderful way to assert absolute authority, to dispense punishment and mercy – could easily be a means of racial discrimination or the suppression of due process rights; the natural antidote was written classification policy. Credentialism was the most difficult to impose and virtually impossible to require at the level of the warden and his top officials, but it was the most crucial from the administrative perspective. Judges were not able to issue a direct command that wardens and guards possess formal credentials, but they could do so, in effect, simply by requiring all the others elements of bureaucratization. The old warden simply could not survive this blizzard of bureaucratic rules. He would constantly run afoul of the courts and, after a while, the state department of corrections would become weary of this steady humiliation and establish a compliance unit to avoid further defeats. The old warden would run afoul of that unit as well. He would become an embarrassment to the system, and like an ancient, tropical creature stranded in the cold, ice age of legal rationalism, he would disappear, to be replaced by someone with a masters degree.

But rights were not mere instrumentalities; rather the rights orientation that was so central to federal judges' attitudes in the 1960s and 1970s provided further motivation to bureaucratize the prisons. A right, because it constitutes a claim one can assert against the prevailing authority, creates a countervailing force to that authority and an opportunity to appeal to outsiders. Nothing could be more antithetical to a rights-oriented ethos than the sacerdotal regime of punishment that Kafka depicts. Similarly, the prebureaucratic prison was a world where the warden's power was complete, whether the verbal formula was that the prisoners were slaves or that the prison administration enjoyed unfettered discretion. Any kindness to the prisoner was a positive act of mercy or forgiveness, and in this lay the paternalistic, God-like power of the warden that promised personal redemption.

Judges were quick to recognize that prisoners' rights of any kind could only be secured through the complete extirpation of the old, prebureaucratic regime. Even the one right that prisoners clearly possessed before the prison reform cases – the right to challenge the validity of their convictions – was frequently denied under the old regime as indicative of a truculent, uncooperative attitude.[258] Other rights, like the basic First Amendment rights to read a book or correspond without censorship, were consistently denied. The reason was not the pragmatic effects that these rights would produce; what made the recognition of these rights inconsistent with the old regime was that they gave prisoners an independent status that could not coexist with a model of absolute official power or privileges by dispensation.

Thus, judges could amplify their generalized sense that the old regime was repugnant with a more specific sense that it was antithical to prisoners' rights of any kind. The remedy was the same process of bureaucratization that the judges were imposing for independent reasons. The concept of prisoners' rights itself was a rather pallid principle with little obvious content, as federal judges discovered when they tried to formulate it in the 1940s and 1950s. How precisely could one conceptualize a regime of rights for people who had been justifiably deprived of so many rights by due process of law? But prisoners' rights became relevant and meaningful when the effort to protect them contributed to the elimination of the prebureaucratic prison. In one sense, Justice Rehnquist was correct in *Hutto v. Finney* when he dissented on the ground that Judge Henley's bureaucratizing remedy went beyond the limits of the rights that the Constitution specified.[259] But in a deeper sense, Rehnquist was less sincere than Henley. It was clear to Henley, as it must have been to Rehnquist, that the old regime in Arkansas could not possibly recognize the rights of prisoners, that any judicial decision granting rights would be nothing more than markings on a piece of paper unless it was accompanied by major structural reform. Thus, the bureaucratic model could be justified as a vast but necessary device for securing the rights that the judges' ideology demanded. In the new bureaucratic prison, individual rights would be protected, not because the concept of bureaucratization grew out of individual rights, but because it established a regime that was consistent with those rights. The underlying motive and the underlying concept was not prisoners' rights, however – it was the destruction of the paternalistic, prebureaucratic regime.

Bureaucratization as a Moral Idea

To be adopted as a coordinating idea, however, bureaucratization had to be more than an antidote to a preexisting model. It had to be regarded as a positive force, a proper way to organize governmental institutions. As a widely dispersed group of decision makers, operating at the limits of their institutional role, judges were unlikely to organize themselves behind a single approach unless that approach was perceived as positively desirable. This creates something of a mystery, because we generally do not view bureaucracy as having independent moral force.

One way to identify the moral force of bureaucracy is to identify it with "rationality." Weber asserts this connection, although he certainly does not regard bureaucratization as morally desirable.[260] But no such claim will be presented here. To begin with, it is not quite clear what "rationality" really means, as debates about psychological, economic, and organizational rationality are legion in philosophy and social science. Even if one were to adopt a prevailing definition, such as the carefully constructed one that Habermas suggests,[261] the resulting argument would be much too abstract to serve as an explanation for judicial behavior. If judges saw bureaucratic governance techniques as morally desirable, it was probably because these techniques fulfilled some value that was more conceptually accessible to them than the rationalization of the social sphere. In fact, bureaucracy has some highly concrete and familiar moral implications. The first, which is specific to the prison reform context, was its role in rehabilitating prisoners, the second was its link to our concept of law, and the third component, the most speculative and the most complex, is the instrumental nature of bureaucracy and the role of instrumentalism in our political morality.

The judges who carried out the prison reform movement seemed to believe that incarceration in a bureaucratized institution would have rehabilitative effects. Thus, the moral force of their first coordinating idea, described in the previous section, enabled them to justify their second. They believed that regular contact with bureaucratic procedures would communicate a sense of order and justice to the prisoners, thereby contributing to their ability to live as law-abiding citizens.[262] At first glance, this notion may seem wildly improbable. Anyone who has dealings with a government bureaucracy is likely to conclude that this experience not only lacks salutary effects, but constitutes the single greatest inducement to violence that an ordinary citizen encounters. It must be remembered, however, that rehabilitation was a deontological principle for prison organization, not an instrumental strategy selected for its empirically demonstrated success. When judges championed the edifying effects of bureaucracy, they were really saying that prisoners should be exposed to a regime that we, as a society, regard as the moral way to organize an institution. They were expressing faith in our own system of governance and disapproval of the old regime's authoritarian paternalism.

At a more pragmatic level, there is some sense in which it was plausible to view bureaucratization as rehabilitative. While a rehabilitative environment is unlikely to make the prisoner a better human being, it may make him a more organized one. Many criminals come from the fringes of society; a bureaucratized prison may be their first experience with a schedule, government officials, written rules, prescribed punishments, and standardized grievance procedures. Learning to survive in this environment may be the most important skill a convict can acquire if he is to move into the social mainstream, get a job, and stay out of trouble. The old prison did not teach this lesson; it was an extension of criminal culture, a legitimized clan or gang where personal contacts meant everything and where rewards and punishments were based on the leader's gratitude, anger, or caprice.[263] In some sense, therefore, judges could well have believed that the bureaucratized prison really is justified by its capacity to rehabilitate, if only by acculturation.

A second moral element to bureaucratization is that it is strongly linked to law, as Weber points out.[264] It is, in large measure, the application of formal legal rules to the problem of governance.*[265] A bureaucratic hierarchy is a legally defined way to organize staff members, and a meritocracy is a legally defined way of selecting and promoting them. Bureaucratic discipline, comprising specified punishments, defined procedures, and comprehensive records is generally homologous with legal discipline. Written policies, the mainstay of bureaucratic organizations, are themselves laws, and allow the system to be subjected to other laws, promulgated by external authorities.[266] For judges, who rely on law for both their legitimacy and their power, such bureaucratic strategies of governance are particularly congenial. In fact, the link between the two is close enough to generate an apparent identity; bureaucracy seems like law itself, and it possesses all the moral force that our concept of legality confers.

The connection between bureaucracy and law quietly and completely transformed the prisoners' rights movement into a quest to reorganize the correctional system. Despite the concern with individual rights of inmates, the language of prison conditions litigation – as articulated by both the plaintiffs' attorneys and the courts – is the language of structural reform and bureaucratic management. The courts asserted that they wanted prisons to comply with a specific set of laws, as established in the Bill of

---

* Anthony Kronman notes that there is a lack of clarity in Weber's use of terms. He describes the legal system of the modern state as "formally rational"; in addition to the much documented uncertainties about the meaning of the term "rational," his use of the term "formal" can mean a system that is either governed by rules or separate from nonlegal considerations. But since both these features are also characteristic of bureaucracy in Weber's view, it remains fair to say that Weber links bureaucracy to law.

Rights, but they were actually imposing law in general, and doing so by means of bureaucratization. The moral force behind bureaucratization thus extends beyond the appeal of any particular legal rules, and connects with the normative appeal of the rule of law as a comprehensive mode of governance.

This may seem paradoxical, for we often contrast bureaucracy and law, condemning the former for conferring broadly defined, uncontrolled power upon government officials.[267] In fact, much of what we claim to dislike about bureaucracy – capriciousness, lack of accountability and unresponsiveness – represents the failure to bureaucratize our institutions sufficiently. Once we do so, we create a web of rules and regulations whose legitimacy stems from the authority of law itself. Written rules and bureaucratic structure replace individual whim or tradition, and organizational goals suppress personalistic prerogatives. The true dangers of bureaucracy are somewhat different; they are the dangers implicit in a system of comprehensive public authority. Bureaucracy can cloak conflict in the guise of consensus and mask power beneath talk of rights and entitlements. It can crush the spirit with a mass of regulations, and drown justice in procedural detail. It can suppress local culture in the name of abstract principle. It can conceal the iron fist inside the velvet glove.*[268] But bureaucracy can also impose a regime of rules and duties that protect, clarify, and standardize, fostering dignity by restraining power and demarcating zones of individual autonomy. It binds people in an institutional framework that simultaneously empowers the weak and constrains the powerful. Thus, if bureaucracy and law are an iron cage that imprisons,[269] they are also a bulwark that protects.

There is a final and still deeper morality to bureaucratic government. As Jürgen Habermas points out, following Weber, the demythologization of society and the formation of modern consciousness establish subsystems of purposive-rational action.[270] These subsystems, which include bureaucratically-organized institutions, are purposive in the sense that they are designed to achieve a particular, socially defined goal; in other words, they are instrumental. This would appear to be the opposite of morality, but there is a strong moral element to it; in fact, instrumentalism is itself

---

* But the suggestion that Fascist or Communist totalitarianism is a natural outgrowth of bureaucracy goes too far. All modern industrial regimes are bureaucratized, so the mere fact that Nazi Germany was bureaucratized only means that atrocities are possible in a bureaucratic regime, not that they are caused, in any real sense, by the regime's bureaucratic structure. Perhaps the Nazis were able to commit their crimes more efficiently because of their bureaucratic apparatus, but there are numerous premodern regimes that rival them in the savagery of their intentions.

a moral notion, at least as it operates in our political context. The point is not the familiar one that any instrumental action must ultimately be traced to a moral one, that there must be a deontological core inside the layers of the instrumental onion.[271] While this is probably true, what makes instrumentalism itself a moral concept is that it imposes limits on the agency that functions as an instrument; that agency must act unifunctionally, in Niklas Luhmann's terms,[272] pursuing a predefined goal. Instrumentalism thus constrains those in immediate control of the instrumentality, and empowers those who give directions to it. This is perhaps the central element in our political morality, and in our commitment to limited government, popular rule, and pluralism. As Bruce Ackerman emphasizes, Americans believe that government is an instrument through which we pursue our collective interests, not some transcendent entity that pursues its own goals independently of the citizens' desires.

While we tend to think of bureaucrats as operating beyond the reach of public control, the instrumentalism of bureaucracy is thus an assertion of public control in the more general sense. When the prison was viewed as an autonomous moral regime, an arena of unconstrained punishment and unpredictable redemption, it was cut off from political control, from social policy and from the law. It was the warden's fiefdom, an insular realm where his will was sovereign and his word supreme. By bureaucratizing prisons, the courts transformed them into instruments of general social policy that were expected to function along purposive-rational lines. They were reconceived as one unit of a hierarchically organized department of corrections, which in turn subjected them to formalized oversight by the state's chief executive. Their need for funds, which often reached bulimic proportions as a result of prison reform, subjected them to further oversight by the legislature. Their connection with the complex network of state administrative agencies subjected them to scrutiny by all the groups that regularly inform, importune, and intimidate those agencies. Thus the prison gates swung open, not to release the inmates, as some prison reform advocates had hoped, but to admit a steady stream of lawyers, reporters, legislative aides, social scientists, part-time educators, doctors, dentists, and psychiatrists.

The instrumentalism of the prison that bureaucratization engendered thus became a means of subjecting prisons to political control. A prison warden could claim that he was expressing the popular will, in the sense of the personal opinions of a majority of citizens as measured by a poll, by instituting a reign of terror against the vicious criminals under his control. The more abstract our notion of the popular will, the more plausible this claim. But when the popular will refers to political control – the actual decision-making process of the courts, legislature, and executive –

it subjects the warden to significant and enforceable constraints. Among those constraints, of course, are the judiciary's own demands that the prison protect the rights of prisoners. The more general notion, which the courts imposed by virtue of bureaucratization, is that the prison must be subject to the constraints imposed by all levels of government.

This morality of bureaucratic constraint is mundane, but certainly familiar. As a society, we generally favor it over alternative strategies for reform, such as a heroic or leadership model. Alexander Maconochie is an appealing figure, but as most people in our culture would point out, one cannot rely on the character of unconstrained individuals. Maconochie, after all, was replaced by John Price, an outright sadist who used his knowledge and purported sympathy for prisoners to perpetuate endless horrors.[274] For every Stateville, whose regime was harsh but just, there was a Cummins Farm; for every Texas convict who was inspired by George Beto to take the righteous path, another was brutalized in one of the dark corners of his clean, well-lighted prison. The modern response is regularity; instead of relying on the character of individual leaders, it establishes systems and routines. Kafka's new commandant, unlike his predecessor, is a faceless figure; against the officer's personal adulation of the old commandant, the explorer offers his approval of the procedures that the new commandant has established.

Bureaucratization as a Diffuse Idea

Although bureaucratization was a specific and positive notion, an ideology that combated the prior era's ideology and that rested on a definitive moral basis, it was not conceived as such. Judges knew that they were championing the rehabilitative model and they discussed it explicitly in their opinions. Sometimes they were forthright about it, sometimes they were apologetic, sometimes they were duplicitous. But they were clearly conscious of it as an issue; it was present in their minds, and although it served the institutional function of coordination, we can account for it without anthropomorphic discourse. In contrast, there are no explicit discussions of bureaucratization in the early prison cases. Bureaucratization was apparently not present in the minds of individual judges, but seems to emerge from decisions that speak in other terms.

The difficulty is to account for this idea without lapsing into anthropomorphism. Individual judges were doing the thinking, yet we identify the results of their efforts in terms that they themselves did not use. As discussed earlier, the idea cannot have been "thought" by the judiciary itself; that is not a meaningful use of the word "thought," but a verbal proxy for an explanation. One possible explanation that readily occurs to any twentieth-century person is that the idea was a subconscious one.

Since Freud, we view the mind as brimming with thoughts, images, and desires of which the person, the ego, is not consciously aware. But there is something suspicious about asserting that a self-conscious thought process like judicial decision making arises from subconscious motivations. Without a link to primal drives, repression, or the other machinery of Freudian theory, the term becomes another verbal proxy. Anything that is not explicitly discussed by a decision maker can be attributed to the decision maker's subconscious, just as any document that does not fit into an established category can be filed under "miscellaneous." But "miscellaneous" tells us nothing about the document, and the judicial subconscious, without more, tells us nothing about the provenance of the bureaucratic model.

A more useful approach is to treat bureaucratization as a diffuse idea. Its totality was present in the minds of the judges, as an image of good governance, but it was a diffuse image that became clear only through its individual elements. The judges explicitly identified all the features of bureaucracy that they actually imposed. Their opinions contained long discussions of procedural due process, not only as a constitutional requirement, but as a means of achieving administrative regularity. They spoke of the need for formalized staff hierarchies in abolishing the trusty systems of the southern prisons. They demanded written policies for food service, medical care, legal services, mail censorship, and a wide variety of other functions to secure compliance with the requirements that they imposed. Their special masters, on the scene and less constrained by formal structures, imposed even more detailed, bureaucratic requirements, of which the judges were aware and often explicitly approved.

There is thus no mystery about the individual elements that composed the bureaucratic ideal. They were present in the consciousness of judges and were explicitly identified in their opinions. The question, rather, is why these separate elements combined in a pattern that could be so readily identified by outside observers. In all likelihood, the reason for this perceptible pattern is that bureaucracy is our basic means of organizing the substructures of our society – our repertoire of governance techniques largely bureaucratic in nature. Each separate issue that arises is likely to be met with a bureaucratic solution because such solutions strike us as the proper way to do things. The term bureaucracy, in other words, simply identifies twentieth-century America's approach to governance, and its unity stems from this culturally embedded strategy. Thus, judges could coordinate their integrative efforts by means of the diffuse institutional conceptualization of properly run, well-managed institutions. The implications of this conceptualization were so clear that there was no need for a more explicit characterization of the overall concept.

Reliance on bureaucratic approaches was particularly natural in reforming an institution whose primary fault lay in its prebureaucratic character. Again, judges never explicitly identified the sins of the old prison as a lack of bureaucratization. But in each specific area, the problem seemed to lie in the personal, discretionary, authoritarian regime that prevailed there, and in each specific area, the antidote was the regularity and accountability that we necessarily rely upon bureaucracy to provide. Discipline was arbitrary and informal, so regular procedures must be instituted, and the results recorded. Medical care was casual and inadequate, so a new department, with credentialed staff, must be established. Trusties must be replaced with professional guards, work with training, punishment with administrative segregation, and paternalism with procedure. The negative example of the old prison made these bureaucratic techniques of governance seem particularly desirable.

Bureaucratic techniques were also natural remedies for judges to impose because of bureaucracy's inherent moral force that infused each of these techniques. While judges viewed a bureaucratized environment as generally rehabilitative, they also traced its potentially rehabilitative effects to specific features such as due process hearings before punishment, professionalized prison guards, and decent living conditions. Similarly, the legal aspect of bureaucratization was embodied in credentializing policies for staff, classification policies, disciplinary rules, grievance procedures, and written manuals for staff and inmates. Bureaucracy's instrumental character found expression in those same rules – rules that required prison officials to punish prisoners in response to specified behaviors, rather than as an instrument of terror or an expression of disdain – in education and vocational training programs, and in the creation of statewide corrections departments to monitor individual prisons. The moral force of bureaucracy was divisible into its component parts because bureaucracy, unlike its quasi-sacerdotal predecessor, is inherently accretive; it does not depend upon a general mood, which can be shattered by particular anomalies, but upon procedures and techniques that can be developed and extended by degrees.

There was thus no need to invoke the general notion of bureaucracy itself, and given our abiding cultural ambivalence about bureaucracy, judges had little incentive to do so. The point of a written opinion, after all, is to legitimize the conclusion that the judge has reached; it is an argument, not an effort to reconstruct the mental process that the judge experienced. To declare that one was trying to bureaucratize the prisons is not a particularly appetizing argument. Consequently, judges tended to retain the ideal of bureaucracy in its diffuse, vaguely identified form. They relied on the familiarity of its individual components, since it really is our dominant form of governance, and on the moral force that these components possessed, without articulating the concept in its entirety. It was the very strength of these features – that bureaucracy is so deeply familiar to us, and so deeply connected to our political morality – that made such indirection possible. The rehabilitative ideal is limited to the penological context and is unfamiliar as a general legal concept, so judges needed to articulate it. But since bureaucracy suffuses our entire legal and administrative system, there is no need to invoke the concept explicitly to coordinate or justify the use of these techniques. Judges were aware of its component parts, and its unity was supplied by their instinctive reliance on it as a general mode of governance.

Our conscious understanding that these component parts are not simply a general concept of good governance, but the more specific process of bureaucratization is a matter of interpretation. Nonjudicial commentators like James Jacobs and Michel Foucault were the first to offer this characterization; they saw judicial intervention as part of the same process that had transformed government operations and private firms, and that represented one of the definitive developments of the twentieth century.[275] The theme was quickly picked up by the law reviews, the popular press, the political critics of the courts, and the prison officials themselves.[276] Thus, they perceived relationships to more general trends that the judges did not see, and their characterization of judicial action as bureaucratizing was the result of that perception. What judges who were immersed in the prison reform process treated as a particularized set of legal rules and remedies, observers saw as part of comprehensive social process.

The prison reform decisions, however, were not a single text, created at a single time, but a set of texts that were continuously developed over the course of two and a half decades. Because of this, the relationship between the authors of those texts and their interpreters was dialogic, as Melvin Eisenberg has noted[277] – the judges could read the interpretations before they created the next version of their text. By virtue of this process, the interpretations had an important effect upon the prison reform process. Judges became aware of the bureaucratizing character of their opinions, and because they were ambivalent about this process, they began to modify their conclusions and their remedies in future opinions.[278] They certainly did not abandon the bureaucratic ideal; despite the negative associations of bureaucracy, it remained our basic mode of governance and retained its moral force. But they became more conscious of its negative aspects and tried to modify their impact. One could regard the judges as responding to criticism in order to avoid political embarrassment, but one could also regard them as having gained new insight into the nature of their actions.

To be sure, there were other reasons for this modification. One reason was a gradual change in the personal attitudes of the judges. With the

Republican Party in power, the new judicial appointees were personally more conservative; if we allow for the lag time that results from the length of a federal judge's tenure, these appointments began to have a significant effect by the mid-1970s. In addition, the doctrinal framework in which judges functioned was changing. A new, conservative mood had dampened the enthusiasm for individual rights, and partially revived the long-dormant doctrines of federalism and the separation of powers.[279] These ideological and doctrinal developments were most dramatically expressed by the Supreme Court, whose personnel probably changed more rapidly than the great mass of federal trial and circuit court judges. The effect of the Supreme Court's decisions, when combined with the lower-court judges' changing attitudes, made these judges more reluctant to find new constitutional rights or to institute comprehensive remedies to vindicate those rights.

But these changes in attitudes and doctrine were amplified by the judges' increasing awareness that their decisions contributed to a previously unperceived pattern of bureaucratization. Beginning in the mid-1970s, there was an observable concern, expressed in the opinions, that judicial remedies will overlegalize the prisons. This is not the old, jurisdictional concern that courts should not intervene; that battle was long ended, and the losing side fully interred. Rather, it was a specific recognition that judicial remedies did in fact produce bureaucratization, and that this had undesired side effects, such as inflexibility, complexity, and the discouragement of staff initiative, that should be minimized whenever possible. Nonetheless, the effect was one of modification, not repudiation. The federal courts in the Burger–Rehnquist era, despite all their reservations, reversals, and tepid affirmances, may have slowed the bureaucratization process, but they did not halt it, and they certainly did not reverse it.

Foucault's *Discipline and Punish*

Although Michel Foucault is one of the commentators responsible for our understanding of modern prisons as bureaucratic institutions, the meaning that he ascribes to bureaucratization is quite different from the one presented in the preceding sections of this chapter. Tracing those differences will further clarify the points that have already been advanced. In addition, it is useful to reconsider Foucault's theory in light of the American prison reform movement. *Discipline and Punish*, Foucault's study of the modern prison, was written in 1975 at the very height of the movement, but he was apparently unaware of these events; he speaks at length of Walnut Street but says nothing about Cummins Farm.[280] It is a matter of some interest to see how Foucault's theory, which is not only an analysis of prisons but a landmark of modern social theory, fits a set of relevant events that he did not consider.

Foucault begins with a discussion of the savage pageantry of torture that prevailed in the premodern era.[281] Unlike Kafka, he does not view torture as an opportunity for the criminal's redemption, but for an exhibition of state power, a demonstration that the king can annihilate those who violate his laws.[282] The Enlightenment brought with it a revulsion toward torture, not because torture is cruel (kindness does not loom large in Foucault's lexicon of motivations) but because of its haphazard inefficiency. "The true objective of the reform movement," he writes, "was not so much to establish a new right to punish based on more equitable principles, as to set up a new 'economy' of the power to punish, to assure its better distribution."[283] To achieve this, the reformers conceived a regime of symbolic punishments that would replace the warlike symbolism of torture with a "gentler," more logical calculus of proportionate penalties. They proposed that "those who abuse public liberty be deprived of their own; those who abuse the benefits of law and the privileges of public office will be deprived of their civil rights; speculation and usury will be punished by fines; theft will be punished by confiscation; 'vainglory' by humiliation; murder by death; fire raising by the stake."[284] In this system, Foucault suggests, "[h]orror is not opposed to horror in a joust of power; it is no longer a symmetry of vengeance, but the transparency of the sign to that which it signifies; what is required is to establish, in the theatre of punishments, a relation that is immediately intelligible to the senses and on which a simple calculation may be based: a sort of reasonable aesthetic of punishment."[285]

But this vision was never to be realized. While the Enlightenment reformers spun their utopian visions, Foucault asserts, powerful forces were rising from the deep, underlying structure of society itself, to move all the functions of governance, including punishment, in an entirely different direction. These were the forces of discipline and institutional organization. They asserted direct control over people's bodies by subjecting them to restrictions of oppressive regularity in space and time. In space, the body was enclosed, divided from others by partitions and assigned to functional locations. In time, it was rigidly scheduled, precisely choreographed to perform its functions and programmed to the fullest possible extent. To keep people under this sort of regime, various techniques were employed, including constant surveillance, rewards and punishments, and examinations to evaluate and document each individual. The school, the hospital, the factory, the military were all organized along these lines.[286] Most modern observers, following Weber, would describe these developments as none other than a rational-purposive system of the modern industrial and administrative state. Foucault's focus, however, is not on rationality, or on instrumental efforts to achieve collective purposes, but on the control of individuals.*[287] For him, Bentham's panopticon, with its all-seeing supervisor in the center and its exposed, partitioned cubicles around the perimeter, in which each occupant performs a rigidly prescribed function, is the paradigmatic image of the modern world.[288] It is a world that dominates the individual by means of subtle, unrelenting technical arrangements, rather than by violent spectacles, a world where power penetrates inside the person, rather than operating as an external force.

The contemporary prison was the product and the quintessential creation of this disciplinary approach in Foucault's view. These "complete and austere institutions"[289] took control of the prisoner's body in space and time, a precise effectuation of the disciplinary model. The sole purpose of the prison was to exert this control, to organize, divide, assign, observe, examine, evaluate, and categorize, rather than to rehabilitate. In fact, Foucault sees the lack of interest in rehabilitation as evidence that prisons were designed to foster delinquency. They did so by the experience to which they subjected the inmates, but also by constructing the concept of delinquency as separate from normal, or standard behavior. "For the observation that prison fails to eliminate crime, one should perhaps substitute the hypotheses that prison has succeeded extremely well in producing delinquency, a specific type, a politically or economically less dangerous – and on occasions usable – form of illegality; in producing delinquents, in an apparently marginal, but in fact centrally supervised milieu; in producing the delinquent as a pathological subject."[290] Reform efforts directed at the "failure" of a prison never produce real changes because the prisons are succeeding in their somber purpose; indeed, the reforms themselves are simply part of a complex power–knowledge system that maintains prisons in their present form.[291]

A comprehensive analysis of *Discipline and Punish* lies beyond the ambit of this study. Within its specific subject area, that is, penal practice, the book has been incisively critiqued as history by Pieter Spierenburg[292] and as sociology by David Garland.[293] For present purposes, the issue is the difference between Foucault's account of bureaucratization and the account presented in this chapter. Foucault's position is that all prisons are inherently bureaucratized, and that their creation overwhelmed the Enlightenment reforms precisely because they reflected the emerging disciplinary culture, the modern machinery of social control. From this, it follows that bureaucratization could not possibly be a means of reforming

---

* As David Garland observes, however, this theme is also to be found in Weber, who points out that many areas of life in modern Europe, most notably the army, exercised an elaborate and minute supervision over individuals.

prisons. Foucault might say that bureaucratization is a natural theme of reform movements, however, because the purpose of these movements is really to maintain the institution as a bureaucratized entity. The position taken here is that many American prisons were not organized along bureaucratic lines prior to 1965, and that the imposition of the bureaucratic model on them produced significant, although far from epochal, reforms.

The difficulty with Foucault's account is that it is highly schematic, reducing complex social and institutional developments to a single theme with a univalent meaning. To the extent that he regards the prison's triumph over the aspirations of eighteenth-century reformers as evidence of its connection with bureaucratic, disciplinary culture, he is over-interpreting. The reformers were philosophers or social theorists who were working as individuals, sketching moral forms of punishment in scholarly isolation. Their views were not explicitly rejected by government officials; for the most part, they were simply unadaptable because they were not conceived and elaborated within an institutional context. At the same time that these reformers were imagining their panoply of penal symbols, other reformers were working quietly but more influentially within the depths of existing social institutions.

As we have seen, these institutions are often governed by ideas, but only ideas that succeeded in coordinating their members' efforts to integrate their personal attitudes with institutional expectations. Clearly, this requirement imposes severe limits on the range of possible reforms. It means that the idea must appeal to a significant majority of the institution's members, not just to an articulate few, and that it must be continuous with the institution's prior rules. Individual thought, in contrast, is flexible and far-ranging; the members of any sophisticated society, as individuals, are capable of imagining virtually any governance technique, certainly any technique that has been employed by another society. But these ideas often cannot be translated into action. The ideas of the Enlightenment reformers, for example, probably lay outside the range of possibilities for Western society to implement. Thus, Foucault reads too much significance into their rejection; in all likelihood, the reformers' ideas were rejected because they were theoretical imaginings that were unconnected with the organic development of real social institutions, not because of some strongly developed countervailing ethos.*[294] Foucault, for all his grids and cynicism, seems to take abstract thought too seriously.

---

* Bentham's grandiose and elaborate plans for his panopticon prison were received with polite bewilderment by the practical politicians of his day, and never acted on. Vermiel's 1781 plan for a punitive city – a sort of Disneyland of punishment with "hundreds of tiny theatres" where those convicted of each type of crime "will receive appropriate punishment under placards identifying the

Conversely, because the range of implemented institutions is so limited, each institution is likely to encompass a rather wide variety of social attitudes. That is, a large number of attitudes, generated with the ease of individual thought, will "map into" a relatively limited set of institutions, rather than each being able to generate an institution of its own. If one starts with a given institution, such as prison, one can plausibly trace its features back to a particular idea. The difficulty is that one can also trace them back to a variety of other ideas – in fact, to all the ideas that could only be realized by attaching themselves to that particular institutional arrangement. These different pathways all exist, but following one or the other only demonstrates the interconnection, not causation or unambiguous association.

Prisons were clearly a multidetermined institution of this nature. For a variety of reasons, execution had become less popular, mutilation less appetizing, and public whipping less entertaining.[295] In England, transportation replaced these for a while, but it had to be abandoned when the transported felons declared their independence or turned into gentlemen and insisted that the further transportation of felons to their country cease.[296] Thus, prisons became the only method of punishment that Western nations were capable of implementing on any significant scale. This suggests that these institutions were fulfilling a wide variety of social purposes, not only discipline and social control, but also humanitarianism, moral instruction of the populace, incapacitation, rehabilitation (however ineffective), and the dishing out of just deserts that the Enlightenment reformers favored.

Foucault's insight that the creation of the modern prison was part of a general process of institutionalization or bureaucratization seems persuasive, as does his view that the purpose of this process was discipline, or control of the body, rather than unalloyed humanitarianism. The accounts of other scholars, such as David Rothman and Michael Ignatieff, are partially consistent with Foucault's.[297] But Foucault fails to demonstrate that this process is unique to modern prisons, or why all modern prisons necessarily reflect this single purpose. During the fifteenth through eighteenth century, for example, several European nations, particularly France, punished criminals by making them serve as galley slaves.[298] If there is some reason why being chained to a bench, pulling an oar in time to a drumbeat, together with one hundred to two hundred other men does not involve discipline or control of one's body, Foucault never

offense and accompanied by trompe-l'oeil scenery to heighten the effect" found a similar reception. Whether the rejection of such fervid fantasies by practical politicians requires any explanation at all is an open question; to take this rejection as indicating major social attitudes, as Foucault does, is a real leap.

provides it for us. Conversely, as this study has shown, prisons in the American South became assimilated to the preexisting model of the plantation. Instead of categorized space and programmed functions, they subjected prisoners to an older model of collective agriculture and personal service to a master. Here, and in other areas, prisons became regimes of patriarchal domination, casual corruption, and personal influence, rather than of rigid rules and uniform surveillance. And interwoven with all this were inefficiency and resource limitations that often led to semianarchy or two-bit totalitarianism.

Just as prison reflected different attitudes, many of them rather distant from bureaucratization, the bureaucratizing instinct that reformed these prisons reflected different attitudes as well. This instinct was no longer needed to create prisons or to assert control over the inconsistent savagery of torture. To say that the process continued to reflect its initial purpose, more than a century after that purpose was achieved, ignores the phenomenological position of the subsequent decision makers who had to choose and justify their actions. Rather, to the generation of the 1960s and 1970s, bureaucracy was not perceived as a means of controlling the criminal – that had been achieved in a past too distant to be salient – but as a means of controlling the prison administration, of making prisons more orderly, and of developing new approaches to rehabilitation. Foucault's unexplained assumption that all governmental agents are part of a single, coordinated power grid forecloses any notion that one set of agents can control another, and can regard such control as their most important exercise of power.

John DiIulio makes the same mistake in his odd description of the pre-*Ruiz* Texas prison system as a bureaucracy;[299] he assumes that the essence of bureaucratization is control over citizens. But citizens were often tightly controlled in the premodern era. Bureaucracy is largely a device for controlling government officials, for turning decentralized discretionary power holders into a hierarchically organized, rule-bound structure. For this reason, progressive administrators like the federal Bureau of Prisons and the American Correctional Association saw bureaucratization as a way of implementing a moral vision of the prison and an antidote to the brutal or repressive regimes that often prevailed in state institutions.

The courts followed the lead of these progressive administrators. They used bureaucratization as a coordinating idea to abolish the old prison and to institute a more moral and legal regime. Although they recognized control of prisoners as a basic requirement, they were not interested in that issue, and it was not the basis of their intervention. There were indeed control problems in the prisons – at the microlevel, escape; at the macrolevel, riot. But these events never served as the basis of court intervention, and the intervention was not designed to reduce or eliminate them. In-

deed, escapes, riots, and security problems generally were used as a counterargument by administrators and appear prominently in judicial
opinions once judges became conscious of and ambivalent about their
bureaucratizing efforts. The driving force behind bureaucracy, in the mid-
twentieth-century context, was not control or discipline of prisoners; it was
control of administrators and the creation of a moral prison. Foucault's
analysis is simply too roughhewn to incorporate this shift in the use of
bureaucratic techniques. The inarticulate social forces he discerns move
in one direction only and do so with a mechanical inevitability that ignores
real complexities of human decision making.

Implementing the Solution, Muddling Through, and Ignoring the Separation of Powers Principle

HAVING CHOSEN THE DOCTRINAL SOLUTION of rehabilitation and bureaucratization, the federal judiciary's next step was to implement its solution. This is precisely what it did, and with a vengeance. Far from limiting themselves to declaring prisons unconstitutional, the judges imposed or approved elaborate remedies whose features ranged from the highest policy to the lowliest details. To say that they "ran" prisons would be an exaggeration, since there was always some sort of state correctional administrator in charge. But they certainly supervised prisons, often with the vigilant intensity of an administrator who has lost faith in the competence of her subordinates.

While this account of judicial policy making is useful for dividing the process into separate categories, it is not always the most convincing description of actual occurrences. Judges did not typically follow the classic model of policy analysis – that is, define the problem, identify the goal, specify alternatives, choose the solution, and implement that solution. More often, they acted incrementally, by intuition; in other words, they muddled through. They did so, in part, because they were apologetic about making policy, but also because an intuitive approach is more common among American policy makers of all kinds, even those who are proud of what they do.

What incrementalism or muddling through means, in essence, is that implementation precedes some of the other stages in the policy-making process. The decision maker imposes a change, usually a delimited one, before selecting a clearly defined set of solutions, and perhaps before settling upon a clearly defined goal. Based on the response to this first implementation, he can discern the goal or the solutions, which can then be used to guide further implementation. This is the sense in which in-

crementalism is related, although not necessarily equivalent, to a hermeneutic approach. It is also possible, however, that the decision maker will
never define either a goal or a solution with any clarity; rather, he will
incrementally adjust his first intervention, and then repeat this adjustment
process over and over, proceeding by "feel" rather than by comprehensive vision.

The early prison reform cases were typically incremental processes.
Courts did not begin with a plan but responded to the problems they
perceived and developed their plan as the case proceeded. Later cases, of
course, could draw upon the solutions that emerged from the earlier,
more incremental ones. Indeed, the very existence of the solution may
have induced them to perceive a problem.[1] Even so, there is a quality of
pure incrementalism to many of the judicial decisions, late as well as early;
having now perceived the problem, the judge proceeds to a specification
of the solution or remedy without much intervening explanation. This is
pure muddling through and, as Lindblom's sobriquet suggests, it often
led to a considerable muddle.

In describing the implementation process of the prison reform cases,
therefore, we are describing two different things. One is the final stage of
the classic policy-making process, and the other is the entire process, in
the incrementalist or muddling-through form. We will not attempt to categorize particular cases as adopting one or the other approach. Indeed,
such a categorization is probably impossible, since the second category is
a fluid one that can range from the complete exclusion of planning to a
slight modification of the classic model. Rather, we will indicate how the
judiciary's implementation efforts simultaneously functioned as the last
stage of the classic policy-making model and as an overall incrementalist
approach.

There is a third aspect to the judiciary's implementation efforts that is
equally pervasive, and that is the criticism that they have invoked. While
commentators condemn judicial policy making in its entirety, they have
treated this administrative aspect of the process as a particular orgy of
volition, where the self-indulgent judge disported without guidance or
constraint. Once the disciplining structure of interpretation has been cast
aside, according to this view, "everything is permitted."[2] Apart from the
vague but widespread sense of judicial policy making as an operational
nothingness, there are two more specific objections to the implementation
aspect of the prison cases: first, that judges cannot be effective when they
stray so far from their established expertise and, second, that they violate
the separation-of-powers principle when they do so. The starting point for
a consideration of these two objections is that they somehow failed to
persuade several hundred federal judges over a period of thirty years. To
be sure, these judges could all have been acting lawlessly and irresponsi-

bly, but an alternative and perhaps more plausible hypothesis is that the objections lacked the force that has been ascribed to them. In fact, as will be shown later, they were never fully applicable to real judges, and have become less applicable still since the advent of the modern administrative state.

The Motivation and Evolution of the Courts' Administrative Role

The basic reason why courts were willing to intervene decisively and comprehensively in the administration of state prisons is that administrative implementation – direct intervention into the ongoing activities of a state or private institution – is an integral aspect of the policy-making process. Once the federal courts perceived state prison conditions as a problem that lay within their purview, and that no other federal institution was prepared to resolve, they embarked upon the enterprise of policy making to reform these institutions. Once embarked upon that enterprise, the implementation aspect of the policy-making process followed naturally.

To be sure, judicial policy making does not necessarily involve judicial implementation. Both the constitutional privacy cases, which culminated in *Roe v. Wade*, and the common law right of privacy cases are clear examples of judicial policy making, but neither includes an implementation element. Roughly speaking, judicial policy making will almost inevitably require implementation when the behavior of public institutions such as prisons, schools, or mental hospitals is concerned, while it can be restricted to mere declaration of a rule when the policy is regulating private conduct. The distinction is far from absolute, however, and nothing in particular turns on it as far as this study is concerned. What is clear is that judicial policy making often involves hands-on implementation, and that this is probably the single most controversial aspect of the entire process. Any exploration or defense of judicial policy making, therefore, must include consideration of the judge as administrator: that is one reason why the prison cases, where administration figures so prominently, were chosen as the subject of this study.

The fact that judicial policy making does not necessarily involve judicial implementation does not mean that implementation is not an inherent element in any policy making effort. Judicial policy making sometimes dispenses with implementation only because the policy-making court need not carry out this effort on its own. Having established a policy, courts can sometimes rely on other agencies or on more traditional forms of judicial action to implement that policy. But there will almost always be some administrative component to the process. Since at least the publication of Richard Neustadt's book, *Presidential Power*, it has been common to observe that few policies are self-executing; indeed, within the last generation a new field of public policy research has emerged to address this issue.[3] Called implementation studies, its defining characteristic is the view that making and implementing policy cannot be treated as separate processes. "Declaration of policies," Pressman and Wildavsky assert in the book that signaled the emergence of this field, "cannot be separated from implementation. . . . Implementation is an extension of policy formulation, and thus has to be factored into the design of programs at the outset."[4]

To say that implementation is an inherent part of policy making does not explain why the federal judiciary adopted its highly activist, administrative approach, however. It would serve as an explanation only if courts were independently motivated to become policy makers, which they were not. Rather, the causal process operated in reverse; courts become policy makers because they experienced the need to implement their orders, just as they became policy makers because they were motivated to impose national standards on divergent institutions.

Moreover, administrative implementation was not the only alternative available to courts that wanted to reform the prisons. They might have carried out their goals through the more traditional remedies that had occurred to them during the hands-off era, such as ordering money damages under the Civil Rights Acts or releasing the inmates adversely affected by improper correctional practices through a writ of habeas corpus. Perhaps they rejected damages because it ultimately would have involved huge public expenditures and done little to correct the continuing institutional problems they perceived. And perhaps they rejected release because, if carried out consistently, it would have violated every actual or imagined function of punishment and engendered widespread public opposition. In all likelihood, however, the reason for their choice of administrative implementation was positive as well as negative. The administrative state has established new norms of governance and new conceptions of the proper role and strategy of any governmental agent, whether legislator, administrator, or judge. It simultaneously generates new understandings of how institutions work and how their behaviors are most effectively transformed. The result was that judges were affirmatively motivated to adopt a managerial approach because they sought to protect the rights of individuals within an organization by enhancing the organization's capacity for rational administration.

But there were also affirmative motivations to avoid a managerial approach. Within the framework of policy making itself, a positive value is attached to incrementalism, or muddling through; judges wanted to take the necessary first step of declaring certain conditions unconstitutional and then see what happened before proceeding with any other action. In addition, a positive value also attaches to the hermeneutic approach; judges did not necessarily know what a global solution would look like, and thus preferred to give prison administrators the chance to articulate some part of that solution. Beyond the constraints of the policy-making framework, judges were also motivated to avoid a managerial approach because it seemed to violate the well-established separation of powers principle; they could minimize this violation by viewing prisoner complaints within the framework of traditional lawsuits. For all these reasons many of the cases began with the judge declaring that the prison had violated the Constitution and allowing the prison administrators to decide how to comply with the announced constitutional requirements. This was essentially the approach adopted by Judge Henley in the Arkansas prison litigation, by Judge Justice in Texas, and by Judge Leahy in Santa Clara County. As the implementation theorists would have predicted, however, it did not meet with success.

One reason a mere declaration of prisoners' rights proved ineffective was the principled resistance of prison administrators. For decades, courts had been proclaiming that they had no jurisdiction over prisons, that convicted felons had simply dropped off the edge of the constitutional earth. The courts had, moreover, given reasons for this policy, ranging from the legal notion that conviction deprived convicts of their rights to the practical one that only prison officials know how to govern a prison. Prison officials were fully aware of this legal position and its rationale, which they found quite persuasive. It is not surprising then, that they regarded the courts' rather sudden turnabout in the late 1960s as unauthorized judicial action, a betrayal of the very principles that courts claimed as their guide.

Another reason the mere declaration of the rights of prisoners did not succeed was unprincipled resistance. No one likes to have their perquisites invaded. For prison wardens, who often wielded the untrammeled power of Oriental satraps, the experience was particularly unwelcome. In their view, freedom from outside supervision was one of the psychic benefits of the job, like the judge's robe or the police officers' gun. When they were suddenly confronted with an outsider's demands, their reaction was, in essence, no.

There was a third, more basic reason why the courts could not change prisons by simply declaring the existing regime unconstitutional. For many wardens, particularly those who had grown up with the plantation model, the notion of prisoners' rights was simply incomprehensible. Even if these officials had wanted to comply with the courts' demands, they would not have known how to do so. The idea that these slaves of the state had rights was totally foreign to their way of thinking; it was a blank wall, a mystery whose contemplation yielded no result beyond astonishment. Of course, the wardens could understand the simple prohibitions; they could eliminate the Tucker telephone, the bread and water diet, the censorship of inmate mail, and, to some extent, they did so. But it required more imagination to conceive of a new order on the basis of a declaration that prisoners had rights, and to recognize that all the elements of the existing order – the trusties, the crude conditions, the use of prisoner labor to support the prison – violated those rights.*

At some relatively early point, therefore, all the judges realized that the conscious and unconscious resistance of the prison administrators rendered traditional approaches ineffective, and that they would need to adopt more interventionist methods. It was as if they had entered the pool at the shallow end and continued to be drawn step by step into deeper water. Although some were more adventuresome than others, none were anxious at the outset to dive in head-first. But they discovered that their orders were ignored or that their actions revealed more deep-seated problems. As they lost patience and gained confidence, they began to issue increasingly detailed orders specifying the concrete steps that needed to be taken. The continued unwillingness or inability of correctional officials to respond led the judges to conclude that problems were still more deeply embedded and resistance more firmly ensconced than they had originally thought. This drew them still deeper into the management of the institutions. At some point, each of the judges came to see the problems as being due to structural inadequacies – the lack of organizational competence, funding, and political accountability. When, in turn, these efforts did not yield sufficient results, the judges went still deeper; they came to appreciate institutional problems not in terms of "mistakes," "neglect," or even failed policies and lack of funding, but as something rooted in organizational structure and leadership. Although they never fully articulated this realization, they proceeded to act on it. Ultimately, they could be seen as engaging in a type of organizational therapy whose purpose was to transform the institution's collective understanding of itself; by incremental stages, they had become comprehensive reform administrators of the state prison systems.

* This conceptual chasm was illustrated by a passing comment made to one of the authors during an interview with the Texas prison authorities in Huntsville, Texas. The interview was conducted in May, 1986, after any overt resistance to the constitutional regime of Judge Justice had ceased. George Beto, an earlier and nearly legendary superintendent, was now an advisor to the system and readily conceded that certain harsh practices, like placing prisoners who refused to work on a diet of bread and water, had been mistaken. Yet he paused at the notion that prisoners should be exempt from farming the system's 160,000 acres of good cropland. "All that land," he mused, "it's a pity not to work it."

The Judicial Imposition of Standards

Because the image of judges as administrators is unfamiliar and perhaps disconcerting, there is a certain instability about it. In their study of modern government, for example, Harold Seidman and Robert Gilmour entitle one chapter "Administration by Judiciary," but they focus largely on fairly traditional cases where judges reviewed administrative action.[5] To fix and sharpen the image of the judge as an actual administrator, it seems best to begin by examining how a more familiar administrator would have functioned in the particular area of prison reform. Suppose a federal agency had been established, by constitutional amendment, to reform all the prisons in America. This agency, resembling a European ministry of justice, would be granted plenary, hierarchial control over the prisons that were previously administered by the states. With all federalism and separation-of-powers questions thus eliminated, how would this hypothetical agency have proceeded in implementing a reform agenda similar to that developed, and ultimately implemented, by the federal courts?

The first task of any agency in approaching a new grant of regulatory jurisdiction of this sort would be to define the nature of its enterprise, combining whatever statutory instructions or suggestions were embodied in the authorizing legislation with a factual assessment of its subject matter. Robert Katzmann distinguishes between proactive agencies that fashion their own initiatives according to an internally developed plan and reactive agencies that receive complaints and resolve them on an individualized basis.[6] The latter approach resembles traditional judicial practice, of course, whereas the former seems more characteristically administrative. Regulatory agencies generally combine the two approaches; even the most proactive agency is likely to derive some information from complaints and feel some obligation to respond to them, while highly reactive agencies will nonetheless engage in planning, investigation, and resource allocation, if only to manage its complaint processing endeavors. Although our hypothetical prison agency might have positioned itself at any point along this continuum, a specific statutory instruction to reform the prisons would have drawn it toward the proactive side of the scale.

What is striking about the prison cases is that the courts, despite the congruence of their traditional practice and a reactive administrative strategy, adopted the sort of proactive approach that would be associated with an aggressively reformist agency. Prior to 1965, of course, they were entirely reactive and, indeed, they rejected virtually all the complaints presented to them without engaging in policy making at all. Once they found themselves drawn into a policy-making process, however gradually, they began to manage the cases in ways that conflict rather dramatically with our traditional image of courts. In Texas, Judge Justice instructed his clerks to select the most characteristic complaints and then recruited an experienced civil rights attorney to fashion them into a comprehensive class action suit. In Arkansas, Judge Henley appointed a series of attorneys, finally settling on the team of Philip Kaplan and Jack Holt who proved so politically effective. Similarly, in Colorado, the ACLU initiated its class action suit against Old Max at the explicit invitation of Judge Kane. In Santa Clara County, Judge Leahy virtually pounced on a crudely written petition from a single prisoner and fashioned a class action suit that ultimately enveloped the entire county jail system. The mixture of proactive and reactive strategies employed by agencies suggests that agencies sometimes act in accordance with our traditional notion of a judge; in the prison cases, the judges moved cautiously in developing their reform agenda, but they acted in accordance with our traditional notion of an administrator.

Having formulated its program, the agency's next task would be to implement the changes that the program demands. The most obvious way for our hypothetical prison reform agency to do so would be to fire all the existing wardens of the southern prisons and to replace them with appointees more sympathetic to reform. Courts could not act analogously, of course, because the federal judiciary has no power to replace state administrative officers. But a federal agency, no matter what its juridical power, would probably find wholesale dismissal of subordinate officials to be impossible as well. Many government employees are protected by civil service rules, and high-ranking employees often have independent power bases that preclude dismissal or even transfer. One need only consider how reluctantly the president dismisses cabinet members, although these officials clearly serve at his will and have virtually none of the due process rights that apply to lower-level officials.

Let us assume then that the federal prison administrators could not dismiss the old wardens or bypass them and replace lower-level employees. Under these circumstances, how would these administrators have transformed the southern prisons? Administrative theory and practice suggest two techniques. First, the federal officials would have decided on the kind of regime they wanted and would have promulgated extensive, detailed instructions to their truculent subordinates. Second, they would have hired a staff of inspectors, answerable to the central office, who would travel to the system's widely dispersed prisons, monitor their progress, enforce the new regulations, and report cases of continued intransigence back to headquarters.[7]

We will consider the promulgation of instructions in the remainder of this section, reserving the question of staff for the section that follows. Continuing the contrast between proactive and reactive styles, federal agencies can generally choose whether to formulate policy through "quasi-judicial" orders or "quasi-legislative" rule making,[8] the former being more incremental and the latter more synoptic. Although traditional modes of legal thought, or perhaps the more mundane lack of a modern vocabulary, leads us to describe these approaches in terms of judicial trials or legislation, they are also, as Colvin Diver has pointed out, basic modes of administrative policy making.[9] The choice between them depends on the agency's general approach, its political situation, the nature of its task, and the attitudes of its regulated parties. Quasi-judicial action enables the agency to proceed incrementally, resolving immediate problems and deferring more distant and uncertain ones; it is generally regarded as a risk-averse strategy and a slower, less ambitious one. Quasi-legislative action, while it can also be performed quite cautiously, has the potential to produce comprehensive and consistent change, risking all the dislocations and opposition that such change will frequently produce.[10]

Whether adjudicatory or legislative style action was selected, our administrative agency would behave in a rather different manner from the standard image of a court in carrying out its program. It would tend to vary the specificity and extent of its instructions in relation to the nature of the particular prison or correctional agency.[11] Some prison administrators would be more intransigent and require more detailed instructions, while others would be more compliant and could thus be granted more discretion. The nature of opposing interest groups would also be a factor. In some cases, there might be a powerful but moderate prisoners' rights group that could negotiate with tractable prison administrators to develop acceptable rules on their own; good administrators often encourage such negotiation processes and then promulgate the results as regulations, an approach that has recently been codified and has become quite fashionable in the environmental and consumer areas.[12] In other cases, the prisoners' rights group could not be relied upon, either because it was too weak to reach a balanced agreement, because its demands were too extreme for moderate prison officials, or because the officials were intransigent and thus unwilling to negotiate. In that case, the administrator would need to act unilaterally, presumably with prior consultation, but without relying on negotiation.

All this, of course, is precisely the pattern that the federal judiciary displayed in the prison reform movement. Precluded from dismissing antagonistic wardens and replacing them with reformers who would respond to broad directives, judges resorted to translating their new doctrine of the rehabilitative, bureaucratic prison into detailed instructions on prison management. The variations in provenance and content of these instructions resemble the variations in administrative orders and regulations. Some judges, like Henley, proceeded incrementally, developing their approach from case to case, while others, like Judge Justice, moved more rapidly to comprehensive orders through a process that resembles classic policy analysis. Some orders were fairly general, permitting prison officials to fill in the details, while others covered every aspect of prison life from soup to nuts (i.e., from nutrition to psychiatric services). In Arkansas, Judge Henley could content himself with rules that gradually became more general and less mandatory as the state's correctional leadership came to accept and ultimately value his involvement. In Texas, where officials were intensely hostile to judicial intervention, Judge Justice felt obligated to stretch them tighter and tighter on the rack of detailed, court-ordered rules. Many cases were settled by negotiation and consent decree, from the least acrimonious, like Arkansas and Georgia, to the most acrimonious, like Texas, but some, like Mississippi, were resolved entirely by judicially fashioned orders.

Administrative agencies possess an additional characteristic; they can engage in strategic behavior, sometimes quite effectively. Thus, their actions are not necessarily to be taken at face value.[13] If the agency perceived that the optimal reform strategy was dismissal of subordinate officials, but was unable to implement this strategy because of legal or administrative constraints, it might try to use its rules to accomplish that ultimate goal. The more comprehensive the regulations, the more assiduously these regulations were enforced, and the more hostile the agency's general demeanor, the more the intransigent official would be tempted to retire, transfer, or seek a new position. Responsible administrators will generally stop short of outright ad hominem harassment, but they tend to feel no obligation to be sympathetic or conciliatory to recalcitrant subordinates.

Once again the courts behaved analogously. Consciously or not, they created a law-suffused environment in which the old-time wardens and their closest associates simply could not survive. The concept of prisoners' rights was too foreign to them, and the supervision by an external authority too distasteful. Even more significantly, these wardens lacked the necessary skills to deal with the courts; they did not know how to tell their stories, how to frame arguments, how to rebut their opponents' claims. Like Cretaceous sauropods, they found themselves inhabiting a hostile world and gradually disappeared, sometimes by voluntary decisions, sometimes by direct action by higher state officials who had grown weary of their ineffectiveness.[14] Texas's truculent correctional leaders, who drew a line in the sand when the *Ruiz* litigation started, were swept off the beach within a few short years, to be replaced with officials from the federal military barracks at Leavenworth and similar facilities. The Santa Clara Board of Supervisors responded with a step beyond replacing personnel; as the litigation progressed it removed jail administration in its entirety from the Sheriff's Office and transferred it into the hands of a "corrections professional." Across the nation, the old wardens were gone in little more than a decade, replaced by progressives of precisely the sort that the courts would have wanted to appoint – college-educated professionals with experience in prison social work and education, rather than in security. These new wardens accepted the judiciary's basic premise about prisoners' rights, they expected outside supervision, and they were comfortable with the legal environment that the courts had created. Like an agency, the courts had used their rule-making and enforcement machinery to achieve the desired but otherwise unattainable goal of replacing subordinates who were unable to "get with the program."

The Judicial Use of Staff

Agency heads are typically generalists selected for political considerations and perhaps for their general competence as administrators, but only occasionally for their substantive expertise. Even if they are experts, their success as administrators rarely depends upon whether they are able to use this expertise effectively. Judges resemble agency heads in this respect; they too are dependent upon others – the parties appearing before them, amicus briefs, and expert witnesses – for substantive expertise. Unlike administrators who command the resources of an extensive bureaucracy, however, a judge is generally limited to a secretary and one or two recent law school graduates. In this situation, the judges did what understaffed administrators often do; they turned to standards that had already been developed by other institutions. As stated in Chapter 5, this approach was partially attributable to the federal judiciary's desire to impose national standards on the states, most notably standards developed by the American Correctional Association and the federal Bureau of Prisons. A contributing explanation, however, is that federal judges turned to these standards because they wanted to impose detailed, administrative-style rules of any sort but lacked the resources to design the rules themselves. As described in Chapter 6, they needed to turn these standards into doctrine by holding that a nonrehabilitational, nonbureaucratic prison violated the Eighth Amendment. In framing specific remedies, however, they could go beyond doctrine, as William Fletcher[15] has pointed out, and impose the nondoctrinal standards of the Bureau of Prisons and the ACA directly.

Borrowing standards from national organizations allowed judges to set benchmarks against which they could compare existing practices and future progress, but it did not provide them with the capacity to monitor that progress, to press deeper into the sources of problems, or to ferret out particularized impediments; for this they needed something closer to an administrative staff. That staff was sometimes supplied by state correctional officials themselves. In the Arkansas case, Commissioner Sarver was quite willing to aid the court, and it was his witnesses, more than those of the complainants, who provided Judge Henley with the most trenchant criticisms and effective diagnoses of problems in the prison system. Commissioner Sarver's own testimony repeatedly drew attention to continuing problems and invited the court to expand its inquiry and to press the legislature for additional resources. In Colorado, a variety of commissions appointed by state officials fully documented the abuses at Old Max; their reports, although produced before the litigation was initiated, became the centerpiece of the plaintiffs' case. The sheriff of the Lincoln, Nebraska, county jail reported to one of the authors several years ago that he had difficulty sleeping because his jail lacked an adequate fire protection system; to calm his nerves, he all but invited the local ACLU attorney to bring a suit challenging this and other conditions he regarded as deficient. In Santa Rosa County, California, federal judge Thelton Henderson had recourse to a different group of existing officials. Having overseen the construction of a new jail facility during a ten-year litigation, he arranged for the grand jury members to tour the new facility. He then invited them to watch for crowding in the new jail after it opened, and to intervene if they learned that inmates were sleeping on the floor or being denied access to basic services.[16]

Obviously, judges could not always rely on the existing correctional staff; indeed, any reformer is more likely to encounter resistance than cooperation from that quarter. Quite often they resorted to another method characteristic of reform administrators. While such administrators generally have permanent staff, they often find these staff members are the problem rather than the solution. Precluded from firing the old-timers by civil service laws and political reality, they might appoint additional staff, loyal to themselves and committed to their vision. But few institutions possess the resources to employ two parallel sets of personnel. Instead, the more usual practice is for the reform administrator to add a small number of direct subordinates in important or highly sensitive positions and to rely on them to catalyze, convert, or discipline the remaining staff members.[17]

The most general way to characterize such new staff is that it provides special assistants to the chief administrator. Special assistants have not been studied carefully in public administration, but they are acknowledged to be widespread and significant.[18] They provide a direct link between a chief administrator, on the one hand, and those charged with administering substantive policies on the other, a link that often bypasses the command structure depicted on the agency's organization chart. Their role is both powerful and ambiguous, and indeed owes much of its power to its ambiguity. Although they may be appointed to deal with selected issues or problems, they generally have few set responsibilities, and within broad parameters are often free to orient their concerns as they see fit.[19] They command few resources of their own, and have little if any formal administrative authority, but they are accorded great deference because they are known to have direct access to the chief executive.* Their authority is not unlimited of course, and if it becomes known that they have exceeded it – if, for instance, they are publicly undercut by their chief – their power and usefulness will rapidly diminish.

This administrative technique was essentially the one adopted by the federal judiciary through its appointment of special masters. Like special assistants in our hypothetical agency, the masters provided judges with loyal managerial subordinates who could facilitate the implementation of their orders. They operated outside the regular administrative hierarchy, but engaged in day-to-day administrative functions that would have been both pragmatically impossible and organizationally inappropriate for judges to perform. Their direct power was generally limited and their jurisdiction vaguely defined, but as designated emissaries of the judge, they often played a decisive role in the reform process.

While a comprehensive study of special masters has yet to be written, there has been a fair amount of attention devoted to their role in recent years. Sturm's study found that masters in prison conditions cases were expected to be fact finders, advisors to the court, enforcement facilitators, mediators, and auditors, although their orders of appointment rarely specified all these functions, let alone attempted to reconcile the incompatible expectations they implied.[20] The result was role confusion and a strain on their legitimacy, which led Sturm to recommend that courts clarify the master's role and incorporate it into their orders of appointment.

On the other hand, David Kirp and Gary Babcock's study of special masters in six school desegregation cases found that nearly identical orders of appointment led to actual work that varied quite significantly.[21] Whatever the initial definition, formal or informal, of their roles, the situation tended to be so fluid that the master's performance was highly contingent upon unforeseen factors, emerging new issues, the chemistry between the judge and special master, and the master's personal style. Much the same point was made by M. Kay Harris and Dudley Spriller in their study of the implementation of court orders in several prison and jail conditions cases.[22] Indeed, both sets of authors underscore the insight that masters inevitably augment their officially prescribed duties with a wide range of informal information-gathering and consulting duties. At some times, their jobs consist largely of selling the courts' orders to the defendants. At other times their function is to serve as consultants to the

---

* This used to be called having the chief executive's ear, but now, through some subtle change in metaphorical physiognomy, it is called "face time."

defendants, advising them how they can most readily satisfy the court's demands. And sometimes, they act like politicians – working quietly behind the scenes in order to forge a consensus among the parties, then going public to rally support for the resulting plan.

There thus seems to be a general sense that masters perform a wide variety of roles that are fluid at their boundaries and only vaguely defined at their core. Both the particular roles and the open-ended manner in which those roles are defined can be readily recognized as features of the special assistant to an agency administrator. We would expect the assistant to provide the administrator with information, to devote full-time attention to the subject of reform, to establish legitimacy as an expert in this subject, and to absorb much of the criticism that the administrator would otherwise receive. Masters performed all of these functions, selecting them, combining them, or alternating between them as the situation changed. Like the special assistants, they acted for their superiors without necessarily speaking for them. Invariably, the judge reserved the right to review the master's work and, if necessary, to disagree with him, to dismiss his ideas, or to dismiss the master himself. This distance served the court well in Arkansas, where Steve La Plante absorbed much of the mounting resentment about the intrusiveness of the court's orders. Judge Eisele could appear to remain above the fray, periodically reminding the defendants that it was "within their reach" to bring the case to a close. Indeed, he could share with them the strong desire to do so, leaving La Plante to point out to them how much remained to do before they reached the end of the proverbial light-terminated tunnel.

We would also expect a competent administrator to use special assistants selectively – as informants always, as consultants and advisors to the tractable, and as supervisors or punishers of the intransigent. Eugene Bardach and Robert Kagan observe, in their study of industrial safety inspectors, that a uniform and formulaic enforcement of the rules, or "going by the book," is generally a poor administrative strategy. It is better, in their view, to induce compliance through compromise and to overlook minor violations in order to achieve more general goals.[23] In cases of outright intransigence, however, the inspector should not only go by the book, but throw it at the obdurate factory manager. This not only punishes the "bad apples," as John Scholz points out in his compliance studies, but indicates to others that forbearance from a maximal enforcement strategy is the reward for tractability.[24]

Of all the states whose prisons were subjected to court order, the bad apple was obviously Texas, and Judge Justice developed the role of his special master, Vincent Nathan, in response. At the height of the struggle, Nathan's staff numbered fourteen – equivalent to a small Texas law firm – who regularly confronted, criticized, and overruled state correctional officials. Nathan's adversarial, uncooperative stance has been much condemned, but it was not the product of either a personality defect or a situation that had spun out of control; rather, it was the stance that most administrators would instruct their special assistants to adopt when trying to reform a highly intransigent bureaucracy.

In other states, when correctional officials were more willing to compromise, special masters followed a more cooperative, advisory approach, showing flexibility in return for broad-level compliance. Steve La Plante in Arkansas and Tom Lonergan in Santa Clara County exemplified this model, although both could certainly turn confrontational when faced with real resistance. Finally, when the bureaucracy was truly cooperative – when the old wardens were gone and the old attitudes had changed – judges tended to reward the state officials with the most desirable special assistant, namely, none at all. Like competent administrators once again, judges who felt that the state officials were willing to comply would either dismiss their master, as in Arkansas and Santa Clara County, or never appoint one, as in Georgia[25] and Colorado.* But this administrative freedom from the irritating presence of an inspector in the field was usually granted as a reward for obedience to the reform agenda that the judges articulated. In sum, the special masters were part of a recognizable administrative strategy, and the variations in their approach, far from being signs of some institutional pathology, generally represented an appropriate response to the varied situations that the courts confronted.

In both their imposition of standards and their use of staff, courts varied between classic policy analysis and incrementalism. To some extent, different cases can be placed in different categories, with Arkansas and Santa Clara being largely incrementalist, while Texas and Colorado, where the judge began with a clearer sense of a general plan, conforming more closely to the classic model. But there is also a sense in which all implementation efforts in these cases simultaneously fulfilled both roles – they served as the last step in the classic model, and they constituted the entirety of a more incremental process.

The Separation of Powers and Judicial Competence

Just as the nationalization of prison standards represented the rejection of the well-regarded principle of federalism, the active implementation of those standards was undertaken in violation of another constitutional fixture: the separation of powers. Like federalism, separation of powers has demonstrated unexpected vitality, as the Supreme Court has continued

---

* In the Colorado litigation, a special master was appointed only to resolve the issue of attorneys' fees – the one issue on which Colorado acted like Texas.

to take this doctrine very seriously. Indeed, while the effects of the Court's federalism decisions have been rather paltry, particularly when contrasted with the grandeur of their rhetoric,[26] separation of powers considerations have led the Court to overturn several major federal statutes dealing with some of our central problems of the day; portions of the Federal Elections Campaign Act,[27] portions of the Balanced Budget and Emergency Deficit Control Act,[28] portions of the Bankruptcy Act,[29] and the legislative veto provision in over two hundred separate statutes[30] have all fallen before the Court's insistence that each branch of government remain within its constitutionally established ambit.[31]

Separation of powers is a complex concept that operates on several different levels. As James Ceasar suggests, a distinction can be made between its application to the "primary powers" of government and to the policy-making process.[32] With respect to primary powers, or government structure, debates about separation of powers have often centered on the choice between a parliamentary and a presidential system.[33] The issue is an interesting one, both for political reform in established democracies and for the thankfully substantial numbers of countries that are adopting democratic regimes, but it does not involve the judiciary, and so need not detain us here. Thus, this chapter does not argue that the federal judiciary's rejection of the separation of powers doctrine represented a total rejection of the concept, as the previous chapter argues with respect to federalism, but only a rejection of it as a limit on the judiciary's range of action. As a result, we do not consider whether separation of powers protects liberty, except for a brief discussion in Chapter 8. The suggestion of Rebecca Brown, Martin Redish, Elizabeth Cisar, and Peter Shane that separation of powers is a means of protecting political freedom is intriguing, but it applies primarily to aggrandizements of power by the legislature or by the executive.[34] Despite complaints about the "imperial judiciary," no one really thinks that the kind of monolithic government that would pose a threat to liberty would arise from an expansion of judicial power.

There is, however, another governmental structure issue that focuses on the judiciary and is often cast in separation of powers terms – the independent status of the courts, or, more specifically, their ability to apply legal rules and binding force to individuals without intervention from other governmental agents. If this is indeed separation of powers, then everyone is in favor of the doctrine, but such support cannot be parlayed into a general approbation of the doctrine's other implications. As an empirical matter, judicial independence is unrelated to the remainder of separation of powers doctrine, because courts in parliamentary regimes such as Britain, New Zealand, and the Netherlands that do not subscribe to the separation of powers doctrine are just as independent as those in the United States. Moreover, as noted in Chapter 1, many important legal issues in our country are decided by administrative law judges, the bankruptcy courts, and the court of claims, all part of the executive branch, without raising major difficulties about the independence of their judgments.[35] As a theoretical matter, the independence of the judiciary possesses its own normative grounding – the individual's right to due process of law[36] – that has no particular connection with separation of powers doctrine. Consequently, judicial independence is more usefully called separation of functions, rather than separation of powers;*[37] it is one of the glories of democratic government, but it has no necessary implications for the scope of the judiciary's role.

Separation of powers doctrine becomes directly relevant to judicial decision making, and a source of current political debate, when we descend from the level of primary powers to that of policy making. At issue here is not the general design of the three, or four branches of government, but their daily interactions, the extent to which their ongoing efforts should be confined within crisply defined roles. The constitutional status of this issue is derived from the introductory provisions of the first three Articles, which grant Congress the legislative power, the president the executive power, and the courts the judicial power. This language clearly demonstrates that the Framers had read Montesquieu, but from the way the terms are currently employed, one might assume that the inspiration was von Clausewitz; each branch is described as invading the other's territory, sometimes by minor border crossings, sometimes by major assaults upon the other's "core." This struggle impacts the federal judiciary in two different ways: first, judges are assigned the task of policing the depredations of the executive or legislative branch against either of the other two, and second, judges are supposed to restrain their own desire to conquer and appropriate the governmental territory beyond the borders of their realm. In thus keeping the peace between the other branches, protecting themselves, and controlling their own aggressive inclinations, the courts assume the vaunted role of a moral combatant, the role in which the United States cast itself during the Gulf War.

This discourse inevitably suggests that strong norms are at stake. But just as many of the standard arguments for federalism actually relate to

---

* There are many other examples of this functional separation principle, some with constitutional implications and some without. Most developed countries separate the money control function of their central bank from elected officials. Technical tasks, like approving a new drug, are often separated as well. The requirement that information which individuals disclose to one government agency, willingly or unwillingly, should be kept private, even from other agencies in the same branch, is also a form of functional separation.

the managerial principle of decentralization, many of the arguments for the separation of powers doctrine relate to the equally managerial principle of functional specialization, or the division of labor. Governments, even premodern governments, cannot be efficiently operated by an undifferentiated body of officials; with the increasing size of the modern state, the division of labor becomes essential. Like decentralization, however, this is a pragmatic, managerial strategy, not a normative principle. Much of the moral force that the separation of powers seems to possess is probably the product of its eighteenth-century origins. As in the case of federalism, pragmatic strategies tended to acquire a certain normative patina at that time because a more managerial discourse had not yet evolved. Indeed, the whole concept of specialization was in its infancy; according to Weber, Durkheim, Talcott Parsons, Niklas Luhmann,[38] and others, the growth of specialization and its penetration into so many different aspects of society is the product of the industrial, bureaucratic system that was just developing in the late eighteenth century. From our present perspective, however, it seems clear that the division of government into separate units serves a largely pragmatic or managerial purpose. Business firms, hospitals, administrative agencies, and almost all other large organizations follow the same organizational pattern, but none claim that this pattern possesses the force of social norms.

The most familiar legal argument for enforcing the separation of powers in fact relates to the managerial technique of specialization. This is the legal process claim that each branch of government possesses intrinsic institutional features that preclude its effective exercise of the powers that are assigned to a different branch.[39] What is at stake here is effectiveness or efficiency, not some normative value like liberty, community, or democracy. The underlying concept is that institutions, like living organisms, are adapted to their own environment, having developed specialized features that are dysfunctional in other settings. An instrumental argument of this nature cannot provide an absolute prohibition against one particular branch of government engaging in activities that we normally associate with another; at most, it offers prudential reasons to proceed with caution. It might be unwise for a polar bear to live in the Sahara, or for a court to undertake administrative functions, but we would hardly call it immoral. And if the bear had no other place to live, or the government had no other institution that could undertake those functions, it would make perfect sense for each of them to do their best, despite the inefficiency.

As Neil Komesar and Oliver Williamson have observed, institutional competence is a relative concept, not an absolute one.[40] There is no transcendental context-free metric by which it can be said that a particular institution is theoretically incapable of carrying out a particular task. The operative issue is whether one institution will do so more or less effectively than another institution, and this will depend upon complex factors that will vary from one situation to another. Williamson points out that human beings are adaptable enough to achieve the same result in a variety of different settings, so that comparative judgments must be based on the particularized costs that these different settings engender.[41]

In making these comparative assessments, it is a mistake to place excessive emphasis on the received categories of executive, legislative, and judicial institutions. These are of great significance for formalist arguments, as will be discussed later, and they acquire pragmatic importance from being ensconced in our political traditions. Nonetheless, the structure of government has changed a great deal since the eighteenth century, and we should not assume that preadministrative demarcations necessarily reflect an accurate categorization of modern governmental institutions. Indeed, the awkwardness of describing our modern state in terms of the traditional model has generated a variety of contemporary observations, usually in the form of jeremiads, about the fourth branch of government, and has probably contributed to our failure to develop either a legal theory or a legal pedagogy for public administration.

Moreover, there is no reason to think that the traditional demarcations are even an accurate categorization of the premodern state. Prior to the seventeenth century, political theorists regarded government as being divided between executive and legislative functions;[42] the perception of three separate functions is the product of the English Civil War.[43] Subsequent thinkers were quite certain that three was the right number, but they were not in agreement about what this number represented. According to Locke, governmental functions were naturally divided into the legislative power, which involved making laws; the executive power, which involved enforcing these laws by punishing their violators; and the federative power, which involved the conduct of external affairs.[44] Montesquieu, a determined trinitarian, established the current division among legislature, executive, and judicial power, but he also restated Locke's taxonomy, dividing the executive between internal law enforcement and external affairs.[45] If his two positions are combined, therefore, there would be four branches, not three. Underlying his apparent confusion is the insight that some of the functions generally described as executive involve the enforcement of enacted law, while others involve rather broad policy or discretionary functions – an insight that is intimately connected with the predominant feature of governance in our modern administrative state. Moreover, there are a number of functions, of which foreign relations is the most notable, that do not obviously fit into one of the recognized categories. As both James Landis and M. J. C. Vile have observed, combining these various functions may preserve the number three, but it does not necessarily represent an accurate political theory.[46]

Once we jettison the idea that our tripartite division of government represents an unambiguous reality, we are left with prudential arguments that the various branches of government function best when limited to their traditional roles. Such arguments, however, are subject to empirical refutation. Empirical analysis of executive and legislative action is a complex subject, raising issues of appointment and removal, delegation and supervision. The concern here is the judiciary and its ability to function in an administrative mode. With respect to the other branches, it is sufficient to observe that any evidence that they will be dangerous or ineffective if they roam beyond their proper ambit does not indicate that judicial peregrinations would raise equivalent difficulties.

The empirical argument that courts should behave "judicially" and not act as administrators appears to be a formidable one, however. It has probably been the dominant belief about courts since the abandonment of substantive due process, and it has not only survived the scholarly bombardment against legal process theory, but thrived on the incoming ordnance. While many contemporary scholars deride the notion that areas of institutional competence can be identified,[47] they champion the institutional incompetence of judges with unprecedented vigor. Their attack has even extended to the area of human rights, where conventional wisdom suggests that courts have been most successful in effectuating public policy. Donald Horowitz's study, *The Courts and Social Policy*,[48] catalogs a long list of limits that impede judges from being effective policy makers, and goes on to argue that any results that do flow from judicial intervention are likely to be counterproductive. Stuart Scheingold develops a similar argument in *The Politics of Rights*[49] about the inability of the courts to effect social change, although he concedes that courts can have a catalytic effect in certain circumstances. Most recently, Gerald Rosenberg in *The Hollow Hope*[50] marshals considerable evidence that courts, by themselves, almost never effect significant social change. Even *Brown v. Board of Education*, the most sacred cow for proponents of judicial activism, produced only marginal nourishment for school desegregation, Rosenberg asserts. Significant change occurred only after Congress and the president took up the cause, and these more effective branches acted in response to civil rights demonstrations, which emerged wholly independent of the federal court decisions.[51]

This general critique of judicial effectiveness has been applied to the prison reform cases by John DiIulio.[52] DiIulio recites the usual list of pragmatic concerns about court intervention: that it was uninformed and unrealistic, that it demoralized the prison staff, and that it produced generally deleterious effects.[53] His discussion goes further; in championing the pre-*Ruiz* Texas prison system as the paragon of correctional adminis-tration,[54] he adopts a position that no other scholar shares. This view can only be explained in terms of DiIulio's preempirical and unexplained admiration for order and, more particularly, for neatness.[55] His praise for the Texas prisons extends not only to the level of discipline they imposed, but also to the prisoners' white uniforms, the care with which towels were distributed, the use of prisoners to wash windows at prison headquarters, and the display of a three and one-quarter foot rawhide belt at that fa-cility.[56] But the peculiarities of his position should not obscure his criticism of court intervention, which allies him with so many other observers of the judicial process.

The theoretical underpinnings for all these works can be found in Lon Fuller's well-known article, "The Forms and Limits of Adjudication."[57] Fuller distinguishes among three forms of social ordering: contracts, where the parties participate by negotiation; elections, where participation comes through voting; and adjudication, where participation involves the presentation of reasoned arguments and structured proofs. Adjudication is impossible without reasoned argument, Fuller maintains, and judicial decisions are impossible without legal standards that can be interpreted and extrapolated. Consequently, agencies cannot rely on an adjudicatory approach in open-ended situations and often respond to the demand they do so by adopting the standards of the regulated party. Courts, on the other hand, are limited to this adjudicatory approach. They can deal with diadic disputes presented by opposing parties, but in what he calls poly-centric situations, involving multifaceted considerations whose conse-quences extend beyond the present parties, adjudication fails.[58] Since policy implementation is inherently open-ended and polycentric, Fuller's model clearly predicts that courts will be ineffective in this role. They will lack the resources to sustain polycentric decision making, and when they try to do so, they will produce substantially inferior results to those achieved by executive or legislative institutions.

Despite the ubiquity of this empirical claim that judges are ineffective policy makers, and despite the claim's impressive intellectual pedigree, it did not persuade the judges in the prison reform cases. The usual expla-nation for this annoying fact seems, once again, to be collective brain fever, but reflection suggests that the federal judiciary was not quite as demented as the theory would imply. The legal process position is based on a number of unexamined and inherently questionable expectations about the nature of judicial policy making. Even more important, it is based on assumptions derived from a traditional model of judicial action, the very model that judges rejected in their policy-making efforts.

To begin with, as Komesar insists,[59] the assumptions about the success or failure of policy making must be understood in relative terms. If we define success as the rapid and inexpensive realization of the precise effects that the policy makers envisioned, then we will not find success on this side of bureaucratic heaven.[60] If we define effective judicial intervention as the comprehensive transformation of government or social institutions without dislocation or delay, success will be equally uncommon. But the mere catalog of disappointments and frustrated expectations cannot be taken as definitive evidence of general failure, any more than a football team's three punts, two turnovers, and two missed field goal attempts can demonstrate that it lost the game. Much of the dissatisfaction with courts as social change agents, as Paul Gewirtz suggests,[61] is derived from the conflation of social change and individual rights that our traditional concept of a court engenders. Courts are supposed to declare rights, particularly in constitutional cases, and rights are supposed to be categorical and universal. When we think of the right to the free exercise of one's religion, our idea is that denial of that right to a single eligible person, or in a single relevant instance, represents a failure. As a matter of legal theory, that is entirely correct. But social change is measured in relative, not categorical terms. A program to provide health care to rural populations or to reduce sexual harassment in the workplace is not counted as a failure if several rural areas remain without services or if incidents of harassment continue to occur. These are, of course, unfortunate, but what matters in assessing whether social programs are effective is the amount of change; if there are dramatic increases in rural health care or dramatic decreases in sexual harassment, the social program would be deemed a great success. In evaluating courts as social change agents, it is only realistic to hold them to the standards we hold other agents, not a theoretical and unachievable standard derived from the concept of rights.

A second point is that social change can rarely be attributed to a single actor or institution. The question whether the court's intervention caused a specific change cannot be answered in the negative by describing the role of other participants; what is relevant is whether the courts were significant players in the process. In fact, the expectation that the courts could effect important changes on their own is not only grandiose, but implicitly rejects the very kind of judicial action that is at issue in the prison cases. If the task of courts is to interpret legal texts, then their actions are essentially self-executing; they can produce their interpretive effects without the participation of other government officials. But if courts are also supposed to make public policy, then implementation becomes part of their task, and this almost always involves shared power and cooperative efforts. There are few studies that attempt to measure the independent impact of traditional policy makers such as the president, Congress, state legislators, city councils, governors, or mayors; the reason, presumably, is that their policy-making efforts inherently involve multiple actors. What is relevant is whether they played a significant role, and this is the only relevant question for judicial policy making as well.[62]

Finally, the prison reform cases were somewhat different from the cases that have tended to dominate concern about the judiciary's power to effect social change. For the most part, those who have explored the impact of courts on social policy have focused on "big" Supreme Court decisions – school desegregation, criminal procedure, reapportionment, abortion, school prayer, and the like. Because the Supreme Court attracts so much attention and possesses so much cachet, we tend to treat it as equivalent to our entire judicial system. In fact, the federal judiciary is a large, complex institution with its branch offices – the trial courts – in every section of the country. As discussed in Chapter 6, in the context of coordination, prison conditions cases were primarily the product of those trial courts. They were part of a jurisprudence of facts, the localized, ground-level efforts of hundreds of separate institutions, each devoting hundreds or thousands of hours to managing or micromanaging specific institutions. An interpretive declaration of the Supreme Court – for example, that prayer in schools violates the Establishment Clause – may not produce much impact, but this does not mean that the detailed orders issued and implemented by trial courts across the nation will be similarly ineffectual.

Much of the belief that the intrinsic structure of courts precludes them from functioning effectively as policy makers stems from these unrealistic expectations – that the proper standard is perfection, that the courts must act alone, and that only Supreme Court decisions count. The remaining basis for this belief is both simpler and deeper. As stated in Chapter 1, many observers assume that the only valid functions of courts are to resolve factual disputes and to interpret authoritative sources of law. As a result, the capacities of courts are assumed to be those of a hypothetical entity limited to fact-finding and interpretation. In his article on the forms and limits of adjudication, Fuller makes precisely this assumption; he treats adjudication as coextensive with judicial action, and then identifies the features of the former – fact-finding and law-interpreting – as the limits of the latter. But this article explicates the forms and limits of the Harvard case law model, not of real courts in a modern administrative state. Real courts are also capable of acting as policy makers, that is, they can create new legal rules in open-ended situations to achieve broadly defined social purposes. When doing so, as Ralph Cavanagh and Austin Sarat point out,[63] they can resolve polycentric problems just like any other policymaker.

Abram Chayes,[64] Colin Diver,[65] Owen Fiss,[66] William Fletcher,[67] Susan Sturm,[68] and others have described the techniques that modern, policy-

making judges use when confronting polycentric problems.* Many of
these are illustrated in the prison cases. Like an administrator confronted
with such problems, judges regularly turned to experts in the field who
had developed solutions through hands-on experience. They had no particular difficulty gaining access to these experts: they encouraged the
plaintiffs to call them as witnesses, they appointed them as special masters,
or they simply read their written work. Administrators also deal with polycentric problems by obtaining information from as many groups as possible, or by convening representatives of these groups to negotiate or
simply interact. Federal judges adopted the same approach, either directly
or through their special masters. They were generally in contact with a
wide range of state prison administrators, and often with other state officials as well. They obtained information about prison conditions directly
from inmates, as well as from the plaintiff's attorneys. In fact, as in Arkansas, Texas, Colorado, and Santa Clara County, the plaintiffs' attorney
was often an appointee of the courts, enlisted for the specific purpose of
enabling the competing groups to negotiate among themselves or with
the judge. Not every affected party had a voice of course; once a plaintiffs'
attorney was in place, the prisoners themselves were frequently ignored.
But failure to include all interested parties is not entirely unknown among
administrative agencies. The significant point is that the courts included
a sufficient variety of parties to go far beyond Fuller's model of a passive
adjudicator receiving the submissions of two contesting parties.

In addition, federal judges, like competent administrators, dealt with
the uncertainty of polycentric situations by proceeding incrementally. Fuller's image of adjudication is that the judge hears the arguments and
issues a definitive order. That is indeed the traditional image of a legal
case, but the prison "cases" were entirely different. As stated earlier,
judges varied in their approach, with some proceeding incrementally and
others proceeding in the more comprehensive fashion characteristic of
the classic model. But they always retained jurisdiction, they always gathered information about the impact of their initial orders, and they always

---

* As discussed in Chapter 1, most of these scholars express serious reservations
  about the legitimacy of these techniques in the process of noting their ubiquity
  and effectiveness. The way many of them resolve the dilemma is to distinguish
  the declaration of rights from the design of remedies, and to acknowledge that
  judges possess more latitude in the remedial area. But, as just described, the
  declaration of remedies is an integral part of the policy-making process; it is one
  stage of the classic model, and an element of every successive effort in the incremental model. This chapter argues, in essence, that the judges' activist stance
  in imposing remedies was legitimate, while Chapter 6 argues that their equally
  activist stance in fashioning new legal rights was also legitimate.

revised their orders on the basis of that information. In short, had judges felt constrained to follow the rules Fuller established for them – rules derived from the case law method designed by C. C. Langdell in the 1870s[69] – they may well have been unable to deal with the polycentric problem of prison reform. But the federal judiciary of the 1970s did not feel so constrained.

In essence, the institutional competence argument for separation of powers is not normative but managerial; it simply restates the standard sociological observation about task specialization in the modern state. The foregoing discussion suggests that it restates this sociological observation rather poorly. Courts are indeed specialized, but they are not so specialized that they are precluded from adopting contemporary styles of governance. Such a preclusion would not be specialization at all, but a separate phenomenon that might be called "conceptual compartmentalization." This phenomenon certainly occurs – in fact, it is the familiar "that's-not-my-department" syndrome – but most people regard it as a defect to be avoided, not a guiding principle to be respected. Indeed, one of the major purposes of specialization is to create clear sources of expertise that can be readily recognized and mobilized as the situation demands. In other words, the division of tasks is supposed to increase interactions, not foreclose it. Modern, specialized physicians, for example, work in teams; the patient with chest pains, instead of being fed herbs, bled, and wrapped in poultices by a premodern solo practitioner, might now be treated by a cardiologist, a cardiovascular surgeon, an anesthesiologist, a nutritionist, and a psychiatrist, all sharing the same epistemological approach to health care despite their various specializations. Similarly, the federal courts, courts though they were, shared contemporary notions about policy making and administration with the other branches of government.

It is true that task specialization often possesses a jurisdictional character, and that prison reform might be regarded as outside the judiciary's jurisdiction. Indeed, that is precisely how judges regarded it during the ascendancy of the hands-off doctrine. But they ultimately took action because they perceived a major social problem that no one else was addressing, and that they could reasonably add to their jurisdiction by invoking the Constitution. To solve the social problem, they had to act in a policy-making mode characteristic of administrators, but that is our dominant style of governance, and nothing about the courts' task specialization precludes them from employing it.

Thus, the implementation stage of judicial policy making consists of the approaches and techniques that are available to all policy makers in the modern, administrative state. In their intensive supervision of state prisons, the federal judges could draw upon a vast and well-established set of methods – methods that had become an integral part of their experience through their interaction with other governmental agents, their previous careers as practicing attorneys, and their general membership in our society. As Dennis Patterson and Steven Winter point out, judicial decision making is a situated practice that always draws heavily on such common understandings.[70] To be sure, not every act of judicial policy making will demand as many of these methods as the judges deployed in the prison cases. But all these methods are available, their use is understood and the occasions where they are relevant are recognizable. There is admittedly no formula or protocol for their application, but that requirement for legitimate governance would return us to the state of nature. The fact is, judges can act as administrators as readily as anyone can perform the activities that are natural to their culture – as readily as medieval clerics discussed theology, as Renaissance explorers sailed ships, as nineteenth-century industrialists built factories, or as judges throughout all these eras interpreted authoritative texts.

The normative aspect of this operational process by which judges act as administrators follows from its contextualized familiarity. We know, by and large, what is involved in being a good administrator. Good administrators should be clear about the ultimate objective and committed to achieving that objective. They should proceed with caution, taking care to consult all relevant parties, but ultimately reaching their own conclusions based on as much information as they can gather and as much practical reason as they can bring to bear. Having decided on a course of action, they should insure that it is carried out, but should avoid allowing frustration or an offended ego to induce the imposition of draconian punishments on the recalcitrant. They should be candid about their ultimate desires, but be willing to engage in strategic action in order to achieve their stated goal. A good policy-making judge should follow the same widely recognized principles when acting in an administrative mode.

While the portrait is somewhat idealized, it is hardly unattainable. Many of the judges who appear in Part I of this study followed these principles rather consistently throughout the arduous, complex operational process that they undertook. Judge Henley was fully familiar with the draconian remedies at his disposal, including civil and criminal contempt and the closure of state institutions, and he invoked them as a threat when he made his abortive or strategic effort to relinquish jurisdiction in *Holt III*, but his basic approach remained as conciliatory as possible. Judge Justice may have veered toward a more heavy-handed style, but he never used his contempt power, despite some powerful temptations to do so, he never stopped consulting with TDC officials, and he ultimately was well regarded by the TDC's reform administration. Other observers, including Bradley Chilton,[71] Ted Storey,[72] Susan Sturm,[73] and Larry Yackle[74] provide similar portraits of the operational process that federal judges followed in the prison cases. Nor is this model limited to the institutional reform arena. Christopher Edley[75] suggests a similar approach for judges when reviewing the policy-making efforts of federal agencies under the Administrative Procedure Act, and Peter Schuck[76] observed these same norms among the judges who handled the mass tort case involving Agent Orange.

Of course, like any norms of official or private behavior, the norms of good judicial policy making will be violated in various cases; no normative principle is definitive and persuasive enough to render its violation inconceivable. The case studies suggest that state courts, rather than federal courts, are the most likely to commit such violations. It was California trial judges who plunged into detailed prison reform without bothering to establish an Eighth Amendment basis for the case, who held prison officials in contempt for disobeying an ambiguous decision, and who issued orders to hire plumbers and to buy bed linens at J. C. Penney; similarly, it was the California trial court judges who refused, en masse, to serve in their county's jail reform case; and it was a California appellate court that concocted a secret deal with the plaintiff and defense attorneys without the knowledge of the trial court judge with whom the case was sub judice. Decisions such as these are probably the product of less talented jurists, less public scrutiny, less staff support, and less judicial independence. Federal judges in Arkansas, Texas, and elsewhere seemed to have acted with more restraint and political sophistication. Of course, studies of other state court cases might reveal similar behavior, just as studies of other federal cases might reveal significant lapses. The point is not that the norms of good administrative action are universal or irresistible, but that they are well recognized, realistic, and frequently achieved.

The Formalist Argument for Separation of Powers

The arguments supporting separation of powers do not all result from conflating this doctrine with the managerial principle of specialization. As in the case of federalism, the doctrine is also supported by several truly normative claims. These claims fall into two familiar categories, one drawn from the language of the Constitution and the other drawn from its functional implications.[77] Traditionally, the linguistic or formal argument conceives the Constitution's references to "executive," "legislative," and "judicial" power as archetypes, preexisting categories of government authority that are assigned to the president, Congress, and the federal courts.[78] The functional argument abjures the metaphysics of formalism and grounds the separation of powers on the role that each branch possesses by virtue of its position in our democratic regime.[79] Again, both arguments raise sweeping questions about the executive and legislative branches that will not be discussed in this study. Although normative arguments are not as readily contained as the empirical argument discussed previously, the narrower focus does not distort their basic contours. The relevance of the formalist claim for judicial action depends on whether the phrase "judicial power" has a meaning that imposes identifiable limits on the federal courts. The relevance of the functional claim depends on whether such limits can be derived from the judiciary's role in our democracy. Neither depends directly on whether the terms "executive power" and "legislative power" have similarly definitive meanings, or on whether those two branches have functional limits.

We will consider the formal argument for separation of powers in this section, reserving the functional arguments for the following one. For the purposes of the present study, there is a short answer to this formalist argument as it applies to the judiciary. Despite the rumbling of various critics, the argument simply does not apply to federal court intervention into state prison systems. Separation of powers is a doctrine that regulates relationships between different branches of the same governmental entity, assigning particular roles to each branch; it says nothing about the relationship of these separate branches to other entities.[80] It is affirmatively the role of the judicial branch to overturn state action that violates the Constitution[81] and there is certainly no doctrine limiting this task to actions of the equivalent state branch, that is, to state judicial action rather than state legislative or executive action.

This answer, while adequate for present purposes, is a bit too quick, however. The federal government runs prisons, just as the separate states do. It has prevailed in the prisoners' rights litigation brought against its institutions – at trial in the Marion cases, on appeal in *Bell v. Wolfish*[82] – and this is not accidental, but a product of prison reform's basic character, as has been discussed in connection with federalism. Nonetheless, the possibility that the federal government could operate prisons in violation of constitutional standards is certainly conceivable. Similarly, state courts are often called on to assess state institutions, as in the Santa Clara County litigation, and most state constitutions provide as much textual or structural support for separation of powers as the federal constitution does.

There is, moreover, a less literal way to understand the formalist objection to judicial policy making. Separation of powers, one can argue, defines not only a jurisdiction but a style of governance. When the Framers wrote the words "judicial power" they had a particular image in mind, an image based on the kinds of tasks that courts performed. Separation of powers, sympathetically interpreted, means that judicial action should remain within those boundaries. Two of the leading critics to invoke this argument against federal court involvement in prison conditions cases are Robert Nagel[83] and Paul Mishkin.[84] Their concern is not simply that the courts have strayed from their platonic essence, but that they have trampled on the natural perquisites of other branches, compelling significant expenditures, a legislative function, and significant administrative changes, an executive prerogative. Far from oblivious to the problems that promoted the courts to intervene, they urge caution, not abdication, and search for ways for courts to protect the rights of individuals in organizational settings while at the same time adhering to a more traditional role. Because of the possibility that federal courts could feel motivated to impose constitutional standards on federal prisons, the frequency with which state courts have in fact been motivated to impose such standards on state prisons, and the general limitations on judicial power that a sympathetic understanding of the formalist argument would involve, this argument must be explored more closely.

To begin with, the formalist approach to constitutional issues generally rests on textualist or originalist interpretation[85] of the Constitution. Textualist interpretation, roughly speaking, involves an examination of the constitutional text as an independent but integrated document, while originalist interpretation seeks to discern the Framers' intentions regarding the text that they created. The difficulty, in this context, is that these strategies provide singularly weak support for the separation of powers doctrine. The constitutional text, after all, never states that the three branches should be separate; it merely names Congress, the president, and the courts as holders of the legislative, executive, and judicial powers respectively, which may be little more than a convenient way of referring to the powers granted or implied.[86] In fact, those powers overlap as a result of the checks and balances incorporated into the document; the presidential veto, the Senate's advice and consent role for treaties and appointments, and the Senate's power of impeachment all suggest that the powers granted by the first three articles should be understood as interrelated rather than as mutually exclusive preserves.[87] There is no coutervailing prohibition in the text against one branch's encroachment on another's territory. Article I, Section 6, does prohibit members of Congress from holding executive offices, but this prohibition is so narrow that it could as readily be read to authorize other interbranch overlaps as to prohibit them. Article I, Section 9, prohibits bills of attainder, which are generally viewed as the imposition of criminal penalties by legislative act.[88] This prohibition is adequately explained by obvious fairness or liberty arguments that are unrelated to separation of powers, an interpretation that is confirmed by its being joined, in the same clause, to the prohibition of ex post facto laws, which raises fairness but not separation of powers concerns.[89] In short, the constitutional text strongly suggests that the powers of three branches regularly overlap, and that only a few specific and readily explicable overlaps are prohibited.

The other mode of formalism, originalist interpretation, also fails to support the strict separation of powers. It seems likely that the checks and balances embodied in the document's provisions were understood at the time to be an explicit rejection of the strict approach. To begin with, one of the classic arguments of intentionalist analysis – "if the drafters wanted to prohibit X, they knew how to do it" – can be invoked against a strict separation argument. Four of the 1776 state constitutions contained explicit separation of powers provisions – Maryland's, for example, declared "that the legislative, executive, and judicial powers of government ought to be forever separate and distinct from each other."[90] Madison, apparently prey to second thoughts about his handiwork, proposed a similar provision to the first Congress, as an amendment to the Constitution, but it was rejected in the Senate.[91] More generally, it is well established that a strict approach to separation of powers was championed by the more radical members of the revolutionary generation as an antidote to the monarchial and aristocratic strands in the English theory of mixed government.[92] By the time of the Constitutional Convention in Philadelphia, however, the difficulties resulting from this position were widely recognized; in particular, strict separation was perceived as providing insufficient coordination among the branches, leading either to legislative domination or to generalized paralysis.[93] Thus, the Framers, relying on the long-standing concept of mixed government, devised a complex set of checks and balances in their effort to establish an effective central government. The portions of the Federalist Papers that address the separation of powers demonstrate only that Madison thought that the concentration of all governmental powers in a single branch was a prescription for tyranny, not that any overlap or mixture of these powers would constitute an equivalent disaster.[94] And, as Victoria Nourse has demonstrated, Madison's primary concern was insuring that one branch could not corrupt and co-opt the members of another, not that the powers of these branches, when exercised by independent, conscientious officials, might overlap each other.[95]

It is possible to argue, as the Supreme Court did in *INS v. Chadha*,[96] that the Constitution only permits those overlaps between the branches that it specifically authorizes, and forbids any others. That is certainly not a textualist argument, however, and there is no particular evidence that it represents the intent of the Framers. In fact, as Erwin Chemerinsky notes, the Framers may well have intended that the structural provisions of the Constitution be read as general guidelines, not as literal prescriptions; in other words, they "intended non-originalism in separation of powers cases."[97] Certainly, the instinct that made them turn to checks and balances – the need for coordinated action to achieve effective governance – would favor the continued and expanded use of such devices. By far the most important development in our governmental structure is the advent of the administrative state, and there the three branches are inevitably intertwined. The administrative agency itself represents a mixture, or indeed a merger, of all three functions, and the control or supervision of that agency demands the participation of all three branches.[98] Separation of powers, being impossible to achieve, tends to yield pointless expressions of anguish or random, quixotic interventions. On the other hand, as Peter Shane, Peter Strauss, and others have pointed out, checks and balances become increasingly relevant as the legislature, executive, and judiciary need not only to check each other, but to supervise an ever growing bureaucratic apparatus.[99]

One of the most hotly contested issues, in recent years, involves independent administrative agencies such as the FCC, the FTC (most people's favorite target), and the Federal Reserve Board (few people's favorite target, given the importance of nonpolitical control of the money supply). A number of scholars argue that these agencies are unconstitutional on separation-of-powers grounds.[100] While the matter is too extensive to be canvassed here, there seems to be little support for the position on either textual or historical grounds, as Martin Flaherty points out.[101] Even if one were to accept the position, however, the main effect would be to authorize presidential removals of the officials he appointed to these agencies. The agencies themselves, with their mixtures of powers, would remain intact, and the disjunction between the constitutionally provided structure and the modern administrative state would be only marginally alleviated.

The separation-of-powers argument is no more convincing when considered with particularized reference to the judiciary. The textual reference to judicial power is as unadorned and elliptical as the equivalent references for the other branches. As for the intent of the Framers, the argument is that courts should be restricted to the role they presumably played in the eighteenth century.[102] Owen Fiss sets forth a response to this argument based on the familiar concept of an evolving Constitution.[103] He argues eloquently that the primary public function of the courts has always been to articulate and clarify public values, rather than merely resolving disputes for the particular participants. What has changed in modern times, he continues, is not the judiciary's function, but the form of its decisions. The transformation from a simple to a complex society and the shift of operative legal units from individuals to organizations has led inevitably to more elaborate remedies. Once a judge could order particular officials to perform a specific function because those individuals themselves were directly responsible for delivery of the service in question. Now, social services are delivered by complex organizations and involve joint action by many separate officials. To secure compliance with the law, judges must become engaged with these organizations, a process that often requires judicial administration. To this, Douglas Laycock adds the observation that equitable relief, far from being an extraordinary remedy available only when money damages are insufficient, has now become the norm in all areas of law.[104] Any traditional presumption against such relief is thus obsolete in light of common law as well as constitutional interpretation.

This is a plausible way to understand the intent of the Framers, even without resorting to the broader interpretive strategies that now represent the dominant approach among contemporary scholars.[105] It is particularly relevant in the context of prisons because prisons did not exist in this country at the time the Constitution was drafted. People were detained in jails when awaiting trial, but the convicted were executed, whipped, fined, or exposed to public contumely. The first American prisons, Walnut Street in Philadelphia and Newgate in New York City, were the product of the decade following the Constitution's adoption, and large institutions with any resemblance to modern prisons would not exist until Auburn and Eastern State penitentiaries were founded some thirty years later.[106] In fact, there were few ongoing state-run institutions of any kind when the Constitution was written, and those that did exist were small and relatively simple. The creation of complex bureaucratic institutions represented a significant expansion of responsibility for any branch of government, and a new conception of collective action. Thus, even if the concept of judicial power was much more limited in 1789, a strong argument can be advanced for the proposition that the Framers' true intentions can only be preserved if those limits are reinterpreted in light of changing circumstances. Certainly commentators on law and politics have made this argument with respect to legislative and executive functions and to the blurring of these branches in the modern state; indeed, such observations are now truisms. To disable courts from dealing with the political and social changes of the past two hundred years is to condemn them to a restricted role that distorts the Framers' true intentions rather than preserving them.

But this well-recognized approach to original intent is not necessary to answer the formalist claim that the judicial power should be limited to the traditional model of passive dispute resolution. Even if one abides by strict intentionalism, and assumes that the Framers intended that each branch of government should be limited to its 1789 role, the passive dispute resolution model remains unpersuasive. The only way the Framers could have had this model in mind when they drafted Article III was by reading the works of the mid-twentieth-century legal process school, not by observing their own contemporary courts. As Martin Shapiro and Gordon Wood have noted, courts have always performed a multiplicity of functions that involve social control and policy implementation.[107] At the time the Constitution was drafted, Wood writes, "judges exercised a broad, ill-defined magisterial authority befitting their social rank; they were considered members of the government and remained intimately involved in politics." Records of quarter sessions judges any time during the eighteenth and nineteenth centuries quickly reveal that a substantial portion of their cases involved claims against government officials for failure to perform public functions.*[108] If the judge found the claim correct, he would respond with orders to perform the omitted functions. Although it is true that government bureaucracy was not so complicated in the eighteenth century, and judicial involvement was consequently simpler, the range of administrative-like functions courts assumed resembles what is found on the dockets of the contemporary federal courts.

Similarly, Theodore Eisenberg and Steven Yeazell have shown that far from being a novelty of late twentieth century, judicial activism, class action suits, and all that is entailed in them possess an ancient and venerable lineage in English law.[109] They were developed during the Middle Ages and used by guilds with great success to pursue a host of economic and social interests. Although their use waned for a period, the modern class action, they argue, stems from an age-old tradition that has never disappeared.

Equity jurisdiction has long acknowledged the courts' frankly administrative role in selected types of issues; far from seeking to curtail judges, it establishes procedures to enhance their performance. Equity judges appoint conservators for the estates of the insane or profligate, receivers for those of the insolvent, and masters to carry out investigations too technical or time-consuming for the court itself.[110] Provisions for judicial adjuncts appointed by the court to aid it in collecting information and overseeing the formulation and implementation of complex orders long predate the rise of the modern welfare state, the modern activist judiciary, and the Federal Rules of Civil Procedure.

Precisely which of these arguments proved persuasive to federal judges, and in what proportions, is impossible to know. But the federal judges clearly were persuaded, for the separation of powers was never a major concern in the prison reform cases. Given that they were dealing with the states, not coordinated federal branches, that the checks-and-balances doctrine pointed in the opposite direction, that social circumstances had

---

* In the late eighteenth century, it was not common for justices in the quarter sessions to appoint "Visiting Committees" to inquire into conditions of local prisons and to adopt policies regulating these prisons. Indeed, the Webbs reported that one of the common criticisms of the judges in this respect was their failure to act aggressively enough and to order substantial improvements in the conditions in the gaols and prisons they superintended.

so clearly changed, and that broad-ranging implementation powers were traditional judicial functions, the judges' imperviousness to formalist arguments for separation of powers is hardly surprising. There were simply too many countervailing factors, whether these were consciously or unconsciously perceived. The formalist argument, whatever its appeal to one dismayed, defiant group of legal scholars, seemed too old-fashioned to impede a major policy-making effort.

The Functionalist Argument for the Separation of Powers

But the normative argument for the separation-of-powers doctrine does not rest exclusively on formalist considerations. Far more important, in terms of contemporary legal scholarship and general political effect, is the functional argument – that the role and position of the courts in our government, rather than any specific textual reference or intentionalist analysis, limit the range of judicial action. The common definition of functionalism, in the separation-of-powers context, is that one branch may venture into the territory of another so long as it does not interfere with the core functions of that other branch.[111] The concept is deeply metaphysical, not so much because the core functions of a given branch are difficult to identify, but because there is no obvious reason why there should be such a prohibition. One could invoke other considerations, such as pragmatic arguments that these deep incursions would be counterproductive, or the formalist argument that they violate the intended constitutional scheme, but once these arguments have been accounted for, the remaining, independent argument is less than clear. Perhaps that is the reason why functionalism, when interpreted in this manner, generally validates the challenged action.[112]

The best interpretation of the functionalist argument is that one branch might disable another branch from functioning effectively, either generally or in one specific area, and thereby deny the people the particular voice, or source of access, that the dominated branch would otherwise provide. Whether this notion really applies to the delimited and mutually agreed-upon provisions that have been featured in Supreme Court cases involving the legislature and the executive is an open question.[113] With respect to judicial depredations, however, the argument has been decisively and formidably characterized by Alexander Bickel as the "counter-majoritarian difficulty."[114] His position, in essence, is that major policy decisions are to be made by officials who are chosen by the people and who represent their will. Of course, those officials need to delegate their power in many circumstances, but they continue to exercise authority over their delegates' actions, and can thus be held accountable for those actions in the forum of public opinion. Similarly, there are some functions

properly insulated from popular control; we want the legislature to declare what constitutes crime, but we do not want it or those subject to its
will to declare whether a specific person is a criminal. In short, we recognize the need for appointees, and even appointees who do not answer
to elected officials. But majority rule, it is argued, means that basic policy
decisions must be made by those officials, not by judges insulated from
electoral process. Prison reform, according to this argument, was the job
of Congress, or the president, or a presidentially appointed agency, but
it was not the job of the judiciary.*[115]

Underlying this countermajoritarian argument, of course, is the belief
that the executive and legislative branches are majoritarian in some significant sense, that they represent the will of the people by virtue of their
electoral status. This belief, almost an article of faith for Bickel, and a
lodestar for other political thinkers ranging from Frederick Hayek to
Theodore Lowi to Allan Hutchinson,[116] has been subjected to intense criticism by several widely disparate branches of modern scholarship. According to public choice theory, elected officials, like the rest of us, are
self-interest maximizers and represent nothing but their own desire to get
reelected. This might yield acceptable results if everyone's vote counted
equally; in fact, due to market failures in the political economy of voting,
cohesive, well-organized special interests exercise disproportionate influence on electoral outcomes.[117] From a very different perspective,
postmodernists challenge the entire concept of representation. Any representation, in their view, inevitably distorts its subject's grounded and
unique actuality, embodying unconscious assumptions that restrict the
subject to its orthodox, readily recognizable meanings.[118] Political representation is precisely such a distortion, spawned by the unfounded assertion that one person represents the views of others and sustained by
manipulation of political symbols through mass media and bureaucratic
systems.[119] Few federal judges are devotees of public choice, and even
fewer are postmodernists, but this correspondence between public choice,
our most positivist approach to political science, and postmodernism, our
most thoroughgoing attack on positivism, suggests that there really may
well be something wrong with the concept of representation.[120]

The prison cases illustrate the nature of this problem. It was clear to
federal judges that prison administrators did not represent, or even claim

---

* Bickel also prescribed a sanction for courts that violate his principle – that they
  will lose their legitimacy. This empirical point, a product of the legal process
  mentality that Bickel represents, is a dubious one, as William Lasser demonstrates, but Bickel's argument does not depend on it. If judicial activism violates
  the underlying scheme of our government, then courts should not be activists,
  even if they can get away with it.

to represent, the will of the people. To be sure, most prisons were headed by appointed officials, who were appointed by an appointed official, who was appointed by an elected official. Despite this gossamer thread of standard political legitimacy, prisons existed in isolation, unnoticed or ignored by the vast majority of citizens and unsupervised by the people's representatives. Some prison systems, such as Texas, assiduously strived for their autonomy, while others, such as Arkansas, simply drifted into it; in neither state, however, did the governor or legislature exercise any significant measure of control until the state was hauled into federal court. Prison policies were set by administrative action, and reflected a self-enclosed world so authoritarian in structure that it resembled nothing any American would recognize as America.

In fact, it was the courts that invoked and relied upon popular opinion. Judges appealed to the public conscience in their written opinions, their evaluation of evidence, their formulation of remedies, and in a variety of less formal ways. They were convinced that if the citizens were confronted with the realities of prison life, particularly in the plantation model prisons, they would be repulsed and would demand reform. In this, the judges were probably correct. Once public attention was focused on the prisons, many of the more extreme practices – the physical abuse, the lack of medical care, the bread and water diets, and the use of armed inmates as guards – became impossible to maintain.

Over time, moreover, the judiciary proved to be quite sensitive to changes in public opinion.[121] The highly interventionist strategy it adopted in the early stages of its efforts reflected the prevailing liberalism of the late 1960s and early 1970s, and the animus against the South that came naturally as a result of the civil rights movement. As more and more state prisons fell under court order, this interventionist approach became institutionalized and, meeting little popular resistance, flourished. By the Reagan era, however, the popular mood had changed and the courts changed with it. They became more cautious, more willing to accept the word of prison officials, more convinced that the worst abuses had been alleviated. As of this writing, we seem to have developed an tolerance, if not a positive affection for, the punitive practices we previously regarded as barbaric; this has been accompanied by an observable loss of enthusiasm among federal judges for prison reform cases, thus confirming the connection between public opinion and judicial action.

In the final analysis, of course, the legislature and the chief executive are more "majoritarian" than the courts, although the difference may be quantitative rather than qualitative. Elections count for something, after all. But there is a deeper problem with the countermajoritarian argument. Even if the courts do not reflect public opinion, the argument is defective because reflection of the popular, or majority, will is not the sole criterion for democratic institutions. As John Rohr puts it, not every major official in a democracy must be chosen by election or directly supervised by an elected official.[122] Instead, a democracy is a set of institutions linked together by accepted rules of priority and interaction in which only some leading officials are selected by popular vote. There may be other criteria we would impose; perhaps a democracy must respect the rights of individuals[123] or be governed by organic law[124] or provide opportunities for expression and participation[125] or establish conditions for rational discourse.[126] But even if we restrict ourselves to a reliance on fair, open elections as the critical determinant, a democracy cannot be said to be a government in which everyone who makes important decisions is elected or truly answerable to elected officials.

Any prior misimpression that elections play a comprehensive role in democratic governance is necessarily removed, as Matthew Adler points out, by the advent of the modern administrative state. Our vast, bureaucratic apparatus is the sinew of modern government and the paradigm for governmental action in the last half of the twentieth century.[127] When the government wants to achieve something, distribute something, or operate something, it generally resorts to an administrative agency. In theory, these agencies operate under instructions from the legislature, and some are supervised by an elected chief executive. But even in juridical terms, most of their members are selected by other unelected bureaucrats, or by examination, whereas independent agencies are not subject to direct supervision by any elected official. In practice, their actions, while enormously important to the citizenry, are too numerous and frequently too technical for the legislators or the chief executive to monitor. They constitute a buzzing infinity of rules, adjudications, exceptions, initiatives, inspections, prosecutions, suggestions, and admonitions whose democratic nature is ensured only by the general government context in which they exist.[128]

The fact that judges are not elected therefore does not mean that they are little islands of totalitarianism in the midst of our democracy. They are part of our limited cultural repertoire for governance, part of our "equipment" in the Heideggerian sense as Brian Leiter suggests.[129] When confronted with a problem like the reform of prisons, we can only solve it by drawing on that repertoire; we must rely on the institutions that are familiar to us.*[130] All these institutions are democratic institutions because they are functioning parts of a democratic government.[131] They all relate, in some fashion, to the populace but none of them expresses the popu-

---

* Heidegger uses the term "ready-to-hand" and his example is a hammer – a device that any person in our culture knows how to use without prior reflection. It seems plausible to suggest that, in the political context, courts are ready-to-hand in exactly this sense.

lace's views in a direct, transparent manner. It is true that judges are appointed, not elected, and that they are not subject to dismissal by elected officials on the basis of their decisions. That is the nature of the judiciary, however, and the judiciary is a basic component of our government.

In adopting an administrative, policy-making role, the courts were following our dominant model of governance. They were able to reform a complex administrative organization because they adopted and adapted that model. Courts existed long before the administrative state and, as we have shown in the previous section, they employed administrative methods in prior times. But this mode of action has been reinterpreted, and thereby expanded and legitimated, by our extensive reliance on administrative agencies. Courts are not agencies, as such, but it is their capacity to act like agencies in appropriate circumstances that makes them fully effectual participants in the modern governmental process.

Underlying the growth of our administrative state is a more basic notion that democratic government is a historically developed institutional structure, not a rationally designed instrumentality to reflect the "will of the people." Federal judges were not deterred from policy implementation by their lack of contact with the popular will because they understood, as practical public officials, there was never really any such thing to begin with. What we call the popular will is in fact constructed by our political institutions. It is the way each institution, as an institution, perceives the desires of the citizenry. The institutions, after all, existed first. England has had a Parliament and a judicial system since the Middle Ages. The concept of a popular will dates from the seventeenth century, and the view that these institutions should be answerable to that popular will was not fully established for another century or two.[132]

If we want to know what people really believe, we can conduct a public opinion poll, but none of our government institutions makes use of these polls for any official purpose. Businesses use them quite religiously for marketing decisions, the media use them to predict elections, candidates use them to plan their campaigns, and social scientists use them to describe society. Clearly, we regard these polls as informative, and we employ them when, as a functional matter, we want to know what people think. Our governmental institutions do not use them very much, and hardly ever as an official basis for decision, because generalized public opinion is not directly relevant to their behavior. These institutions have their own structured way of interacting with the public, and of constructing our conception of a politically relevant popular will. When we speak of the popular will, in the political sense, we do not mean public opinion, but these varied mechanisms for public interaction with established governmental structures.

All these governmental institutions, whether elected or appointed, interact with the public in ways that are too complex to be described as simply majoritarian. Thus, the courts are not some sui generis, countermajoritarian exception to an otherwise majoritarian government. Rather, they are one standard component of our democratic regime as it has evolved through time. They have their own feedback mechanisms, which grant them as much legitimacy as any other branch. One can imagine a government, ruled by nonelected officials known as "judges," who exercised comprehensive power, and had no sense of being responsible to the populace. That would indeed be a nondemocratic regime. But that is not what we have, nor something toward which we move when judges take a policy-making or administrative role as they did in the prison reform cases.

Conclusion

THROUGH THE VARIEGATED PRISM of a single, but extended, group of cases, we have now provided a description of judicial policy making, and an account of its legitimacy as one mode of judicial action. This chapter summarizes our conclusions and speculates about their general implications. It begins with a summary description of judicial policy making, as revealed by the prison reform cases, and a brief effort to generalize this description to other situations. It then explores the argument for the legitimacy of judicial policy making at a more general level, noting connections among the three chapters in Part II.

The argument for the legitimacy of judicial policy making has some rather important implications. As stated at the outset, the common assumption that this widespread, albeit semisubterranean form of ordinary public decision making violates established legal principles such as federalism, the separation of powers, and the rule of law is implausible as a matter of basic sociology. We have argued for the opposite conclusion – that the admitted divergence between the judiciary's actions and accepted legal principles reveals an underlying weakness in those principles. That weakness is inherent, but it has been exacerbated by the rise of the modern administrative state.

In this chapter, we argue that the deeper connections among these principles reflect a particular vision of law and of the state. Judicial policy making, by virtue of its brute existence, thus casts doubt not only on the individual principles, but on the general image of law and government from which they are derived. In other words, the prison reform cases, as the high-water mark of judicial policy making, have something to teach us about the political world in which we live. This subject is obviously a vast one, and we will not explore it in any comprehensive fashion. Our goal is not to develop a new theory of the state, but simply to identify some of the broader implications of the prison reform cases that have served as the subject of this study.

The Nature of Judicial Policy Making

Policy making is the process by which a public official reaches a decision on the basis of a judgment that the decision will produce beneficial results. In the executive and legislative areas, this simple definition appears virtually tautological – on what other basis, after all, should an official make decisions? The issue that receives the most attention is the scope of the official's authority, that is, the area within which a decision maker is authorized to seek these beneficial results. But, in reality, many of the tasks that public officials must perform are not policy making but interpretation; the decisions are governed by written texts whose language the official is required to understand and obey. This is sometimes obscured by the hierarchical structure of executive agencies, which allows verbal orders to replace written texts as the source of authority. Nonetheless, interpretation is an important part of the executive decision-making process.*

With respect to judges, of course, the situation is the opposite. Interpretation is regarded as so central to the decision-making process that policy making is ignored, or more frequently, treated as an act of impropriety. But the combination of judgment, obedience, initiative, and consequentialism that renders executive decision making a mixture of policy making and interpretation produces the same mixture in judicial decision making. This phenomenon is not limited to the administrative era; judges, in the Anglo-American tradition at the very least, have always been at least partially consequentialist, and have often been obligated or motivated to make decisions in the absence of any textual guidance.

Because interpretation and policy making mix together, texts are often interpreted in light of the social consequences of the interpretation, while policy is often made with the assistance of related legal texts. But, as argued in Chapter 1, the two functions are distinguishable. In their policy-making mode, to be sure, judges still look to text – through a process of interpretation – to establish their jurisdiction, or power, over a given subject area. But having identified the subject, and demarcated its boundaries, they then pay no further attention to the text, generally because the text conveys no useful information. Instead they proceed to impose stan-

---

* We leave to one side the interesting but unnecessarily dramatic question of the extent to which executive and legislative agencies are obligated to interpret the Constitution.

dards, to implement changes, and to develop rules based on judgments of social benefit. The interpretive process can also generate new legal rules, but it does so on the basis that those rules are somehow contained in or implied by the text, not on the basis of the desirable results they will produce.

The difference between policy making and interpretation is generally apparent from examining the rationale that appears in the opinion and the result the judge has reached. When the judge is interpreting a legal text, the opinion will be replete with textual references, and will attempt to link those references to the result by linguistic analyses, historical accounts of meaning, more general analysis of structure, purpose, or the drafters' intent, and citations of prior decisions that relied on these interpretive techniques. When the judge is making public policy, such references will be absent, and in their place will be discussions of moral norms, social principles, nonlegal sources, nonauthoritative legal texts, and citations of prior decisions that feature such discussions. The decisions in the prison reform cases are dramatic demonstrations of this approach. Results are somewhat more difficult to judge, but even a thorough going skeptic about the inherent meaning of texts will generally acknowledge that there is a delimited set of conclusions that people in a given society will recognize as possible readings of the text. When the result lies outside that set, it is either an error or the product of a noninterpretive process such as policy making. This is not to suggest that the skeptics are necessarily correct in their claim that texts themselves have no inherent meaning. The point, rather, is that even if they are correct, the results of policy making are still distinguishable from the results of an interpretive process.

While judges generally do not acknowledge that they are engaged in policy making, it is difficult to believe that these observable differences in their opinions and results do not have a phenomenological correlative. When they sit down to write opinions like *Roe v. Wade*,[1] *Griswold v. Connecticut*,[2] *Hennigsen v. Bloomfield Motors*,[3] or the prison reform cases, they must have the subjective sense that they are doing something different from the interpretation of a text. Certainly, none of their decisions in any of these cases fooled any educated observer, and it seems difficult to believe that the judges really fooled themselves. Despite this awareness, their general unwillingness to state that they are engaged in policy making need not be ascribed to cynicism or duplicity. Rather, it stems from the absence of a legitimate legal discourse that supports the judicial policy-making process. The role expectations that govern their behavior demand that they remain within the bounds of legitimate discourse. Those expectations, however, only prohibit them from saying that they are making policy, and not from actually doing it. The result is that judges will continue to make policy in certain circumstances, and that they will continue to be circumspect, and perhaps insincere about it, until a legal discourse for judicial policy making is developed.

The most basic element of such a legal discourse is a dispassionate and usable description of the process by which judicial policy making takes place. This study develops a description by adopting several of the standard accounts of policy making that have been used for nonjudicial decision makers. According to the classic account, the decision maker should define the problem, identify a goal, generate alternatives, select the alternative that provides the best solution, and implement that alternative. Many observers find this account unrealistic; in their view, policy makers proceed incrementally, trying out partial solutions and then using the response to their last intervention to develop the next partial solution. Still another approach is derived from hermeneutic theory, where the decision maker oscillates between part and whole, deriving particularized solutions from a general perception of the problem, and then altering that general perception on the basis of the chosen solution.

These descriptions, despite their nonjudicial provenance, seem to fit judicial policy making rather well. In the prison cases, for example, the judges can be described as having perceived a fairly well defined problem – the divergence of many state prisons from national standards – and to have responded by establishing the obvious goal. They also implemented the solution they selected, despite severe resource constraints, scholarly condemnation, and their own lack of a convincing rationale. At the same time, some of the judges can be described as proceeding incrementally, implementing limited changes either directly or through their special masters, and choosing their next step on the basis of the results they produced, and the information they learned. The hermeneutic description is less familiar and in certain ways more abstract, but it seems as applicable to judges as to other decision makers, and has been used in this study to explain the judges' motivations.

The two stages in the classic model that cannot be applied to judicial decision making directly and unambiguously are the articulation of alternatives and the selection of solutions. The reason is not merely the judiciary's general preference for incrementalism, but the fact that these alternatives and solutions are necessarily framed in doctrinal terms. This doctrinal framework distinguishes judicial policy making from executive policy making and, indeed, is characteristic of, if not unique to, the judicial process. That is the reason why it was necessary, in this study, to explicate the two middle steps in the classic policy-making model at great length, when the other steps – problem definition, goal identification, and implementation – could be characterized with a one-sentence definition and compared directly with their executive equivalents.

Since the purpose of this study is to explain the ways in which judicial policy making resembles policy making by other branches, and is an ordinary mode of governmental action, we emphasize the similarity between the process of creating legal doctrine and the process of generating alternatives and choosing a solution. If one wanted to emphasize the way in which judicial policy making was distinct – the way one knows, by examining a summary of the decision, that it was made by a judge, not an administrator – one would focus on the differences that appear in these two middle stages. In the administrative or executive process, the generation of alternatives remains a vaguely comprehended mystery, as creative processes so often are, but the selection of solutions is the arena for many of the process's most characteristic methodologies, such as cost–benefit analysis. In the judicial process, the creation of new doctrine is similarly characteristic. Perhaps it should not be divided into generating alternatives and choosing solutions at all, but treated as a sui generis totality, and the analogue of both these steps in the classic policy-making model.

In any event, the equivalence of a doctrinally related process to one aspect of these policy-making models clarifies the argument advanced at the outset of this study. Judges are simply wrong when they assert that they do not engage in policy making. Legal scholars are wrong when they say that judicial policy making is exceptional, or incoherent, or avoidable by better legal reasoning. But political scientists are also wrong when they say that judicial policy making is no different from policy making by the other branches and represents a complete abandonment of legal doctrine. As has been demonstrated, it is a complex process that engages and connects with legal doctrine, and that expresses its results in terms of legal doctrine, but that the doctrine does not explicitly control or constrain.

Because doctrinal creation is so central to and so distinctive of judicial policy making, it might be used to distinguish between different types or categories of this process. Chapter 6 divided the coordinating ideas, which represent the crucial element in doctrinal creation, into labeling, analogy, metaphor, and institutional conceptualization. The most notable distinction, as suggested by this study, is between institutional conceptualization and the other three categories. Such conceptualizations address the structures of the administrative state in a direct, context-specific manner. In addition, they are closely, albeit not inevitably, linked to an implementation process that is carried out by the judiciary itself. Analogies, metaphors, and labels are not necessarily specific to an institution, although they can be, and do not typically involve implementation by the judiciary itself, although this too can vary. They constitute the mode of policy making that predates the administrative state and characterizes the development of the common law.

Within this category one could make further distinctions. No effort will be made to do so here, however, because the category lies outside our case study and would require a sustained, detailed analysis. Perhaps metaphors and analogies could be distinguished from labels, as representing a larger and less predictable departure from existing doctrine. Perhaps the more relevant distinction is between those new doctrines, whether labels, analogies, or metaphors, that represent an expected next stage in the development of doctrine and those that are orthogonal to existing doctrine. Alternatively, one could look at the origin of the coordinating idea – this would now include institutional characterizations as well – and distinguish among ideas that were generated by scholars, those generated by the people subject to the rule, such as merchants or administrators,[4] and those generated by the judiciary itself. But further analysis would be required to determine whether any of these distinctions could be sustained, and whether they serve any useful purpose.

The Desuetude of Structural Constraints

The abiding sense of illegitimacy about judicial policy making goes well beyond the lack of a description, however; indeed, it may explain this lack, for the description that has been suggested in this study is drawn from the most familiar sources. As stated in Chapter 1, and elaborated in the three chapters of Part II, judicial policy making seems to violate a number of well-established legal principles, including federalism, the separation of powers, and the rule of law itself. The first two may be described as structural principles because they relate to the general design of government and to the role and relationship of its component parts. The latter is a substantive principle, prescribing the way each governmental decision maker should perform the functions that the structure of the government prescribes.

In Chapters 5 and 7, we argued that the structural principles of federalism and the separation of powers gain their apparent force and continuing appeal by being conflated with the managerial strategies of decentralization and specialization. To the extent that federalism and the separation of powers rest on normative arguments, both doctrines are inapplicable in our nationwide administrative era. Attempts to revive them may serve to mount an indirect challenge to that administrative state, but the very indirection of the challenge suggests its unreality. We are much more likely to turn the clock back 500 million years by bombing ourselves into the protoplasmic slime than we are to turn it back 120 years to the preadministrative era. Federal judges certainly sensed this, which is the reason this middle-aged, middle class, middle-of-the-road group of people was willing to ignore supposedly established doctrine.

The fact that the desuetude of both federalism and the separation of powers spring from the very same source suggests that there may be connections between them that we have not considered in our separate discussion of those principles. This section will briefly explore two such connections, one pragmatic and the other epistemological.

In the eighteenth century, many people perceived political regimes as the interaction of opposing forces. This was particularly true of thinkers such as Hobbes, Locke, and Montesquieu, who exercised the greatest influence upon the founders of our own republic. As E. P. Panagopoulos demonstrates,[5] these thinkers were deeply affected by the most striking intellectual achievement of their era, the physical theories of Isaac Newton. Galileo had found mechanistic explanations for mundane events like swinging pendulums and falling objects; Newton developed more decisively mechanistic explanations for the sun, the moon, the planets, light, and motion – the stuff of poems and the work of God. This Newtonian world consisted of discrete and independently operating forces that counterbalanced one another. A moving object comes to rest when opposed by another object; the Earth describes its path around the Sun because its momentum is balanced by the Sun's gravitational attraction. Similarly, the political regime was comprised of discrete forces – the legislative, executive, and judicial power within the national government, the national government and the state governments in the general polity. To control these nonconscious forces, one needed to balance them against one other. Each branch of government would constrain the power of the other two, while the national and state governments would constrain each other. Separation of powers and federalism are doctrines that reflect this conception of governance.

Underlying this perceived interplay of forces within the political regime was the larger interplay of forces in society at large. Human beings pursued their interests or their inclinations unless constrained by other human beings, and the result of this interaction was invariably conflict. To control such conflict and to establish a well-ordered regime, one needed to balance them against each other in the governmental process, and then balance the opposing force of government against them all. Thus, the basic purpose of government was to keep the peace within the nation and to protect it from enemies beyond its borders, not to improve or enrich the citizens. Improvement and enrichment were subjects of serious concern at the time, but people looked to religion, secular morality, private education, philanthropy, the growth of knowledge, and, increasingly, the market to achieve these beneficial ends.*[6]

---

* Recent scholarship about this period often focuses on the republican ideal, in which citizens participate in government and achieve true fulfillment of their personhood through such participation. This scholarship is a useful antidote to

The penitentiaries that developed during the 1820s, 1830s, and 1840s were among America's first divergences from this eighteenth-century model. While undoubtedly instruments of punishment, like the gallows, stocks, and lashes of the prior era, they were also explicitly designed to improve the prisoners, to make them better people. It is certainly no accident that development of penitentiaries was contemporaneous with debate over Henry Clay's American Plan, which represented a consciously designed program to improve the national economy by direct intervention, rather than simply encouraging it with tariffs or free trade. These were adumbrations of America's administrative state, a governmental transformation that arrived when the overwhelming power of the railroads vis-à-vis the small towns and small companies they served led to an irresistible demand for coordinated regulation.[7] In the century since that first, decisive choice of a managerial response, we have created a new mode of governance, one that rests on premises that differ markedly from the Newtonian, eighteenth-century premises of the Framers.

In operational terms, we now expect government to play a positive role in improving people's lives and in managing the economy. To achieve these more proactive programmatic goals, we have fashioned a regulatory system based on the idea that good government does not emerge from a mechanical balance of opposing forces, but from the conscious, coordinated effort of a central authority that represents our entire political community. Thus, this regime is national in scope and regulates areas that were previously regarded as the separate jurisdiction of the states. In addition, it combines all modes of governmental power – rulemaking, adjudication, and implementation – in pursuing its regulative programs.

The pragmatic reason courts tend to ignore federalism and the separation of powers, therefore, is that these principles no longer describe the governmental system in which they exist or the model of governmental action that modern government embodies.[8] To the extent that these principles continue to be relevant at all, it is as a traditional version of equally pragmatic concerns – decentralization in the case of federalism, and specialization in the case of separation of powers. But because the principles are now part of a pragmatic calculus of governance, they no longer carry normative force, and simply serve as elements in a complex analysis. The demand that courts continue to be constrained by these structural principles, particularly when other branches have abandoned them, simply excludes the courts from the modern governmental process. This may

easy characterizations about eighteenth century liberalism, and it may even be true. At most, however, it suggests that citizens were expected to find meaning, or fulfillment, by devoting time and energy to governmental service, not that government was expected to secure a good life for its citizens.

appeal to those who disagree with the substantive policies of modern government, a position that possesses increasing rhetorical appeal but thus far not enough serious support to produce significant change. Federal judges did not disagree with these substantive policies, however, certainly not in the 1960s and 1970s. They are part of the modern administrative state, not critics of it, and they fulfill their role within that context. Under certain circumstances that role involves public policy making; as our state has become increasingly administrative and managerial, judicial policy making has become both more necessary for judges to produce effects and more legitimate as a general model of governmental action.

These operational changes have been accompanied by epistemological ones. The most significant, perhaps, is that we have factored people back into our explanatory system. The study of governmental structure and behavior is now regarded as a branch of social science. As its name suggests, social science began with the same Newtonian aspirations as seventeenth- and eighteenth-century political philosophers; its founder, Auguste Comte, believed that people were as predictable as pendulums, and saw society developing in a magisterial succession of inevitable stages.[9] Herbert Spencer proposed a similar theory, reinforced by Darwin's success in bringing biological evolution into the Newtonian framework.[10] As time went on, however, social science developed in a different direction. Anthropology, psychology, sociology, and other "human sciences" revealed a vast and variegated range of human behavior, while political scientists began incorporating these insights into their theory of government. At present, when we want to explain the political process, we speak of individual motivation, interest groups, voter attitudes, and social belief systems. This is not to suggest that mechanistic models are entirely gone; the general systems branch of organization theory, for example, models government agencies as cybernetic systems. But the dominant approach is to focus on the interplay between individuals and institutions. When we think about government, therefore, we no longer see discrete, independently operating entities, like "the executive," "the legislative," or "the judiciary." Rather we see complex organizations that interact with each other through a wide range of individual behaviors. When we think about control, we no longer envision opposing powers, but mechanisms of public accountability, information exchange, direct supervision, and organizational restructuring.

Since these functional and epistemological transformations are quite apparent, those who continue to champion structural doctrines such as federalism or the separation of powers need some counterargument. The most widespread one, as suggested in Chapters 5 and 7, is that the advent of the modern state threatens basic values such as liberty, community, or democratic legitimacy, and that federalism and the separation of powers provide a necessary bulwark against the continued erosion of these values.[11] But to provide such protection by invoking principles that are no longer operationally relevant or conceptually coherent is a poor strategy indeed. Moreover, even if we could somehow reconstruct these bygone principles of government, they would not serve our purposes; they tolerate too many depredations of the very values they purportedly protect. The liberty that could be obtained by permitting states to resist federal intervention would be purchased by the tyranny that these states could impose on their insulated domains; the democracy that could be obtained by keeping executive power free of legislative and judicial intervention would leave the exercise of those powers subject to all the particular distortions in democracy that executive agencies so frequently impose.

Fortunately, we do not need to rely upon outmoded, partial strategies to preserve important values, for we have modern comprehensive ones. The most notable can be described, for simplicity's sake, as checks and balances. Essentially the opposite of federalism or the separation of powers, it invokes the complex overlap and interplay among different governmental organizations, with different tasks and jurisdictions.[12] At the operational level, it is fully congruent with the positive proactive stance that modern government assumes, for it protects our liberties by permitting a dynamic interaction among rival, programmatic agencies. At the conceptual level, it is linked to the engineering principle of redundancy, to the organizational principle of administrative supervision, and to the social science principle that human beings are controlled through human interaction.

To be sure, separation of powers possesses a premodern precursor that is every bit as Newtonian in concept as the separation of powers – the seventeenth-century English theory of a balanced constitution.[13] But governmental mechanisms do not become obsolete merely on the basis of their ancient lineage. The point, rather, is that they do not become relevant and usable in a modern administrative state by virtue of that lineage. Each mechanism must be judged by its contemporary performance; if one is beginning with the governmental furniture delivered by tradition, each inherited item must be judged by its ability to fit the place we currently inhabit. Separation of powers translates into the empirical necessity of governmental specialization, but provides no useful method for protecting liberty; checks and balances, however, translates into supervision and redundancy, the dominant mechanism by which modern bureaucracies are restrained, and by which the liberty of the people who are subject to these bureaucracies is preserved. To achieve this translation, however, the Newtonian discourse must be jettisoned, and the concept must be reconfigured in the dynamic, interactive terms of modern governance.

In the prison reform cases, the courts did not act as despots but as friends of liberty and as agents of our national community. They ignored federalism and the separation of powers – and provided checks and balances – by imposing federal power on the states and judicial power on administrative agencies. They thus restrained and controlled state agencies that might otherwise have continued to perpetrate obscure but grinding tyrannies on a group of people who were subject to unsupervised control. The federal courts were controlled in turn by the continued existence of those states and agencies; they "took over" the prisons, in a very real sense, but they did so only as supervisors, not as absolute and unconstrained authorities. They checked, and they were checked in turn, and thus enacted the essential dynamic of modern democratic government.

The Transformation of the Rule of Law

The rule of law, as suggested in Chapter 6, is not so readily consigned to the preadministrative era as federalism or the separation of powers. As the size of government and the range of its concerns expand, as it surrounds and interpenetrates the structure of civil society and private life, the need for constraint, for the subjugation of bureaucratic discretion to generally established rules, becomes increasingly insistent. In Chapter 6, we argued that judicial policy making does not violate the rule of law. Judges are constrained by the internal dynamics of the policy-making process, specifically the need to implement policy by means of ideas that coordinate individual judges' efforts to integrate personal attitudes and preexisting doctrine. These ideas must themselves be recognizable as law and, once established, act as the same sort of constraint as the preexisting doctrine that was one element in their formulation. We further argued that the institutional conceptualization of the rehabilitative, bureaucratic prison, however managerial it seemed, was in fact recognizable as law.

As stated at the beginning of Chapter 6, the rule of law means many different things; we treat it, in this study, as the idea that government decision makers should be subject to some external control that is general, clear, well-accepted and congruent with the legal order that applies to private citizens. Dicey's definition incorporates this principle, but also includes the idea of equality before the law.[14] Joseph Raz adds the independence of the judiciary, judicial supervision of the executive and legislative branches, and the accessibility of courts to ordinary citizens,[15] while John Rawls adds the similar treatment of similar cases, the possibility of compliance, and natural justice.[16] Lon Fuller's morality of law, which includes prohibitions against ex post facto law, contradictory laws, and laws that are impossible to obey can be fairly regarded as another definition.[17] We take no position, in this study, on the relative merits of these definitions;

the reason we ignore their additional requirements is not because they are unimportant, but because they are not implicated in an analysis of judicial policy making. Obviously, when observers express a concern that judicial policy making such as the prison reform cases violates the rule of law, they are not talking about the independence of the judiciary or the accessibility of the courts. Neither are they talking about ex post facto or contradictory laws, because there is no particular reason that such laws would be produced by judicial rather than executive or legislative policy making. The rule-of-law concern about judicial policy making is that judges are operating without constraint to produce a body of variable, unpredictable, and personally motivated orders.

The general formulation of the rule of law that raises questions about judicial policy making is advanced most forcefully by F. A. Hayek in *The Road to Serfdom*,[18] and recently reargued at length by Geoffrey de Q. Walker.[19] Hayek defines the rule of law, or, as he puts it, the Rule of Law, as the principle "that government in all its actions is bound by rules fixed and announced before – rules which make it possible to foresee with fair certainty how authority will use its coercive powers in given circumstances."[20] This shares with the definition stated earlier the idea that government decision makers must be subject to control or constraint, but adds the additional element that the control must be exercised by fixed rules stated in advance. Judicial policy making clearly violates Hayek's definition; our argument for its conformance with the rule of law is that this definition should be rejected in favor of the less demanding definition that we have proposed.

Although Hayek readily acknowledges that *The Road to Serfdom* was directed to English readers, and more particularly to his concerns about the British Labour Party,[21] his book has had enormous resonance in the United States, particularly with respect to American constitutionalism. The reason probably lies within America's collective – if we may use this term in connection with Hayek – political experience. Although recent scholarship has emphasized the radical nature of the ideas that animated the American Revolution,[22] one must also recognize the radicalism of the Revolution itself, as a political event. In 1776 all of Europe's nation-states were ruled by kings, kings who still laid claim to the attributes of divinity. It is true, of course, that the English had killed their king a century and a quarter previously, that they had replaced him with a succession of increasingly insubstantial foreigners, and that Pope could refer to the predecessors of George III, the ruling king in 1776, by writing "in vain decried and curst, still Dunce the Second reigns like Dunce the First."[23] But kings still supplied a sense of solidity to political regimes, and Revolution bore the taint of lèse majesté. By 1789, America seemed to have brought off its revolution with civil society intact, but the twin demons of anarchy and tyranny haunted people's minds;[24] by the time the first presidential term under the new Constitution was complete, heads were rolling at the Tuilleries, and only the nation's insularity protected it from the horror with which all Europe regarded the continuing carnage.

It was natural, then, for Americans to look to the Constitution as a source of fixed and reliable standards that would replace the king and protect them from the threat of anarchy or dictatorship. The Constitution not only serves as a transcendent constraint on ordinary politics, but provides definitive answers for the bewildering and threatening questions of political morality. It is seen as the source of such rules and thus becomes an ultimate authority that will protect us from ourselves and provide the stability we sacrificed when we cut ourselves off from our ancestral authority and our ancestral source of law.[25]

But Hayek's definition, despite its constitutional resonances, represents a premodern conception of the rule of law, just as federalism and the separation of powers represent a premodern conception of governmental structure. Rules are conceived as a countervailing force to the discretion, or capriciousness, of governmental agents; in America, the Constitution serves as the force that opposes the violations of our democratic faith in which politicians would otherwise indulge. If one branch violates these rules, which, after all, cannot enforce themselves, another branch must animate them to restore the balance. This is the connection between federalism, separation of powers, and the rule of law, and explains why the latter two are linked in Raz's definition.[26]

The difficulties with this position, as with the structural constraints, are both operational and epistemological. In operational terms, the positive role of the state that was discussed earlier precludes the declaration of fixed, preestablished rules; a hands-on administrator like the Environmental Protection Agency, the Federal Reserve Bank, or the federal courts when they decided the prison reform cases needs much more flexibility. Regulation is an intimate, albeit not affectionate, process of negotiation, threat, bargaining, compromise, and confrontation that cannot be subjected to fixed, preestablished rules without becoming either excessively lax or excessively harsh. It is dynamic, rather than mechanistic, and the rigid boundaries that are argued for by Hayek, Walker, and less coherently, by Theodore Lowi,[27] would do little other than secure its ineffectiveness.

Hayek is quite aware of this opposition, which he presents, with characteristic perceptiveness, as a conflict between centralized planning and the rule of law;[28] as in so many other cases, however, his rhetorical momentum carries him well beyond his target. In technical, economic terms, he errs in assuming that the only market failure that threatens the efficiency of competition is monopoly. Hayek concedes that regulation is required to prevent monopoly, although he argues, with some force, that monopoly is not a naturally stable market structure, and that its dramatic development in the late nineteenth century was often the result of governmental policy.[29] But Hayek's economics has been rendered seriously obsolete by the subsequent realization that market failures often stem from externalities and information asymmetries, not monopoly, and that the market is further limited by the phenomenon of public goods.[30] These failures and limitations are the source of much of our regulatory state, such as environmental protection, securities laws, and the national parks. Thus, Hayek assumes that any regulations that are not designed to prevent monopolization will necessarily displace efficient competition and take us down the primrose path to serfdom; in fact, they are generally designed to correct other forms of market failure. For Hayek.to describe this regulation as "planning," by which he means centralized planning of the Soviet *gosplan* variety,[31] is simply incorrect.

A deeper problem with Hayek's rule-of-law idea involves the structure of the modern administrative state. As stated here, and in the previous section, this state engages in conscious and coordinated policy making to achieve collective purposes and to correct market failures. The term "state," however, is a gross generalization; what is really involved is a complex interplay of governmental institutions that operate on different levels and affect the citizenry in different ways. All these institutions, from the legislature to the "street-level bureaucrats,"[32] make policy, and all exercise constraints on one another through an interacting process that is conventionally described as checks and balances. Of course the legislature, with its juridical power of command, controls and constrains welfare caseworkers, but that control is filtered through several layers, each of which can augment, alter, or deflect it. And the caseworkers also constrain the legislature, for their capabilities and embedded patterns of behavior will determine the possibilities for effective legislation. Thus, the idea that government officials can only be constrained and disciplined by preestablished, explicitly stated rules is a seriously impoverished picture of the modern state's operational structure. The idea that rules must move downward through a hierarchy is equally impoverished; quite often, it is guidelines and authorizations that move downward, while the rules are generated by lower-level officials who apply them to private parties.[33] Hayek, Walker, Lowi, and Raz are still tied to the premodern concept that all rules emerge from the legislature and are enforced by courts; their rule-of-law concept simply fails to make contact with the nature of modern, administrative governance.

From the epistemological perspective, the idea of fixed, preestablished rules is equally outdated. To begin with, it relies on a concept of rules that seems naive in terms of modern thought. Margaret Radin has critiqued this concept based on Wittgenstein's analysis of rules and language use,[34] while Frances Mootz has done so on the basis of Gadamer's hermeneutics.[35] To these persuasive critiques, we would add the observation that modern social theory focuses on human actors, rather than on structural devices. As Robert Post observes, democracy must be understood as a substantive value, not a procedural mechanism.[36] The constraints it generates reside within people's minds and in the intersubjective process by which social attitudes are mediated. Here too, the constraints that constitute the rule of law are not fixed, preestablished rules, but the understandings that emerge from shared values and ongoing interactions. In other words, these constraints, together with the constitutional provisions to which they are attributed, are elements of our social or collective memory. They have no existence outside of ourselves.

These insights of contemporary social theory indicate that the equating of constraints with rules is mistaken at both the constitutional and the quotidian levels. The Constitution cannot be regarded as a set of preestablished rules, but only as a set of internalized attitudes that have evolved over time. It is these same attitudes that mediate the day-to-day interactions among government institutions, simultaneously empowering and constraining public officials. People possess these attitudes because they have internalized them as part of their socialization process; they follow them, despite the presence of countervailing attitudes and motivations, because to do so constitutes appropriate role behavior.

A modern version of the rule of law, therefore, incorporates the concept of constraint, but jettisons the idea that the constraint must necessarily consist of fixed, preestablished rules. To locate the sources of constraint, we must examine contemporary attitudes and governmental arrangements. We must observe the process by which government agents reach decisions, and supervise, discipline, and influence – or, in older terminology, check and balance – one another. They may well perceive some of the controls they wield, or are subject to, as rules, but these rules will be components of their social attitudes, not external forces that act upon those attitudes.

As stated, this perspective is consistent with modern social theory and it is also consistent with the actual operation of the modern administrative state. It is not surprising that social theory and administrative practice should be consistent, for the two are likely to be cocausally related. Theory reflects political reality, even without adopting a Marxist-inspired superstructure analysis, because it expands the range of the conceivable. The activist state that was developed under the lash of necessity turns out to possess a variety of mechanisms to avoid the tyranny that the Framers' generation feared from coordinated central government, as well as the more recently identified terrors of Weber's iron cage. The exploration of these mechanisms has taught theorists that oppression can be contained by supervision and culture, instead of formal mechanisms. Conversely, theory informs practice, and while scholars often succumb to a self-induced sense of cynicism, concluding that theory has no effect on practice or is merely an apology for power, a balanced assessment suggests that its effects are significant, though rarely determinative. The more we learn about political behavior, the more we realize that its control is a complex, dynamic process that can be illuminated and improved with modern social theory.

Reliance on attitudes, culture, and complex supervisory mechanisms rather than on the grand structure of government may appear to be an insubstantial or unreliable way to protect freedom, but there is really nothing else. We like to imagine that constitutional rules function as an external constraint, or an impersonal force, and that they prescribe a structure in which elected officials declare rules that function as a further, equally impersonal constraint. But this is only our social mythology, a burnt conceptual offering to placate the forces of disorder and to excuse the fact that we owe our origin as a nation to the disorder of a revolution. We have no difficulty recognizing that other people's myths are internal to their belief system; the equivalent insight about our own myths is a bit more difficult to accept. Nonetheless, we must do so if we are to develop a realistic account of our modern state and of the way in which the rule of law functions in that context.

The Constrained Nature of Judicial Policy Making

The first section of this chapter summarized our description of judicial policy making; having discussed the desuetude of structural constraints, and the transformation of the rule of law, we can now complete our summary of its legitimacy. As stated, judicial policy making seems to violate some vaunted legal principles: federalism, separation of powers, and the rule of law. But the first two, we have argued, are not genuine norms of modern governance, but managerial strategies that can be properly ignored when it is practical to do so. The rule of law remains a valid norm, and an important one, but it has been transformed by administrative reality and modern social theory from the requirement of fixed and preestablished rules to one of socially embedded constraints on the actions of government officials. Judicial policy making generally conforms to these constraints.

Judicial policy making begins with the perception of a problem and the identification of a goal. This is generally motivated by a moral imperative of some sort, an insistent belief that some observed condition violates a well-recognized, important social norm. Although attitudes vary from one person to the next, most conscientious and well-socialized decision makers are capable of examining their own attitudes and distinguishing idiosyncratic beliefs from widely held norms. Of course, judges can make mistakes, delude themselves, or act irresponsibly, but that is true for anyone who wields public authority. The solution is not to deny them the authority they need to perform their role, and certainly not to grant them that authority but deny that it exists. Rather, errors are best minimized by supervision, a bureaucratic-sounding principle that in fact has long been embodied in the design of the judiciary. The isolated judge who figures so prominently in jurisprudence is to be found only in what Weber describes as Kadi-justice;[37] virtually all modern judiciaries, including the federal judiciary and the judiciary of every state, consist of many individuals, organized in several levels, with the upper levels deciding cases in multi-member panels. This is a reasonably good system to counteract idiosyncratic beliefs.

In discussing the moral imperatives that triggered the prison reform cases, this study focused heavily on the national character of these imperatives. The observation seems linked to the particular characteristics of the prison reform issue, specifically the felt need to extirpate the slave plantation model that had flourished in the southern states, and the structural relationship between federal courts and state-run institutions. In fact, the force behind the federal court intervention suggests that the national character of the moral imperative is a general feature of judicial policy making. The courts in the prison reform cases were prepared to ignore the countervailing principle of federalism because our community is national, because the nation as a whole is the arena in which prevailing political norms arise. Norms must thus be national if they are to possess the motivating force to initiate the policy-making process. Dworkin speaks of doctrine as possessing gravitational force;[38] the inherent meaning of this image, in the twentieth century, is that norms enable courts to pull away from existing doctrine when their motive power is sufficient to generate an escape velocity. That power can only be provided by norms that are shared by the entire political community.

Much has been made of the judge's moral sense by legal scholars,[39] but it functions here only as a precondition, not a complete justification. The mere possession of an identifiable motive, after all, is a condition of sanity, not legitimacy. Its main effect is to ensure that policy making will be initiated only with a certain sense of seriousness, as administrations initiate a rule-making process. In other words, it is a threshold condition, a way of differentiating judicial policy making from the more common, but not more characteristic, actions of fact-finding and interpretation. Its constraining force, though limited, is real and results from social attitudes and hierarchial supervision, not from governmental structure.

The substantive constraints that limit the judicial policy-making process do not flow directly from social norms, but rather are inherent in the techniques by which that process is performed. This would seem to follow from the institutional fact that no one supervises courts but other courts, so that any enforceable constraint must be an aspect of judicial decision making. In more conceptual terms, the judiciary can be viewed, in Luhmann's and Teubner's models, as an autopoietic system that generates the rules for evaluating its own actions, and self-consciously engages in the application of those self-generated rules.[40] But the interrelationship of techniques and constraints also has a political dimension; it is part of the real meaning of self-government, and thus linked directly to the rule of law. The phrase "self-government" is often taken to mean that the people of our nation govern themselves, but if this implies that they exercise any real supervision over government officials, it can be nothing more than a high school civics bromide. Certainly, the people choose some of their leaders, but those chosen leaders, and others whom the people do not choose, must also govern themselves, in the sense that they internalize constraints upon their actions. Self-government cannot operate through elections without also operating through internalized constraints. Michels' iron law of oligarchy – that elected and appointed leaders become self-perpetuating elites[41] – would yield not only oligarchy but unbounded tyranny without internalized constraints, for the power granted to modern government officials would quickly enable them to crush the supposedly sovereign populace. It may be uncomfortable for us to recognize that the Madisonian machinery of countervailing forces is not sufficient to preserve democracy, but the modern understanding of political and social systems clearly indicates that organizations depend upon embedded norms, and that human agents are most powerfully controlled by their internalized beliefs. The reason judges are willing to make public policy, despite the apparent prohibitions on this enterprise, is that they sense that this policy-making process is internally constrained. They feel they are governed, although no outside actor is governing them, and that they are thus conforming to the rule of law.

These governing constraints appear at both the doctrinal creation and the implementation stage of the policy-making process. At the former stage, a judge cannot concoct a new rule on the basis of his own predilections; not only would it be reversed by a higher court, or distinguished by lower ones, but the judge himself would end up looking like an idiot, something no sane person would risk, not even for the pleasure of imposing his personal views on others. Rather, new legal rules are generated through a complex process that conforms to well-established institutional patterns.

To explore the techniques that characterize this process, it would seem natural to begin with the legislative and executive branches, where rule-making is prevalent and well accepted. We do so in this book, using the classic model of policy analysis, but this model breaks down when it comes to the difficult question of precisely how policy makers think of new ideas; we lack a clear sense of the operational process by which such ideas are conceived, selected, and operationalized. One reason for this is that we are so scornful of legislators and administrators; to speak of their creative or intellectually imaginative achievements seems like hopeless naiveté. To be sure, many legislators or administrators are indeed venal, uninterested, perpetually inebriated, or downright stupid, and are no more capable than molluscs of developing new ideas. The same is true, however, for people who decide they want to paint, and yet alongside all the canvasses that have been justifiably deposited in the garbage lie some of the greatest glories of the human spirit. Similarly, there are at least some extremely talented legislators and administrators, and perhaps a few of genius. Many of the concepts by which we live and work, including antitrust, affirmative action, unfair and deceptive trade practices, deposit insurance, and factory emissions standards are relatively recent creations of legislative or administrative action. But few scholars study this creative process; most believe it is exclusively political, as if the mere desire for reelection was sufficient to generate such truly formative ideas.

Thus, this study, while it advances the claim that judicial policy making is simply one variant of the general policy-making approach of modern government, cannot rely on any close analogy to other policy-making efforts in describing the actual process of creating doctrine. Instead, it focuses on the judiciary's own behavior. The process begins because most judges possess both a strong desire to fulfill the expectations that their role imposes on them and a strong desire to implement their own beliefs. When the two conflict, they will try to integrate them by articulating a new rule. But relying on individually stated rules violates role expectations as the judges themselves well know, so they will be further motivated to seek ideas that coordinate their own integrative efforts with those of other judges. Those coordinating ideas constitute new doctrine, at least in areas when the supreme court of the jurisdiction has not acted by command.

The constrained nature of this process is inherent in its internal dynamics. The process can only begin when the beliefs involved are widely held. An individual judge may possess idiosyncratic norms, but most will know enough to exclude those from the courtroom; a few will not, but unless they are in the unusual situation of holding the deciding votes in their jurisdiction's supreme court, they will be reversed or ignored. These beliefs need not be limited to the compelling norms that initiate the entire process: as in the prison cases, judges are likely to be more circumspect when deciding whether to enter the lists than they are once they find themselves in the midst of battle. In more phenomenological terms, the judge will find herself confronting an issue where her attitudes diverge from existing doctrine. She will first decide whether those attitudes justify an effort to achieve beneficial results without guidance from a specific legal text; if she decides they do, she will proceed directly to an effort to achieve that result by drawing on her attitudes and on the general body of legal doctrine. A larger and less carefully considered set of attitudes is likely to become involved at this point. Nonetheless, the two sorts of attitudes are closely related. They constrain the process at both stages because judges are socialized to possess a delimited set of attitudes and professionally trained to treat even those attitudes with caution and restraint.

Having been initiated, the conceptual process of judicial policy making only generates a result through a coordinating idea that meets the rather demanding conditions of realization, delimitation, and directionality. What is needed is an image that is both vivid and recognizably legal, that moves doctrine far enough to satisfy most judges' current beliefs without moving it too far, and that conforms to the general trend of legal developments in the relevant field; in short, the idea must persuade a widely dispersed, individualistic group of judges that it resolves their own dilemmas in a manner consistent with the expectations of their role. Clearly, it is difficult to frame such ideas, and only certain ones will serve this purpose. The judges' experience of both effort and constraint is derived from these inherent limitations.

When all is said and done, therefore, the process of judicial policy making is constrained by legal doctrine. But this does not mean that there exists some specific legal rules, or even principles behind a rule, that prescribes the decision that the judge ultimately reaches. A process of that sort reflects a premodern view of law, premodern in the dual sense that it predates the advent of the activist state and that it represents an antiquated epistemology of legal rules. Rather, doctrine constrains as one element in a dynamic, interacting process; the need to maintain contact with existing doctrine, to stretch it without snapping it, is one of several conditions for effective judicial policy making.[42] The effect of doctrine is neither unambiguous nor unaccompanied by other forces, but it is distinctive, and makes judicial policy making different from policy making by other governmental institutions.

When the coordinating idea consists of an institutional conceptualization, as it did in the prison cases, there is an additional set of constraints involving the implementation process. Since judges know, in advance, that they will probably need to implement that new doctrine, they must develop one that they perceive as implementable at the doctrinal creation stage. This means that it must be comprehensible to those in the affected institution, and must represent an incremental change. No institutional conceptualization that lacks these attributes is likely to coordinate the integrative effort of the very practical group of people who populate American judiciaries.

Incrementalism, like belief, thus appears at several stages of the policy-making process. Its heuristic role in policy making – Lindblom's muddling through – has been extensively observed and used as a subsidiary frame-work in this study. But incrementalism also represents a specific, substantive constraint on the judicial policy-making process, a need to institute change by degrees, to remain in contact with preexisting structures when one moves in new directions. It operates with respect to doctrine, which is the internal, or autopoetic aspect of judicial decisions, and also with respect to the external institutions that these decisions affect. In both these roles it serves as an aspect of the rule of law, for, in the modern state, law not only means judicially enforced legal doctrine but also the rules and regulations that govern public institutions. The incrementalism of judicial policy making means that it must incorporate both bodies of law at the same time that it produces change. As Robert Pushaw suggests, the case or controversy requirement – one of the very few limits on judicial decision making that is actually stated in the Constitution – enforces this incremental approach.[43] This is not to endorse the weirdness of the current Supreme Court's standing doctrine;[44] the requirement that the judiciary proceed on a case-by-case basis imposes substantive instrumentalism as a constraint, even in cases raising broad issues that the court has endeavored to exclude.

The final stage of the judicial policy-making process, implementation, generates a separate set of constraints, even beyond those that are anticipated at the doctrinal creation stage and incorporated into the new doctrine. Operationally, the techniques of judicial policy making resemble the operational techniques of any other governmental agency. Administrative policy makers initiate programs, impose rules, negotiate regarding the compliance with those rules, appoint inspectors to monitor compliance, bedevil recalcitrant parties with sanctions or onerous requirements, oscillate between confrontation and conciliation, and mobilize support from a variety of outside forces. Judicial policy makers rely on similar techniques. They too initiate programs, although we generally regard them as more passive; one of the striking features of the case studies is the proactive role that the judges adopted in initiating and directing the cases that they ultimately adjudicated. They try one solution and, if it proves unsuccessful, they switch to another. They impose rules, negotiate with the parties, appoint monitors, mobilize support, and use intervention to punish recalcitrant parties. Not all these techniques are used in every policy-making situation, of course. Sometimes, courts, like agencies, limit themselves to declaring rules, as they did in the common law and constitutional right of privacy cases. But all the techniques are available to the judiciary and, in extreme situations like the prison reform effort, all of them will be used.

But if judges are able to deploy a wide variety of implementation techniques that we traditionally regard as administrative, they are also constrained by the institutional attributes of these techniques, attributes born of both intrinsic limits and shared understandings. A government can free itself from certain operational constraints by taking proprietary control of a given subject area, as the federal government has done with the armed forces, the national parks, the financial institution that controls the money supply, and the prisons that fall within its jurisdiction. Most often, however, American governments leave direct control in other hands and exercise their policy-making power through a regulatory process that remains subject to a wider range of limitations. Courts always follow this second approach, even in areas that provide the best evidence for a judicial "takeover"; daily operations in their areas of policy making invariably remain in the hands of private or other governmental institutions. Judicial administration, therefore, always involves negotiations, persuasion, and the recruitment of allies from within and without the subject institution. Indeed, it is notable that federal judges rarely ever invoked their ultimate sanction – the contempt power – just as federal administrative agencies rarely invoke similarly draconian sanctions such as funding cut-offs, deposit insurance cancellation, or dissolution of a corporation. Instead, it is the possibility of these sanctions, and the application of more minor, less legally defined penalties such as inspections, publicity, and detailed instructions, that are employed to punish recalcitrance and induce compliance.

Thus, there exists a deeply understood cultural experience with administrative implementation techniques. These techniques are multifarious and can fall with heavy weight upon the obdurate, but they are delimited. The limitations cannot be stated with precision at the present time because insufficient attention has been given to them, at least in legal terms. Prevailing legal theories are directed toward statutory limits on administrative action and toward textual limits on interpretive judicial decision making. The mechanisms of administrative intervention are equally constrained, however, and those constraints are apparent in practice, even if they are not yet sufficiently defined in theory. The aggressive judicial intervention into prisons appears unconstrained only if one believes that courts are operating in some sort of moral and practical void once they venture beyond interpretation or beyond the modes of action recognized by the 1950s legal process school.

Despite all these constraints upon judicial policy making, the question of legitimacy still lingers. The one constraint that cannot act upon this process is fidelity to authoritative texts, for the whole purpose of the enterprise is to create and apply new legal doctrine. This fidelity to texts is often regarded as the sine qua non of judicial legitimacy, because it is the means of binding judges to the people's will, as expressed by their elected representatives. The built-in constraints of judicial administration and doctrine creation may be equally effective, but they seem to emerge from a different source. As previously discussed, however, the idea that the popular will is an operative concept of modern democracy is an extremely doubtful proposition. Our machinery of state is generally designed as a series of constrained institutions, whose powers are limited and whose general purposes are prescribed, not as a means of translating public opinion into governmental policy. This is not merely because elections are an ineffective means of communicating the popular will, although that is certainly true. It is because we are a massive modern state, not a Greek polis or a New England village. The tasks of governance are too complex and the scale of society too vast to admit any process of direct governance, no matter how fair or effective our elections. The legitimacy of modern government must be understood in other terms.

While public governance is not a viable principle in a modern state, popular sovereignty retains more force. The people cannot manage their own government, but the argument can certainly be made that they should retain the ultimate control over its structure by speaking through the Constitution, and the ultimate control over its broadest policies by speaking through their elected representatives. Judicial policy making does not violate this principle, however; textually defined jurisdiction cabins policy making within both constitutional and statutory boundaries. These texts do not control the content of judicial policy making, but they do define the areas in which the courts have jurisdiction. The words of the Eighth Amendment establish that punishment is a matter of constitutional concern, and thus the proper province of constitutional courts, even if they do not establish anything else. Of course, such textual grants of jurisdiction must be interpreted; it is at least arguable that the amendment applies only to the type of sentence, for example. But this only places judicial policy making in the same position as more traditional modes of judicial action, and preserves the principle of popular sovereignty to the extent that it is preserved by any judicial decision.

The precise relationship between judicial policy making and popular sovereignty could be formulated in terms of intent; when the people or the legislature provides a general grant of jurisdiction to the courts, they intend that the courts engage in policy making. There is something artificial about this approach, however. A better formulation is that policy making is an intrinsic or in-dwelling element of the judicial process, that when courts are granted jurisdiction the potentiality of policy making is inherent in that grant. Part of the meaning of a court, as that institution is understood in our culture, is that it will make public policy under the constrained conditions that have been described earlier. This approach conforms to the realities of the modern state and to the insights of modern social theory: the contrary position conflicts with both of these.

Any normative account of a governance modality must allow for evaluation and critique; it must enable observers to carry out a discussion about whether the particular decision was made well or badly, even if there are no definitive criteria for that determination. Much of legal scholarship, for example, evaluates the quality of judicial interpretations. The account of judicial policy making presented here allows for the same sort of discussions. An analysis of judicially developed policy could begin by questioning the court's moral imperative. Was the value that the court invoked or implied a deeply felt, national norm, or was it a more idiosyncratic attitude of the particular judge? Was the stated policy genuinely based upon that value? Second, the analysis could question the choice of a solution. Did the court articulate a coordinating idea that truly integrated the national norm with existing doctrine? An idea that failed this test would probably fail to persuade other courts as well, but the critique might be stated before the decision's effect on other courts was known, or the deciding court might be a supreme court exercising its hierarchical power. Moreover, an observer might attempt to demonstrate that a more effective coordinating idea was available, just as observers now demonstrate the possibility of preferable interpretations. Finally, an observer might ask whether the implementation efforts that the courts employed emerged from the newly articulated doctrine, whether it translated that doctrine into operational reality in the most effective manner, and whether it remained within the bounds of accepted practice or situational prudence in doing so.

The fact that the discussion of coordinating ideas in this chapter incorporated the institutional character of courts raises a complex issue for evaluative efforts, but it is an issue that is equally troublesome for evaluations of interpretive decisions. This is the issue of the scholar's audience.[45] With respect to coordinating ideas, is the scholar addressing a single judge or the judiciary as a whole? If she is addressing a single judge, then the attitudes of other judges, and not simply the scholar's assessment of the best decision, must be factored into the analysis. This seems awkward, perhaps because it merges "is" and "ought," perhaps because it reduces the scholar's recommendation from policy to strategy, at least in part. But if the scholar is addressing the judiciary as a whole, then the dynamics of the coordination process are obscured, and the phenomenological reality of the judge's position, as an individual decision maker, is lost. In evaluations of interpretation, however, the same problem arises. Interpretations must also be adopted by the entire institution, even though the text may provide conceptual unity that must otherwise be provided by coordination. Thus, the emphasis on the courts as institutions in the analysis presented here merely brings to the forefront an unsolved problem for scholarship about judicial decision making in general.

But the issue of the judge as a potential audience for scholarly evaluations of judicial policy making presents an additional complexity: the judiciary's extreme reluctance to acknowledge the existence of this mode of action and to articulate the rules that guide it. This can be attributed to a conscious program of mystification, if one is in a conspiratorial mood, but the secret has been out for so long that the supposed conspirators would resemble children who stay curled up in their hiding place after they have been discovered. There seems to be an epistemological element as well, a lack of concepts or vocabulary with which to describe the policy-making process.

In fact, the reason judges are reluctant to acknowledge their policy-making role is not because of any convincing countervailing norm, but precisely because they lack an established vocabulary by which this role can be described. To some extent, the vocabulary for judicial policy making can be borrowed from the administrative process, as our dominant image of government, and can be elaborated by studying the interaction of that image with the specific features of judicial action such as the institutional features of the courts and the need to translate norms or standards into legal doctrine. Unfortunately, that vocabulary is not fully developed. While most people accept the idea that the legislative and executive branches are policy makers for a vast administrative state, a great deal of ambivalence about that role remains, as is apparent from the most cursory consideration of contemporary politics. This ambivalence has focused normative or prescriptive accounts of policy making on general issues of its legitimacy, rather than on more detailed inquiries about how it can be accomplished more effectively. Consequently, this study has relied on fairly descriptive, nontheoretical accounts of the policy-making process, and devised its own theory for the particular problem of doctrine creation. As research on the administrative state develops, however, there will undoubtedly be further insights that can be applied to judicial policy making.

There is, however, a remaining mystery that resides in this approach. While modern administrative practice has certainly increased the visibility of governmental policy making, it did not invent the policy-making process. All branches of government, including courts, acted as policy makers in the preadministrative era, albeit not as frequently or comprehensively. It is disconcerting that we have been required to draw upon concepts derived from the administrative era to describe a process that predates that era by several centuries, at least. Does this mean that it would have been impossible to describe judicial policy making at an earlier time, despite the fact that it was being practiced? Are the concepts we associate with the administrative state more central to the process of governance than we believe?

These questions go beyond the limits of this study. What seems clear is that a proper understanding of the administrative, policy-oriented nature of our present government establishes the basis for a clearer understanding and a more realistic approach to the judicial policy-making process. One purpose of this study is to bring this process into the light, in both the descriptive sense of recognizing its existence, and the normative sense of demonstrating its legitimacy. To do so, we must abandon a good deal of our current mythology about the judicial process. That may be difficult, but it was also difficult for our predecessors to stop dancing around a bonfire and painting themselves blue. Time goes on, however; judicial policy making will not be abandoned, and it can be improved only if it is acknowledged. Although the administrative state did not create judicial policy making, its advent provides a new opportunity to explore the possibilities of this widespread but much disparaged mode of governance.

Coda: Assessing the Successes of Judicial Prison Reform

The Problem of Assessment

This concludes our study of judicial policy making. We have argued that policy making is a standard mode of judicial action, and that the familiar criticisms of its legitimacy are overly simplistic, particularly in the context of a modern administrative state. To demonstrate these points, we have examined one of the most dramatic examples of judicial policy making – the prison reform cases of the past three decades. In these cases, the federal courts made public policy by imposing national standards on state prisons, by implementing standards through administrative action, and by fashioning new legal doctrine. The question that remains, however, is whether all this effort, legitimate though it may have been, produced a good result. Was its net result an improvement in American prisons or in American society at large?

As we announced in advance in Chapter 1, we cannot answer this question. We can, however, explain why we cannot answer it. We can also do the next best thing, which is to summarize the impact of the prison conditions cases and to speculate about the future of corrections and correctional reform now that the judicial effort seems to have run its course.

Any devotee of prison movies is familiar with the scene in which an inmate, generally the protagonist, finds himself on line in the prison cafeteria, confronting a food server, whether a staff member or inmate, who despises him. The two men glare at each other for a moment. Then, the server, with a malignant smirk, dishes out a particularly scrofulous piece of meat, or tosses a dollop of mashed potatoes into the protagonist's coffee.

Situations of this sort occurred at the Alameda County Jail prior to the time when a federal district court held that conditions at the jail were unconstitutional.[1] In addition to arbitrary food service, the court found that the food was made from substandard ingredients, was cold when served, and was prepared by ill-trained personnel in a kitchen with leaky sewer pipes that ran across the ceiling. Sheriff Charles Plummer, whose office supervised the facility, was initially incensed at being sued, but he quickly realized that the suit could help him to obtain a long-planned but yet unbuilt new jail – in fact, it could help him obtain a jail that was considerably better than the long-planned, yet unbuilt one. So, in a mood of apparent contrition, he helped write specifications into the consent decree that went well beyond anything the court would have ordered. Some years later, when the sheriff showed one of the authors around his new facility, he evinced particular pride in both his strategy and the resulting kitchen. The kitchen was indeed impressive – full of white, tiled surfaces and shiny metal equipment, stocked with nutritious supplies, and presided over by a newly hired dietician. But the pièce de resistance was the food delivery system. Meals were placed in styrofoam trays, packed in metal warming units, and delivered to inmates on a computer-controlled, driverless trolley, which automatically uncoupled one of its carts in front of each of the jail's housing units.

The Alameda County Jail Automated Food Delivery Robot is a product of the judicial prison reform process. Is it a success? Clearly, it provides inmates with warmer, more appetizing food than the old system and all but eliminates the possibility of arbitrary servings, since portions are standardized and distribution mechanized. Staffing costs are reduced by automation and confrontations between inmates are decreased. Thus, the robot and the judicial decision that produced it seem to meet both the humanitarian's demand for decent living conditions and the administrator's demand for more control; in David Rothman's phrase, it satisfies both "conscience and convenience."

But this does not prove that the Food Delivery Robot should be counted as a success. Although outside observers would probably regard it as a better way to treat inmates, the inmates might not agree. They might prefer to break up the day's monotony by walking down the corridors to the cafeteria and eating in a central dining hall, despite the cold food and the danger of getting mashed potatoes in their coffee. This preference may not rank very high in public policy terms, but it is linked with deeper and more far-reaching concerns. Many of the most highly touted Progressive era reforms were designed to relieve the crushing monotony of prison life. Prison administrators implicitly acknowledge this monotony as the most severe consequence of incarceration by using it, in the form of administrative segregation, to discipline unruly inmates. The critics of Marion Penitentiary and other supermaximum prisons point to the monotonous, heavily controlled environment as the major human rights violation that occurs within these formidable institutions.[2] Oscar Wilde identified it, together with recurrent diarrhea, as the greatest indignity to which he was subjected in the British prisons.[3] More generally, Foucault's implicit criticism of penitentiaries focuses on the mechanized, automated, and oppressively complete control that they impose. Being served food by a robot could certainly be regarded as an element in that regime, and might be even more objectionable in a jail than a prison.

If those concerned about the rights of prisoners would voice these criticisms, those who demand harsher punishment for criminals might raise an opposite concern, at least if the robot were to be used in a prison. It might seem trivial and spiteful to insist that cold food is part of a convicted felon's just deserts, but again there is a larger issue. Incarcerating criminals for extended periods is a relatively recent idea, having gained ascendancy in England and North America only in the late eighteenth century. From the outset there was fierce opposition to this new form of punishment. Why, opponents asked, should undeserving criminals be provided housing, food, and perhaps even employment at public expense when so many law-abiding people lacked those amenities? A common answer was to assure skeptics that prisoners would be confined under unappealing conditions, one of the few promises in prison administration that has rarely been broken. Rusche and Kirchheimer, writing from a Marxist perspective, regard this insistence that prisoners be worse off than anyone else as a universal principle of punishment in Western society.[4]

The robot, which provides a food service equivalent to that provided airline passengers or factory workers, and better than that provided many elementary school students, might thus be viewed as inappropriate for prisons. One might assume that this would not be true in jails, at least for presumptively innocent inmates awaiting trial. In fact, little solicitude has been shown for jail inmates on this basis, perhaps because cost issues lie at the root of the concern that prisoners are being "coddled," perhaps because of the factually accurate, although legally unsupportable assumption that most arrestees are guilty and will end up in prison anyway. Certainly, public resistance to providing excessive amenities for prisoners and detainees looms large in many politicians' minds. Almost every prison administrator, no matter how tough, would like to give all the inmates a television, not only because it would occupy their time but because it would be so easy to punish them by taking the television away. In most places, however, this would be politically unacceptable, conjuring up images of the prison as a "posh resort" or "country club." We can safely assume that the "will of the people" would be equally opposed to the Food Delivery Robot.

Thus, court orders that require decent or comfortable conditions will not necessarily be seen as a success, even if both prisoners and administrators favor them. Judgments about the success or failure of judicial action clearly depend upon one's underlying values. This does not foreclose thoughtful analysis and debate, but it precludes the easy characterizations of specific results as successful or unsuccessful. To be sure, all issues in the human sciences are subject to such normative disagreement. Correctional policy may be particularly controversial however, since the dispersion of views is unusually wide and the intensity with which they are held is unusually high. There hardly seems to be anyone in America, no matter how ignorant of actual prison conditions, who does not have strong opinions on the subject.

Despite these disagreements, the enterprise of measuring empirical effects remains a useful one, but it must be carried out with caution. The disagreements tend to insinuate themselves into the definition of the research problem, the terminology in which the problem is expressed, and the interpretation of the results. Consider, for example, the debate about whether judicial intervention into prisons has produced increased levels of "violence." The way the research project is formulated suggests certain normative commitments, and the very concept of violence embodies many of those same commitments. For John DiIulio, with his concern for order, authority, and neatness, violence refers to attacks by one inmate on another.[5] Both Steve Martin and Sheldon Ekland-Olson,[6] and Ben Crouch and James Marquart,[7] beginning from a human rights orientation, would include the unauthorized use of force by guards in their definition of violence. The obviously different results that these approaches generate can both be useful, but they will breed confusion unless we are clear about their underlying premises. Neither one can answer categorical questions about the success of judicial intervention, because the answer to that question requires sustained normative inquiry into the purposes of prisons and of punishment in general that will control, rather than being controlled by, the collection of empirical data.

The focus of this book has been somewhat different. What seems most striking to us about the Alameda County Jail Automated Food Delivery Robot is not its effects upon the prisoners – all social policies have such effects – but the process leading to its creation. The robot was a product of a comprehensive order issued by the federal judge for the complete restructuring of the Alameda County Jail. As a result, a new facility was financed and constructed based on detailed specifications contained in the court order. Policy making of this nature is not part of our existing theory of judicial action. The litigation leading to the order is equally disconcerting; instead of an adversarial contest between the parties, advancing opposing positions from which a single truth emerges, there was, as in Santa Clara County, an essentially collusive arrangement between the plaintiffs' attorney and the sheriff.

These events are easy to condemn by making widely accepted but unsupported assumptions about the role of courts and the nature of law. This book has tried to avoid these assumptions and to explore the judicial process in our modern administrative state more dispassionately. As a descriptive matter, it has identified the policy-making function that judges undertake and the variety of strategic actions that are natural and perhaps intrinsic to that function. As a normative matter, it has argued that judicial policy making, strategies and all, is consistent with the concept of law that the modern state engenders. This is the success that the analysis identifies – that the courts succeeded in consistently and legitimately making public policy. Some people will agree with the policies they made in the prison cases and some will disagree; assessing those positions is the subject for a different book. But people disagree about the policies that Congress makes, and that disagreement is rarely seen as a ground for depriving Congress of its policy-making function. The courts performed no worse than Congress; they were players in the game, and did as well as any other governmental participants.

What the Courts Accomplished

Although we cannot provide a global judgment of the federal judiciary's success or failure in the prison reform cases, we can identify the major impacts that the courts produced. The first and most obvious was the extension of well-recognized constitutional rights to prisoners – access to courts, freedom of speech, freedom of religion, and due process. This has not been emphasized in our study because it is not directly related to the theme of judicial policy making. Judicial decisions granting prisoners the right to receive books of their choice, to be served food that comports with the dietary restrictions of their religion, or to receive a rudimentary hearing before being subjected to serious punishment for alleged misbehavior could have been based on the familiar process of interpreting the Constitution's language, reasoning by analogy and extending principles established for other institutions to the prison setting. Of course, most of these interpretations are controversial, but they are interpretations nonetheless; that is, they could be credibly regarded as drawing their content from a legally binding text. One right, moreover, is a noncontroversial interpretation; it is certain that a prisoner should not be precluded or seriously restricted from challenging the validity of his conviction because he is in prison as a result of that conviction.[8] Although these more specific, constitutional rights of prisoners do not require judicial policy making, they are nonetheless results of judicial policy making in the prison reform cases. Their recognition was a by-product of the more comprehensive supervision that the policy-making efforts of the courts imposed.

Of course, one can question the practical significance of the various rights that prisoners secured as a result of the prison reform cases. Free speech for prisoners does not necessarily grant them reasonable access to the outside world, freedom of religion is often subordinated to security concerns, and disciplinary hearings generally validate the administration's action. Some of these rights, moreover, might have emerged from a non-judicial process of professionalization and standard setting had the judges never been involved. Nonetheless, the fact remains that due to the prison reform cases, virtually all prisoners now have certain rights and privileges that few possessed thirty years ago, and that many prison administrators would have found inconceivable.

Another direct effect of the prison reform cases was the abolition of the South's plantation model. In 1965, southern prisons were distinctly different from those in other parts of the United States; by the 1980s this was no longer the case. Precisely how much value one attaches to this change depends upon one's views. Some observers might share John DiIulio's preference for well-run plantation-style prisons, while others might view all American prisons as so repressive that the variation in form is insignificant. But whatever one's evaluation of the change, it seems clear that a distinct, extensive change had been effectuated by the federal courts.

The change in correctional strategy may be compared with the abolition of de jure segregation in the South. Andrew Hacker, Douglas Massey, and Nancy Denton,[9] among others, argue that black Americans remain segregated in many ways, in all parts of the nation. Nonetheless, the abolition of de jure segregation – legally separate schools, exclusion from public places, separate treatment on public transport – is a palpable and an important change. The courts played a role in that process, but so did Congress and the president; according to Gerald Rosenberg, the impact of the other branches dwarfed that of the courts.[10] In the case of prison reform, however, the federal judiciary was the dominant actor; no other branch of the federal government was involved to any significant extent, a situation that continues to the present day.

This is not to say that courts acted entirely on their own. As discussed in Chapter 5, reform movements were initiated in several southern states. In Florida, the effort was carried to completion without comprehensive court orders and indeed before courts began an active role in conditions cases. In other states, such as Louisiana, it fizzled, but nonetheless indicated that there were forces in these states that would support the judicial effort. Once the courts issued their orders, moreover, they found allies from both inside and outside the prison system. In Arkansas, Commissioner Sarver saw judicial intervention as a way to educate his own sub-ordinates and to gain more support from the legislature and the governor; in Santa Clara County, Sheriff Winter may have made a similar assessment. The Texas legislature ultimately tired of the correctional system's intransigence and supported the reform process. Throughout the nation, the media and other public opinion leaders often rallied behind the federal courts. As stated, the courts probably could not have produced the changes that they did without these in-state allies. Nonetheless, the courts were often the primary agents, by almost anyone's definition of institutional change, and the abolition of the plantation model is a definite result of their efforts.

But the extension of constitutional rights to prisoners and the abolition of the plantation model were not the sole results of the prison reform cases. In fact, they were embedded in several larger, albeit more diffuse effects. These are more difficult to discern because they helped consolidate reforms that had been heavily promoted by correctional officials during the previous twenty-five years. Nonetheless, judicial involvement made a noticeable difference, accelerating reform in certain cases, consolidating it in others, enabling it to defeat strong countervailing influences in others still. The nationwide impact of the prison reform cases can thus be characterized as a part, but an important part, of larger trends in correctional administration. In particular, the cases were an important contribution to three major developments: the emergence of a national corrections profession, the formulation of national standards for corrections, and the general bureaucratization of state prisons.

Prison litigation enhanced and accelerated the process of professionalization by providing a new and important forum for the ideas of national correctional leaders who had long advocated reform. Far from relying on radical opponents of imprisonment, the plaintiffs' attorneys regularly sought out the views of the best and the brightest leaders in the correctional field and urged the courts to embrace their positions.[11] In case after case, the same small handful of nationally known experts was called upon to serve as witnesses, to advise the court, and to act as special masters or compliance officers. These experts were quick to take advantage of the bully pulpit that the courts were providing. The litigation enabled them to speak forcefully, not just to like-minded colleagues as they had in the past, but to judges, state legislators, governors, and newspaper editors. Their names may have not become household words, but James Bennett, Allen Breed, John Conrad, Thomas Lonergan, Kenneth Schoen, and a handful of other corrections professionals gained new and influential audiences as a result of the prison reform cases. As director of the National Institute of Corrections, Allan Breed joined forces with the Federal Judicial Center to develop a program to train and certify special masters and a handbook for judges who were involved in conditions cases. From his position with the Edna McConnell Clark Foundation, Kenneth Schoen, former commissioner of corrections for Minnesota, provided generous funding for the litigation efforts of Al Bronstein and the ACLU's National Prison Project and promoted a host of other prison reforms. Former California corrections administrator John Conrad was a member of the court-appointed Visiting Committee dealing with Alabama's prisons and wrote numerous articles in correctional journals about the value of constitutionally based reforms in prisons. And the testimony of James Bennett, a former director of the federal Bureau of Prisons, led judges, state corrections officials, and others to regard the bureau as a model to be emulated. Litigation did not create this group of experts, nor did it change their views, but it did serve to amplify their voices dramatically.

Litigation also promoted a new generation of correctional administrators who embraced the views of these national leaders and accepted the role of the courts in overseeing conditions in their institutions. As described in Chapter 7, state prisons constituted one of the last public institutions to be exempt from standard civil service requirements and modern bureaucratic structure. They continued to be led by "good ol' boys" who were recruited through a system of patronage and promoted by an informal, discretionary process. Although this form of organization was being eroded by forces wholly independent of the prisoners' rights movement, litigation accelerated the trend by requiring knowledgeable wardens and assistant wardens who could defend institutional practices, and by imposing intolerable preserves on the outraged, outmaneuvered relics of the plantation economy and the sacerdotal sensibility.

Below the level of warden and assistant warden, similarly significant staffing changes resulted from the prison reform cases. Inmate trusties were replaced with government employees and existing guard positions were filled by more educated, more highly trained, and, in general, more professional employees. Many corrections departments established the position of compliance coordinator or litigation coordinator to deal with lawsuits or court orders. These positions served as liaisons between the corrections administrators and the attorneys, usually from the state attorney general's office who represented them, and thus played a crucial role in explaining legal requirements to the correctional administrators and explaining correctional practices to the state attorney. Far from being dead-end jobs designed to insulate prison administrators from the courts or to churn out vacuous public relations copy and compliance documents, these positions were often filled by articulate professionals who gained valuable knowledge and experience, which they used as springboards for advancement.[12] Indeed, such liaison positions have become so common that the American Correctional Association and the National Jail Association have established separate membership sections for "compliance co-ordinators."

In these and a host of other ways, litigation has promoted professionalization and facilitated opportunities for a new generation of administrators and staff who embraced a nationally oriented correctional perspective, consistent with the orientation of the federal courts. Of course, this does not mean that the new generation has welcomed judicial intervention or agreed with it; indeed, most have found much to criticize in court orders and consent decrees. But even in their opposition, they are comfortable with the idea of prisoners' rights, bureaucratic organization, and rehabilitative efforts. They may chafe at the intrusions and the increased paperwork, but they take the new regime in stride and accept, if not welcome, much of what the courts have forced upon them.

The second major trend that the prison reform cases strongly reinforced was the development and implementation of national standards for corrections. The history of standard setting in American criminal justice administration has yet to be written, but the general contours of the process are well known. It was initiated by concerns over the virtually unfettered discretion of criminal justice officials. Beginning in the 1870s, the National Prison Association, as the American Correctional Association (ACA) was then called, adopted a set of "principles" that over the years has evolved into detailed standards. The ACA has assiduously promoted these standards, and indeed used them as ways to gain professional recognition and institutional stature. Concern about discretion came to the forefront in the mid-1950s through the work of the American Bar Foundation's Survey of the Administration of Criminal Justice under University of Wisconsin Professor Frank Remington, and through the writings of Kenneth Culp Davis of the University of Chicago.[13] This concern increased during the 1960s, as the American Law Institute began drafting the Model Code of Pre-Arraignment Procedure to offer guidance for rationalizing pretrial release and bail decisions,[14] and the American Bar Association (ABA) initiated a major study entitled Standards for the Administration of Justice.[15] Encouraged by the national climate and, more immediately, by funding from the Law Enforcement Assistance Administration (LEAA), three professional associations began promulgating standards involving corrections in the following decade. The ABA's Standards for the Administration of Justice project was expanded to include jails and prisons. The U.S. Department of Justice established a National Advisory Commission on Criminal Justice Standards and Goals, which in turn began developing standards for all components of the criminal justice process.[16] LEAA funded the Commission on Accreditation of the ACA, whose express purpose was to develop national standards for prison administration and to institute a national accreditation program as a way of fostering professionalization of the field.

Two of these three efforts eventually withered away, although their influence was far from insubstantial. The ABA produced twelve volumes before abandoning its effort in 1977 when its general assembly was unable to reach agreement on the results. The draft reports, however, have influenced both legislation and court decisions and are frequently cited. The Department of Justice's Standards and Goals project lost its support during the cutbacks under the Reagan administration, but not before some of its results were incorporated into department policy, influencing its stance toward intervention in prison conditions suits and helping shape provisions in the Civil Rights for Institutionalized Persons Act (CRIPA).[17] The third effort, however – the ACA's standards setting and accreditation project – continues to this day. The ACA receives ongoing support from the National Institute of Corrections, and virtually every correctional administrator agrees that its standards have become increasingly accepted as the prevailing norm.[18] One measure of this effort's success is that the ACA's "Division of Standards and Accreditation" had approved and published nineteen separate sets of standards as of 1994, for "Small Jails," "Juvenile Facilities," "Boot Camps," "Correctional Administration," and the like, and was active in reviewing correctional facilities in all fifty states and in performing accreditation reviews in many of them.[19]

Nor was the process of standards setting in corrections limited to associations of lawyers or criminal justice professionals. The American Medical Association, the American Architectural Association, the American Public Health Association, the Joint Committee on Accreditation of Hospitals, the National Fire Protection Association, and the National Association of Heating, Refrigeration and Air Conditioning Engineers have all promulgated standards regarding their respective areas of expertise that apply, explicitly or implicitly, to correctional institutions. These efforts often have had far-reaching reverberations even beyond their particular provisions. Standards pertaining to food service, medical care, education, access to legal materials, ventilation, and heating often not only specify the nature of the substantive service to be provided – the type of food and number of calories, for example – but also imply further standards pertaining to the qualifications and training of the staff required to provide those services.

These standard-setting efforts predate judicial involvement in prison reform, and many of them possess an independent history that can be traced without reference to the courts. In fact, the judicial decisions may seem to be a result of the standard-setting process, since described in Chapter 5; from the outset in prison condition cases, courts borrowed heavily from standards promulgated by national organizations in framing their own remedies, and were motivated to intervene, in part, because such standards were available.* But the causal relationship is at times reversed. While the American Correctional Association possesses a good deal of prestige among correctional officials, it is nonetheless a voluntary organization. The National Association of Heating, Refrigeration and Air Conditioning Engineers carries somewhat less weight; as for the American Bar Association, it is well known what the general public thinks of lawyers. A federal district court, however, speaks with the entire authority of the United States government. When combined with a willingness to implement new standards, as described in Chapter 6, this becomes a rather formidable inducement for change. Some prison systems complied with court orders only reluctantly, a good many complained, and a few told lies, but there is not a single case of outright disobedience in the entire annals of the judicial prison reform process.

Moreover, while judicial intervention was partially encouraged by existing standard-setting efforts, additional standard setting was encouraged by the judicial intervention that relied on it. A variety of factors motivate organizations to develop standards: the self-interest of the members, the institutional needs of the organization itself, and even, as Ross Cheit has shown, the desire of technically skilled professionals to produce beneficial effects.[20] But most people sing more loudly when the audience is larger; whatever motivations are operative, they are likely to be amplified by the possibility that the resulting standards will become federal law. The prison reform cases gave the standard-setting organizations an additional audience; beyond their own members, who were already convinced, their members' employers, who did not always listen, and the legislatures, which did not always care, these organizations could now speak to federal judges, probably the most prestigious group of public officials in America.

The two trends just noted – the emergence of a national corrections profession and the formulation of national standards for corrections – were closely related to a final trend, the bureaucratization of state prisons. Chapter 6 discussed bureaucratization's role as a coordinating idea that judges used to conceptualize a new model for state prisons. One reason it could serve as a coordinating idea was because it was implementable; that is, it was connected to existing prison practices. The judiciary's use

---

* Indeed, the 1959 edition of ACA's *Manual of Correctional Standards* devotes one chapter to the "Legal Rights of Probationers, Prisoners and Parolees," and warns that if correctional administrators cannot guarantee these rights, then it is likely that the courts will. Indeed, the manual outlines, somewhat sympathetically, the sort of civil rights case that was eventually brought. This ACA discussion in 1959 predates similar discussions in law reviews by several years, and Judge Henley's ruling in Arkansas by ten.

of the idea was thus made possible by the prior existence of an extraju-
dicial trend toward bureaucratization; here too, however, the trend was
amplified by judicial intervention.

Bureaucratization produced two apparently divergent but in fact complementary results: in Samuel Walker's phase, "it tamed the system"[21] by
securing the rights of prisoners and by increasing the accountability and
efficiency of the prison. As suggested in Chapter 6, bureaucratization was
seen by courts as a means of eliminating the quasi-sacerdotal premodern
prison and replacing it with a regime consistent with prisoner's rights. But
this regime not only protects individual inmates; it also strengthens institutional hierarchy, efficiency, and effectiveness. It enables the organization to: clarify goals, improve accountability, reduce particularism, gather
and interpret information, recruit more and better-skilled employees, add
new technologies, and extract more resources from the larger environment. Thus, bureaucratization fosters more evenhandedness and demands
better conditions while simultaneously enhancing the organization's capacity to govern.

Even bitter critics of bureaucracy have long acknowledged its effectiveness. Subjects accept it as inevitable and perhaps even legitimate; they are
willing to submit to its authority, minimizing the need for direct coercion
and increasing the effectiveness of its control, as Foucault has pointed
out. These effects are readily observed in the newly constitutionalized prisons for the most part; prisoners are more willing to submit to evenhanded
bureaucratic authority than to capricious demands and brutal, unpredictable punishments. The prison with well-understood rules, standardized
practices, and impersonal administration is more efficient and effective as
a means of control than is brute force or even charismatic authority. An
occasional leader with exceptional abilities may achieve better results with
a premodern organization, but the average prison will be more chaotic
and diffuse under this regime. To the extent that judicial prison reform
protected prisoners by enhancing rational-legal organization, it also
strengthened the prison's capacity for control.

This double-edged feature of prisoners' rights litigation helps explain
why, after their initial hostility to the judicial intervention and the short-
term disruptions it sometimes involved, so many prison administrators
came to welcome it. It may also help explain why judicial intervention was
at its zenith during the time when the campaign to promote efficiency
and expand prison capacity was also at its height. Far from being antithetical to each other, the prison reform cases, the Department of Justice's
Law Enforcement Assistance Administration project that provided funding
to enhance system efficiency, and the American Correctional Association's
campaign to professionalize correctional administration were part of the
same general process of nationalization of prison policy and rationaliza-

tion of correctional practices. As a group, correctional agencies became more effective in pursuing their central missions, more powerful in commanding a greater share of public resources, and more innovative in controlling their inmate populations and in expanding their capacities. Judicial intervention is not the only reason for this system-on-steroids quality of modern correctional departments, and it may not even be the primary one. But by insisting on more bureaucratic structures, and thus more efficient and more powerful forms of organization, the courts have certainly contributed to this development.

The increased efficiency that resulted from the prison reform decisions is apparent from many of the case studies in Part I. In Arkansas, administrators in the newly reconstituted prison system are more powerful – even as the inmates are much better off – than they were earlier, when the prisons were run by a small group of corrupt officials and a large number of brutal inmate guards who depended upon terror to maintain a semblance of order. Similarly, in Santa Clara County, the new Department of Corrections – headed by a professional correctional administrator, guided by several volumes of written policies, and possessing well-defined lines of authority, an efficient classification system, more options for pretrial release and sentencing, and a massive new jail – is a much more powerful institution than the informal organization headed by the bumbling sheriff who preceded it. And no one would dispute the fact that Marion Prison, the federal institution that was given a clean constitutional bill of health by a federal judge, imposes an extraordinarily strict and effective regime of control.

There is, of course, wide variation within the bureaucratic rule of law. It can be cumbersome and repressive, hyperformalistic and self-defeating, or it can be responsive and flexible. In the correctional setting there is always the danger that it can overprotect inmates at the expense of authority, or insufficiently protect them in deference to that same authority. Needless to say, some bureaucratic styles are better than others; this is the insight into law offered by Nonet and Selznick in their book, *Law and Society in Transition*,[22] and it is John DiIulio's central message about prison governance.[23] But despite the value of more carefully nuanced accounts, it must be kept in mind that the conditions cases were not about fine-tuning bureaucratic structures but about imposing a rudimentary bureaucratic approach where very little existed before. No doubt, judges often got the fine points wrong; their accomplishment was that they hewed a crude but functional design from damaged stone, not that they fashioned a perfectly proportioned figure.

Max Weber anticipated all this.[24] He saw the value, indeed the necessity, of rational-legal bureaucracy in a modern, complex society, and he appreciated the power, the predictability, the protection for individuals, and the harnessing of energy that rational bureaucracy produces. But he also saw the rigidity, impersonalism, domination and control that it implies. Thus he came to regard the development as a mixed blessing, an ongoing and insoluble dilemma that would continue to beset modern societies. The modern constitutional prison is a mixed blessing of precisely this sort. Conditions and practices are much improved and the constitutionalization of the process assures that these improvements are likely to be permanent. But the mission of prisons and jails remains safety and security by means of a tight system of control. Judicial reform has, on balance, enhanced the ability of officials to pursue this mission: they are now more, not less, effective and efficient. As such, the courts may have contributed to an increased willingness to rely on prisons and even to the increasing oppressiveness that results from the development of supermaximum institutions. Perhaps nowhere else is Weber's metaphor of the "iron cage" so apt as it is with respect to the modern, constitutional prison. The jailbird is constrained, but not chained; in erecting the iron cage of bureaucracy, the federal courts have provided both protection for the prisoner and a structure for his more efficient incarceration.

What the Courts Did Not Accomplish

A full understanding of the courts' impact on American prisons requires an assessment of what they did not accomplish, as well as what they did. The best way to assess the lack of accomplishment in any enterprise – a potentially limitless inquiry – is to consider the expectations of the participants. In the prison reform cases, these participants include the prisoners' rights advocates, the prisoners, and the prison administrators. The judges were also involved, of course, and they generally achieved what they expected, although they also constructed their expectations in light of their achievements. Their views have been discussed at length, however, in the preceding pages; the concern here is how those views and their implementation were perceived by other actors.

Prisoners' rights advocates generally became directly involved in the judicial prison reform process as plaintiffs' attorneys. Not all the attorneys who litigated the prison cases were affiliated with the prisoners' rights movement, but many were, and they are the ones with an identifiable point of view. They were often heavily influenced by the abolitionist movement in Europe and they passionately believed in establishing alternatives to incarceration. In their view, litigation was a means of achieving this objective. By forcing states to bear the cost of maintaining constitutional prisons, they hoped that state decision makers would embrace less costly, noncustodial alternatives. One leading correctional reformer and prisoners' rights advocate described a two-pronged "pincer strategy": continued litigation to drive up the costs of prisons and active promotion of alternatives as the remedy for these increased costs.

Like most efforts by sincere, well-meaning people to outmaneuver their opponents, this one failed miserably. The per capita cost of imprisonment did indeed increase as a result of the judicial demand that prisoners be treated decently; the most dramatic increases, of course, came in the southern states, where the entire purpose of reform was to eliminate the plantation model, with its aspirations to run self-supporting institutions, and to replace it with a funded, bureaucratic agency.[25] But as these cost increases occurred, there was a simultaneous growth in prison populations. The bulk of this growth, moreover, did not result from rising crime rates or changing demographics, but from consciously adopted social policies that placed more felons in prison and increased the length of their sentences. As a result, expenditures rapidly spiraled upward, placing ever more serious burdens on state budgets. For some reason, American politics had generated a thirst for incarcerating criminals that was largely insensitive to the economic costs involved.*[26]

While the reformers' strategy thus turned out to be a dismal failure, it was premised on a correct understanding of the judicial policy-making process. The reformers accurately predicted that courts could, and would, make social policy in the proper circumstances, and that this policy would result in increased per prisoner costs. They also predicted that judicial policy making could not prescribe new alternatives for the punishment of convicted felons. Here too they were correct; as indicated in Chapters 6, 7, and 8, the judicial policy-making process is thoroughly incremental, and precludes the sort of comprehensive planning from which new alternatives could emerge. Even in the prison cases, perhaps the high-water mark of judicial policy making in America, the courts derived their standards from the best-run prisons or from a national corrections association. They conceptualized and justified those standards through a process of doctrine creation that is inherently limited to changes that are incremental with respect to existing law and dependent on implementable conceptualizations of an institution that are incremental with respect to that institution. They developed and elaborated them by implementing them in ongoing situations. Thus, one thing that the courts most certainly did not accomplish was the creation of novel approaches to the punishment of criminals.

* During the twenty-five-year period from 1970 to 1995, the prison population in the United States nearly quadrupled, and there were corresponding increases in jails, probation, and juvenile custody. Although there are a number of useful efforts to begin to come to grips with this near sea change in the use of imprisonment, it is likely that the complete explanation must await future historians of American crime policy.

Unfortunately for the reformers, the political branches, which probably possessed the capability of developing alternatives, lacked the motivation to do so. The result was that incarceration remained our dominant – indeed, our almost universal – approach to punishing serious offenders, and the rising costs that judicial prison reform imposed were grimly but willingly accepted by an ever more punitively minded populace.

The second group of participants in prisons are, of course, the prisoners themselves. One would need to be a committed revolutionary to want to satisfy all the prisoners' expectations; on the other hand, many of the reforms that were adopted were motivated by a genuine concern for prisoners and attempted to secure their decent treatment. Precisely what prisoners wanted, within the obvious constraints of their situation, is not clear, however, and in this lack of clarity lies an important feature of judicial prison reform. Throughout the process, only minimal efforts were made to determine what was important to the prisoners themselves. The plaintiffs' attorneys, whether they were part of the prisoners' rights movement or whether they were previously unconnected with that movement and recruited by the court, tended to assume that they knew what was best for prisoners. Litigation proceeded with prisoners as passive witnesses, not real clients, and agreements were struck among the plaintiffs' attorneys, the defense attorneys, the correctional administrators, and the judge. Special masters were generally concerned with securing administrative compliance with court orders, not with assessing the actual desires of the prisoners.

None of this is particularly surprising, of course, but it does conflict with much of the current legal thinking about lawyer–client relationships. Some scholars have emphasized the role of client autonomy,[27] while others propose a client-centered model for the professional relationship.[28] Prison litigation necessarily involved a large, disparate group of clients, rather than a single individual, but Stephen Ellman,[29] David Luban,[30] Deborah Rhode,[31] and William Simon[32] provide various models for securing client autonomy and client-centered approaches under these circumstances. To be sure, some scholars still argue for the more traditional, paternalistic approach, but the idea of the lawyer as authority, who simply assumes he knows what is best for the client, is currently rejected by almost all observers.[33] That seems to be the idea that controlled the prison cases, however. These cases, although their subject matter was the well-being of the prisoners, were legally complex interactions among various professionals, with very little involvement of the actual prisoners.

It is difficult to know what was lost or not accomplished as a result of the virtual exclusion of prisoner-clients from the decision-making process. Legal writers often speak of the empowerment, respect, and sense of responsibility that flows from a client-centered model. Such virtues, although certainly desirable for almost any other group of people, may only have been a source of trouble when the clients were convicts; on the other hand, it might have improved their behavior in the institutions and even possessed some rehabilitative effect. Moreover, there may have been subgroups within the general prisoner population who had special needs that were ignored due to the absence of a client-centered approach. One such group may have been women, whose relatively low numbers and nonviolent behavior have often caused prison administrators to overlook them, particularly since these administrators are predominantly male.

The third group of participants in the correctional system comprises prison administrators. If it is a bit odd to talk about meeting the expectations of prisoners, it may seem even stranger to talk about meeting the needs of administrators, who were, after all, being sued on the grounds that their practices violated the Constitution. For one group of administrators – the old-time wardens – the courts neither met their needs nor wanted to; they were the enemy and the implicit objective was to get rid of them. But as we have seen, the more progressive administrators either viewed the courts as allies or were able to conclude a truce with them that traded their discretion for increased resources and a tighter organizational structure.[34] Judges were eager to meet the needs of these administrators; with no aspirations to transform radically or to abolish prisons, they quailed at their own intrusions on behalf of prisoners, and were reassured when they could combine those efforts with ways of strengthening a good administrator's power.

Even modern, forward-looking prison administrators complain about the problems of judicial intervention, of course. The concern here is not with the difficulties associated with the courts' accomplishments, which have been discussed at length, but with the limitations to which those accomplishments were subject. While the judicial intervention often solved the administrators' problems involving inadequate facilities, food service, medical care, educational services, and vocational training, many problems remained. Violence among prisoners, while probably not caused by judicial intervention, was certainly not resolved by it; indeed, the 1970s and 1980s saw the rise of prison gangs, a problem courts rarely addressed and did nothing to control. The physical design of prisons has been another continuing problem, as planners try to balance the conflicting demands of security, staff safety, inmate welfare, and, of course, expense. Although courts sometimes ordered and often encouraged the construction of new facilities, they did not offer any substantial guidance regarding their design.

Most significant of all, the courts never provided any real help with the single greatest problem facing prison administrators – the inmate population explosion. During the 1970s and 1980s, America engaged in an orgy of incarceration; the nation's rate of imprisonment soared past that of such dubious regimes as Cuba, prereform South Africa, and the former Soviet Union to the highest level of any major nation. Its absolute number of prisoners now exceeds one million,[35] the largest in the world with the possible exception of the People's Republic of China. Just as the general population explosion in third world nations tended to swallow up advances in agriculture, health, housing, and sanitation, so America's prison population explosion has tended to erode many of the gains in prison conditions that have resulted from new facilities, the rehabilitative model, and the bureaucratization of the administrative structure. Cells designed for one person now hold two or three, school rooms and gymnasiums have been converted into dormitories, tent camps and trailer parks for inmates have sprouted in the prison yard, training and rehabilitation programs have been either overwhelmed with participants or restricted to small fractions of the eligible inmates, and prison officials have been compelled to shift from management to coping strategies.[36]

In one of the cases described in Part I – Santa Clara County – crowding was the major issue from the outset; in three others – Texas, Arkansas, and Colorado – it quickly became a central focus as both the courts and prison officials found that the growth in inmate population impacted virtually every aspect of the judicial orders. Judges tried to deal with the problem by ordering new construction and by imposing stringent population caps on existing facilities, thereby triggering early releases from sentences and expanded pretrial release. Many judges searched desperately for faster ways to bring arrestees to arraignment and trial, new forms of pretrial supervision, and alternatives to custodial sentences. In Texas, for example, Judge Justice's actions led the state legislature to enact a statute establishing maximum prison capacity and authorizing the department to grant early releases as needed, a provision that was used frequently after its adoption. It led state administrators to reclassify institutions and experiment with the use of private "return to custody" facilities to house low-risk inmates. But it also led the department to find ways to delay acceptance of newly sentenced offenders, a move that helped TDC maintain its population cap but kept offenders in even more crowded county jails. Neither judges overseeing prison conditions litigation nor correctional officials have found a way to control "intake," and those who do, legislators and judges, have, for various reasons, not been willing to do so. Thus many prisons and jails manage their populations with court-ordered ad hoc early release decisions that will no longer be in effect once the court terminates its jurisdiction. Elsewhere, the effort to control prison populations led to new and unusual alliances. In Los Angeles, the ACLU and the county sheriff's department joined together to sue the municipal court judges, seeking a federal court order forcing them to accelerate arraignments so that arrestees would not need to be held so long in the crowded county jail. In several states, corrections officials quietly counseled state legislatures against increasing lengths of sentences, although such advice, as prison population increases suggest, has usually fallen on deaf ears.

Ultimately, it is not clear that the judges were any more adept at coping with the problems of crowding than were the prison administrators themselves. By setting population limits, even if they were only temporary, they did generate pressure to locate funds for new facilities and to intensify the search for alternative forms of sentencing and custody. But those efforts were largely stopgap measures, and they were soon swept aside by the continuing deluge of prisoners. Whether it is reasonable to expect the courts to resolve a problem of this magnitude is an open question; the point here is simply that they did not do so.

The Future of Imprisonment in America

If one compiles a balance sheet of what the courts accomplished in the prison reform cases and what they failed to accomplish – again abjuring undefined, categorical judgments of success or failure – it appears that the judiciary's performance was both extraordinary and inadequate. It was extraordinary because it represented a consistent development and implementation of social policy in an area where no other policy maker was prepared to act. It established clear standards and produced definitive results which have now become fully integrated into American corrections. But it was inadequate because it solved only some of the severe and numerous problems in this field. These problems have been documented at length; there are few fields, it seems safe to say, where observers from all parts of the political spectrum agree so fully in their assessment of near total failure. In all probability, these judgments are overly harsh, and result from the same vagueness about evaluative criteria that was noted earlier. But that does nothing to controvert the widespread recognition that America's prisons remain a major social problem.

What are the solutions to this problem, and which social institutions will develop and implement them? Judicial intervention seems to have reached its limit. While many more prisons and jails will undoubtedly be sued, and some of those will become subject to court order, it seems unlikely that any dramatic new approaches will emerge from the process. The reason is not only the more restrictive criteria that the Supreme Court has imposed in cases such as *Whitney v. Albers*[37] and *Wilson v. Seiter*.[38] It is, ironically, that the critics of judicial policy making are correct: courts are inherently limited in the scope of the solutions that they can effectuate.

As this study has indicated, judicial capacities are an order of magnitude greater than most observers have assumed. Courts can implement social policy and they can effectively transform large administrative institutions. But they have their limits, the most notable – which has also been discussed at length – being the inherent incrementalism of the judicial policy-making process. In order to develop and implement more far-reaching, comprehensive solutions to the problem of corrections, we will need to look to different institutions.

One institution that comes naturally to mind comprises the political branches of the federal government, whose previous inaction was in part responsible for the judicial intervention. In fact, Congress has already taken an important step to which we have adverted already – the enactment of the Civil Rights of Institutionalized Persons Act of 1980 (CRIPA).[39] CRIPA is designed to protect the rights of persons in prisons, jails, mental hospitals, and juvenile detention facilities. Patterned on several other civil rights statutes, it gives the Department of Justice the power to initiate federal civil rights litigation challenging conditions that exist "pursuant to a pattern or practice of resistance by state officials."[40] The designated purpose of such suits is to correct conditions that are so "egregious or flagrant" as to deprive inmates of their rights, privileges, and immunities secured by the U.S. Constitution and federal law. Unlike some other civil rights acts, CRIPA contains several provisions that promote alternatives to litigation. Before filing a suit, federal officials must notify the state of their intentions, detail their allegations, consult with appropriate state or local officials to apprise them of opportunities for technical assistance from the federal Bureau of Prisons, and employ "informal methods of conference, conciliation, and persuasion."[41] CRIPA requires a court to postpone prisoner-initiated civil rights petitions for up to ninety days if there is an administrative grievance system in the prison that meets minimum standards established by the Department of Justice. The Act also provides a process to certify those institutions which meet the specified standards.

CRIPA was not the first time the federal executive-branch officials became involved in trying to effect changes in jails and prisons through litigation. In 1974 Judge Justice had successfully requested the Department of Justice to intervene in order to supplement the limited investigatory and legal resources available to the plaintiffs' attorney, an action that was upheld on appeal. In two other cases, *Battle v. Anderson*[42] and *Gates v. Collier*,[43] the Department of Justice acted in a similar capacity, and its involvement was also upheld. But federal district court judges dismissed at least two similar suits on the grounds that the Department of Justice had no statutory authority to bring the cases. Indeed, it was this ambiguity that led Drew Days, then assistant U.S. attorney general for civil rights, to press for passage of CRIPA, a bill that had been on the back burner in the House Judiciary Committee for several years.

Although CRIPA explicitly authorizes federal involvement in litigation challenging conditions in state and local correctional systems, it was nearly stillborn and has yet to gain vigor. The act was passed in the waning months of the Carter administration and the Department of Justice immediately appointed attorneys to staff the new section. They in turn quickly brought a number of suits challenging conditions in various institutions and set about developing standards for the certification of institutions. But this flurry of activity quickly ended under the Reagan administration as the Civil Rights Division within the Department of Justice did a near about-face and sought to reduce, if not altogether eliminate, federal civil rights actions. No one in the Reagan, Bush, or Clinton administrations has sought to breathe life into CRIPA. But, if somnolent in operation, it nonetheless remains something of a sleeping giant, and provides impressive evidence that Congress has recognized and approved judicial policy making in corrections.

Congress, however, has spoken with multiple voices. Although CRIPA seemed to acknowledge the legitimacy of litigation, its aim was to reduce litigation by pressing state and local institutions to improve conditions and internal grievance procedures. And since its enactment, public distaste for prisoner suits has continued to grow. With the advent of a Republican-controlled Congress in 1994 and a Democratic president who was intent on preempting the tough-on-crime issue, restriction of prisoners' rights became a matter of national consensus. The result was three new laws specifically designed to limit prisoner litigation and prisoners' rights.

The first, enacted in 1994, is a provision of the Violent Crime Control and Enforcement Act, known as the Helms amendment.[44] It requires individual prisoners to prove that crowding violates their Eighth Amendment rights before a court can find the prison overcrowded, thus tying the court's remedy to a specific constitutional violation. This approach was extended to all prison issues in 1996 by the Prison Litigation Reform Act (PLRA).[45] The PLRA prohibits federal courts from ordering changes in prisons and jails unless the court first finds that an inmate's federal rights have been violated. Even then, the law requires that any relief be "narrowly drawn" and that "the least intrusive means necessary to correct the violation" be followed in fashioning a remedy.[46] The PLRA further provides that the court order shall be terminated upon request after two years, unless the court makes an affirmative finding that the relief still conforms to these conditions,[47] and that the court may not enter a consent decree that fails to conform with them.[48] Special masters must be chosen with the participation of the parties and paid with funds appropriated to the judiciary.[49] All of this is explicitly designed to limit the scope of conditions cases and to enable corrections officials to modify existing orders in accordance with those limitations.[50]

Perhaps the most important purpose of the Helms amendment and the PLRA, however, is the implicit one – to restrict judicial policy making in the prison reform area. Policy making, it will be recalled, is not characterized by a complete willingness to ignore legal texts, but by the use of those texts as a grant of jurisdiction, rather than as a source of standards. Justice Rehnquist, as the sole dissenter when an order in the very first totality of conditions case came before the Court, was astute enough to perceive this aspect of policy making. He wrote: "I fear that the Court has allowed itself to be moved beyond the well-established bounds limiting the exercise of remedial authority by the federal district courts."[51] Rehnquist sensed that the use of wide-ranging remedies, not tied to some interpretation of a specific legal text, was the essence of judicial policy making. Congress, at least implicitly, sensed this as well in enacting the restrictive legislation. Yet the two laws do not indicate a rejection of judicial policy making; at most, they indicate that Congress, after some thirty years, has reached the point of disagreeing with the courts on this particular policy, just as Rehnquist had disagreed at the outset. Nor do they really indicate disagreement, for the courts themselves have engineered virtually the very same retrenchment through the Supreme Court decisions in *Wilson v. Seiter*[52] and *Ruffo v. Inmates of the Suffolk County Jail.*[53]

In fact, the statutes can be regarded as a validation of judicial policy making in three different ways. First, Congress went no further than the Court itself had gone; there was no support for removing prison cases entirely from federal court jurisdiction, as there had been to remove loyalty security cases from their jurisdiction during the McCarthy era.[54] Second, Congress's ability to take action of this sort demonstrates that the courts are not nearly so imperial, or unstoppable, as their critics have claimed, even when grounding their authority on the Constitution. When they breach the separation of powers and engage in administrative action, Congress, which can control administrative agencies if it chooses, can control the courts as well. Finally, the fact that Congress decided to control the courts, as well as the fact that it did so after the courts no longer needed to be controlled, indicates the strength of the one structural principle that constitutes a living aspect of our law – checks and balances. It is the overlaps between the branches – here Congress's ability to control the judiciary's jurisdiction, but also its power to confirm or to reject new judicial appointments – that represent the process by which one branch constrains another.

It is not clear how much real effect these laws will have. As a practical matter, many of the mega-conditions cases that were initiated in the 1970s had already been terminated or were already winding down by 1994 or

1995, and there was general consensus that new suits attacking an array of conditions were not likely to emerge. As a matter of legal doctrine, the Supreme Court had already scaled back prison conditions doctrine and prisoners' rights. Those parts of the doctrine that have not been scaled back are well recognized, having been created nearly thirty years ago and elaborated during the two decades that followed. Limiting courts to remedies that emerge from existing legal doctrine is not particularly restrictive of prison reform since the reach of current doctrine, even in its modified form, is quite extensive. It is certainly not as restrictive as it would have been had the same law been passed in 1965, before the doctrine was created.

The ability of correctional officials to reopen consent decrees is potentially more significant. This has always been a controversial issue because there is often no authoritative judicial determination as to the nature and scope of legal or constitutional violations, and thus no tight link between liability and remedy. Indeed, it is for this reason that Owen Fiss and others have inveighed "against settlement," arguing that approval of settlements undermines judicial authority and fails to advance important "public values."[55] However until the Court decision in *Ruffo*, now reinforced by the PLRA, such issues were largely academic – the provisions in court-approved consent decrees were generally inviolable. It seems quite possible that a number of the decrees in place could be reopened and substantially revised.* It should be recalled, however, that many of these decrees now constitute the regime in place, and are the reason why the current warden, or a person like him, was appointed to the position. The Alameda County Jail Automated Food Delivery Robot was written into a consent decree, and probably goes beyond any demonstrable constitutional requirement. It was not placed there by the plaintiffs, however, but by Charlie Plummer, the crafty sheriff who was the defendant in the case.

Still another expression of Congress's current mood is the Anti-

---

* In some cases, a strong argument can be made for modification on the basis of changed circumstances. For example, in the mid-1970s California corrections officials agreed to a liberal exercise regime for inmates on death row. At the time there were less than one hundred inmates on death row, and corrections officials anticipated that the death penalty would be either declared unconstitutional by the courts or abolished by the state legislature. But times change, and in the early 1990s, there were over 350 inmates on an increasingly crowded death row. Accordingly corrections officials asked the court to modify provisions in the long-standing consent decree regarding frequency and length of exercise for prisoners, asserting that the original provisions to which they had agreed went well beyond any constitutional minimum, and citing increased crowding as the basis for their request. The court agreed, and reduced the exercise requirements for these inmates.

Terrorism and Effective Death Penalty Act of 1996,[56] designed to restrict the use of habeas corpus petitions. This act tightens the requirement that prisoners exhaust their state remedies and places procedural hurdles in the way of those inmates who attempt to file more than one petition. Its provisions were challenged on the grounds that they deprived the Supreme Court of its appellate jurisdiction in violation of Article III of the Constitution, but a unanimous Supreme Court swept aside such arguments and upheld the law.[57] It is likely that this law will achieve its intended effect of reducing prisoner habeas corpus petitions and expediting executions. But by itself it is likely to have only limited impact on prison conditions litigation, since most such cases arise under the civil rights law. Still, this law, coupled with other congressional action and rulings by the federal courts in the late 1980s and 1990s, clearly reveals a marked decline in public support for rights and reform.

While CRIPA and these other laws represent divergent inclinations, this legislation has produced an important cumulative effect: to draw the federal government ever deeper into state and local crime policy. In the 1970s, the Democratic-controlled Congress took a first big step, with its insistence on categorical rather than block grants under the Law Enforcement Assistance Administration.[58] A short time later, Congress and the Department of Justice supported efforts to establish "national standards" for criminal justice, including correctional standards. This was followed by CRIPA, which authorized the Department of Justice to use its resources to sue prisons who violated Eighth Amendment standards. And in the 1994 Violent Crime Control and Law Enforcement Act, a Republican-controlled Congress authorized funds for state and local correctional programs, but placed a host of conditions on them.[59] The act, as amended, declared "a national need for additional prison and jail capacity so that violent offenders can be removed from the community and the public can be assured that these offenders will serve a substantial portion of their sentences," and conditioned receipt of federal funds upon a showing that "violent offenders serve a substantial portion of the sentences imposed," that sentences must be "designed to provide sufficiently severe punishment for violent offenders, including violent juvenile offenders," that prison time served is "appropriately related to the determination that the inmate is a violent offender and for a period of time deemed necessary to protect the public."[60] Other conditions required states to show that they had increased the average length of sentences for those convicted of violent crimes, and that they had enacted laws to recognize the rights of crime victims, to expand drug testing programs, and to incarcerate more drug users. The 1994 act also expanded the role and functions of the National Institute of Corrections (NIC) and the national Office of Juvenile Justice and Delinquency Prevention (OJJDP), two research and training units in the Department of Justice. Similar legislation appropriating funds for law enforcement also specified conditions for the receipt of these funds.[61]

Thus in series of steps over twenty-five years, culminating in the 1994 Crime Act, actions by all three branches created a policy making role for the national government in the area of crime and corrections. This follows a time-honored tradition. Now policies of state and local criminal justice agencies, like those of state and local departments of highways, education, and the like, can be affected in significant ways by conditions attached to funding provided by Congress. However, when national standards are not met, the courts may be called upon to act.

A second institution that might effect a transformation in American corrections is private enterprise. This immediately brings to mind the much discussed issue of privatizing existing institutions, or building new, private institutions in the standard mode.[62] The ethical and jurisprudential issues raised by these institutions are so interesting that both their present scope and potential impact tend to be exaggerated. At present, there are relatively few private prisons and the explosive growth of public prisons has tended to decrease their proportions. In addition, even if there were more, the resulting change would probably be fairly minor, since privatization is essentially a compliance mechanism, not a real innovation. A privately run prison is generally nothing more than an ordinary prison with different supervisors; many state-run prisons already contract out food and medical services, so "going private" may not mean much more than removing the guards from the civil service system. The concept of a prison run for profit might conjure up more dramatic images – perhaps gainful employment for prisoners whose improved morale would translate into the need for less strict security; or perhaps a reincarnation of convict leasing or of the plantation model prison. There is no indication that anyone knows how to create the first of these models, however, and as long as the federal courts are open, no one will be allowed to recreate the latter.

The real potential of private enterprise lies less in the area of privatization than in the area of innovation. Historically, many of the innovations in punishment techniques have come from private entrepreneurs. The transportation of felons from England to North America, which began in 1607 and continued up until the Revolutionary War, was an innovation conceived of and carried out by entrepreneurs at minimal cost to the state. Often characterized as an "alternative" to the death penalty, it was much more. Before transportation gained popularity, only a small handful of the felons sentenced to death were in fact hanged; after transportation, ten or twenty times as many suffered the civil death of transportation. Thus transportation greatly increased the capacity of the state to punish and it revolutionized eighteenth-century crime policy. But it was not a result of any well-developed public plan; it emerged from the efforts of entrepreneurs seeking to take advantage of simple technology and to make a profit by selling English convicts into limited-term slavery in labor-short North America.[63]

One most promising trend at present involves the use of technology for security and monitoring purposes. With electronic devices establishing a secure perimeter around the prison and tracking prisoner movements inside, planners may be able to reduce their present reliance on concrete and steel. Of course, this might simply provide cheaper ways to build traditional prisons; the electrified wire fence that has replaced masonry walls at most prisons represents an existing use of electricity at least, if not electronics. But electronic controls might also enable planners to create more normal-looking environments for prisoners, and to provide more flexibility in the institution's internal arrangements.

A further step involves electronic monitoring outside of institutions. Private firms have already developed electronic bracelets that set off an alarm at a central monitoring station if the wearer deviates from a prescribed path. Devices of this sort could effectuate the restriction of liberty characteristic of modern punitive sanctions, but do so in a variety of non-institutional settings, including daytime work in the community, incarceration in a nonsecure halfway facility, and house arrest. Whether such settings could be used as an alternative to existing prisons involves a great deal more than technology, however. It is not difficult to imagine punishing juveniles, mothers of young children, parents generally, or nonviolent first offenders in this manner, but it is equally possible that the current punitive mood will continue, and electronic monitors will be used only to increase surveillance of parolees, and not to alter our basic level and method of incarceration.*[64]

At this juncture, therefore, the future course of incarceration in America is uncertain. But this does not indicate that judicial intervention into prisons was unwise, since it failed to resolve the problem; rather, it emphasizes the real nature of the courts' accomplishment. Thirty years ago, the courts were still maintaining their long-established policy of ignoring the conditions in American prisons, despite the pleas that they regularly received from prisoners. Then, rather suddenly, a combination of factors motivated them to change their approach; for the last thirty years, they have spearheaded the effort to reform American corrections. While other national institutions avoided the issue, and state institutions generally failed to act, the federal judiciary served as the dominant policy maker.

---

* There is some considerable evidence to suggest that the distinction between punishment and law enforcement functions is becoming blurred as correction officials become more active in surveillance.

It abolished the plantation model, extirpated a number of serious, widely condemned abuses that sprang from that model or from other sources, promulgated a detailed code of minimal treatment conditions, and oversaw the implementation of that code in a large number of institutions. Perhaps most significantly, it carried the banner that other institutions had dropped or were not prepared to lift – the banner of human decency and of a collective willingness to seek solutions for one of our most serious social problems.

By reviewing this thirty-year effort we can learn something about courts as institutions and about law itself. We can learn that courts are policy makers, as well as fact-finders and interpreters. While certain disadvantages attend their efforts in this capacity, the courts have certain strengths as well, and are fully able to function in this dominant mode of modern governmental action. We can also learn how outmoded our conceptions of law and government have become. The principles of federalism or the separation of powers that are supposed to limit federal courts lack normative force at present. The rule of law retains its force, but only as a functional concept of internally generated constraint, and not as a set of external principles that produce predictable results.

All these changes are a result of our modern, administrative state. It is that state that makes prisons possible as mechanisms for the punishment of offenders, and it is that same state that generates the conceptual possibilities that enable us to solve the problems that these prisons present. The future solutions to the problems posed by prison thus lie somewhere within the governmental structure that created them. This is only natural, since prisons are our own creations, not external forces. The task is to find that solution and the institutions that can implement it. The courts are no longer likely to do so, as they have for the past thirty years, but they have certainly provided an example of the flexibility, pragmatism, and creativity that will be needed in this effort.

Notes

1. INTRODUCTION

1. Lawrence Baum, *American Courts: Process and Policy*, 295–358 (1990); Robert Dahl, "Decision-Making in a Democracy: The Supreme Court as a National Policy-Maker," 6 J. Public Law 279 (1957); Lee Epstein & Joseph F. Kobylka, *The Supreme Court and Legal Change: Abortion and The Death Penalty* (1992); John Gates & Charles Johnson, eds., *The American Courts: A Critical Assessment* (1991); Henry Glick, *Courts, Politics and Justice*, 352–418 (3d ed., 1993); Charles Johnson & Bradley Canon, *Judicial Policies: Implementation and Impact* (1984); Jack Peltason, *Federal Courts in the Federal System* (1955); Victor Rosenblum, *Law as a Political Instrument* (1955); C. K. Rowland & Robert A. Carp, *Politics and Judgments in Federal District Courts* (1996); Jeffrey Segal & Harold Spaeth, *The Supreme Court and the Attitudinal Model*, 1–31 (1993); Glendon Schubert, *Judicial Policy Making: The Political Role of Courts* (rev. ed., 1974); Harold Spaeth, *Supreme Court Policy Making: Explanation and Prediction* (1979); S. Sidney Ulmer, *Courts, Law, and Judicial Processes* (1981); Barbara Yarnold, *Politics and the Courts: Toward a General Theory of Public Law* (1990).
2. Raoul Berger, *Government by Judiciary* (1977); Alexander Bickel, *The Least Dangerous Branch: The Supreme Court at the Bar of Politics* (1962); Ronald Dworkin, "Hard Cases," 88 Harvard L. Rev. 1057 (1975); Colin Diver, "The Judge as Political Powerbroker: Superintending Structural Change in Public Institutions," 65 Va. L. Rev. 43 (1979); Ronald Dworkin, *Law's Empire* (1986); Rolf Sartorius, *Individual Conduct and Social Norms*, 181–210 (1975); Herbert Wechsler, "Toward Neutral Principles in Constitutional Law," 73 Harv. L. Rev. 1 (1959).
3. Anthony Kronman, *The Lost Lawyer*, 321–51 (1993); Owen Fiss, "The Bureaucracy of the Judiciary," 92 Yale L. J. 1442 (1983); Owen Fiss, "Against Settlement," 93 Yale L. J. 1073 (1984); Stephen Landsman, "The Decline

of the Adversary System: How the Rhetoric of Swift and Certain Justice Has Affected Adjudication in American Courts," 29 Buff. L. Rev. 487 (1980); Wade McGree, "Bureaucratic Justice: An Early Warning," 129 U. Pa. L. Rev. 777 (1981); Todd Peterson, "Restoring Structural Checks on Judicial Power in the Era of Managerial Judging," 29 U.C. Davis L. Rev. 41 (1995); Judith Resnick, "Managerial Judges," 96 Harv. L. Rev. 374 (1982); Joseph Vining, "Justice, Bureaucracy and Legal Method," 80 Mich. L. Rev. 248 (1981).

4. J. M. Balkin, "Deconstructive Practice and Legal Theory," 96 Yale L. J. 743 (1987); Clare Dalton, "An Essay in the Deconstruction of Contract Doctrine," 94 Yale L. J. 997 (1985); Morton Horowitz, *The Transformation of American Law, 1780–1860* (1977); Allan Hutchinson, "Democracy and Determinacy: An Essay on Legal Interpretation," 43 U. Miami L. Rev. 743 (1989); Allan Hutchinson, *Dwelling on the Threshold: Critical Essays on Modern Legal Thought* (1988); Mark Kelman, Interpretive Construction in Substantive Criminal Law," 33 Stan L. Rev. 591 (1981); Gary Peller, "The Metaphysics of American Law," 73 Cal. L. Rev. 1151 (1985); Joseph Singer, "The Player and the Cards: Nihilism and Legal Theory," 94 Yale L. J. 1 (1984); Mark Tushnet, *Red, White and Blue: A Critical Analysis of Constitutional Law* (1988); Mark Tushnet, "Following the Rules Laid Down: A Critique of Interpretivism and Neutral Principles," 96 Harv. L. Rev. 781 (1983); Roberto Unger, *The Critical Legal Studies Movement* (1986).

5. Jerome Frank, *Law and the Modern Mind*, 32–41 (1930); Glick, *supra* note 1, at 2–7; Segal & Spaeth, *supra* note 1, at 4–7; Spaeth, *supra* note 1, at 1–8; E. W. Thomas, "A Return to Principle in Judicial Reasoning and an Acclamation of Judicial Autonomy," 93 Victoria Wellington Univ. L. Rev. Monograph No. 5, at 16 (1993).

6. Stephen Carter, *The Confirmation Mess*, 54–84 (1994); Donald Lively, "The Supreme Court Appointment Process: In Search of Constitutional Roles and Responsibilities," 59 S. Cal. L. Rev. 551 (1986); William Ross, "The Questioning of Supreme Court Nominees at Senate Confirmation Hearings: Proposals for Accommodating the Needs of the Senate and Ameliorating the Fears of the Nominees," 62 Tulane L. Rev. 109, 168–71 (1987); Gary Simson, "Taking the Court Seriously: A Proposed Approach to the Senate Confirmation of Supreme Court Nominees," 7 Constitutional Commentary 283 (1990).

7. Herbert Jacob, *Justice in America* (1964); Herbert Jacob, "Trial Courts in the United States: The Travails of Exploration," 17 L. & Soc. Rev. 407 (1983).

8. Epstein & Kobylka, *supra* note 1, at 8.

9. See, e.g., Richard Abel, "Western Courts in Non-Western Settings: Patterns of Court Use in Colonial and Neo-Colonial Africa," in *The Imposition of Law* (S. B. Burman & B. E. Harrell-Bond, eds., 1979); William Felstiner, Richard Abel L. & Austin Sarat, "The Emergence and Transformation of Disputes: Naming, Blaming, and Claiming," 15 L. & Soc. Rev. 631 (1980–81); Lynn Mather & Barbara Yngvesson, "Language, Audience, and the Transformation of Disputes," 15 L. & Soc. Rev. 775 (1980–81); Lynn Mather, "Policy

Making in State Trial Courts," in *The American Courts: A Critical Assessment* (J. B. Gates & C. A. Johnson, eds., 1991).

10. See, e.g., John Kingdon, *Agendas, Alternatives, and Public Policies* (1984); H. W. Perry, *Deciding to Decide: Agenda Setting in the United States Supreme Court* (1991); Nelson Polsby, *Political Innovation in America* (1984); Jack Walker, "The Diffusion of Innovations among the American States," 68 Am. Pol. Sci. Rev. 880 (1969); Jack L. Walker, "Setting the Agenda in the U.S. Senate: A Theory of Problem Selection," 7 British J. of Pol. Sci. 423 (1977); Jack Walker, "The Diffusion of Knowledge, Policy Communities and Agenda Setting," in *New Strategic Perspectives on Social Policy* (J. Tropman, M. Dluhy, & R. Lind, eds., 1981).

11. William Eskridge, *Dynamic Statutory Interpretation* (1994); William Eskridge, "Public Values in Statutory Interpretation," 137 U. Pa. L. Rev. 1007 (1989); Thomas Grey, "Do We Have an Unwritten Constitution?" 27 Stan. L. Rev. 703 (1975); Thomas Grey, "The Constitution as Scripture," 37 Stan L. Rev. 1 (1984); D. Neil MacCormick & Robert Summers, *Interpreting Statutes: A Comparative Study*, 518–21 (1991); Cass Sunstein, *After the Rights Revolution: Reconceiving the Regulatory State* (1990).

12. Abraham Chayes, "The Supreme Court, 1981 Term – Foreword: Public Law Litigation and the Burger Court," 96 Harv. L. Rev. 4 (1982); Phillip Cooper, *Hard Judicial Choices* (1988); Owen Fiss, *The Civil Rights Injunction* (1978); Owen Fiss, "The Supreme Court, 1978 Term – Foreword: The Forms of Justice," 93 Harv. L. Rev. 1 (1979); William Fletcher, "The Discretionary Constitution: Institutional Remedies and Judicial Legitimacy," 91 Yale L. J. 635 (1982); Donald Horowitz, *Courts and Social Policy* (1975); Susan Sturm, "Resolving the Remedial Dilemma: Strategies of Judicial Intervention in Prisons," 138 U. Pa. L. Rev. 805 (1990).

13. Bruce Ackerman, *We the People* (1991); Louis Lusky, *By What Right* (1975).

14. Philip Bobbitt, *Constitutional Interpretation* (1991); Benjamin Cardozo, *The Nature of Judicial Process* (1921); Robert Dahl, *supra* note 1; William Lasser, *The Limits of Judicial Power* (1988); Robert Post, *Constitutional Domains: Democracy, Community, Management*, 15–18 (1995); Martin Shapiro, *Law and Politics in the Supreme Court* (1964); Martin Shapiro, *Courts: A Comparative and Political Analysis* (1981); Stuart Scheingold, *The Politics of Rights* (1974); Tushnet, *Red, White and Blue, supra* note 4. See also Marc Galanter, Frank Palen & John Thomas, "The Crusading Judge: Judicial Activism in Trial Courts," 52 S. Cal. L. Rev. 699 (1979) (judges engage in policy making for a variety of different reasons).

15. Cardozo, *supra* note 14, at 113 ("If you ask how [the] judge is to know when one interest outweighs another, I can only answer that he must get his knowledge just as the legislator gets it, from experience and study and reflection, in brief from life itself").

16. Roger Traynor, "The Limits of Judicial Creativity," 63 Iowa L. Rev. 1, 7 (1977) ("I believe the primary obligation of a judge, at once conservative and creative, is to keep the inevitable evolution of the law on a rational course. [R]eason, and not merely the rulebook, [is] the soul of law"). For an insightful discussion of Traynor's theory of judicial policy making, see

John Poulos, "The Judicial Philosophy of Roger Traynor," 46 Hastings L. J. 1643 (1995); John Poulos, "The Judicial Process and the Substantive Criminal Law: The Legacy of Roger Traynor," 29 Loyola (L.A.) L. Rev. 428 (1996).

17. Michael Perry, *The Constitution, the Courts and Human Rights*, 98 (1982) ("noninterpretive review represents the institutionalization of prophecy").

18. Frank, *supra* note 5, at 252 (the "civilized administration of justice" is achieved by "a mind free of childish emotional drags, a modern mind," emphasis omitted).

19. Clifford Geertz, *Local Knowledge: Further Essays in Interpretive Anthropology* (1983); Ihab Hassan, *The Postmodern Turn* (1987); Jean-Francois Lyotard, *The Postmodern Condition: A Report on Knowledge* (G. Bennington & B. Massouri, trans., 1984); Gianni Vattimo, *The End of Modernity, Nihilism and Hermeneutics in Post-Modern Culture* (1988).

20. E.g., Cooper, *supra* note 12; Horowitz, *supra* note 12; Gerald Rosenberg, *The Hollow Hope: Can Courts Bring about Social Change?* (1991); Shapiro, *Courts, supra* note 14; Robert Wood, ed., *Remedial Law When Courts Become Administrators* (1990).

21. 381 U.S. 479 (1965); 410 U.S. 113 (1973). The general consensus has been that the right of privacy decisions, particularly *Roe v. Wade*, are not coherent interpretations of the Bill of Rights, as the opinions claim. Critics refer to these decisions as "substantive due process," but in reality they are judicial policy making. See Robert Dixon, "The 'New' Substantive Due Process and the Democratic Ethic: A Prolegomenon," 1976 B.Y.U. L. Rev. 43; Epstein & Kobylka, *supra* note 1; Richard Epstein, "Substantive Due Process by Any Other Name: The Abortion Cases," 1973 Sup. Ct. Rev. 159; John Ely, "The Wages of Crying Wolf: A Comment on *Roe v. Wade*," 82 Yale L. J. 920 (1973); Louis Henkin, "Privacy and Autonomy," 74 Colum. L. Rev. 1410 (1974); Ira Lupu, "Untangling the Strands of the Fourteenth Amendment," 77 Mich. L. Rev. 981 (1979); Henry Monaghan, "The Constitution Goes to Harvard," 13 Harv. C.R. – C.L. L. Rev. 116 (1978).

22. *Pavesich v. New England Life Insurance Co.*, 122 Ga. 190, 50 S.E. 68 (1905) (right to privacy); *Haelan Laboratories, Inc. v. Topps Chewing Gum, Inc.*, 202 F.2d 866 (2d Cir. 1953) (right of publicity); *Factors, Inc. v. Pro Arts, Inc.*, 579 F.2d 215 (2d Cir. 1978) (same); *Zacchini v. Scripps-Howard Broadcasting Co.*, 443 U.S. 564 (1977) (same). For a comprehensive discussion, see J. Thomas McCarthy, *The Rights of Publicity and Privacy* (1987).

23. E.g., *Stromberg v. California*, 283 U.S. 359 (1932); *Schenck v. United States*, 249 U.S. 47 (1919); *Masses Publishing Co. v. Patten*, 244 F. 535 (1917). These decisions, and others of their period, created free-speech doctrine; the constitutional clause had never been used to invalidate legislation prior to that time. See Zachariah Chafee, *Free Speech in the United States* (1941); Harry Kalven, *A Worthy Tradition*, 125–89 (J. Kalven, ed., 1988); Gerald Gunther, *Learned Hand: The Man and the Judge*, 151–70 (1994). The doctrine's development continues to the present, e.g., *New York Times v. Sullivan*, 376 U.S. 255 (1964) (public figures doctrine); *Miller v. California*,

413 U.S. 15 (1973) (community standards doctrine for obscenity). See Post, *supra* note 14.

24. E.g., *Halderman v. Pennhurst State School & Hospital*, 446 F. Supp. 1295 (E.D. PA 1977), *aff'd on other grounds*, 612 F.2d 84 (3d Cir. 1979), *rev'd and remanded*, 451 U.S. 1 (1981); *Wyatt v. Stickey*, 325 F. Supp. 781 (M.D. Ala. 1971), *modified*, 344 F. Supp. 373 & 344 F. Supp. 387 (M.D. Ala. 1972), *aff'd in part, reversed and remanded in part sub nom.*, *Wyatt v. Aderhold*, 503 F.2d 1305 (5th Cir. 1974).

25. E.g., *Standard Oil of N.J. v. U.S.*, 221 U.S. 1 (1911) (rule of reason); *White Motor Co. v. United States*, 372 U.S. 253 (1963) (same); *United States v. Socony-Vacuum Oil Co.*, 311 U.S. 150 (1940) (price fixing); *Interstate Circuit, Inc. v. United States*, 306 U.S. 208 (1949).

26. *Henningsen v. Bloomfield Motors, Inc.* 32 N.J. 358, 161 A.2d 69 (1959); *Greenman v. Yuba Power Products, Inc.*, 59 Cal. 2d 57, 377 P.2d 897 (1963).

27. See *Glidden Co. v. Zdanok*, 370 U.S. 530 (1962).

28. *American Insurance Co. v. Canter*, 26 U.S. (1 Pet.) 511 (1828) (Marshall, C. J.) (courts in Florida territory).

29. See *Solorio v. United States*, 483 U.S. 435 (1987).

30. See *Thomas v. Union Carbide Agricultural Prods.*, 473 U.S. 568 (1985) (arbitration under Federal Insecticide, Fungicide and Rodenticide Act); *Commodity Futures Trading Comm'n v. Schor*, 478 U.S. 833 (1986) (administrative adjudication under Commodity Exchange Act); Paul Bator, "The Constitution as Architecture: Legislative and Administrative Courts under Article III," 64 Ind. L. J. 233 (1990); Richard Fallon, "Of Legislative Courts, Administrative Agencies, and Article III," 101 Harv. L. Rev. 915 (1988).

31. R. Dworkin, *supra* note 2, at 1057, 1067–73.

32. See Stuart Nagel, *Policy Evaluation: Making Optimal Decisions* (1982); Carl Patton & David Sawicki, *The Policy Analysis Process: Basic Methods of Policy Analysis and Planning*, 26–38 (1986); Edith Stokey & Richard Zeckhauser, *Thinking about Policy Choices: A Primer for Policy Analysis*, 5–6 (1978).

33. Charles Lindblom, "The Science of Muddling Through," 19 Publ. Admin. Rev. 79 (1959); see David Braybrooke & Charles Lindblom, *A Strategy of Decision: Policy Evaluations as a Social Process* (1963).

34. See Richard E. Palmer, *Hermeneutics*, 77–81, 84–88, 118–21 (1969).

35. Hans-Georg Gadamer, *Truth and Method*, 162–73, 235–305 (G. Barden & J. Cumming, trans., 1975). Gadamer derives his generalization of hermeneutics from Heidegger, see *id.* at 225–40, Martin Heidegger, *Being and Time*, 188–95 (J. Macquarrie & E. Robinson, trans., 1962).

36. Anthony Giddens, *The Constitution of Society: Outline of the Theory of Structuration* (1984).

37. Charles Fox & Hugh Miller, *Postmodern Public Administration* (1995). For a similar approach to industrial design, see Michael Piore, Richard Lester, Fred Kofman & Kamal Malck, *The Organization of Product Development*, 3 Industrial & Corporate Change (1994).

38. Bobbitt, *supra* note 14; Steven Burton, *An Introduction to Law and Legal Reasoning* (1985); William Eskridge & Philip Frickey, "Statutory Interpretation as Practical Reasoning," 42 Stan. L. Rev. 321 (1990); Daniel Farber

& Philip Frickey, "Practical Reason and the First Amendment," 34 UCLA
L. Rev. 1615 (1987); Anthony Kronman, "Alexander Bickel's Philosophy
of Prudence," 94 Yale L. J. 1567 (1985); Dennis Patterson, "The Property
of Interpretive Universalism: Toward a Reconstruction of Legal Theory,"
72 Tex. L. Rev. 1 (1993); Suzanna Sherry, "Civic Virtue and the Feminine
Voice in Constitutional Adjudication," 72 Va. L. Rev. 543 (1986); Cass
Sunstein, "Interest Groups in American Public Law," 38 Stan. L. Rev. 29
(1985); Vincent Wellman, "Practical Reasoning and Judicial Justification:
Toward an Adequate Theory," 57 U. Colo. L. Rev. 45 (1985).

39. Bobbitt, *supra* note 14.
40. Steven Winter, "The Constitution of Conscience," 72 Tex. L. Rev. 1805
(1994).
41. Gadamer, *supra* note 35, at 235–45, 345–66; Heidegger, *supra* note 35, at
58–63, 182–210.
42. The phrase derives from Peter Berger & Thomas Luckman, *The Social
Construction of Reality: A Treatise in the Sociology of Knowledge* (1966). The
underlying approach can be fairly described as the dominant methodological theme in modern scholarship. In addition to the works of Heidegger and Gadamer, see Terry Eagleton, *Literary Theory* (1983); Murray
Edelman, *Constructing the Political Spectacle* (1988) (political science); Paul
Feyerabend, *Against Method* (1975) (natural science); Stanley Fish, *Is There
a Text in This Class?* (1980) (literature); Harold Garfinkel, *Studies in Ethnomethodology* (1984) (sociology); Clifford Geertz, *The Interpretation of Culture* (1973) (anthropology); Thomas Kuhn, *The Structure of Scientific
Revolutions* (2d ed., 1970) (natural science); David McCloskey, *The Rhetoric
of Economics* (1985); Alfred Schutz, *The Phenomenology of the Social World*
(1972) (sociology). For other discussions at the epistemological level, see
Richard Bernstein, *The Restructuring of Social and Political Theory* (1978);
Willard Quine, *Pursuit of Truth* (1990); Willard Quine, *Word and Object*
(1960); Hillary Putnam, *Reason, Truth and History* (1981); Peter Winch, *The
Idea of Social Science* (1958). For challenges to this approach, see James
Harris, *Against Relativism* (1992); Thomas Nagel, *The View from Nowhere*
(1986).
43. Heidegger, *supra* note 35, at 99–114.
44. J. M. Balkin, "Ideological Drift and the Struggle over Meaning," 25 Conn.
L. Rev. 869 (1993); Horowitz, *supra* note 4; Hutchinson, "Democracy and
Determinacy," *supra* note 4; Hutchinson, *Dwelling on the Threshold, supra*
note 4; Peller, *supra* note 4; Segal & Spaeth, *supra* note 1; Spaeth, *supra*
note 1, Tushnet, *Red, White and Blue, supra* note 4; Tushnet, "Following
the Rules Laid Down," *supra* note 4; Unger, *supra* note 4; Yarnold, *supra*
note 1.
45. The leading statement is Wechsler, *supra* note 2.
46. See note 4, *supra*.
47. See, e.g., Harry Edwards, "Public Misperceptions concerning the 'Politics'
of Judging: Dispelling Some Myths about the D.C. Circuit," 56 U. Colo.
L. Rev. 619 (1985); Alvin Rubin, "Doctrine in Decision-Making: Rationale
or Rationalization," 1987 Utah L. Rev. 357 (1987). For a more modulated

and thoughtful version of this argument, see Jon Newman, "Between Legal Realism and Neutral Principles: The Legitimacy of Institutional Values," 72 Cal. L. Rev. 200 (1984).

48. Guido Calabresi, *A Common Law for the Age of Statutes*, 92–101 (1982); Melvin Eisenberg, *The Nature of the Common Law* (1988); John Ely, *Democracy and Distrust*, 4–5, 76–69 (1980); William Fletcher, "The General Common Law and Section 34 of the Judiciary Act of 1789: The Example of Marine Insurance," 97 Harv. L. Rev. 1513 (1984); Harlan F. Stone, "The Common Law in the United States," 50 Harv. L. Rev. 4 (1936).

49. Thomas Grey, "Langdell's Orthodoxy," 45 U. Pitt. L. Rev. 1 (1993). For an effort to restate this position in a muted, modern form, see Geoffrey Walker, *The Rule of Law*, 162–70 (1988).

50. George Keeton, *The Norman Conquest and the Common Law* (1966); Frederick Pollock & Frederic Maitland, *The History of English Law, vol. 4, Before the Time of Edward I* (2d ed., 1968).

51. See William Holdsworth, *A History of English Law*, 252–93 (1903–38); see generally Daniel Coquillette, *Ideology and Incorporation III: Reason Regulated – The Post-Restoration English Civilians, 1653–1735*, 67 B.U. L. Rev. 289 (1987).

52. See J. G. A. Pocock, *The Ancient Constitution and the Feudal Law*, 30–55 (1957).

53. Fletcher, *supra* note 48; Horowitz, *supra* note 4; Craig Klafter, *Reason over Precedents: Origins of American Legal Thought* (1993).

54. Bickel, *supra* note 2; Fredrich A. Hayek, *Law, Legislation and Liberty* (1979); Theodore Lowi, *The End of Liberalism* (2d. ed., 1979).

55. David Nachimas & Daniel Rosenbloom, *Bureaucratic Government USA* (1980); Glenn Robinson, *American Bureaucracy: Public Choice and Public Law* (1991); Robert Stillman, *The American Bureaucracy* (1987); James Q. Wilson, *Bureaucracy* (1989). The seminal work, of course, is Max Weber, *Economy and Society*, 956–1005 (G. Roth & C. Wittich, eds., 1978).

56. MacCormick & Summers, *supra* note 11. See *id.* at 37–40 (Argentina), 78–82 (Germany), 131–32 (Finland), 218–20 (Italy), 268–69 (Poland), 313–14 (Sweden), 362–64 (United Kingdom). See Aleksander Peczenki, *On Law and Reason*, 24–26 (1989).

57. H. L. A. Hart, *The Concept of Law*, 121–50 (1966). See also Aharon Barak, *Judicial Discretion* (Y. Kaufman, trans., 1989) (distinguishing among easy, intermediate, and hard cases); Frederich Schauer, "Easy Cases," 58 S. Cal. L. Rev. 399 (1985).

58. See David Richards, "Rules, Policies, and Neutral Principles: The Search for Legitimacy in Common Law and Constitutional Adjudication," 11 Ga. L. Rev. 1069 (1977).

59. Bobbitt, *supra* note 14.

60. Fiss, *Forms of Justice, supra* note 12.

61. Frank Michelman, "Foreword: Traces of Self-Government," 100 Harv. L. Rev. 1 (1986).

62. Michael Perry, *The Constitution in the Courts* (1993); Michael Perry, *The Constitution, the Courts and Human Rights* (1982).

63. Cass Sunstein, "Interest Groups in American Public Law," 38 Stan L. Rev. 29 (1985).

64. Tushnet, *Red, White and Blue, supra* note 4.

65. Philip Bobbitt, *Constitutional Fate,* 59–73 (1982); Tushnet, *Red, White and Blue, supra* note 4, at 1–87.

66. See note 15 *supra.*

67. *Standard Oil Co. of New Jersey v. United States, supra* note 25.

68. See generally David Armor, *Forced Justice: School Desegregation and the Law* (1995); David Kirp, *The Idea of Racial Equality in American Education* (1982); Christine Roselli, *The Carrot or the Stick for Desegregation Policy* (1990); J. Harvie Wilkinson, *From Brown and Bakke, the Supreme Court and School Integration, 1954–1978* (1979); Mark Yudof, "School Desegregation: Legal Realism, Reasoned Elaboration, and Social Science Research in the Supreme Court," 42 L. & Contemp. Prob. 57 (1978).

69. See Chapter 2.

70. *Talley v. Stephens,* 247 F. Supp. 683 (E.D. Ark. 1965).

71. E.g., *Holt v. Sarver,* 309 F. Supp. 362 (E.D. Ark. 1970); 300 F. Supp. 825 (E.D. Ark. 1969). See Chapter 3.

72. National Prison Project, *Status Report,* updated January 1995, 1–2.

73. *Id.* at 2.

74. See Chapter 9.

75. See Kingdon, *supra* note 10.

76. Blake McKelvey, *American Prisons: A History of Good Intentions,* 1–11 (1977); David Rothman, *The Discovery of the Asylum: Social Order and Disorder in the New Republic,* 45–78 (2d. ed., 1993); cf. Michael Ignatieff, *A Just Measure of Pain: The Penitentiary in the Industrial Revolution, 1750–1850,* 15–43 (1978) (absence of prisons in Britain). Pieter Spierenburg, in *The Prison Experience* (1991), argues that prisons on the continent emerged considerably earlier, but neither he nor anyone else has advanced this argument with respect to the American colonies or the early United States.

77. See, e.g., *Turner v. Safley,* 482 U.S. 78 (1987), *Sandin v. Connor,* 515 U.S. 472 (1995).

78. *Helling v. McKinney,* 509 U.S. 25 (1993).

79. *Farmer v. Brennan,* 511 U.S. 825 (1994). See also *Lynce v. Mathis,* 117 S. Ct. 891 (1997) (unanimously holding that good time orders cannot be cancelled retroactively).

80. Justice Thomas concurred only in the judgment. *Id.* at 1990.

81. The list comes from Justice O'Connor's opinion in *Gregory v. Ashcroft,* 111 S. Ct. 2395 (1991). See Chapter 5, "Instrumental Arguments for Federalism."

82. *Brown v. Board of Education,* 347 U.S. 483 (1954); *Miranda v. Arizona,* 384 U.S. 436 (1966); *Roe v. Wade,* 410 U.S. 113 (1973).

83. Ben Crouch & James Marquart, *An Appeal to Justice* (1989); James Jacobs, *Stateville: The Penitentiary in Mass Society* (1977).

84. John DiIulio, *Governing Prisons* (1987); William Taylor, *Brokered Justice* (1993).

85. Brad Chilton, *Prisons under the Gavel: The Federal Court Takeover of Georgia*

Prisons (1991); Steve Martin & Sheldon Ekland-Olson, *Texas Prisons* (1987); Larry Yackle, *Reform and Regret: The Story of Federal Judicial Involvement in Alabama Prison System* (1989); Robert Wood, supra note 20.

86. For a concurring view, see Susan Sturm, "Resolving the Remedial Dilemma: Strategies of Judicial Intervention in Prisons," 138 U. Pa. L. Rev. 805 (1990).

87. Montesquieu, *The Spirit of the Laws* (D. Carruthers, trans., 1977). For the view that Montesquieu's view of British politics was a misinterpretation, see M. J. C. Vile, *Separation of Powers*, 76–97 (1967).

88. Richard Epstein, *Takings: Private Property and the Role of Eminent Domain* (1985); Fredrich A. Hayek, *The Road to Serfdom* (1944); Robert Nozick, *Anarchy, State and Utopia* (1974).

89. Hayek, *supra* note 88, at 72–73; Walker, *supra* note 49.

90. Francis Mootz III, "Is the Rule of Law Possible in a Postmodern World?" 68 Wash. L. Rev. 249 (1993); Francis Mootz III, "Rethinking the Rule of Law: A Demonstration that the Obvious Is Plausible," 61 Tenn. L. Rev. 69 (1993); Margaret Radin, "Reconsidering the Rule of Law," 69 B. U. L. Rev. 781 (1989).

91. Charles Warren & Louis Brandeis, "The Right to Privacy," 4 Harv. L. Rev. 193 (1890). See McCarthy, *supra* note 22 at §§ 1.3 & 1.4.

92. See note 23 *supra*.

93. *Standard Oil Co. of New Jersey v. United States*, supra note 25. According to Lawrence Sullivan, *Handbook of the Law of Antitrust*, 172 (1977), Chief Justice White "took the opportunity in *Standard Oil* to announce what has come to be known as the 'rule of reason,' a new and more general rubric under which the legality of concerted arrangements was to be evaluated."

94. E.g., *Hussey v. Jacob*, 1 Ld. Raym. 86, 91 Eng. Rep. 954 (1969); *Miller v. Race*, 1 Burr. 452, 97 Eng. Rep. 398 (1758); *Tyndal v. Brown*, 99 Eng. Rep. 1033 (K.B. 1786). See Cecil Fifoot, *Lord Mansfield*, 82–117 (1936); William Holdsworth, *Some Makers of English Law*, 160–75 (1938); David Lieberman, *The Province of Legislation Determined*, 111–17 (1989); James Oldham, *The Mansfield Manuscripts and the Growth of English Law in the Eighteenth Century*, 602–4 (1992); James Rogers, *The Early History of the Law of Bills and Notes* (1995); Edward Rubin, "Learning from Lord Mansfield: Toward a Transferability Law for Modern Commercial Practice," 31 Idaho L. Rev. 775 (1995).

95. Niccolo Machiavelli, *The Prince*, §§ 4–8 (L. Ricci, trans., E. Vincent, ed., 1935).

96. James Buchanan & Gordon Tullock, *The Calculus of Consent* (1962); Dennis Mueller, *Public Choice* (2d ed., 1989); David Mayhew, *Congress: The Electoral Connection* (1974); Mancur Olson, *The Logic of Collective Action* (1965); see Daniel Farber & Philip Frickey, *Law and Public Choice* (1991).

97. William Eskridge, "Reneging on History? Playing the Court/Congress/President Civil Rights Game," 29 Cal. L. Rev. 613 (1991); Herve Moulin, *Game Theory for the Social Sciences* (1986); Peter Ordeshook, *Game Theory and Political Theory* (1986); Peter Ordeshook & Thomas Schwartz, "Agendas and the Control of Political Outcomes," 81 Am. Pol. Sci. Rev. 180 (1987);

Daniel Rodriguez, "The Positive Political Dimension of Regulatory Reform," 72 Wash. U. L. Q. 1 (1994).

98. See sources cited in note 1, *supra.*

99. Paul Brest, "The Fundamental Rights of Controversy: The Essential Contradictions of Normative Constitutional Scholarship," 90 Yale L. J. 1063 (1981); George Fletcher, "Two Modes of Legal Thought," 90 Yale L. J. 970 (1981); Edward Rubin, "The Practice and Discourse of Legal Scholarship," 86 Mich. L. Rev. 1835 (1988); Mark Tushnet, "Legal Scholarship: Its Causes and Cures," 90 Yale L. J. 1205 (1981).

100. M. Eisenberg, supra note 48; William Eskridge & Philip Frickey, "The Supreme Court, 1993 Term: Foreword – Law as Equilibrium," 108 Harv. L. Rev. 27 (1994); Tracey George & Lee Epstein, "On the Nature of Supreme Court Decision Making," 86 Am. Pol. Sci. Rev. 323 (1992); Kent Greenawalt, "Discretion and the Judicial Decision: The Elusive Quest for the Fetters That Bind Judges," 75 Colum. L. Rev. 359 (1975); Sidney Shapiro & Richard Levy, "Judicial Incentives and Indeterminacy in Substantive Review of Administrative Decisions," 44 Duke L. J. 1049 (1995); Charles Yablon, *Justifying the Judge's Hunch: An Essay on Discretion* (1990); Paul Gewirtz, introduction in Karl Llewellyn, *The Case Law System in America* (M. Ansaldi, trans., 1989).

2. AN OVERVIEW OF JUDICIAL PRISON REFORM

1. United States ex rel. *Atterbury v. Ragen,* 237 F.2d 953 (7th Cir. 1956), *cert. denied,* 353 U.S. 964 (1957).

2. James Jacobs, *Stateville: The Penitentiary in Mass Society,* 15–51 (1977).

3. 237 F.2d at 954.

4. *Id.* at 954–55.

5. *Id.* at 955, quoting *Siegel v. Ragen,* 180 F.2d 785 (7th Cir.), *cert. denied,* 339 U.S. 990 (1950).

6. *Id.* quoting United States ex rel. *Morris v. Radio Station* WENR, 209 F.2d 105, 107 (7th Cir. 1953). This opinion was also written by Judge Duffy, and also involved an inmate at Stateville. The reason the named defendant was a radio station is that the station regularly recorded a program at the penitentiary, using inmates as announcers and narrators; Morris claimed that he had been denied the opportunity to audition for a role in the program because he was black.

7. *Id.* quoting *Morris,* 209 F.2d at 107, which in turn quotes *Stroud v. Swope,* 187 F.2d 850, 851 (9th Cir. 1951).

8. The phrase apparently originated in Fritch, *Civil Rights of Federal Prison Inmates* (1961) and was introduced into academic legal discourse in Note, "Beyond the Ken of the Courts: A Critique of Judicial Refusal to Review the Complaints of Convicts," 72 Yale L. J. 506 (1963).

9. 42 U.S.C. § 1981 *et seq.*

10. *Attebury* was originally treated as a habeas petition by the district court,

which appointed an attorney to represent the prisoner. The attorney then informed the judge that the action was in fact a Civil Rights Act suit for damages and requested permission to withdraw, which the judge granted.

11. William Duker, *A Constitutional History of Habeas Corpus*, 12–63 (1980); W. Holdsworth, *A History of English Law*, vol. 9, 104–22; Clarke Forsythe, "The Historical Origins of Broad Habeas Corpus Review Reconsidered," 70 Notre Dame L. Rev. 1079, 1092–1101 (1995); Jim Thomas, *Prisoner Litigation*, 74–81 (1988).

12. Duker, *supra* note 11, at 126–56; Forsythe, *supra* note 11, at 1101–17. The current statute is 28 U.S.C. § 2241. Habeas corpus for federal prisoners was provided for by the Judiciary Act of 1789, Ch. 20 § 14, 1 Stat. 73, 81–82, and was extended to state prisoners generally in 1867, Ch. 28, § 1, 14 Stat. 385. Federal prisoners now proceed under 28 U.S.C. § 2255, an equivalent postconviction remedy. See *United States v. Hayman*, 342 U.S. 205 (1952); *Kaufman v. United States*, 394 U.S. 217 (1969).

13. Forsythe, *supra* note 11; Ann Woodhandler, "Demodeling Habeas," 45 Stan. L. Rev. 575 (1993). For the view that the 1867 statute always had a broader meaning, see James Liebman, "Apocalypse Next Time? The Anachronistic Attack on Habeas Corpus/Direct Review Parity," 92 Colum. L. Rev. 1997 (1992) (arguing that the habeas statute had a broader scope); Gary Peller, "In Defense of Federal Habeas Corpus Relitigation," 16 Harv. C.R. - C.L. L. Rev. 579 (1982) (same).

14. 237 U.S. 309 (1915).

15. 261 U.S. 86 (1923).

16. United States ex. rel. *Atterbury v. Ragen*, 237 F.2d 953, 955 (7th Cir. 1956). See *Platek v. Aderhold*, 73 F.2d 173 (5th Cir. 1934); *Sarshik v. Aderhold*, 142 F.2d 676 (5th Cir. 1944); *Snow v. Roche*, 143 F.2d 718 (9th Cir. 1944); *Powell v. Hunter*, 172 F.2d 330 (10th Cir. 1949); *Stroud v. Swope*, 187 F.2d 850 (9th Cir. 1951); *Garcia v. Steele*, 193 F.2d 276 (8th Cir. 1951); United States ex rel. *Morris v. Radio Station WENR*, 209 F.2d 105 (7th Cir. 1953); *Eaton v. Bibb*, 217 F.2d 446 (7th Cir. 1955); *Harris v. Settle*, supra note 6.

17. *McNally v. Hill*, 293 U.S. 131 (1934); *In re Pinaire*, 46 F. Supp. 113 (N.D. Tex. 1942); *Snow v. Roche*, supra note 16; *Johnson v. Dye*, 175 F.2d 250, 257 (3d. Cir.), *rev'd per curiam* 338 U.S. 864 (1949) (O'Connell, J. concurring); *Williams v. Steele*, 194 F.2d 32 (8th Cir. 1952).

18. *Ex parte Barnard*, 52 F. Supp. 102 (E.D. Ill. 1943); *Kelly v. Dowd*, 140 F.2d 81 (7th Cir. 1944); *Johnson v. Dye*, 338 U.S. 864 (1949); *Johnson v. Matthews*, 182 F.2d 677 (D.C. Cir. 1950); *Ross v. Middlebrooks*, 188 F.2d 308 (9th Cir. 1951); *Sweeney v. Woodall*, 344 U.S. 86 (1952).

19. 344 U.S. 443 (1953). See generally Paul Bator, "Finality in Criminal Law and Federal Habeas Corpus for State Prisoners," 76 Harv. L. Rev. 441 (1963); Curtis Reitz, "Federal Habeas Corpus: Postconviction Remedy for State Prisoners," 108 U. Pa. L. Rev. 461 (1960).

20. United States ex rel. *Jackson v. Ruthazer*, 181 F.2d 588 (2d Cir. 1950). The only way to obtain a federal court hearing in these circumstances was a certiorai petition to the U.S. Supreme Court.

21. *Monroe v. Pape*, 365 U.S. 167, 212–16 (1961) (Frankfurter, J., dissenting); Marshall Shapo, "Constitutional Tort: *Monroe v. Pape*, and the Frontiers Beyond," 60 Nw. U. L. Rev. 277 (1965); Eric Zagrans, "Under Color of *What* Law: A Reconstructed Model of Section 1983 Liability," 71 Va. L. Rev. 499 (1985).
22. 313 U.S. 299 (1941).
23. 325 U.S. 91 (1945).
24. *United States v. Jones*, 207 F.2d 785, 786–87 (5th Cir. 1953): "[P]aradoxical as it may seem, the defendant was whipping these prisoners under color of law, although doing it in violation of law. Color of law, as used in the statute, means pretense of law: it may include, but does not necessarily mean, under authority of law." The tone of this explanation suggests that the view the Court was rejecting was widely held.
25. 365 U.S. 167 (1961).
26. See Steven Winter, "The Meaning of 'Under Color of' Law," 91 Mich. L. Rev. 323 (1992).
27. Owen Fiss, *The Civil Rights Injunction* (1978). Injunctions had been used by federal courts at the turn of the century in labor disputes, e.g., *In re Debs*, 158 U.S. 564 (1895), but there was a widespread sense that this use was unwise or illegitimate.
28. 403 U.S. 388 (1971).
29. The Court specifically held that the Eighth Amendment was incorporated in *Robinson v. California*, 370 U.S. 660 (1962), a nonprison case invalidating a law which criminalized the status of being a narcotics offender. The leading case on incorporation generally was *Mapp v. Ohio*, 367 U.S. 643 (1961); the one that brought the controversy to an effective close was *Duncan v. Louisiana*, 391 U.S. 145 (1968).
30. 329 U.S. 459 (1947). Moreover, in reversing the Third Circuit decision in *Johnson v. Dye*, 175 F.2d 250 (3d Cir.), *rev'd per curiam* 338 U.S. 864 (1949), which specifically declared the Eighth Amendment to be incorporated, the Court cites only a case involving exhaustion of state remedies of habeas corpus, thus making no apparent objection to the Third Circuit's Eighth Amendment holding.
31. Louisiana ex rel. *Frances v. Resweber*, 329 U.S. 459, 468 (1947) (Frankfurter, J., concurring). Justice Frankfurter, along with Justice Harlan, was the chief proponent of the position that the due process clause contains a general proscription of uncivilized state action, rather than simply incorporates the specific provisions of the Bill of Rights.
32. *Ex parte Barnard*, 52 F. Supp. 102 (E.D. Ill. 1943); *Siegel v. Ragen*, 180 F.2d 285 (7th Cir. 1950); *Bryant v. Harrelson*, 187 F. Supp. 738 (S.D. Tex. 1960); *Blythe v. Ellis*, 194 F. Supp. 139 (S.D. Tex. 1961).
33. *Ex parte Barnard*, 52 F. Supp. 102 (E.D. Ill. 1943); *Kelly v. Dowd*, 140 F.2d 81 (7th Cir. 1944); *Siegel v. Ragen*, 180 F.2d 785 (7th Cir. 1950); *Eaton v. Bibb*, 217 F.2d 446 (7th Cir. 1955); *Application of Hodge*, 262 F.2d 778 (9th Cir. 1958); United States ex rel *Knight v. Ragen*, 337 F.2d 425 (7th Cir. 1964).
34. United States ex rel. *Atterbury v. Ragen*, 237 F.2d 953, 955 (7th Cir. 1956).

35. *Id.*
36. *Sarshik v. Aderhold,* 142 F.2d 676 (5th Cir. 1944); *Shepherd v. Hunter,* 163 F.2d 872 (10th Cir. 1949); *Numer v. Miller,* 165 F.2d 986 (9th Cir. 1948); *Dayton v. Hunter,* 176 F.2d 108 (10th Cir. 1949); *Stroud v. Swope,* 187 F.2d 850 (9th Cir. 1951); *Garcia v. Steele,* 193 F.2d 276 (8th Cir. 1951); *Adams v. Ellis,* 197 F.2d 483 (5th Cir. 1952); *United States v. Radio Station WENR,* 209 F.2d 105 (7th Cir. 1953); *Curtis v. Jacques,* 130 F. Supp. 920 (W.D. Mich. 1954); *Application of Hodge,* 262 F.2d 778 (9th Cir. 1958); United States ex rel. *Knight v. Ragen,* 337 F.2d 425 (7th Cir. 1964).
37. *Platek v. Aderhold,* 73 F.2d 173 (5th Cir. 1934); *Coffin v. Reichard,* 143 F.2d 443 (6th Cir. 1944); *Shepherd v. Hunter,* 163 F.2d 872 (10th Cir. 1947); *Eaton v. Bibb,* 217 F.2d 446 (7th Cir. 1955); *Application of Hodge,* 262 F.2d 778 (9th Cir. 1958); *Austin v. Harris,* 226 F. Supp. 304 (W.D. Mo. 1964).
38. 143 F.2d 443 (6th Cir. 1944).
39. *Id.* at 444.
40. *Id.* at 445.
41. *Williams v. Steele,* 194 F.2d 32, 33–34 (8th Cir. 1952). As late as 1970, a case law review of habeas corpus doctrine stated that "[N]o other circuit purports to follow *Coffin.*" "Developments in the Law – Federal Habeas Corpus," 83 Harv. L. Rev. 1038 (1970).
42. 77 F. Supp. 477 (E.D. In. 1948).
43. 101 F. Supp. 285 (D.C. Alaska 1951).
44. *I Am a Fugitive from a Chain Gang* (Warner Brothers, 1932).
45. 175 F.2d 250 (3d Cir.), *rev'd per curiam* 338 U.S. 864 (1949).
46. *Id.* at 256, note 12.
47. *Id.*
48. *Id.* at 256.
49. *Id.* at 257, note 1 (O'Connell, J., concurring).
50. 338 U.S. 864 (1949).
51. *Ex parte Hawk,* 321 U.S. 114 (1944).
52. 344 U.S. 86 (1952).
53. *Id.* at 92.
54. *Harper v. Wall,* 85 F. Supp. 783 (D.N.J. 1949); *Application of Middlebrooks,* 88 F. Supp. 943 (S.D. Cal. 1950).
55. In general, prisoners seem to have been reading these decisions rather assiduously. There is also a tendency for particular institutions to generate a disproportionate number of complaints, perhaps due to the presence of an inmate "writ writer." Alcatraz federal penitentiary and Stateville in Illinois seem to be the leaders in the 1950s. In the early 1960s, Lorton Federal Penitentiary in Virginia became a major source as a result of Black Muslim activity.
56. *Miller v. Overholer,* 206 F.2d 415 (D.C. Cir. 1953); *Austin v. Harris,* 226 F. Supp. 304 (W.D. Mo. 1964).
57. *Miller v. Overholder,* Id.); *Threatt v. North Carolina,* 221 F. Supp. 858 (W.D.N.C. 1963).
58. United States ex rel. *Westbrook v. Randolph,* 259 F.2d 215 (7th Cir. 1958); *Evans v. Cunningham,* 335 F.2d 491 (4th Cir. 1964). These are not prison

conditions cases, but there is no reason to think that the same reasoning would not have been applied.

59. *United States v. Jones*, 207 F.2d 108 (7th Cir. 1953); *Redding v. Pate*, 220 F. Supp. 124 (N.D. Ill. 1963); United States ex rel. *Hancock v. Pate*, 223 F. Supp. 202 (N.D. Ill. 1963).

60. *Robinson v. California*, 370 U.S. 660 (1962) (not a prison conditions case, but its application to such cases was undeniable); *Redding v. Pate*, 220 F. Supp. 124 (N.D. Ill. 1963).

61. *Coleman v. Johnson*, 247 F.2d 273 (1957); *Threatt v. North Carolina*, 221 F. Supp. 858 (W.D.N.C. 1963); *Stone v. McGinnis*, 334 F.2d 906 (2d Cir. 1964).

62. *Fullwood v. Clemmer*, 295 F.2d 171 (D.C. Cir. 1961); *Austin v. Harris*, 226 F. Supp. 304 (W.D. Mo. 1964); *Edwards v. Duncan*, 355 F.2d 993 (4th Cir. 1966).

63. *Application of Hodge*, 262 F.2d 778 (9th Cir. 1958); *Bryant v. Harrelson* 187 F. Supp. 738 (S.D. Tex. 1960); *Hadfield v. Bailleaux*, 290 F.2d 632 (9th Cir. 1961); *Blythe v. Ellis*, 194 F. Supp. 139 (S.D. Tex. 1961); *Harris v. Settle*, 322 F.2d 908 (8th Cir. 1963); United States ex rel. *Knight v. Ragen*, 337 F.2d 425 (7th Cir. 1964). Presumably, there are also many unpublished decisions that dismissed the prisoner's complaint.

64. The legislation was debated throughout the late 1950s and early 1960s. See John Martin, *Civil Rights and the Crisis of Liberalism: The Democratic Party, 1945–76* (1979); Charles Whalen & Barbara Whalen, *The Longest Debate: A Legislative History of the 1964 Civil Rights Act* (1985).

65. Blake McElvey, *American Prisons: A History of Good Intentions*, 69, 76, 208–9 (1977); Estelle Freedman, *Their Sisters Keepers*, 25–29 (1984); David Rothman, *The Discovery of the Asylum*, 85, 104 (2d ed., 1990); William Taylor, *Brokered Justice*, 18, 94, 125 (1993).

66. Prior to the Black Muslim cases, there appears to be only one claim of religious discrimination, *Kelly v. Dowd*, 140 F.2d 81 (7th Cir. 1944), which involved a Jehovah's Witness. In *McBride v. McCorkle*, 44 N.J. Super 468, 130 A.2d 881 (1957), the prisoner was denied the opportunity to receive communion, but only because he was in the prison's isolation wing, not because the New Jersey prison authorities had any concerns about Catholic religious observance.

67. E.g., *Cantwell v. Connecticut*, 310 U.S. 296 (1940); *Braunfield v. Brown*, 366 U.S. 599 (1961).

68. *Childs v. Pegelow*, 321 F.2d 487 (4th Cir. 1963); *Cooper v. Pate*, 324 F.2d 165 (7th Cir. 1963), *rev'd per curiam*, 387 U.S. 546 (1963).

69. *Price v. LaVallee*, 293 F.2d 233, 235 (2d Cir. 1961); see *Fullwood v. Clemmer*, 295 F.2d 171 (D.C. Cir. 1961); *Sewell v. Pegelow*, 291 F.2d 196 (1961); *Sostre v. McGinnis*, 334 F.2d 906 (2d Cir. 1964); *Banks v. Haveaner*, 234 F. Supp. 27 (1964).

70. 324 F.2d 165 (7th Cir. 1963).

71. *Id.* at 167.

72. *Id.* at 166–67.

73. 378 U.S. 546 (1963), citing *Pierce v. LaVallee*, 293 F.2d 233 (2d Cir. 1961); *Sewell v. Pegelow*, 291 F.2d 196 (4th Cir. 1961).

74. James Jacobs, "The Prisoner's Rights Movement and Its Impact," in *New Perspectives on Prisons and Imprisonment*, 33, 36 (J. Jacobs, ed., 1983).
75. See, for example, the remedies envisioned in Note, *supra* note 8; Note, "Constitutional Rights of Prisoners: The Developing Law," 110 U. Pa. L. Rev. 985 (1962); Note, "Black Muslims in Prison: Of Muslim Rites and Constitutional Rights," 62 Colum. L. Rev. 1488 (1962).
76. 247 F. Supp. (E.D. Ark. 1965).
77. *Holt v. Sarver* (*Holt II*), 309 F. Supp. 362 (E.D. Ark. 1970); *aff'd*, 442 F.2d 304 (8th Cir. 1971).
78. *Gates v. Collier*, 349 F. Supp. 881 (N.D. Miss. 1972), *aff'd*, 501 F.2d 1291 (5th Cir. 1974).
79. *Battle v. Anderson*, 376 F. Supp. 402 (E.D. Okla. 1974), *aff'd*, 564 F.2d 388 (10th Cir. 1977).
80. *Costello v. Wainwright*, 397 F. Supp. 20 (M.D. Fla. 1975), *vacated on other grounds*, 539 F.2d 547 (5th Cir. 1976), *rev'd and remanded*, 430 U.S. 325 (1977).
81. *Louisiana v. Edwards*, 547 F.2d 1206 (5th Cir. 1977).
82. *Pugh v. Locke*, 406 F. Supp. 318 (M.D. Ala. 1976), *aff'd in substance sub nom. Newman v. Alabama*, 559 F.2d 283 (5th Cir. 1977), *rev'd in part and remanded sub nom. Alabama v. Pugh*, 438 U.S. 781 (1978).
83. All three of the nonstate systems are subject to comprehensive court orders. See *Inmates of D.C. Jail v. Jackson*, 416 F. Supp. 119 (D.D.C. 1976); *Twelve John Does v. District of Columbia*, 855 F.2d 874 (D.C. Cir. 1988); *Morales Feliciano v. Romero Barcelo*, 497 F. Supp. 14 (D.P.R. 1979); *Barnes v. Government of the Virgin Islands*, 415 F. Supp. 1218 (D.V. 1 1976).
84. For a summary of prison litigation, see *American Civil Liberties Union (ACLU) National Prison Project (1995)*, reprinted in *Prisoners and the Law* (Ira Robbins, ed., 1996), App. B at 109.
85. See Wayne N. Welsh, *Counties in Court* (1995).
86. *Watson v. Ray*, 90 F.R.D. 143 (S.D. Iowa 1981).
87. *Johnson v. Levine*, 450 F. Supp. 648 (D. Md. 1978); *Nelson v. Collins*, 455 F. Supp. 727 (D. Md. 1978), *aff'd in part sub nom. Johnson v. Levine*, 588 F.2d 1378 (4th Cir. 1978); *Washington v. Keller*, 479 F. Supp. 569 (D. Md. 1979).
88. *American Civil Liberties Union*, *supra* note 84, at App. B 109–110.
89. See, e.g., *Walker v. Blackwell*, 411 F.2d 23 (5th Cir. 1969) (access to religious literature, even if inflammatory; communication with religious leaders); *O'Malley v. Brierly*, 477 F.2d 785 (3d Cir. 1973) (access to priest); *Barnett v. Rodger*, 410 F.2d 995 (D.C. Cir. 1969) (special diet); *Wojtazak v. Cuyler*, 480 F. Supp. 1288 (E.D. Pa. 1979) (access to religious services while in protective custody). For a summary of the doctrine as it developed during this period, see Comment, *The Religious Rights of the Incarcerated*, 125 U. Pa. L. Rev. 812 (1977).
90. E.g., *Cruz v. Beto*, 405 U.S. 319 (1972) (Buddhism); *Knuckles v. Prasse*, 435 F.2d 1255 (3d Cir. 1970) (Islam); *Northern v. Nelson*, 315 F. Supp. 687 (N.D. Cal. 1970) (Islam); *Konigsberg v. Ciccone*, 285 F. Supp. 585 (W.D. Mo. 1968), *aff'd*, 417 F.2d 161 (8th Cir. 1969) (Judaism). For cases on the limits of the principle, see *Theriault v. Carlson*, 339 F. Supp. 375 (N.D. Ga. 1972),

vacated and remanded, 495 F.2d 390 (5th Cir. 1974) (CONS); *Remmers v. Brewer,* 361 F. Supp. 537 (S.D. Iowa 1973), *aff'd,* 494 F.2d 1277 (8th Cir. 1974) (CONS); *Kennedy v. Meachan,* 382 F. Supp. 996 (D. Wyo. 1974), *vacated and remanded,* 540 F.2d 1057 (10th Cir. 1976) (Satanism).

91. *Procunier v. Martinez,* 416 U.S. 396 (1974), *overruled by Thornburgh v. Abbott,* 490 U.S. 401 (1989) (censorship of incoming and outgoing mail); *LeVier v. Woodson,* 443 F.2d 360 (10th Cir. 1971) (communication with state officials); *Nolan v. Fitzpatrick,* 451 F.2d 545 (1st Cir. 1971) (communication with news media); cf. *Main Road v. Ayteh,* 522 F.2d 1080 (3d. Cir. 1975) (prisoners do not have a general right of personal access to the media, but such access cannot be regulated on the basis of the particular content of the communication). See Note, "Mail Censorship and the First Amendment," 81 Yale L. J. 87 (1971).

92. *Lee v. Washington,* 390 U.S. 333 (1968); *McClelland v. Sigler,* 456 F.2d 1266 (8th Cir. 1972); *Board of Managers v. George,* 377 F.2d 228 (8th Cir. 1967).

93. The leading case is *Wolff v. McDonnell,* 418 U.S. 539 (1974), discussed later. Prior to *Wolff,* some of the decisions on this issue were *Howard v. Smyth,* 365 F.2d 428 (4th Cir. 1966); United States ex rel. *Campbell v. Pate,* 401 F.2d 55 (7th Cir. 1968); United States ex rel. *Miller v. Twomey,* 479 F.2d 701 (7th Cir. 1973); *Workman v. Mitchell,* 502 F.2d 1201 (9th Cir. 1974). For an assessment of the decisions during this period, see William Babcock, "Due Process in Prison Disciplinary Proceedings," 22 B.C. L. Rev. 1009 (1981); Thompson Gooding, "The Impact of Entitlement Analysis: Due Process in Correctional Administrative Hearings," 33 U. Fla. L. Rev. 151 (1981); Note, "Searching for a Liberty Interest: The Prisoner's Right to Due Process," 61 Neb. L. Rev. 382 (1982).

94. *Johnson v. Avery,* 393 U.S. 483 (1969) (jailhouse lawyers); *Bounds v. Smith,* 430 U.S. 817 (1977) (law libraries); *Wolff v. McDonnell,* 418 U.S. 539 (1974); *Wainwright v. Coonts,* 409 F.2d 1337 (5th Cir. 1969); *Sigafus v. Brown,* 416 F.2d 105 (7th Cir. 1969); *Souza v. Travisono,* 368 F. Supp. 459 (D. R.I. 1973), *aff'd,* 498 F.2d 1120 (1st Cir. 1974). See Raymond Lin, "A Prisoner's Constitutional Right to Attorney Assistance," 83 Colum. L. Rev. 1279 (1983).

95. American Civil Liberties Union, *The Rights of Prisoners* (1985); Sheldon Krantz, *The Law of Corrections and Prisoners' Rights in a Nutshell* (1988); Michael Mushlin, *Rights of Prisons* (2d ed., 1993); John Palmer, *Constitutional Rights of Prisoners* (4th ed., 1991); James Potts & Alvin Bronstein, *Prisoners' Self Help Litigation Manual* (1976); Robbins, *supra* note 84; Sheldon Krantz, *The Law of Corrections and Prisoners' Rights* (3d ed., 1986) (casebook).

96. See Robbins, *supra* note 84, App. B.

97. *Pugh v. Locke,* 406 F. Supp. 318 (M.D. Ala. 1976), *aff'd in substance sub nom. Newman v. Alabama,* 559 F.2d 283 (5th Cir. 1977), *rev'd in part and remanded sub nom. Alabama v. Pugh,* 438 U.S. 781 (1978). For descriptions of the case, see Larry Yackle, *Reform and Regret* (1989); Ira Robbins & Michael Buser, "Punitive Conditions of Prison Confinement: An Analysis of *Pugh v. Locke* and Federal Court Supervision of State Penal Administration under The Eighth Amendment," 29 Stan. L. Rev. 893 (1977).

98. See Chapter 3, (on Arkansas).
99. *Gates v. Collier*, 349 F. Supp. 881 (N.D. Miss. 1972), *aff'd*, 501 F.2d 1291 (5th Cir. 1974). See William Taylor, *Brokered Justice* (1993).
100. *Plyler v. Evatt*, C.A. No. 82-876-0 (D.S.C. January 8, 1985). See *Plyler v. Leeke*, 804 F.2d 1251 (4th Cir. 1986).
101. *Grubbs v. Bradley*, 552 F. Supp. 1052 (M.D. Tenn. 1982).
102. See Chapter 2.
103. *Guthrie v. Evans*, C.A. No. 73-3068 (S.D. Ga. 1973) (Georgia State Prison in Radsville); *Cason v. Seckinger*, No. 84-313-1-MAC (M.D. Ga. 1984). See Bradley Chilton, *Prisons under the Gavel* (1991).
104. *Williams v. Edwards*, 547 F.2d 1206 (5th Cir. 1977) (Louisiana State Prison at Angola); *Hamilton v. Morial*, 644 F.2d 351 (5th Cir. 1981).
105. *Costello v. Wainwright*, 397 F. Supp. 20 (M.D. Fla. 1975), *vacated on other grounds*, 539 F.2d 547 (5th Cir. 1976) (en banc). There have also been conditions suits against individual Florida facilities, *LaMarca v. Turner*, 995 F.2d 1526 (11th Cir. 1993). As discussed in Chapter 5 ("The Judiciary's Motivation"), however, enlightened leadership enabled Florida to avoid the more extensive judicial intervention to which its neighbor states were subjected.
106. *Small v. Martin*, No. 85-987-CRT (E.D. N.C. 1988) (most of the state prisons); *Hubert v. Ward*, No. C-E-80-414-M (W.D. N.C. 1985) (thirteen road and farm camps).
107. See *ACLU*, *supra* note 84, at App. B 109-42.
108. *Cagle v. Hutto*, No. 79-0515-R (E.D. Va. 1979) (State Prison at Powhattan); *Brown v. Hutto*, No. 81-0853-R (E.D.Va. 1985) (State Prison at Mecklenburg). See Paul Keve, *The History of Corrections in Virginia* (1986).
109. Paul Keve, *Prisons and the American Conscience: A History of U.S. Federal Corrections* (1991). See Chapter 4, on the Marion Penitentiary.
110. *Wolfish v. Levi*, 439 F. Supp. 114 (S.D. N.Y. 1977). For clarity, we use the well-known caption of the Supreme Court's decision throughout. The facility is called the Metropolitan Correctional Center.
111. *Wolfish v. Levi*, 573 F.2d 118 (2d Cir. 1978).
112. *Bell v. Wolfish*, 441 U.S. 520 (1979). See Ira Robbins, "The Cry of *Wolfish* in the Federal Courts: The Future of Federal Judicial Intervention in Prison Administration," 71 J. Crim. L. & Criminology 211 (1980).
113. William Taggart, "Redefining the Power of the Federal Judiciary: The Impact of Court-Ordered Prison Reform on State Expenditures for Corrections," 23 L. & Soc. Rev. 241 (1989).
114. For a thoughtful discussion of the extent to which federal courts should actually mandate state expenditures, see Gerald Frug, "The Judicial Power of the Purse," 126 U. Pa. L. Rev. 715 (1978).
115. E.g., *Lee v. Washington*, 390 U.S. 333 (1968); *Johnson v. Avery*, 393 U.S. 483 (1969) (rights of jailhouse lawyers); *Procunier v. Martinez*, 416 U.S. 396 (1974) (censorship of mail); *Cruz v. Beto*, 405 U.S. 319 (1972) (equal rights for minority religions).
116. 418 U.S. 539 (1974).
117. *Id.* at 555–56.

118. *Gates v. Collier*, 501 F.2d 1291, 1295 (5th Cir. 1974).
119. 418 U.S. at 556.
120. *Id.* at 558–72.
121. 397 U.S. 254 (1970).
122. *Morrissey v. Brewer*, 408 U.S. 471 (1972) (parole); *Gagnon v. Scarpelli*, 411 U.S. 778 (1973) (probation).
123. Of course, the due process rights of prisoners became an important element of the prison reform process on its own. See generally Susan Herman, "The New Liberty: The Procedural Due Process Rights of Prisoners and Others under the Burger Court," 59 N.Y.U. L. Rev. 482 (1984).
124. 429 U.S. 97 (1976). See Eric Neisser, "Is There a Doctor in the Joint? The Search for Constitutional Standards for Prison Health Care," 63 Va. L. Rev. 921 (1977).
125. 429 U.S. at 105.
126. 429 U.S. at 115.
127. *Hutto v. Finney*, 437 U.S. 678 (1978).
128. *Id.* at 680.
129. *Id.* at 689–700, 704–10.
130. *Id.* at 711.
131. Pub. L. No. 96-247 (1980), codified at 42 U.S.C. § 1997 *et seq.* (1996).
132. Thomas, *supra* note 11, at 58–59.
133. Jim Thomas, "The "Reality" of Prisoner Litigation: Repackaging the Data," 15 New Eng. J. on Crim. & Civil Confinement 27, 34 (1989). Thomas's book contains more complete data, see Thomas, *supra* note 11, at 60–61, 261–72, but we use the figures from his study because the periodization corresponds more closely to the one we use in the text.
134. Thomas, *supra* note 11, at 34.
135. 441 U.S. 520 (1979).
136. *Id.* at 525.
137. *Id.* at 562.
138. See Henry M. Hart Jr. & Albert Sacks, *The Legal Process*, 696, 1009–11 (William Estridge Jr. & Philip Frickey, eds., 1994); Lon Fuller, *The Morality of Law*, 152–85 (1964).
139. 452 U.S. 337 (1981).
140. *Chapman v. Rhodes*, 434 F. Supp. 1007 (S.D. Ohio 1977), *aff'd*, 624 F.2d 1099 (6th Cir. 1980).
141. 452 U.S. at 344–47, 353–61 (Brennan, J., concurring in the judgment).
142. *Id.* at 345.
143. *Id.* at 347. The cases were *Estelle v. Gamble*, 429 U.S. 97 (1976), which involved the provision of medical services, and *Hutto v. Finney*, 437 U.S. 678 (1978), which involved the legitimacy of a thirty-day limit on punitive isolation and an award of attorney's fees. Both prison systems, of course, were embroiled in massive totality-of-conditions litigation at the time *Rhodes* was being decided. See Chapter 3.
144. 452 U.S. at 347.
145. *Id.* at 353.

146. On Chapman's impact, see James Robertson, "When the Supreme Court Commands, Do the Lower Courts Obey? The Impact of *Rhodes* on Correctional Litigation," 7 Hamline L. Rev. 79 (1988).
147. *Thornburg v. Abbott*, 490 U.S. 401 (1989). See Megan McDonald, "*Thornburg v. Abbott*: Slamming the Prison Gates on Constitutional Rights," 17 Pepp. L. Rev. 1011 (1990).
148. *Sandin v. Connor*, 115 S. Ct. 2293 (1995).
149. *Lewis v. Casey*, 116 S. Ct. 2293 (1995).
150. *O'Lone v. Estate of Shabazz*, 482 U.S. 342 (1987). See Matthew Blischak, "*O'Lone v. Shabazz*: The State of Prisoners' Religious Free Exercise Rights," 37 Am. U. L. Rev. 453 (1988).
151. *Rufo v. Inmates of Suffolk County Jail*, 502 U.S. 367 (1992).
152. 501 U.S. 294 (1991). For commentary on this case, see Arthur Berger, "*Wilson v. Seiter*: An Unsatisfying Attempt at Resolving the Imbroglio of Eighth Amendment Prisoners' Rights Standards," 1992 Utah L. Rev. 565; Russell Gray, "*Wilson v. Seiter*: Defining The Components of and Proposing a Direction for Eighth Amendment Prison Condition Law," 41 Am. U. L. Rev. 1339 (1992).
153. 475 U.S. 312 (1986).
154. *Id.* at 320–22, 324–26. *Id.* at 323.
155. 501 U.S. at 302.
156. *Id.* The deliberate indifference standard comes from *Estelle v. Gamble*, 429 U.S. 97, 106 (1976) and, as in the *Estelle* case, the Court summarized with approval the rationale of Louisiana ex rel. *Francis v. Resweber*, 329 U.S. 459 (1947), the insufficient electricity case.
157. 501 U.S. at 310.
158. 113 S. Ct. 2475 (1993).
159. 114 S. Ct. 1970 (1994).
160. *Id.* at 1975 (quoting the court of appeals).
161. See, e.g., *Gates v. Wilson*, 39 F.3d 1439 (9th Cir. 1994); *Madrid v. Gomez*, 889 F. Supp. 1146 (N.D. Cal. 1995); *Porter v. Finney*, 857 F. Supp. 65 (D. Kan. 1994); *Glover v. Johnson,* 850 F. Supp. 592, 862 F. Supp. 180 (E.D. Mich. 1994).
162. See, e.g., *Ruffo v. Inmates of the Suffolk County Jail*, 502 U.S. 365 (1992) (modification of consent decree is appropriate when decree proves to be unworkable because of unforeseen obstacles or when enforcement of decree without modification would be detrimental to public interest).
163. 18 U.S.C. § 3626 (1995).
164. P.L. 104–134 (1996), 110 Stat. 1328–66, to be codified at 18 U.S.C. § 1326, 42 U.S.C. § 1997.
165. See Shelly Geballe & Martha Stone, "The New Focus on Medical Care Issues in Women's Prison Cases," 15 J. Nat'l Prison Project 1 (1988); Rosemary Herbert, "Women's Prisons: An Equal Protection Evaluation," 94 Yale L. J. 1182 (1985); Susan Hoffman, "On Prisoners and Parenting: Preserving the Tie That Binds," 87 Yale L. J. 1408 (1978).

3. TWO CLASSIC PRISON REFORM CASES: ARKANSAS AND TEXAS

1. The historical summary is based on: Arkansas Department of Corrections, *A Brief History of the Arkansas Department of Corrections,* (1985); James Ferguson, *A History of the Arkansas Penitentiary* (1965).
2. Ferguson, *supra* note 1, at 9.
3. This description, like much of the information about the litigation's effect on the Arkansas prisons, is based on interviews conducted by the authors at Cummins Farm on January 2, 1992, with A.L. Lockhart, commissioner of the Arkansas Department of Corrections, and with other Arkansas prison officials. For a description of Mississippi's Parchman Farm, a rather similar institution, see David Oshinsky, *Worse Than Slavery,* 135–55 (1996).
4. See *Talley v. Stephens,* 247 F. Supp. 683 (E.D. Ark. 1965); *Jackson v. Bishop,* 268 F. Supp. 804 (E.D. Ark. 1967); *Holt vs. Carver,* 300 F. Supp. 825 (E.D. Ark. 1969).
5. 247 F. Supp. 683 (E.D. Ark. 1965).
6. *Id.* at 684.
7. 268 F. Supp. 804, 806 (E.D. Ark. 1967); *vacated* 404 F.2d 571 (8th Cir. 1968).
8. *Jackson v. Bishop,* 404 F.2d 571, 580 (8th Cir. 1968).
9. *Id.*
10. 400 F.2d 1185 (8th Cir. 1969).
11. Authors' interview with Judge Eisele, Little Rock, Arkansas, January 3, 1992. (Judge Eisele was Rockefeller's campaign manager in his first race for the governorship, and later his chief of staff.)
12. For a general description, see Mary Parker, "Judicial Intervention on Correctional Institutions: The Arkansas Odyssey" (Ph.D. dissertation: Sam Houston State University, 1983).
13. Eisele interview, *supra* note 11.
14. 300 F. Supp. 825 (E.D. Ark. 1969). This suit was probably encouraged by Sarver. Lockhart Interview, *supra* note 3.
15. See Parker, *supra* note 12; authors' interview with Mary Parker, Little Rock, January 3, 1992.
16. 300 F. Supp. at 832.
17. *Arkansas Gazette,* February 21, 1970, at 8, col. 4, cited in Parker, *supra* note 12.
18. Parker, *supra* note 12, at 336.
19. 309 F. Supp. 362 (E.D. Ark. 1970).
20. Authors' interview with Jack Holt, Chief Justice, Arkansas Supreme Court, January 6, 1992.
21. *Arkansas Gazette,* February 20, 1970, p. 1, col. 1.
22. *Holt v. Sarver* (*Holt II*), 309 F. Supp. 362, 365 (E.D. Ark. 1970).
23. The figures in the footnote are found at *id.* at 373.
24. *Id.* at 381.

25. *Id.* at 381–82.
26. *Id.* at 382.
27. *Id.* at 385.
28. *Holt v. Sarver*, 442 F.2d 304 (8th Cir. 1971).
29. *Holt v. Hutto*, 363 F. Supp. 194 (E.D. Ark. 1973).
30. *Id.* at 198.
31. *Id.* at 216.
32. *Id.*
33. *Id.* at 217.
34. *Finney v. Arkansas Board of Corrections*, 505 F.2d 194, 215 (8th Cir. 1975).
35. *Id.* at 199.
36. *Id.* at 215.
37. *Finney v. Hutto*, 410 F. Supp. 257 (E.D. Ark. 1976).
38. Dudley Spiller & M. Kay Harris, *After Decision: Implementation of Judicial Decrees in Correctional Settings*, 64 (1977).
39. *Hutto v. Finney*, 437 U.S. 678 (1978).
40. Lockhart interview, *supra* note 3; Parker interview, *supra* note 15.
41. For an account of this process, see Parker, *supra* note 12.
42. Eisele interview, *supra* note 11.
43. *Finney v. Marbry*, 455 F. Supp. 756 (E.D. Ark. 1982).
44. *Id.* at 758.
45. *Id.* at 777.
46. Eisele interview, *supra* note 11.
47. Federal Rules of Civil Procedure, Rule 53 (b). David Kirp & Gary Babcock, "Judge and Company: Court-Appointed Masters, School Resegregation and Insitutional Reform," 72 Ala. L. Rev. 313 (1981); Theodore Eisenberg & Stephen Yeazell, "The Ordinary and Extraordinary in Institutional Litigation," 93 Harv. L. Rev. 465 (1980).
48. See Susan Sturm, "Mastering Intervention in Prisons," 88 Yale L. J. 1062 (1979).
49. Parker, *supra* note 12.
50. *Id.*
51. Eisele interview, *supra* note 11.
52. *Id.*
53. *Id.*
54. Lockhart interview, *supra* note 3.
55. Frank R. Kemerer, *William Wayne Justice: A Judicial Biography*, 358 (1991).
56. *Id.* at 358.
57. *Id.* at 359.
58. *Id.*
59. For an account of this process, see *id.* at 359–361.
60. *In re W. J. Estelle, Jr.*, 516 F.2d 480 (5th Cir. 1975).
61. There are several excellent descriptions of the prelitigation Texas prisons and the ensuing litigation: Ben Crouch & J. W. Marquart, *An Appeal to Justice: Litigated Reform of Texas Prisons* (1989); Steve Martin & Sheldon Ekland-Olson, *Texas Prisons: The Walls Came Tumbling Down* (1987). Another account, which has received widespread attention, is John Di-

Iulio, *Governing Prisons: A Comparative Study of Correctional Management* (1987). The authors' questions about DiIulio's interpretation appear in Malcolm Feeley & Edward Rubin, "Prison Litigation and Bureaucratic Management," 17 L. & Soc. Inquiry 125, 137–43 (1992).

62. Martin & Ekland-Olson, *supra* note 61, at 19–20.
63. *Id.* at 15–23.
64. *Id.* at 9–25; Crouch & Marquart, *supra* note 61, at 13–46.
65. Crouch & Marquart, *supra* note 61, at 35.
66. *Id.* at 40.
67. *Id.* at 42–43.
68. *Id.* at 43.
69. Author's interview with George Beto, Huntsville, Texas, May 9, 1986.
70. Martin and Ekland-Olson, *supra* note 61, at 175–77.
71. *Ruiz v. Estelle*, 503 F. Supp. 1265, 1378 (S.D. Tex. 1980).
72. *Id.* at 1381.
73. Martin and Ekland-Olson, *supra* note 61, at 176–77.
74. *Ruiz v. Estelle*, 503 F. Supp. 1265 (S.D. Tex 1980).
75. Crouch & Marquart, *supra* note 61, at 127; Martin & Ekland-Olson, *supra* note 61, at 183.
76. 452 U.S. 337 (1981).
77. *Ruiz v. Estelle* (S.D. Tex. 1981) (Memorandum Opinion, July 24).
78. Author's interview with O. L. McCotter, Huntsville, Texas, May 9, 1986; Beto interview, *supra* note 69.
79. Martin & Ekland-Olson, *supra* note 61, at 198.
80. *Id.* at 189 *Id.* at 196.
81. *Id.* at 196.
82. *Ruiz v. Estelle*, 688 F.2d 266 (1982).
83. Crouch & Marquart, *supra* note 61, at 235.
84. Crouch & Marquart, *supra* note 61, at 199.
85. *Id.* at 201.
86. *Id.* at 221.
87. Crouch & Marquart, *supra* note 61, at 149. See also McCotter interview, *supra* note 78.
88. Samuel Jan Brackel, "Mastering Legal Access Rights of Prisoners," 12 New Eng. J. of Crim. and Civ. Confine. 69 (1986).
89. The statute described in the footnote is Texas Prison Management Act, General and Specialized Laws, 68th Legislature, Regular Session (1982), codified as amended at Vernon's Texas Codes Ann. § 449 (West 1990 & Supp. 1997).
90. *Ruiz v. Estelle* (S.D. Tex. 1992) (Memorandum Opinion, December 11, 1992).
91. *Id.* at 33.
92. 502 U.S. 367 (1992).
93. 503 U.S. 467 (1992).
94. See *United States v. Swift & Co.*, 286 U.S. 106 (1932).

4. THREE VARIATIONS ON THE THEME: COLORADO STATE PENITENTIARY, THE SANTA CLARA COUNTY JAILS, AND MARION PENITENTIARY

1. Colo. Rev. Stat. §17-24-102(1) (a), (b), (c), (d) (1978).
2. Colo. Rev. Stat. §24-90-107 (1) (a) (1973).
3. *Ramos v. Lamm*, 485 F. Supp. 122, 137 (1979).
4. *Id.* at 142.
5. *Id.* at 142.
6. *Id.* at 137, 140.
7. *Id.* at 46.
8. *Id.* at 133.
9. *Id.* at 134.
10. *Id.* at 133.
11. *Id.*
12. *Id.*
13. Author's interview with Brad Rockwell, Legal Affairs Coordinator, Colorado Department of Corrections, Canon City, Colorado, June 6, 1989.
14. On the status of transitional workers, see *Ramos v. Lamm*, 485 F. Supp. at 138.
15. *Ramos v. Lamm*, 485 F. Supp. at 561.
16. 441 U.S. 520 (1979).
17. Cited in *Ramos v. Lamm* 485 F. Supp. at 129.
18. *Ramos v. Lamm* 485 F. Supp. at 133.
19. *Ramos v. Lamm*, *supra* note 3.
20. *Id.* at 140.
21. *Ramos v. Lamm*, 485 F. Supp. at 144.
22. *Id.* at 156.
23. *Id.* at 170.
24. *Id.* at 168.
25. *Ramos v. Lamm*, 713 F.2d 546 (1983).
26. The language quoted in the footnote from the dissenting opinion appears at *id.* at 560.
27. *Ramos v. Lamm*, Civil Action 77-K-1093 (N. D. Colo., August 7, 1985, at 3 (consent order).
28. *Ramos v. Lamm*, Civil Action 77-K-1093 (N. D. Colo., November 29, 1985) (Legal access plan).
29. *Ramos v. Lamm*, Civil Action 77-K-1093 (N. D. Colo., March 27, 1986) (Memorandum opinion and order).
30. *Ramos v. Lamm*, Civil Action 77-K-1093 (N. D. Colo. September 18, 1987) (Agreement and stipulation for order).
31. *Ramos v. Lamm*, Civil Action 77-K-1093, N. D. of Colo., December 8, 1987) (Order approving stipulation for closure of care).
32. For a history and analysis of jail litigation, see Wayne Welch, *Counties in Court: Jail Overcrowding and Court-Ordered Reform* (1995).

33. State Board of Correction, *State of the Jails in California* (1987) (Report no. 4 1986 Jail Profile Data Summary. Sacramento: Board of Corrections Jail Planning and Construction Div.).

34. *Batchelder v. Geary*, Civil Action No. 71-2017, N. D. Calif. March 1972) (Memorandum opinion).

35. Letter from Joseph Durant, Deputy County Counsel, to the Board of Supervisors, May 15, 1975.

36. *Fischer v. Winter*, Civil Action 79-1843, (N.D. Calif. March 25, 1980).

37. Subsequently, this suit was expanded and amended to challenge crowded conditions in the Women's Detention Facility; *Fischer v. Geary*, Civil Action No. 72-2208, (N. D. Calif. October 5, 1976). These efforts resulted in a consent decree, which required the county to add ninety-six new beds to its facility by April 1, 1984. This target was met.

38. 1978 Cal. Stat. ch 24, §23; codified in Cal. Const. § XIIIA.

39. As the sole Republican in any of the countywide elected offices, Winter was also active as his party's standard-bearer at various events.

40. The jail case was closely followed by two peninsula newspapers from the outset, the *San Jose Mercury News* and the *Times Tribune.* See articles in the *San Jose Mercury News* February 7, 1981, B1 Law & Order 11:D7–8; February 17, 1981, B1 Law & Order 11:D9; February 18, 1981, B1 Law & Order 11:D10; February 12, 1981, B1 Law & Order 11:G11–12; January 11, 1981, B1 Law & Order 12:A10.

41. Amended Petition for Writ of Habeas Corpus, Court Record, April 28, 1981.

42. *Branson v. Winter* (Sup. Ct. Cty. of Santa Clara, No. 78807).

43. *Branson v. Winter* (Sup. Ct. Cty. of Santa Clara, No. 78807) Notice of DeNovo Hearing, Memorandum of Points and Authorities in Support, Declaration Pursuant to CCP 170.6, Court Record, February 17, 1982.

44. Research assistant's interview with Judge David W. Leahy, San Jose, California, June 29, 1988.

45. Research assistant's interview with Ellen Matteucci, San Jose, California, August 10, 1988.

46. *Id.*

47. *San Jose Mercury News,* March 18, 1982.

48. *Fischer v. Geary, supra* note 37.

49. These limits and other related decisions are described in *Branson v. Winter* (Sup. Ct. Cty. of Santa Clara, No. 78807). (Settlement Agreement, Appendix A, Court Record, June 8, 1983

50. All of the major players in the case, including Judge Allen, described such actions, although of course they cast them in different lights. Research assistant's interviews with Judge Bruce Allen, San Jose, California, July 17, 1988; Matteucci interview, *supra* note 45.

51. *Branson v. Winter,* Case No. 78807, Santa Clara County, Superior Court, Order 10, Court Record, March 19, 1982.

52. Order 16C, Court Record, February 7, 1983.

53. On the elective nature of the sheriff, see Cal. Gov. Code § 24009 (West 1988 & Supp. 1997).

54. Research assistant's interview with County Executive, Sally Reed, San Jose, California, June 29, 1988.
55. *Id.*
56. *San Jose Mercury News,* December 4, 1982, B1 Law & Order 86:Fn-G1.
57. *San Jose Mercury News,* December 8, 1982, B1 Law & Order 106:Fn-G1, Sidney Hill.
58. *San Jose Mercury News,* December 1, 1983, B11 Law & Order 58.
59. Compliance Report, *Branson v. Winter,* November 2, 1983.
60. Matteucci interview, *supra* note 45.
61. *Branson v. Winter,*(Sup. Ct. Cty. of Santa Clara, No. 78807) (Settlement Agreement, June 8, 1983).
62. Author's Interview with Steven Woodside, Deputy County Counsel, San Jose, California, June 29, 1988.
63. Author's interview with Thomas Lonergan, San Jose, California, September 12, 1989.
64. *Branson v. Winter,* (Sup. Ct. Cty. of Santa Clara, No. 78807) (Compliance Report Nov. 2, 1983).
65. *Branson v. Winter* (Sup. Ct. Cty. of Santa Clara, No. 78809) (Order of Reference, Nov. 2, 1983). Order of Reference, Court Record, November 2, 1983.
66. Author's interview with Judge Eugene Premo, San Jose, California, June 29, 1988.
67. Lonergan interview, *supra* note 63.
68. *Branson v. Winter* (Sup. Ct. Cty. of Santa Clara, No. 78809) (County Plan for Special Confinement Cells, Nov. 4, 1983).
69. *San Jose Mercury News,* January 5, 1984, B4 Law & Order 12:D8–9.
70. *Branson v. Winter* (Sup. Ct. Cty. of Santa Clara, No. 78809) (Memo. Opinion and Order, Dec. 20, 1985).
71. *Id.,* (Order for Contempt, March 16, 1987).
72. *Id.* (Stipulation and Order, April 27, 1987).
73. Author's Interview with Judge Spurgeon Avakian, San Jose, California, June 28, 1988.
74. *Wilson et al. v. Santa Clara County Superior Court,* Ct. of App., Sixth App. Dist., No. H 002840 (September 17, 1987).
75. Lonergan interview, *supra* note 63.
76. Comprehensive Plan for Inmate Population Management, November 1988, Santa Clara County Department of Corrections, at 1–3.
77. Reed interview, *supra* note 54.
78. *Federal Bureau of Prisons: Facilities,* 4 (1991).
79. *Id.*
80. *Bruscino v. Carlson,* 854 F.2d 162, 164 (7th Cir. 1988); Michael Dorman, "The Toughest Prison in America," *Newsday,* March 31, 1985 63; Fay Bowker & Glenn Good, "From Alcatraz to Marion to Florence: Control Unit Prisons in the United States," in *Cages of Steel,* 134–37 (W. Churchill & J. J. Vander Wall, eds., 1992). *Cages of Steel* is a collection of essays written by self-declared political and prisoners' rights activists. It is one-sided, but so are many other sources in this field, and it contains much useful information.

81. A detainer is a warrant filed by one jurisdiction against a person in the custody of another jurisdiction for the purpose of obtaining control over that person once the custodial jurisdiction has released him. Leslie Abramson, *Criminal Detainers* (1979).

82. James A. Johnston, *Alcatraz: Island Prison*, 12–24 (1949); Paul Keve, *Prisons and the American Conscience*, 173–80 (1991). Johnston was the first warden of Alcatraz.

83. Joseph Conrad, *Victory*, 1 (1914).

84. Johnston, *supra* note 82, at 25–88. Stroud kept birds at Leavenworth, where he had been previously incarcerated. The impression that he kept birds at Alcatraz is largely the result of one motion picture, *The Birdman of Alcatraz* (Hecht/United Artists, 1962) in which Burt Lancaster played Stroud.

85. See Keve, *supra* note 82, at 176.

86. *Escape from Alcatraz* (Paramount, 1979).

87. David Ward & Allen Breed, "The United States Penitentiary, Marion, Illinois: A Report to the Judiciary Committee, U.S. House of Representatives," reprinted in *Marion Penitentiary, Oversight Hearing before the Subcommittee on Courts, Civil Liberties, and the Administration of Justice of the Committee on the Judiciary*, House of Representatives, 99th Cong., 1st Sess., 1985, at 9. This report was commissioned by Congress as part of its oversight process.

88. Paul Keve reports, based on information from Myrl Alexander, director of the Bureau of Prisons from 1964 to 1970, that Marion had always been intended to serve as a successor to Alcatraz. None of the Alcatraz inmates was transferred to Marion at the time it opened, however. Keve, *supra* note 82, at 187.

89. Dowker & Good, *supra* note 80, at 132–33; Jessica Mitford, *Kind and Usual Punishment: The Prison Business*, 134–35 (1973). This program was called Control and Rehabilitation Effort, which gave it the reassuring acronym CARE.

90. Ward & Breed, *supra* note 87, at 10–11.

91. Keve, *supra* note 82, at 193–94; Ward & Breed, *supra* note 87, at.

92. Author's interview with Gary Henman, Warden, Marion Penitentiary, May, 1991.

93. Timothy Flanagan, "Prison Labor and Industry," in *The American Prison: Issues in Policy and Research* 135, 146–47 (L. Goodstein and D. MacKenzie, eds., 1989). The General Accounting Office reported that 60% of employed federal prisoners were working in jobs that provided services to their own institution. U.S. General Accounting Office, *Improved Prison Work Programs Will Benefit Correctional Institutions and Inmates* (1982).

94. Ward & Breed, *supra* note 87, at 1–13; Bill Dunne, "The U.S. Prison at Marion: An Instrument of Oppression," in *Cages of Steel, supra* note 199, at 40–44. Dunne, formerly a prisoner at Marion, writes with acknowledged anger, but his account often agrees with Ward & Breed.

95. Dunne, *supra* note 94, at 44–47; Victor Gonzales, "The New Alcatraz,"

Chicago, February 1986, 121, reprinted in *Oversight Hearing, supra* note 87, at 685.

96. *Abel v. Miller,* No. 80–2848 (7th Cir., May 18, 1982), reprinted in *Oversight Hearing, supra* note 87, at 516–27.

97. *Bono v. Saxbe,* 450 F. Supp. 934 (E.D. Ill. 1978).

98. On prison gangs generally, see United States Department of Justice, *Prison Gangs: Their Extent, Nature and Impact on Prisons* (1985) (George Camp, principal investigator).

99. A detailed portrait of Silverstein, based on personal interviews, can be found in Pete Earley, *The Hot House: Life Inside Leavenworth Prison* (1992). Earley reports that, unlike several leading Nazis, Silverstein is not even part-Jewish; the surname comes from Thomas's stepfather.

100. *Id.* at 229–30; *U.S. v. Silverstein,* 732 F.2d 1338 (7th Cir. 1984).

101. Earley, *supra* note 99, at 230–32.

102. *Id.* at 232–39; *U.S. v. Fountain,* 768 F.2d 790 (7th Cir. 1985); *Bruscino v. Carlson,* No. CV 84-4320 (S.D. Ill., August 15, 1985), *adopted,* 654 F. Supp. 609 (S.D. Ill. 1987), reprinted in *Oversight Hearing, supra* note 87, at 350–515; Dorman, *supra* note 80, at 361; Keve, *supra* note 82, at 194–95; Ward & Breed, *supra* note 87, at 14. According to Dunne, *supra* note 94, at 48–52, Fountain was not engaged in a murder competition with Silverstein but, like Silverstein, had developed a personal antagonism toward the guard he ultimately killed.

103. *Bruscino v. Carlson,* No. CV 84-4320, *supra* note 102, at 362; Dunne, *supra* note 80, at 52; Ward & Breed, *supra* note 87, at 14–15.

104. *Bruscino v. Carlson,* No. CV 84-4320, *supra* note 102, at 364–71; Keve, *supra* note 82, at 194–95, 198; Ward & Breed, *supra* note 87, at 15–19.

105. Keve, *supra* note 82, at 197; Ward & Breed, *supra* note 87, at 19, 42–46 (reprinting text of Warden's memoranda on B-Unit operations); Henman interview, *supra* note 92.

106. *Bruscino v. Carlson,* 654 F. Supp. 609, 612 (S.D. Ill. 1987).

107. *Bono v. Saxbe,* 450 F. Supp. 934 (E.D. Ill. 1978).

108. *Bono v. Saxbe,* 462 F. Supp. 146 (E.D. Ill. 1978).

109. *Bono v. Saxbe,* 620 F.2d 609, 614 (7th Cir. 1980).

110. *Id.* at 615, 617. This drew a dissent from one judge, who stated, "I do not consider the mere difference in wattage to raise a constitutional question requiring judicial intervention." *Id.* at 619.

111. *Bono v. Saxbe,* 527 F. Supp. 1182 (S.D. Ill. 1980).

112. *Bono v. Saxbe,* 527 F. Supp. 1187 (S.D. Ill. 1981).

113. *Abel v. Miller,* No. 80–2448 (7th Cir., May 18, 1982), reprinted in *Oversight Hearing, supra* note 87, 516–24.

114. *Abel v. Miller,* No. 82–5280 (S.D. Ill., June 19, 1985), reprinted in *Oversight Hearing, supra* note 87, 525–37.

115. *Garza v. Miller,* 688 F.2d 480 (7th Cir. 1982).

116. *Id.* at 487.

117. *Bruscino v. Carlson,* No. CV 84–4320 (S.D. Ill., August 15, 1985), *supra* note 102.

118. *Id.* at 372–73.
119. *Id.* at 376. For the contrary view, see Dunne, *supra* note 94, 52–57.
120. *Bruscino v. Carlson, supra* note 102, at 478.
121. *Id.* at 479.
122. 28 U.S.C. §636(b)(1) (1992). This is the procedure by which the magistrate is designated by the judge, rather than by consent of the parties.
123. *Bruscino v. Carlson,* 654 F. Supp. 609, 612 (S.D. Ill. 1987); see *Bono v. Saxbe,* 527 F. Supp. 1182, 1185–86 (S.D. Ill. 1980).
124. *Bruscino v. Carlson,* 854 F.2d 162 (7th Cir. 1988).
125. *Campbell v. Miller,* 787 F.2d 217 (7th Cir. 1986). James Foreman was the trial judge in this case as well.
126. *Miller v. Henman,* 804 F.2d 421 (7th Cir. 1986). The case was also tried by Magistrate Meyers.
127. Pursuant to 28 U.S.C. § 636(c) (1992), the judgment in a trial conducted by a magistrate designated through the consent of the parties may be appealed directly to the U.S. Court of Appeals.
128. *Caldwell v. Miller,* 790 F.2d 589 (7th Cir. 1986).
129. *Id.* at 599.
130. *Oversight Hearings, supra* note 87, at 334–49. For example, "It is the have-nots who populate the prisons. . . . The message is that crime is caused by bad individuals. . . . Our attention is turned away from the real causes of crime. Instead we are encouraged to blame the individual and since most of the blaming is directed toward Black people, this leads to the criminalizing of an entire people. . . . Political prisoners like George Jackson spoke very clearly to the role that prisons played in the government's effort to contain and destroy Black people's freedom struggle" (342–43). More recent views of the Marion Prisoners' Rights Project, later renamed the Committee to End the Marion Lockdown, can be found in their publication Walkin' Steel (1992 to present).
131. *Bruscino v Carlson,* No. CV 84-4320, *supra* note 118, at 453, 457–58, 462, 464–65.
132. *Bruscino v. Carlson,* 654 F. Supp. 609, 612 (S.D. Ill. 1987); author's interviews with Warden Gary Henman, Legal Advisor Van Vandiver, and Paralegal Randy Davis, Marion, Illinois, May 1991. The previous warden, Jerry Williford, and Bureau Director Norman Carlson, took the same position regarding congressional investigation. See *Oversight Hearings, supra* note 87, at 163–64.
133. Author's interview with Van Vandiver.
134. *Bruscino v. Carlson,* No. CV 84–4320, *supra* note 102, at 465.
135. *Caldwell v. Miller,* 790 F.2d 589, 597–99 (7th Cir. 1986).
136. *U.S. v. Fountain,* 768 F.2d 790 (7th Cir. 1985); *U.S. v. Silverstein,* 732 F.2d 1338 (7th Cir. 1984). See *id* at 1342–43 (Posner's rational actor analysis of a psychopathic killer); Earley, *supra* note 99, at 121–24 (Atlanta Penitentiary incident).
137. *Bruscino v. Carlson,* No. CV 84–4320, *supra* note 102, at 476.
138. *Id.* at 467.
139. *Id.* at 366.

140. Henman interview, *supra* note 132. According to Henman, Marion can be viewed "as a fresh start, as well as the end of the line."
141. *Bruscino v. Carlson*, No. CV 84-4340, *supra* note 102; *Bruscino v. Carlson*, 854 F. 2d 162, 167–68 (7th Cir. 1988); Ward & Breed, *supra* note 87.
142. Author's interview with Howard Eisenberg, currently dean, University of Arkansas at Little Rock School of Law.
143. Dowker & Good, *supra* note 80.
144. *Id.* The Marianna unit will replace a women's control unit at Lexington, Kentucky, Federal Correctional Institution, which is now closed. This unit survived a constitutional challenge to its conditions of confinement, but the court did hold that transferring two women to this unit because of their political views violated their first amendment rights. *Baraldini v. Meese*, 691 F. Supp. 432 (D.D.C. 1988).
145. Dowker & Good, *supra* note 80; Fay Dowker & Glenn Good, "The Proliferation of Control Unit Prisons in the United States," J. Prisoners on Prisons (1993).
146. *Madrid v. Gomez*, No. C90-3094 – TEH (N.D. Cal., January 1, 1995).
147. American Friends Service Committee, "The Lessons of Marion" (1985), reprinted in *Oversight Hearings*, *supra* note 87, at 172–215; *The Human Rights Watch Global Report on Prisons*, 247 (1993).

5. DEFINING THE PROBLEM, IDENTIFYING THE GOAL, AND REJECTING THE PRINCIPLE OF FEDERALISM

1. *Gregory v. Ashcroft*, 501 U.S. 452 (1991) (invoking federalism concerns to interpret Age Discrimination in Employment Act as inapplicable to state court judges).
2. *United States v. Lopez*, 115 S. Ct. 1624 (1995) (invalidating Gun-Free School Zones Act of 1990 as exceeding Congress's power under the Commerce Clause).
3. Specifically any habeas corpus case, even one asserting that one's trial was unfair, is brought against the person holding the petitioner in custody, that is, the prison warden. See Chapter 3, on Arkansas.
4. *Holt v. Sarver*, 309 F. Supp. 362, 381–82 (E.D. Ark. 1970).
5. E.g., *Sweeney v. Woodall*, 344 U.S. 86 (1952); *Ex parte Pickens*, 101 F. Supp. 285 (D.C. Alaska 1951).
6. See Blake McKelvey, *American Prisons: A Study of American Social History Prior to 1915* ([1936] 1972); David Rothman *The Discovery of the Asylum*, 79–108 (rev. ed., 1990).
7. John DiIulio, *No Escape*, 104 (1991); Raymond Hawkins & Geoffrey Alpert, *American Prison Systems*, 183–229 (1989); McKelvey, *supra* note 6, at 299–321; Rothman, *supra* note 6, at 107–8.
8. David Rothman, *Conscience and Convenience: The Asylum and Its Alternatives in Progressive America*, 117–58 (1980).
9. DiIulio, *supra* note 7, at 126–47 (Patuxent experiment); Hawkins & Alpert,

supra note 7, at 413–16; Helen Blatte, "State Prisons and the Use of Behavior Control," 4 Hastings Center Rep. 11 (September, 1974); Norman Carlson, "Behavior Modification in the Federal Bureau of Prisons," 1 New Eng. J. Prison L. 155 (1974) (token economy); Michael Milan & John McKee, "The Cellblock Token Economy: Token Reinforcement Procedures in a Maximum Security Correctional Institution for Adult Male Felons," 9 J. Applied Behav. Analysis 253 (1976); William Gaylin & H. Blatte, "Behavior Modification in Prisons," 13 Am. Crim. L. Rev. 11 (1975); Roger Wolfe & Dominic R. Marino, "A Program of Behavioral Treatment for Incarcerated Pedophiles," 13 Am. J. Crim. L. 69 (1975) (Connecticut Correctional Institution experiment); "Hearings on Behavior Modification Programs in the Bureau of Prisons before the Subcommittee on Courts, Civil Liberties and the Administration of Justice of the House Committee on the Judiciary," 93d Cong. 2d Sess. 46–55 (1974) (START Program, using Tier system).

10. Ben Crouch & James Marquart, *An Appeal to Justice*, 15–16 (1989); Steven J. Martin & Sheldon Ekland-Olson, *Texas Prisons: The Walls Came Tumbling Down*, 5 (1987); Mark Carleton, *The Politics of Punishment*, 4 (1971); David Oshinsky, *Worse Than Slavery* (1996); William Taylor, *Brokered Justice*, xii, 77 (1993).

11. Edward Ayers, *The Promise of the New South: Life after Reconstruction*, 92–95, 195–202 (1992); Eric Foner, *Reconstruction: America's Unfinished Revolution, 1863–1877*, 405–9 (1988); Ronald Davis, *Good and Faithful Labor: From Slavery to Sharecropping in the Natchez District, 1860–1890* (1982); Lawrence Goodwyn, *The Populist Movement*, 20–27 (1978); Roger Ransom & Richard Sutch, *One Kind of Freedom: The Economic Consequences of Emancipation*, 120–64 (1977); Gavin Wright, *Old South, New South: Revolutions in the Southern Economy since the Civil War*, 64–98 (1986).

12. Goodwyn, *supra* note 11, at 23; Oshinsky, *supra* note 10, at 116–19.

13. Carleton, *supra* note 10, at 8–11 (Louisiana); Thorsten Sellin, *Slavery and the Penal System*, 138–41 (1976); Taylor, *supra* note 10, at 12–30 (Mississippi). This was also true of Arkansas, as discussed in Chapter 3. It was not true of Texas, however. Martin & Ekland-Olson, *supra* note 10, at 5.

14. Carleton, *supra* note 10, at 13; Sellin, *supra* note 13, at 134–38.

15. Edward Ayers, *Vengeance and Justice*, 34–72 (1984); Ayers, *supra* note 11, at 154–55; Carleton, *supra* note 10, at 16–573; Tessa Gorman, Note, "Back on the Chain Gang: Why the Eighth Amendment and the History of Slavery Proscribe the Resurgence of Chain Gangs," 85 Calif. L. Rev. 441, 448–52 (1997); Paul Keve, *The History of Corrections in Virginia*, 72–87 (1986); McKelvey, *supra* note 6, at 197–216; Sellin, *supra* note 13, at 145–62; Taylor, *supra* note 10, at 31–54; Larry Yackle, *Reform and Regret: The Story of Federal Judicial Involvement in the Alabama Prison System*, 9–10 (1989).

16. Carleton, *supra* note 10, at 45.

17. *Ruffin v. Commonwealth*, 62 Va. 720, 790 (1871).

18. U.S. Constitution, Amendment XIII ("Neither slavery nor involuntary servitude, except as a punishment for a crime whereof the party shall have been duly convicted, shall exist in the United States. . . .").

19. Bradley Chilton, *Prisons under the Gavel*, 17–19 (1991); Crouch & Marquart,

supra note 10, at 21–24; Carleton, *supra* note 10, at 137; Martin & Ekland-Olson, *supra* note 10, at 5–23; Yackle, *supra* note 15, at 9–10.

20. See, e.g., Carleton, *supra* note 10, at 137–40; Chilton, *supra* note 19, at 15–17; Crouch & Marquart, *supra* note 10, at 21–24, 69–74; Oshinsky, *supra* note 10, at 144–49; Taylor, *supra* note 10, at 55–76. Georgia, Louisiana, and Texas prisoners all resorted to self-mutilation to escape from the demands of the work schedule.

21. For a riveting first person account of this regime, see Albert Sample, *Racehoss: Big Emma's Boy* (1984).

22. See, e.g., Carleton, *supra* note 10, at 139–44, 181; Crouch & Marquart, *supra* note 10, at 35, 44; Taylor, *supra* note 10, at 112–15, 162–63; Yackle, *supra* note 15, at 10–11.

23. See, e.g., *Holt v. Sarver*, 300 F. Supp. 825 (E.D. Ark. 1969), *aff'd*, 442 F.2d 304 (8th Cir. 1971); Taylor, *supra* note 10, at 183–92; *Gates v. Collier*, F. Supp. 881 (N.D. Miss. 1972), *aff'd*, 501 F.2d 1291 (5th Cir. 1974); Carleton, *supra* note 10, at 135–66; Martin & Ekland-Olson, *supra* note 10, at 9–23; Yackle, *supra* note 15, at 11–13.

24. See, e.g., Eugene Genovese, *Roll, Jordon, Roll: The World the Slaves Made*, 285–324 (1972); Kenneth Stampp, *The Peculiar Institution: Slavery in the Ante-Bellum South*, 34–85 (1956). Cf. Richard Fogel & Stanley Engerman, *Time on the Cross: The Economics of American Negro Slavery*, 107–57 (1974).

25. See, e.g. Carleton, *supra* note 10, at 92–93; Crouch & Marquart, *supra* note 10, at 15; McKelvey, *supra* note 6, at 214.

26. Oshinsky, *supra* note 10, at 139; interview with Ronald Dobbs, Warden, Tucker Unit, Arkansas Department of Corrections, Little Rock, January 3, 1991; interview with James H. Bird, Public Relations Officer, Texas Department of Corrections, Huntsville, Texas, May 9, 1986; Taylor, *supra* note 10, at 85.

27. See Dobbs Interview, *supra* note 26; Bird interview, *supra* note 26; Carleton, *supra* note 10, at 144–45; Taylor, *supra* note 10, at 90.

28. See Genovese, *supra* note 24, at 327–65; Stampp, *supra* note 24, at 59; Austin Steward, *Twenty-two Years a Slave and Forty Years as a Free Man*, 17–21 (1867).

29. Crouch & Marquart, *supra* note 10, at 85–116; John DiIulio, *Governing Prisons*, 206–12 (1987); Oshinsky, *supra* note 10, at 140–41; Taylor, *supra* note 10, at 90–92, 139–42. In *Holt v. Sarver*, 309 F. Supp. 362, 373 (E.D. Ark. 1970), the Court stated that the "trusties run the prison. They not only guard other inmates; they also perform many administrative tasks normally performed by free world people, and their authority over other convicts of lesser rank is great."

30. Genovese, *supra* note 24, at 10–22, 356–88; Stampp, *supra* note 24, at 40–44; William Van Deburg, *The Slave Drivers* (1979).

31. Quoted in Stampp, *supra* note 24, at 40–41.

32. Frederick Law Olmsted, *A Journey in the Seaboard Slave States*, 436–37 (1856).

33. Genovese, *supra* note 24, at 370–71; Van Deburg, *supra* note 30, at 15.

34. Genovese, *supra* note 24, at 374–81; Stampp, *supra* note 24, at 151–53; Van

Deburg, *supra* note 30, at 14. Genovese argues that black drivers betrayed their compatriots much less often than has been assumed. He leaves no doubt, however, that they were expected to play this role.

35. Sellin, *supra* note 13, at 136–38; see also James Oakes, *The Ruling Race*, 159 (1982).

36. Genovese, *supra* note 24, at 63–67, 307–8; Oakes, *supra* note 35, at 159–60; Stampp, *supra* note 24, at 171–77. The personal narratives of those subjected to slavery confirm this. See, e.g., Frederick Douglas, *Narrative of the Life of Frederick Douglas: An American Slave* (1845); Solomon Northup, *Twelve Years a Slave* (1853); Steward, *supra* note 28.

37. As Frederick Douglas says: "It would astonish one, unaccustomed to a slaveholding life, to see with what wonderful ease a slaveholder can find things, of which to make occasion to whip a slave." Douglas, *supra* note 36, reprinted in *The Classic Slave Narratives*, 302 (H. Gates ed., 1987).

38. Olmsted, *supra* note 32, at 47.

39. DiIulio, *supra* note 29, at 100. See Oshinsky, *supra* note 10, at 149–51.

40. Regarding Vardaman's hunting practices, see Oshinsky, *supra* note 10, at 100; Taylor, *supra* note 10, at 74–75.

41. Olmsted, *supra* note 32, at 160–561; Stampp, *supra* note 24, at 189–590.

42. Frederick Law Olmsted, *A Journey in the Back Country*, 214–15 (1856).

43. Bird interview, *supra* note 26.

44. Ayers, *supra* note 11; McKelvey, *supra* note 6; Rothman, *supra* note 6; Rothman, *supra* note 8.

45. McKelvey, *supra* note 6.

46. In addition to the Arkansas and Texas litigation, see, e.g., *Williams v. Edwards*, 547 F.2d 1206 (5th Cir. 1977) (Louisiana); *Gates v. Collier*, 349 F. Supp. 881 (N.D. Miss. 1972), *aff'd*, 501 F.2d 1291 (5th Cir. 1974); *Pugh v. Locke*, 406 F. Supp. 318 (M.D. Ala. 1976), *aff'd as modified sub nom. Newman v. Alabama*, 559 F.2d 283 (5th Cir. 1979), *reversed in part on other grounds*, 438 U.S. 781 (1978).

47. See, e.g., *Talley v. Stephens*, 247 F. Supp. 683, 687 (E.D. Ark. 1965); *Holt v. Sarver*, 300 F. Supp. 825, 829 (E.D. Ark. 1969); *Ruiz v. Estelle*, 503 F. Supp. 1265, 1301 n. 76 (S.D. Tex. 1980) (inmates beaten when they refused to work).

48. See, e.g., *Ruiz v. Estelle*, 679 F.2d 1115, 1140–42, 1149–50 (5th Cir. 1982); *Williams v. Edwards*, 547 F.2d 1206 (5th Cir. 1977); *Newman v. Alabama*, 503 F.2d 1320 (5th Cir. 1974); *Campbell v. Beto*, 460 F.2d 765, 768 (5th Cir. 1972); *Gates v. Collier*, 501 F.2d 1291, 1300–4 (5th Cir. 1974); *Pugh v. Locke*, 406 F. Supp. 318, 322–24 (M.D. Ala. 1976).

49. See, e.g., *Williams v. Edwards*, 547 F.2d 1206, 1208–9 (5th Cir. 1977); *Gates v. Collier*, 501 F.2d 1291, 1306–8 (5th Cir. 1974) *Ruiz v. Estelle*, 503 F. Supp. 1265, 1288–98 (S.D. Tex. 1980).

50. See, e.g., *Talley v. Stephens*, 247 F. Supp. 683, 687–90 (E.D. Ark. 1965); *Ruiz v. Estelle*, 503 F. Supp. 1265, 1299–1303 (S.D. Tex. 1980).

51. See, e.g., *Tillery v. Owens*, 907 F.2d 418 (3d Cir. 1990), *cert. denied*, 112 S. Ct. 243 (1991) (double celling at State Correctional Institution at Pitts-

burgh was cruel and unusual punishment when considered in light of the totality of conditions prevailing in the prison); *Ramos v. Lamm*, 639 F.2d 559 (10th Cir. 1980), *cert. denied*, 450 U.S. 1046 (1981) (Colorado maximum security prison violates constitutional standards, but district court order closing facility is vacated in light of state's ongoing efforts); *Todaro v. Ward*, 565 F.2d 48 (2d Cir. 1977) (medical care at New York women's prison violates constitutional standards); *Stewart v. Rhodes*, 473 F. Supp. 1185 (E.D. Ohio 1979), *aff'd*, 785 F.2d 210 (6th Cir. 1986) (preliminary injunction prohibiting Ohio prison from segregating prisoners by race and from using body restraints).

52. Ayers, *supra* note 11; Foner, *supra* note 11, at 405–10; Eric Foner, *Nothing but Freedom: Emancipation and Its Legacy* (1983); Gerald Jaynes, *Branches without Roots* (1986); Leon Litwack, *Been in the Storm So Long*, 336–449 (1978); John Mandle, *Not Slave, Not Free* (1992); Edgar Tristam Thompson, *Plantation Society, Race Relations in the South* (1975); Michael Wayne, *The Reshaping of Plantation Society: The Natchez District, 1869–1880* (1983); Wright, *supra* note 11.

53. 347 U.S. 483 (1954).

54. See John Giglio, *The Presidency of John F. Kennedy*, 159–87 (1991). Kennedy's level of commitment was a disappointment to many civil rights leaders, *id*; Victor Navask, *Kennedy Justice* (1971), but the mere fact that these leaders had the expectations that they did suggests that the presidency had come to be regarded as a source of support for the civil rights struggle.

55. Pub. L. 88–352, 78 Stat. 241 (1964) (codified in scattered sections of 42 U.S.C.). On the relative effectiveness of congressional action in this area, see Gerald Rosenberg, *The Hollow Hope: Can Courts Bring About Social Change?* (1991).

56. 367 U.S. 643 (1961).

57. 370 U.S. 660 (1960).

58. 365 U.S. 167 (1961).

59. 347 U.S. at 495.

60. *Holt v. Sarver* (*Holt II*), 309 F. Supp. 362, 381 (E.D. Ark. 1970).

61. David Garland, *Punishment and Modern Society*, 216–225 (1990); Pieter Spierenburg, *The Spectacle of Suffering* (1984). See Norbert Elias, *The Civilizing Process*, vol. 1, *The History of Manners*; vol. 2, *State Formation and Civilization* (1994).

62. See Elias, *supra* note 61, at 447–54.

63. Philip Bobbitt, *Constitutional Fate: Theory of the Constitution* (1982).

64. Ronald Dworkin, *Taking Rights Seriously* (1978); Ronald Dworkin, *Law's Empire* (1988); Ronald Dworkin, The Forum of Principle," 56 N.Y.U. L. Rev. 462 (1981).

65. Owen Fiss, "Foreword: The Forms of Justice," 93 Harv. L. Rev. 1 (1979); Owen Fiss, "Against Settlement," 93 Yale L. J. 1073 (1984); Owen Fiss, "The Death of Law?" 72 Cornell L. Rev. 1 (1986).

66. Michael Perry, *The Constitution, the Courts and Human Rights* (1982).

67. See, e.g., *Bounds v. Smith*, 430 U.S. 817, 820 (1973); *Battle v. Anderson*, 447

F. Supp. 516 (E.D. Okla. 1977); *Gates v. Collier,* 349 F. Supp. 881, 897 (N.D. Miss. 1972); *Landman v. Royster,* 333 F. Supp. 621, 647 (E.D. Va. 1971).

68. See, e.g., *Ruiz v. Estelle,* 503 F. Supp. 1265, 1307 n. 84, 1311 n. 93 (S.D. Tex. 1980); *Holt v. Sarver,* 309 F. Supp. 362, 365 (1970).

69. For a brief account of the founding of the NPA, see McKelvey, *supra,* note 6.

70. American Correctional Association, Manual of Correctional Standards, 6–10 (1959).

71. McKelvey, *supra* note 6, at 172–89.

72. American Correctional Association, *Manual of Correctional Standards* (1946).

73. American Correctional Association, *supra* note 7. The association now publishes a variety of volumes on different aspects of corrections. For the most recent version of its principal volume, see American Correctional Association, Standards for Adult Correctional Institutions (3d ed., 1990). See generally, Dale Sechrest, "Adopting National Standards for Correctional Reform," 46 Fed. Probation, No. 2, at 18 (1982).

74. *Id.* at 129, 129–31.

75. *Id.* at 137–40.

76. See Malcolm M. Feeley, "Federal Courts in the Political Process," in *Courts in the Political Process: Jack W. Peltason's Contribution to Political Science* (Austin Ranney ed., 1996).

77. American Correctional Association, *supra* note 71, 1–16.

78. E.g., James V. Bennett, Retired Director, federal Bureau of Prisons; Austin H. McCormick, Executive Director of the Osborne Association. Chapters 11–24 of the *Manual of Standards* are entitled, respectively, "The Physical Plant," "Custody, Security and Control," "Discipline," "Health and Mental Services," "Food Services," "Classification," "Counseling, Casework, and Clinical Services," "Education," "Recreation," "Library Services," "The Religious Program," and "Institutional Employment." Almost all of these issues, and roughly in this order, were addressed, in Judge Henley's opinion in *Holt v. Sarver.*

79. Paul Keve, *Prisons and the American Conscience,* 36–112 (1991); Todd Clear & George Cole, *American Corrections,* 140–47 (1986); McKelvey, *supra* note 6, at 290–321.

80. Keve, *supra* note 79, at 91–112.

81. See Clear & Cole, *supra* note 79, at 535; Pete Earley, *The Hot House: Life Inside Leavenworth Prison,* 55–57 (1992); Keve, *supra* note 79, at 155–72, 214–44.

82. *Jackson v. Bishop,* 268 F. Supp. 813–94 (E.D. Ark. 1967).

83. Deborah Stone, *Policy Paradox and Political Reason* (1988).

84. Carleton, *supra* note 10, at 151–79.

85. For a brief discussion of Florida as a Southern "exception," see Malcolm M. Feeley, "The Significance of Prison Conditions Cases: Budgets and Prisons," 23 L. and Soc. Rev. 273 (1989).

86. *Id.* at 279.

87. Carleton, *supra* note 10, at 179–88.

88. *Williams v. Edwards,* 547 F.2d 1206, 1208 (5th Cir. 1977) (quoting district court opinion).
89. *Id.* at 1219. The court of appeals remanded with instructions that the district court should take further action on overcrowding.
90. *Id.* at 1209.
91. E.g., *Pell v. Procunier,* 417 U.S. 817 (1974); *Wolff v. McDonnell,* 418 U.S. 539 (1974); *Meachum v. Fano,* 427 U.S. 215 (1976); *Jones v. North Carolina Prisoners' Labor Union,* 433 U.S. 119 (1977); *Rhodes v. Chapman,* 452 U.S. 337 (1981); *Hewitt v. Helms,* 459 U.S. 460 (1983); *Olim v. Wakinekona,* 461 U.S. 238 (1983). This tendency continues to the present, although with somewhat more extensive retrenchments, e.g., *Kentucky Department of Corrections v. Thompson,* 490 U.S. 454 (1989); *Washington v. Harper,* 494 U.S. 210 (1990); *Wilson v. Seuter,* 501 U.S. 294 (1991). On the divisions within the Court on this issue, see David Rudenstine, "Judicially Ordered Social Reform: Neofederalism and Neonationalism and the Debate over Political Structure," 59 S. Cal. L. Rev. 451 (1986).
92. E.g., *Procunier v. Martinez,* 416 U.S. 396 (1974); *Estelle v. Gamble,* 429 U.S. 97 (1976); *Bounds v. Smith,* 430 U.S. 817 (1977); *Hutto v. Finney,* 437 U.S. 678 (1978); *Vitek v. Jones,* 445 U.S. 480 (1980). This tendency continues as well, e.g., *Hudson v. McMillan,* 503 U.S. 1 (1992); *Helling v. McKinney,* 113 S. Ct. 2475 (1993); *Farmer v. Brennan,* 62 U.S.L.W. 4446 (June 6, 1994).
93. *Wolff v. McDonnell,* 418 U.S. 539, 555–60 (1974).
94. Law Enforcement Assistance Administration Act, Pub. L. No. 89–197, 79 Stat. 828 (1965); Civil Rights of Institutionalized Persons Act, Pub. L. No. 96–247, 94 Stat. 349 (1980), codified at 42 U.S.C. §§ 1997a–1997j.
95. See American Civil Liberties Union National Prison Project, reprinted in *Prisoners and the Law* (Ira Robbins, ed., 1996), App. B.
96. 441 U.S. 520 (1979).
97. 490 U.S. 401 (1989), overruling *Procunier v. Martinez,* 416 U.S. 396 (1974).
98. Seth Kreimer, "Allocational Sanctions: The Problem of Negative Rights in a Positive State," 132 U. Pa. L. Rev. 1294 (1984).
99. Samuel Beer, *To Make a Nation,* 20–25 (1993); Malcolm M. Feeley & Edward Rubin, "Federal-State Relations and Prison Administration," in *Power Divided,* 63, 63–64 (H. Scheiber & M. Feeley, eds., 1989); Kim Scheppele, "The Ethics of Federalism," in *Power Divided, supra,* 51, 52; Seth Kreimer, "The Law of Choice and the Choice of Law: Abortion, the Right to Travel, and Extraterrestial Regulation in American Federalism," 67 N.Y.U. L. Rev. 451, 463 (1992); Robert Post, "Chief Justice William Howard Taft and the Concept of Federalism," in *Federalism and the Judicial Mind* 53, 64–66 (H. Scheiber, ed., 1992).
100. Peter Blau & Richard Scott, *Formal Organizations* (1962); Ernest Dale, *Organization,* 104–30 (1967); Manfred Kochen & Karl Deutsch, *Decentralization: Sketches toward a Rational Theory* (1980); Walter Morris, *Decentralization in Management Systems* (1968); Kenneth Arrow & Leonid Hurweiz, "Decentralization and Computation in Resourse Allocation," in *Essays in Economics and Econometrics,* 34 (R. Phouts, ed., 1960).
101. Akhil Reed Amar, "Some New World Lessons for an Old World," 58 U.

Chi. L. Rev. 483, 498 (1991); Martin Diamond, "On the Relationship of Federalism and Decentralization," in *Cooperation and Conflict: Readings in American Federalism*, 72, 74 (Daniel Elazar, Robert Caroll, Edward Levine, & David St. Angelo, eds., 1969); Feeley & Rubin, *supra* note 99; Andrzej Rapaczynski, "From Sovereignty to Process: The Jurisprudence of Federalism after *Garcia*," 1985 Sup. Ct. Rev. 341, 408-14. For articles that simply assume the equivalence of these principles, see, e.g., Michael McConnell, "Federalism: Evaluating the Founders' Design," 54 U. Chi. L. Rev. 1484, 1500-7 (1987); Richard Posner, "The Constitution as an Economic Document," 56 Geo. Wash. L. Rev. 4, 13-15 (1987); Richard Stewart, "Federalism and Rights," 19 Ga. L. Rev. 917 (1987).

102. Ann Althouse, "Federalism, Untamed," 47 Vand. L. Rev. 1207 (1944); William Bennett, *American Theories of Federalism*, 10 (1964); Daniel Elazar, *American Federalism: A View from the States*, 2 (3d ed., 1984); Carl Friedrich, *Constitutional Government and Democracy*, 224-26 (4th ed., 1968); Kenneth Wheare, *Federal Government*, 11 (3d ed., 1953); Robert Leach, *American Federalism*, 1-10 (1970); Scheppele, *supra* note 99, at 54.

103. Jonathan Macey, "Federal Deference to Local Regulators and the Economic Theory of Regulation: Toward a Public-Choice Explanation of Federalism," 76 Va. L. Rev. 265 (1990).

104. Beer, *supra* note 99, at 308-40; see Akhil Reed Amar, "The Consent of the Governed: Constitutional Amendment outside Article V," 94 Colum. L. Rev. 457, 469 (1994); Jack Rakove, "The First Phases of American Federalism," in *Comparative Constitutional Federalism* (Mark Tushnet, ed., 1990). For a somewhat tendentious argument for the states-first approach, see Raoul Berger, *Federalism: The Founders' Design* (1987).

105. John Hope Franklin, *From Slavery to Freedom*, (2d ed., 1956); Leon Litwack, *North of Slavery*, 3-20 (1961); Fogel & Engerman, *supra* note 24, at 29-37. On the Quakers, see Thomas Drake, *Quakers and Slavery in America* (1950).

106. *Younger v. Harris*, 401 U.S. 37, 44 (1971).

107. *Gregory v. Ashcroft*, 111 S. Ct. 2395, 2399-2400 (1991). See also *FERC v. Mississippi*, 456 U.S. 742, 788-90 (1982) (O'Connor, J., dissenting).

108. 111 S. Ct. at 2399-2400.

109. *Gregory v. Ashcroft*, 111 S. Ct. 2395 (1991); *New York v. United States*, 112 S. Ct. 2408 (1992). See Althouse, *supra* note 102; William Eskridge & John Ferejohn, "The Elastic Commerce Clause: A Political Theory of American Federalism," 47 Vand. L. Rev. 1355 (1994).

110. Murray Edelman, *Political Language: Words That Succeed and Policies That Fail* (1977); Murray Edelman, *The Symbolic Uses of Politics* (1964).

111. 115 S. Ct. 1624 (1995).

112. 117 S. Ct. 2365 (1997).

113. See 115 S. Ct. at 1629-30.

114. 115 S. Ct. at 1631-33. Deborah Merritt perceives the *Lopez* decision as similarly limited in scope, perhaps even more so, but argues that it possesses real, rather than symbolic, significance because it indicates that there remains a category of truly intrastate activity. Deborah Merritt,

"Commerce!" 94 Mich. L. Rev. 674 (1995). Other commentators have also focused on the Court's notion that it can review the quality of congressional findings, see Barry Friedman, "Legislative Findings and Judicial Signals: A Positive Political Reading of *United States v. Lopez*," 46 Case W. Res. L. Rev. 757 (1996); Philip Frickey, "The Fool on the Hill: Congressional Findings, Constitutional Adjudication, and *United States v. Lopez*," 46 Case W. Res. L. Rev. 695 (1996); Harold Krent, "Turning Congress into an Agency: The Propriety of Requiring Legislative Findings," 46 Case W. Res. L. Rev. 731 (1996).

115. Thomas Dye, *Politics in States and Communities* (1977); Nicholas Henry, *Governing at the Grassroots* (1980); Barry Karl, *The Uneasy State* (1983); Leach, *supra* note 102; William Riker, *Democracy in the United States* (2d ed., 1965). On the problems of participation in an administrative context, see Jim Rossi, "Participation Run Amok: The Costs of Mass Participation for Deliberative Agency Decisionmaking," 92 Nw. U. L. Rev. (1997).

116. Roberto Unger, *False Necessity: Anti-Necessitarian Social Theory in the Service of Radical Democracy,* 475–76 (1986); Gerald Frug, "Decentering Decentralization," 60 U. Chi. L. Rev. 253 (1993). Mechanisms of this nature were a central feature of the federal War on Poverty. See, e.g., Joel Handler, *Reforming the Poor: Welfare Policy, Federalism and Morality* (1972); Frances Fox Piven & Richard Cloward, *Regulating the Poor: The Functions of Public Welfare,* 248–84 (1971); James Sundquist, *Making Federalism Work* (1969); David Zaretsky, *President Johnson's War on Poverty* (1986). This is not to suggest that the local participation aspects of the War on Poverty were a howling success, but only to indicate that efforts to encourage participation are as likely to come from the central government as from governments that are "closer" to the people.

117. Richard Briffaut, "What about the 'ism?': Normative and Formal Concerns in Contemporary Federalism," 47 Vand. L. Rev. 1303 (1994); Richard Briffaut, "Our Localism: Part I – The Structure of Local Government Law," 90 Colum. L. Rev. 1 (1990).

118. See Steven Calabresi, "A Government of Limited and Enumerated Powers: In Defense of *United States v. Lopez*," 94 Mich. L. Rev. 752 (1995). Calabresi argues that federalism, not nationalism, supports electoral democracy; this will be true, however, only if there is a national policy favoring elections and a decentralized political system.

119. *Gregory v. Ashcroft,* 111 S. Ct. 2395, 2399 (1991). See Richard Epstein, "Exit Rights under Federalism," 55 L. & Contemp. Prob. 149 (1992); Richard Stewart, "Federalism and Rights," 19 Ga. L. Rev. 917 (1987). See in general Albert Hirschman, *Exit, Voice and Loyalty* (1970).

120. Charles Tiebout, "A Pure Theory of Local Expenditures," 64 J. Pol. Econ. 416 (1956).

121. William Oates, *Fiscal Federalism* (1972); Richard Posner, *Economic Analysis of Law,* ch. 26 (3d ed., 1986); Frank Easterbrook, "Antitrust and the Economics of Federalism," 26 J. L. & Econ. 23 (1983); Epstein, *supra*

note 119; Alan P. Hamlin, "The Political Economy of Constitutional Federalism," 46 Pub. Choice 187 (1984); Alice Rivlin, "Strengthening the Economy by Rethinking the Role of Federal and State Government," 5 J. Econ. Persp. 3 (1991); Carol Rose, "Planning and Dealing: Piecemeal Land Contracts as a Problem of Local Legitimacy," 71 Cal. L. Rev. 837 (1983).

122. David Wildasin, *Urban Public Finance* (1986); James Buchanan & Charles Goetz, "Efficiency Limits of Fiscal Mobility: An Assessment of the Tiebout Hypothesis," 1 J. Pub. Econ. 25 (1972); Robert Inman & Daniel Rubinfeld, "A Federalist Constitution for an Imperfect World: Lessons from the United States," in *Federalism: Studies in History, Law and Policy*, 79, 84–86 (H. Scheiber, ed., 1988).

123. Inman & Rubinfeld, *supra* note 122, at 79.

124. Eric Nordlinger, *Decentralizing a City: A Study of Boston's Little City Halls* (1972). For a discussion of the process by which people choose a residential neighborhood within a city, see Brian Berry & John Kasarda, *Contemporary Urban Ecology*, 126–31 (1977) (major factors include income, age, life-style preference, employment).

125. *Hunter v. City of Pittsburgh*, 207 U.S. 161, 178–79 (1907). For subsequent reaffirmations, see *Holt Civic Club v. Tuscaloosa*, 439 U.S. 60, 70–72 (1978); *Sailors v. Board of Educ.*, 387 U.S. 105, 108 (1967); *Reynolds v. Sims*, 377 U.S. 533, 575 (1964). See generally John Forrest Dillon, *Commentaries on the Law of Municipal Corporations* (5th ed., 1911); Elazar, *supra* note 102, at 202–8. Indeed, the Supreme Court's approach to federalism may actually weaken the power of local governments to bargain with the national government. See M. David Gelfand, "The Burger Court and the New Federalism: Preliminary Reflections on the Roles of Local Government Actors in the Political Dramas of the 1980s," 21 B.C. L. Rev. 763 (1980).

126. For the arguments referred to in the footnote, see Charles Fried, "Federalism – Why Should We Care?," 6 Harv. J. L. & Pub. Pol'y 1, 2 (1982); Lino Graglia, "In Defense of Federalism," 6 Harv. J. L. & Pub. Pol'y 23 (1982).

127. See, e.g., Peter Dodd & Richard Leftwich, "The Market for Corporate Charters: 'Unhealthy' Competition versus Federal Regulation," 53 J. Bus. 259 (1980); Frank Easterbrook, "Managers' Discretion and Investors' Welfare: Theories and Evidence," 9 Del. J. Corp. L. 540 (1984); Frank Easterbrook & Daniel Fischel, "Voting on Corporate Law," 26 J. L. & Econ. 395 (1983).

128. See, e.g., Lucian Bebchuk, "Federalism and the Corporation: The Desirable Limits on State Competition on Corporate Law," 105 Harv. L. Rev. 1435 (1992); William Cary, "Federalism and Corporate Law: Reflections upon Delaware," 83 Yale L. J. 663 (1974); Alan N. Greenspan, "The Constitutional Exercise of the Federal Police Power: A Functional Approach to Federalism," 41 Va. L. Rev. 1019, 1047–48; Jerry Mashaw & Susan Rose-Ackerman, "Federalism and Regulation," in *The Reagan Reg-*

ulatory Strategy: An Assessment, 111 (George Eads & Michael Fix, eds., 1984).

129. See, e.g., Morton Grodzins, *"The American System"* (D. Elazar, ed., 1966); James Gardner, "The Failed Discourse of State Constitutionalism," 90 Mich. L. Rev. 761 (1992).

130. Daniel Elazar makes much of the variations in state culture, but the differences he observes are in fact quite small by worldwide standards. See Elazar, *supra* note 102. See also Ira Sharkansky, *Regionalism in American Politics* (1970). For example, Elazar offers an admittedly impressionistic chart ranking states by their degree of political cohesiveness. Elazar, *supra* note 102, at 19–20. The most cohesive states, in 1980, were Alaska, Utah, Montana, Nevada, South Carolina, Tennessee, and Vermont; the least cohesive were New York, New Jersey, Connecticut, Ohio, Missouri, Michigan, Maryland, and Illinois. Virtually all the variability in this list would seem explicable by a single factor: how much of the state's population resides in a large metropolitan area, and particularly in a large metropolitan area that is divided among several states (New York City, Cincinnati, St. Louis, Kansas City, Detroit, Washington, D.C., and Chicago). States whose large metropolitan areas lie entirely within the state, such as California, Colorado, Georgia, Massachusetts, Texas, Washington, and Florida, rank in the middle, while those that are predominantly rural rank at the top. There are a few exceptions to this rule (Tennessee and Minnesota rank higher than expected). But Elazar's chart seems to demonstrate that we really have a highly uniform political culture, in which people throughout the nation respond to the same kinds of phenomena, rather than several political cultures which vary by region.

131. Fried, *supra* note 126; Lewis Kaden, "Politics, Money and State Governments: The Judicial Role," 79 Colum. L. Rev. 847, 854–55 (1979); Arthur MacMahon, "The Problems in Federalism," in *Federalism: Mature and Emergent* 3, 10–11 (A. MacMahon, ed., 1962); Deborah Merritt, "The Guarantee Clause and State Autonomy: Federalism for a Third Century," 88 Colum. L. Rev. 1 (1988).

132. *New State Ice Co. v. Liebmann,* 285 U.S. 262, 311 (Brandeis, J., dissenting).

133. Regarding Chinese policy, as discussed in the footnote, see Harry Harding, *China's Second Revolution: Reform after Mao* (1987); Jonathan Spence, *The Search for Modern China,* 673–74 (1990).

134. Briffault, *supra* note 117, at 1326; Rapaczynski, *supra* note 101, at 408–12; Susan Rose-Ackerman, "Risk-Taking and Reelection: Does Federalism Promote Innovation?" 9 J. Legal Stud. 593 (1980); cf. James Gardner, "The States-as-Laboratories: Metaphor in State Constitutional Law," 30 Val. L. Rev. 475 (1996) (concept does not make sense for state court judges).

135. William Baumol, *Economics, Environmental Policy, and the Quality of Life* (1979); Richard Musgrave & Polly Musgrave, *Public Finance in Theory and Practice,* 47–81 (4th ed., 1984); Mancur Olson, *The Logic of Collective Action* (1965).

136. On the National Center for State Courts, see *The National Center for State Courts, Annual Report* (1972). The center publishes studies of the state courts; see, e.g., William Hewitt, Geoffrey Gallos, & Barry Mahoney, *Six Courts That Succeed* (1990); John A. Martin & Elizabeth A. Prescott, *Appellate Court Delay* (1981); Barry Mahoney, *Changing Times in Trial Courts* (1988). On the National Institute for Corrections, see U.S. Department of Justice, *National Institute of Corrections, Annual Program Plan* (published annually). The Institute runs its own training programs; see National Institute for Corrections, *Training Programs Conducted by the National Academy of Corrections* (1987). It also publishes studies; see Richard Howard, *Designs for Contemporary Correctional Facilities* (1985); Joan Petersilla & Steven Turner, *Guideline-Based Justice: The Implications for Racial Minorities* (1985).

137. Akhil Reed Amar, "Of Sovereignty and Federalism," 96 Yale L. J. 1425, 1444–51, 1492–1520; Beer, *supra* note 99, at 295–301, 386–88; William Livingston, *Federalism and Constitutional Change*, 7–10 (1956); Mark Tushnet, *Red, White and Blue: A Critical Analysis of Constitutional Law*, 9–12 (1988); Charles Cooper, "Limited Government and Individual Liberty: The Ninth Amendment's Forgotten Lessons," 4 J. L. & Pol. 63 (1987); John M. Harlan, "Thoughts at a Dedication: Keeping the Judicial Function in Balance," 49 A.B.A. J. 943 (1963); Kaden, *supra* note 131, at 849–56; Geoffrey Miller, "Rights and Structure in Constitutional Theory," 8 Soc. Phil. & Pol'y 196, 205–9 (1991).

138. Michael Mann, *The Sources of Social Power*, vol. 1, 1–32 (1986); Brian Barry, "Power: An Economic Analysis," in *Power and Political Theory*, 67 (B. Barry, ed., 1976); Robert Dahl, *The Concept of Power in Behavioral Science*, 201 (1957); Herbert Danziger, "Community Power Structure: Problems and Continuities," 29 Am. Soc. Rev. 707 (1964); John Elster, "Some Conceptual Problems in Political Theory," in *Power and Political Theory*, *supra*, at 245; William Riker, "Some Ambiguities in the Notion of Power," 58 Am. Pol. Sci. Rev. 341 (1964).

139. See Beer, *supra* note 99, at 295–301; Elazar, *supra* note 102, at 2; Amar, *supra* note 137, at 1444–51; Miller, *supra* note 137, at 207–8.

140. Deborah Merritt, "Three Faces of Federalism: Finding a Formula for the Future," 47 Vand. L. Rev. 1563 (1994); Saikrishna Bangalore Prakash, "Field Office Federalism," 79 Va. L. Rev. 1957 (1993). According to Jesse Choper, genuine threats to state autonomy are unlikely because of the structural role that states play in the national government, e.g., the fact that our national legislature is composed of state representatives. Jesse Choper, *Judicial Review and the National Political Process* (1980); Jesse Choper, "The Scope of National Power vis-à-vis the States: The Dispensibility of Judicial Review," 86 Yale L. J. 1552 (1977). See also Herbert Wechsler, "The Political Safeguards of Federalism: The Role of the States in the Composition and Selection of the National Government," in *Principles, Politics and Fundamental Law*, 49 (1961). For critiques of the structural argument, see Larry Kramer, "Understanding Federalism," 47 Vand. L. Rev. 1485, 1503–14 (1994); Mark Tushnet,

"Why the Supreme Court Overruled *National League of Cities*," 47 Vand. L. Rev. 1623 (1994).

141. See Lawrence Lessig & Cass Sunstein, "The President and the Administration," 94 Colum. L. Rev. 1, 45–46 (1994).

142. Leach, *supra* note 102, at 26–27. For an example, see Charles Cooper, "The Demise of Federalism," 20 Urban Lawyer 239 (1988).

143. See Sarah Sun Beale, "Too Many and Yet Too Few: New Principle to Define the Proper Limits for Federal Criminal Jurisdiction," 46 Hastings L. J. 979 (1995); Kathleen Brickley, "Criminal Mischief: The Federalization of American Criminal Law," 46 Hastings L. J. 1135 (1995); John Jeffried & John Gleason, "The Federalization of Organized Crime: Advantages of Federal Prosecution," 46 Hastings L. J. 1095 (1995); Rory Little, "Myths and Principles of Federalization," 46 Hastings L. J. 1029 (1995); Franklin Zimring & Gordon Hawkins, "Toward a Principled Basis for Federal Criminal Legislation," *The Annals: The Federal Role in Criminal Law*, vol. 545, 15A (January 1996).

144. Samuel Beer, "The Modernization of American Federalism," 3 Publius 49 (1973); Daniel Elazar, "Cursed by Bigness or Toward a Post-Technocratic Federalism," 3 Publius 239 (1973); Richard Stewart, "Pyramids of Sacrifice? Problems of Federalism in Mandating State Implementation of National Environmental Policy," 86 Yale L. J. 1196 (1977).

145. Kramer, *supra* note 140, at 1504.

146. Edward Corwin, "The Passing of Dual Federalism," 36 Va. L. Rev. 1 (1950); Harry Scheiber, "American Federalism and the Diffusion of Power: Historical and Contemporary Perspectives," 9 U. Tol. L. Rev. 619, 628–36 (1978); David Walker, *Toward a Functioning Federalism*, 46–95 (1981). Raoul Berger argues, in effect, that the dual federalism was the intention of the Framers. Raoul Berger, *The Founder's Design* (1987). Even if one accepts the rather simplistic interpretive strategy he propounds, however, the evidence of the Framers' real intentions on this issue are far from clear. See H. J. Powell, "The Modern Misunderstanding of Original Intent," 54 U. Chi. L. Rev. 1513 (1987). The fact that dual federalism was the practical arrangement of governmental authority for the nation's first seven decades does not mean that it was inscribed as a norm in the Constitution.

147. Scheiber, *supra* note 146, at 636–43. The reality thus corresponded to the theory propounded by Kenneth C. Wheare; see Wheare, *supra* note 102.

148. Morton Grodzins, *supra* note 129, at 60–88; Morton Grodzins, "The Federal System," in *American Federalism*, 13 (A. Wildavsky, ed., 1967).

149. Stephen Gardbaum, "Rethinking Constitutional Federalism," 74 Tex. L. Rev. 795 (1996); Daniel Elazar, *The American Partnership* (1962); William Graves, *American Intergovernmental Relations: Their Origins, Historical Development and Current Status* (1964); Leach, *supra* note 102, at 25–82; Samuel Huntington, "The Founding Fathers and the Division of Powers," in *Area and Power: A Theory of Local Government* (A. Maass, ed., 1959); Scheiber,

supra note 146; Stewart, *supra* note 144; Joseph Zimmerman, *Contemporary American Federalism* (1992).

150. Unfunded Mandates Reform Act, Pub. L. No. 104-4, 109 Stat. 48 (1995), codified at 2 U.S.C. § 658, 1501–57 (1977); Personal Responsibility and Work Opportunity Act of 1996, Pub. L. No. 104–93 110 Stat. 2105 (1996), codified at 42. U.S.C. §§ 601–15.

151. There have been a number of thoughtful articles in recent years arguing that increases in federal power can upset the balance between the federal government and the states. See, e.g., Lynn Baker, "Conditional Federal Spending after *Lopez*," 95 Colum. L. Rev. 1911 (1995); H. Jefferson Powell, "Enumerated Means and Unlimited Ends," 94 Mich. L. Rev. 651 (1995); Donald Regan, "How to Think about the Federal Commerce Power and Incidentally Rewrite *United States v. Lopez*," 94 Mich. L. Rev. 554 (1995); Saikrishna Prakash, "Field Office Federalism," 79 Va. L. Rev. 1957 (1993). These articles, however, rely on the concept of a preexisting balance, typically derived from some sort of originalist theory of constitutional interpretation. They do not argue that the states are being undermined or destroyed in any absolute sense.

152. Franz Neumann, *The Democratic and the Authoritarian State*, 216–32 (1957).

153. Issah Berlin, *Four Essays on Liberty* (1969); Duncan Kennedy, "Form and Substance in Private Law Adjudication," 89 Harv. L. Rev. 1685, 1745–51 (1976); Robert Paul Wolff, *The Poverty of Liberalism*, 89–93 (1968).

154. Amar, *supra* note 137; Akhil Reed Amar, "Using State Law to Protect Federal Constitutional Rights: Some Questions and Answers about Converse – 1983," 64 U. Colo. L. Rev. 159 (1993); Akhil Reed Amar, "Five Views of Federalism: 'Converse-1983' in Context," 47 Vand. L. Rev. 1229 (1994).

155. Adeno Addis, "Individualism, Communitarians and the Rights of Ethnic Minorities," 67 Notre Dame L. Rev. 615 (1991); Martha Minow, *Putting Up and Putting Down: Tolerance Reconsidered, Comparative Constitutional Federalism*, 77 (M. Tushnet, ed., 1990); Vincent Ostrom, "Federal Principles of Organization and Ethnic Communities," in *Federalism and Political Integration*, 73 (D. Elazar, ed., 1979).

156. Richard Rorty, "Postmodern Bourgeois Liberalism," 80 J. Phil. 583 (1983).

157. Stanley Fish, *Is There a Text in This Class?* (1980).

158. Michael Walzer, *Spheres of Justice* (1983); Michael Walzer, *Exodus and Revolution* (1985).

159. Michael Sandel, *Liberalism and the Limits of Justice* (1982).

160. Wolff, *supra* note 153.

161. See, e.g., Hannah Arendt, *The Human Condition* (1958).

162. Bernard Barber, *Strong Democracy* (1984).

163. J. G. A. Pocock, *The Machiavellian Moment* (1975).

164. Philip Selznick, *The Moral Commonwealth: Social Theory and the Promise of Community* (1992).

165. See, e.g., Robert Bellah, Richard Madsden, William Sullivan, Ann Swidler & Steven Tipton, *Habits of the Heart* (1985).
166. Cass Sunstein, "Beyond the Republican Revival," 97 Yale L. J. 1539 (1988).
167. Frank Michelman, "Law's Republic," 97 Yale L. J. 1493 (1988).
168. Wolff, *supra* note 153, at 187–92. See also Peggy Rosenthal, *Word and Values*, 219–50 (1984). Wolff's use of this term is somewhat different. He states that affective community "is the reciprocal consciousness of a shared culture[.]" *Id.* at 187. In exploring the possibility of an affective community, however, he refers to reciprocal relationships between individuals. *Id.* at 182–83. We use his term to describe the set of such relationships within a group.
169. *Id.* at 192–93; see Bruce Ackerman, *Social Justice in the United States* (1980); Jürgen Habermas, *The Theory of Communicative Action*, 8–43, 273–337 (T. McCarthy, trans., 1984). Wolff would call this one form of affective community, reserving the term "political community" for a society in which "each member of society must recognize his fellow citizens as rational moral agents and must freely acknowledge their right (and his) to reciprocal equality in the dialogue of politics." Wolff, *supra* note 153, at 192. As Wolff acknowledges, this is an aspiration.
170. Sandel, *supra* note 159, at 147–54.
171. Baker Brownell, *The Human Community: Its Philosophy and Practice for a Time of Crisis* (1950).
172. Robert Nisbet, *Communities and Power: A Study in the Ethics of Order and Freedom* (1962).
173. Robert Park, *Human Communities* (1952).
174. Stephen Gardbaum, "Law, Politics and the Claims of Community," 90 Mich. L. Rev. 685 (1992).
175. David Konig, *Law and Society in Puritan Massachusetts, 1629–1692* (1979).
176. Kathryn Abrams, "Kitsch and Community," 84 Mich. L. Rev. 941 (1986); Frug, *supra* note 116, at 301–3; Edward Rubin, "Nazis, Skokie, and the First Amendment as Virtue," 74 Cal. L. Rev. 233, 252–56 (1986).
177. See Tushnet, *supra* note 137, at 42 n. 64 ("In a world in which the so-called community school boards in New York City would have represented populations in 1967 only slightly smaller than the population of the entire state of New York in 1790, . . . the 'states' that were protected in *National League of Cities* are not the same entities the framers had in mind . . ."); Gardner, *supra* note 134, at 837 ("the communities in theory defined by state constitutions simply do not exist").
178. Minow, *supra* note 155; Ostrom, *supra* note 155; Rapaczynski, *supra* note 101.
179. Nathan Glazer, "The Constitution and American Diversity," in *Forging Unity Out of Diversity*, 60 (R. Goldwin, A Kaufman, & W. Schambra, eds., 1989). As Glazer points out, Utah is something of an exception, having been founded, and continuing to be dominated, by members of a distinct religion. See *id.* at 64. But the Mormons are a recent group who emerged

from a period of general turmoil in American Protestantism, and they have no distinguishing features apart from their religious commitment. Thus, while they undoubtedly represent a true community, there are many bonds linking them to the national community as well.

180. On the essentially geographic character of federalism see, e.g., Ramesh Dikshit, *The Political Geography of Federalism* (1975); Ivan Duchacek, *Comparative Federalism: The Territorial Dimension of Politics* (1970); C. Friedrich, *supra* note 102, at 188–227; William Livingston, *Federalism and Constitutional Change* (1956). Of course, this does not mean that there is a perfect correspondence between geographical divisions and juridical subunits, even in truly federal regimes. See Richard L. Watts, *New Federations: Experiments in the Commonwealth*, 67–69 (1966).

181. Gardner, *supra* note 134, at 823, 827–30.

182. Jürgen Habermas, *The Structural Transformation of the Public Sphere* (T. Burger, trans., 1989).

183. Gardner, *supra* note 134, at 823, 827–30.

184. Paul Sniderman, *A Question of Loyalty* (1981).

185. Ackerman, *supra* note 169.

186. Ayers, *supra* note 11, 9–33; David Bruce, *Violence and Culture in the Antebellum South* (1979); B. Wyatt Brown, *Southern Honor: Ethics and Behavior in the Old South* (1982).

187. 478 U.S. 186 (1986).

188. Kramer, *supra* note 140.

189. David Hollinger, "How Wide the Circle of the 'We?' American Intellectuals and the Problem of Ethnicity since World War II," 98 Am. Hist. Rev. 317 (1993); Frederich Schauer, "Easy Cases," 58 S. Cal. L. Rev 399, 399 n. 1. (1985); Peter Schuck, "Immigration Law and the Problem of Community," in *Clamor at the Gates*, 285 (N. Glazer, ed., 1985); James B. White, "Law as Language: Reading Law and Reading Literature," 60 Tex. L. Rev. 415, 442–43 (1992).

190. Amar, *supra* note 137; Amar, *supra* note 101.

191. 198 U.S. 45 (1905).

192. Morris Cohen, "The Basics of Contract," 46 Harv. L. Rev. 553 (1933); John Hart Ely, *Democracy and Distrust*, 14–21 (1980); Gerald Gunther, "Foreword: Search of Evolving Doctrine on a Changing Court: A Model for a Newer Equal Protection," 86 Harv. L. Rev. 1 (1972); Charles Warren, "The New Liberty under the Fourteenth Amendment," 39 Harv. L. Rev. 431 (1926).

193. *Skinner v. Oklahoma*, 316 U.S. 535 (1942).

194. *Rochin v. California*, 342 U.S. 165 (1952).

195. *Myer v. Nebraska*, 262 U.S. 390 (1923).

196. *Bolling v. Sharpe*, 347 U.S. 497 (1954).

197. *Pierce v. Society of Sisters*, 268 U.S. 510 (1925).

198. *Aptheker v. Secretary of State*, 378 U.S. 500 (1964).

199. *Griswold v. Connecticut*, 381 U.S. 479 (1965).

200. 298 U.S. 587 (1936).

201. 410 U.S. 113 (1973).

202. Gerald Rosenberg, supra note 55 at 175–201.

203. Ely, *supra* note 192.

204. Contemporary decisions that arguably revive this aspect of substantive due process, albeit in equal protection clothing, include *Zobel v. Williams*, 457 U.S. 55 (1982); *Metropolitan Life Ins. Co. v. Ward*, 470 U.S. 869 (1985); *Williams v. Vermont*, 472 U.S. 14 (1985); *Allegheny Pittsburgh Coal Co. v. County Commission*, 488 U.S. 366 (1989). See Robert McCloskey, "Economic Due Process and the Supreme Court: An Exhumation and Reburial," 1962 Sup. Ct. Rev. 34; J. M. Hetheryton, "State Economic Regulation and Substantive Due Process of Law," 53 Nw. U. L. Rev. 13, 226 (1958); Cass Sunstein, "Naked Preferences and the Constitution," 84 Colum. L. Rev. 1689 (1984); James Strand, Note: "State Economic Substantive Due Process: A Proposed Approach," 88 Yale L. J. 1487 (1979).

6. CREATING DOCTRINE, CHOOSING SOLUTIONS, AND TRANSFORMING THE RULE OF LAW

1. Melvin Eisenberg, *The Nature of Common Law* (1988).

2. Duncan Kennedy, "Freedom and Constraint in Adjudication: A Critical Phenomenology," 36 J. Legal Educ. 518 (1986).

3. Douglas Hay, *Albion's Fatal Tree: Crime and Society in England and the Eighteenth Century* (1975); George Riley Scott, *The History of Corporal Punishment: A Survey of Flagellation in Its Historical, Anthropological and Sociological Aspects* (1938).

4. With respect to punishment, see David D. Cooper, *The Lesson of the Scaffold* (1974); Peter Gay, *The Enlightenment: An Interpretation*, vol. 2 (1969); Pieter Spienenburg, *The Spectacle of Suffering* (1984); Franco Venturi, *Utopia and Reform in the Enlightenment* (1971). With respect to investigatory torture, see John Langbein, *Torture and the Law of Proof: Europe and England in the Ancient Regime* (1977); Mirjan Damaska, "The Death of Legal Torture," 87 Yale L. J. 860 (1978).

5. Larry Berkson, *The Concept of Cruel and Unusual Punishment* (1975); Anthony Granucci, "Nor Cruel and Unusual Punishments Inflicted: The Original Meaning," 57 Cal. L. Rev. 839 (1969). Granucci argues that the Framers' view was actually a misunderstanding of the English original, which proscribed excessive punishment, but not necessarily torturous ones.

6. Adam Hirsch, *The Rise of the Penitentiary* (1993); Blake McKelvey, *American Prisons: A History of Good Intentions*, 6–11 (1977); David Rothman, *The Discovery of the Asylum: Social Order and Disorder in the New Republic*, 45–78 (2d ed., 1993). The same was true in England. Michael Ignatieff, *A Just Measure of Pain: The Penitentiary in the Industrial Revolution, 1750–1850* (1978).

7. 113 S. Ct. 2474, 2484 (Thomas, J., dissenting).

8. *Id.* at 2483–84.

9. John DiIulio, *Governing Prisons: A Comparative Study of Correctional Management* (1987).

10. Robert Wood, ed., *Remedial Law: When Courts Become Administrators* (1990).

11. Bradley Chilton, *Prisons under the Gavel: The Federal Court Takeover of Georgia Prisons* (1991).

12. Larry Yackle, *Reform and Regret: The Story of Federal Judicial Involvement in the Alabama Prison System* (1989).

13. A. V. Dicey, *Introduction to the Study of the Law of the Constitution*, 202–3 (10th ed., 1961); Friedrich A. Hayek, *The Road to Serfdom*, 80–81 (15th ed., 1994); Mortimer Kadish & Sanford Kadish, *Discretion to Disobey*, 40–45 (1973). In recent years, scholars have advanced more elaborate definitions, incorporating requirements of judicial independence, legal stability, and the accessibility of courts. Lon Fuller, *The Morality of Law*, 33–94 (rev. ed. 1969); John Rawls, *A Theory of Justice*, 235–43 (1971); Joseph Raz, "The Rule of Law and Its Virtue," 93 Law Q. Rev. 195 (1977), reprinted in *Liberty and the Rule of Law*, 3 (R. Cunningham, ed., 1979); Geoffrey Walker, *The Rule of Law*, 1–48 (1988); Richard Fallon, " 'The Rule of Law' as a Concept in Constitutional Discourse," 97 Colum. L. Rev. (1977). All these definitions include the core idea that the government official must be subject to some kind of legal constraint. This is the aspect of the rule of law that doctrinal creation potentially threatens. The relationship between the various definitions of the rule of law and the issue of judicial policy making is explored further in Chapter 8.

14. Alexander Bickel, *The Least Dangerous Branch*, 16–23 (1962).

15. Phillip Bobbitt, *Constitutional Fate* (1982); Steven Burton, *An Introduction to Law and Legal Reasoning* (1985); Ronald Dworkin, *Taking Rights Seriously* (1978); Eisenberg, *supra* note 1, at 14–42. Not surprisingly, thoughtful judges who write about the decision-making process acknowledge the judge's role in creating doctrine and justify it in these terms. See, e.g., Aharon Barak, *Judicial Discretion* (1989); Benjamin Cardozo, *The Nature of the Judicial Process*, 98–141 (1921); Jon Newman, "Between Legal Realism and Neutral Principles: The Legitimacy of Institutional Values," 72 Cal. L. Rev.; E. W. Thomas, "A Return to Principle in Judicial Reasoning and an Acclamation of Judicial Autonomy," Victoria U. Wellington L. Rev., Monograph 5 (1993); Sol Wachtler, "Judicial Lawmaking," 65 N.Y.U. L. Rev. 1 (1990). Of course, shared cultural values can also be a source of injustice. See Richard Delgado & Jean Stefancic, "Norms and Narratives: Can Judges Avoid Serious Moral Error?" 69 Tex. L. Rev. 1929 (1992).

16. Herbert Hart & Albert Sacks, *The Legal Process: Basic Problems in the Making and Application of Law*, 139–44 (W. Eskridge & P. Frickey, eds., 1994).

17. See William Eskridge & Gary Peller, "The New Public Law Movement: Moderation as a Postmodern Cultural Form," 89 Mich. L. Rev. 707, 711–37 (1991); Edward Rubin, "The New Legal Process, The Synthesis of Discourse and the Microanalysis of Institutions," 109 Harv. L. Rev. 1393 (1996); Anthony Sebok, "Misunderstanding Positivism," 93 Mich. L. Rev. 2054, 2105–17 (1995).

18. Zachariah Chafee, *Free Speech in the United States* (1941); Mark Denbeaux, "The First Word of the First Amendment," 80 Nw. U. L. Rev. 1156, 1207–20 (1986); Harry Kalven, *A Worthy Tradition*, 125–89 (J. Kalven, ed., 1988); Gerald Gunther, "Learned Hand and the Origins of Modern First Amendment Doctrine: Some Fragments of History," 27 Stan. L. Rev. 719 (1975); G. Edward White, "The First Amendment Comes of Age: The Emergence of Free Speech in Twentieth-Century America," 95 Mich. L. Rev. 299 (1996). The first significant judicial decision on the subject was *Masses Publishing Co. v. Patten*, 244 F. 535 (2nd Cir. 1917) (Hand, J.). *Schenck v. United States*, 249 U.S. 47 (1919), was the Supreme Court's first pronouncement, articulating the famous clear and present danger test. That is certainly First Amendment doctrine, but, of course, the case upholds the challenged statute. In fact, free-speech doctrine in the sense of a doctrine, which would invalidate state legislation on free-speech grounds, developed entirely in dissenting opinions during the period from 1919 to 1930. It did not command a majority of the court until *Stromberg v. California*, 283 U.S. 359 (1931). See also Lucas Powe, *The Fourth Estate and the Constitution IX* (1991). ("Surprising though it may seem, for all practical purposes the modern constitutional law of freedom of the press began with the Supreme Court's constitutionalization of libel in *New York Times v. Sullivan* (1964)").

19. Cardozo, *supra* note 15, at 167–71.

20. Martin Shapiro, "Decentralized Decision-Making in the Law of Torts," in *Political Decision-Making* 44 (S. Ulmer, ed., 1970); Martin Shapiro, *Courts: A Comparative and Political Analysis* (1981). Modern organization theory offers a range of illuminating models of institutions, but rarely addresses the institution's ability to generate ideas. Of the classic branches of organization theory, the human relations school tends to emphasize individual behavior and to treat the organization as possessing few behaviors of its own – see, e.g., Chris Argyris, *Personality and Organization* (1957); George Homans, *The Human Group* (1950); Charles Perrow, *Complex Organizations: A Critical Essay* (2d ed., 1979); Philip Selznick, *Leadership in Administration* (1957) – while systems theory tends to treat institutional behaviors as largely autonomous of individuals, see, e.g., Stafford Beer, *Cybernetics and Management* (1964); Jay Galbraith, *Organization Design* (1977); Karl Weick, *The Social Psychology of Organizing* (2d ed., 1979). These approaches provide considerable insight into institutional behavior, but do not attempt to explain institutional ideas. Decision theory seems more promising, with its emphasis on the interaction of individual thought processes and institutional settings; see, e.g, James March & Johan Olsen, *Rediscovering Institutions* (1989); James March & Johan Olsen, *Ambiguity and Choice in Organizations* (1976); Herbert Simon, *Administrative Behavior* (2d ed., 1957). But its emphasis has been the institution's capabilities and limitations in carrying out tasks, not its creation of ideas. Even the new institutionalism, despite its efforts to link individual motivation to institutionalism behavior, has not addressed this topic directly, although there are indications that it offers a promising approach for doing so. See,

e.g., Paul DiMaggio & Walter Powell, "The Iron Cage Revisited: Institutional Isomorphism and Collective Rationality in Organization Fields," in *The New Institutionalism in Organizational Analysis* (W. Powell & P. DiMaggio, eds., 1991); Paul DiMaggio, "State Expansion and Organizational Fields," in *Organization Theory and Public Policy*, 147 (R. Hall & R. Quinn, eds., 1983).

21. Mary Douglas, *How Institutions Think* (1986).

22. A notorious version in the legal context is the attribution of intentionality to legislatures, or to even more amorphous groups such as "The Framers." This is a belief that remains very much alive. See, e.g., Raoul Berger, *Government by Judiciary: The Transformation of the Fourteenth Amendment* (1977); Andrei Marmore, *Interpretation and Legal Theory* (1992); Jack Rakove, *Interpreting the Constitution: The Debate over Original Intent* (1990). Devastating theoretical criticisms have been leveled at the concept, see, e.g., Ronald Dworkin, *Law's Empire*, 312–37 (1986); Eben Moglen & Richard Pierce, "Sunstein's New Canons: Choosing the Fictions of Statutory Interpretation," 57 U. Chi. L. Rev. 1203, 1209–15 (1990); Mark Tushnet, *Red, White and Blue: A Critical Analysis of Constitutional Law*, 23–45 (1988); Max Radin, "Statutory Interpretation," 43 Harv. L. Rev. 863 (1930); Jeremy Waldron, *Legislators' Intent and Unintentional Legislation* (1998).

23. James Buchanan & Gordon Tullock, *The Calculus of Consent* (1962); John Ferejohn, *Pork Barrel Politics* (1974); David Mayhew, *Congress: The Electoral Connection* (1974); William Niskanen, *Bureaucracy and Representative Government* (1971); Mancur Olson, *The Logic of Collective Action* (1965).

24. Edward Rubin, "Beyond Public Choice: Comprehensive Rationality in the Writing and Reading of Statutes," 66 N.Y.U. L. Rev. (1991).

25. Joel Grossman, "Social Background and Judicial Decisions: Notes for a Theory," 29 J. Pol. 29 (1967); Glendon Schubert, *The Judicial Mind: The Attitudes and Ideologies of Supreme Court Justices, 1946–1963* (1965); Glendon Schubert, *Quantitative Analysis of Judicial Behavior* (1954); Jeffrey Segal & Harold Spaeth, *The Supreme Court and the Attitudinal Model* (1993); Harold Spaeth, *Supreme Court Policy Making* (1979); Sidney Ulmer, "The Analysis of Behavior Patterns in the Supreme Court of the United States," 22 J. Pol. 429 (1960); Harold Lasswell, *Power and Personality* (1958).

26. John Gruhl, "The Supreme Court's Impact on the Law of Libel: Compliance by Lower Federal Courts," 33 W. Pol. Sci. Q. 518 (1980); Fred Kort, "Predicting Supreme Court Cases Mathematically: An Analysis of the Right to Counsel Cases," 57 Am. Pol. Sci. Rev. 1 (1957); Fred Kort, "Content Analysis of Judicial Opinions and Rules of Law," in *Judicial Decisionmaking*, 153 (G. Schubert. ed., 1963); Charles Johnson, "Law, Politics, and Judicial Decision Making: Lower Court Uses of Supreme Court Decisions," 21 L. & Soc. Rev. 325 (1987); Ronald Kahn, *The Supreme Court and Constitutional Theory, 1953–1993* (1994). See also H. W. Perry, *Deciding to Decide: Agenda Setting in the United States Supreme Court* (1991) (jurisprudential considerations more important than strategic ones in the decision to take certiorari).

27. Paul Brest, "State Action and Liberal Theory: A Casenote on *Flagg Brothers*

v. Brooks," 130 U. Pa. L. Rev. 1296 (1982); Morton Horowitz, *The Transformation of American Law, 1780–1860* (1977); Duncan Kennedy, "The Structure of Blackstone's Commentaries," 28 Buff. L. Rev. 205 (1979); Karl Klare, "Judicial Deradicalization of the Wagner Act and the Origins of Modern Legal Consciousness, 1937–1941," 62 Minn. L. Rev. 265 (1978); Mark Tushnet, "Following the Rules Laid Down: A Critique of Interpretation and Neutral Principles," 96 Harv. L. Rev. 781 (1983); Robert Unger, *The Critical Legal Studies Movement* (1986).

28. Regina Austin, "Sapphire Bound!" 1989 Wis. L. Rev. 539; Kimberly Crenshaw, "Race, Reform, and Retrenchment: Transformation and Legitimation in Anti-discrimination Law," 101 Harv. L. Rev. 1331 (1988); Charles Lawrence, "The Id, the Ego, and Equal Protection: Reckoning with Unconscious Racists," 39 Stan. L. Rev. 317 (1987).

29. Richard Posner, *The Economic Analysis of Law* (4th ed., 1992); John C. Goodman, "An Economic Theory of the Evolution of the Common Law," 7 J. Legal Stud. 393 (1978); George Priest, "The Common Law Process and the Selection of Efficient Rules," 6 J. Legal Stud. 65 (1977).

30. Phillip Bobbitt, *Constitutional Interpretation* (1991); Bobbitt, *supra* note 15; R. Dworkin, *supra* note 22; Eisenberg, *supra* note 1; Owen Fiss, "Objectivity and Interpretation," 34 Stan. L. Rev. 739 (1982).

31. Karl Llewellyn, *The Common Law Tradition: Deciding Appeals* (1960).

32. John Poulos, "The Judicial Philosophy of Roger Traynor," 46 Hastings L. J. 1643 (1995); John Poulos, "The Judicial Process and Substantive Criminal Law: The Legacy of Roger Traynor," 29 Loy. L.A. L. Rev. 429 (1996).

33. Dworkin, *supra* note 15.

34. Eisenberg, *supra* note 1.

35. William Eskridge, *Dynamic Statutory Interpretation* (1994).

36. Kent Greenawalt, *Law and Objectivity* (1992).

37. Richard Posner, *The Federal Courts: Crisis and Reform* (1985); Richard Posner, "What Do Judges and Justices Maximize? (The Same Thing Everybody Else Does)," 3 Sup. Ct. Econ. Rev. 1 (1993).

38. Frederich Schauer, "Easy Cases," 58 S. Cal. L. Rev. 399 (1985); Frederich Schauer, "Giving Reasons," 47 Stan. L. Rev. 633 (1995).

39. Kennedy, *supra* note 2. Kennedy derives his sense of phenomenology from Sartre; see *supra* note 2, at 518 n. 1. Sartre is more commonly categorized as an existentialist, and thus a direct follower of Heidegger, rather than of Husserl; see William Barret, *Irrational Man* 239–63 (1958); H. J. Blackmun, ed., *Reality, Man and Existence: Essential Works of Existentialism,* 302–49 (1985); Abraham Kaplan, *The New World of Philosophy,* 97–128 (1961). However, Heiddeger disagreed with Sartre's approach; see Martin Heidegger, "Letter on Humanism," reprinted in Martin Heidegger, *Basic Writings,* 189 (D. Krell, ed., 1977). However, it is fair to regard Sartre as a phenomenologist because virtually all continental philosophy, and certainly Heidegger, was heavily influenced by Husserl.

40. Alisdair MacIntyre, *Whose Justice? Which Rationality?* (1988).

41. James March & Johan Olsen, *Rediscovery Institutions,* 25–26 (1989).

42. See, e.g., Peter Blau & Richard Scott, *Formal Organizations* (1962); Sanford

Dornbusch & W. Richard Scott, *Evaluation and the Exercise of Authority* (1975); Robert Merton, *Social Theory and Social Structure* (2d ed., 1952); Milton Rokeach, *Beliefs, Attitudes and Values: A Theory of Organization and Change* (1968); John Thibaut & Harold Kelley, *The Social Psychology of Groups* (1959). With respect to the judiciary, see Henry Glick, *Courts, Politics and Justice*, 305–8 (3d ed., 1993).

43. Niklas Luhmann, *The Sociology of Law*, 49–61 (1985).

44. The distinction between formal and informal rules comes from human relations theory. Homans, *supra* note 20; F. J. Roethlisberger & William Dickson, *Management and the Worker* (1939).

45. Erving Goffman, *The Presentation of Self in Everyday Life* (1959).

46. On the centrality of language to human thought, see H. G. Gadamer, *Truth and Method*, 345–498 (G. Barden & J. Cumming, trans., 1988); Martin Heidegger, *Being and Time*, 188–224 (J. Macquarrie & E. Robinson, trans., 1962); A. R. Louch, *Explanation and Human Action* (1969); Hillary Putman, *Representation and Reality* (1988).

47. Paul Feyerabend, *Three Dialogues on Knowledge* (1991).

48. Harold Garfinkel, *Studies in Ethnomethodology* (1984); Alfred Schutz, *Collected Papers* (1962).

49. Edmund Husserl, *The Crisis of European Sciences and Transcendental Phenomenology*, 163–64 (David Carr, trans., 1970).

50. See Shapiro, *Decentralized Decisionmaking*, *supra* note 20.

51. Eisenberg, *supra* note 1.

52. Stanley Fish, *Is There a Text in This Class?* (1980); Karl Llewellyn, *The Bramble Bush*, 66–69 (1951); Tushnet, *supra* note 22; Anthony D'Amato, "Legal Uncertainty," 71 Cal. L. Rev. 1 (1983); David Kairys, "Law and Politics," 52 Geo. Wash. L. Rev. 243 (1984); Sanford Levinson, "Law As Literature," 60 Tex. L. Rev. 373 (1982); Gary Peller, "The Metaphysics of American Law," 73 Cal. L. Rev. 1151 (1985); Joseph Singer, "The Player and the Cards: Nihilism and Legal Theory," 94 Yale L. J. 1 (1984).

53. Greenawalt, *supra* note 36 (some legal questions are clear, but others depend upon a mixture of political and moral views); H. L. A. Hart, *The Concept of Law*, 120–50 (1961) (rules are generally open to some ambiguity, but are not entirely indeterminate); William Eskridge, *Dynamic Statutory Interpretation*, 5–80 (1994) (meaning of rules determined by interaction of text and interpreter); Owen Fiss, "Objectivity and Interpretation," 34 Stan. L. Rev. 739 (1982) (interpretive community generates "disciplining rules" that constrain interpretation); Kenneth Kress, "Legal Indeterminacy," 77 Cal. L. Rev. 283 (1989) (level of indeterminacy is only moderate); Newman, *supra* note 15 (institutional values guide interpretive process that is discretionary, but not indeterminate); Dennis Patterson, "Law's Pragmatism: Law as Practice & Narrative," 76 Va. L. Rev. 937 (1990) (meaning of rule is determined by practical judgments based on textual language); Robert Post, "The Relatively Autonomous Discourse of Law," in *Law and the Order of Culture*, vol. 7 (R. Post, ed., 1991) (the meaning of rules is determined by social practices that incorporate relatively autonomous rules).

54. Berger, *supra* note 22 (original intent of the Framers is determinate); Dworkin, *supra* note 22 (there exists a best interpretation for most legal texts); Dworkin, *supra* note 15 (correct interpretation can be derived from prevailing moral principles); Michael Moore, "A Natural Law Theory of Interpretation," 58 S. Cal. L. Rev. 277 (1985) (definitive answers can be derived from universally valid moral principles); Schauer, *supra* note 38 (many legal texts have definitive meanings, and most have a core of definitive meaning); Frederich Schauer, "Formalism," 97 Yale L. J. 509 (1988) (definitive rules constraining decision makers can be stated in linguistic form).
55. The source discussed in the footnote is David Rhode & Harold Spaeth, *Supreme Court Decision Making*, 72–76 (1976).
56. For general explorations of the issue, see, e.g., Meir Dan-Cohen, "Responsibility and the Boundaries of the Self," 105 Harv. L. Rev. 959 (1992); Erving Goffman, *Encounters* (1961); Harry Frankfurt, *The Importance of What We Care About* (1988); George Herbert Mead, *Mind, Self and Society* (1934); Charles Taylor, *Sources of the Self: The Making of Modern Identity* (1989).
57. Peter Berger & Thomas Luckman, *The Social Construction of Reality* (1966); Michel Foucault, *The Order of Things* (1970); Heidegger, *supra* note 39; Mead, *supra* note 56.
58. Glick, *supra* note 42; Sheldon Goldman & Thomas Jahnige, *The Federal Courts as a Political System* (3d ed., 1985); Segal & Spaeth, *supra* note 25; Spaeth, *supra* note 25; Ulmer, *supra* note 25. Glendon Schubert discusses both the attitudes and ideologies of judges, treating the latter as "macroattitudes." Glendon Schubert, *Human Jurisprudence*, 199–202 (1975). His analysis of decisions is based on attitudes, however, Schubert, *supra* note 25 at 203–11.
59. Dworkin, *supra* note 22; Dworkin, "Hard Cases," 88 Harv. L. Rev. 1057 (1975), reprinted in Dworkin, *supra* note 15, at 81; Eisenberg, *supra* note 11; Bobbitt, *supra* note 15; Bobbitt, *supra* note 30; Michael Perry, *The Constitution, the Courts, and Human Rights* (1982).
60. Allan Hutchinson, *Dwelling on the Threshold: Critical Essays on Modern Legal Thought* (1988); Allan Hutchinson, "Democracy and Determinacy: An Essay on Legal Interpretation," 43 U. Miami L. Rev. 541 (1989); William Simon, "Visions of Practice in Legal Thought," 36 Stan. L. Rev. 469 (1984); Singer, *supra* note 52; Tushnet, *supra* note 22.
61. Austin, *supra* note 28; Crenshaw, *supra* note 28; Lawrence, *supra* note 28.
62. Glick, *supra* note 42, at 328–30.
63. Kennedy, *supra* note 2.
64. Dworkin, *supra* note 22, Dworkin, *supra* note 15.
65. Michael Sandel, *Liberalism and the Limits of Justice*, 135–47 (1982); Stanley Fish, "Working on the Chain Gang: Interpretation in the Law and Literary Criticism," in *The Politics of Interpretation* (W. T. Mitchell, ed., 1983); Charles Fried, "Sonnet LXV and the Black Ink of the Framers' Intention," 100 Harv. L. Rev. 751 (1987); Allan Hutchinson, "Indiana Dworkin and Law's Empire," 96 Yale L. J. 637 (1987); Kenneth Kress, "Legal Reasoning and Coherence Theories: Dworkin's Rights Thesis, Retroactivity, and the Linear Order of Decisions," 72 Cal. L. Rev. 369 (1984); Cornelius Mur-

phy, "Dworkin on Judicial Discretion: A Critical Analysis," 21 U.C. Davis L. Rev. 767 (1988); John Stick, "Literary Imperialism: Assessing the Results of Dworkin's Interpretive Turn in Law's Empire," 34 UCLA L. Rev. 371 (1986).

66. Dworkin, *supra* note 15, at 105–30; Dworkin, *supra* note 22, at 238–354.
67. Victor Hugo, "My Visit to the Concierge," in *The Last Day of the Condemned Man and Other Prison Writings*, 133, 134 (G. Woollen, trans., 1992).
68. Charles Dickens, *Little Dorritt*, ch. 8 (1857).
69. On the value of adopting this approach, rather than treating judicial decisions as part of a disembodied legal process, see Peller, *supra* note 52; Pierre Schlag, "The Problem of the Subject," 69 Tex. L. Rev. 1627 (1991).
70. William James, *Pragmatism* (1907), reprinted in *The Writings of William James: A Comprehensive Edition*, 376, 382–83 (J. McDermott, ed., 1967).
71. Robert Cover, *Justice Accused: Antislavery and the Judicial Process* (1975).
72. See Kennedy, *supra* note 2; Thomas, *supra* note 15.
73. Schauer, "Giving Reasons," *supra* note 38.
74. E.g., *Platek v. Aderhold*, 73 F.2d 173 (5th Cir. 1934); *Snow v. Roche*, 143 F.2d 718 (9th Cir. 1944) (involving Alcatraz); *Siegel v. Ragen*, 180 F.2d 785 (7th Cir.), *cert. denied*, 339 U.S. 990 (1950); *Adams v. Ellis*, 197 F.2d 483 (5th Cir. 1952); *Curtis v. Jacques*, 130 F. Supp. 920 (W.D. Mich. 1954); *Application of Hodge*, 262 F.2d 778 (9th Cir. 1958); *Hatfield v. Bailleaux*, 290 F.2d 632 (9th Cir.), *cert. denied*, 368 U.S. 862 (1961).
75. E.g., *Gordon v. Garrson*, 77 F. Supp. 477 (E.D. Ill. 1948) (failure to provide medical care); *Sweeney v. Woodall*, 344 U.S. 86 (1952); (beating, excessively hard work, and coerced sexual relations); *United States v. Jones*, 207 F.2d 785 (1953) (whipping); *Coleman v. Johnston*, 247 F.2d 273 (7th Cir. 1957) (lack of medical care leading to amputation of leg); *Bank v. Havener*, 234 F. Supp. 27 (E.D. Va 1964) (denial of privileges to Black Muslims).
76. E.g., *Snow v. Roche*, 143 F.2d 718 (9th Cir. 1944) (habeas corpus available only when conviction was illegal); *Powell v. Hunter*, 172 F.2d 330 (10th Cir. 1949) (same); *Sweeney v. Woodall*, 344 U.S. 86 (1952) (fugitive from chain gang must exhaust remedies in state from which he fled); United States ex rel. *Attebury v. Ragen*, 237 F.2d 953 (7th Cir. 1956) (civil rights act does not apply to prison complaints about beatings, deprivation of food, and solitary confinement without clothing or blankets; prisoner should pursue common-law remedies); *Harris v. Settle*, 322 F.2d 908 (8th Cir. 1963) (habeas corpus generally not available to supervise prison conditions).
77. 143 F.2d 443, 445 (6th Cir. 1944).
78. 324 F.2d 165 (7th Cir. 1963), *rev'd*, 378 U.S. 546 (1964).
79. See James Jacobs, *New Perspectives on Prisons and Imprisonment*, 36–41 (1983). On remand, the court of appeals enjoined the prison from banning Black Muslim religious activity, but this decision was limited in scope and was not reached until 1967. 382 F.2d 518 (7th Cir. 1967).
80. 370 F.2d 135 (4th Cir. 1966).
81. *Id.* at 136.
82. *Id.* at 141.
83. *Id.*

84. 101 F. Supp. 285 (Terr. Alaska 1951).
85. *Id.* at 286–87.
86. *Id.* at 289.
87. *Id.* at 289–90.
88. Benjamin Cardozo, *Paradoxes of Legal Science*, 1–30 (1928); Eisenberg, *supra* note 1, at 10–12; Fuller, *supra* note 13, at 63–91; Anthony Amsterdam, "The Void-for-Vagueness Doctrine in the Supreme Court," 109 U. Pa. L. Rev. 67 (1960); Thomas Currier, "Time and Change in Judge Made Law: Prospective Overruling," 51 Va. L. Rev. 207 (1965).
89. Argyris, *supra* note 20; Rosabeth Kanter, *The Change Masters: Innovation for Productivity in the American Corporation* (1985); Edwin Hollander & James Julian, *Studies in Leader Legitimacy, Influence and Innovation, in Group Process*, 115 (L. Berkowitz, ed., 1978). There has been some discussion of late about creating institutions that are biased toward change rather than stability – see, e.g., Roberto Unger, *False Necessity*, 395–595 (1987) – but people are probably most enthusiastic about that approach when they disagree with the particular institution's present views.
90. The quotation in the footnote is from Edmund Husserl, *Ideas*, 140–41 (W. R. Gibson, trans., 1962) (emphasis in original).
91. See, e.g., Guido Calbresi, *A Common Law for the Age of Statutes*, 172–81 (1982); Joseph Goldstein, *The Intelligible Constitution* (1992); Gerald Gunther, "The Subtle Vices of the Passive Virtues: A Comment on Principle and Expediency in Judicial Review," 64 Colum. L. Rev. 1 (1964); Alan Hirsch, "Candor and Prudence in Constitutional Interpretation," 61 Geo. Wash. L. Rev. 858 (1993); Scott Idleman, "A Prudential Theory of Judicial Candor," 73 Tex. L. Rev. 1307 (1995); John Kircher, "Judicial Candor: Do As We Say, Not As We Do," 73 Marq. L. Rev. 421 (1990); Robert Leflar, "Honest Judicial Opinions," 74 Nw. U. L. Rev. 721 (1979); David Shapiro, "In Defense of Judicial Candor," 100 Harv. L. Rev. 731 (1987); Martin Shapiro, "Judges as Liars," 17 Harv. J. L. & Pub. Pol'y 155 (1994); Nicholas Zeppos, "Judicial Candor and Statutory Interpretation," 78 Geo. L. J. 353 (1989).
92. Warren Bennis, *Beyond Bureaucracy* (1966); Paul Lawrence & Jay Lorsch, *Organization and Environment* (1986); Alvin Toffler, *The Third Wave* (1980); Ronald Lippit, "The Changing Leader-Follower Relationships of the 1980s," 18 J. Applied Behav. Sc. 395 (1982).
93. Chris Argyris, *Integrating the Individual and the Organization* (1964); Kanter, *supra* note 89; Karl Lewin, *Resolving Social Conflicts* (1948).
94. Argyris, *supra* note 20; Bennis, *supra* note 93; Edwin Hollander, *Leaders, Groups and Influence* (1964). To the extent that the leader can control the subordinate, it is by transforming the subordinate's construction of reality. See Weick, *supra* note 20.
95. This rapid rise may result from the political significance of the case at hand; see, e.g., *Buckley v. Valeo*, 424 U.S. 1 (1976); *New York Times Co. v. United States*, 403 U.S. 713 (1971) (Pentagon Papers Case); *Youngstown Sheet & Tube Co. v. Sawyer*, 343 U.S. 579 (1952). Or it may result from the Supreme Court's willingness to rule decisively on some particular subject;

see, e.g., *INS v. Chadha*, 462 U.S. 919 (1983) (holding legislative veto un-constitutional in politically insignificant case, after relatively little litigation in the lower courts); *Jones v. Alfred H. Mayer Co.*, 392 U.S. 409 (1967) (holding 42 U.S.C. § 1982 valid under Thirteenth Amendment after a ruling by one circuit involving a single private citizen).

96. 392 U.S. 409 (1968).

97. See, e.g., Alexander Aleinikoff, "A Case for Race Consciousness," 91 Colum. L. Rev. 1060, 1118–20 (1991) (recommending general shift to Thirteenth Amendment to combat discrimination); Akhil Reed Amar, "The Case of the Missing Amendments: *R.A.V. v. City of St. Paul*," 106 Harv. L. Rev. 124 (1992) (recommending use of Thirteenth Amendment against hate speech); Akhil Reed Amar, "Forty Acres and a Mule: A Republican Theory of Minimal Entitlements," 13 Harv. J. L. & Pub. Pol'y 37 (1990) (recommending use of Thirteenth Amendment as a general tool for social justice); Akhil Reed Amar, "Child Abuse as Slavery: A Thirteenth Amendment Response to DeShaney," 105 Harv. L. Rev. 1359 (1992); Douglas L. Colbert, "Liberating the Thirteenth Amendment," 30 Harv. C.L.-C.R. L. Rev. 1 (1995) (recommending general use of Thirteenth Amendment in race-related cases and other human rights situations); Douglas L. Colbert, "Challenging the Challenge: Thirteenth Amendment as a Prohibition against the Racial Use of Peremptory Challenges," 76 Cornell L. Rev. 1 (1990): Charles H. Jones, "An Argument for Federal Protection against Racially Motivated Crimes: 18 U.S.C. § 241 and the Thirteenth Amendment," 21 Harv. C.R.-C.L. L. Rev. (1986); Andrew Koppelman, "Forced Labor: A Thirteenth Amendment Defense of Abortion," 84 Nw. U. L. Rev. 480 (1990); Joyce E. McConnell, "Beyond Metaphor: Battered Women, Involuntary Servitude and the Thirteenth Amendment," 4 Yale J. L. & Feminism 207 (1992); James Gray Pope, "Labor and the Constitution: From Abolition to Deindustrialization," 65 Tex. L. Rev. 1071 (1987); Lea S. VanderVelde, "The Labor Vision of the Thirteenth Amendment," 138 U. Pa. L. Rev. 437 (1989). See generally Guyora Binder, "Did Slaves Author the Thirteenth Amendment? An Essay in Redemptive History," 5 Yale J. L. & Human. 471 (1993) (redemptive value of treating the Thirteenth Amendment as a central element in constitutional law).

98. *Bobilin v. Board of Educ.*, 403 F. Supp. 1095 (D. Haw. 1975) (mandatory cafeteria duty in school is not a badge or incident of slavery); *NAACP v. Hunt*, 891 F.2d 1555 (11th Cir. 1990) (flying confederate flag on Alabama state capitol dome was not a badge or incident of slavery); *Steirer v. Bethlehem Area School Dist.*, 789 F. Supp. 1337 (E.D. Pa. 1992) (requiring students to perform sixty hours of community service between start of ninth grade and completion of twelfth was not a badge or incident of slavery); *In re Herberman*, 122 B.R. 273 (W.D. Tex. 1990) (treating income accruing to debtor after he filed Chapter 11 case as property of the estate except to the extent of a reasonable salary due to debtor as compensation for his services as professional employee is not a badge or incident of slavery); *Jane L. v. Bangerter*, 794 F. Supp. 1537 (D. Utah 1992) (prohibition of abortions does not subject women to a badge on incident of slavery); *Sharp*

v. State, 245 Kan. 749, 783 P.2d 343 (1989), *cert. denied*, 498 U.S. 822 (1990) (appointment of lawyer to represent indigent defendant is not a badge or incident of slavery).

99. Edward Purcell, Jr., *The Crisis of Democratic Theory: Scientific Naturalism and the Problem of Value*, 74–77 (1973); Thomas Grey, "Langdell's Orthodoxy," 45 U. Pitt. L. Rev. 1 (1983); Duncan Kennedy, "Toward a Historical Understanding of Legal Consciousness: The Case of Classical Legal Thought in America, 1850–1940," 3 J. Res. L. & Soc. (1980); Robert Gordon, "Legal Thought and Practice in the Age of American Enterprise, 1870–1920," in *Professions and Professional Ideologies in America* (G. Geison, ed., 1983).

100. For early criticism, see, e.g., Jerome Frank, *Law and the Modern Mind* (2d ed., 1949); Felix Cohen, "Transcendental Nonsense and the Functional Approach," 35 Colum. L. Rev. 809 (1935); Robert Hale, "Coercion and Distribution in a Supposedly Non-Coercive State," 38 Pol. Sci. Q. 470 (1923); Karl Llewellyn, "A Realistic Jurisprudence – The Next Step," 30 Colum. L. Rev. 431 (1930); Roscoe Pound, "Mechanical Jurisprudence," 8 Colum. L. Rev. 605 (1908). The criticism continues to the present day; see, e.g., Roberto Unger, *The Critical Legal Studies Movement*, 1–14 (1989); Peller, *supra* note 52; Schlag, *supra* note 52, at 1632–62; Robert Weisberg, "The Calabresian Judicial Artist: Statutes and the New Legal Process," 35 Stan. L. Rev. 213, 232–34 (1983).

101. Steven Burton, *An Introduction to Law and Legal Reasoning* (1985); Daniel Farber & Philip Frickey, "Practical Reason and the First Amendment," 34 UCLA L. Rev. 1615 (1987); Daniel Farber, "The Inevitability of Practical Reason: Statutes, Formalism, and the Rule of Law," 45 Vand. L. Rev. 533 (1992); Anthony Kronman, "Alexander Bickel's Philosophy of Prudence," 94 Yale L. J. 1567 (1985); Frank Michelman, "Foreword: Traces of Self-Government," 100 Harv. L. Rev. 4 (1986); Patterson, *supra* note 33; Suzanna Sherry, "Civic Virtue and the Feminine Voice in Constitutional Adjudication," 72 Va. L. Rev. 543 (1986); Vincent Wellman, "Practical Reasoning and Judicial Justification: Toward an Adequate Theory," 57 U. Colo. L. Rev. 45 (1985).

102. See W. Brian Arthur, "Competing Technologies, Increasing Returns, and Lock-In by Historical Events," 99 Econ. J. 116 (1989); W. Brian Arthur, "Self Reinforcing Mechanisms in Economics," in *The Economy as an Evolving Complex System* (P. Anderson, K. Arrow & D. Pines, eds., 1988); William Barnett & Glenn Carroll, "How Institutional Constraints Affected the Organization of Early U.S. Telephony," 9 J. L. Econ. & Org. 98 (1993); Paul David, "Clio in the Economics of QWERTY," 75 Am. Econ. Rev. 332 (1985); Oliver Williamson, *The Economic Institutions of Capitalism*, 236–40 (1985). For a critique of this idea when applied to technological innovation, see Stephen J. Liebowitz & Stephen Margolis, "The Fable of the Keys," 33 J. L. & Econ. 12 (1990).

103. Martin Shapiro, *Courts: A Comparative and Political Analysis* (1981).

104. See Shapiro, "Decentralized Decisionmaking," *supra* note 20; Roger Traynor, "The Limits of Judicial Creativity," 63 Iowa L. Rev. 1 (1977);

John Poulos, "Judicial Philosophy," *supra* note 32, at 1702–5; John Poulos, "Judicial Process," *supra* note 32, at 509–15. Cf. Robert Pushaw, "Justiciability and Separation of Powers: A Neo-Federalist Approach," 81 Cornell L. Rev. 393 (1996) (viewing case or controversy requirement as an inherent constraint on otherwise broad judicial authority).

105. Calabresi, *supra* note 91, at 129–31 (1982). For a critique see Weisberg, *supra* note 100, at 221–30.
106. Eskridge, *supra* note 53.
107. Llewellyn, *supra* note 31.
108. Burton, *supra* note 101, at 25–40.
109. Eisenberg, *supra* note 1, at 83–96.
110. Steven Winter, "Transcendental Nonsense, Metaphoric Reasoning, and the Cognitive Stakes for Law," 137 U. Pa. L. Rev. 1105 (1989); Steven Winter, "Death Is the Mother of Metaphor," 105 Harv. L. Rev. 745 (1992) (reviewing Thomas Grey, *The Wallace Stevens Case: Law and the Practice of Poetry* (1991)); Steven Winter, "The Meaning of 'Under Color Of' Law," 91 Mich. L. Rev. 323 (1992).
111. Cass Sunstein, *Legal Reasoning and the Political Process* (1996); Cass Sunstein, "On Analogical Reasoning," 106 Harv. L. Rev. 743 (1993).
112. Roberto Unger, *What Should Legal Analysis Become?* (1996). There is also extensive interest in these techniques, particularly analogy, among European legal thinkers. See, e.g., Aleksander Peczenik, *On Law and Reason*, 392–404 (1989); Theodor Viehweg, *Topics in Law* (W. Durham, trans., 1993); Cees W. Maris, "Milking the Meter – On Analogy, Universalizability and World Views," in *Legal Knowledge and Analogy*, 71 (P. Nerhot, ed., 1991); Giuseppe Zaccaria, "Analogy As Legal Reasoning – The Hermeneutic Foundation of the Analogical Procedure," in *Legal Knowledge and Analogy, supra*, at 42.
113. There are also numerous discussions of the metaphorical structure of thought in general. See Jacques Derrida, *Margins of Philosophy*, 224–70 (Alan Bass, trans., 1982); George Lakoff, *Women, Fire, and Dangerous Things* (1987); George Lakoff & Mark Johnson, *Metaphors We Live By* (1980); Andrew Ortony, ed., *Metaphor and Thought* (2d ed., 1993); Paul Ricoeur, *The Rule of Metaphor: Multi-Disciplinary Studies in the Creation of Meaning in Language* (R. Czerny, trans., 1977); Richard Rorty, *Essays on Heidegger and Others*, 9–26 (1991). While much of this is illuminating, the argument threatens to become somewhat uninteresting because it does not explain what nonmetaphorical speech and thought could possibly be like, as least for ordinary discourse (as opposed to mathematics). As used here, metaphor is not either the general use of concrete concepts or a figure of speech, but the use of a nonliteral or nondeductive concept as a basic element in a legal argument.
114. John Serle, "Metaphor" in Ortony, *supra* note 113, at 83.
115. Martha Minow & Elizabeth Spelman, "Passion for Justice," 10 Cardozo L. Rev. 37, 39–48 (1988).
116. See, e.g., *Dombrowski v. Pfister*, 380 U.S. 479, 487 (1965) ("The chilling effect upon the exercise of First Amendment rights may derive from the

fact of persecution, unaffected by the prospects of success or failure"). Having been articulated, the term becomes available for use as a fixed element of constitutional argument. See, e.g., *Virginia State Board of Pharmacy v. Virginia Consumer Council,* 425 U.S. 748, 777 (1976) (Stewart, J., concurring) ("The advertiser's access to the truth about his product and its price substantially eliminates any danger that governmental regulation of false or misleading price or product advertising will chill accurate and nondeceptive commercial expression").

117. Charles Warren & Louis Brandeis, "The Right to Privacy," 4 Harv. L. Rev. 193 (1890).

118. *Haelen Laboratories v. Topps Chewing Gum,* 202 F.2d 866 (2d Cir. 1953).

119. *Frost v. Railroad Commission,* 271 U.S. 583, 593–94 (1926); *Speiser v. Randall,* 357 U.S. 513 (1958); *Sherbert v. Verner,* 374 U.S. 398 (1963); *Pickering v. Board of Education,* 391 U.S. 563 (1968).

120. Established by *Carrington v. Rash,* 380 U.S. 89 (1965); *Shapiro v. Thompson,* 394 U.S. 618, 631 (1969); *Stanley v. Illinois,* 405 U.S. 645 (1972); *Vlandis v. Kline,* 412 U.S. 441 (1973); *Cleveland Board of Education v. La Fleur,* 414 U.S. 632 (1974): abandoned in *Weinberger v. Salfi,* 442 U.S. 749 (1978). See Jerry Mashaw, "Administrative Due Process: The Quest for a Dignatory Theory," 61 B.U. L. Rev. 885, 896–98 (1981).

121. James Frazier, *The Golden Bough,* ch. 22 (1922); C. Levi-Strauss, *The Savage Mind* (1962).

122. Fish, *supra* note 52.

123. Fiss, *supra* note 53.

124. Schauer, "Easy Cases," *supra* note 38. Schauer's position is open to challenge, of course; see Sanford Levinson, "What Do Lawyers Know (and What Do They Do with Their Knowledge)?: Comments on Schauer and Moore," 58 S. Cal. L. Rev. 441 (1991); James Nickels, "Uneasiness about Easy Cases," 58 S. Cal. L. Rev. 477 (1985); David Richards, "Interpretation and Historiography," 58 S. Cal. L. Rev. 489, 516–22 (1985). Indeed, these critiques probably represent our dominant approach to the interpretive process. But the point being made here is not that certain cases are really easy, in the sense that they yield determinate and justifiable outcomes, but that they are perceived as easy by the majority of judges.

125. Nicoli Gogol, *The Overcoat* (1841). Similar depictions from the same era include Nicoli Gogol, *The Inspector General* (1836); Dickens, *supra* note 68, ch. 10 ("Containing the whole science of government," which describes the Circumlocution Office).

126. Gadamer, *supra* note 46, at 305–41.

127. Cardozo, *supra* note 15, at 98–141.

128. Bobbitt, *supra* note 30.

129. Dennis Patterson, *Law and Truth* (1997); Dennis Patterson, "The Poverty of Interpretive Universalism: Toward a Reconstruction of Legal Theory," 72 Tex. L. Rev. 1 (1993); Dennis Patterson, "Conscience and the Constitution," Colum. L. Rev. 270 (1993) (review of Bobbitt, *supra* note 30).

130. Steven Winter, "Incommesurability in Constitutional Law," 78 Cal. L. Rev. 1441 (1990).

131. Niklas Luhmann, *Social Systems* (1992); Niklas Luhmann, "The Creative Uses of Paradoxes in Law and Legal History," 15 J. L. & Soc'y 153 (1988); Niklas Luhmann, "The Self-Reproduction of Law and Its Limits in Dilemmas of Law," in *The Welfare State* (G. Teubner, ed., 1985).

132. Gunther Teubner, *Law as an Autopoietic System* (1993); Gunther Teubner, "How the Law Thinks: Towards a Constructivist Epistemology of Law," 23 L. & Soc. Rev. 727 (1989); Gunther Teubner, "Evolution of Autopoietic Law," in *Autopoietic Law: A New Approach to Law and Society* (G. Teubner, ed., 1987).

133. Teubner, *Law as a Autopoietic System, supra* note 132, at 35.

134. Kadish & Kadish, *supra* note 13, at 66–94; Francis Mootz III, "Rethinking the Rule of Law: A Demonstration That the Obvious Is Plausible," 61 Tenn. L. Rev. 69 (1993); Francis Mootz III, "Is the Rule of Law Plausible in a Postmodern World," 68 Wash. L. Rev. 249 (1993); Margaret Radin, "Reconsidering the Rule of Law," 69 B.U. L. Rev. 781 (1989).

135. Lawrence Baum, *American Courts, Process and Policy* (2d ed., 1990); Glick, *supra* note 42; Goldman & Jahnige, *supra* note 58. For recognition of this fact in legal sources, see Eskridge, *supra* note 35; Poulos, "Judicial Philosophy," *supra* note 32, at 1710–15; Poulos, "Judicial Process," *supra* note 32, at 531–35.

136. See Evan Caminker, "Why Must Inferior Courts Obey Superior Court Precedents," 46 Stan. L. Rev. 817 (1994); Lewis Kornhauser, "Positive Theory as Conceptual Critique: A Piece of a Pragmatic Agenda," 68 S. Cal. L. Rev. 1595 (1995); Lewis Kornhauser, "Modelling Collegial Courts I: Path Dependence," 9 Int'l. Rev. L. & Econ. 169 (1992); Lewis Kornhauser, "Modelling Collegial Courts II: Legal Doctrine," 8 J. L. Econ. & Org. 441 (1992).

137. Bobbitt, *Constitutional Fate, supra* note 15, at 167–68 ("A judge who never felt the constraints of the various modalities, who felt that any decision could be satisfactorily defended, would be very foolish or very unimaginative.... [But the] United States Constitution formalizes a role for the conscience of the individual sensibility by requiring decisions that rely on the individual moral sensibility when the modalities of argument clash"); Ronald Dworkin, *A Matter of Principle*, 17 (1985) ("So a judge following the rights conception must not decide a hard case by appealing to any principle that is in that way incompatible with the rule book of his jurisdiction. But he must still decide many cases on political grounds, because in these cases contrary moral principles directly in point are each compatible with the rule book"); Joseph Raz, *The Authority of Law*, 186 (1979) ("There is an indefinite number of different modifications of every rule conforming to the two conditions spelt out above. The court's obligation, however, is to adopt only that modification which will best improve the rule").

138. Dworkin, *supra* note 15, at 105–30.

139. Robert Graves, *The Greek Myths*, §§ 123–34 (rev. ed., 1960).

140. *Id.* at § 148.
141. See, e.g., Michael Gerhardt, "The Role of Precedent in Constitutional Decisionmaking and Theory," 60 Geo. Wash. L. Rev. 68, 138 (1991); Paul Gewirtz, "Remedies and Resistance," 92 Yale L. J. 585, 670–72 (1983); Arthur Miller, "On the Choice of Major Premises in Supreme Court Opinions," 14 J. Publ. L. 251, 257 (1965). These discussions focus on multimember panels, rather than on the judiciary as a whole, and there the role of compromise may be larger relative to the role of conceptual coordination. For somewhat contradictory views, see *supra* note 136 (law and economics analysis of multimember judiciaries).
142. Cf. Patricia Williams, "The Obliging Shell: An Informal Essay on Formal Equal Opportunity," 87 U. Mich. L. Rev. 2128 (1989). Gadamer's discussion of the horizon appears at *supra* note 46, at 267–74.
143. Eskridge, *supra* note 35; William Eskridge, "Dynamic Statutory Interpretation," 135 U. Pa. L. Rev. 1479 (1987); William Eskridge, "Politics without Romance: Implications of Public Choice Theory for Statutory Interpretation," 74 Va. L. Rev. 275 (1988).
144. Alexander Aleinikoff, "Updating Statutory Interpretation," 87 Mich. L. Rev. 20 (1988).
145. Bruce Ackerman, *We the People* (1991).
146. Bobbitt, *supra* note 30.
147. Eisenberg, *supra* note 1.
148. Thomas, *supra* note 15, at 75.
149. David Danelski, "The Influence of the Chief Justice in the Decisional Process of the Supreme Court," in *The Federal Judicial System*, 158 (T. Jahnige & S. Goldman, eds., 1968); Glick, *supra* note 42, at 338–45; Goldman & Jahnige, *supra* note 58, at 149–58; Walter Murphy, *Elements of Judicial Strategy* (1964).
150. 410 U.S. 113 (1973). See Daniel Farber & Philip Frickey, *Law and Public Choice*, 145–53 (1991).
151. Alexander Bickel, *The Least Dangerous Branch: The Supreme Court at the Bar of Politics* (1962).
152. *Id.* at 23–34, 244–72.
153. *Id.* at 111–98.
154. Lea Brilmayer, "The Jurisprudence of Article III: Perspective on the 'Case or Controversy' Requirement," 93 Harv. L. Rev. 287 (1979); Calabresi, *supra* note 91, at 18–20; Gerald Gunther, "The Subtle Vices of the 'Passive Virtues' – A Comment on Principle and Expediency in Judicial Review," 64 Colum. L. Rev. 1 (1964); Martin Redish, *The Federal Courts in the Political Order*, 89–136 (1991); cf. Jan Deutsch, "Neutrality, Legitimacy, and the Supreme Court: Some Interactions between Law and Political Science," 20 Stan. L. Rev. 169 (1968) (Bickel's prudential approach points toward an interdisciplinary understanding of all Supreme Court decision making).
155. Robert Cover, "Nomos and Narrative," 97 Harv. L. Rev. 4, 40–44 (1983).
156. This is the first reason for certiorari review stated in the Rule of the Supreme Court. Rule 10.1(a), 493 U.S. 1097, 1106 (1989). There is evi-

dence that the Court actually follows this rule. Gregory Caldeira & John Wright, "Organized Interests and Agenda Setting in the U.S. Supreme Court," 82 Am. Pol. Sci. Rev. 1109 (1988); Arthur Hellman, "Case Selection in the Burger Court: A Preliminary Inquiry," 60 Notre Dame L. Rev. 947, 1014–20 (1985); Perry, *supra* note 26, at 127–28; Siegel & Spaeth, *supra* note 25, at 199–202; Sidney Ulmer, "The Supreme Court's Certiorari Decisions: Conflict as a Predictive Variable," 78 Am. Pol. Sci. Rev. 901 (1984). Conflict thus serves as a cue for granting review; see Joseph Tannenhaus, Marvin Schick, Michael Muraskin & David Rosen, "The Supreme Court's Certiorari Jurisdiction: Cue Theory," in *Judicial Decision Making* (G. Schubert, ed., 1963). But see Marie Provine, *Case Selection in the United States Supreme Court* (1980) (selection process too complex to be reduced to yes/no).

157. This is, in effect, the third reason given in the Rule for granting certiorari. Rule 10.1(c), 493 U.S. at 1106. See Hellman, *supra* note 156, at 1040–41; Perry, *supra* note 156, at 271–84; Donald Songer, "Concern for Policy Outputs as a Cue for Supreme Court Decisions on Certiorari," 41 J. Pol. 1185 (1979); Ulmer, *supra* note 156.

158. On the federal government's role in triggering Supreme Court review, see Hellman, *supra* note 156, at 1020–24; M. Provine, *supra* note 156, at 87; Tannenhaus et al., *supra* note 156; Sidney Ulmer, William Hintze & Louise Kirklosky, "The Decision to Grant or Deny Certiorari: Further Consideration of Cue Theory," 6 L. & Soc. Rev. 637 (1972). In one of the only cases decided against a federal facility, the Second Circuit found certain conditions in the New York City federal jail unconstitutional. When the solicitor general filed a certiorari petition, the Supreme Court granted the petition and reversed. *Bell v. Wolfish*, 441 U.S. 520 (1979).

159. Francis Mootz III, "Is the Rule of Law Possible in a Postmodern World?" 68 Wash. L. Rev. 249 (1993); Francis Mootz III, "Rethinking the Rule of Law: A Demonstration That the Obvious Is Plausible," 61 Tenn. L. Rev. 69 (1993).

160. See Owen Fiss, "The Supreme Court, 1978 Term – Foreword: The Forms of Justice," 93 Harv. L. Rev. 1 (1979).

161. *Youngberg v. Romeo*, 457 U.S. 307 (1982); *Pennhurst State School & Hospital v. Halderman*, 612 F.2d 84 (3rd Cir. 1979), *rev'd.* 451 U.S. 1 (1982); 673 F.2d 647 (1982), rev'd 465 U.S. 89 (1984); *Society for Good Will to Retarded Children, Inc. v. Cuomo*, 737 F.2d 1239 (2d. Cir. 1984); *Welsch v. Likins*, 550 F.2d 1122 (8th Cir. 1977); *Wyatt v. Aderholt*, 503 F.2d 1305 (5th Cir. 1974) (affirming *Wyatt v. Stickney*, 344 F. Supp. 373, 387 (M.D. Ala. 1972)); *Krecht v. Gillman*, 488 F.2d 1136 (8th Cir. 1973); *Rouse v. Cameron*, 373 F.2d 451 (D.C. Cir. 1966).

162. Adolph Meyer, *The Collected Papers of Adolph Meyer* (E. Winters, ed., 1975).

163. Charles Beers, *A Mind That Found Itself* (4th ed., 1917).

164. Regarding the right to treatment discussed in the footnote, see Morton Birnbaum, "The Right to Treatment," 46 A.B.A. J. 499 (1960); see Morton Birnbaum, "A Rationale for the Right," 57 Geo. L. J. 752 (1969); Morton Birnbaum, "Some Comments on 'The Right to Treatment,'" 13

Arch. Gen. Psychiatry 34 (1965). The case the Supreme Court decided is *Youngberg v. Romeo*, 457 U.S. 307 (1982).

165. Pub. L. No. 89–197, 79 Stat. 828 (1965).

166. 423 U.S. 362 (1976).

167. Ronald Coase, "The Federal Communications Commission," 2 J. L. & Econ. 1 (1959); Alfred Kahn, *The Economics of Regulation*, vol. 2, 173–210 (1971); Warren Schwartz, "Comparative Television and the Chancellor's Foot," 47 Geo. L. J. 655 (1959); Glen Robinson, "The FCC and the First Amendment: Observations on 40 Years of Radio and Television Regulation," 52 Minn. L. Rev. 67 (1967).

168. McKelvey, *supra* note 6, at 14–31; Rothman, *supra* note 6, at 79–108.

169. Francis Cullen & Kenneth Gilbert, *Reaffirming Rehabilitation*, 73–81 (1982); Ernest Hoag & Edward Williams, *Crime, Abnormal Minds, and the Law* (1923); Thomas Osborne, *Society and Prisons* (1916); Rothman, *supra* note 6, at 43–201; William White, *Crime and Criminals* (1933).

170. Estelle Freedman, *Their Sister's Keepers: Women's Prison Reform in America, 1830–1930*, 109–57 (1984). Nicole Rafter, *Partial Justice: Women, Prisons and Social Control*, 53–82 (1990); Rothman, *supra* note 6, at 205–89.

171. John Bender, *Imagining the Penitentiary*, 11–43 (1987); Leon Radzinowicz, *A History of the English Criminal Law and Its Administration from 1750*, vol. 1 (1948) G. Scott, *A History of Corporal Punishment* (1938); Thorsten Sellin, *Slavery and the Penal System*, 30–112 (1976); Pieter Spierenburg, *The Spectacle of Suffering* (1984).

172. Britton, bk. I, ch. 12 (F. Nichols, trans., 1865); Thomas Hobbes, *Leviathan*, ch. 28 (1651). See Ralph Pugh, *Imprisonment in Medieval England*, 1–56 (1970) (citing Braxton, Britton, and Glanville).

173. Pugh, *supra* note 172, at 1–56; T. Sellin, *supra* note 171, at 43–112; Pieter Spierenburg, *The Prison Experience* (1991).

174. Sellen, *supra* note 171, at 43–112.

175. Harry Barnes, "The Historical Origin of the Prison System in America," 12 J. Am. Inst. Crim. L. & Criminology 36 (1921); Rothman, *supra* note 6, at 57–78.

176. Harry Barnes, *The Story of Punishment: A Record of Man's Inhumanity to Man* (1930); Rothman, *supra* note 6, at 79–108. For parallel developments in Britain, see Bender, *supra* note 171, and Ignatieff, *supra* note 6; for continental Europe, see Michel Foucault, *Discipline and Punish* (1977); Spierenburg, *supra* note 171, at 183–99; Spierenburg, *supra* note 173.

177. Victor Turner, *The Forest of Symbols* (1967); Victor Turner, *The Ritual Process: Structure and Anti-Structure* (1969). This in turn is based on Arnold Van Gerrep, *Rites of Passage* (M. Vizedom & G. Chaffee, trans., 1960).

178. Bender, *supra* note 171.

179. *Id.* at 27.

180. *Id.* at 33–61.

181. But see Graeme Newman, *Just and Painful: A Case for the Corporal Punishment of Criminals* (1985). See Jonathon Simon, "Back to the Future: Newman on Corporal Punishment," 1985 A.B.F. Res. J. 927.

182. Barnes, *supra* note 176; Cullen & Gilbert, *supra* note 169, at 45–83 (1982);

T. E. Erikson, *The Reformers: A Historical Survey of Prisoner Experiments in the Treatment of Criminals* (1976); Rothman, *supra* note 6, at 117–58, 379–421.

183. E.g., *Kelly v. Dowd*, 140 F.2d 81 (7th Cir. 1944); *U.S. v. Radio Station WENR*, 209 F.2d 105 (7th Cir. 1953); *Morris v. Igoe*, 209 F.2d 108 (7th Cir. 1953); *Lee v. Tahash*, 352 F.2d 970 (8th Cir. 1965).

184. E.g., *Sewell v. Pegelow*, 291 F.2d 196 (4th Cir. 1961); *Pierce v. LaVallee*, 293 F.2d 233 (2d Cir. 1961); *In re Ferguson*, 55 Cal. 2d 663, *cert. denied sub. nom. Ferguson v. Heinze*, 368 U.S. 864 (1961).

185. *Powell v. Hunter*, 172 F.2d 330 (10th Cir. 1949); *Siegel v. Ragen*, 180 F.2d 785 (7th Cir); *cert. denied*, 339 U.S. 990 (1950); *Banning v. Looney*, 213 F.2d 771 (10th Cir. 1954); *Bryant v. Harrelson*, 187 F. Supp. 738 (S.D. Tex. 1960).

186. *U.S. v. Radio Station WENR*, 209 F.2d 105 (7th Cir. 1953); *Nichols v. McGee*, 169 F. Supp. 721 (N.D. Cal.), *appeal dismissed*, 361 U.S. 6 (1959); *Harris v. Settle*, 322 F.2d 908 (8th Cir. 1963).

187. *In re Rider*, Volume # Cal. App. 797 (1920); *Ex parte Snyder*, 62 Cal. App. 697, 217 P.2d 777 (1923); *Ex parte Hull*, 312 U.S. 546 (1941) (prison rule prohibiting inmate from filing habeas corpus petition is invalid).

188. William Taylor, *Brokered Justice*, 83–88, 138, 160 (1993).

189. 347 U.S. 483 (1954).

190. Taylor, *supra* note 188, at 83–84, 89, 160.

191. *Ex parte Terell*, 47 Okla. 92, 287 P. 753 (1930); *Miller v. Overholser*, 206 F.2d 415 (D.C. Cir. 1953). For the courts' palpable confusion about the scope of the writ, see *Thomas v. Cavell*, 158 F. Supp. 19 (W.D. Pa. 1957); *Harris v. Seattle*, 322 F.2d 908 (8th Cir. 1963). But see *Sellers v. Cloone*, 530 F.2d 199, n. 5 (8th Cir. 1976) ("The denial of all rehabilitative training to a prisoner who can benefit therefrom is violative of the prisoner's constitutional rights").

192. *Holt v. Sarver*, 309 F. Supp. 362, 379 (1970). See also *Hamilton v. Schiro*, 338 F. Supp. 1016, 1018 (E.D. La. 1970); *Craig v. Hocker*, 405 F. Supp. 656, 697–80 (D. Nev. 1975) (cruel and unusual punishment to place inmates under the age of twenty-one in administrative segregation for their protection "with slight opportunity for education, training, or rehabilitation;" they should be placed in more appropriate institutions); *Pugh v. Locke*, 406 F. Supp. 318, 330 (M.D. Ala. 1976), *aff'd and remanded sub. nom. Newman v. Alabama*, 559 F. 2d 283 (5th Cir. 1977), *rev'd in part on unrelated grounds sub. nom. Alabama v. Pugh*, 438 U.S. 781 (1987); *Barnes v. Government of Virgin Islands*, 415 F. Supp. 1218, 1229 (D.V.I. 1976); *Laaman v. Helgemoe*, 437 F. Supp. 269, 319 (D.N.H. 1977); *Ramos v. Lamm*, 485 F. Supp. 122, 147 (D. Colo. 1979) *aff'd in part and set aside in part on unrelated grounds*, 639 F. 2d 559 (10th Cir. 1980), *cert. denied*, 450 U.S. 1041 (1981).

193. *Id.* See *id.* at 380–81 (condemning degrading and disgusting conditions as inconducive to rehabilitation). See also *Wolff v. McDonnell*, 418 U.S. 539, 563 (1974) (arguing both pros and cons of due process) and at 2990–91 (Marshall, J., concurring and dissenting); *Milter v. Twomey*, 479

F.2d 701, 712 & n. 23 (7th Cir. 1971) *cert. denied sub. nom. Gutierrez v. Dept. of Public Safety*, 414 U.S. 1146 (1974); *Landman v. Royster*, 333 F. Supp. 621 (1971).

194. 365 U.S. 167 (1961). See, e.g, *Palmigiano v. Garrahy*, 599 F. Supp. 956, 986 (D.R.I. 1977) (ordering defendant to "make available as soon as possible access, on a voluntary basis, . . . to educational programs"); *Laaman v. Helgemoe*, 437 F. Supp. 269, 294–96 (D.N.H. 1977); *Barnes v. Government of Virgin Islands*, 415 F. Supp. 1218, 1227, 1233–34 (D.V.I. 1976) (ordering Virgin Island prison to provide "meaningful rehabilitative opportunities . . . failing which I shall sentence all offenders to mainland institutions"); *Holt v. Sarver*, 309 F. Supp. 362, 362 (E.D. Ark. 1970), *aff'd*, 442 F. 2d 304 (8th Cir. 1971).

195. *Holt v. Sarver*, 309 F. Supp. at 382–85.

196. For cases rejecting a constitutional right to rehabilitation, see *Pell v. Procunier*, 417 U.S. 817 (1974); *United States v. Brown*, 381 U.S. 437 (1965); *Williams v. New York*, 337 U.S. 241, 248 (1949); *Anderson v. Nosser*, 438 F.2d 183, 190 (5th Cir. 1971), *modified on rehearing en banc*, 456 F.2d 835 (1972), *cert. denied*, 409 U.S. 848 (1972); *Benson v. United States*, 332 F.2d 288, 292 (5th Cir. 1964); *Jackson v. Bishop*, 404 F.2d 571, 580 (8th Cir. 1968) (Blackmun, J.); *Diamond v. Thompson*, 364 F. Supp. 659, 667 (M.D. Ala. 1973); *Brenneman v. Madigan*, 343 F. Supp. 128, 142 (N.D. Cal. 1972); *Finney v. Arkansas Board of Corrections*, 505 F.2d 194, 209 (8th Cir. 1974); *Miller v. Carson*, 401 F. Supp. 835, 900 (M.D. Fla. 1975); *Battle v. Anderson*, 376 F. Supp. 402 (E.D. Okla. 1974); *Inmates of Allegheny County Jail v. Pierce*, 612 F. 2d 754 (3rd Cir. 1979); *James v. Wallace*, 406 F. Supp. 318 (M.D. Ala. 1978); *Morris v. Travisono*, 499 F. Supp. 149 (D.R.I. 1980); *Albirti v. Sheriff of Harris Co., Tex.*, 406 F. Supp. 649 (S.D. Tex. 1975); *Ohlinger v. Watson*, 652 F. 2d 775, 28 (9th Cir. 1980). A few cases, however, did hold that prisoners have a constitutional right to rehabilitation. In *People v. Feagley*, the California Supreme Court ruled that a statutory scheme that imprisoned habitual sex offenders for an indeterminate period was unconstitutional if it failed to include rehabilitative efforts. 14 Cal. App. 3d 338, 535 P.2d 373 (1975).

197. *Ramos v. Lamm*, 485 F. Supp 122 (D. Colo. 1969).

198. See, e.g., *Hamilton v. Schiro*, 338 F. Supp. 1016, 1018 (E.D. La. 1970); *Craig v. Hocker*, 405 F. Supp. 656, 697–80 (D. Nev. 1975) (cruel and unusual punishment to place inmates under the age of twenty-one in administrative segregation for their protection "with slight opportunity for education, training, or rehabilitation;" they should be placed in more appropriate institutions); *Pugh v. Locke*, 406 F. Supp. 318, 330 (M.D. Ala. 1976), *aff'd and remanded sub. nom. Newman v. Alabama*, 559 F. 2d 283 (5th Cir. 1977), *rev'd in part on unrelated grounds sub. nom. Alabama v. Pugh*, 438 U.S. 781 (1987); *Barnes v. Government of Virgin Islands*, 415 F. Supp. 1218, 1229 (D.V.I. 1976); *Laaman v. Helgemoe*, 437 F. Supp. 269, 319 (D.N.H. 1977); *Ramos v. Lamm*, 485 F. Supp. 122, 147 (D. Colo. 1979) *aff'd in part and set aside in part on unrelated grounds*, 639 F. 2d 559 (10th Cir. 1980), *cert denied*, 450 U.S. 1041 (1981).

199. See e.g., *Wolff v. McDonnell*, 418 U.S. 539, 563 (1974) (arguing both pros and cons of due process) and at 2990–91 (Marshall, J., concurring and dissenting); *Milter v. Twomey*, 479 F.2d 701, 712 & n. 23 (7th Cir. 1971), *cert. denied sub. nom. Gutierrez v. Dept. of Public Safety*, 414 U.S. 1146 (1974); *Laaman v. Helgemoe*, 437 F. Supp. 269, 291–94, 317–18 (D.N.H 1977); *Landman v. Royster*, 333 F. Supp. 621 (1971).

200. See, e.g., *Gates v. Collier*, 501 F.2d 1291 (5th Cir. 1974); *Palmigiano v. Garrahy*, Supp. 956, 986 (D.R.I. 1977) (ordering defendant to "make available as soon as possible access, on a voluntary basis, . . . to educational programs"); *Laaman v. Helgemoe*, 437 F. Supp. 269, 294–96 (D.N.H. 1977); *Barnes v. Government of Virgin Islands*, 415 F. Supp. 1218, 1227, 1233–34 (D.V.I. 1976) (ordering Virgin Island prison to provide "meaningful rehabilitative opportunities . . . failing which I shall sentence all offenders to mainland institutions"); *Holt v. Sarver*, 309 F. Supp. 362, 362 (F.D. Ark. 1970), *aff'd*, 442 F. 2d 304 (8th Cir. 1971); *Jones v. Wittenbemp*, 330 F. Supp. 707, 717 (N.D. Ohio 1971).

201. *Ruiz v. Estelle*, 503 F. Supp. 1265 (E.D. Tex. 1980).

202. *James v. Wallace*, F. Supp. 1177 (M.D. Ala. 1974); *Ramos v. Lamm*, 639 F.2d 559, 568 (10th Cir. 1980) (Colorado); *Battle v. Anderson*, 564 F.2d 388, 395 (10th Cir. 1977) (Oklahoma); *Finney v. Arkansas Bd. of Corrections*, 505 F.2d 194, 202 (8th Cir. 1974) (medical care); *Newman v. Alabama*, 503 F.2d 1320, 1333 (5th Cir. 1974) (medical care); *Ruiz v. Estelle*, 503 F. Supp. 1265, 1282 (S.D. Tex. 1980) (overcrowding impedes rehabilitation); *Capps v. Atiyeh*, 495 F. Supp. 802, 811 (D. Ore. 1980) *vacated*, 652 F. 2d 823 (9th Cir. 1981) (same); *Palmigiano v. Garrahy*, 443 F. Supp. 956, 971 (D.R.I. 1977) (rehabilitation impossible without drug abuse treatment); *Laaman v. Helgemoe*, 437 F. Supp. 269, 319 (D.N.H. 1977) (medical classification); *Barnes v. Government of Virgin Islands*, 415 F. Supp. 1218, 1235 (D.V.I. 1976) (ordering drug and alcohol treatment); *James v. Wallace*, 406 F. Supp. 318, 325–26 (M.D. Ala. 1976); *Gates v. Collier*, 349 F. Supp. 881, 893 (N.D. Miss. 1972).

203. E.g., *Rouse v. Cameron*, 373 F.2d 451 (D.C. Cir. 1966); *Pennsylvania Ass'n for Retarded Children v. Commonwealth*, 334 F. Supp. 1257 (E.D. Pa. 1971), *modified*, 343 F. Supp. 279 (E.D. Pa. 1972); *Wyatt v. Stickney*, 325 F. Supp. 781 (M.D. Ala. 1971), *modified*, 344 F. Supp. 373 & 344 F. Supp. 387 (M.D. Ala. 1972); *Halderman v. Pennhurst State School & Hospital*, 446 F. Supp. 1295 (E.D. Pa. 1977), *affirmed on other grounds*, 612 F.2d 84 (3d Cir. 1979), *rev'd and remanded*, 451 U.S. 1 (1981); *Romeo v. Youngberg*, 644 F.2d 147 (3d Cir. 1980), *vacated and remanded*, 457 U.S. 307 (1982). The Supreme Court's opinion in *Romeo* endorsed the right to treatment, but vacated the appellate court decision on the ground that the professional judgment of the institution's administrator was presumptively valid.

204. 430 U.S. 651 (1977). Justice White, in dissent, made the memorable observation that "if it is constitutionally impermissible to cut off someone's ear for commission of murder, it must be unconstitutional to cut off a child's ear for being late to class." *Id*. at 684.

205. See Ackerman, *supra* note 145.

206. E.g., *Reitman v. Mulkey*, 387 U.S. 369 (1967) (invalidating constitutional provision that permitted private homeowners to discriminate when selling their homes); *Swan v. Charlotte McKlenburg Board of Education*, 402 U.S. 1 (1971) (comprehensive desegregation of public school district: *Wisconsin v. Yoder*, 406 U.S. 205 (1972) (forbidding the application of compulsory education law to Amish because it would interfere with their religious practice); *Stanton v. Stanton*, 421 U.S. 7 (1975) (invalidating statute that required parental support for males until the age of twenty-one and females until the age of eighteen); *Hampton v. Mow Sun Wong*, 426 U.S. 88 (1976) (invalidating federal Civil Service Commission's prohibition of aliens from competitive civil service).

207. *Miranda v. Arizona*, 384 U.S. 436 (1966) (forbidding use of confessions without prior warning of rights); *Reynolds v. Simms*, 377 U.S. 533 (1964) (holding independently of racial considerations, representation in some legislatures is unconstitutional); *Goldberg v. Kelly*, 397 U.S. 254 (1970) (requiring oral hearing before benefits termination).

208. *Shapiro v. Thompson*, 394 U.S. 618 (1969).

209. Cullen & Gilbert, *supra* note 169, at 258–60.

210. Regarding Progressive ideas in southern states, see Mark Carleton, *The Politics of Punishment*, 151–64 (1971); Taylor, *supra* note 188, at 138–40.

211. 377 U.S. 533 (1964).

212. American Friends Service Committee, *Struggle for Justice* (1971); Robert Martinson, "What Works? Questions and Answers about Prison Reform," 24 Pub. Int. 25 (1974); Diane Lipton, Robert Martinson & James Wilks, *The Effectiveness of Correctional Treatment* (1975). See also William Bailey, "Treatment: An Analysis of One Hundred Correctional Outcome Studies," 57 J. of Crim. L., Criminology & Police Sci. 153 (1966); Lee Sechrest, Susan White & Eric Brown, *The Rehabilitation of Criminal Offenders* (1979).

213. Francis Allen, *The Decline of the Rehabilitative Ideal*, 9 (1981).

214. Fydor Dotoyevsky, *The House of the Dead*, 41 (C. Garnett, trans., 1959).

215. Cullen & Gilbert, *supra* note 169, at 247–53, 261–63.

216. Norvell Morris, *The Future of Imprisonment*, 12–27 (1974).

217. Pete Earley, *The Big House*, 58 (1992) (quoting Norman Carlson, director of the Bureau of Prisons); George Playfair, *The Punitive Obsession*, 212 (1971) (quoting the governor of Hull Prison, England); Author's interview with Gary Herman, Warden, U.S. Penitentiary at Marion. See Cullen & Gilbert, *supra* note 169, at 258–60.

218. American Friends Service Committee, *supra* note 212; David Greenberg, *The Problem of Prisons* (1970); Jessica Mitford, *Kind and Usual Punishment: The Prison Business* (1973); Herbert Morris, "Persons and Punishment," 53 Monist 475 (1968); Norvell Morris & James Jacobs, "Proposals for Prison Reform" (Public Affairs Pamphlet 510, Public Affairs Comm. 1974); Andrew von Hirsch, *Doing Justice: The Choice of Punishments* (1976).

219. For criticisms of indeterminate sentencing, see Allen Dershowitz, "Indeterminate Confinement: Letting the Therapy Fit the Harm," 123 U.

Pa. L. Rev. 303 (1974); David Fogel, *We Are the Living Proof: The Justice Model for Corrections* (2d ed., 1979); Marvin Frankel, *Criminal Sentences: Law without Order* (1972); David Greenberg, "Rehabilitation Is Still Punishment," 32 Humanist 29 (1972); Mitford, *supra* note 218, at 87–103.

220. DiIulio, *supra* note 9; Fogel, *supra* note 219; Newman, *supra* note 181; von Hirsch, *supra* note 218.

221. Karl Menninger, *The Crime of Punishment* (1969).

222. Ivan Pavlov, *Lectures on Conditioned Reflexes*, vol. 2, *Conditioned Reflexes and Psychiatry* (H. Gantt, trans., 1941); Ivan Pavlov, *Selected Works* (1955); Yuri Frolov, *Pavlov and His School* (1938); William W. Sargant, *Battle for the Mind*, 51–75 (1957).

223. William Walters Sargant, *supra* note 222, at 68 (reporting comment made by Pavlov to an American psychologist).

224. John DiIulio, *No Escape*, 126–47 (1991); Robert Hawkins & Geoffrey Alpert, *American Prison Systems*, 413–16 (1989); Helen Blatte, "State Prisons and the Use of Behavior Control," 4 Hastings Center Rep. 11 (September, 1974); Norman Carlson, "Behavior Modification in the Federal Bureau of Prisons," 1 New Eng. J. Prison L. 155 (1974) (token economy); Michael Milan & John McKee, "The Cellblock Token Economy: Token Reinforcement Procedures in a Maximum Security Correctional Institution for Adult Male Felons," 9 J. Applied Behav. Analysis 253 (1976). William Gaylin & H. Blatte, "Behavior Modification in Prisons," 13 Am. Crim. L. Rev. 11 (1975); Roger Wolfe & Dominic Marino, "A Program of Behavioral Treatment for Incarcerated Pedophiles," 13 Am. J. Crim. L. 69 (1975) (Connecticut Correctional Institution experiment); "Hearings on Behavior Modification Programs in the Bureau of Prisons before the Subcommittee on Courts, Civil Liberties and the Administration of Justice of the House Committee on the Judiciary," 93d Cong., 2d Sess. 46–55 (1974) (START Program, using Tier system).

225. *The Manchurian Candidate* (United Artists 1962) (based on the novel by Richard Condon).

226. See references in note 224 *supra*.

227. John Heath, *Torture and English Law: An Administrative and Legal History from the Plantagenets to the Stewarts* (1982); Edward Peters, *Torture* (1985); M. Ruthven, *Torture: The Grand Conspiracy* (1978). For contemporary examples, see Amnesty International, *Torture in the Eighties* (1984); Florence Kandell, *Torture and Other Cruel, Inhuman and Degrading Treatment or Punishment in Relation to Detention and Imprisonment* (1977).

228. For the virtues of the just deserts model, see John Conrad, "Where There's Hope There's Life," in *Justice as Fairness: Perspectives on the Justice Model*, 3 (D. Fogel & J. Hudson, eds., 1981); DiIulio, *supra* note 9, at 259–63.

229. James Jacobs, *Stateville: The Penitentiary in Mass Society*, 105–37 (1977).

230. Max Weber, *Economy and Society*, vol 1, 956–90 (G. Roth & C. Wittich, eds., 1968).

231. Max Weber, "Bureaucracy," in *From Max Weber: Essays in Sociology*, 196, 203. H. Gerth and C. W. Mills (eds./trans.). See also, *McCray v. Burrell*,

516 F.2d 357 (4th Cir. 1975); *Wright v. McMann*, 387 F.2d 519 (2d Cir. 1967); *Toussaint v. McCarthy*, 597 F. Supp. 1388 (N.D. Cal. 1984); *Gates v. Collier*, 501 F.2d 1291 (5th Cir. 1976); *Spain v. Procunnier*, 600 F.2d 189 (9th Cir. 1979).

232. Weber, *supra* note 231, at 198–204. See also *Gates v. Collier*, 501 F.2d 1291 (5th Cir. 1974); *Holt v. Sarver*, 309 F. Supp. 362 (E.D. Ark. 1970); *Robert v. Williams*, 302 F. Supp. 972 (N.D. Miss. 1969); *Ruiz v. Estelle*, 503 F. Supp. 1265 (S.D. Tex. 1980).

233. The leading case is *Estelle v. Gamble*, 429 U.S. 97 (1976). For a review of the standards used to determine unconstitutional denial of medical services, see Michael Cameron Friedman, "Cruel and Unusual Punishment in the Provision of Prison Medical Care: Challenging the Deliberate Indifference Standard," 45 Vand. L. Rev. 921 (May 1992).

234. *Pugh v. Locke*, 406 F. Supp. 318 (M.D. Ala. 1976); *Gates v. Collier*, 501 F.2d 129 (5th Cir. 1974); *Holt v. Sarver*, 309 F. Supp. 362 (E.D. Ark. 1970); *Ruiz v. Estelle*, 679 F.2d 115 (5th Cir. 1982).

235. *Sandin v. Connor*, 45 S. Ct. 2293, 2299 (1995).

236. Weber, *supra* note 230, at vol. 1, 215–41; vol. 2, 1114–18. Weber, of course, draws a direct contrast between charismatic and bureaucratic authority.

237. Robert Hughes, *The Fatal Shore*, 498–505 (1986).

238. *Brubaker*, TCD Productions (1980).

239. Chilton, *supra* note 11; Ben Crouch & James Marquart, *An Appeal to Justice* (1989); Jacobs, *supra* note 229, Jacobs, *supra* note 79, at 20–23, 54–55; Steve Martin & Sheldon Ekland-Olson, *Texas Prisons* (1987); Taylor, *supra* note 188, 193–232 (1993); Yackle, *supra* note 12.

240. Weber, *supra* note 230.

241. Michael Crozier, *The Bureaucratic Phenomenon*, 3 (1964); Charles Goodsell, *The Case for Bureaucracy*, 2–11 (1982); Kenneth Meier, *Politics and Bureaucracy*, 3–4 (2d ed., 1987); Robert Stillman, *The American Bureaucracy*, 3–20 (1987).

242. E.g., *Willner v. Committee on Character and Fitness*, 373 U.S. 96 (1963) (license to practice law); *Suglin v. Kauffman*, 418 F.2d 163 (7th Cir. 1969) (college disciplinary proceedings); *Holmes v. New York City Hous. Auth.* 398 F.2d 262 (2d Cir. 1968) (liquor license); *Dixon v. Alabama State Board of Edu.*, 294 F.2d 150 (5th Cir.), *cert. denied*, 368 U.S. 930 (1961) (college disciplinary proceedings); *Great Lake Airlines, Inc. v. CAB*, 294 F.2d 217 (D.C. Cir. 1961) (airline licenses); *Copper Plumbing and Heating Co. v. Campbell*, 290 F.2d 368 (1961) (opportunity to compete for government contracting). The process had actually begun earlier, see *Hannegan v. Esquire, Inc.*, 327 U.S. 146 (1946) (second-class mail privileges); *Stoehower v. Board of Higher Educ.*, 350 U.S. 551 (1956) (government job), but it assumed the definitive form of a trend or movement in the 1960s.

243. *Goldberg v. Kelly*, 397 U.S. 254 (1970) (holding that an oral hearing is required prior to a temporary suspension of welfare benefits).

244. Lawrence Tribe, *American Constitutional Law*, 685–768 (2d ed., 1988); Al-

fred Aman & William Mayton, *Administrative Law*, 147–98 (1993). See also *Ruiz v. Estelle*, 503 F. Supp. 1265, 1350–58, 1365–67 (S.D. Tex. 1980); *Finney v. Hutto*, 410 F. Supp. 251, 272–74 (F.D. Ark. 1976); *James v. Wallace*, 406 F. Supp. 318, 330 (M.D. Ala. 1976); *Craig v. Hayler*, 405 F. Supp. 656, 662–64 (D. Nev. 1975); *Rarefield v. Leach*, slip op. no. 10282 (D.N.M. 1974) (available on Lexis); *Battle v. Anderson*, 376 F. Supp. 402, 421–22, 430–31 (E.D. Okla. 1974); *Gates v. Collier*, 349 F. Supp. 881, 895 (N.D. Miss. 1972); *Landman v. Royster*, 333 F. Supp. 621 (E.D. Va. 1971); *Carrothers v. Follette*, 314 F. Supp. 1014 (S.D. N.Y. 1970).

245. *Goldberg v. Kelly*, 397 U.S. 254 (1970); *Matthews v. Eldridge*, 424 U.S. 319 (1976). See Jerry Mashaw, *Due Process in the Administrative State* (1985); Frank Michelman, "Formal and Associational Aims in Procedural Due Process," *Nomos XVIII: Due Process* (J. Pennock & J. Chapman, eds., 1977). The scope of due process rights has been the subject of extensive controversy. See Cynthia Farina, "Concerning Due Process," 3 Yale J. L. & Feminism 189 (1991); Edward Rubin, "Due Process and the Administrative State," 72 Cal. L. Rev. 1044 (1984); Rodney Smolla, "The Reemergence of the Right-Privilege Distinction in Constitutional Law: The Price of Protecting Too Much," 35 Stan. L. Rev. 69 (1982); Timothy Terrel, " 'Property,' 'Due Process,' and the Distinction between Definition and Theory in Legal Analysis, " 70 Geo. L. J. 861 (1982). See also *Ruiz v. Estelle*, 503 F. Supp. 1265, 1303–4, 1306 (S.D. Tex. 1980); *Holt v. Sarver*, 309 F. Supp. 366, 373–75, 383–85 (E.D. Ark. 1970).

246. For an analysis of how Supreme Court decisions enhanced the organizational capacity of police, see Jonathon Simon and Jerome Skolnick, "Federalism, the Exclusionary Rule, and the Police," in *Power Divided: Essays on the Theory and Practice of Federalism*, 78–88 (H. Scheiber & M. Feeley, eds., 1989). On the importance of judicial rulings that structured discretion and "tamed" the system, see Samuel Walker, *Taming the System: The Control of Discretion in Criminal Justice, 1950–1990*, (1993). See also *Campbell v. Beto*, 460 F.2d 765 (5th Cir. 1972); *Ruiz v. Estelle*, 503 F;. Supp. 1265 (S.D. Tex. 1980); *Finney v. Hutto*, 410 F. Supp. 251, 258–61 (E.D. Ark. 1976) *aff'd*, 548 F. 2d 740 (8th Cir. 1977), *aff'd sub. nom. Hutto v. Finney*, 437 U.S. 678 (1978); *Battle v. Anderson*, 376 F. Supp. 402, 424, 434 (E.D. Okla. 1974).

247. See also Lauren Edelman, "Legal Environments and Organizational Governance: The Expansion of Due Process in the Workplace," 95 Am. J. of Soc. 1401–40 (1990); Elizabeth Chambeliss & Howard S. Erlanger, "Legal Ambiguity and the Politics of Compliance: Affirmative Action Offices' Dilemma," 13 L. and Pol'y 73–87 (1991); Lauren Edelman, Howard S. Erlanger & John Lande, "Employers' Handling of Discrimination Complaints: The Transformation of Rights in the Workplace," 27 L. and Soc. Rev. 497–534 (1993).

248. David Garland, *Punishment and Modern Society*, 180–89 (1990).

249. Franz Kafka, "In the Penal Colony," in Franz Kafka, *The Penal Colony: Short Stories and Short Pieces*, 191 (Wilkes Muir & Edwin Muir, trans., 1961).

250. *Id.*

251. *Id.* at 204.
252. *Id.* at 198.
253. *Id.* at 216.
254. *Id.* at 218–22.
255. Joseph Conrad, *Victory,* 1 (1914).
256. John DiIulio, *Governing Prisons,* 104–117 (1987); Jacobs, *supra* note 239, at 29; Crouch & Marquart, *supra* note 239, at 40. (1989).
257. Taylor, *supra* note 188, at 193–232.
258. *Ex parte Hull,* 312 U.S. 546 (1941) (invalidating regulation in Michigan prison that required review of habeas petitions by prison officials); Jacobs, *supra* note 229, at 37.
259. 437 U.S. 678, 711–14.
260. Weber, *supra* note 231, at vol. 2, 755–76, 883–85. See Jürgen Habermas, *The Theory of Communicative Action,* vol. 1, 143–271 (T. McCarthy, trans., 1981); Herbert Marcuse, "Industrialization and Capitalism," in *Sociology Today,* 133 (O. Stammer, ed., K. Morris, trans., 1971); Claus Offe, *Disorganized Capitalism,* 300–3 (1985); Ann Swidler, "The Concept of Rationality in the Work of Max Weber," 43 Soc. Inquiry 35 (1977).
261. Habermas, *supra* note 260, at vol. 1, 1–102.
262. See, e.g., *Holt v. Hutto,* 363 F. Supp. 202 (E.D. Ark. 1973).
263. Crouch & Marquart, *supra* note 239, at 60–84; Jacobs, *supra* note 229, at 38–45; Taylor, *supra* note 188, at 165–92. See also Albert Sample, *Racehoss: Big Emma's Boy* (1984).
264. Weber, *supra* note 230, at vol. 1, 216–17; vol. 2, 655–57, 850–55; from Max Weber, *supra* note 231, 216–21. See Max Albrow, *Bureaucracy* (1970); Reinhart Bendix, *Max Weber: An Intellectual Portrait,* 417–30, 481–86 (1977); Meier, *supra* note 241, at 42–108; Stillman, *supra* note 241.
265. Weber, *supra* note 230, at vol. 3, 973–87; Anthony Kronman, *Max Weber,* 92–95 (1983).
266. Jerry Mashaw, *Bureaucratic Justice* (1983); Meir, *supra* note 241; Stillman, *supra* note 241; Weber, *supra* note 230, at 956–89; James Q. Wilson, *Bureaucracy,* 332–45 (1989).
267. Peter Aranson, Ernest Gellhorn & Glen Robinson, "A Theory of Legislative Delegation," 68 Cornell L. Rev. 1 (1982); Kenneth Davis, *Discretionary Justice* (1969); Michael Lipsky, *Street-Level Bureaucrats* (1980); Theodore Lowi, *The End of Liberalism* (rev. ed., 1979); Schwartz, *supra* note 167; Karl Wittfogel, *Oriental Despotism* (1957).
268. Bendix, *supra* note 264, at 431–37; Herbert Jacoby, *The Bureaucratization of the World* (1973); David Nachimas & David Rosenbloom, *Bureaucratic Government USA* (1980); Frances Piven & Richard Cloward, *Regulating the Poor* (1971); Erich Strauss, *The Ruling Servants* (1961); Ludwig Von Mises, *Bureaucracy* (1944); Weber, *supra* note 230, at 987–93, 1148–56. The link between bureaucracy and Nazism is asserted in David Luban, Alan Strudler & David Wasserman, "Moral Responsibility in the Age of Bureaucracy," 90 Mich. L. Rev. 2348 (1992); also Strauss, *supra* note 268; Von Mises, *supra* note 268.
269. Weber, *supra* note 230, at 810–14; Kronman, *supra* note 265, at 93–95.

270. Habermas, *supra* note 260, at 143–271.
271. *Id.* at 254–67. Habermas's argument is actually more complex: he asserts that the deontological core is separated from particular legal instrumentalities by the positivistic approach to law, and thus more readily subjected to normative, public debate.
272. Luhmann, *supra* note 43, at 238–39. See Niklas Luhmann, *The Differentiation of Society* (S. Holmes & C. Larmore, trans., 1982).
273. Bruce Ackerman, *Social Justice in the Liberal State* (1980).
274. Hughes, *supra* note 237, at 543–51.
275. Foucault, *supra* note 176; Jacobs, *supra* note 229.
276. See also Owen Fiss, "The Forms of Justice," 93 Harv. L. Rev. 1 (1979); Abram Chayes, "The Role of Judges in Public and Litigation," 89 Harv. L. Rev. 1281 (1976); Nathan Glazer, "Judicial and Social Policy," in *The Judiciary in a Democratic Society,* 67 (L. J. Thebridge, ed., 1979); Colin Diver, "The Judge as Political Powerbroker: Superintending Structural Changes in Public Institutions," 65 U. Va. L. Rev. 43 (1979); Bradley Chilton, *supra* note 11.
277. Eisenberg, *supra* note 1, at 96–99.
278. For instance, as Judge Eisele gained more confidence in the administrators in the Arkansas Department of Corrections, he stepped back and gave them more leeway, and at times modified earlier orders to accommodate new developments.
279. E.g., *New York v. United States,* 112 S. Ct. 2408 (1992) (federalism); *Gregory v. Ashcroft,* 111 S. Ct. 2395 (1991) (federalism); *Bowsher v. Synar,* 478 U.S. 714 (1986) (separation of powers); *INS v. Chadha,* 462 U.S. 919 (1983) (separation of powers).
280. Foucault, *supra* note 176, at 123–36.
281. *Id.* at 3–6.
282. *Id.* at 32–69.
283. *Id.* at 80.
284. *Id.* at 105.
285. *Id.* at 105–6. See generally *id.* at 104–14.
286. *Id.* at 135–94.
287. The reference in the footnote is to Garland, *supra* note 248, at 177–80.
288. Foucault, *supra* note 176, at 195–228.
289. *Id.,* title of part 4, ch. 1.
290. *Id.* at 277.
291. *Id.* at 257–92.
292. Spierenburg, *supra* note 171. Spierenburg's main point is that Foucault's model of sudden transition is not confirmed by investigation. Instead, public executions continued until the 1860s, well after the penitentiary was established, while serious mutilation disappeared in the early seventeenth century, long before Foucault's disciplinary society appeared (*id.* at viii). In another work, Spierenburg demonstrates that prisons evolved in continental Europe during this earlier period, and also before the transition that Foucault constructs. See also Pieter Spierenburg, *supra* note 171.

293. Garland, *supra* note 248, at 131–75. Garland's principal criticism is that Foucault's emphasis on power leads to the view that prisons are an efficient mechanism for social control, that they produce delinquents, and that failed efforts to reform them are simply part of the control process. In fact, Garland argues, "There are elements of the penal system which either malfunction and so are not effective as forms of social control, or else are simply not designed to function as control measures in the first place" *ID.* at 162. The political debate about penal policy is a genuine one, and the persistence of prisons emerges from a complex interplay of social and political forces.

294. Michael Fry, "Bentham and English Penal Reform," in *Jeremy Bentham and the Law*, 20, 53–55 (G. Keeton & G. Schwarzenberger, eds., 1948); L. J. Hume, "Bentham's Panopticon: An Administrative History – II," 16 *Historical Studies* 36 (1974); Mary Mack, *Jeremy Bentham: An Odyssey of Ideas, 1748–1792*, 402–4 (1963).

295. Spierenburg, *supra* note 4. Spierenberg suggests that the change in attitude can be explained by Norbert Elias's theory of developing sensibilities. See Norbert Elias, *The Civilizing Process*, vol. 2, *The Process of State Formation and Nation Building* (E. Jephcott, trans., 1994).

296. Hughes, *supra* note 237, at 363–67, 559–80.

297. Ignatieff, *supra* note 6; Rothman, *supra* note 6.

298. Sellin, *supra* note 171, 43–55.

299. John DiIulio, *Governing Prisons*, 236–41 (1987). This conflicts with other accounts of the Texas prisons such as Crouch & Marquart, *supra* note 239; Martin & Ecklund-Olson, *supra* note 239. See also Malcolm M. Feeley and Edward Rubin, "Prison Litigation and Bureaucratic Development," 12 L. and Soc. Inquiry 125 (1992).

7. IMPLEMENTING THE SOLUTION, MUDDLING THROUGH, AND IGNORING THE SEPARATION OF POWERS PRINCIPLE

1. Fydor Dostoyevsky, *The Brothers Karamazov*, vol. 1, 309 (D. Magarshack trans. 1958).

2. Deborah Stone, *Policy Paradox and Political Reason* (1988).

3. Eugene Bardach, *The Implementation Game* (1977); Eugene Bardach & Robert Kagan, *Going by the Book* (1982); Keith Hawkins & John Thomas, eds., *Enforcing Regulation* (1984); Jeffrey Pressman & Aaron Wildavsky, *Implementation* (1973); Richard Newstadt, *Presidential Power: The Politics of Leadership* (1960) (original edition); John Scholz, "Cooperation, Deterrence, and the Ecology of Regulatory Enforcement," 18 L. & Soc. Rev. 179 (1984).

4. Pressman & Wildavsky, *supra* note 3, at 3.

5. Harold Seidman & Richard Gilmour, *Power: From the Positive to the Regulatory State*, 136–65 (4th ed., 1986).

6. Robert Katzmann, *Regulatory Bureaucracy: The Federal Trade Commission's Antitrust Policy* (1979).

7. For an account of how "Washington" managed the far-flung U.S. Forest Service, see Herbert Kaufman, *The Forest Service* (1964).

8. Christopher Edley, *Administrative Law: Rethinking Judicial Control of Bureaucracy*, 36–48 (1990); William Mayton, "The Legislative Revolution of the Rulemaking versus Adjudication Problem in Agency Lawmaking," 1980 Duke L. J. 103; Glen Robinson, "The Making of Administrative Policy: Another Look at Rulemaking and Adjudication and Administrative Procedure Reform," 118 U. Pa. L. Rev. 485 (1970); David Shapiro, "The Choice of Rulemaking on Adjudication in the Development of Administrative Policy," 78 Harv. L. Rev. 921 (1965). The distinction is codified in the Administrative Procedure Act, 5 U.S.C. §§ 553, 556, 557 (1988).

9. Colin Diver, "Policymaking Paradigms in Administrative Law," 95 Harv. L. Rev. 393 (1981).

10. Colin Diver, "The Optimal Precision of Administrative Rules," 93 Yale L. J. 65 (1983).

11. David Braybrooke & Charles Lindblom, *A Strategy of Decision* (1963); Edward Stokey & Richard Zeckhauser, *A Primer for Policy Analysis* (1978); Aaron Wildavsky, *Speaking Truth to Power* (1979); Charles Lindblom, "The Science of 'Muddling Through,'" 19 Pub. Ad. Rev. 78 (1959).

12. Negotiated Rulemaking Act of 1990, Pub. L. No. 101–648, § 3(a), 104 Stat. 4969, codified at U.S.C. §§ 561–70 (1993 Supp.); Philip Harter, "Negotiating Regulations: A Cure for Malaise," 71 Geo. L. J. 1 (1982); Henry Perritt, "Negotiated Rulemaking before Federal Agencies: Evaluation of Recommendations by the Administrative Conference of the United States," 74 Geo. L. J. 1625 (1986); Henry Perritt, "Negotiated Rulemaking and Administrative Law," 38 Admin. L. Rev. 471 (1986).

13. Scholz, *supra* note 3; Robert Kagan & John Scholz, "The Criminology of the Corporation and Regulatory Enforcement Strategies," in Hawkins & Thomas, *supra* note 3, at 67.

14. On the indirect effects of legal environments upon organizations, see Lauren Edelman, "Legal Ambiguity and Symbolic Structures: Organizational Meditation of Civil Rights Law," 97 Am. J. Soc. 1531 (1992); Paul DiMaggio & Walter Powell, "The Iron Cage Revisited: Institutional Isomorphism and Collective Rationality in Organizational Fields," 48 Am. Soc. Rev. 147 (1983).

15. William Fletcher, "The Discretionary Constitution: Institutional Remedies and Judicial Legitimacy," 91 Yale L. J. 635 (1982).

16. Judge Thelton Henderson, Talk to the Solano County Grand Jury, County Jail, Santa Rosa, California, May 14, 1990.

17. See, e.g., James Q. Wilson, *Bureaucracy: What Government Agencies Do and Why They Do It*, 218–234 (1989).

18. See, e.g., Martha Weinberg, *Managing the State*, 32–33, 63–67 (1977); Harold Wilensky, *Organizational Intelligence: Knowledge and Power in Government and Industry*, 48–57, 171–81 (1967); Herbert Kaufman, *Administrative Feedback: Monitoring Subordinates' Behavior*, 4–15 (1973).

19. On the role of special assistants as policy analysts, see Aaron Wildavsky, *Speaking Truth to Power* (1979).
20. Susan Sturm, Note, "Mastering Intervention in Prisons," 88 Yale L. J. 1062 (1979); see also Susan Sturm, "A Normative Theory of Public Law Remedies," 79 Geo. L. J. 1355, 1371–79 (1991).
21. David Kirp and Gary Babcock, "Judge and Company: Court-Appointed Masters, School Resegregation and Institutional Reform," 72 Ala. L. Rev. 313–98 (1981).
22. M. Kay Harris & Dudley Spriller, *After Decision: Implementation of Judicial Decrees in Correctional Settings* (1976).
23. Bardach & Kagan, *supra* note 2, at 80–119.
24. Scholz, *supra* note 3; Kagan & Scholz, *supra* note 3.
25. Bradley Chilton, *Prisons under the Gavel: The Federal Takeover of Georgia Prisons* (1991).
26. See Chapter 5.
27. *Buckley v. Valeo*, 424 U.S. 1 (1976). Federal Elections Campaign Act, Pub. L. No. 92–225, 86 Stat. 3 (1972), surviving sections codified at 2 U.S.C. § 431 *et seq.*
28. *Bowsher v. Synar*, 478 U.S. 714 (1986). Balanced Budget and Emergency Deficit Control Act, popularly known as Gramm-Rudman Act, Pub. L. No. 99–177, 99 Stat. 1038 (1985), surviving sections codified at 2 U.S.C. § 901 *et seq.*
29. *Northern Pipeline Constr. Co. v. Marathon Pipe Line Co.*, 458 U.S. 50 (1982). Bankruptcy Act of 1978, Pub. L. No. 95–598, 92 Stat. 2549 (1978), surviving sections on bankruptcy judges codified at 28 U.S.C. §151 *et seq.*
30. *INS v. Chadha*, 462 U.S. 919 (1983). See *id.* at 1002 (White J., dissenting) ("This decision has invalidated in one fell swoop provisions in more laws enacted by Congress than the Court had cumulatively invalidated in its history").
31. In addition, the issue was intensively debated in several recent cases, e.g., *Morrison v. Olson*, 487 U.S. 654 (1988) (removal of independent prosecutor by Congress); *Mistretta v. United States*, 488 U.S. 361 (1989) (creation of sentencing commission in judicial branch). The two seminal separation-of-powers cases of the administrative era are *Myers v. United States*, 272 U.S. 52 (1926), which held that Congress may not limit the president's removal power and *A.L.A. Schechter Poultry Corp. v. United States*, 295 U.S. 495 (1935) which invalidated Roosevelt's National Recovery Act on delegation grounds. *Myers* was limited, if not overruled, by *Humphrey's Executor v. United States*, 295 U.S. 602 (1935); *Schechter* has never been overruled explicitly, but is considered effectively displaced as a result of cases such as *FCC v. Sanders Brothers R.S.*, 309 U.S. 470 (1940); *National Broadcasting Co. v. United States*, 319 U.S. 190 (1943); *Amalgamated Meat Cutters v. Conally*, 337 F. Supp. 737 (D.D.C. 1971). It seems safe to say that the separation-of-powers doctrine, while very much alive, is also very much confused. See Rebecca Brown, "Separated Powers and Ordered Liberty," 139 U. Pa. L. Rev. 1513 (1991); Erwin Chemerinsky, "A Paradox without a Principle: A Comment on the Burger Court's Jurisprudence in Separation of Powers Cases," 60 S. Cal. L. Rev. 1083 (1987); E. Donald Elliot, "Why Our Sep-

aration of Powers Jurisprudence Is So Abysmal," 67 Geo. Wash. L. Rev. 506 (1989); William Gwyn, "The Indeterminacy of the Separation of Powers and the Federal Courts," 57 Geo. Wash. L. Rev. 474 (1989).

32. James Caesar, "In Defense of Separation of Powers," in *Separation of Powers – Does It Still Work?*, 168 (R. Goldwin & A. Kaufman, eds., 1986).

33. E.g., Samuel Beer, *Britain against Itself: The Political Contradictions of Collectivism* (1982); S. Beer & A. Ulams, eds., *Patterns of Government*, (3d ed., 1973); Erwin Chemerinsky, "The Question's Not Clear, but Party Government Is Not the Answer," 30 Wm. & Mary L. Rev. 411 (1989); J. Sundquist, "The Question *Is* Clear, and Party Government *Is* the Answer," 30 Wm. & Mary L. Rev. 425 (1989); Lloyd Cutler, "To Form a Government," in *Separation of Powers, supra* note 32, at 1; Charles Hardin, *Constitutional Reform in America: Essays on the Separation of Powers* (1989); Donald Price, *America's Unwritten Constitution: Science, Religion, and Political Responsibility* (1983); Thomas Sargentich, "The Limits of the Parliamentary Critique of Separation of Powers," 34 Wm. & Mary L. Rev. 679 (1993); Thomas Sargentich, "The Contemporary Debate about Legislative–Executive Separation of Powers," 72 Cornell L. Rev. 430 (1987).

34. Brown, *supra* note 31, at 1513; Martin Redish & Elizabeth Cisar, " 'If Angels Were to Govern:' The Need for Pragmatic Formalism in Separation of Powers Theory," 41 Duke L. J. 449 (1991); Peter Shane, "Independent Policymaking and Presidential Power: A Constitutional Analysis," 57 Geo. Wash. L. Rev. 596 (1989). Brown connects the separation-of-powers notion directly to the protection of individual rights, while Shane and Redish and Cisar take the somewhat more traditional view that it protects democratic government in general.

35. Richard Fallon, "Of Legislative Courts, Administrative Agencies, and Article III," 101 Harv. L. Rev. 915 (1988); Jeffrey Lubbers, "Federal Administrative Law Judges: A Focus on Our Invisible Judiciary," 33 Admin. L. Rev. 109 (1981); Richard Pierce, "Political Control versus Impermissible Bias in Agency Decisionmaking: Lessons from *Chevron* and *Mistretta*," 57 U. Chi. L. Rev. 481 (1990); Martin Redish, "Legislative Courts, Administrative Agencies and the Northern Pipeline Decision," 1983 Duke L. J. 197 (1983).

36. Martin Redish & Lawrence Marshall, "Adjudicatory Independence and the Values of Procedural Due Process," 95 Yale L. J. 455 (1986). The authors express concern about the independence of administrative law judges, but their solutions are salary protection and tenure provisions, not transfer to the judicial branch. *Id.* at 499–500.

37. Michael Asimow, "When the Curtain Falls: Separation of Functions in the Federal Administrative Agencies," 81 Colum. L. Rev. 759 (1981); Peter Strauss, "The Place of Agencies in Government: Separation of Powers and the Fourth Branch," 84 Colum. L. Rev. 573, 622–25 (1984); Paul Verkuil, "Separation of Powers, The Rule of Law and the Idea of Independence," 30 Wm. & Mary L. Rev. 301 (1989).

38. Emile Durkheim, *The Division of Labor in Society* (W. D. Halls, trans., 1984);

Niklas Luhmann, *A Sociological Theory of Law*, 238–41 (E. King & M. Albrow, trans., 1985); Talcott Parsons, "An Outline of the Social System," in *Theories of Society*, vol. 1, 30–79 (T. Parsons, et al., eds., 1961); Max Weber, *Economy and Society* (G. Roth & C. Witrich, eds., 1978).

39. William Banks, "Efficiency in Government: Separation of Powers Reconsidered," 35 Syracuse L. Rev. 715 (1984); D. Frohnmayer, "The Separation of Powers: An Essay on the Vitality of a Constitutional Idea," 52 Ore. L. Rev. 211 (1973); William Gwyn, *The Meaning of the Separation-of-Powers* (1965); Henry Hart & Albert Sacks, *The Legal Process: Basic Problems in the Making and Application of Law* (W. Eskridge & P. Frickley, eds., 1995); Edward Levi, "Some Aspects of Separation of Powers," 76 Colum. L. Rev. 371 (1976). On the role of this argument in the legal process movement, see Edward L. Rubin, "The New Legal Process, The Synthesis of Discourse, and the Microanalysis of Institutions," 109 Harv. L. Rev. 1393, 1394–98 (1996).

40. Neil Komesar, *Imperfect Alternatives* (1994); Oliver Williamson, "Transaction Cost Economics and Organization Theory," in *Organization Theory: From Chester Barnard to the Present and Beyond*, 207 (O. Williamson, ed., 1995).

41. Williamson, *supra* note 40, at 217.

42. M. J. C. Vile, *Constitutionalism and the Separation of Powers*, 27–38 (1967).

43. George Lawson, *An Examination of the Political Part of Mr. Hobbes: His Leviathan* (1967); John Sadler, *Rights of the Kingdom* (1649). See W. B. Gwyn, *The Meaning of Separation of Powers*, 37–65 (1965); Vile, *supra* note 42, at 53–58.

44. John Locke, *Second Treatise of Government*, ch. 12 (C. B. Macpherson. ed., 1980).

45. Montesquieu, *The Spirit of the Laws, Book XI* (T. Nugent, trans., 1949).

46. James Landis, *The Administrative Process*, 47–50 (1938); Vile, *supra* note 42, at 87.

47. Karl Lowenstein, *Political Power and the Governmental Process* (2d ed., 1965); Paul Gewirtz, "Realism in Separation of Powers Thinking," 30 Wm. & Mary L. Rev. 343 (1989); Cass Sunstein, "Constitutionalism after the New Deal," 101 Harv. L. Rev. 421 (1987); Peter Strauss, "When the Judge Is Not the Primary Official with Responsibility to Read: Agency Interpretation and the Problem of Legislative History," 66 Chi.-Kent L. Rev. 321 (1990). For an interesting effort to breathe new life into this mode of analysis, see Komesar, *supra* note 40.

48. Donald Horowitz, *The Courts and Social Policy* (1977).

49. Stuart Scheingold, *The Politics of Rights* (1974).

50. Gerald Rosenberg, *The Hollow Hope: Can Courts Bring about Social Change?* (1991).

51. For similar arguments, see Nathan Glazer, "Towards an Imperial Judiciary?," 41 Public Interest 104 (1975); Lino Graglia, *Disaster by Decree: The Supreme Court's Decisions on Race and Schools* (1976); Harold Spaeth, *Supreme Court Policymaking* (1979); Robert Wood, *Remedial Law* (1990).

52. John DiIulio, *Governing Prisons: A Comparative Study of Correctional Management* (1987).
53. *Id.* at 212–31. See also Wood, *supra* note 51; W. Taylor, *Brokered Justice: Race, Politics and Mississippi, 1798–1992*, 214–22 (1993).
54. DiIulio, *supra* note 52, at 99–118.
55. Malcolm M. Feeley & Edward Rubin, "Prison Litigation and Bureaucratic Development," 17 L. & Soc. Inquiry, 125, 137–43 (1992).
56. DiIulio, *supra* note 52, at 100, 139–53.
57. 92 Harv. L. Rev. 353 (1978).
58. *Id.* at 393–404. Fuller's concept of polycentric problems is derived from Michael Polyani, *The Logic of Liberty: Reflections and Rejoinders* (1951).
59. Komesar, *supra* note 40.
60. Edley, *supra* note 8, at 259; Malcolm M. Feeley, "Hollow Hopes, Flypaper, and Metaphors," 17 L. and Soc. Inquiry 745 (1992); Susan Sturm, "The Legacy and Future of Corrections Litigation," 142 U. Pa. L. Rev. 639, 654 (1993).
61. Paul Gewirtz, "Remedies and Resistance," 92 Yale L. J. 585 (1983).
62. Joel Handler, *Social Movements and the Legal System: A Theory of Law Reform and Social Change* (1978); Feeley, *supra* note 60; Peter Schuck, "Public Law Litigation and Social Reform," 102 Yale L. J. 1763 (1993); Sturm, *supra* note 60, at 655–57.
63. Ralph Cavanagh & Austin Sarat, "Thinking about Courts: Toward and Beyond a Jurisprudence of Judicial Competence," 14 L. & Soc. Rev. 371 (1980); Austin Sarat, "Judicial Capacity: Courts, Court Reform, and the Limits of the Judicial Process," in *The Analysis of Judicial Reform*, 31 (P. DuBois ed., 1982).
64. Abram Chayes, "The Role of the Judge in Public Law Litigation," 89 Harv. L. Rev. 1281 (1976).
65. Colin Diver, "The Judge as Political Pawnbroker: Superintending Structural Change in Public Institutions," 65 Va. L. Rev. 43 (1979).
66. Owen Fiss, "The Forms of Justice," 93 Harv. L. Rev. 1 (1979).
67. William Fletcher, "The Discretionary Constitution: Institutional Remedies and Judicial Legitimacy," 91 Yale L. J. 697 (1982).
68. Sturm, "A Normative Theory," *supra* note 20, at 1355.
69. See Thomas Grey, "Langdell's Orthodoxy," 45 U. Pitt. L. Rev. 1 (1983); Dennis Patterson, "Langdell's Legacy," 90 Nw. U. L. Rev. 196 (1995).
70. Dennis Patterson, "The Poverty of Interpretive Universalism: Toward a Reconstruction of Legal Theory," 72 Tex. L. Rev. 1 (1993); Steven Winter, "Indeterminacy and Incommensurability in Constitutional Law," 78 Cal. L. Rev. 1441 (1990).
71. Chilton, *supra* note 25.
72. Theodore Storey, "When Intervention Works: Judge Morris E. Lasker and the New York City Jails," in *Courts, Corrections and the Constitution: The Impact of Judicial Intervention on Prisons and Jails*, 138–72 (J. DiIulio ed., 1990).
73. Sturm, "Measuring Intervention," *supra* note 20.

74. Larry Yackle, *Reform and Regrets: The Story of Federal Judicial Involvement in the Alabama Prison System* (1989).

75. Edley, *supra* note 8.

76. Peter Schuck, *Agent Orange on Trial* (1986).

77. On the formalist–functional distinction, see Brown, *supra* note 31, at 1522–29; Harold Krent, "Separating the Strands in Separation of Powers Controversies," 74 Va. L. Rev. 1253, 1254–57 (1988); Geoffrey Miller, "Independent Agencies," 1986 Sup. Ct. Rev. 41, 52–54; Sunstein, *supra* note 47, at 493–96; Peter Strauss, "Formal and Functional Approaches to Separation-of-Powers – A Foolish Inconsistency?" 72 Cornell L. Rev. 482 (1987); the rejection of these two claims is identified by Sunstein as a third approach to the separation of powers, which he labels "Holmesian."

78. See Steven Calabresi & Kevin H. Rhodes, "The Structural Constitution: Unitary Executive, Plural Judiciary," 105 Harv. L. Rev. 1155 (1992); John Fitzgerald, *Congress and the Separation of Powers* (1986); Lee S. Lieberman, "*Morrison v. Olson*: A Formalist Perspective on Why the Court Was Wrong," 38 Am. U. L. Rev. 313 (1989); Gary Lawson, "The Rise and Rise of the Administrative State," 107 Harv. L. Rev. 1231 (1994); G. Lawson, "Territorial Governments and the Limits of Formalism," 78 Cal. L. Rev. 853 (1990).

79. See Harold Bruff & Ernst Gellhorn, "Congressional Control of Administrative Regulation: A Study of Administrative Vetoes," 90 Harv. L. Rev. 1369 (1977); Douglas Kmiec, "Of Balkanized Empires and Cooperative Allies: A Bicentennial Essay on the Separation of Powers," 37 Cath. U. L. Rev. 73 (1987); Peter Shane, "Presidents, Pardons, and Prosecutors: Legal Accountability and the Separation of Powers," Yale L. & Pol'y Rev. 361 (1993); David Schoenbrod, *Power without Responsibility* (1993); Sunstein, *supra* note 47.

80. Lawson, *supra* note 43, at 858; Thomas Sargentich, "The Contemporary Debate about Legislative–Executive Separation of Powers," 72 Cornell L. Rev. 430 (1987).

81. *Baker v. Carr*, 369 U.S. 186, 210 (1962); *Elrod v. Burns*, 427 U.S. 347, 352 (1976); David Rudenstine, "Judicially Ordered Reform: Neofederalism and Neonationalism and the Debate over Political Structure," 59 S. Cal. L. Rev. 451, 480 (1986).

82. 441 U.S. 520 (1979).

83. Robert Nagel, "Separation of Powers and the Scope of Federal Equitable Remedies," 30 Stan. L. Rev. 661 (1978); Robert Nagel, "Controlling the Structural Injunction," 7 Harv. J. Law & Pub. Pol'y 395 (1984).

84. Paul Mishkin, "Federal Courts as State Reformers, " 35 Wash. & Lee L. Rev. 949 (1978).

85. For recent, sophisticated versions of the argument, see Stephen Carter, "From Sick Chicken to Synar: The Evolution of Subsequent De-Evolution of the Separation of Powers," 1987 B.Y.U. L. Rev. 719; Miller, *supra* note 77.

86. Bruce Ackerman, "Liberating Abstraction," 59 U. Chi. L. Rev. 317 (1992); Gerhardt Casper, "An Essay in Separation of Powers: Some Early Versions

and Practices," 30 Wm. & Mary L. Rev. 209 (1989); Louis Fisher, "The Allocation of Powers: The Framers' Intent," in *Separation of Powers in the American Political System* (B. Knight, ed., 1989); Shane, *supra* note 79.

87. Louis Fisher, *The Politics of Shared Power* (1981); Yvette Barksdale, "The President and Administrative Value Selection," 42 Am. Univ. L. Rev. 273 (1993); Peter Shane, "Legal Disagreement and Negotiation in a Government of Laws: The Case of Executive Privilege against Congress," 71 Minn. L. Rev. 461 (1987).

88. *Fletcher v. Peck*, 10 U.S. (6 Cranch) 87, 132–37 (1810) (Marshall, J.); *The Federalist*, no. 44 (Madison); Joseph Story, *Commentaries on the Constitution of the United States* 210 (4th ed., 1873).

89. Both practices, for example, are included in Lon Fuller's list of actions that would violate our concept of law on moral grounds. Lon Fuller, *The Morality of Law*, 46–49, 51–63 (rev. ed., 1969).

90. Gordon Wood, *The Creation of the American Republic*, 150–51 (1969).

91. *Papers of James Madison*, vol. 12, 202 (C. Hobson & R. Rutland, eds., 1979); Richard Kay, *Adherence to the Original Intentions in Constitutional Adjudication: Three Objections and Responses*, 82 Nw. U. L. Rev. 226, 271–72 (1988); Edward Dumbauld, *The Bill of Rights and What It Means Today*, 33–44 (1957).

92. Vile, *supra* note 42, at 136–41; Wood, *supra* note 90, at 150–53.

93. Vile, *supra* note 42 at 157–62. Wood's discussion of this subject is somewhat unclear. See supra note 90, at 547–55. He identifies checks and balances as a dominant theme, but seems to equate it with strict separation of powers. The reason he does so, perhaps, is that his major emphasis is on the effort to strengthen the executive and judicial departments, thereby avoiding legislative supremacy. Both checks and balances and strict separation would achieve that goal, so the distinction between the two may not seem significant to Wood from this perspective.

94. *The Federalist*, nos. 47 and 48 (Madison).

95. Victoria Nourse, "Toward a 'Due Foundation' for the Separation of Powers: The Federalist Papers As Political Narrative," 74 Tex. L. Rev. 447 (1996).

96. 462 U.S. 919 (1983).

97. Chemerinsky, *supra* note 33, at 1108. Chemerinsky points out that recent Supreme Court decisions use a strict originalist approach in assessing Congressional action, and a nonoriginalist or evolutionary approach in assessing presidential action, without offering any reason for this bifurcation. See generally H. Jefferson Powell, "The Original Understanding of Original Intent," 98 Harv. L. Rev. 885 (1985); Suzanna Sherry, "The Founders' Unwritten Constitution," 54 U. Chi. L. Rev. 1127 (1987).

98. Asimow, *supra* note 37; Edley, *supra* note 8, at 236–39; Pederson, "The Decline of Separation of Functions in Regulatory Agencies," 64 Va. L. Rev. 991 (1978); Richard Stewart, "Beyond Delegation Doctrine," 36 Am. U. L. Rev. 323 (1987); Sunstein, *supra* note 47, at 446–47; Strauss, *supra* note 47.

99. Susan Bandes, "Reinventing *Bivens:* The Self-Executing Constitution," 68 S. Cal. L. Rev. 289, 311–22 (1995); Edley, *supra* note 8, at 236–39; Shane, *supra* note 34; Strauss, *supra* note 37, at 616–21, 640–67.

100. See, e.g., Harold Bruff, "On the Constitutional Status of the Administrative Agencies," 36 Am. U. L. Rev. 491 (1987); Calabresi & Rhodes, *supra* note 78; Steven Calabresi & Saikrishna Prakash, "The President's Power to Execute the Laws," 104 Yale L. J. 541 (1994); Miller, *supra* note 77. For contrary views, see Lawrence Lessig & Cass Sunstein, "The President and the Administration," 94 Colum. L. Rev. 1 (1994); Shane, *supra* note 87; Strauss, *supra* note 77.

101. Martin Flaherty, "The Most Dangerous Branch," 105 Yale L. J. 1725 (1996).

102. Raoul Berger, *Government by Judiciary: The Transformation of the Fourteenth Amendment* (1977); Alexander Bickel, "The Original Understanding and the Segregation Decision," 69 Harv. L. Rev. 1 (1955); Robert Bork, "The Impossibility of Finding Welfare Rights in the Constitution," 1979 Wash. U. L. Q. 695; Henry Monaghan, "Our Perfect Constitution," 56 N.Y.U. L. Rev. 353 (1981); William Rehnquist, "The Notion of a Living Constitution," 54 Tex. L. Rev. 693 (1976).

103. Owen Fiss, "Objectivity and Interpretation," 34 Stan. L. Rev. 739 (1982); See also Fiss, *supra* note 66; Sunstein, *supra* note 47, at 493–94.

104. Douglas Laycock, *The Death of the Incomparable Injury Rule* (1991).

105. Larry Alexander, "Painting without Numbers: Noninterpretive Judicial Reviews," 8 U. Dayton L. Rev. 458 (1983); Phillip Bobbitt, *Constitutional Fate: Theory of the Constitution* (1982); Stephen Carter, "Constitutional Adjudication and the Indeterminate Text: A Preliminary Defense of an Imperfect Muddle," 94 Yale L. J. 821 (1985); Thomas Grey, "Do We Have an Unwritten Constitution?" 27 Stan. L. Rev. 703 (1975); Frank Michelman, "Politics and Values or What's Really Wrong with Rationality Review," 13 Creighton L. Rev. 487; Michael Perry, "The Authority of Text, Tradition and Reason: A Theory of Constitutional Interpretation," 58 S. Cal. L. Rev. 551 (1985); Cass Sunstein, "Public Values, Private Interests, and the Equal Protection Clause," 1982 Sup. Ct. Rev. 127. For a discussion and critique of all interpretive theories based on evolving moral standards, see Mark Tushnet, *Red, White and Blue: A Critical Analysis of Constitutional Law* (1988).

106. W. Lewis, *From Newgate to Dannemora: The Rise of the Penitentiary in New York, 1796–1848* (1965); Blake McKelvey, *American Prisons: A History of Good Intentions*, 1–35 (1977); David Rothman, *The Discovery of the Asylum*, 45–56 (2d ed., 1990).

107. Martin Shapiro, *Courts: A Comparative and Political Analysis* (1981); Gordon Wood, *The Radicalism of the American Revolution*, 323–24 (1991).

108. See Sidney Webb & Beatrice Webb, *English Prisons under Local Government*, 50–52 (1922; rev. ed., 1963). For a more general treatment of the power of judges to affect the conditions of public services, see Charles Haar and Daniel Fessler, *Fairness and Equity: Law in the Service of Equality* (1986).

109. Theodore Eisenberg & Stephen Yeazell, "The Ordinary and the Extraordinary in Institutional Litigation," 93 Harv. L. Rev. 465 (1980).

110. See Webb & Webb, *supra* note 108; see also Robert Black, "The Origins of Structural Reform: Federal Judges in the Late Nineteenth Century" (paper on file at the Center for the Study of Law and Society, 1983).

111. Brown, *supra* note 31, at 1527–29; Redish & Cisar, *supra* note 34, at 490–91; Sargentich, *supra* note 33, at 433; Sunstein, *supra* note 47, at 494–96.

112. See, e.g., *Mistretta v. United States*, 488 U.S. 361 (1989); *Morrison v. Olson*, 487 U.S. 654 (1988).

113. E.g., *Mistretta v. United States*, 488 U.S. 361 (1989) (sentencing commission located in judicial branch); *Morrison v. Olson*, 487 U.S. 654 (1988) (special prosecutor appointed by judiciary); *Bowsher v. Synar*, 478 U.S. 714 (1986) (budget officer removable by Congress); *INS v. Chadha*, 462 U.S. 919 (1983) (legislative veto exercised without presidential approval); *Buckley v. Valeo*, 424 U.S. 1 (1976) (some members of Federal Election Commission appointed by congressional officers).

114. Alexander Bickel, *The Least Dangerous Branch: The Supreme Court at the Bar of Politics*, 16–23 (1962).

115. *Id.* at 23–33. See also Geoffrey Miller, "Rights and Structure in Constitutional Theory," 8 J. Philo. & Pol'y 196 (1991); Redish & Cisar, *supra* note 34. See William Lasser, *The Limits of Judicial Power* (1988).

116. Frederick D. Hayek, *Law and Legislation*, 3 vols. (1973–79); Allan Hutchinson, *Dwelling on the Threshold: Critical Essays on Modern Legal Thought* (1988); Allan Hutchinson & Patrick Monahan, "Democracy and the Rule of Law," in *The Rule of Law: Ideal or Ideology*, 97 (A. Hutchinson & P. Monahan, eds., 1987); Theodore Lowi, *The End of Liberalism* (2d ed., 1979). Hayek is an archconservative, Lowi a liberal of sorts, and Hutchinson a radical identified with the critical legal studies movement.

117. James Buchanan & Gordon Tullock, *The Calculus of Consent* (1962); John Ferejohn, *Pork Barrel Politics* (1974); Morris Fiorina, *Congress: Keystone of the Washington Establishment* (1977); David Mayhew, *Congress: The Electoral Connection* (1974); Barry Weingast, "Regulation, Reregulation, and Deregulation: The Political Foundations of Agency Clientele Relationships," 44 L. & Contemp. Probs. 147 (1981). Dennis Mueller, *Public Choice* (2d ed., 1989), provides a general overview. For critical analysis, see Dennis Farber & Philip Frickey, *Law and Public Choice* (1991); Einer Elhauge, "Does Interest Group Theory Justify More Intrusive Judicial Review," 101 Yale L. J. 31 (1992); Edward Rubin, "Beyond Public Choice: Comprehensive Rationality in the Writing and Reading Statutes," 66 N.Y.U. L. Rev. 1 (1991).

118. Roland Barthes, *The Pleasure of the Text* (1975); Jean Baudrillard, *Simulations* (1983); Alain Touraine, *Return of the Actor: A Social Theory in Post-industrial Society* (1988).

119. Stanley Aronowitz, "Postmodernism and Politics," in *Universal Abandon? The Politics of Postmodernism* (A. Ross, ed., 1988); Jean Baudrillard, *In the Shadow of the Silent Majorities* (1983); A. Norton, *Reflections on Political Iden-*

tity (1988); Harry Redner, "Representation and the Crisis of Post-Modernism," 20 Pol. Sci. & Politics 673 (1987); R. B. J. Walker, *One World, Many Worlds* (1988).

120. See Barry Friedman, "Dialogue and Judicial Review," 91 Mich. L. Rev. 577, 629–43 (1993); Steven Winter, "An Upside/Down View of the Countermajoritarian Difficulty," 69 Tex. L. Rev. 1991, 119–25 (1991).

121. On the judiciary's responsiveness to public opinion generally, see David Adamany & Joel Grossman, "Support for the Supreme Court as National Policymakers," 5 L. & Pol'y Q. 405 (1983); Larry Baum, "Measuring Policy Change in the U.S. Supreme Court," 82 Am. Pol. Sci. Rev. 905 (1988); Robert Dahl, "Decisionmaking in a Democracy: The Supreme Court as a National Policymaker," 6 J. Pub. L. 279 (1957); Donald Lively, *Judicial Review and the Consent of the Governed* (1990); Thomas Marshall, *Public Opinion and the Supreme Court* (1989); William Mishler & Reginald Sheehan, "The Supreme Court as a Countermajoritarian Institution? The Impact of Public Opinion on Supreme Court Decision," 87 Am Pol. Sci. Rev. 87 (1993); Glendon Schubert, *The Constitutional Polity* (1970); Jeffrey Segal, "Measuring Change on the Supreme Court: Examining Alternative Models," 29 Am. J. Pol. Sci. 461 (1985).

122. John Rohr, *To Run a Constitution: The Legitimacy of the Administrative State* (1986); Robert Pushaw, "Justiciability and Separation of Powers: A Neo-Federalist Approach," 81 Cornell L. Rev. 393 (1996).

123. Feredrick A. Hayek, *The Constitution of Liberty*, 103–17 (1960).

124. Joseph Raz, *The Concept of a Legal System* (2d ed., 1980).

125. Robert Dahl, *Dilemma of Pluralist Democracy: Autonomy and Control* (1982).

126. Bruce Ackerman, *Social Justice in the Liberal State* (1980); Jürgen Habermas, *The Structural Transformation of the Public Sphere: An Inquiry into a Category of Bourgeoisie Society*, 222–35 (T. Burger, trans. 1991); Jürgen Habermas, *Legitimation Crisis*, 113–17 (T. Burger, trans., 1975).

127. Matthew Adler, "Judicial Restraint in the Administrative State: Beyond the Countermajoritarian Difficulty," 145 U. Pa. L. Rev. 759 (1997).

128. Barksdale, *supra* note 87; Strauss, *supra* note 77; Nicholas S. Zeppos, "Legislative History and the Interpretation of Statutes: Toward a Fact-finding Model of Statutory Interpretation," 76 Va. L. Rev. 1295, 1311–12 (1990).

129. Brian Leiter, "Heidegger and the Theory of Adjudication," 106 Yale L. J. 253 (1996).

130. Martin Heidegger, *Being and Time*, 91–122 (J. Macquarrie & E. Robinson, trans. 1962).

131. Akhil Reed Amar, "Philadelphia Revisited: Amending the Constitution outside Article V," 55 U. Chi. L. Rev. 1043, 1085 (1988); Erwin Chermerinsky, "Foreword: The Vanishing Constitution," 103 Harv. L. Rev. 43 (1989); Dahl, *supra* note 121; Friedman, *supra* note 120, at 629–43, 653–80.

132. Habermas, *supra* note 126, at 89–140.

8. CONCLUSION

1. 410 U.S. 113 (1973).
2. 381 U.S. 479 (1965).
3. 32 N.J. 358, 161 A.2d 69 (1959) (holding that modern market practices create an implied warranty of merchantability for consumer products).
4. On the derivation of legal standards from the people subject to the law, see Robert Cooter, "Decentralized Law for a Complex Economy: The Structural Approach to Adjudicating the New Law Merchant," 144 U. Pa. L. Rev. 1643 (1996); Richard Danzig, "A Comment on the Jurisprudence of the Uniform Commercial Code," 27 Stan. L. Rev. 671 (1975); Edward Rubin, "Learning from Lord Mansfield: Toward a Transferability Law for Modern Commercial Practice," 31 Idaho L. Rev. 775 (1995).
5. Epaninondas Panagopoulos, *Essays on the History and Meaning of Checks and Balances,* 161–66 (1985). He quotes a discussion at the Philadelphia convention among John Dickinson, James Wilson, and James Madison regarding federal–state relations in which all three made reference to the planets. *Id.* at 164–65. See also Michael Kammen, *A Machine That Would Go of Itself* (1986).
6. Frank Michelman, "Foreword: Traces of Self-government," 100 Harv. L. Rev. 4 (1990); J. G. A. Pocock, *The Machiavellian Moment* (1975); J. G. A. Pocock, "Virtues, Rights and Manners: A Model of Political Thought," 9 Pol. Theory 353 (1981); Cass Sunstein, "Interest Groups in American Public Law," 38 Stan. L. Rev. 29 (1985); Suzanna Sherry, "Civic Virtues and the Feminine Voice in Constitutional Adjudication," 72 Va. L. Rev. 543 (1986).
7. David Rothman, *The Discovery of the Asylum* (2nd ed., 1990).
8. M. J. C. Vile, *Constitutionalism and the Separation of Powers,* 5–7 (1967); Paul Gewirtz, "Realism in Separation of Powers Thinking," 30 Wm. & Mary L. Rev. 343 (1987).
9. Auguste Comte, *A General View of Positivism* (J. Bridges, trans., 1958).
10. Herbert Spencer, *Illustrations of Universal Progress: A Series of Discussions* (1864).
11. With respect to the separation of powers and liberty, a topic that is not discussed in our text, see Rebecca Brown, "Separated Powers and Ordered Liberty," 139 U. Pa. L. Rev. 1513 (1991); Peter Quint, "The Separation of Powers under Nixon: Reflections on Constitutional Liberties and the Rule of Law," 30 Duke L. J. 1 (1981); Martin Redish & Elizabeth Cisar, " 'If Angels Were to Govern:' The Need for Pragmatic Formalism in Separation of Powers Theory," 41 Duke L. J. 449 (1991); cf. Steven Calabresi & Jane Larsen, "One Person, One Office: Separation of Powers or Separation of Personnel," 79 Cornell L. Rev. 1045 (1994).
12. Jesse Choper, *Judicial Review and the National Political Process* (1980).
13. Vile, *supra* note 8, at 120–71.
14. A. V. Dicey, *Introduction to the Study of the Law of the Constitution,* 179–92 (1908).

15. Joseph Raz, "The Rule of Law and Its Virtue," 93 L. Q. Rev. 195 (1977); reprinted in Robert Cunningham, ed., *Liberty and the Rule of Law*, 3 (1979).
16. John Rawls, *A Theory of Justice*, 235–43 (1971).
17. Lon Fuller, *The Morality of Law*, 33–94 (rev. ed., 1969).
18. Fredrich A. Hayek, *The Road to Serfdom* (15th ed., 1994).
19. Walker does not discuss Hayek at length, but his extended diatribes against legislation and administration seemed inspired by this source; he uses Critical Legal Studies, a relatively weak movement within legal scholarship and hardly a political movement at all, as a stand-in for the misguided socialists who incite so much of Hayek's fury. See Geoffrey de Q. Walker, *The Rule of Law* (1988).
20. Hayek, *supra* note 18, at 80. Hayek specifically links this with Dicey's related definition.
21. *Id.* at xxvii (preface to the 1956 paperback edition).
22. See Bernard Bailyn, *The Ideological Origins of the American Revolution* (rev. ed., 1992); Gordon Wood, *The Creation of the American Republic, 1776–1786* (1969); Gordon Wood, *The Radicalism of the American Revolution* (1991).
23. Alexander Pope, *The Dunciad Book I*, ll. 4–5 (1727), reprinted in *Selected Poetry and Prose* 380 (W. Wimsatt, ed., 1965).
24. See Wood, *Creation, supra* note 21, at 391–564.
25. This is only implied in Hayek's book. He is writing for an English audience and, quite understandably, does not address American constitutionalism. When he speaks about government in all its actions "being bound by fixed rules announced in advance," he seems to be speaking primarily of rules that the legislature imposes on executive officials; the only rule he treats as being binding on the legislature is the obligation to articulate fixed rules.
26. Raz, *supra* note 15.
27. Theodore Lowi, *The End of Liberalism*, 295–310 (rev. ed., 1979). Lowi recommends "juridical democracy" where no important actions could be taken without specific authorization by the legislature. This reveals not only an excessive pessimism about the ability of administrators to follow the law and to act responsibly, but an even more questionable optimism about the ability of a legislature to make all the major decisions necessary for the operation of a modern government.
28. Hayek, *supra* note 18, at 80–95.
29. *Id.* at 49–62.
30. James Buchanan, *The Demand and Supply of Public Goods* (1969); Robert Cooter & Thomas Ulen, *Law and Economics*, 45–49, 108–17 (1988); Allen Kneese & Charles Schultze, *Pollution, Prices and Public Policy* (1975).
31. Hayek, *supra* note 18, at 38–45. As he notes, planning, in the general sense, is required for any form of effective government, but he uses it as a defined term for the methodology of socialism.
32. See Michael Lipsky, *Street-Level Bureaucrats* (1980).
33. On the complexity of command structures within bureaucracies, see, e.g., Paul Di Maggio & Walter Powell, "The Iron Cage Revisited: Institutional Isomorphism and Collective Rationality," in *The New Institutionalism in Or-*

ganizational Analysis, 63 (W. Powell & P. DiMaggio, eds., 1991); Anthony Giddens, *The Constitution of Society: Outline of the Theory of Structuration* (1984); John Meyer & Brian Rowan, "Institutionalized Organizations: Formal Structure as Myth and Ceremony," in *The New Institutionalism in Organizational Analysis, supra*; Harold Seidman & Robert Gilmour, *Politics, Position, and Power* (1986); Herbert Simon, *Administrative Behavior* (1957); Oliver Williamson, *Transaction Cost Economics and Organization Theory,* in *Organization Theory: From Chester Barnard to the Present and Beyond,* 207 (Oliver Williamson, ed., 1995); James Wilson, *Bureaucracy* (1989).

34. Margaret Radin, "Reconsidering the Rule of Law," 69 B.U. L. Rev. 781 (1989).

35. Francis J. Mootz III, "Rethinking The Rule of Law: A Demonstration That the Obvious Is Plausible," 61 Tenn. L. Rev. 69 (1993); Francis J. Mootz III, "Is the Rule of Law Possible in a Postmodern World," 68 Wash. L. Rev. 249 (1993) (reviewing Walker, *supra* note 19).

36. Robert Post, *Constitutional Domains: Democracy, Community, Management* (1995).

37. Max Weber, *Economy and Society: An Outline of Interpretive Sociology,* vol. 2, 976–80 (G. Roth & C. Wittich, eds., 1978).

38. Ronald Dworkin, *Taking Rights Seriously,* 110–23 (1978).

39. E.g., Phillip Bobbitt, *Constitutional Fate* (1982); Dworkin, *supra* note 38; Ronald Dworkin, "The Forum of Principle," 56 N.Y.U. L. Rev. 469 (1981); Owen Fiss, "Foreword: The Forms of Justice," 93 Harv. L. Rev. 1 (1979); Michael Perry, *The Constitution, The Courts and Human Rights* (1982).

40. Niklas Luhmann, *Social Systems* (J. Bednarz, trans., 1995); Gunther Teubner, *Law As an Autopoietic System* (Zenon Bankowski, ed., & Anne Bankowska & Ruth Adler, trans., 1993).

41. Robert Michels, *Political Parties* (E. Paul & C. Paul, trans., 1962).

42. See Melvin Eisenberg, *The Nature of the Common Law* (1986); John Poulos, "The Judicial Philosophy of Roger Traynor," 46 Hastings L. J. 1643, (1995).

43. Robert Pushaw, "Justiciability and Separation of Powers: A Neo-Federalist Approach," 81 Cornell L. Rev. 393 (1996). See also Poulos, *supra* note 42, at 1710–13.

44. For notorious examples, see *Lujan v. Defenders of Wildlife,* 504 U.S. 555 (1992); *Simon v. Eastern Kentucky Welfare Rights Org.,* 426 U.S. 26 (1976); *Worth v. Seldin,* 422 U.S. 490 (1975). For commentary, see William Fletcher, "The Structure of Standing," 98 Yale L. J. 221 (1988); Cass Sunstein, "What's Standing after *Lujan?* Of Citizen Suits, 'Injuries,' and Article III," 91 Mich. L. Rev. 163 (1992); Cass Sunstein, "Standing and the Privatization of Public Law," 88 Colum. L. Rev. 1432 (1988).

45. See Edward L. Rubin, "What Does Prescriptive Legal Scholarship Say and Who Is Listening to It: A Response to Professor Dan-Cohen," 63 U. Colo. L. Rev. 731 (1992); Edward L. Rubin, "The Practice and Discourse of Legal Scholarship," 86 Mich. L. Rev. 1835 (1988).

9. CODA: ASSESSING THE SUCCESSES OF
JUDICIAL PRISON REFORM

1. *Smith et al. v. Dyer et al.*, Nos. 74184, 63779, 76086, 750121 (Cal. Super. Ct., County of Alameda, August 15, 1983).
2. Fay Bowker & Glenn Good, "From Alcatraz to Marion to Florence: Control Unit Prisons in the United States," in *Cages of Steel*, 134 (W. Churchill & J. J. Vander Wall, eds., 1992); Bill Dunne, "The U.S. Prison at Marion: An Instrument of Oppression," in *Cages of Steel*, at 40.
3. Oscar Wilde, "Letter to the Daily Chronicle," May 27, 1897, reprinted in O. Wilde, *The Soul of Man and Prison Writings*, 159, 163 (1990); "Letter to the Daily Chronicle," March 23, 1898, reprinted in *id.* at 190, 191–92.
4. George Rusche and Otto Kirchheimer, *Punishment and Social Structure* ([1939] 1968), at 84–109, 138–45.
5. John DiIulio, *Governing Prisons* (1987).
6. Steve Martin & Sheldon Ekland-Olson, *Texas Prisons: The Walls Came Tumbling Down* (1987).
7. Ben Crouch & James Marquart, *An Appeal to Justice* (1989).
8. See *Ex parte Hull*, 312 U.S. 546 (1941); *Ex parte Terrill*, 287 P. 753 (Okla. Crim. Ct. App. 1930).
9. Andrew Hacker, *Two Nations: Black and White, Separate, Hostile, Unequal* (1992); Douglas Massey & Nancy Denton, *American Apartheid: Segregation and the Making of the Underclass* (1993).
10. Gerald Rosenberg, *The Hollow Hope: Can Courts Bring about Social Change?* (1991).
11. See Malcolm M. Feeley, "The Federal Courts in the Political Process," in *Courts and the Political Process: Jack Peltason's Contributions to Political Science* (Austin Ranney, ed., 1995).
12. In the early 1970s, Texas Department of Corrections attorney Steve Martin helped coordinate the state's defense in *Ruiz*; shortly thereafter he found himself on a short list of candidates for the director's position. In California, Anthony Newland, a correctional officer working on his Ph.D. in public administration, was assigned to serve as the department's litigation coordinator, acting as liaison between the department and forty-seven attorneys in the state attorney general's office; after a short stint in this position he was appointed superintendent of Vacaville Correctional Unit, which houses over four thousand medium security inmates in one of the largest prisons in the world, and he has been mentioned as a possible future director of the California Department of Corrections. In Colorado, the legal liaison officer appointed in the aftermath of *Ramos v. Lamm* stayed on to draft departmental regulations which further rationalized the department's structure.
13. For a good account of the effort to "tame discretion" by structuring decision making by standards, see Samuel Walker, *Taming the System: The*

Control of Discretion in Criminal Justice, 1950–1990 (1993). American Correctional Association, *Manual of Correctional Standards* (various years, 1940–90).

14. American Law Institute, *Model Code of Pre-Arraignment Procedure* (1975).
15. American Bar Association, *Standards for Criminal Justice,* (2d ed., 1980).
16. *U.S. National Advisory Commission on Criminal Justice Standards and Goals* (1973).
17. Pub. L. No. 96–247, 94 Stat. 349 (1980), codified at 42 U.S.C. § 1997 *et seq.* (1994).
18. See B. James George, "The Case for Correctional Accreditation," in *Prisoners and the Law,* 18–19 (I. Robbins, ed., 1996); Lynn Sanders Branham, "Accreditation: Making A Good Process Better," in *Prisoner's and Law, supra,* at 18–41.
19. American Correctional Association, *supra* note 13.
20. Ross Cheit, *Setting Safety Standards: Regulation in the Public and Private Sector* (1990).
21. Samuel Walker, supra note 13.
22. Philipe Nonet & Philip Selznick, *Law and Society in Transition* (1977).
23. DiIulio, *supra* note 5.
24. Max Weber, *Economy and Society,* vol. 2, 941–1005, 1158–1211 (Gueuther Roth & Claus Wittich, eds., 1968).
25. William Taggart, "Redefining The Power of the Federal Judiciary: The Impact of Court-Ordered Prison Reform on State Expenditures for Corrections," 23 L. & Soc. Rev. 241 (1989).
26. See Franklin Zimring & Gordon Hawkins, *The Scale of Imprisonment* (1991); John Irwin & James Austin, *It's about Time: America's Imprisonment Binge* (1994).
27. Stephen Pepper, "Autonomy, Community and Lawyers' Ethics," 19 Cap. U. L. Rev. 939 (1990); Stephen Pepper, "The Lawyer's Amoral Ethical Role: A Defense, a Problem and Some Possibilities," 1986 A.B.F. Res. J. 613; Mark Spiegel, "Lawyering and Client Decisionmaking: Informed Consent and the Legal Profession," 128 U. Pa. L. Rev. 41 (1979).
28. David Binder, Paul Bergman, & Susan Price, "Lawyers as Counselors: A Client-Centered Approach," 35 N.Y.L. Sch. L. Rev. 29 (1990); Lucie White, "Subordination, Rhetorical Survival Skills and Sunday Shoes: Notes on the Hearing of Mrs. G.," 38 Buff. L. Rev. 1 (1990).
29. Stephen Ellman, "Lawyering for Justice in a Flawed Democracy," 90 Colum. L. Rev. 116 (1990).
30. David Luban, *Lawyers and Justice* (1988); David Luban, "Paternalism and the Legal Profession," 1981 Wis. L. Rev. 454 (1981).
31. Deborah Rhode, "Class Conflicts in Class Actions," 34 Stan. L. Rev. 1183 (1982).
32. William Simon, "Lawyer Advice and Client Autonomy: Mrs. Jones's Case," 50 Md. L. Rev. 213 (1991).
33. See Douglas Rosenthal, *Lawyer and Client: Who's in Charge?* (1974) (referring to the lawyer as authority as the "traditional" approach); Richard

Wassertrom, "Lawyers as Professionals: Some Moral Issues," 5 Human Rights 1 (1975).

34. For an assessment of the impact of prison litigation on prison administration by a thoughtful prison administrator, see Anthony Newland, "Managing Prison Conditions-of-Confinement Litigation: Lessons for California Administrators" (Ph.D. Thesis, Department of Public Administration, Golden Gate University, 1990).

35. U.S. Department of Justice, Bureau of Justice Statistics, *Prisoners in 1996*.

36. See Robert McKay, "Overcrowding," in *Prisoners and the Law, supra* note 18, at 6–3; Zimring & Hawkins, *supra* note 26. But see Jeffrey Bleich, "The Politics of Prison Crowding," 77 Cal. L. Rev. 1125 (1989) (complaints about crowding used by administrators to obtain additional funding).

37. 475 U.S. 312 (1986).

38. 501 U.S. 284 (1991). See also the various cases cutting back on specific constitutional rights: *Thornburg v. Abbott*, 490 U.S. 401 (1989) (free speech); *Sandin v. Connor*, 115 S. Ct. 2293 (1995) (due process); *Lewis v. Casey*, 116 S. Ct. 2174 (1995) (access to legal materials); *O'Lone v. Estate of Shabazz*, 482 U.S. 342 (1987) (free exercise of religion).

39. Pub. L. No. 96–247 (1980), codified at 42 U.S.C. § 1998 *et seq.* (1994).

40. 42 U.S.C. § 1997c.

41. *Id.* at § 1997(b)(2).

42. 376 F. Supp. 402 (E.D. Okla. 1974).

43. 349 F. Supp. 881 (N.D. Miss. 1972).

44. Pub. L. No. 103–322 (1994), 108 Stat. 1827, codified at 18 U.S.C. § 3626 (1994).

45. Pub. L. 104–134 (1996), 110 Stat. 1328–66, to be codified at 18 U.S.C. § 1326, 42 U.S.C. § 1997. The act is part of the Omnibus Appropriations Bill of 1996.

46. *Id.* at § 3626(a)(1). The same restrictions extend to injunctive relief. *Id.* at § 3626(a)(2).

47. *Id.* at § 3626(b). Orders entered before the enactment of PLRA can be terminated two years after its enactment. Once the court has continued its order, the parties can move for termination on a yearly basis.

48. *Id.* at § 3626(c).

49. *Id.* at § 3626(f).

50. PLRA also places limitations on the judicial release of prisoners, *id.* at § 3626(a)(3), and makes numerous, though limited, changes in CRIPA.

51. *Hutto v. Finney*, 437 U.S. 678, 711 (1978).

52. 501 U.S. 294 (1991).

53. 502 U.S. 367 (1992).

54. See S. 2646, 85th Cong., 1st Sess. (1957) (the Jenner-Butler bill); Walter Murphy, *Congress and the Court* (1962).

55. Owen Fiss, "Against Settlement," 93 Yale L. J. 1073 (1984).

56. Pub. L. No. 104–132, 110 Stat. 1217.

57. *Felker v. Turpin*, 116 S. Ct. 2333 (1996).

58. For a discussion of LEAA, see Malcolm M. Feeley & Austin Sarat, *The Policy Dilemma* (1983).

59. Pub. L. 103–322 (1994).

60. FY 1997 Department of Justice Appropriations Act (Pub. L. 104–208, 100 Stat. 3009, H.R. 3610).

61. Edward Byrne Memorial State and Local Law Enforcement Assistance Formula Grant, Pub. L. 103–232 (1994).

62. For a comprehensive discussion, see Ira Robbins, "Privatization of Corrections: The Legal Dimensions of Private Incarceration," in *Prisoners and the Law, supra* note 18, at 22–3, 22–33.

63. For a discussion of this instance of privatization of corrections as a revolutionary innovation, see Malcolm M. Feeley, "The Privatization of Punishment in Historical Perspective," in *Privatization and Its Alternatives* (W. Gormley, ed., 1991).

64. See Malcolm M. Feeley & Jonathan Simon, "The New Penology: Notes on the Emerging Strategy of Corrections and Its Implications," 30 *Criminology* 449 (1992).

Author Index

Subject Index